THE CAMBRIDGE COMPANION

ROUSSEAU

Each volume in this series of companions to major philosophers contains specially commissioned essays by an international team of scholars, together with a substantial bibliography, and will serve as a reference work for students and
nonspecialists. One aim of the series is to dispel the intimi-
dation such readers often feel when faced with the work of a
difficult and challenging thinker.

Universally regarded as the greatest French political theorist and philosopher of education of the Enlightenment and
probably the greatest French social theorist *tout court*,
Rousseau was an important forerunner of the French Revolution, although his thought was too nuanced and subtle
ever to serve as mere ideology. This is the only volume that
systematically surveys the full range of Rousseau's activities
in politics and education, psychology, anthropology, religion,
music, and theater.

New readers will find this the most convenient and accessible guide to Rousseau currently available. Advanced students and specialists will find a conspectus of recent developments in the interpretation of Rousseau.

Patrick Riley is Oakeshott Professor of Political and Moral
Philosophy at the University of Wisconsin – Madison., and
Professore a Contratto, Facoltà di Giurisprudenza, Univer-
sità degli Studi di Bologna.

The Cambridge Companion to
ROUSSEAU

Edited by Patrick Riley
University of Wisconsin – Madison
and
Università degli Studi di Bologna

CAMBRIDGE
UNIVERSITY PRESS

PUBLISHED BY THE PRESS SYNDICATE OF THE UNIVERSITY OF CAMBRIDGE
The Pitt Building, Trumpington Street, Cambridge, United Kingdom

CAMBRIDGE UNIVERSITY PRESS
The Edinburgh Building, Cambridge CB2 2RU, UK
40 West 20th Street, New York, NY 10011-4211, USA
10 Stamford Road, Oakleigh, VIC 3166, Australia
Ruiz de Alarcón 13, 28014 Madrid, Spain
Dock House, The Waterfront, Cape Town 8001, South Africa

http://www.cambridge.org

First published 2001

Printed in the United States of America

Typeface 10/13 Trump Medieval   *System* LaTeX 2$_\varepsilon$ [TB]

A catalog record for this book is available from the British Library.

Library of Congress Cataloging in Publication Data
The Cambridge companion to Rousseau / edited by Patrick Riley.
p.   cm. – (Cambridge companions to philosophy)
Includes bibliographical references and index.
ISBN 0-521-57265-7 – ISBN 0-521-57615-6 (pbk.)
1. Rousseau, Jean Jacques, 1712–1778. I. Riley, Patrick, 1941–
II. Series.
B2137 .C27   2001
194 – dc21   2001018430

ISBN   0 521 57265 7   hardback
ISBN   0 521 57615 6   paperback

CONTENTS

ACKNOWLEDGMENTS

My chief debt is to Terence Moore, senior Humanities Editor at Cambridge University Press (New York office), who asked me to edit *The Cambridge Companion to Rousseau* in 1995 and who has displayed an admirably long-suffering patience in waiting for the volume to materialize. It is a real joy to work with so understanding and helpful an editor. (I am particularly grateful to him for bending the rules of the *Cambridge Companion* series by permitting republication of celebrated Rousseau essays by the late Judith N. Shklar and George A. Kelly; I learned everything I know about Rousseau from them (and from John Rawls) and was determined to have them in the present *Companion*. Ill health prevented Rawls himself from contributing what would have been a splendid chapter.)

I am of course grateful to all the other contributors to the *Companion*; many of them put aside pressing work to produce their contributions. No editorial uniformity was imposed on them: I simply asked each to do what he or she knows and loves best, and I think that the outcome justifies such faith and confidence.

I am grateful to my son, Professor Patrick Riley, Jr., of the Department of French at Colgate University, for undertaking his fine translation of Jean Starobinski's remarkable chapter, "The Motto *Vitam Impendere Vero* and the Question of Lying."

For typing and other technical help I am grateful to Ms. Laura Weeks, who has taken on more than a fair share of labor for this *Companion*. Without her constant effort the book would not exist.

I am grateful to the National Gallery of Scotland, Edinburgh, for kindly permitting the reproduction of the Ramsay portrait of Rousseau that adorns the *Companion's* cover.

Finally I acknowledge my own companion, Joan A. Riley, who for 35 years has made all of my work possible; without her support I would have achieved little indeed.

Patrick Riley
Cambridge, Massachusetts
October, 2000

CONTRIBUTORS

CHRISTOPHER BROOKE is Senior Tutor in Political and Moral Philosophy at Magdalen College, Oxford University. His work is on early-modern Stoicism and on 17th-century Augustinianism.

C.N. DUGAN is a Tutor at St. John's College in Annapolis, Maryland. His dissertation was on political education in Plato's *Laws*, and he is presently preparing a version of this work for publication.

VICTOR GOUREVITCH is Professor (Emeritus) of Political Philosophy at Wesleyan University. He is the editor of the Rousseau volumes in the Series, Cambridge Texts in the History of Political Thought, and the author of numerous chapters and articles on Rousseau.

MARK HULLIUNG is Professor of History at Brandeis University. He is the author of *Rousseau: The Autocritique of Enlightenment* (Harvard University Press) and of a book on Machiavelli.

THOMAS KAVANAGH is Professor of French Literature at the University of California, Berkeley. He is the author of *Writing the Truth: Authority and Desire in Rousseau* (University of California Press).

CHRISTOPHER KELLY is Professor of Political Science at Boston College. He is the author of *Rousseau's Exemplary Life: The Confessions as Political Philosophy* (Cornell University Press) and is co-editor (with Roger D. Masters) of *Rousseau's Collected Writings* (University Press of New England).

THE LATE GEORGE ARMSTRONG KELLY was Visiting Professor of Political Philosophy at Johns Hopkins University. He was the author of *Idealism, Politics and History* (Cambridge University

Press), *Hegel's Retreat from Eleusis* (Princeton University Press), and many chapters and articles.

GERAINT PARRY is Professor of Government at the University of Manchester, England. He is the author of numerous works on the philosophy of education (especially on Rousseau).

PATRICK RILEY is Oakeshott Professor of Political and Moral Philosophy at the University of Wisconsin (Madison). He is the author of *The General Will before Rousseau* (Princeton University Press) and of *Leibniz' Universal Jurisprudence: Justice as the Charity of the Wise* (Harvard University Press).

SUSAN MELD SHELL is Professor of Political Science at Boston College. She is the author of several books on Kant (Toronto and Chicago) and is at work on a book on *Punishment.*

THE LATE JUDITH N. SHKLAR was Professor of Government at Harvard University. She was the author of *Men and Citizens: A Study of Rousseau's Social Theory* (Cambridge University Press), of *Ordinary Vices* (Harvard University Press), and of a study of Hegel's *Phenomenology* (Cambridge).

JEAN STAROBINSKI is Professor in the Department of Modern French Language and Literature at the University of Geneva, Switzerland. He is the author of *Transparence et l'Obstacle,* a psychological and even psychoanalytical study of Rousseau.

TRACY STRONG is Professor of Political Science at the University of California, San Diego. He is the author of *Jean-Jacques Rousseau: The Politics of the Ordinary* (Sage) and of numerous Nietzsche studies. He was for many years the editor of *Political Theory.*

ROBERT WOKLER is Senior Lecturer at the University of Exeter, England. He is the author or editor of four books on Rousseau, including *Rousseau* (Oxford Unviersity Press) and *Rousseau and Liberty* (University of Manchester Press).

1 Introduction: Life and Works of Jean-Jacques Rousseau (1712–1778)

There is no need to recommend the writings of Jean-Jacques Rousseau: the greatest of all critics of inequality, the purest social contract theorist of the eighteenth century (and simultaneously the deepest critic of contractarianism after Hume), the greatest writer on civic education after Plato, the most perceptive understander of mastery and slavery after Aristotle and before Hegel, the finest critic of Hobbes, the most important predecessor of Kant, the most accomplished didactic novelist between Richardson and Tolstoy, the greatest confessor since Augustine, the author of paradoxes ("the general will is always right" but "not enlightened") that continue to fascinate or infuriate.

Rousseau's extensive range and intensive depth have been best brought out by Judith Shklar, in the Postscript to her celebrated *Men and Citizens*:

What did his contemporaries recognize as great in him, even those who reviled him as a charlatan and a *poseur*? He lived among the most intelligent and competent literary judges. Why did they think that he was so remarkable? His eloquence was universally recognized. Admirers and bitter enemies alike agreed that Rousseau was the most eloquent man of his age. His style is overwhelming. Rousseau, Diderot eventually said, was what one says of the poor draftsman among painters: a great colorist. Rousseau's literary powers were indeed phenomenal and to understand him fully one must give more than a passing thought to how he wrote. There is, however, another quality that his contemporaries did not recognize, partly because they shared it. That is the scope of Rousseau's intellectual competence. Even among his versatile contemporaries he was extraordinary: composer, musicologist, playwright, drama critic, novelist, botanist, pedagogue, political philospher, psychologist. That is not unimpressive. There is nevertheless even more in Rousseau's intellectual scope that seems notable now, though it did not strike his fellow intellectuals. They tended only to marvel at his suspect novelties and "paradoxes." We can marvel at the catholicity of Rousseau's social philosophy.

The range of his social thought, much more than his specific admiration for them and for antiquity in general, makes Rousseau an heir of Plato and Aristotle, and a part of the intellectual world they created. That is what one means when one speaks of Rousseau's writings as an aspect of European high culture. It is also what makes him a major, rather than a minor, figure in the history of political theory. The battle between the ancients and the moderns was not really decided in favor of the latter until after the French Revolution. Until then pagan antiquity was admired and known in all its details even by those who adopted a decidedly modern philosophic and scientific outlook. In Rousseau's time the attraction of an un- and pre-Christian world was particularly great. Everyone who was educated at all, and by whatever means, was familiar with classical literature. It defined intellectuality, set it limits and its style. The standard of relevance raised by ancient philosophy still prevailed, even when its content no longer did. Eager to out-do the ancients, Rousseau and his fellows nevertheless emulated them all the more intensely, because all the topics that Plato and Aristotle had touched upon had to be reconsidered. Rousseau was no slavish imitator of either one, but he accepted their example, their vision of what was involved in social theory, without a question. The importance which psychological, pedagogic, artistic, ethical and religious ideas play in his philosophical ensemble and their inseparability from politics, all demonstrate an adherence to a literary and philosophic culture which had its roots in antiquity and of which Rousseau was one of the last representatives. The scope of his theory, therefore, demands that all its aspects be studied without allowing later categories of thought to cut out what was essential for him. There is, moreover, a judgment here also. For surely Rousseau is so penetrating and convincing because his was so comprehensive a structure of ideas about man and society.

Jean-Jacques Rousseau was born in the Calvinist stronghold of Geneva on June 28, 1712, the second son of the watchmaker Isaac Rousseau and his wife Susan; both parents were "citizens" of Geneva, and Rousseau styled himself *citoyen de Genève* until his final renunciation of citizenship in 1764. Rousseau's mother died ten days after his birth, leaving him initially in the care of his father – with whom the child read (and then perpetually cherished) Plutarch's *Lives* of the greatest Greeks and Romans; later he was brought up by a puritanical aunt who (he admitted in the *Confessions*) did much to warp his sexuality. In 1722 Isaac Rousseau fled Geneva after a quarrel, and the ill-educated Jean-Jacques had to be apprenticed – first to a notary, then to an engraver.

In March, 1728, Rousseau missed the Genevan city curfew, found himself locked outside the gates, and wandered on foot to Annecy in Savoy – where he was taken in by Mme. de Warens, Rousseau's protector and then (1733–40) lover. In the provincial salon of Mme. de Warens (*"Les Charmettes"*), Rousseau acquired the education he had lacked in Geneva (Plutarch apart); one gets some sense of his autodidactic passion from his poem, *Le Verger des Charmettes*:

> Tantot avec Leibniz, Malebranche et Newton,
> Je monte ma raison sur un sublime ton,
> J'examine les lois des corps et des pensées,
> Avec Locke je fais l'histoire des idées.

Mme. de Warens, who specialized in finding Catholic converts, sent the young Rousseau to Turin, where he renounced his inherited Calvinism and converted to the Roman church; he even briefly attended a seminary for priests, until a Catholic ecclesiastic attempted to seduce him (as we again learn in the *Confessions*). Returning to Les Charmettes, he lived with *maman*, completed his education, and undertook his earliest writings – including the remarkable *Chronologie universelle* (ca. 1737), with its eloquent praise of Fénelon's charitable moral universalism.

Beginning in 1740, the now superbly educated Rousseau began to serve as a tutor, moving north to Lyon and living in the house of M. de Mably, whose children he instructed. However, in Lyon, above all, he met M. de Mably's two elder brothers – Étienne Bonnot (later the Abbé de Condillac, with Voltaire the greatest "Lockean" in post-Regency France) and the Abbé de Mably. This was the beginning of Rousseau's connection to the Paris *philosophes*, with whom he would later (and permanently) have a love–hate relationship. At this same time Rousseau became a considerable composer, music theorist, and music copyist; in later years he would represent himself as a simple Swiss republican who earned a living as a musical craftsman.

In 1742 Rousseau moved definitively northward to Paris, carrying with him a new system of musical notation, a comedy, an opera, and a collection of poems. (Even at this comparatively early date his sheer range was in evidence: If he eventually came to be known as a psychologist, group psychologist, and eloquently accusing *moraliste*, he was one of the last and latest "Renaissance men.") In Paris Rousseau eked out a precarious living by tutoring, writing, and copying music; for a brief period (1743–44) he served, not very happily, as Secretary to the French ambassador in Venice – an interlude that he mordantly described in his later *Lettres écrites de la montagne* (1764). Most importantly for his career as a man of letters, he met and befriended Denis Diderot, soon-to-be editor of the great *Encyclopédie* (who would ultimately commission Rousseau's first great writing on civic "general will," the *Économie politique* of 1755).

It was while visiting Diderot in prison (for alleged impiety) in 1749 that Rousseau *became* Rousseau (as we now know him) by deciding to write an essay for a prize competetion sponsored by the Académie de Dijon – dealing with the question whether morals had been harmed or advanced by the rebirth (*renaissance*) of the arts and sciences. Rousseau won the prize with the so-called *First Discourse*, in which he defended Spartan–Roman civic *généralité* against the Athenian literary "tyranny" of poets and orators; the *Discourse* made a European reputation, even attracting the criticism of the King of Poland, and from this period forward Rousseau was a leading citizen, however reluctantly, of the *République des lettres* (as Voltaire maliciously reminded him).

In 1752 his opera, "*Le devin du village*" ("The Village Soothsayer") was performed at the court of Louis XV at Versailles; at roughly the same time his black comedy, "Narcissus, the Lover of Himself" was given in Paris at the Theatre Français. As a good *citoyen de Genève*, Rousseau refused a royal pension, continuing his republican self-support as a musician by publishing his *Letter on French Music* in 1753; the *Lettre*, with its strong defense of Italian simplicity against French elaborateness, led to a collision with Rameau, the greatest French composer of the day.

Rousseau's *Discourse on the Origins of Inequality among Men*, the so-called *Second Discourse*, was completed in May, 1754; it is his most radical work and urges that existing government is a kind of confidence trick on the part of the rich, who persuade the poor that it is universally and equally advantageous to be subjected to law and to political order. (For the French Revolution this was the "true" Rousseau.) In June, 1754, Rousseau left Paris for a visit to his native Geneva, where he reconverted to Calvinism and had his civic rights restored; the year 1755 saw the publication of *Inégalité* and the *Économie Politique* (the *Third Discourse*). In 1756 Rousseau moved to the countryside, taking up residence at l'Hermitage, the country seat of Mme. d'Épinay; this inspired Diderot's sarcastic epigram, "a fine citizen a hermit is," and marked the start of the weakening of Rousseau's ties to the *philosophes* – a process accelerated by his 1758 "Lettre to M. d'Alembert," which opposed the latter's scheme to found a theater in Geneva. (Plato-like, Rousseau urged that such a theater would be inimical to civic virtue and good morals and that Molière's "*Misanthrope*" would have a deleterious effect.)

To the year 1758 can also be assigned the magnificent, uncompleted fragment called *L'état de Guerre* (*The State of War*), Rousseau's most brilliant and scathing critique of Hobbes and Hobbism. Taking over observations first made by Descartes and Leibniz (*Theodicée*, 1710), Rousseau insists that Hobbes has simply mistaken badly socialized, ill-educated Englishmen for "natural" men, leading to Hobbesian unquestionable "sovereignty" as the only antidote to rapacious appetitiveness: Looking out his London window, Hobbes "thinks that he has seen the natural man," but he has really only viewed "a bourgeois of London or Paris." Hobbes, for Rousseau, has simply inverted cause and effect; he has mistaken a bad effect for "natural" depravity.

In the late 1750s Rousseau labored on (but never published) the superb *Lettres morales* (for Sophie d'Houdetot) and then produced his vast epistolary novel, *Julie, ou la Nouvelle Heloïse* (published 1761), with its celebrated account of a small ideal society, Clarens, superintended by the godlike, all-seeing M. de Wolmar. The novel was a runaway best-seller, the greatest literary success since Fénelon's *Telemachus, Son of Ulysses* in 1699.

In May, 1762, Rousseau brought out two of his greatest but most ill-fated works: *The Social Contract* and *Émile*. Both were condemned and publicly burned in Paris, at the behest of Archbishop Christophe de Beaumont (and with the acquiesence of the *Parlement* of Paris); Rousseau, under order of arrest, fled to Geneva (only to find the same works condemned and burned there). Against charges of impiety leveled by the Genevan public prosecutor – alleging the dangerousness of Rousseau's "natural" theology in *Émile*'s "Profession of Faith of the Savoyard Vicar" – Rousseau composed and published his trenchant *Letters Written from the Mountain*, in which he defended ancient "civic" religion, and insisted that Christianity produces good men whose other-worldliness makes them "bad citizens." (This of course only increased the furor against him, and he took refuge in the Prussian enclave of Neuchâtel.) Renouncing his Genevan citizenship definitively, Rousseau occupied himself by writing a *Constitution* for recently liberated Corsica; increasingly threatened, his paranoia aggravated by genuine danger, Rousseau accepted the offer of British refuge from David Hume, although he soon came to see the benevolent Scot as part of the "league of malignant enemies" bent on his destruction. After an unhappy period in England – which nonetheless yielded the great Ramsay portrait now in the National Gallery at Edinburgh – Rousseau returned incognito to France, living under the assumed name of Renou. (While living under this assumed name, Rousseau finally married his longtime companion, Thérèse Levasseur, by whom he had fathered – if the *Confessions* are to be believed – five children, all supposedly abandoned in a foundling hospital.)

The *Confessions* themselves increasingly occupied Rousseau's time, and he often read substantial fragments of this work-in-progress in sympathetic aristocratic *salons*. In 1772 he produced the remarkable *Gouvernement de Pologne* as part of an effort to avert partition by Prussia, Austria, and Russia; the book combines intelligent constitutional reforms with Rousseau's most glowing account of Spartan and Roman-republican civic virtue. And in the same year he wrote (without publishing) the brilliantly innovative *Rousseau juge de Jean-Jacques*, in which he bifurcated himself and had one half comment on the other half – schizophrenia turned into a literary genre.

In 1777 Rousseau wrote his last great confessional work, *The Reveries of a Solitary Walker*, which begins with the celebrated words, "Here I am, then, alone on the earth, no longer having any brother, or neighbor, or friend, or society except myself." A year later, while in refuge on an aristocratic estate at Erménonville (north of Paris) and while engaging in his beloved botanical studies, Rousseau died quite suddenly on July 2, 1778; he was originally buried in a quasi-Roman sarcophagus on the Isle of Poplars at Erménonville, but at the height of the French Revolution his ashes were translated, in a dramatic torchlight procession, to the Pantheon and placed next to the remains of his nemesis Voltaire (1794).

"Given the range of his erudition, the depth of his reflection, and the variety of his interests," writes the eminent Rousseau scholar Roger D. Masters, "it is hardly surprising that Rousseau's influence has changed markedly over time."

In the eighteenth century, he was the *enfant terrible* of the Enlightenment, denying the legitimacy of the status quo while challenging the concept of progress. In the nineteenth century, he was more often viewed either as the apostle of the French Revolution or as the founder of the romantic movement. For twentieth-century critics, he is often praised as the founder of the western democratic tradition or vilified as a forerunner of totalitarianism. This very range of interpretation suggests that his thought cannot be reduced to a single stereotype or category: Rousseau – like Plato, Hobbes, or Marx – deserves to be considered as one of the most profound and complex political thinkers in the history of the West.

What the twenty-first century will make of the *citoyen de Genève* remains, of course, to be seen. But no imaginable transmogrification, however it may reshape Rousseau, will succeed in diminishing his stature as one of the half-dozen supreme political–moral theorists of the last two and a half millennia.

2   A General Overview

THE UNREDEEMED FUTURE AND THE POLEMIC AGAINST KNOWLEDGE

In tracing the genesis of the modern historical consciousness, Rousseau must be understood both as a point of departure and as a deliberate foil. He is neither an idealist – insofar as we can ascribe any consistent philosophical position to him – nor a metaphysician of the historical process. Yet it is with him that this discussion must begin. Because our focus is on political theory, only Rousseau can clarify our procedures; Leibniz or Hume might serve if our attention were elsewhere. There is no pretense, however, of making a full critical survey of Rousseau's unique and complex contributions to moral and political thought in this brief treatment.

For Rousseau, nature is a wise guide, man is an open question, and history is a tale of horror. These three elements form, at the outset, a chemistry of ambiguous potential. As man is free because he commands his own will, exclusive of his intelligence or station in life and because each child born into the world or each act must be regarded as a perpetual beginning,[1] the possibility of salvation – in the act, in the individual, or in the community – cannot be cosmically foreclosed. If history is woeful, it is not authoritative. "Man," exhorts the Savoyard vicar, "look no further for the author of evil; that author is you. No evil exists but that which you make or suffer; both are your works."[2] "By new associations," urges the first draft of the *Social Contract*, "let us correct, if we can, the shortcomings of the general association." The *Social Contract* carries us still more pressingly it would seem, away from defeatism: "... while a people is forced to obey and obeys, it does well; once it can shake off the yoke, and shakes it off, it does still better."[3] Rousseau is, in this sense, a philosopher of hope, a prophet of action. As such he contributed his share to the ideals of the French Revolution, to the optimism of the Romantic movement, and to a whole school of interpretation, which can be summarized in the following words of Gustave Lanson: "The idea of progress, the great idea of the century, inspires all the work of Jean-Jacques: He seems to deny its reality only so as to announce its possibility more loudly, its necessity more demandingly."[4]

Yet, setting aside all anticipations, Rousseau is much more a philosopher of despair: "Nature has made everything in the best way possible; but we want to do better still, and we spoil everything." Precisely for the same reasons that hope remains, salvation is most unlikely: "...the vices that make our social institutions necessary are the same that make their abuses inevitable." Moreover, man hastens the deterioration of everything he sets his mark on, except in the rarest of cases. Rousseau is fundamentally the philosopher of the note in the bottle thrown out to sea. "I like to flatter myself," he jotted among his papers, "that some day there will be a statesman who is [also] a citizen...that by some lucky chance he will cast his eyes on this book [i.e., the *Social Contract*], that my loose ideas will inspire in him more useful ones, that he will devote himself to making men better or happier.... My writing has been guided by this fantasy...."[5] The citizen of Geneva knew the odds. But better, as he wrote in *Emile*, his "land of chimeras" than the "land of prejudices" of his readers. Rousseau conceived models. There is a huge gap between a model and a method. Whatever redemption Rousseau held out for the individual, the domestic unit, or the society of sovereign equality he hemmed in with insuperable provisos or felt atavistically compelled to dynamite.[6]

It is indeed possible to regard Rousseau's writings as a fundamental attack on man as a history-making animal. The poignant truth of the matter is that "man is good and men are wicked." History is a dangerous striving to be avoided. You may not shine among the annals of the nations, he told the Corsicans, but you will win a greater prize: You will be happy. And yet man *is* that history-making animal, willing himself above and beyond nature, the coherent universal order in which "everything is renewed and nothing degenerates."[7] Man's fate is partly a result of his mortality, but in the species (contrary to Kant) it is due to his corruption. Rousseau, passionately concerned with the puzzle of man, viewed his perplexity against the background of time, the moral and physical destroyer. In this regard (inspired by his reading and experience), Rousseau has a deeply classical and anti-Christian time sense. Nature is complete and does not aspire toward a vindication. Like most of the intellectual tradition in which he worked and unlike the later Germans whom he partly inspired, he is profoundly antiteleological. "I judge the order of the world," the Savoyard vicar says, "although I am ignorant of its end."[8] If the image of the clock and the master clockmaker appealed to this *horloger apprenti*, it is the ordered competence of the machine and not its ability to tick away the time of life toward a more perfect future that he appreciated. For Rousseau, the human clock, the clock of peoples, the universal clock all run down; we service them for better or worse. The main thing is to obey the inner clock of nature and to discard our modern European timepieces. In a score of passages he seconded the sentiment of Montaigne: "We are never at home; we are always beyond it. Fear, desire or hope drive us toward the future and deprive us of the feeling and contemplation of what it is."[9]

Rousseau undertakes the puzzle of history from the most antitheoretical of angles: moral self-certainty.[10] Thus he inaugurates a new tendency to moralize history, not merely as a thesaurus of examples – though the Plutarchian strain is prominent – but also as a sequence of states of the human system of faculties, depicted as a kind of challenge – response pattern between sense and sensibility over time. Much of Rousseau's historical equipment is derivative; however, his combinations and emphases have much to do with his peculiar social and existential position, of whose "uniqueness" he was so intolerably well aware. It is scarcely too much to say that Rousseau attempted the first methodical liaison between the sense of world process and individual psychological tensions, a sort of "phenomenology." This is not to link him explicitly with Hegel, whose own *Phenomenology* analyzed a consciousness that achieves concrete social content and passes beyond society in order to judge it, or with the modern neo-Freudians, whose concern with civilization and its neuroses is etched with the data of the industrial epoch and a different picture of man. Nevertheless, these and others can be regarded as Rousseau's successors. His own effort may be viewed as the despairing quest for unity by a man who accepted neither the

Christian correlation of individual and historical destiny in the Last Judgment nor the secularist assurances of natural harmony so much in vogue about him.

Rousseau connected the historical growth of knowledge with the corruption of wisdom. On the opening page of his first published work, this treatment is, to all intents, clarified: "It is not knowledge that I am flaying (*que je maltraire*)... it is virtue I am defending."[11] For our purpose we shall pass over the fact that virtue meant a number of contradictory things to Rousseau.[12] What we should notice is that in establishing this priority Rousseau will reject all knowledge that gets in the way of virtue; he will extol and claim to teach "useful" wisdom. Now, this tradition, which can be traced in post-classical intellectual history from the *Idiota* of Nicholas of Cusa, is far from novel[13]; it is in fact an aspect of that very Enlightenment from which Rousseau takes his leave. But heretofore it had been used chiefly as a rhetorical weapon against Church dogmatism and intolerance – the metaphysics of priestly authority and public obedience – and not to attack the new structures of secular thought. Rousseau's reaction (here we cannot help but be reminded of Book III of *Gulliver's Travels*) is to put both in the same boat. Both, in their instigation of pride and fear, were at war with virtue; both, as Rousseau would later conclude, were even capable of uniting in a single fanaticism bent on capturing the inner citadel of the conscience.[14]

Thus Rousseau announced his characteristically sharp separation of *science and sagesse; science*, at best, is for the few who can "bring together great talents and great virtues."[15] Let the rest leave well enough alone; half-educated people are both slaves to their illusions and promoters of the modern European personality split. Standards of public morality and human values cannot be set to accommodate genius. But it is conceivable that men might be "wise." Rousseau will refer *sagesse* to the seat of virtue, the conscience, which creates no *lumières* but rather activates man's cosmic sense of proportion. He will put moral truth ahead of all speculative fact; or, rather, it will be made the unifying fact, the test and core of all reality. All method in Rousseau flows from this principle. And though his writings are charged with defeatism, he was convinced that he had recovered the way of wisdom: In an age when philosophy had destroyed, he was the single writer who had built solidly.[16]

"Sophisticated" knowledge was to Rousseau a compendium of conceited feints, of false lights, of "ideologies," not, of course, in the modern Mannheimian sense, but with regard to his belief that the fashionable doctrines of his age were simple elaborate projections of *amour-propre*, rooted in the vain wishes of their proponents to be exalted in the esteem of others,[17] above all natural affinities,[18] and to seek unmerited laurels from posterity.[19] Philosophy would sell out mankind for a drop of honor.[20] By contrast, Rousseau believed himself to be the least ideological of men. He was the expounder of "facts" – the pure facts of interior certitude – and not of "systems."[21] "Readers," he exclaims in a characteristic vein, "never forget that he who is speaking is neither a scholar nor a philosopher, but a simple man, a friend of the truth, unprejudiced, without a system...."[22] As such, he was a self-appointed mediator between those carnivorous extremes, the Church and the free-thinking intelligentsia, "mad wolves ready to tear each other to pieces in their rage."[23] His brain teemed with religious peace plans.[24] If he entered the intellectual fracas at all, it was to fly to the aid of virtue, though under compulsion to use the weapons of his adversaries. This is explained at some length in one of the polemics resulting from the *First Discourse*. Here Rousseau compares his reluctant immersion in controversy to the role of St. Justin Martyr and other early Christian apologists: "They had to take up the pen in self-defense."[25]

Effusive and hypersincere, the pose is surely irritating. Rousseau annoyed his acquaintances by staking out a claim in the Parisian world of high culture while roaring at its shallowness and affecting strange habits. Like most other literary *fauves*, this "simple man" used levels of discourse that were far from homely even while he was conceding nothing to the epitomes of modern learning beyond an occasional Bacon or Newton that could be afforded.[26] But if he had committed any fault, it was not by joining in the overbearing pursuit of the *libido sciendi*, but rather by carrying his own self-conscious citizen virtue to absurdities that deepened his misery and abused his personality.[27]

History, never a point of departure for Rousseau (except as the projection of souvenir and chagrin), becomes the problematic means of extending the experience of personal tension to the race as a whole. It is a plot. The plot cannot be halted, because "individuals die, but collective groups know no death. The same passions live on, and their burning hatred, as immortal as the Demon who inspires them, acts always in the same way."[28]

Thus we will not find Rousseau embarked on any effort to systematize the known facts of human social experience for any detached purposes of comparison and conclusion. He will not collect data and ask their meaning. Rather, his procedure will be the opposite: to use conjectural or probable data to verify his own sensitive convictions. "To discover the connections between things," he writes, "I studied the relation of each thing to myself: from the two known terms I learned to find the third; to know the universe through all that might interest me, I had only to know myself."[29] This is, in fact, the singular method of the *Second Discourse*: "... it is history's job, when there is a history, to give the facts linking [two known points]; it is philosophy's job, where history is wanting, to determine apparent facts which can link them."[30] Rousseau's "age of gold" is thus arrived at by "philosophy," which for him is the logic that the heart knows to be true. Regarding the "heuristic" and "naturalistic" aspects of the *Second Discourse*, I shall comment ahead. Here it is sufficient to note that his most extended research into human development is bounded by "facts" joined by a deductively "necessary" sequence of phenomena.

In *Emile*, Rousseau goes as far as to attack the recording of history itself and to defend the notion that our impressions of the past should be used to further sound education, not to cultivate our theoretical knowledge.[31] Here he departs from the more neutral position of a *philosophe* like d'Alembert, who regarded history as a laboratory and wished it to regale posterity with a dispassionate spectacle of virtues and vices.[32] The virtues alone would be best. Though he had earlier argued with regard to the Spartans that virtue is its own reward,[33] he now sees the possibility that history might be used as a Trojan horse to carry virtue within the walls of the enemy. Our conception of the past might be used to challenge its bitter unfolding. Rousseau gives these views quite straightforwardly: "... we have no idea how to draw the truth out of history ... as if it mattered much whether a fact was true, so long as it could furnish useful instruction. Sensible men should look on history as a tissue of fables with very appropriate moral lessons for the human heart."[34] It is another case, another vain hope, of drawing the remedy from the source of evil. And yet Rousseau, almost against his will, has a view of history to propose.

A PHENOMENOLOGY OF DESPAIR

Rousseau's philosophical substructure commands our attention. His point of departure, as is well known, is the empiricist theory of knowledge, the impingement of sense data on latent faculties, and the awakening of the human psychological mechanism to these external bombardments. Empiricism, as opposed to rationalism, has the implicit tendency to develop the historical viewpoint.[35] The logic of the mind is not prefigured. Sense experience gives not a simultaneous manifold of insight but a temporal sequence of indiscriminate events, leading to the combination of simple ideas and the labored ascent from particular to abstract thought. Locke and Condillac were of course not concerned with the question of historical genesis but with the problem of how we know and how far we can know.[36] The Lockean *tabula rasa* is swiftly written on; the Condillacian statue is activated with dispatch. But Rousseau, whose interests were quite different, very properly asked the question, What happens if, because of literal human isolation, the complex ideas of reason are very long in forming? Because he had already decided that the source of evil was in man's social communication and that a core of goodness or innocence lay behind that, he inevitably historicized the problem beyond the requirements of a theory of knowledge.

The symbols used with such dexterity by Rousseau had also been invoked by Locke in his attack on innate ideas. What is the essence of man? Locke had asked; and he had cited reports of savages with tails, women with beards, etc., to show that there were no easy assumptions, that we could know only "nominal" essences.[37] Rousseau, too, was searching for that essence, and he became convinced that one must go far behind anything the philosophers had imagined to judge it.[38] There were two possibilities: a hypothetical brute-man, living in a state that had "perhaps never existed," or a child unexposed to society. Look at a young child, Locke had challenged; where will you possibly discover those famous "innate ideas," especially practical–moral ones?[39] I shall take a child, Rousseau contended; I will discover there no ideas of God, or of duty, or of complex reason, but I will show you freedom from that stain of corruption. Here the concern of *Emile* joins that of the *Discourse*, forming commensurate fields of speculation – similes might be the proper word.

Rousseau, the methodological individualist, uses the human physical unit as his center of reference and extends the analogy to his interpretation of corporate bodies.[40] He writes, "Whoever knew perfectly the inclinations of each individual could foresee all their combined effects in the collective body (*corps du peuple*)."[41] Using a child who stands for all men,[42] Rousseau will be able to rerun a controlled experiment of the *Second Discourse* to prove that salvation is conceivable if society does not close in.

Rousseau accepted the pain–pleasure principle as the instinctual foundation of moral analysis.[43] Indeed, pain and evil are often one for Rousseau. He continued to the end to wonder whether avoidance of all contact that had the chance of being painful (i.e., human contact) was not the best way of settling the question, How shall I act?[44] But for one who believed as he did in the positive and indwelling presence of corruption in the human heart, a simple hedonism could not suffice. For one thing, it could not sustain that sometimes gruesome heroism in which he periodically set so much store. This dilemma runs throughout his writings and adds much to their ambiguity. Where, as in the growth of a child or in the development of the species, there is the preliminary mechanism of moral formation but, as yet, no completed activation of reason and personality, hence no full-fledged imputability, the empiricist procedures are useful: They furnish the original standard of innocence and establish the *why* of evil. But they do not really expose the character of evil itself. Evil may be brought on by external modifications wrought on the *amour de soi* and the subsequent growth of cancerous passions,[45] but "it is the abuse of our faculties which makes us unhappy and wicked. ... Moral evil is incontestably of our doing, and physical evil [pain] would be nothing without our vices, which have made us sensitive to it."[46] Here, a much more traditional and "rationalist" formulation of the problem of evil comes into play, one that depends no longer on the description of the "*lente succession des choses*" but rather on a stationary analysis of the moral equipment of rational man. Shorn of an earlier metaphysics, shorn of the Christian mechanism of sin and grace, shorn especially of the intellectualist disposition to relate virtue to knowledge, Rousseau's position rescues the soul (and the will) from physics in order to make evil and virtue plausible.[47]

Beginning the second volume of the *Confessions* with many gaps in his notes, letters and literal recollection of events, Rousseau comments "I have only one faithful guide upon which I can depend: the chain of feelings which have marked the development of my being...."[48] The journey of "being" measured by the souvenirs of "feeling": This is Rousseau's central notion of historical process. Feeling is "fact," and it reaches over wide distances where *science* cannot follow. If "feeling is existence" and means not the mere activity of the five senses but the inward capacity to judge the truth lying outside, "the distinctive faculty of being able to give meaning to the word *is*,"[49] then presumably no other method is more certain.

Rousseau is not against reason. But reason is highly corruptible; the passions distort it into self-serving "*raisonnements*."[50] Though reason enables us to know the truth, only conscience can make us *love* it, i.e., regard it as an end in itself.[51] But though conscience is indestructible, it flickers feebly in the souls of the mass of modern men, "Europeans" and "bourgeois," "masters" and "slaves," where it is "smothered by [overbearing passions]" and remains only "a word used for mutual deception."[52] Man has forsaken the "errorless" order of nature, and conscience "speaks the language of nature which everything has caused us to forget."[53]

Rousseau believed that he had been spared from these baleful consequences. He stood removed from the whole human spectacle, from brute to philosopher, so that he could take it all in and declare "I have understood."[54] Never had premeditated evil approached his heart[55]; always, even if he sustained the demands of virtue less well than others, he had known how to "return to the order of nature."[56] He had preserved his earliest integrity[57]: His education had modified him but little.[58] He was therefore qualified to speak.

He historicized empiricism; but once he had descriptively brought the system to completion and man had, so to speak, become "man" in the imputable-rational sense, he adopted the severer techniques of seventeenth-century moralism, minus, of course, its visionary theologies. But it is now conscience, and not reason, that sustains truth-seeking action.[59] "Take away the *sentiment interieur*," he declared, "and I defy all the modern philosophers together to prove to Berkley [sic] the existence of [physical] bodies."[60] In a thoroughly "rationalist" manner, the inner certitude establishes the outer fact; but the judgment is now moral (what Rousseau often calls "useful"), not *more geometrico* and theoretical. The *je qui pense* is no longer the philosophical construction of an impersonal and universal reason, but the sensitive *moi qui existe*, the man in whom nature still speaks, in the instance Rousseau himself, by extension the Romantic artist. Truth remains externally grounded, but the subject must "love" it, which is precisely what the philosophers, with their *furor systemicus*, do not do: They aspire to instruct others, not themselves.[61] Even one's own mistake, sincerely arrived at, is worth more than the truth of another's authority.[62] Thus the personal history of a man of unspoiled feeling, fusing with his sensibility honest observations and the impeccable disclosures of men of the stripe of Plutarch and Fénelon, becomes, in some profound sense, a revelation of the millenial shocks of the human condition.

A fragment from the time of the *Second Discourse* discloses, "I studied man in himself, and saw or thought I saw finally within his constitution [Rousseau's customary word for the 'changeable' aspect of humanity][63] the true system of nature, which people have not failed to call my own, even though to establish it I simply removed from man what, according to my demonstration, he had acquired for himself."[64] Finally, at about the time of the writing of *Emile*, the citizen of Geneva makes his view more explicit: "I conceive of a new kind of service to man: to offer them the faithful image of one of them so that they may learn to know themselves."[65] If man is the "*dernière étude du sage*,"[66] Rousseau never doubted that he was the one to undertake it. And he spent much of his last years retracing, dissecting, and transfiguring his own existence, seeking to justify man through his labyrinth of tribulation and neurotic anguish. Compulsively he asked, "Am I alone good and wise among mortals?"[67] This was the "error most to be feared," against which he had warned in *Emile*.[68] But throughout his life Rousseau shuttled between the extremes of feeling archetypically human and wholly unique, an oscillation reflected in his divided loyalty to the common man and the sublime hero, the solidaristic *cité* and the solitary wanderer, Emile and his tutor.

To ignore the subjectivist foundation – and incentive – of Rousseau's research and to attribute to him any "scientific" experimentalism obviously passes wide of the mark. But there is also an opposite error to be avoided: that of taking his positions as simply "metahistorical."[69] According to this view, history becomes a metaphor for moral judgment, a figurative embellishment lightly gowning a diatribe against the gathered evils of contemporary man.

Not all aspects of this problem can be treated here. But there are compelling reasons against the notion that the "facts" of the *Second Discourse* are simply *écartés*.[70] To be sure, "one must not take [these] inquiries. . . for historical truths, but only for hypothetical and conditional lines of reasoning."[71] Conjecture is conjecture, and the reach of the Church is long. Moreover, Rousseau's intellectual milieu had two conflicting tendencies with regard to history, nowhere more sharply defined than in his own writings. In the first place, "nature" was often absolutely opposed to "history" for the purpose of establishing civil liberties based on "natural right" as against prescriptive tyrannies. But, in the second place, "history" was thrown against "revelation" or religious authority in order to loosen the chains of ecclesiastical obedience.[72] The Pelagianizing Rousseau was no less concerned with the latter than the former problem, and he needed history as a tool to deal with it. History, not primordial guilt, was the clue to corruption. It was the immense continuum stretching between man's anthropological innocence and his social misery. Seen in this light, it is improbable that Rousseau intended a relinquishment of fact to fancy. His materials are characteristic of the literary social science of the epoch. Even today (cf. Lewis Mumford), in which artifacts are lacking, the interpreter scruples to imagine or resorts to the evidence of myth and poetry. Kant, a distinguished anthropomoralist himself and a tendentious examiner of Rousseau's arguments, was not incorrect in writing, "The experimental moralist will be fair-minded enough not to classify M. Rousseau's propositions as merely fine fancies before having tested them out."[73]

Rousseau saw historical process both as a deformation that man, first victimized by excessive contact and competition for scarce goods and reciprocal approval, gradually imposed on himself and as a nexus of sociopolitical growth cycles analogous to the human experience of youth, maturity, and decrepitude. There is at least some ambiguity between these two interpretations, encouraging the hesitation between cosmopolitan and particularistic values so profound in his works. It is perhaps convenient to see the first image (forcefully expressed in the *Second Discourse* and in texts like the "Lettre à Philopolis") as a refutation of the most optimistic and "progressivist" strains of the Enlightenment – ideas found especially in the writings of St.-Pierre, Grimm, Turgot and, somewhat more guardedly, d'Alembert. Unlike these men, Rousseau feared the future.

He inveighed often against the sacrifice of the present for uncertain gains.[74] "In the long run all men become similar, but the order of their progress is different," he writes[75]; this is not meant as an encouragement. Perhaps the Russians will overrun Europe, to be followed by the Tartars.[76] Above all, he is concerned to show that *science* is destructive to *sagesse*. In his *Reply to the King of Poland*, he argues thus at considerable length over the field of postclassical European history.[77] The polemic is aimed chiefly at the Church, but Rousseau makes it amply clear that the free-thinking philosophers come under the same rubric. Indeed, he regarded the two camps as even capable of uniting in a single fanaticism, as had happened in China.[78] It is difficult to comprehend why certain historians still persist in claiming Rousseau as "progressivist." *Perfectibilité* is a bitter irony, and "progress" is surely what history is *not* or, better, an expression of the human condition run amok.[79]

The problem of man is thus the problem of evil, not sin, and evil is fundamentally psychic pain. Evil is to be sought for in history among men, not in the mysterious designs of the creation. Theology, among its other abuses, begs the question by making corruption its own cause. Thus Rousseau challenges Archbishop Cristophe de Beaumont: "...I concluded that it was not necessary to imagine man wicked because of his nature, when one could assign the origin and progress of his wickedness."[80] The defense of *Emile* continually verges toward a vindication of the *Discourse on Inequality* because Rousseau saw the two works as complementary explorations of the same issue.

Of course, the *Second Discourse* was not intended as a philosophical disquisition on the development and function of the faculties of the will and understanding. Rousseau shuddered at being called a philosopher. He had a burning message of grievance addressed, as he well knew, not to an academy but to dissolute Parisians and (as he then fancied) respectable Genevans. Thus, when an able scholar of the sources of the work writes, "Rousseau sought to provide the experimental history of societies,"[81] the definition sounds a little cool. Rousseau had a personal heartache. Yet we may agree that Rousseau regarded his research as "*conjecturale mais vraisemblable*...."[82] No other sequence of argument, he felt, could bridge the lacuna between natural goodness and social corruption: "...upon the principles I have just established, it would be impossible to form any other

n that would give the same results or from which I could draw
the same conclusions."[83] Somehow the composite of brute flesh and
corrupted spirit that he perceived in humanity had not just appeared
ready-made, as the legal philosophers seemed to argue. As the child
is father to the man, so are the instincts to the moral and rational
equipment of a later age. Hereupon, Rousseau created one of the most
fruitful but least tempting visions of humanity ever put forward. For
he said straight out that anthropological man was good but that historical man had become perverse, that the development that made
virtue possible had also given rise to supreme viciousness, and that
a history attributable somehow to human violation had become a
decisive blockade to human fulfillment. This denial of the efficacity
of civilization profoundly challenged the later adepts of history who
fell under Rousseau's influence.

Conceivably, this is the first moment in European thought when,
without theological contrivance or scholastic obfuscation, the enormous contradiction of man as moral *and* as historical agent is posed
without diluting either of the two terms to suit the other. Hence-
forward, theodicies and natural orders (style of the Physiocrats) will
not suffice. Man is, as Rousseau believed, both responsible and victimized. The tragic irony is that he has truly become a victim before
becoming responsible. The tormented hope is that his responsibility
could conceivably provide a method of escaping his victimization.

To understand the first point – which is no doubt inseparable from
Rousseau's early-developed feelings about his own destiny[84] – it is
convenient to go back to the *Second Discourse*. Here, the problem
of the generation of evil is most ambiguous. Ideas of morality, we
are told, arise only when habitual and regular contact among human beings is established.[85] Long before this, however, a sequence
of events and modifications is established that foreshadows society,
morality, and corruption. Man is, to begin with, created with potential capacities of will and perfectibility.[86] Thus he is presumably,
even in nature, a creature that begins to reason from acorn to oak in
order to subserve his hunger. But, according to Rousseau, despite his
innate proclivities, he might never have used his will for more than
animal satisfaction, might never have "perfected himself" one iota,
might never have groped his way toward reason and reflection.[87]
On the other hand, nature, "ever the same order...[with] ever the
same revolutions,"[88] cannot be brought to account for engendering

progress. Consequently, there is need for a *tertium quid*, chance, represented generally by Rousseau as "unnatural" modifications in nature.[89] Chance forces man beyond himself to obtain what he needs, to become imaginative and *prévoyant*. It makes him enter into competition with other animals and finally into conflict and cooperation with his own kind; it drives him into unfavorable geographical milieux; it deflects him into specialized ways of life, in which he loses a part of his integrity for the sake of necessity or advantage. Rousseau's recourse to the notion of chance as the instigator or trigger for human development is not only a serious departure from his conviction of the plentitude and "goodness" of nature, but also underscores the profoundly antiteleological implications of this particular work.[90]

Later, when Rousseau comes to lavish his enthusiasm on that point in evolution, that "age of gold" in which many have allegedly achieved a happy balance of need and want, a psychological notch equidistant from reason and instinct, it is again some *"funeste hasard"* that launches the species on its further course.[91]

Spangled throughout this speculative narrative are the minor nodes of varied significance. Man early learns to fear death.[92] He raises himself above the other animals by slaying them and wearing their pelts.[93] Finally, he begins to commingle with his fellows, to compare and judge and to desire preference and approval.[94] It seems that vision itself ("of all the senses the least separable from the judgments of the mind")[95] conspired to betray man into the snares of pride.[96] Starobinski brilliantly interprets the supreme irony with which Rousseau treats the primary form of social contact. That very primitive feast, described with such loving detail in the *Essai sur les origines des langues* and echoes in the *Second Discourse*, which consecrates the birth of love and community, also unleashes the demon of *amour-propre*.[97] Equality is effectively lost when independence is lost: the syllables *aimez-moi* and *aidez-moi* are the first verbal links in man's perennial chains.[98]

The foregoing is not intended to serve as an adequate summary of the *Second Discourse*, even up to the point at which "all our faculties [are] developed, memory and imagination [set] in play, vanity stimulated, reason made active, and mind evolved practically to the limit of its possible perfection," that is to say, at which "rationalism" can be called into being to redress the inadequacy of "empiricism."[99] We are only concerned to ask: Is man imputable for any part of this course of events? And the answer is, of course, that he is not; no more than a child is responsible for bad handling. What has been described is "pre-evil." Man has entered the clutches of development unknowingly; like the gates of Geneva and of the monastery at Turin, the barriers of his retreat have been fatally closed. Against infernal novelty, order is helpless. Human history is the record of the abolition of patterns of order; morality and legality will be the conceivable tools for the recovery of order. But man becomes responsible only after he has been victimized, corrupted in his helpless minority.

Let us repeat: For Rousseau the riddle of life was essentially a question of the journey of "being" interpreted by the instrument of "feeling." The corollary questions that most preoccupied him were: Am I not, as my whole inner being tells me but as the slanders of others deny, spared from evil? How is it that such gross wickedness thrives around me, seemingly perpetuated by the process of social communication itself? From this fundamental *point de départ* we pass to such propositions as "If, as I feel, I am good, than man must be good." *Evil takes time.* The extrapolation of personal experience into the social world is, of necessity, a historical problem. Man has been corrupted in history and is trapped in the consequences of this fact. He has fought free from God and nature and constructed the world from his own (mostly deplorable) desires. What can he then do?

There is a customary answer. In the words of one analysis, "salvation must be immanent in history."[100] This logically follows on what has been said and yet is curiously misstated in terms of Rousseau's vision and beliefs. A fair correction might be put this way: Salvation, if salvation there be (and so as not to give up all human dignity, we must never renounce its possibility), will be a human act against history or, as I put it earlier, an attempt to substitute for the historical pattern of corruption the natural pattern of birth, growth, and decline, which is also the rhythm of the human heart. To say that salvation must be immanent in history comes perilously close to arguing that history (driven by spirit, nature, providence, or whatever) unfolds toward salvation. But by no stretch of the imagination can Rousseau be made to entertain such a notion. The "pre-Kantian" version of Rousseau founders precisely on this most critical of issues: the sense of the world and the destiny of the human race. "Man is very strong when he is content to be what he is."[101] That simple statement, almost tautological, is the foundation for the only kind of "salvation" Rousseau really believed in.

IMAGES OF INTEGRATION

Emile: *The Encyclopedic Image*

If we do not accept either the view that commits Rousseau to a total unconcern with history or that which attributes to him a belief in the goal of historical salvation, we are obliged to locate some middle ground that can illustrate the historical tension of his thought and, if possible, relate his intellectual constructions to a historical context. There are three sequences of examination that I would propose. These could be called the "juridical" perspective of the *Social Contract*, the "customary-defensive" solution of *Corsica* and some of the other writings, and the "comprehensive" demonstration of *Emile*. These sequences are neither discrete nor correlative.

Emile, which Rousseau rightly thought his masterwork, sets what I shall call the pattern of "triplicity" against the "dualism" or "bipolarity" so frequently noted in Rousseau's moral and social doctrines.[102] *Emile*, as we have seen, is correlative to the general problem of human development in time. Controlled education and rampantly uncontrolled history are set against each other to show what Everyman might have been; "chimera" is posed against "prejudice." In Rousseau's case, however, we have both correlation and inversion: "good" education against "bad" history. That is enough to set the Genevan off very clearly from prophets of progress like Lessing, who spoke of the "education of mankind" as if, despite travails, history had proved the good handmaiden of human evolution.

In developing the idea of triplicity I shall recall the earlier distinction made between Rousseau's genetic-historical treatments of the human condition and his purposively rationalist-analytical ones. In the first category fall the *Second Discourse* and *Emile*, although it is important to note that each contains passages of the latter sort. The second category would comprise the first part, generally, of the *Second Discourse*, the *Social Contract*, and parts of the *Emile*, most notably the *Profession de foi*. It is not hard to establish the distinction. The first sort of writing is temporally grounded and displays the triple pattern *instinct–morality–law;* passages of the second type, interludes that "interrupt" the development of man, depend on dual analytical contrasts, respectively those between the real man of nature and the "natural man" of the philosophers, between law and lawlessness, and between the moral and the physical sense apparatus. As for the temporal exemption of the latter group, it is obviously not entirely pristine: Not only are human concepts riveted to time, but the "chimera" of social harmony seems to be pitted against time's very relentlessness.

In the "dual" sections Rousseau's emphasis is on "contrast and analytic exploration"; in the "triple" ones it is on the "*lente succession des choses.*" Of course, except in the case of the *Social Contract,* the divisions I have made are not thoroughly obvious. But it is significant that Rousseau has provided three analytical set pieces that probe the nature of the three major stages of human development. Each man possesses, after all, three interwoven systems of action, the sensual-physical, the moral–spiritual, and the legal–political, depending on the primacy of three stabilizers, the senses and natural instincts, the moral conscience, and the general will. Chronologically developed, each has its role to play in the completed individual. Thus it is no less interesting that each "system's" description–one directly inserted, the others in *précis*–is found incorporated in the structure of *Emile,* a work that is itself keyed on evolution.[103] If the previous suppositions are useful in understanding Rousseau's doctrinal center of gravity, one might conclude that *Emile* is the capstone or "encyclopedia" of Rousseau and that his other writings must be interpreted in the light of this relationship. This is, to be sure, not a magic formula for resolving contradictions that stubbornly resist all academic ingenuity. It may at least be a means of weighing them against each other.

"Make man whole and you will make him as happy as he can be. Give him entirely to the state, or leave him entirely to himself."[104] Rousseau sounded that trumpet call more than once. After all, he preferred being a "man of paradox" to being a "man of prejudice." But he did not intend simply to rest with the impossible. His own preference was for some intermediate solution, as is evident in his dedication of the *Second Discourse* to the magistrates of Geneva and in passages like the following: "Our sweetest [form of] existence is relative and collective, and our true self (*moi*) is not entirely inside us."[105] The word relative here seems to be a kind of rehabilitation of the "*moi relatif*," damned in *Emile* as the agent of *amour-propre*.[106] In any case it sometimes passes unnoticed that *Emile* is not simply a forceful exposition of the individualist side of Rousseau's paradox: Rather, it is an experimental resolution of both terms. The passage in which this is asserted deserves to be exhumed:

> ... what will a man brought up uniquely for himself become for others? If perhaps the double object proposed could be combined in a single one, a great obstacle to man's happiness would be removed with the removal of man's contradictions.[107]

The Rousseauian ideal is, in fact, a man who is both for himself and for others, and *Emile* is intended to show whether such a supposition is possible. Emile will be neither a solitary hedonist fleeing social pain nor a "denatured" Gaius or Lucius, but will somehow bestride both positions. Unlike the unhappy universal victims of the *Second Discourse* (who had no *gouverneur* to ward off the *funestes hasards* of history), he will presumably run the race right. But he will not be natural in the sense that a primitive is "natural": he will be a savage trained to live in cities, because he has learned to *think*.[108] If, lacking a *patrie*, he cannot be a citizen (and it is doubtful that modern Europe would make him a statesman), he will at least be a law-abiding spectator.[109] *Emile*, then, is Rousseau's vision of how nature might be projected into society without the awful wrench that most men suffer.

There are, as I have suggested, three divisions to this work. The first part, containing the education of sense experience and a long analysis of the senses (including the "sixth" *sensus communis* or simple reason) culminates in the third book, in which sense experience creates the basis for the premoral judgments that form the substructure of all knowledge. There the methodology of the relations of the self to the sheerly physical objects of existence is set forth: the symbol is Robinson Crusoe, the motor is *il faut que je vive*.[110] Rousseau never allowed his moral preoccupations to disguise his primary concern over the maldistribution of the physical necessities of life. With the fourth book, "we finally enter the moral order ... man's second step"[111]; the *grande leçon* is the *Profession de foi*. In the fifth book, Emile is initiated to domestic life as well as the consequences of living in a civil community; he will be a parent and a citizen: "... after having considered himself in his physical relations with other beings and moral relations with other men, he has still to consider himself in his civic relations with his fellow citizens."[112]

Man would be defective without his "triplicity," which he develops as he ages but, once grown up, generally uses chaotically, with psychological and physical damage to himself and others. Emile is the "chimera" set against this pessimism: As his styles of order change with increased age, responsibility, and *connaissances*, he will pass smoothly between levels of existence without the cruel contradictions of logic or the millenial disorder that history has spread in its wake. He will be able to suffer the knowledge of evil and remain good. In him the psychological, moral, and political faculties will be perfectly joined. He will be man and citizen without division or mutilation. He will be the person sufficient until himself, farmer, husband, father, companion, bearer of the general will – the "citizen who decides only according to his own judgment"[113] – even *Weltbürger*. Man's true destiny was to be all these things.

Emile, however, is not history, but literature. If not a fiction, it is a fancy; and Rousseau was well aware of this. Although he was undeniably pleased to gain disciples for his precepts, he had no expectation that a world of "natural men" would ever be brought into being. "You can teach the people [all you like]," he replied to a correspondent, "but you will make them neither better nor happier."[114] Rousseau, after all, was not writing a treatise on education, but a curious, original document about *"le bonheur ou le malheur du genre humain,"*[115] an antihistory as well as a proof that evil is neither supernatural nor hereditary.

The child Emile represents the way man might have been if God had brought him out of nature into society instead of abandoning him before the portals of his human vocation. The freedom and responsibility that were to become the cornerstone of Kantian ethics are measured by Rousseau against a deism of despair in which man alone among phenomenal beings has been torn from the natural order. That is why we must, beyond the equality of respect that the conscience enjoins, beyond the mathematical equations of the just *polis*, have tutors, legislators, Wolmars, *"devins du Village,"* Claude Anets, God-surrogates for the precariousness of this earthly life, ordainers, symbols of order.[116] That is why we must also have the cement of custom, levels of autarky, "noble lies," civil religions, and, indeed, the fictional but forceful personality of the state. Above all, we must have, to the extent of the possible, self-control, whether it is the virtue that comes by force or the less demanding routine of the natural, unspoiled inclination.

Emile, the hothouse plant, is thus really a completed perspective, not a reconstructed humanity. He is mankind only until he comes among men. Personalized at last when he is thrust into the world, he then encounters that society of the *Second Discourse* to which his entire education had been a challenge. It proves immediately to be an unequal combat. For all this, Emile does not join the villainous tormentors. Instead, he retreats to the last outpost of psychological endurance, already prefigured in his training,[117] a stoical reduction of voluntary evil to physical law: "Was I not born slave of necessity? What new yoke can men place upon me?"[118] Emile's final answer was evidently also Rousseau's. "The man of nature," he writes, "learns in every affair to bear the yoke of necessity and submit to it."[119] *Emile* is thus Rousseau's essay on truth and failure, man against man, education against history, ending in a freedom that becomes elliptical and repressive. The completed vision is a vision of impasse. A man has been made for a community of equals, but has not found it. Can we imagine a community that is made for men?

The Social Contract: The Image of Legal Morality

In the "triple" scheme of *Emile*, "natural man" is, as we have suggested, an appropriate and balanced system of instinct, morality, and legality. Each element is in its place, and none is precisely paramount because each is indispensable and, alone, each is insufficient. In the whole man these aspects are built upon each other and interwoven in the personality. Nevertheless, both in individual growth and in the psychological act of volition, the moral conscience would appear to have an intermediary role. Developing out of the primary instincts, in which it is evidently latent or "innate" and often described by Rousseau as the "voice of nature," it is also the "love of order" or of "virtue," the prelude to a rational and just system of social relationships.[120] The conscience (assisted by reason) is in some sense the link between nature and spirit. However, this faculty, most precious and important to the human condition, is also the feeblest and most precarious: As the "voice of nature," it is choked off by the unremitting interplay of desire and need; as the "love of order," it is faulted by man's insatiable penchant to have himself preferred above others, to vaunt his glory and his commodities, to tyrannize. In history, nature has been mortgaged by the time morality appears. Conscience was not given to man to ward off expected trials, but rather developed with, and as a result of, those experiences. Conscience conveys the "natural law" to the rare individual who has *sagesse*.

For Emile, educated to be *sage*, the concern of the conscience is central. "The eternal laws of nature and order do exist," he is told. "For the wise man they take the place of positive law; they are written in the depths of his heart by the conscience and by reason: to them he should hearken if he is to be free."[121] But even Emile, as he acquires the responsibilities of parenthood and citizenship, will pass from the tutelary (or meditative) condition of contemplating the love of man to the close-quarters relationship of a community. Here is echoed the tension between Rousseau's highly personal defense of solitude ("When one lives alone, one loves men better; we are attached to them by a tender interest, our imagination develops the charms of society..."[122]) against Diderot's barb ("Only the wicked man lives alone"[123]) and his idealization of the small republic of his birth ("where all the members [should] know each other"[124]). Emile must now learn, despite his *sagesse*, to owe, not to nature, but to his country "the morality of his actions and the love of virtue."[125] The paradox is that in an order without evil (a *siècle d'or*), conscience would not be necessary (indeed could scarcely have developed), whereas in the actual order of men, conscience is ineffective in keeping the peace. In fact, if taken as the rule of general order, it will simply lead to the discomfiture and injury of good men.[126] Instead of the "divine instinct," it is the laws of the land, even the "simulacrum of laws," that "give [a man] the courage to be just, even among the wicked" and "teach him to rule himself." Evidently, this "legal" morality is quite opposed to the earlier "moral" morality whereby, through the agency of conscience, "[man] discovers his real interest in being good, in doing good far from the gaze of men, and *without being forced to by the laws* [my italics], in being just in the sight of God, in doing his duty even if it should cost him his life...."[127] We might, however, explain the paradox in the form of an aphorism: Natural law without sanctions is social impotence; positive law without morality is social injustice. Legal morality is designed to supervene on the arbitrary combat of restraint and self-interest, virtue and *amour-propre*, which is the actual result of free will, by furnishing the sanctions provided for by the artificial, though general, will of a community.

The triple action of *Emile* is thereupon compressed into the dual analytical mechanism of the *Social Contract*, law and lawlessness, state and statelessness. Morality (as analyzed in the *Profession de foi*) does not disappear in this perspective, but it is dispersed between the "order of nature" for which the state attempts to provide a surrogate and the "legal order" by which the popular state, thought a "general will," attempts to condition itself to virtue. For the characteristic "double man" of Christian moralism, the man of instinct and rational morality, Rousseau had already in *Emile* suggested the substitution of a "triple man," the man of instinct, morality, and law. "Triple man" would succeed if he lived in a world of respectful "triple men," but even Emile is made to bear the woe that no such world exists, no world social and natural at the same time, no *"heureuse Salente,"* no "general society of mankind."

Consequently, Rousseau returns to a juridical "duality" in which, however, the postulates of morality have been subsumed, collectivized, and turned into a "general will"[128] whose superiority over the personal conscience as a guarantor of order is established both by its physical power to coerce through the consensus of the community and through its psychological power to divert man's outer directedness away from the mirror of preference and vanity and toward the common task.[129] Here Rousseau suppresses the ideal of personal morality, not because it is formal, as in Hegel's general critique of Kant's *Moralität*, but because it is feeble.

The sense of Rousseau's juridical analysis is expressed particularly by two well-known passages from the *Social Contract*. In the first of these the duality is dramatically presented:

This passage from the state of nature to the civil state produces in man a very remarkable change, substituting justice for instinct in his conduct, and giving his actions the morality that they previously lacked. Only then, with the voice of duty replacing physical impulse and law replacing appetite, is man, who up to that time had been only self-regarding, forced to act on different principles and to consult his reason before listening to his inclinations.[130]

In the second passage, the reason for that compression is made clear:

That which is good and in conformity with order is so by the nature of things and independent of human convention. All justice comes from God, he alone is its source; but if we could receive it from so high up, we would need neither government nor laws... for want of natural sanction the laws of justice lack force (*sont vaines*) among men....[131]

One may very easily put Rousseau in contradiction here by inquiring how, if divine justice (natural law) is not merely empty speculation, the transfer from instinct to morality could result solely from the political act. And of course the answer must be that the genetic and analytical strains of his thought are pitted against each other at this point. Some legal analysts have exploited this confusion to insist that the Rousseauian pact of association is null and meaningless if it represents a common undertaking of premoral beings.[132] But it must be recognized that Rousseau has said elsewhere that a (prepolitical) *société commencé* possesses a *"moralité commençante"*[133] and that moral relationships begin, in effect, with the act of visual comparison: "As soon as a man compares himself to others he necessarily becomes their enemy.... There is the primitive and radical contradiction...."[134] We can see the confusion somewhat by presuming that Rousseau intended not to place the origins of moral life within the state by mere rhetoric, but to insist that only the bonds of political association could create the structural guarantee for a *"moralité bonne."* We should remember, too, that he was concerned to prove, against Diderot, that political society was a pure convention, not a natural development.

The *Social Contract* is not history but logic. Indeed, it denies all explanations of social conditions, being rather an explanation of how the maximum of juridical and moral integrity (of individuals) could be preserved in the light of those conditions. Still, it has some peculiar connections with the historical perspective. Like *Emile*, it is an antihistory, flinging not only the standard of political right but the accusation of delinquent development against virtually all governments, despite its pragmatic passages and protective overtones of abstract discourse. It implies that if there is no public virtue, this is a direct consequence of the way men have formed their political associations. It is a gloomier antihistory than *Emile* because, far from assuming the image of uncorrupted man, it takes as its point of departure the precivil (or, by extrapolation, "prelegitimate") "war of

all against all" described in the *Second Discourse* and, by implication, transfers this war to the level of political communities rather
than that of the mere strivings of individuals to be preferred.[135] That
leads, paradoxically, to both greater abstraction and greater realism.
The entire marathon of humanity is not to be problematically rerun,
only its darker half.

Even this "squaring of the circle" does not escape from the burden
of history. The remarkable book I, Chap. ii of the *Geneva Manuscript*
("De la société générale du genre humain") attempts to phase out
the "philosophical" history of the *Second Discourse*, which had suggested prerational and prepolitical nodes of order and had invoked accident to account for their demolition. Now man, clearly destined for
civil society by a virtually Hobbesian necessity, suffers only enough
of a break with isolated brutishness as is required to define a life-
or-death choice. Gone is the cherished "age of gold," "...always a
condition foreign to the human race, either for our having failed
to recognize it when it was possible to enjoy it, or for having lost it
even when it has been possible to know it."[136] This delight forsworn,
man is now compelled to choose the civic order that can alone inspire him to conscientious virtue, "the most delicious feeling of the
soul." No doubt there is a wrench here, elaborated more finely in
Rousseau juge de Jean-Jacques, between ideals of logic and emotion,
duty and innocence. But, as Emile is told by his tutor, "lawfulness
(*le droit*) does not bend before human passions"[137]; and it is "droit
politique" that Rousseau is intent on establishing. It is not so much
that Rousseau has arbitrarily demolished the *siècle d'or* (whose legacy
he will continue to discover in the solid independence of small peasant communities), but that he has recognized the gap of awareness between the natural *per se* and the reflective yearning for the natural.[138]
The simple soul, absorbed in his routine, cannot step back from it to
measure his felicity. Memory and imagination, those sources of our
hopes, fears, and woes, also secure what pleasures are to be had from
life. And, as Rousseau writes with reference to Emile's "*sensibilité
naissante*" of the happy paleolithics, "There are ages in human life
which are made so as never to be forgotten."[139] The adolescents of
the world had never acquired a consciousness of their fortunate years
but we can stand on the high ground of experience and regret in order
to commemorate such blessedness, which we still sense in "fertile
fields," "festivals," and "country games": "People treat the golden

age as a chimera, and so it will be always for the man whose heart and taste are spoiled.... What then must be done to bring it back to life? A single, but impossible thing: to love it."[140]

It has been suggested that Rousseau failed to include *Geneva Manuscript* Book I, Chap. ii in his final version of the *Social Contract* because, as a personal polemic waged with Diderot over the universality of reason and the rational accessibility of a standard of natural right, it seemed out of place in a deductive essay on *"droit politique."* In any case, by the time we reach *Social Contract* Book II, Chaps. vii–x (also included in the *Geneva Manuscript* in a single large chapter called "Du peuple á instituer"), we are resolutely back in the realm of history and all too aware of the catalog of limitations that the *"succession des choses"* imposes on the ideal of civic order. Now it would seem that just communities are not simply vaulted out of a crumbling world of nature in which dependence has caused men to pool their strength; they require a deliberate pause between socialization and legislation, no longer represented as a "wrench" between instinct and duty, brutishness and reason, but as a transformation of natural simplicity into the rational–legal order. Hereupon, Rousseau cites two cases: the Russians, who have been "civilized" ineptly and too early,[141] and the Corsicans, who, alone among the peoples of Europe, are ripe for institutions of freedom. With these examples, the shadow of history once again crosses the monochrome landscape of *"droit politique."* We are thus prepared by the most corruscating sort of antihistory for the historical limitations of political justice as Rousseau conceived it.

Corsica: The Customary-Defensive Image

This third pattern of possibility, which I have labeled customary defensive, is Rousseau's most consistent effort to come to grips with the historical problem of a "good" political development. It is his most tangible. The customary-defensive solution is prefigured by the historical intrusions on the *Social Contract*. The key is to be found in a displacement of emphasis from virtue to habit and from ethics to natural morality, indeed from institutions to custom. This shift of emphasis is, in itself, a source of prime Rousseauian confusion, because we are given variously to understand that custom as unquestionable attachments from nature[142] and yet that, no less than the work of formal legislation, it must be the concern and challenge of that superior and misty figure who forms a people and, in Rousseau's term, "denatures" it.[143] We are left uncertain as to whether, like the austere, political virtue described elsewhere by Rousseau, it is a socialized transformation. Probably it was vaguely intended to have connections with both, in a manner that Rousseau never made very clear. We see, for example, in one passage that it has appeared as a substitute for moral conscience: "The law acts only externally, governing the actions; custom (*les moeurs*) alone penetrates within and directs the operations of will."[144] Custom, according to the *Social Contract*, is the fourth and most important sort of law[145]; by extrapolation, it may even underlie that so-called *voix céleste* that teaches each citizen "to act according to the maxims of his own judgment and to avoid being in contradiction with himself."[146] "When philosophy has once taught a people to despise its customs," we are told, "it soon discovers the secret of bypassing its laws."[147] But custom is apparently, in the perspective of the *Social Contract*, as artificial an acquisition as positive legislation itself: That sort of people fit for legislation is "one which has neither customs nor superstitions deeply rooted."[148] It is Lycurgus who made the Spartans and Moses who created the Jews.

Nonetheless, we get a quite different picture from Rousseau's treatment of the *Project for Corsica*. Here the anteriority of custom to law and the connection between nature and custom is emphasized, and the trick is apparently to bring a "natural" people unmutilated into the political world. It is very much as if a colony of *siécledoriens*, threatened not by *funeste hasard* but by the proximity of civilization, was enjoined to freeze its patterns of social behavior in defense against outside contamination

In hypothesizing this historical liaison between the natural and the political by means of the bridge of socialization (a people "already bound by some tie of origin, interest or convention"[149]), Rousseau permits himself a reminiscence about the destiny of the early Swiss. In the "Lettre à d'Alembert" he had first painted their idyllic portrait: "In [his] youth, on the outskirts of Neufchatel..." he had seen "...a mountain entirely covered with dwellings, each in the midst of its land, so that those houses, as equally spaced as the fortunes of their owners, at once gave the numerous inhabitants of that mountain the inner contemplation of withdrawal and the charms of society."[150]

The *Corsica* manuscript further explains that "this people...had no virtues because, having no vices to conquer, it acted well at no cost; it was good and just without even knowing what justice and virtue were."[151] This is the model for the Corsicans. There are lessons for them, too, because whereas once "the uniformity of [Swiss] life took the place of law," it later happened that contact with other peoples "made them admire what they should have despised," inaugurating *amour-propre*, inequality, and corruption. In Rousseau's judgment, "the Corsicans are still almost in the sound and natural state."[152] Before the fate of the Haut-Valaisians catches them, they must cross the frail bridge to organized political life, because, in words written for another context, "there is no longer time to draw us outside of ourselves, when once the *moi humain* concentrated in our hearts takes on that contemptible activity that absorbs every virtue...."[153]

Whether or not Rousseau really imagined himself as a legislator for Corsica is a moot point. He had both misgivings and temptations: After all, he was the man who could find his own traits in both the patient and the healer, in Saint-Preux, and in the mentor of Emile.[154] He seems to have hedged the issue in his own mind:

...in order to live quietly there, I made up my mind to abandon, *at least to all appearances* [my italics], the work of legislation, and in order to repay my hosts in some measure for their hospitality, to confine myself to writing their history on the spot, with the reservation of quietly acquiring the information necessary to make me of greater use to them, if I saw any prospect of success.[155]

Nonetheless, the fragments of his *Project* resound with the hope of taking advantage of the opportune historical moment to thrust this people outside of European history and into a "natural" history all its own. And despite frequent references to republican Rome (especially where economic policy is discussed), the grave and spectral virtues of antiquity will not be the pole star for the Corsicans:

I will not preach morality to them, I will not prescribe virtues for them; but I shall put them in such a position that they will have virtues without knowing the word, and that they will be good and just, scarcely knowing what justice and goodness are. [156]

In short, the Corsicans, in their isolation from the wickedness of Europe, are to be much like Rousseau himself in his flight from "intolerance and fanaticism," children of an order in which nature is not so much supplanted but strengthened by political institutions: "Noble people, I have no wish to give you artificial and systematic laws of man's invention, but to bring you back beneath the laws of nature and order, which alone command the heart and do not tyrannize the will."[157] To "have virtues without knowing the word" is to surrender the boon of virtue for the sake of immunity to vice and thus to surrender conscience; to be "beneath the laws of nature and order" is somehow to recapture that symmetrical distance between instinct and reason that verified man's orderly place in the cycles of nature and yet already bespoke his privileged position in the creation. Custom now becomes the spring of the will, and the will is so conditioned that it ceases to aspire beyond the rectitude of custom. Like de Tocqueville, Rousseau saw societies essentially regulated "by the feelings, the beliefs, the ideas, the habits of heart and mind of the men who compose them,"[158] not by the documentary passion of recurrent constitutional assemblies. "There will never be a good and solid constitution unless the law rules over the hearts of the citizens," he reminded the Poles.[159] The passion for order had to come first, and that conviction was essentially rooted in a series of attitudes related to the will and sometimes called custom, a core of communal being, "which should be tampered with only with extreme circumspection."[160]

But the problem is more complicated than this. Rousseau stood halfway between believing that customs, developed in a *"nuit des temps,"* were a primitive substrate for positive law and order and that there was a genuine necessity for legislators, "gods on earth," who from mysterious depths of skill dispensed law and custom at prime historical moments, miraculously forming *"peuples"* from mere *"peuplades."* The one feeling derived from Rousseau's own historical perception of "rustic feasts," "village games," and "joyful harvest," the other from his indebtedness to Machiavelli, Montesquieu, and, above all, Plutarch and the classics. He attempted to join both visions by seeing in the patriotic festival and other exhibitions of civic solidarity the emotional remnant – or should one say, equivalent? – of a primal and spontaneous community and by formulating a theory of *"droit politique"* that would reassert men's independence vis-à-vis each other while binding them equally beneath laws of general adoption and application. The essay on Poland, particularly, is full of the first preoccupation.

Rousseau was torn between a conviction of the need for order and authority in the light of the fundamental weakness of man and an overpowering sense of the corrupt inclinations of authority measured against the fundamental goodness of man. The solution then was to imagine a type of alien authority that disinterestedly created order under which a still uncorrupted man could then be placed and could, within limits of natural devolution, prosper. Such is the situation of the legislator and the inchoate *"peuplade."* Unquestionably, the parallel with the tutor and the child, reinforced by the classical correlation of education and laws and by Rousseau's own wishful reflections on his early years, affected this portrait. Nor should we fail to notice that, like the eighteenth-century *deus absconditus*, legislator and tutor withdraw from their creation once it has been completed, leaving behind a human product of custom, law, and education that it is now man's responsibility to guide and preserve.

Rousseau's demigods are, in one sense, creators but, in another, interpreters and intermediaries. Despite the mathematical clarity with which Rousseau presented his either/or images of "man and citizen," we have seen that his real preference was for a combination of the social and personal that would avoid contradiction, a *"moi relatif"* untinged with *amour-propre*. This required the assimilation of the independence of nature to the mutuality of communal life. In effect, his demigods of authority redirect nature into new patterns of order rather than abolish it completely. To speak of the antithesis of nature and political society in Rousseau is to recognize the deep dilemma between independence and community that underlay his thoughts. But to coronate this antithesis as his last word is to misconstrue him. In this regard, the term denature is unfortunate because it suggests dehumanization rather than the humanizing redirection of a corruptible impulse. The more accurate slogan, also used by Rousseau, is that art makes reparation of the evils consequent to the breakdown of the natural order.[161] This is the task of the mysterious figure of authority: to ensure the continuity of nature in a new perspective, to create, if one pleases, a "second nature," but not one that is a substitution for that older and more fundamental principle, but rather one that saves it from its own cumulative and destructive defects. The old Adam is not forsworn, for it comes again to birth at every moment of human time, the carrier at first of helplessness and soon thereafter, if unchecked, of vanity and license, but also of those imperishable assets that bad society stifles, independence and innocence.

Conscience is an individual affair upon which one might construct a society of the wise or a republic of the just. Custom, on the other hand, achieves – or might achieve – the bond of a people who share an "origin, interest or convention." Made formal in the state, it is nevertheless also a link with nature, drawing, as Rousseau thought he perceived among the Corsicans, the "simplicity of nature" into the system of "needs" inaugurated by society. If it be argued that Rousseau vaunted ethnic particularism as against the ideal of "natural" cosmopolitanism, the "general society" proclaimed by the intellectual republic of Europe of his day, it should be remembered that he admired the particularism of rural Switzerland, of Corsica, and, later, of Poland, because he believed them close to the spirit of the popular and "natural," to feasts, rites, and occurrences of millennial origin, not because he rejected the criterion of "humanity" so abundantly acknowledged in *Emile*. Politics, for Rousseau, meant making a tradition out of nature by giving civic foundations to a once-spontaneous enterprise. The wise legislator shapes his materials as he can. But where intolerable inequality presides over the political act, the state will be similarly misshapen and thus no happy meeting of art and nature.

Unlike later theories that owe much to Rousseau's moral–juridical analysis, this presupposes no purposeful unfolding of the state toward goals of justice and freedom, no explicit destiny for socialized man to develop his culture and intellect, no meeting of the nations in a cosmopolitan world order. Rather, there is an insistent correlation between origins and ideals, isolation and innocence, wisdom and immobility, and politics and the natural life cycle. Far from "standing on the shoulders of the ancients" or striving for a perfectibility in the species, men and peoples run the same race over and over, mostly for the bad; and if they transmit any accumulated knowledge to descendants, compatriots, or foreigners, it is almost inevitably corrupt. Though each life is a fresh start, the bad currency tends to drive out the good. Circumstances might save Corsica from this horror of history; she might meet her "salvation in time." But it will involve putting her in a museum.

Having with some care explored three approaches of Rousseau to the question of evil in history, of which the first probably represents his most personal and comprehensive treatment, we are better able to savor his pessimism and to disown critical attributions of "progressivism." He composed lengthy antihistorical treaties with flourish and genius in order to demonstrate that human development was, for the most part, a comfortless anomaly. What, then, could one do? Remake humanity or human institutions? Substitute a "good history" for a bad? *Recommence à zéro*? Scarcely, in view of the prevailing forces. In the present state of morality, anarchy was more to be feared than injustice. In the end, there is no answer but perseverance and counterpressure against the vortex. The "*moi*" must move within the sphere of its competence. If no wider field of expansion can be imagined, it becomes a task to place oneself "in order," "adding no other chains to those which nature and the laws impose."[162] In effect, the only barrier to history was order itself.

Order and Disorder

"What sweeter felicity," asks the Savoyard vicar, "than to feel ordered in a system where everything is good?"[163] Although the vicar's remark commends the divine order, which is, for Rousseau, effectively the order of nature, here is a motto for all the researches of this brilliant and disturbed man into the requirements for human peace and well-being. Order, however, did not have the fundamental meaning of authority, but of justice.[164] Rousseau indeed extolled superhuman symbols of authority that could create order or cure disorder, but he was far from cherishing human authority as such, except when, as "love of virtue," it redressed violations. Justice, on the other hand, carried overtones of equality and cohesiveness, of harmony and integrity within a given sphere of operation, as well as the fear of problematic extension in time or space. For Rousseau, there were essentially concentric circles of order, most valid at the greatest circumference, most intense and reliable at the narrowest.

If history is the record of *perfectibilité* and, more especially, of "*la prévoyance...* which bears us ceaselessly beyond ourselves... the true source of all our wretchedness,"[165] order is the idea that reasserts "nature" or attempts to reorient history to a natural rhythm. Order is that style of human affairs in which reason becomes possible, because reason's determinations are essentially directed toward a static field of analysis in which the components tend to remain as given. Where order prevails, life can be encompassed, worked out, and savored.[166] In this sense, Rousseau is surely a rationalist.

Once more, Rousseau's anxiety for order mounts from the depths of his personality and experience. Throughout his life, but acutely in his later years, Rousseau was tortured both by the sense of time, which played on his memory and imagination, and of space, which both affronted his ego with limits and drew it out to unsafe distances.[167] To these issues was intimately related his groping for unity or a center of order, akin to Paradise, where, as he put it, "...I shall be me without contradiction, without division,"[168] and to his notion of psychological balance, defined as "the perfect equalization of power and will."[169]

Rousseau's final position, "less a morality of action than of abstinence,"[170] was less a solipsism than an infinite retreat. Projecting his own consciousness upon the world, he did not aspire to draw the entire world back into the ego. He still found time to praise virtue, even if he could not rise to it, or the solidarity of games and feasts, even if he felt alone.[171] In *Emile* he had written, "Everywhere that there is feeling and intelligence there is some moral order. The difference is that the good man orders himself in relation to the whole, and that the wicked man orders the whole in relation to himself. The one makes himself the center of all things; the other measures his radius and holds himself at the circumference."[172] Rousseau's own radius had finally shrunk to a point where center and circumference were congruent, where memory and imagination had fallen in on the undifferentiated moment; the man himself had become the god of a miniscule cosmos.[173] By his earlier definition, Rousseau had passed beyond good and evil.

But his literary career had been a frantic groping for other solutions of order: the private and eternal order of God "who can because he so wills"[174]; the order of nature "whose first motions are always right"; the hypothetical order of primal, instinctive man; the order of the *siècle d'or*, equidistant between reason and instinct; the societal order of being "just and virtuous without knowing the meaning of justice and virtue"; the "denatured" order of the patriotic *polis*; the domestic order of the Wolmars at Clarens; the juridical order of "laws above men"; the precarious moral order of the very wise; and the wistful order of the "*homme nouveau*," *pret à tout*, even slavery in Algiers; even that facetious but meaningful "*Hobbisme le plus parfait*";[175] not to mention those particularistic solutions for societies at middrift in their political life. For every kind of order there was a price to be paid – ignorance, self-limitation, psychological sublimation, arrested development, inaction, the chains of society, or the forfeit of reason – but there was the consolation of feeling intact, sustained at a point of balance and not driven in two directions.

This does not mean, however, that order was a pick-and-choose proposition. One did not, could not, go back to superannuated solutions.[176] Nor could one wish to sacrifice the hazards of moral life for a subhuman security. History and consciousness denied that alternative.[177] The destructive liberty of the savage or of the child is curtailed by his weakness; but our only hope is to curtail it with a reason that is too often fatally corrupted. In view of this situation, and because man is now just as destined to live in a community as if his instincts had commanded it, Rousseau found himself hesitating between logical and psychological answers to the problem of order. The logical answer, prefiguring Kant and his successors, is in the alchemical transformation of the law of freedom into a law of necessity:

If the laws of nations, like those of nature, could have an inflexibility which no human force could ever defeat, man would then return to a dependence on things; in the republic there would be combined all the advantages of the natural and civil conditions; to the liberty that keeps man from vice would be added the morality that raises him to virtue.[178]

This is what Rousseau called squaring the circle. He had no more confidence in its achievement than would a geometer. Nor is the logic of the proposition really very evident once one plunges beneath its brittle "metaphysical" veneer. The cruel metaphorical play on the triple meaning of the word "law" (physical, moral, juridical), unhappily a temptation in the major European languages and undoubtedly an important clue to the Western mind, has encouraged both noble and evil ideological consequences that need not be spelled out here. In effect, one is trying to correlate forms of order that are, respectively, natural and coercive (necessary), natural and noncoercive (injunctive), and artificial and coercive (admonitory and punitive). It is difficult to see how a "dependence on things" can be moral or how "the liberty that keeps man from vice" (self-sufficiency) can be combined with "the morality that raises him to virtue" (society, implying the eternal possibility of vice).

Rousseau would seem to be saying that we escape moral harm by escaping moral relations. But we must remember that Rousseau's natural order is more an animism than a mechanism (as indeed was Diderot's). "Mortals," he could exclaim, "you are not abandoned; nature lives on."[179] This "vast ocean of nature"[180] in which we draw breath adds beauty, tranquillity, and innocence to the diurnal course of the Newtonian cosmos; *"douce félicité"* softens the acute angles of the geometer's exercise. Above all, Rousseau postulates kinds of order in which there is some vitalizing principle, not merely an automatic conjugation of the "private vices–social virtues" variety. They have no "laws of motion" but are the antithesis of that relentless, if self-contained, mobility. "The great maxim of Madame de Wolmar," we read, "is to favor no changes in condition, but to contribute to the happiness of each one in his own."[181] In *Emile* he comes down hard on the same point.[182] "Because of my attachment for [your constitution], I would have wished that nothing could change it," he tells the Genevans.[183] His ornate catalog of exaggerative compliments in the Dedication of the *Second Discourse* – freedom, longevity, staticity, virtue, modesty, piety, friendship, gentleness of climate – come probably as close to his psychological center of gravity as any passage written before this final embitterment.[184] Here, time is domesticated but not assassinated, space is restricted but not driven within the ego, custom and will, law and liberty are harmonzied. *"Puisse durer toujours...!"* He could exclaim. But the search in the crevasses of history had turned up only a chimera.

"[Man] realizes form," wrote Schiller, "when he creates time, and contrasts the changeable with the permanent, the manifoldness of the world with the eternal unity of his ego; he gives a form to matter when again he abolishes time, maintains permanency in change, and subjects the manifoldness of the world to the unity of his ego."[185] Despite Rousseau's acknowledged role as midwife to the Romantic movement, he had never believed that man could do so much. Should man's strength ever carry him to the brink of mastering historical time, nature would not then accept the imprint of the ego's newfound unity; rather, the ego, historically torn between capacity and desire, would be healed by glimpsing the true shape of nature. Man might conceivably become just and wise – an artist – by submitting to his reintegration, but not by assembling nature in forms to satisfy his expansive will. Rousseau and Schiller agree on the necessity for a recaptured harmony of art and nature. Where they differ – and it is the whole distinction between a future open to man's willful designs and one foreclosed by the accumulated travesties of *perfectibilité* – is in the plausibility of the attempt. Yet Rousseau's very doctrines would prove a dynamite to force the future, whereas Schiller later attempted to cover his ears from that explosion.

Rousseau came in his turn to be possessed by history and modern factionalism. Split away from their precarious private core, his doctrines led in oblique directions and, in the opinion of some post-Marxian critics, led nowhere – except to an intangible "petty bourgeois" or preindustrial solution already denied in advance by forces of change embedded in the Old Regime.[186] On the other hand, Rousseau's radical protest lodged deeply in the febrile sensitivities of a whole younger generation of intellectuals and *roturiers*, aspirants for the discordant acquisitions of respect, autonomy, power, and order – for mastery over a history that, they thought, had cheated them blind.

Daniel Mornet writes of the *collèges* toward 1770: "Public exercises testify that history is becoming more than a chronology or a pretext for moral sermons. One discovers a real curiosity about customs and a taste for thinking about the life of nations and governments."[187] He is speaking roughly of the graduating class of the Brissots and the Robespierres. According to the testimony of these men and many others, it was Rousseau who laid the groundwork for this would be action. Rousseau stepped beyond the Enlightenment – beyond reason into feeling. Shortly after his death he began his conquest of the France that had spurned and persecuted him. Robespierre received the living word from his lips in 1778[188]; but the Jean-Jacques mania was no respecter of causes, and Marie Antoinette and her children accomplished the pilgrimage to Erménonville in their turn.[189] Rousseau taught men that they were "good" apart from social station and intellect, paradoxically good in both their independence and solidarity.[190] These lessons come, of course, from *Emile* and the discourses; Mornet "has not managed to collect ten pieces of evidence concerning readers who, before 1789, received a strong impression from [the *Social Contract*]."[191] It is only after the first shock of liberty that the political Rousseau is "discovered," by means of Sieyès, Marat, and others.

According to Rousseau, history blocked justice because it carried man expansively away from nature in a fatal reciprocity of moral and physical demand and satisfaction, spreading mastery and slavery in its wake. This corruption was itself superimposed on a natural life cycle of peoples, measured by political criteria and modeled on the biological career of the individual. Somehow, Rousseau believed, the viciousness of man could be overcome only in the youth of his undertakings and then only through extraordinary tutelage. He had, however, severely questioned the legality of all political relationships, and had remarked that peoples were sometimes granted a *"seconde naissance"*: Sparta and Rome among them.

That is the script by which the most fervent Montagnard ideologists understood the Revolution that they had to make. They would return France to "nature" and to a *seconde naissance*. "If nature created man good," declared Robespierre, "he must be brought back to nature."[192] It is not simply a juridical demand. Saint-Just, though his political ideals varied considerably between 1791 and 1794, played unceasingly with similar notions: "... an enslaved people which suddenly emerges from tyranny will not return to it for a long time, because freedom has found new, uncultured, violent souls...."[193] In short, where Rousseau had seen masters and slaves, the leaders of the Terror proclaimed the hidden "natural" of a French people ready to burst from ancient bondage. Though "despotism corrupts...the most intimate feelings of the oppressed" and though "a people is critically situated when it passes suddenly from slavery to freedom, when there is contradiction between its customs and habits and the principles of its new government," "the [French] *peuple*, that large, industrious class... is untouched by the causes of depravation which has doomed... those of a superior condition.... It is closer to nature."[194] In Robespierre's rhetoric, it is as if Rousseau's legendary Corsicans had been transplanted to Picardy and the Ile de France. And as Rousseau never failed to enjoin isolation on the peoples of his choice – for the sake of solidarity and justice – so Robespierre put forward a similar barrage of arguments again the Girondin appetite for war and cosmopolitan fraternity in 1792.[195] To use a Thucydidean metaphor, the Robespierristes remind us of Sparta after the Persian wars; by contrast, the Brissotins are Alcibiadean. Or, taking a modern parallel, they were respectively the Stalinists and Trotskyites of their own revolution.

Granting this link with Jacobin and *sans-culotte* lyricism, there is definitely something about Rousseau's concatenation of moods that evades the equation. In the end, he stands alone. There is a vast distance, not to be measured by decades or kilometers, between the Isle of Poplars and the Panthéon, between Arcadia and the Hôtel de Ville. That something is pathos, passivity, and regret. It is a matter of non-expectation. Rousseau's adieu to his century was not in favor of the next, but in favor of a *temps mort* or a *nulle part*, a place of childhood denied by history, denied by the fate of growing old. "Will," writes the philosopher Louis Lavelle, "converts the future into a sensuous present, while memory converts the past into a spiritual present." Further, "will is, in a certain sense, the reverse of memory; it makes a perception out of the image, just as memory makes an image out of the perception."[196] Despite his defense of the will, Rousseau is fundamentally an apostle of the memory: his perceptions become images. Still, he is at a point of tension, trying to resolve the contradictory triads of "past-memory-regret" and "future-will-desire" into a perfect present, in which , as he puts it, "each moment is a perpetual beginning." Sociologically, this attitude has a good deal of resemblance to what Georges Gurvitch has labeled the sense of "erratic time": "...a time of uncertainty par excellence where contingency is accentuated...the present appears to prevail over the past and the future, with which it sometimes finds it difficult to enter into relations."[197] Rousseau's political disciples of the Montagne will take the decisive step of transforming "memory" into "will" across the a temporal *kairos* of the "recommencement" (whose aptest symbol is the Revolutionary calendar). And this will mean, once the deed is accomplished, a future; with that future a past; and with the past a history, a new "*nuit des temps*," new heroes, a new *cité*. In a matter of time, that history can join the "old" history that has never ceased. Progress can achieve a double boon. But Rousseau himself did not cut this Gordian knot; he did much to call attention to it.

CONCLUSION

Rousseau positioned man against history, in one sense, and, in still another, he placed man in a history he could not summon or command. That much connects him with current moods and problems. His sensitive communication of the experience of human disruption touches a world in which millions have felt disrupted in the two centuries since he put down his pen. We are no longer optimists, even in the Kantian sense: The diversity of the world and the enormity of our acts have oxidized the apodictic moral law. The roughshod upward crusade of Fichte is not ours. Neither is the turbulent but sovereign security of Hegel. We look around in the fascinating junkyard of our artifacts and we try to find ourselves. For this task Rousseau is an eminent companion.

Rousseau did not solve problems, but he transmitted some of the most important ones across the debris of history in works that we read for insight more than for system. He did not possess formal philosophical equipment, although he intellectualized basic notions far more than he cared to admit. He was frankly a neurotic, but he was also a sociological neurotic of the most productive kind. His ideology is so subtle and, in operational terms, contradictory that it has founded no party, especially no *internationale*. Unlike Burke, he preferred "chimeras" to "prejudices;" unlike the idealists he despaired of their realization, even in an ethical time beyond sensual time.

The ruler can learn from Rousseau that his legitimacy is at best precarious. The subject can learn that he owns by right a modest portion of the judgment that makes all rulers nervous and that he owes a modicum of respect to his fellows, who participate equally in the judgment. The democrat can find here the substantial psychological basis for his principles. If democracy becomes a merely passive reflex – a parody of what Constant would later call modern liberty – Rousseau is on hand to berate. If cosmic Whiggery ("modernization," development, etc.) carries us away, he is there to warn. Rousseau directs us neither toward Hobbesian fatality nor toward the hypocrisy of secular sainthood, but he does focus in a profoundly original way on the problem of how men act, usually less than well, and how they cause each other to suffer in the social order. All this is to say that, in an age of change, an age of enormous complacency and enormous claims, Rousseau may have been the greatest realist of all.

ENDNOTES

1 Not by his natural forces; cf. *Discours sur l'Inégalité*, O.C. III, 135–6. Citations from Rousseau are identified as follows: O.C. = *Oeuvres complètes* (eds. Bernard Gagnebin and Marcel Raymond, 3 vols.,

Paris, 1959–64); Vaughan = *Jean-Jacques Rousseau: The Political Writings* (ed. C.E. Vaughan, 2 vols. Cambridge University Press, 1915); C.G. = *Corréspondance générale de Jean-Jacques Rousseau* (ed. Théophile Dufour, 21 vols., Paris, 1924–32); *Émile* = *Émile ou de l'éducation* (eds. François and Pierre Richard, Paris, 1961`).

2 *Emile*, IV, 342.

3 *Contrat social (première version)*, II, ii, O.C. III, 288. The "general association" refers to the "natural socialability" theorized by Diderot in his article "Droit naturel." See *Contrat social*, I, i, O.C. III, 352.

4 Gustave Lanson, *Histoire de la Littérature Française* (Paris, 1895), p. 770. For a modified version of the argument, see Ernst Cassirer, *The Question of Jean-Jacques Rousseau* (trans. Peter Gay, Principia, Bloomington, 1963), p. 105: "We cannot resist progress but, on the other hand, we must not simply surrender to it.... "

5 *La Nouvelle Héloïse* (hereafter N.H.), V, vii, O.C. II, 610; *Inégalité*, O.C. III, 187; "Lettre à Philopolis," O.C. III, 232. See "Lettre à Vernet," 29 Nov. 1760, C.G. v, 271–2: "Nothing can slow down the progress of evil.... Luxury advances: there is general decline; there is the pit where sooner or later everything perishes"; *Fragments politiques*, O.C. III, 474; cf. *Rêveries d'un promeneur solitaire*, O.C. III.

6 Rousseau's most finished and deliberate writings end or are tinctured with a note of despair: cf. N.H. vi, xii, O.C. II, 740–1, for Julie's unresolved problem of love and society, ending in death; *Solitaires*, Didier, IV, 296, for Emile's defeat and attempt to reconcile liberty and submission ("... he who knows best how to will all that [harsh necessity] commands in the freest, because he is never forced to act against his will"); and, for our purposes, most significantly in *Contrat social (première version)*, II, iii, O.C. III, 318–26; *Contrat social* II, x, *ibid.*, pp. 389–91, in which he finds the just society swiftly sabotaged by the remarkable set of conditions that must preside at the establishment of a national civil community, satisfied alone for Corsica, and goes so far as to speak of "the impossibility of finding the simplicity of nature joined to the needs of society."

7 Compare *Inégalité*, note ix, O.C. III, 202; *Rousseau juge de Jean-Jacques*, I, O.C. I, 687; *Projet pour la constitution de la Corse*, O.C. III, 947; "Lettre à M. de Franquières," C.G. XIX, 56.

8 *Emile*, IV, 332; cf. *Ibid.* II, 215; *Confessions*, VIII, O.C. I, 363. Also, Ernst Cassirer, *Question* (Peter Gay, Principia, Bloomington, 1963), p. 41.

9 Michel de Montaigne, "Our Feelings Continue Beyond This Life," in *Essays* (trans. E.J. Trechmann, Modern Library New York, 1946), p. 9; cf. *Emile*, II, 67.

10 This is what the Savoyard vicar means when he says "Sometimes I have
good sense, and I have always loved truth... all I need do is expose what I
think in the simplicity of my heart," *Emile*, IV, 320. On Rousseau's concept of truth as equivalent to sincerity, see Judith N. Shklar, "Rousseau's
Two Models: Sparta and the Age of Gold," *Political Science Quarterly*
(March 1966), p. 25. For the universality of the moral standard, see "Lettres morales," V, C.G. III, 365–6, *Emile*, IV, 351.

11 *Discourse sur les sciences et les arts*, O.C. I, 6.

12 Virtue means essentially conscientious action against one's inclinations.
It can encompass everything from taking care of one's parents ("Lettre
à un jeune homme," Winter, 1758, C.G. III, 329) to slaughtering one's
children for the good of the state (*Dernière Réponse*, O.G. III, 88); cf.
Rêveries, VI, O.C. I, 1053; *Emile*, V, 567.

13 Compare *Emile*, III, 184: "The point is not in knowing what is, but what
is useful..." Regarding Rousseau's own learning (cf. *Confessions*, VI,
O.C. I, 234–45, and *Le Verger de Madame de Warrens, ibid.* II, 1124–9), I
would agree with Jean Fabre, " *Réalité et utopie dans la pensée* politique
de Rousseau," *Annales*, XXXV (1959–62), 220: "I think that Rousseau
had rather good learning but not up to... the level of erudition of his
age." Compare Henri Gouhier, "*Ce que le vicaire doit à Descartes,*"
Annales, XXXV, 141. Also Bertrand de Jouvenel, "Essai sur la politique
de Rousseau," introduction to *Du contrat social* (Droz, Geneva, 1947),
citing Seneca, p. 35.

14 *Confessions*, XI, O.C. I, 567.

15 *Observations*, O.C. III, 39. Rousseau is not far from Hobbes in this;
cf. *Leviathan*, v: "yet they that have no *science* are in better and
nobler condition with their natural prudence than men that by mis-
reasoning, or by trusting that reason wrong, fall upon false and absurd general rules." However, Rousseau is thinking of conscience, not
prudence.

16 *Rousseau juge de Jean-Jacques*, I, O.C. I, 728; "Lettre à Moultou,"25
April 1762, C.G. VII, 191.

17 "Lettre à Franquières," C.G. XIX, 61: "The philosopher needs to be exalted in the eyes of man, but in the eyes of God the just man prevails."

18 *Préface à Narcisse*, O.C. II, 967.

19 Rousseau hit a nerve of his contemporaries; cf. Diderot, "Lettres à
Falconet," in *Oeuvres complètes* (eds. J. Assézat and M. Tourneaux,
20 vols., Paris, 1875–7), XVIII, 179–80: "O sages of Greece and Rome...
how blissful to my mind it would be if I could raise my statue in the
midst of yours and imagine that those one day stopping before it would
feel the delicious transports that you inspire in me."

20 *Emile*, IV, 323.

21 *Ibid.* II, 107; III, 192, 203; IV, 285, 305.

22 *Ibid.* II, 107; also "Lettre à Duchesne," 24 May 1760, C.G. V, 109.

23 *Confessions*, IX, O.C. I, 435; cf. *Emile*, IV, 386: "Dare to confess God among the philosophers; dare to preach humanity to the intolerants"; "Lettre á Vernes,"1761, C.G. VI, 158: "The devout Julie is a lesson for the philosophers and so is the atheist Wolmar for the intolerants."

24 Compare "Lettre à Beaumont," Didier, IV, 204 ff.; "Lettre à Usteri," C.G. IX, 234: "How taken I am with this plan of a catholic, a really catholic religion."

25 *Observations*, O.C. III, 46.

26 Leo Strauss, in *Natural Right and History* (University of Chicago Press, Chicago, 1953, pp. 260–1), is mistaken in claiming that Rousseau preached intellectual elitism behind the back of his democracy. He simply gave genius its due without drawing political onclusions. Judith N. Shklar's interpretation of Rousseau's authoritarian streak is more profound: see "Rousseau's Images of Authority," *American Political Science Review* (December 1964), pp. 919–32.

27 See *Confessions*, VIII, O.C. I, 362; IX, 416–17. At Rousseau's first success as a writer, he became "intoxicated" with a "blaze of virtue... which for forty years had not emitted the smallest spark." Finally, "special circumstances... restored [him] to nature, above which [he] had tried to raise [himself]." Also, *Rêveries*, VIII, *ibid.* p. 1079.

28 *Rêveries*, I, *ibid.* p. 998.

29 *Solitaires*, Didier, IV, 259.

30 *Inégalité*, O.C. III, 163.

31 *Emile*, IV, 282 ff. One should not overlook the classicism of this conception; cf. Xenophon, *Anabasis*, v, *in fine* "it is noble, as well as just and pious, and more pleasant to remember the good things rather than the bad ones."

32 Compare D'Alembert's article "Elémens des sciences," *Encyclopédie*, v, 495–6; *Preliminary Discourse to the Encyclopedia* (trans. R.N. Schwab; Mac Millan, New York, 1963), pp. 34–5.

33 *Observation*, O.C. III, 83–6.

34 *Emile*, II, 172 n.; cf. *Fragment: Histoire de Lacédémoine*, O.C. III, 545; *Rêveries*, IV, O.C. I, 1029.

35 On this point, cf. R.G. Collingwood, *The Idea of History* (Oxford University Press, Oxford, 1946), pp. 59–76; L. Lévy-Bruhl, "The Cartesian Spirit and History," in *Philosophy and History: The Ernst Cassirer Festschrift* (eds. R. Klibansky and H.J. Paton, Oxford 1936, Oxford University Press, pp. 191–6), emphasizes the antihistorical spirit of rationalism. These are of course only general tendencies.

36 Compare J. Starobinski, introduction to *Inégalité*, O.C. III, liii, lv: "They

hardly cared to project their hypothesis into the temporal depths of human history."

37 John Locke, *An Essay Concerning Human Understanding* (ed. A. Campbell Fraser, 2 vols., Dover New York, 1959), II, Book, III, vi, 22, pp. 73 ff.

38 *Inégalité*, O.C. III, 132.

39 Locke, *Essay*, I, Book I, iii, I–5, pp. 92–4.

40 Compare *Emile*, I, 41; IV, 312 and notes. For the corporate extension, See "Lettre à d'Alembert sur les spectacles," Didier, I, 285: "Mankind is one, I confess; but men modified by religions, governments, laws, customs, prejudices, climates become so different from each other that we must no longer seek among us for what is good for men in general, but what is good for them in a given time or country." The inspiration is of course from Montesquieu; cf. *Lettres Persanes*, XXIV.

41 *Ibid.* IV, 286. This "psychologism" is a typical feature of liberal thought; cf. J.S. Mill, *System of Logic*, VI, vii, para. I: "Human beings in society have no properties but those which are derived from, and may be resolved into, the laws of the nature of individual man."

42 *Ibid.* I, 12: "We must generalize our views, and consider in our pupil the abstract man, the man exposed to all the accidents of human life."

43 Compare *inter alia, ibid.* III, 200: "The happiness of natural man consists in not suffering"; v, 565: "... pain and vice are inseparable, and man becomes wicked only when he is unhappy."

44 *Rousseau juge de Jean-Jacques*, II, O.C. I, 855.

45 *Emile*, IV, 247.

46 *Ibid.* IV, 341. The problem of the nature of evil in Rousseau is closely connected with his conception of education and his refusal to base his political theory on the notion of harmoniously legislated self-interest. In these respects, his most direct antagonist is Helvétius. For a brilliant discussion, see D.W. Smith, *Helvétius: A Study in Persecution* (Oxford University Press, Oxford, 1965), pp. 172–84, esp. pp. 175–9.

47 *Rousseau juge de Jean-Jacques*, II, O.C. I, 805; also, *Inégalité*, O.C. III, 141–2.

48 *Op. cit.* VII, 278.

49 *Emile*, IV, 326

50 "Lettres morales," II, C.G. III, 352.

51 *Emile*, I, 48.

52 "Lettre à Beaumont," Didier, IV, 362–3.

53 *Emile*, IV, 355; "Lettres morales," VI, C.G. III, 369.

54 Compare *Confessions*, I, O.C. I, 5: "I feel my heart and I know men."

55 *Rêveries*, IV, O.C. I, 1028.

56 *Ibid.* VIII, 1075–9.

57 *Ibid.* IV, 1025.

58 *Rousseau juge de Jean-Jacques*, II, O.C. I, 799. This, of course, does not mean that Rousseau was without self-doubt; cf. *Confessions*, I, *ibid.* p. 31.

59 Compare *Emile*, IV, 348: "Too often reason deceives us...but the conscience never deceives; it is man's true guide." See Iring Fetscher, "Rousseau's Concept of Freedom in the Light of his Philosophy of History," *Nomos* IV (Columbia University Press , New York, 1962),

60 "Lettre à Franquières," C.G. XIX, 54.

61 *Emile*, IV, 285.

62 *Ibid.* p. 323

63 Compare Notes to *Inégalité*, O.C. III, 1294.

64 *Fragment biographique*, O.C. I, 1115.

65 *Mon portrait*, O.C. I, 1120.

66 *Emile*, II, 219.

67 *Réveries*, III, O.C. I, 1020.

68 *Emile*, IV, 292.

69 Compare Henri Gouhier, "Nature et histoire dans la pensée de Jean-Jacques Rousseau," *Annales*, XXIII (1953–5), p. II.

70 See J. Starobinski's introduction, O.C. III, liii–liv, and notes, p. 1302 and *passim*.

71 *Inégalité*, O.C. III, 133.

72 See especially, René Hubert, *Les sciences sociales dans l'Encyclopédie* (Félix Alcan, Paris, 1923), pp. 23–6.

73 "Note on the Wanderer Jan Kommarnicki," in *Gesammelte Schriften* (Akademieausgabe, 24 vols., Berlin, 1902–64), II, 489.

74 Compare *Solitaires*, Didier, IV, 289.

75 *Essai sur l'origine des langues*, Didier, II, 362.

76 *Contrat social*, II, viii, O.C. III, 386.

77 *Observations*, O.C. III, 43–56.

78 *Confessions*, IX, O.C. I, 435; XI, *ibid.* p. 567.

79 Compare *Rousseau juge de Jean-Jacques*, I, O.C. I, 687; also *Emile*, IV, 342: "Take away our evil progress...and all is well."

80 "Lettre à Beaumont," Didier, IV, 393–4.

81 Jean Morel, "Recherches sur les sources du Discours sur l'inégalité," *Annales*, v, 131.

82 *Ibid.* 132.

83 *Inégalité*, O.C. III, 162.

84 Notably his adolescent experience of returning too late to Geneva to be admitted through the gates (*Confessions*, I, 42: " *Il était trop tard*"), which launched him on the world; re-echoed in the closing of the monastery gates at Turin (*ibid.* II, 60). See also his experience with the

manuscript of the *Dialogues*, when he was barred from the high altar of Notre Dame, where he wished to entrust it to Providence (*Histoire du précédent écrit*," O.C. I, 978–80); and the final detemporalization of this theme, indicating submission, in *Rêveries*, I, 998: "*il est trop tard.*"

85 *Inégalité*, O.C. III, 170; cf. *Fragments, ibid.* pp. 404–5; "It is certain that from this [human] commerce are born their vices and virtues and generally their whole moral being."

86 *Inégalité*, O.C. III, 141–2.

87 *Ibid.* 162.

88 *Ibid.* 144.

89 *Ibid.* 162, 171; *Langues*, IX, Didier, II, 357: "The associations of men are in large part the work of accidents of nature."

90 Whether or not men were destined to live in society according to Rousseau depends very much on what meaning one gives to destiny. In *Inégalité*, chance is the culprit, but see "Lettres morales," V, C.G. III, 367; *Emile*, IV, 354; *Fragments*, O.C. III, 504–5.

91 *Inégalité*, O.C. III, 171.

92 *Ibid.* p. 143; cf. "Lettres morales," V, C.G. III, 367.

93 *Inégalité*, O.C. III, 140. Rousseau sees prefigured in man's assertion of primacy among the animals the inequality within his own species (p.166). This is very different from Kant's opinion of the "fourth and final step which reason took". Compare "Conjectural Beginning of Human History," in *Kant on History* (ed. L.W. Beck, Library of Libral Costs, Indianapolis, 1963), p. 58.

94 *Inégalité*, O.C. III, 170.

95 *Emile*, III, 153.

96 *Inégalité*, O.C. III, 169: "Each began to look at the others, and to want to be looked at himself..."

97 Starobinski stresses the irony: "...thus is aroused the overbearing desire to be preferred, the comparison that makes us attentive to others only if we can surpass or displant them. Unanimity is lost in the same ceremony that seems to celebrate it." Notes to *Inégalité*, O.C. III, 1344.

98 *Langues*, X, Didier, II, 363.

99 *Inégalité*, O.C. III, 174.

100 Lionel Gossman, "Time and History in Rousseau," *Studies on Voltaire and the Eighteenth Century*, XXX (1964), esp. pp. 338–45.

101 *Emile*, II, 65.

102 See the brilliant essay by Jean Wahl, "La bipolarité de Rousseau," *Annales*, XXXIII (1953–5), pp. 49–55.

103 Aside from the *Profession de Foi, Emile*, II, 137–74, on the senses, and V, 585–96, the *précis* of the *Social Contract*.

104 *Fragments*, O.C. III, 510; cf. *Emile*, I, 9–10.

105 *Rousseau juge de Jean-Jacques*, II, O.C. I, 813.

106 *Emile*, IV, 290.

107 *Ibid*. I, II.

108 *Ibid*. III, 240; IV, 306.

109 *Ibid*. III, 227; V, 606

110 *Ibid*. III, 200, 211, 224.

111 *Ibid*. IV, 278.

112 *Ibid*. V, 581. Rousseau makes elsewhere (III, 185) the more conventional distinctions of the necessary, the useful, the good; the triad – sensuous, intellectual, moral – informs the interpretation of Paul Duproix, *Kant et Fichte et le probléme de l'éducation* (Felix alcan, Paris, 1895), p. 74.

113 *Contrat social*, II, iii, O.C. iii, 372.

114 "Lettre à H. Tscharner," 29 April. 1762, C.G. VII, 202.

115 Preface to *Emile*, pp. 2–3; cf. "Lettre à Philibert Cramer," 13 October 1764, C.G. XV, 339.

116 Fully covered in J. N. Shklar, "Rousseau's Images of Authority," *op. cit.*

117 Especially in the long "dialogue" of *Emile*, v, 603–7.

118 *Solitaires*, Didier, IV, 295. Interestingly, Emile, who leaves his country and is cast adrift on the world (p. 290), has virtually the same feelings as those of Schiller in 1784; "I have lost my country and exchanged it for the vast universe,"quoted by Maurice Boucher, *La révolution de 1789 vue par les écrivains Allemands* (Presses Universitaires de France, Paris, 1954), p. 34.

119 *Rousseau juge de Jean-Jacques* , II, O.C. I, 864; Cf. *Réveries*, VIII, *ibid.* p. 1077.

120 Compare *Emile*, IV, 320. Conscience "stubbornly follows the order of nature against all the laws of men".

121 *Emile*, V, 605.

122 "Lettres morales," VI, C.G. III, 370.

123 Compare *Confessions*, IX, O.C. I, 455.

124 Dedication to *Inégalité*, O.C. III, 112.

125 *Emile*, V, 605.

126 *Contrat social*, II, vi, O.C. III, 378.

127 *Emile*, IV, 389.

128 On Rousseau's conception of the "general will" and the origin of the term, see Paul-L. Léon, "Rousseau et l'idée de la volonté générale," *Archives du droit public et de la science politique*, Nos. 3–4 (1936), pp. 148–200; Irving Fetscher, *Rousseaus politische Philosophie* (Luchterhand Neuwied, 1962), pp. III ff.; B. de Jouvenel, "Essai," *op. cit* pp. 105–14; Georges Gurvitch,"Kant and Fichte als Rousseau-Interpreten," *Kant-Studien*, XXVII (1922) pp. 151–3. No less than the Rousseauian state itself, the "general will" is conventionalistic.

129 Compare *Emile*, IV, 303: "Let us extend *amour-propre* to others, thereby transforming it into virtue." This is what a "general will" makes routine; cf. in this connection Rousseau's stress on opinion (*Contrat social*, II, xii, 394) and on public surveillance (*Montagne*, VIII, 845), important ideas among the Paris setions in years II and III of the Revolution.

130 *Contrat social*, I, viii, O.C. III, 364.

131 *Ibid.* II, vi, 378. God's effective justice relates to the *post mortem*; cf. "Lettre à l'Abbé de Carondelet," 4 March, 1764, C.G. x, 341: "Take away eternal justice and the prolongation of my being after this life, and I would see in virtue nothing but madness masked by a fine name."

132 Compare Raymond Carré de Malberg, *Contribution à la théorie générale de l'Etat* (L. Tenin Paris, 92 vols. 1920–2), I, 6i ff.; and Franz Haymann, "La loi naturelle dans la philosophie politique de J.-J. Rousseau," *Annales*, xxx, 65–109.

133 *Inégalité*, O.C. III, 170.

134 *Fragments*, O.C. III, 478.

135 *Contrat social*, I, vi, O.C. III, 360.

136 *Contrat social* (première version.), I, ii, O.C. III, 283.

137 *Emile*, V, 597.

138 Rousseau's wishful image of the *siècle d'or*, which permeates most of his writings, even the Spartan ones (cf. *Sciences et arts*, p. 22), expresses an alchemization of psychology into history. See especially his rendition of this theme in the air "*Les consolation des miséres de ma vie*," O.C. II, 1169–70: "*Mais qui nous eut transmis l'histoire/De ces tems de simplicité ?*"

139 Emile, IV, 398. cf. V, 550, clearly an idealization of childhood: "If you would extend the effect of a fortunate education over a whole lifetime, prolong the habits of childhood into early manhood; when your pupil is what he ought to be, keep him the same from then on." Also v, 565.

140 *Ibid.* V, 606.

141 Rousseau's dislike of Peter the Great was proportional to the adulation heaped on that monarch by Voltaire and the Encyclopedists; cf. Damilaville's, article "Vingitiéme," *Encyclopédie*, XVII, 856; "The Russians were a people before the reign of Tsar Peter. The prodigious changes wrought by the genius of this great man make them a more civilized but not a new people."

142 Compare *Emile*, I, 8.

143 *Contrat social*, II, xii, O.C. III, 394.

144 *Fragments*, O.C. III, 555. cf. Montaigne, "Of Custom," *Essays*, p. 96: "The laws of conscience, whose origin we attribute to nature, are born rather from custom." This is, of course, implicit in the linguistic

parallels: *ethos–ethika* (Greek) and *mos–moralis* (Latin). Rousseau's distance from a later liberal tradition is underlined by this position; cf. J.S. Mill, "On Liberty," in *The Philosophy of John Stuart Mill* (ed. Marshall Cohen, Modern Library, New York, 1961), p. 192: "... the magical influence of custom, which is not only, as the proverb says, a second nature, but is continually mistaken for the first."

145 *Contrat social*, II, xii, O.C. III, 394.

146 *Economie politique*, O.C. III, 248.

147 *Préface à Narcisse*, O.C. II, 971.

148 *Contrat social*, II, x, O.C. III, 309.

149 *Ibid.*

150 "Lettre à d'Alembert," Didier, 329.

151 *Corse*, O.C. III, 914–15.

152 *Ibid.* 950.

153 *Economie politique*, O.C. III, 259.

154 *Rousseau juge de Jean-Jacques*, II, O.C. I, 778.

155 *Confessions*, XII, O.C. I, 651. Also, "Lettre à Buttafuoco,"22 Sept. 1764, in Vaughan, II, 356: "The very idea [of legislating] rouses my soul and transports me.... But... zeal does not supply the means, and the desire is not the power."

156 *Corse*, O.C. III, 948; cf. *Emile*, III, 223. Rousseau's own expectation was undoubtedly more complex. In *Confessions*, XII, 648, he speaks of the Corsicans "*naissantes vertus*," which might some day equal those of Sparta and Rome.

157 *Ibid.* 950.

158 De Tocqueville to Corcelle, 17 Sept. 1853. Cited in Richard Herr, *Tocqueville and the Old Regime* (Princeton University Press, Princeton, NJ 1962), p. 35.

159 *Pologne*, O.C. III, 955.

160 *Ibid.*

161 *Contrat social* (Première version.), I, ii, O.C. III, 288.

162 *Emile*, V, 567, 603.

163 *Ibid.* IV, 357.

164 *Ibid.* IV, 342: "... the love of order which preserves [order] is called justice." Also, *Confessions*, IX, O.C. I, 327: "The justice and uselessness of my complaints left in my mind the seeds of indignation against our foolish civil institutions, whereby the real welfare and true justice are always sacrificed to an apparent order, which is really subversive of all order...." In a more theoretical vein, *Emile*, IV, 344.

165 *Emile*, II, 67.

166 Compare "Lettres morales," II, C.G. III, 350: "... for want of knowing how we ought to live we all die without having lived," cf. *Confessions*,

IX, O.C. I, 426: "I saw myself reaching the gates of old age, and dying without having lived."

167 These observations are much indebted to two brilliant studies by Georges Poulet: *Etudes sur le temps humain* (Plon Paris, 1949), pp. 158–93, and *Les métamorphoses du cercle* (Plon Paris, 1961), pp. 102–32. Also of interest is Mark J. Temmer, *Time in Rousseau and Kant* (Droz, Geneva and Paris, 1958).

168 *Emile*, IV, 358.

169 *Ibid.* II, 64.

170 *Rousseau juge de Jean-Jacques*, II, O.C. I, 855.

171 For example, *Rêveries*, IX, O.C. I, 1085: "Is there sweeter satisfaction than to see a whole people joyful on a festival day...?"

172 *Emile*, IV, 356.

173 *Ibid.* IV, 347 "... the goodness of man is love of his fellows and the goodness of God is love of order", Cf. *Rêveries*, I, O.C. I, 999: "Everything outside me is henceforth foreign to me." In *Emile*, IV, 344, he writes, "I know that the identity of the ego is given continuity only by the memory."

174 *Emile*, III, 347.

175 Compare "Lettre à Mirabeau," 26 July 1767, C.G., XVII, 157.

176 Compare *Inégalité*, O.C. III, 193.

177 Original nature contains the seeds of its own destruction, because "the first law of nature is the concern of self-preservation," *Emile*, II, 223.

178 *Ibid.* II, 71.

179 *Emile*, IV, 432.

180 *Rêveries*, VII, O.C. I, 1066.

181 N.H., V, ii, O.C. II, 536.

182 *Emile*, I, 12.

183 *Montagne*, VI, O.C. III, 809.

184 *Inégalité* O.C. III, 112 ff.

185 F. Schiller, *Letters on the Aesthetic Education of Mankind*, 11th letter, in *The Esthetic Letters, Essays, and the Philosophical Letters* (trans. J. Weiss, Boston, 1845), p. 51.

186 For example, E. J. Hobsbawm, *The Age of Revolution, 1789–1848* (London, The Ctholic Series, Weidenfeld Nicholson, 1962), p. 293.

187 Daniel Mornet, *Les origines intellectuelles de la Révolution française* (5th ed., A.Colin, Paris, 1954), p. 329.

188 *Ibid.* 416.

189 *Ibid.* 227.

190 Compare R. Hubert, *Sciences sociales* (Paris, Félix Alcan, 1923), p. 364.

191 Mornet, *Origines*, p. 96.

192 Maxmillien Robespierre, *Oeuvres complétes* (10 vols., Georges Thomas,

Nancy, 1910–67), *Lettres à ses commentans*, 2nd series, no. 2 (10 Jan. 1793), V, p. 207.

193 Louis Antoine Léon de Saint-Just, *Oeuvres* (ed. Jean Gratien, Editions de la Cité Universelle, Paris, 1946), pp. 91–2.

194 Robespierre, *Défenseur de la Constitution*, no. 4, O.C. IV, 113–15; also *Lettres*, no. 4, V, 20.

195 See H. A. Goest-Bernstein, *La politique extérieure de Brissot et des Girondins* (Félix Alcan, Paris, 1912), passim, and Georges Michon, *Robespierre et la guerre révolutionnaire, 1791–1792* (M. Rivière et cie, Paris, 1937). Also, Albert Mathiez, *La révolution française et les étrangers* (*La Renaissance du livre*, Paris, 1918), pp. 158 ff.

196 Louis Lavelle, *Du temps et de l'éternité* (A. Michel, Paris, 1945), p. 283.

197 Georges Gurvitch, The Spectrum of Social Time (Kluwer, Dordrecht, The Netherlands, 1964), pp. 31 ff.

3   Rousseau, Voltaire, and the Revenge of Pascal

THE OLD MISANTHROPE AND THE NEW

At the end of his *Lettres philosophiques* (1734), Voltaire attempted to refute Pascal, the thinker all the *philosophes* regarded as their arch-nemesis. It was profoundly disturbing to Voltaire, the author two years later of the world-affirming poem *"Le mondain,"* that Pascal did not start with the philosophy of Port Royal and then work out-ward, as expected, to his condemnation of the social world. For such a conventional Christian maneuver the *philosophes* were, of course, well prepared. Rather, Pascal did something far more threatening: He spoke as a worldling and a skeptic who had eventually retreated to the shelter of Port Royal. Pascal, who might have been a forerunner of the *philosophes*, chose instead to reject in advance the dreams of Voltaire, Diderot, and company.

All through the eighteenth century Pascal continued to haunt the French Enlightenment. Holbach, as late as the 1770s, still found it necessary to quarrel with the author of the *Pensées*; Condorcet, when editing Pascal's works, renewed the old debate; Voltaire throughout his life, and even in his last year, launched sally after sally at the writer who frightened him every time he – a hypochondriac – felt ill.[1]

Only one threat to the *philosophes* was even greater than that pre-sented by Pascal. The worst of all possible worlds was for one of the insiders of the "party of humanity" to offer the reading public a set of findings, arrived at through the "philosophy of the Enlightenment," that duplicated Pascal's. The author of the *Pensées* had challenged the French Enlightenment from outside its borders; Rousseau threat-ened it from within.

"I dare side with humanity against this sublime misanthrope,"[2] wrote Voltaire when he set out to refute Pascal's *Pensées* in the early 1730s. Beginning two decades later and lasting till his dying day, Voltaire constantly attacked another "misanthrope," Jean-Jacques Rousseau. If Pascal was a difficult foe, all the more so was Rousseau, a leading spokesperson of the cause of humanity. Unwavering in his opposition to the reign of prejudice and oppression, unrelenting in his quest for furthering human autonomy, Jean-Jacques was not easily dismissed. That Rousseau, regular contributor to the *Encyclopédie*, long-time best friend of Diderot, go-between who introduced Diderot to Condillac, undisputed leader of the *philosophes* in the quarrel over French versus Italian music – that such a figure should reject society was a potentially devastating blow to the philosophical movement, which was dedicated to the proposition that salvation is here and now, in the temporal world and through the good graces of society.

The *philosophes* eventually succeeded in drumming Rousseau out of their ranks, but how could they ever hope to deny he was one of their own? The intellectual genres to which he contributed were unquestionably theirs, his philosophical assumptions theirs, too. The *Discourse on the Sciences and Arts* is obviously modeled on the *Age of Louis XIV*, no matter that Rousseau's conclusions are antithetical to Voltaire's. Both the *Discourse on Inequality* and the *Essay on the Origin of Languages* build on Condillac's *Essay on the Origin of Human Knowledge*. And *Emile* completes what Locke began in *Some Thoughts Concerning Education*.

Time and again Rousseau published a work that used the intellectual resources of the *philosophes*, only to conclude that the social world was too corrupt to reform. Time after time the *philosophes* overlooked his indiscretions – until he united his theory with his practice by leaving Paris. "It was on the 9th of April, 1756," he recalled in his *Confessions*, "that I left Paris, never again to live in a city."[3] Not long thereafter the *philosophes* found that they had no choice but to rid themselves of Rousseau by casting him outside the human species: Jean-Jacques was a "monster," a misanthrope, an enemy of the human race.

Wounded by the accusations of his erstwhile companions, Rousseau struggled in each of his autobiographical writings for an explanation of his self-exile: at first his excuse is illness, then his love of independence, next his need to flee men in order to love mankind, finally his need to flee humans in order to avoid hating them.[4] By far his most ingenious strategy was to accept the role of misanthrope while rewriting Molière's script. Rousseau agreed that someone who hates humanity is a "monster"; he insisted, however, that we draw a distinction between the despicable man who reviles humanity and the admirable person who, "precisely because he loves his fellow creatures, hates in them the evils they do to one another."[5] Caring only to please and flatter *le monde*, Molière created a misanthrope so petty, spiteful, and untrue to himself that a corrupt society could avenge itself against its accuser by laughing him off the stage. Rousseau's revised edition of the "*Misanthrope*," in sharp contrast, would dramatize the tragic fate that awaits anyone willing to speak the truths to his degraded contemporaries that they needed to hear.

Rousseau consistently repudiated the notion of original sin, and indeed always resisted admitting the very idea of sin to his philosophy. Neither Arnauld nor anyone else at Port Royal, nor Pascal on its fringes, figured as a reference point in his thoughts on religion. Yet Rousseau conjured up, through the resources of the Enlightenment, as bleak a view of social relations as Pascal's or that of any of the more orthodox Jansenists. From the standpoint of the *philosophes*, Rousseau might just as well have been the reincarnation of Pascal; better that than for one of their kind to discover, even without invoking God, the Fall, or sin, that this world is a vale of tears.

Rousseau may have been a tormented man, but he was even more the torment of the *philosophes*. They had not yet succeeded in finding a way to dispose of Pascal when Jean-Jacques appeared on the scene; misanthropy thereafter had a new face made in the image of the Enlightenment itself.

One way to account for Rousseau's central place in the Enlightenment is to tell the story of Pascal, Voltaire's response, and Rousseau's subsequent rehabilitation, by means of the philosophy of the Enlightenment, of thoughts echoing Pascal's on *la condition humaine*.

VOLTAIRE ANSWERS PASCAL

In an irony that Providence might savor, it was the skeptic Voltaire who brought Pascal's *Pensées* to prominence in the eighteenth century. Two giants of religious thought in the seventeenth century,

Bossuet and Malebranche, had ignored Pascal[6]; and Arnauld went through Pascal's text with scissors and paste, doing his best to pass on to posterity a safe, dull, and bland edition of the *Pensées*.[7] The Pascal that Port Royal cherished was the author of the Jesuit-baiting, casuistry-hating *Lettres écrites à un provincial*, not the author of the disturbing *Pensées*. Had it not been for the last chapter of Voltaire's *Lettres philosophiques*, the ghost of Pascal would not have periodically haunted the philosophes.

Say what one may about Voltaire, call him shallow as so many have, yet it was he who refused to be duped by Port Royal's expurgated edition of the *Pensées*. No matter that the conniving editors, in reworking the text, put the theology first, Pascal's vision of the human condition second; Voltaire reversed and corrected the order in the course of commenting on the *Pensées*, placing the human condition first, the theology second. In doing so he invited the *philosophes* to read the text as originally intended, a remarkable accomplishment given that neither Voltaire nor anyone outside Port Royal had access to an uncorrupted copy of the *Pensées*.

How could Voltaire, the skeptic and worldling, empathize so well with Pascal, the religious zealot? Perhaps Voltaire understood that both he and Pascal shared a debt to the great skeptic Montaigne; or perhaps Voltaire recognized how readily Pascal, like Montaigne, might have been a forerunner of the *lumières*. Pascal was an experimental scientist who rejected Descartes' proof by pure reason that a vacuum cannot exist. Pascal appreciated both the possibilities and the limitations of *l'esprit de géométrie*, was a pioneer in studies of the mathematics of probability, and showed his flair for applied science by organizing a bus service and designing a calculating machine. Unlike those living within Port Royal, he wrote as someone familiar with the *honnête homme*, the *mondain*, the libertine. Only one thing more is necessary to complete the picture of Pascal, the might-have-been *philosophe*, his explicit admission that happiness is our legitimate desire.[8] For such a man to throw himself into the arms of the "hidden God" was, Voltaire realized, especially menacing.

Pascal's gambit was to end rather than begin with the dogma of original sin. Without the mystery of original sin, a doctrine repugnant to human notions of justice, we can never hope to understand ourselves[9] or find asylum from the miseries of existence. Such he

attempted to prove, building his case by pointing to our divided, dis-
tracted, empty, and unhappy selves. A conglomeration of the lowest
and the highest, the human self is haunted by memories of the wholeness and the bliss that marked it before the Fall.[10] In Christianity, and
only in Christianity, can we discover "the cause of our weaknesses,
the treatment that can cure them, and the means of obtaining such
treatment."[11]

The major symptoms of our illness are that we can never sit still,[12]
cannot find satisfaction in ourselves, and seek to flee from our noth-
ingness, to fill the void within by endlessly chasing after desires that
once satisfied, immediately yield to successive desires[13] rather than
providing the inner peace for which we yearn. Our human condition
is one of inconstancy, boredom, anxiety,[14] and is marked by relentless
efforts to escape from ourselves by means of an unbroken succession
of meaningless diversions. Absorbed in past or future, never living
in the present, our lives end before we have begun to live. "We never
actually live, but only hope to live, and since we are always planning
how to be happy, it is inevitable that we should never be so."[15]

To those who would seek in others the esteem they lack in themselves, Pascal issues the stern reminder that "if everyone knew what
others said about him, there would not be four friends in the world."[16]
Look beneath the surface of our social relations, Pascal cajoles the
reader, and dare to discover that "man is nothing but disguise, falsehood, and hypocrisy, both in himself and in regard to others."[17]

Saint Augustine had spoken of two cities formed by two loves,
"the earthly by the love of self, even to the contempt of God; the
heavenly by the love of God, even to the contempt of self."[18] Pascal
agreed that the reign of self-love explains why "human relations are
based on mutual deception":

[A person] wants to be the object of men's love and esteem and sees that
his faults deserve only their dislike and contempt. . . . He conceives a deadly
hatred for the truth which rebukes him and convinces him of his faults. . . .
He takes every care to hide his faults both from himself and others.

Politeness, civility – all the social graces – are founded on an implicit agreement to tell others what they wish to hear: "We hate the
truth and it is kept from us; . . . we like being deceived and we are
deceived."[19]

If humans are the "glory" no less than the "refuse" of the universe, that is because "thought constitutes the greatness of man."[20] Brilliant scientist that he was, Pascal never doubted that the accomplishments of mathematicians and physicists are remarkable. However, scientific reason lets us down in our time of metaphysical and moral need[21]; and our everyday reason also fails, defeated in the interminable civil war between reason and the passions. "All our reasoning amounts to surrendering to passion," and we are left at odds with, and divided against, ourselves.[22]

Reason enables us to know many things, but it cannot provide us with the insight into ourselves that we are eager to avoid. We refuse to look within for fear of what we might see; "nothing could be more wretched than to be ... reduced to introspection with no means of diversion."[23] For beings as wretched as human kind, advances in the accumulation of knowledge will never include self-knowledge, as we do wish to know who we are.[24]

Much of Voltaire's response hinged on showing that what Pascal had depicted as dire and depressing was harmless and insignificant if placed within the sensationalist philosophy of John Locke. Of course, we live outside ourselves because, according to Locke, "ideas can only come from outside.... Hence man is either outside himself or an imbecile."[25] By the same token, "enjoyment can only come from outside. We cannot receive sensations or ideas except through external objects, as we can only feed our bodies by bringing into them foreign substances which turn into our bodies."[26]

In general, Voltaire finds that our physical and emotional health depends on rejecting all versions of Christian dualism, whether Pascal's or the Cartesian separation of body and mind found in the Jansenist Arnauld or the Oratorian Malebranche. Wrapping himself in Locke's epistemology and psychology, Voltaire argues that no one can withdraw his soul from the world, for where our body is, so too is our mind. It follows that when Pascal, Arnauld, and Malebranche chastised humans for not turning inward, for failing to divorce themselves from the world, they uttered nonsense. "Our condition is precisely to think about outside things, with which we have a necessary connection.... To think about oneself, apart from all natural things, is to think of nothing at all."[27]

As a loyal disciple of Locke, Voltaire was not disturbed by Pascal's complaint that humans are incomprehensible beings. Had not Locke shown that we know neither body nor mind,[28] that we cannot ascend from sense–experience to metaphysical wisdom – and yet we understand enough to cope, get by, and solve problems? Reason, including scientific reason, is probabilistic and instrumental, permitting us to muddle through and pursue our happiness, whatever form it takes. Why should we ask for or expect anything more?

Nor need a good Lockean lose any sleep over Pascal's observation that we can never relax and enjoy the moment. Locke's *tabula rasa* rules out original sin as the explanation, and other chapters of the *Essay Concerning Human Understanding* rule in the proposition that a certain feeling of uneasiness, of unquenchable desire, keeps us going,[29] Without our habit of sinking into boredom, we should vegetate and be useless. Born to act, for us to yearn for inactivity is a death wish.[30]

The cure for our supposedly divided selves, Voltaire suggested, may be found in the very *amour-propre* that Christian thought diagnosed as a deadly remedy. A morality of self-love does not divide us in two, a higher and a lower self, nor does it ask that we repress our wants, needs, and desires; all it asks is that we accept the inevitable, that in all our actions we never forget ourselves. To embrace self-love instead of condemning it is to be whole and entire, at one with ourselves and on good terms with others.

It is as impossible for a society to be formed and be durable without self-interest as it would be to produce children without carnal desire. . . . It is love of self that encourages love of others, it is through our mutual needs that we are useful to the human race. That is the foundation of all commerce, the eternal link between men. Without it not a single art would have been invented, no society of ten people formed.[31]

Pascal could not be more mistaken in his assertion that "the bias toward self is the beginning of all disorder . . . in politics and economics."[32] In point of fact, a proper penal code rests on self-interest, as does trade.

To condemn selfishness categorically, as Pascal does, is to damn ourselves to find nothing but disappointment in the midst of the very social existence that permits each individual to seek happiness through interacting with others. To demand selflessness is to make inhuman demands, to lose one's humanity, to create the monster one has claimed to discover in the human creature. Finally, it is to denature oneself and then to cry with anguish about not fitting into the scheme of nature.

Paris, to Voltaire, was the best refutation of Pascal; Paris, that wondrous city where the social art has been perfected and the joy of life is constantly on splendid display. Two years after publishing his refutation of the *Pensées*, Voltaire wrote the final line to *Le Mondain*: "Paris to me's a paradise."

WHY JEAN-JACQUES LEFT PARIS

Throughout the eighteenth century, Paris was the place to visit and, better yet, the place to reside. All the members of the party of humanity, whatever their nationality, came to Paris, the beacon of light in the age of enlightenment: Hume came from Scotland, Holbach from Germany, Galiani from Italy, and, of course, Rousseau from Switzerland, to name only a few. Many, like Diderot, found excuses to avoid traveling outside Paris and France, except when absolutely necessary. When Galiani was forced to return to Italy, he recognized that moment as the low point of his career. Yet Rousseau, after living there for several years, chose to leave at the precise moment he "arrived" as a man of letters.

Much as the *philosophes* hated to admit it, Rousseau's withdrawal was a perfectly logical conclusion to his reflections. Paris, as the *philosophes* said, was the emblem, pride, and pinnacle of civilized life. However, the worth of civilized life was precisely what Jean-Jacques had questioned in such noteworthy writings as the *Discourse on the Sciences and Arts* and the *Discourse on Inequality*. In the course of launching his assault on our so-called "progress," Rousseau also vindicated Pascal's devastating portrayal of the human condition: reenter in the pages of Rousseau the Pascal-like notions of the divided self, the chase after a perpetually fugitive happiness, the enslavement of reason to the most unworthy passions, the loss of one's very self on the part of selfish human beings.

Pascal had argued that we do not want self-knowledge and could not understand our natures if we tried, so thoroughly have we constructed a "second nature that destroys the first."[33] Voltaire answered that we do not need and are not equipped to have self-knowledge. Thereupon Rousseau reminded the *philosophes* that unless knowledge of nature was supplemented by knowledge of human nature, the theory of natural right collapses: "It is ignorance of the nature of man that throws so much uncertainty and obscurity on the true definition of natural right."[34]

Rousseau begins the *Discourse on Inequality* by reminding us that "Know thyself," the inscription of the temple of Delphi, is the most important and the most unheeded of moral precepts. Then, in his notes, he quotes Buffon, whose *Natural History* was recognized as one of the pillars upon which the French Enlightenment rested. The first part of the quotation from Buffon might have pleased Voltaire:

Whatever interest we may have to know ourselves, I am not sure whether we do not know better everything that is not ourselves. Provided by nature with organs destined uniquely for our preservation, we use them only to receive foreign impressions, we seek only to extend beyond ourselves, and exist outside ourselves.

Thus far one might think that Buffon's position was the same that Voltaire had taken against Pascal in the final letter of his *Lettres philosophiques*. But the rest of the quotation from Buffon is a decided blow to Voltaire.

Too busy multiplying the functions of our senses and augmenting the external range of our being, we rarely make use of that internal sense which reduces us to our true dimensions.... However, it is this sense we must use if we wish to know ourselves; it is the only one by which we can judge ourselves. But how can this sense be made active and given its full range? ... [I]t has been dried out by the fire of our passions; heart, mind, sense, everything has worked against it.[35]

Without realizing it, Buffon had slammed the door to Voltaire and opened it to Rousseau. On Buffon's authority, self-knowledge is as essential as it is elusive.

Buffon was willing to toss off a provocative comment but unwilling or unable to build upon his initial insight. Rousseau, on the other hand, played Buffon's passing comments for all they were worth, which was a great deal, amounting to a deep criticism of the outlook of the *philosophes*. The reason why we live outside ourselves comes to light, Rousseau argues, when we realize that the world the senses encounter is social as well as natural. It is not enough, therefore, to say that after repeated exposure to trees the mind formulates the concept of the tree. The empiricist epistemology of Locke and Condillac must be supplemented by a social epistemology. Locke's empiricism correctly suggests that we learn from comparing one sensation with another. What he failed to note is the extent to which the mind develops in the course of one person's learning to compare his or her self with others.

Amour-propre, or self-love, is not a physical instinct as Voltaire thought, nor is it an instance of the conservation of energy as Holbach affirmed, nor of the laws of movement as Helvétius held.[36] No good Lockean should abandon the *tabula rasa* and postulate innate ideas or forces so quickly. To complete Locke's program of research, we must follow Rousseau in seeking out the events that implanted selfishness in the human psyche, beginning with the pride that followed the first capture or killing of an animal: At the moment of victory the hunter glanced at himself with pride "and considering himself in the first rank as a species, he prepared himself from afar to claim first rank as an individual."[37]

Soon, perhaps at the first festive dance, individuals were comparing themselves with one another, each hoping to find the scale on which to score the highest marks, each fearing to be judged on a scale chosen by others:

People grew accustomed to assembling in front of the huts or around a large tree; song and dance, true children of love and leisure, became the amusement or rather the occupation of idle... men and women. Each one began to look at the others and to want to be looked at himself....[38]

Not psychic strength but chronic self-doubt drives us to seek the approval of others. Nothing more characterizes our selfishness than how it feeds on the insecurities of our socially acquired selves. The less we belong to ourselves, the more we demand that others reassure us, even to the point of preferring us to themselves, which can never be.[39]

Rousseau's view is that society gives us our very sense of self, our "I," and then robs us of personal autonomy. It is on encountering the look of others than we turn back and discover ourselves, only to spend the rest of our lives seeing ourselves through the eyes of others, chasing after but never catching up with ourselves:

The savage lives within himself; the sociable man, always outside of himself, knows how to live only in the opinion of others; and it is, so to speak, from their judgment alone that he draws the sentiment of his own existence.

Once he has become a social being, a human is "always active, sweats, agitates himself, torments himself incessantly," whereas in the presocial state a human wants "only to live and remain idle."[40]

In his search for and discovery of a time when we could sit still, Rousseau sounds like Pascal, with the difference that the latter was thinking of the Garden of Eden, Rousseau of the brutish but innocent state of nature. Whereas Pascal blames sin, Rousseau – to the consternation of the *philosophes* – blames society. In Pascal's thought a society that revolves around deception and self-deception is the effect of a corrupt human nature, in Rousseau's a corrupt society is the cause and a debased human nature the effect.

One can well imagine how vexed the *philosophes* must have felt each time they read Rousseau's latest publication. He began as they did, with a denial of original sin, an affirmation of Locke's *tabula rasa*, a claim not only that human nature was originally innocent but that it was naturally good (*bonté*). He shared their hatred of the Catholic Church and seconded their view that the cloistered life of monks and nuns is unnatural. However, in the social relations to which the *philosophes* turned to find the joy of existence, Rousseau consistently discovered the vindication of Pascal's depiction of the human condition. Julie, the heroine of Rousseau's novel *La Nouvelle Héloïse*, needs religion – not Pascal's religion to be sure, but she does seek the assurance of a life to come because this life is so very hollow.

The parallels between the positions staked out by Pascal and those later taken by Rousseau are remarkable. Pascal had lamented that "we never keep to the present. We recall the past; we anticipate the future.... We are so unwise that we wander about in times that do not belong to us, and do not think of the only one that does."[41] Much the same position was taken by Rousseau, who thought the capacity to live in the present the prerogative of humans in the state of nature.[42] Quite otherwise is our fate once we have become social beings. Saint-Preux, the leading man of *La Nouvelle Héloïse*, who longs for the woman Julie once was but is no more, was Rousseau's most powerful depiction of the capacity of nostalgia to ruin a life.[43] What he is, so are we all, if less dramatically. We all live in the past – or the future – and are never present to ourselves.

Again, like Pascal, Rousseau held that our wants, desires, and needs outpace our capacity to fulfill them; hence we are cursed to unhappiness. Every desire satisfied produces new desires, as Pascal foresaw. Once we have entered into society, our limited natural needs are less important to us that the unlimited artificial needs that social intercourse induces. Seeing what others have, we always need one thing more. In the very remote past, when we were animals, our desires did not exceed our physical needs; imagination, a product of social interaction, did not yet exist.[44] Now, however, our removal from nature to society has had the result of overheating our imaginations. We can never have enough, and hence we can never know the happiness that was ours when we still belonged to nature.

The divided self is another concept common to Pascal and Rousseau. Soul against body, reason against passions, the spark of divinity against carnal desire, are the divisions with which Pascal struggled. Rousseau's divisions flow from the contrast between the *amour de soi* (love of self) that is naturally given to us and the *amour-propre* (selfishness) into which our natural drives are transformed by society. Humans in the state of nature are similar to other animals insofar as they express love of themselves by seeking to avoid pain and to safeguard their well-being. They are not selfish, however; they do not compare themselves with other persons, they do not suffer from envy or petty pride. On the contrary, they instinctually empathize with others who suffer, pity being one of the few innate traits of human nature.

Contemporary evidence of how love of self combines with concern for others may be seen in the practice of breast-feeding, which is why Rousseau did his best – and with some success – to convince aristocratic women to stop using wet nurses. The mother acts as agent of our not entirely lost natural selves when she breast-feeds her child; she acts as the agent of our socially acquired selves when, some years later, she sends her offspring into the world with the imperative, "Achieve." Out of love the mother breast-feeds, out of love she wishes her maturing child social success – but this second love is no longer the expression of nature. The mother is herself divided between her natural and social selves and, with the best of intentions, she passes her inner division on to her children.

Usually we escape from inner division, if at all, only by capitulating to *amour-propre*. Attempts to listen to our "inner voice" rarely succeed because what we take for "nature's gentle voice" is in reality the voice of society that "stifles humanity in men's hearts by awakening personal interest."[45] Our human condition, after society has denatured us, is woeful indeed: "Our needs bring us together in proportion as our passions divide us, and the more we become enemies of our fellow men, the less we can do without them."[46] Rousseau's position is reminiscent of Pascal's and even more of another seventeenth-century advocate of Jansenism. Pierre Nicole preceded Rousseau in depicting a self-regulating society, functioning effectively, no matter that each individual human member lived in estrangement from himself and from his fellows. Given our sinful selves, we cannot hope for a social order that rests on the principle of charity, Nicole believed.[47] Julie agrees (except for sin) but nevertheless practices charity on a daily basis, doing her best to save a few souls from the miseries of society.

Pascal and Rousseau share at least one more conviction: Both believe that reason, which should grant us autonomy, has surrendered to debased passions. "One no longer finds anything except the ugly contrast of passion which presumes to reason and understanding in delirium,"[48] Rousseau complained in words that recall Pascal's earlier verdict that "all our reasoning comes down to surrendering to feeling." In reason as it functions when released from the passions Pascal saw proof of the possibility of human greatness. Likewise Rousseau thought that for reason to live up to its potential it would have to outgrow its tainted origins. On a Lockean view we begin to reason when we compare objects with one another and on Rousseau's amended view those comparisons are of ourselves with other humans; which is to say, reason and *amour-propre* are born together in the mental development of the human species.

How, then, can we have one without the other, reason without *amour-propre*? That was the question Rousseau faced. If the *siècle des lumières* had not led to enlightenment, he did not draw conclusion that we should abandon the quest for an alternative to the rule of religious fanaticism and intolerance, or that we should thereupon agree that humans will never achieve autonomy. Rather, Rousseau needed reason to launch an alternative to the standard program of enlightenment, as represented by Voltaire.

Too good a Lockean to seek a human reason purified of the senses, too much the *philosophe* to think metaphysical and certain truths available to human reason, Rousseau knew what he had to do if he was to find the means to ponder and write the great works containing his program for an alternative Enlightenment, *La Nouvelle Héloïse,*

Emile, and the *Social Contract*. He had to flee Paris; only thus could he free himself from the socially induced passions that clouded his earthbound and sensual reason.

Reason cannot rise above the surrounding environment. By leaving Paris Rousseau could distance himself from society without making the mistake of trying to rise above it, which, as Voltaire had said against Pascal, is impossible, so deeply has society left its imprint on our being. Rousseau simply moved to the outskirts of Paris, far enough away to give reason its chance, but near enough to compete with the *philosophes* for the minds and souls of the public.

WHOSE GENERAL WILL?

Perhaps no concept is more strongly attached to Rousseau's reputation as a social and political thinker than that of the "general will." However, the history of the concept of the general will begins long before Rousseau, dating back to seventeenth-century Christian thought, in which it was most systematically developed by Malebranche but initially sketched in the notebook entries of Pascal's *Pensées*. In his reflections on the "general will," Rousseau secularized the concept and transformed it from a divine to a civic concept.[49]

If Pascal's thoughts on the "general will" stand in the background when Rousseau approaches the topic, Diderot's are in the foreground. Rousseau's first significant encounter with the concept of the general will came when he responded to Diderot's article for the *Encyclopédie*, "Natural Right (*Droit naturel*)," which placed the "general will" at the center of moral reflection. Rousseau dismantled Diderot's general will in a brief section entitled "On the General Society of the Human Race," written for the first version of the *Social Contract*. Those pages did not appear in the final version; but in his novel *La Nouvelle Héloïse*, as we shall see, Julie covers much the same ground and enters a plea for a return to religion. The story of Rousseau's general will constitutes another vital chapter in the saga of Jean-Jacques' uncanny capacity to remain within the Enlightenment while strongly criticizing it in terms that sound as if Pascal were taking his revenge.

Probably Diderot was thinking of Hobbes in "Natural Right" when he asked whether a "violent reasoner," a strictly self-interested and calculating person "tormented by violent passions," can be restored to morality. Can such a being, out to serve his interest at the expense of everyone else's, be converted to ethical existence by appealing to what is most distinctive in his makeup: his reason and his membership in the *genre humain*? Both these traits may be put to moral use, Diderot suggested, through placing the question of right and wrong "before the entire human race..., since the good of all is the only passion it has. Particular wills are suspect... but the general will is always good." For each individual the general will is "a pure act of understanding in the silence of the passions"; for the collectivity it is "the general will of the species." Whatever wants and needs characterize humanity and are therefore in the interests of every human should be deposited under the rubric of "natural right," Diderot argued.[50]

Rousseau countered Diderot by showing that in societies as presently constituted there is no possibility of silencing the "violent reasoner." Shall we appeal, as Diderot did in imitation of Pufendorf, to what we share with all humans? That strategy is bound to fail: in the first instance because whatever is desired by all is in limited supply for each one, in the second because it is our differences from other persons that our vain, weak selves wish to assert. Rousseau reminded the *philosophes* of what they, defenders of the passions against repressive Christian ethics, had always known: that our passions come first, reason later and as little more than the servant of the passions. Reason never silences the passions, and the passions to which it listens are not those naturally given but such as have been implanted by corrupt society.

In any case a rational understanding of the good of the species matters not at all if my personal good remains in doubt. "It is not a matter of teaching me what justice is, but of showing me what interest I have in being just," writes Rousseau in the name of the "independent man," his expression for Diderot's "violent reasoner." The rationally self-interested actor, if he exists, will understand that he had better do the vile deeds to others that they will do to him, should he fail to strike the first blow. What is the rational course, if not to ally with the strong so as to share the spoils they extract from the weak? "The proof that this is how the enlightened and independent man would have reasoned is that this is how every sovereign society accountable for its behavior only to itself does reason."[51]

"The term *human race* suggests only a purely collective idea which assumes no real union among the inhabitants who constitute it," concluded Rousseau after carefully examining Diderot's article. A morality of the general will cannot be sustained, Rousseau argued, unless it is given political embodiment in a civic republic. Diderot's essay *"Droit naturel"* appeared in the fifth volume of the *Encyclopédie;* Rousseau's vision of a civic general will was published in the same volume under the heading *"Économie politique."*

In his essay on political economy published in the *Encyclopédie,* Rousseau sketched a civic way of life, a plan for the political education of the many, which would make the renewal of the general will our daily task. Rousseau described a society dedicated to public affairs, a world in which social activities were, as in the ancient *polis,* fundamentally political in nature. We must be citizens first and foremost, cradle to grave: "The instant of our birth should be the beginning of the performance of our duties." The familial unit in such a setting should be charged with a public mission: "The Romans' virtue... turned all their homes into as many schools of citizens."[52] Our reward for devotion to the common good is that we love our duty and ourselves; obligation and inclination are united, and the divided self created by society meets with a political cure. Patriotism makes us whole, if not complete.

Rousseau preferred a social order in which humans were not asked to rise above themselves, one in which civic virtue is unnecessary. "Happy are the peoples among whom one can be good without effort and just without virtue,"[53] Rousseau sighed. Alas, such peoples, save for a few Swiss mountain dwellers and the downtrodden inhabitants of Corsica, no longer exist.[54] Nonrepressive virtue is impossible, now that *amour-propre* has exiled the natural goodness of *amour de soi* to the outermost limits of the psyche. Under present circumstances the "will of all" would signify the exaltation of the reign of *amour-propre* rather than the triumph of the "general will." Reluctantly but necessarily, Rousseau was driven to reintroduce the morality of the higher self. For us to enjoy doing the right thing, we must constantly be pulled out of our selves in an incessant whirl of civic rituals. *Laissez-faire, laissez-passez,* are the slogans of the historically acquired lower self. True freedom, freedom from base passions, freedom of self-mastery, comes solely to citizens who consent to be "forced to be free."

Not coercion but subtle psychological pressure is what Rousseau has in mind: In a well-regulated republic, he repeatedly advises, "every citizen shall feel the eyes of his compatriots upon him every moment of the day."[55] The *philosophes* counted on the internalized eyes of others,[56] not on the eyes of God as in Christian thought, to hold us morally accountable; Diderot and Holbach could arrive at such a view, however, only by forgetting that living to please the members of a corrupt society was what got us into trouble in the first place. Only when the eyes always watching us are those of fellow citizens are we likely to overrule the lower self, countered Rousseau.[57]

The more Rousseau set forth his civic conception of the general will, the more his language sounded as if it were borrowed from Pascal. In the *Pensées* we learn that to "tend toward the general" through absorption in the body of Christ is to witness the transfiguration of *amour-propre*:

To be a member is to have no life ... except through the spirit of the body.... We love ourselves because we are members of Christ. We love Christ because he is the body of which we are members. All are one.[58]

Strikingly similar is the civic virtue that Rousseau charged with the mission of sustaining the general will:

It is certain that the greatest miracles of virtue have been produced by patriotism. By combining the force of egoism with all the beauty of virtue, this sweet and ardent sentiment gains an energy which, without disfiguring it, makes it the most heroic of all the passions.[59]

Inside the sentiment of patriotism lies a concealed syllogism, only the major premise of which is ever uttered: My country is great and admirable. Unstated are both the minor premise of my membership and the conclusion that I, too, am admirable. Yet, despite its origins in *amour-propre*, patriotism makes us willing to sacrifice our very lives for something larger than ourselves.

Pascal and Rousseau agree again in their descriptions of the misery that awaits us whenever our self-love is left to itself rather than being transformed by the general will, whether of the body of Christ or the body politic. "The separated member believes itself to be a whole," writes Pascal, "... and tries to make itself its own center and body. But it wanders about and becomes bewildered at the uncertainty of its existence." Rousseau's comments on membership and nonmembership in civic life are strikingly reminiscent of Pascal's religious phraseology: "Your true republican is a man who imbibed love of the fatherland ... with his mother's milk. That love makes up his entire existence.... The moment he is alone, he is nothing."[60]

What are we to do if, as is almost always the case, the public assemblies of a republic have nothing to do with our daily lives? Julie knows how to state the arguments of "dangerous reasoners" with perfect lucidity. She grants the "common utility" of virtue, but asks,

what does that matter compared with my particular interest, and which in the end concerns me more, that I should attain happiness at the expense of others or they should attain theirs at my expense? If fear of shame or punishment prevents me from acting badly for personal benefit, I have only to do wrong in secret and virtue will no longer have anything to say to me.

In the eyes of God she finds a substitute for the eyes of citizens:

Adore the Eternal Being.... It is he who never ceases to cry to the guilty that their secret crimes have been seen, and who says to the forgotten just person, Your virtues have a witness.[61]

Julie's faith, in which no one is guilty of original sin and all will eventually be saved, is incompatible with Pascal's. Yet her seemingly optimistic religion is noteworthy for asserting a new version of his desperate "wager": "Supposing this immense being does not exist, it still would be good to occupy ourselves constantly with him, in order to be more master of ourselves and happier."[62] It is her conviction that this world can never be saved from itself that drives Rousseau's heroine to place all her bets on religion. Pascal might have understood Julie; the *philosophes* decided to misunderstand her.

We can reconcile interest and virtue by trying, in defiance of history and with little hope of success, to re-create Sparta in the modern world, as Rousseau proposed in his political writings. Or reconciliation can be effected through the appeals to eternity that, Julie realizes, are closer to hand. Most assuredly, however, we cannot merge interest and virtue, as Voltaire, Diderot, and the *philosophes* wished, through glorifying *la vie mondaine*. Voltaire would answer Pascal by pointing to life in Paris; Julie will spend her life avoiding the greatest city of France and Europe.

In his own mind Rousseau was always the good son of the Enlightenment. However, to the *philosophes*, he was the great conjurer who gave Pascal a second life even more injurious to their cause than the first.

ENDNOTES

1 René Pomeau, *La religion de Voltaire* (Librairie Nizet, Paris, 1956), p. 237.
2 Voltaire, *Lettres philosophiques* (Garnier-Flammarion, Paris, 1964), p. 160.
3 *Confessions*, p. 403. Unless otherwise noted, citations to Rousseau are to the Pléiade edition of the *Oeuvres complètes*. The *Confessions* and other autobiographical writings are found in Vol. I.
4 *Mon portrait*, p. 1125; *Lettres à Malesherbes*, pp. 1130, 1132, 1144; *Reveries*, p. 1066.
5 *Lettre à d'Alembert* (Garnier-Flammarion, Paris, 1967), pp. 96–97.
6 J. S. Spink, *French Free-Thought from Gassendi to Voltaire* (Athlone, London, 1960), p. 312.
7 Mara Vamos, "Pascal's *Pensées* and the Enlightenment," *Studies on Voltaire and the Eighteenth Century*, 97, 17–145 (1972).
8 *Pensées*, ed. Brunschvicg, 425, 465.
9 *Ibid.* 434.
10 *Ibid.* 425.
11 *Ibid.* 430.
12 *Ibid.* 131, 129.
13 *Ibid.* 109.
14 *Ibid.* 127.
15 *Ibid.* 172.
16 *Ibid.* 101.
17 *Ibid.* 100.
18 Augustine, *City of God*, XIV, 28.
19 *Pensées*, 100.
20 *Ibid.* 346, 434.
21 *Ibid.* 67.
22 *Ibid.* 274, 412.
23 *Ibid.* 164; 139–143.
24 *Ibid.* 144, 377.
25 *Lettres philosophiques*, Letter 25, No. 23.
26 *Ibid.* No. 35.
27 *Ibid.* No. 37.
28 *Ibid.* No. 56.

29 Locke, *Essay Concerning Human Understanding*, ed., A. C. Fraser, Book II, Chap. xx, No. 6; Chap. xxi, No. 31 (Dover).

30 *Lettres philosophiques*, No. 23.

31 *Ibid*. No. 11.

32 *Pensées*, 477.

33 *Ibid*. 93.

34 "*Discours sur l'origine et les fondements de l'inégalité parmi les hommes,*" in *Oeuvres complètes*, Vol. III, 124. Hereafter cited as *2nd Discourse*.

35 *Ibid*. 195–196.

36 Voltaire, *Lettres philosophiques*, Letter 25, No. 11; Holbach, *Système de la nature* (G. Olms, Hildesheim, 1966), Vol. I, p. 59; Helvétius, *De l'esprit*, Book I, Chap. 4; Book II, Chap. 2; Book III, Chap. 6.

37 *Ibid*. 166.

38 *Ibid*. 169.

39 *Emile*, in *Oeuvres complètes*, IV, 493.

40 *2nd Discourse*, 192–193.

41 *Pensées*, 172.

42 *2nd Discourse*, 144.

43 Judith Shklar, *Men and Citizens: A Study of Rousseau's Social Theory* (Cambridge, University Press, Cambridge, 1969), Chap. 4 ("Images of Authority").

44 *2nd Discourse*, 143–144.

45 *Du contrat social (première version)*, in *Oeuvres complètes*, Vol. III, pp. 284–284. Hereafter cited as *Geneva MS*.

46 *Ibid*. 282.

47 Nicole, "De la Charité et de l'amour-propre," in *Oeuvres philosophiques de Nicole* (Hachette, Paris, 1845).

48 *2nd Discourse*, 122.

49 Patrick Riley, *The General Will before Rousseau: the Transformation of the Divine into the Civic* (Princeton University Press, Princeton, NJ, 1986).

50 Diderot, *Oeuvres* (Éditions Robert Laffont, Paris, 1995), Vol. III, pp. 43–47.

51 *Geneva MS*, 281–289.

52 *Discours sur l'économie politique*, in *Oeuvres complètes*, Vol. III, pp. 260, 262. Hereafter cited as *Political Economy*.

53 *Emile*, 468.

54 *Projet de constitution pour la Corse*, in *Oeuvres complètes*, Vol. III; *Lettre à d'Alembert*.

55 *Considérations sur le gouvernement de Pologne*, in *Oeuvres complètes*, Vol. III, p. 1019; see also p. 968. Hereafter cited as *Poland*.

56 For example, Diderot, "*Le Fils naturel,*" Act V, Scene 3.
57 *Lettre à d'Alembert,* 131, 237.
58 *Pensées,* 477, 483.
59 *Political Economy,* 255.
60 *Pensées,* 483; *Poland,* 966.
61 *La Nouvelle Héloïse,* in *Oeuvres complètes,* Vol. II, pp. 358–359.
62 *Ibid.*

PATRICK RILEY
(IN MEMORIAM JUDITH N. SHKLAR)

4 Rousseau, Fénelon, and the Quarrel between the Ancients and the Moderns

The great Rousseau scholar Judith Shklar was usually more concerned with Rousseau's striking originality – as a psychologist, as a
pre-Freudian group psychologist, as the very prototype of the *homme
revolté* – than with his intellectual debts. "His enduring originality
and fascination," she urges in *Men and Citizens*, "are due entirely to
the acute psychological insight with which he diagnosed the emotional diseases of modern civilization."[1] However, she made two
large exceptions in favor of Locke and Fénelon: She thought that
Rousseau's debt to the psychological theory of Locke's *Essay* was
huge and central and that his debt to Fénelon's political and moral
thought was equally massive. For Rousseau owed to Fénelon nothing less than the legitimation of his obsession with Graeco–Roman
antiquity: If an early Genevan reading of Plutarch set off this propensity, it was Fénelon's *Telemachus* (1699) and *Letter to the French
Academy* (1714) that confirmed and dignified it; thus Fénelon's "Roman" *auctoritas* and *gravitas* were worth a great deal. In Shklar's
view, Rousseau owed to Fénelon (above all) the notion of seeing
and using two ancient "models" of social perfection – a prepolitical "age of innocence" and a fully political age of legislator-caused
civic virtue – as foils to modern egoism and corruption.[2] Fénelon's
familiar utopias of "*Bétique*" (celebrating pastoral innocence) and of
"*Salente*" (depicting legislator-shaped civisme) in *Telemachus* were,
for Shklar, echoed in Rousseau's "happy family" (in *La nouvelle
Héloïse* and *Lettre à d'Alembert*) and in his Spartan–Roman "fantasies" (in *Government of Poland* and the *Social Contract*). Small
wonder, then, that Shklar should direct us toward "Rousseau's admiring remarks about Fénelon" in the *Confessions*, in *Rousseau juge*

78

de Jean-Jacques, in the *Rêveries d'un promeneur solitaire,* and in *Émile.*[3]

However, none of this can become clear enough until Fénelon's social thought is exposed to the light of present day. Rousseau may have known it by heart, as Shklar herself was later to do – but we no longer do. And therefore the first task is to recover those facets of Fénelonianism that Rousseau found irresistible.

François de Salignac de La Mothe-Fénelon was born in Perigord in 1651, the son of an aristocratic provincial family that was distinguished but threadbare. Ordained a priest in 1675, he was within three years given an important ministry in the Church – that of spiritual guide to the "New Catholics" (ex-Huguénots) in northern France. This ministry lasted for a decade (1678–89) and was crowned by the publication of the treatise *On the Education of Girls* (1687), which first revealed Fénelon's classicizing taste for the ancient pastoral simplicity depicted by Virgil in the *Aeneid* and *Georgics.* By this time the Abbé Fénelon had caught the eye of Bossuet, the most powerful French ecclesiastic of the Grand Siècle; and for the Bishop of Meaux, Fénelon produced his *Réfutation de Malebranche* (ca. 1687–88), which attacked Malebranche's notion of a "Cartesian" *Providence générale* operating through simple, constant, universal laws, and sustained Bossuet's notion (outlined in the *Histoire universelle*) of a *Providence particulière* that had furnished David and Solomon to ancient Israel and Louis XIV to modern France. In 1689 he was named tutor to Louis' grandson, the Duc de Bourgogne (1682–1712), and it was for his royal pupil that he was soon to write *Telemachus, Son of Ulysses* (ca. 1693–95) and the *Dialogues of the Dead.* Rhetorically the high point of Fénelon's "court" period was his speech on being received into the Académie Française (1693), with its fulsome praise of the Sun King. The Archbishopric of Cambrai followed in 1695, carrying with it the titles of Duke and Prince of the Holy Roman Empire.[4]

However, in the late 1680s Fénelon had also become deeply interested in the quietistic notion of a "disinterested love of God" free of hope for personal happiness – a disinterested interest fanned by the mystical pieties of his friend Mme. Guyon. His insistence that one must "go out of oneself," even "hate oneself," finally eventuated in the *Maxims of the Saints on the Inner Life* (1697) – a work in which

Fénelon argued for five degrees of "purity" or "disinterestedness" in human love of God. At the lowest end of the scale one finds the love of God, not for himself but for "the goods which depend on his power and which one hopes to obtain": This Fénelon contemptuously calls "purely servile love." One small notch above this Fénelon places loving God, not for "goods" that he can provide but as the "instrument" of our salvation; even this "higher" love, however, is still "at the level of self-love." At the third and the fourth levels Fénelon finds a mixture of self-love and true love of God; but what really interests him is the fifth and highest degree, the "pure love" of God that one finds only in "saints." "One can love God," Fénelon urges, "from a love which is pure charity, and without the slightest mixture of self-interested motivation." In such a love, Fénelon adds, neither the "fear of punishment" nor the "hope of reward" plays any part at all.[5] As is well known, Bossuet and others – including Malebranche, in his *Traité de l'amour de Dieu* – argued that Fénelon's "disinterested" love excluded all hope of salvation, as well as all fear of justified punishment and thus subverted Christianity: Fénelon's work was finally placed in the Index in March, 1699. In this condemnation the prime mover was Bossuet, now Fénelon's greatest detractor: "To detach oneself from himself to the point of no longer desiring to be happy, is an error which neither nature, nor grace, nor reason, nor faith can suffer."[6]

A month later *Telemachus* was printed, without Fénelon's permission, through "the infidelity of a copyist." Louis XIV had already banished the "chimerical" Fénelon to his Cambrai diocese in 1697, and with the double disaster of 1699 – condemnation at Rome followed (within a few weeks) by publication of the "Homeric" novel that Louis considered an attack on his faults – Fénelon was divested of his pension and of his tutorship of the Duc de Bourgogne. He never set foot in Versailles, or even Paris, again.

With the premature death in 1712 of the Duc de Bourgogne, whom Fénelon had carefully educated to be an enlightened successor to his grandfather, Fénelon's hopes for a renewed France collapsed like a house of cards. His *Demonstration de l'existence de Dieu* (1713) was a work of pure theology; and, indeed, had Fénelon not been a royal tutor for ten years, *Telemachus* and the *Dialogues of the Dead* would almost certainly never have come into existence. Conscientiously administering his half-Flemish diocese even as Louis XIV made perpetual war on its borders, constantly engaging in a wide-ranging correspondence as spiritual counselor, Fénelon died, prematurely worn out, in January, 1715. To this day many French Fénelonians view the Archbishop of Cambrai as a saint and martyr, the victim of the "interested" high politics of Louis XIV, Bossuet, and the Roman *curia*.

The year 1716 saw the posthumous publication of the magnificent *Letter on the Occupations of the French Academy* (written in 1714), in which Fénelon contributed to the "quarrel between the ancients and the moderns" by offering glowing praise of Homer, Plato, Demosthenes, Virgil, and Cicero and insisting that "it is our insane and cruel vanity, and not the noble simplicity of the ancients, which needs to be corrected." It was that "noble simplicity" that he had tried to illustrate in the demi-Platonic myths of *"Bétique"* and *"Salente,"* in *Telemachus*:

When the ancient poets wanted to charm the imagination of men, they conducted them far from the great cities; they made them forget the luxury of their time, and led them back to the age of gold; they represented shepherds dancing on the flowered grass in the shade of a grove, in a delightful season, rather than agitated hearts, and great men who are unhappy in virtue of their very greatness.[7]

Telemachus may have contributed to Fénelon's downfall, but the book was spectacularly successful: indeed the most-read literary work in eighteenth-century France (after the *Bible*). Cherished and praised by Rousseau, it was first translated into English in the very year of its publication and was retranslated by no less a figure than the novelist Tobias Smollett in 1776. (In Rousseau's *Émile* the eponymous pupil is given *Robinson Crusoe* as his sole adolescent reading, then Fénelon's *Telemachus* on reaching adulthood – a striking concession from one who thought almost all literature morally suspect.)

Without doubt the two most important pieces of French political theory at the turn of the eighteenth century are Bossuet's *Politics Drawn from the Very Words of Holy Scripture* (completed in 1704) and Fénelon's *Telemachus*.[8] However, whereas Bossuet offered the greatest of all defenses of divine right monarchy – in which Louis XIV's rule is unbrokenly descended from Abraham's covenant with God in *Genesis* ("kings shall come out of you") – Fénelon by contrast theorized what might be called a "republican" monarchy in which the key notions are simplicity, labor, the virtues of agriculture, the absence of luxury and splendor, and the elevation of peace over war and aggrandizement. This proto-Rousseauian, demilitarized "Spartanism" led Louis XIV, of course, to read *Telemachus* as a satire on his luxuriousness and bellicosity, and Fénelon fell permanently from official favor. Fénelon combines monarchical rule with republican virtues in a unique way: After him Montesquieu was to draw a necessary connection between monarchy and "war and the enlargement of dominion" and to separate monarchy by a categorical gulf from republican simplicity and "virtue," and Rousseau was to restore a more nearly Fénelonian view of "republican monarchy" in his glowing Plutarchian encomium of Lycurgus – in a Sparta not just temporally and geographically but *morally* distant from Versailles.

It was no accident that Rousseau so greatly admired Fénelon's fable: For like *Émile*, *Telemachus* is the story of the moral and political education of a young man by a knowledgeable and virtuous tutor. Whereas Émile, however, is in some sense Everyman, the tutor in *Telemachus*, Mentor, is preparing a young prince to succeed Ulysses at Ithaca. (As Rousseau says, "Émile is not a king, nor am I god, so that we are not distressed that we cannot imitate Telemachus and Mentor in the good they did.") Fénelon himself, in a letter from 1710, indicates his objective in writing Telemachus for his royal pupil, the Duc de Bourgogne:

As for *Telemachus*, it is a fabulous narration in the form of an heroic poem like those of Homer and of Virgil, into which I have put the main instructions which are suitable for a young prince whose birth destines him to rule. . . . In these adventures I have put all the truths necessary to government, and all the faults that one can find in sovereign power.[10]

Louis XIV, for his part, saw nothing but the alleged "faults" of sovereign power in *Telemachus* – faults that Fénelon describes at length in his account of misrule by Idomeneus, former King of Crete. (Because Idomeneus kills his own son and is deposed and exiled, one can understand Louis's displeasure!) One of Mentor's long speeches to the slowly reforming Idomeneus (now King of Salente) in Book X of *Telemachus* must have been read by Louis XIV as a veiled, mythologized version of what Fénelon would have wanted to say to, or rather against, Versailles:

Have you sought after people who were the most disinterested, and the most likely to contradict you ... to condemn your passions and your unjust feelings? No, no: let us see whether you will now have the courage to be humiliated by the truth which condemns you.

You have exhausted your riches; you have never thought of augmenting your people, nor of cultivating fertile lands. Was it not necessary to view these two things as the two essential foundations of your power – to have many good people, and well-cultivated lands to nourish them? It would require a long peace to favor the multiplication of your people. You should never think of anything but agriculture and the establishment of the wisest laws. A vain ambition has pushed you to the very edge of the precipice. By virtue of wanting to appear great, you have let yourself ruin your true greatness. Hasten to repair these faults; suspend all your great works; renounce this display which would ruin your new city; let your people breathe in peace.[11]

That second paragraph, particularly, could be invisibly woven into Rousseau's *Social Contract*, Book II, Chap. 11: "Devote your whole attention to agriculture, which causes man to multiply, and drive out the arts and crafts." (To be sure, both Fénelon and Rousseau have their roots in Cato's *De Rustica*, with its praise of Cincinnatus's virtues and its equation of moneylending with murder.)

But Fénelon did not put such speeches into the mouth of Mentor only: at every turn, and in every chapter, the *inventions de la vanité et de la molesse* are denounced. In Book VII, having escaped the seductions of Calypso, Mentor and Telemachus are told a story of the land of Bétique by Adoam – who reveals that the luxuries of Greece and Egypt are anathema in that simple prepolitical land:

Among these people (Adoam says) we found gold and silver put to the same use as iron – for example, as plowshares.... They are almost all shepherds or laborers (who practice only) those arts necessary for their simple and frugal life.... When one speaks to them of peoples who have the art of making superb buildings, furniture of gold and silver, fabrics ornamented with embroideries and with precious stones, exquisite perfumes ... they reply in these terms: "These people are very unfortunate to have used up so much labor and industry in order to corrupt themselves. This superfluity softens, enervates, torments those who possess it: it tempts those who are without it to want to acquire it through injustice and violence. Can one call good a superfluity which serves only to make men evil?" ... It is thus, Adoam went on, that those wise men spoke, who learned their wisdom only by studying mere nature.[12]

(Rousseau must have remembered this Fénelonian inversion of the usual value of precious metals when, in the "Government of Poland," he suggested awarding gold medals to the lowest public benefactors, silver ones to those who contribute more, and plaques of steel to those who most advance the general good.[13])

The unfortunate outgrowths of "vanity and flabbiness" are set in even higher relief by Fénelon's account of the austere and noble pleasures of "just kings" who live in the eternal daylight of the Elysian fields. In Book XIV of *Telemachus*, Telemachus is ferried across the river Styx by Charon, where he sees rulers "who have governed men wisely" enjoying "a happiness infinitely greater than that of the rest of men who have loved virtue on earth":

Neither blood-covered war nor cruel envy which bites with a venomous tooth, and which bears vipers wound around its middle and its arms, nor jealousy, nor mistrust, nor fear, nor vain desires, ever approach this happy abode of peace.... A pure and gentle light surrounds the bodies of these just men and covers them in its rays like a vestment.[14]

Here, of course, the *Champs Elysées* take on some of the coloration of a Christian Heaven – even if Fénelon's avowed models are Homer and Virgil.

However, what is least "Homeric" – and also most Rousseauian – is the transformation of the notion of "heroism" in *Telemachus*. The nominal hero, of course, is Telemachus – the son of a greater hero, Ulysses. But the true hero of Fénelon's work is certainly Mentor: It is he who educates and restrains a Telemachus who could easily degenerate into another Idomeneus. The true hero for Fénelon is not the wanderer on an Odyssey to Ithaca, nor a *Louis le Grand* who sacrificed real goods to apparent ones; the true hero is the moral–civic educator who "denatures" natural egoists – the man whom Rousseau later called "the true miracle" in the *Social Contract*. The proof comes at the very end of Telemachus: Mentor undergoes a metamorphosis and is revealed as Minerva (goddess of wisdom), and the book ends abruptly before Telemachus is shown being reunited with Ulysses. The hero has already been resolved into pure Wisdom: The nominal hero barely reaches Ithaca.

What that true hero teaches is a political version of Fénelon's quietistic "disinterested love of God"; just as one truly loves God only by renouncing self-interested *amour-propre* (the hope for personal salvation), so too for Fénelon the "idea of pure disinterestedness dominates the political theories of all ancient legislators." In antiquity "it was not a matter of finding happiness in conforming to that order but, *au contraire*, of devouring oneself for love of that order, perishing, depriving the self of all resources." Fénelon completes this thought with a wonderful passage that Rousseau must have had in mind when he wrote his discourse on *Political Economy* for Diderot's *Encyclopédie* sixty years later: "All these [ancient] legislators and philosophers who reasoned about laws presupposed that the fundamental principle of political society was that of preferring the public to the self – not through hope of serving one's own interests, but through the simple, pure disinterested love of the political order, which is beauty, justice, and virtue itself." If one "brackets" God out of Fénelonian thought, the Rousseauian "civic" ideal is more than half in place. And what is displaced is virtually everything imagined or accomplished by Louis XIV. That is clearest, perhaps, in Fénelon's *On Pure Love*":

> Nothing is so odious as this idea of a heart always occupied with itself: nothing delights us so much as certain generous actions which persuade the world (and us) that we have done the good for love of the good, without seeking ourselves therein. Self-love itself renders homage to this disinterested virtue, by the shrewdness with which it tries to take on the appearance of it – so true is it that man, who does not bring himself about, is not made to seek after himself, but to exist solely for him who has made him. His glory and his perfection consist in going out of himself (*sortir de soi*), in forgetting himself, in losing himself, in being swallowed up in the simple love of infinite beauty.[15]

The central truth about Fénelon, then, is that the whole of his practical thought – religious, moral, political – is held together by the notion of disinterested love, of "going out of oneself" in order to lose oneself in a greater Beyond (or, in the case of God, Above). The disinterested love of God, without self-interest and hope for benefits, is pure "charity" (as in Pascal's *Pensées*, in which "the self is hateful" and charity is "of another order")[16]; the disinterested love of one's neighbor is "friendship" (as in Cicero's *De Amicitia*); the disinterested love of the *polis* is a proto-Rousseauian ancient civic virtue. On this view of the moral world, an austere Pascalian *charité* and a Platonic "sublimated" *eros* meet. Small wonder that Fénelon, a brilliantly sympathetic classical scholar, loved the *Symposium* and *Phaedrus* with nonconcupiscent passion.[17]

Because one cannot hope to point out every parallel between Fénelon and Rousseau, the best course is to bring out affinities between Fénelon's last work, the *Letter on the Occupations of the Académie Française*, and Rousseau's first, the *Discourse on the Arts and Sciences* (1750), the work that made Rousseau Rousseau.

Fénelon's *Letter* was written soon before his death in January, 1715, and was posthumously published in the following year. It is the *summa* of his thought, drawing together his favorite themes. However, above all the *Letter* is celebrated as the most important turn-of-the-eighteenth-century contribution to the "the quarrel between the ancients and the moderns" – the quarrel to which Rousseau was soon to contribute so much.

That quarrel itself, however, has a limited side and a much broader significance. The limited quarrel was French, took place mainly from 1685 to 1715, and was fairly narrowly literary; the broader and more important quarrel was pan-European and political. The "large quarrel" goes back at least to Machiavelli's claim in *The Discourses* that the golden age of ancient Roman civic virtue remains a perfect model for intelligent imitation by modern men, whenever *fortuna* affords the opportunity,[18] and extends forward in time – after Rousseau's ardent "Spartanism"[19] – to Benjamin Constant's celebrated essay on ancient versus modern liberty in the post-Napoleonic period. The quarrel between the ancients and the moderns then had a very long "run," and it included phenomena as significant as Poussin's and Lorrain's paintings of Greek and Roman pastoral felicity at the very moment of Louis XIV's glittering Versailles ascendancy.

Fénelon was an important contributor to that large political–cultural quarrel stretching from Machiavelli to Rousseau to Constant – though his *Letter* was nominally concerned with a more parochial fight within the Académie Française (between the classicist Boileau and the modernist Fontenelle, for example). Fénelon's *Letter*, to be sure, deals with the local and narrow issues of the day – such as the question of whether French is less adequate and expressive than Greek and Latin or whether the rhyme schemes of Corneille are more forced and stilted than those of Sophocles. However, in subordinating the "insane and cruel vanity" of the moderns to the "noble simplicity" of the ancients, in praising Homer, Virgil, Plato, Demosthenes, and Cicero as nearly perfect models, Fénelon went well beyond Parisian academic quarrels about rhetoric and diction to offer a general encomium of pre-Christian civilization.

That is of course paradoxical, as Fénelon was not only a Christian but an Archbishop. But his view (in the *Maximes des saints*) was that most modern Christians love God from a base and "interested" motive (hope for personal salvation), whereas the ancients *disinterestedly* loved the *polis* and sacrificed themselves for it. For Fénelon the Christians have the right object (God) but the wrong motive (self-love); the ancients had a lower if estimable object (the city) but a worthy motive (disinterested affection). Here only Fénelon's own words in the *Letter* will do:

> Those who cultivate their reason and who love virtue – can they compare the vain and ruinous luxury which in our times is the plague of morality and the shame of the nation, with the happy and elegant simplicity which the ancients place before our eyes?
>
> Virgil, who saw all the magnificence of Rome from close up, turned the poverty of the King Evander into the grace and the ornament of his poem [*The Aeneid*].... Virgil even goes to the point of comparing a free, peaceable and pastoral life with the voluptuous actions, mixed with trouble, which come into play with great fortunes. He imagined nothing happy except a wise mediocrity, in which men would be secure from the desire for prosperity, and [full of] compassion for the miseries of others.[20]

It is easy enough to see why Rousseau so cherished Fénelon and made Fénelon's *Telemachus* (with its quasi-Platonic utopias of pacific and agricultural simplicity) the only book that Émile is encouraged to read on reaching adulthood. (To be sure, one can understand the dismay of Archbishop Beaumont of Paris: Émile is not given Scripture, or even Bossuet's *Politics from Scripture*; he is given a "Greek" work bearing the subtitle *Continuation of the Fourth Book of the Odyssey*. He is given Tertullian standing on his head: If we have Greece, what need of Jerusalem?) If, indeed, Rousseau had died in the early 1750s, before the writing of *Inequality* and the *Social Contract*, leaving the *Discourse on the Arts and Sciences* as his main legacy, he would now probably be thought of as a minor if eloquent embroiderer of familiar Fénelonian themes. For the

First Discourse (1750) is Rousseau's first contribution to the quarrel between the ancients and the moderns; with its magnification of Spartan and Roman republican civic virtue and its denigration of Athenian aestheticism, it is an extension of the view that Fénelon had made famous in his 1714 *Letter*. It is almost as if Rousseau, on the road to Vincennes to visit Diderot in prison, were thinking of these Fénelonian lines:

Nothing so much marks a declining nation as this disdainful luxuriousness which rejects the frugality of the ancients. It is this depravity which over-turned Rome. . . . I love a hundred times better the poor Ithaca of Ulysses than a city [Imperial Rome] shining through so odious a magnificence. Happy the men who content themselves with pleasures which cost neither crime nor ruin; it is our insane and cruel vanity and not the noble simplicity of the ancients which needs to be corrected.[21]

Because Fénelon's *Letter* is so proto-Rousseauian, Jean-Jacques needed only to enlarge a long familiar subordination of modernity to antiquity in *Arts and Sciences*; mainly he needed to add Cato and Brutus to the Socrates whom Fénelon had already made a civic saint. He did this, in effect, by collapsing Socrates into Cato and Brutus: Socrates is now the only acceptable Athenian, but that is because he willingly died for the sake of the laws. The Platonic Socrates who hears the harmony of the spheres and sees the psyche as a Pythagorean geometrizing echo of a consonant *kosmos* yields to Socrates the civic martyr in the *Crito*. Socrates displays "the general will one has as a citizen."[22]

However, that last phrase reveals what is not yet present in the *First Discourse*. If what is ancient, à la Fénelon, is fully "there" in the *First Discourse*, what has not yet appeared is modern (indeed Lockean) "voluntary agreement" as the basis of legitimate government in the *Social Contract*.[23] There must be voluntariness as something morally crucial before "general will" can be a will of a particular kind, and that voluntariness is Augustinian/Christian – as is Rousseau's stress on "conscience" in the *Lettres Morales* and his insistence on the final arrival of adult moral autonomy at the end of Émile's denaturing, transformative education.[24] The civic *généralité* of Roman–Spartan antiquity has not yet been fused in the *First Discourse* with the autonomy and "will" of *Inequality* and the works that succeed it. Indeed, the key term *volonté générale* does not even appear until the *Discourse on Political Economy*.[25]

In time, Rousseau's thought became far richer and more complex, but the final worry is whether that thought is as coherent as it is complex – whether Fénelonian, Plutarchian, Lockean, Roman, Christian, Platonic, Machiavellian, Spartan, and Augustinian strands really cohere. Whether Rousseauian thought is truly a *corpus* or just a basket of enthused-over *disjecta membra* is what is at issue. At the time of the *First Discourse* Rousseau was in his neo-Fénelonian vein: That is why he places Ovid on his title page ("here I am the barbarian because they do not understand me"); later he sought (and sometimes achieved) an equilibrium between ancient "generality" and modern voluntarism. And that is why the general will "expresses everything he most wanted to say."[26]

Fénelon's *Letter*, then, made a crucial contribution to one of the greatest ongoing modern disputes. If he was certainly no Machiavellian, he loved Rome as ardently as the celebrated Florentine did, and he bequeathed that love to the most intense and eloquent of modern "romanists," Rousseau.

Now that the links between Fénelon and Rousseau have been brought out – the devotion to Greek and Roman antiquity, the subordination of self-love to a larger general good – it is important too to stress the things which separate them; and the main thing that distances them is the crucial difference between "generality" and true "universality." If the mature Rousseau consistently sought after a civic "general will" valid only for Sparta or Rome *en particulier* – so that "the general will one has as a citizen" is precisely particular with respect to the entire *genre humain* – Fénelon remained a believer in a Dantean universal *respublica christiana* held together by universal charity or "disinterested" love. (Unorthodox as Fénelon may have been, he was not about to deny Christian universalism; and indeed he and Leibniz were the last figures of the first rank to adhere to the ideals of Dante's *De Monarchia*).

To be sure, the young Rousseau had at one time clung to the venerable idea of a *morale universelle*. In an early, unpublished manuscript called *Chronologie universelle, ou histoire générale du temps* (ca. 1737) he had appealed to Fénelon's notion of a universal Christian republic:

We are all brothers; our neighbors ought to be as dear to us as ourselves. "I love the human race more than my country," said the illustrious

M. de Fénelon, "my country more than my family and my family more than myself." Sentiments so full of humanity ought to be shared by all men.... The universe is a great family of which we are all members.... However extensive may be the power of an individual, he is always in a position to make himself useful ... to the great body of which he is a part. If he can [do this] he indispensably ought to.[27]

Later, of course – most notably in his attack on Diderot's notion of a reason-ordained "universal morality" in the first version of the *Social Contract* – Rousseau would abandon the *universelle* in favor of the *générale* and exchange the *respublica christiana* for more modest republics, such as Sparta, Rome, and Geneva. That is especially clear in the first of the *Lettres écrites de la montagne* (1764), in which Rousseau shows very clearly that his concern is to produce a civic general will that is peculiar to some particular nation, not a Fénelonian universal will for the good of the whole human race – even if this entails abandoning Christianity as a universal religion:

All the ancient religions, not excepting that of the Jews, were national in origin, appropriated to, and incorporated in, the state; forming the basis, or at least making a part of the legislative system.

Christianity, on the contrary, is in its principles a universal religion, having nothing exclusive, nothing local, nothing peculiar to one country any more than to another. Its divine author, embracing all mankind in his boundless charity, came to remove those barriers that separated the nations from each other, and to unite all mankind in a people of brethren....

National religions are useful to a state ... but they are hurtful to mankind in general.... Christianity, on the contrary, by making men just, moderate and peaceable is very advantageous to society in general, but it weakens the force of the political spring [and] ... breaks the unity of the moral body.[28]

Rousseau ends this passage with a radical claim that proves how little he finally favored Christian universalism: "Christianity ... inspires humanity rather than patriotism, and tends rather to the forming of men than of citizens." In the end, for Rousseau, no *morale universelle* – whether given by Christ or Reason – can help in the transformation of natural men into denatured citizens. The *générale* must be (somewhat) *particulière*.

Admittedly in the *Political Economy*, a comparatively early transitional work, Rousseau seems to vacillate between *universalité* and *généralité*. There he first says that "any body politic" is "a moral being that has a will," and that "this general will which always tends to the preservation and welfare of the whole and of each part, and which is the source of the law, is ... the rule of what is just and unjust." But this "rule of justice," Rousseau immediately adds, although "infallible" for citizens within a particular polity, "can be defective with [respect to] foreigners." This is simply because "the will of the state, though general in relation to its [own] members, is no longer [such] in relation to other state and their members." At this early point, however, Rousseau was not yet ready to say (as he does in the *Lettres écrites de la montagne*) that humanity must yield to patriotism, that men matter less than citizens; thus, having begun by making the general will the will of some particular body politic, Rousseau falls back on the more-or-less Fénelonian thought that "the large town of the world becomes the body politic, of which the law of nature is always the general will, and the various states and peoples are merely individual members."[29] In his mature, fully confident, and radically civic works, that last echo of the *Chronologie universelle*, of a Dantean–Fénelonian Christian *respublica* under Thomist natural law, finally vanishes altogether: After *Inequality*, there is usually no natural law with which the general will can be equated, and after the *Lettres écrites de la montagne* and the "Government of Poland" the "various states" are no longer "members" of a world body politic. In the *Political Economy* there is still some vacillation between the polis and the cosmopolis, the general and the universal; later that vacillation gave way to a radical constancy.

If, then, disinterested love of "Fénelonianism" will not explain everything in Rousseau, it nonetheless accounts for a great deal; at a minimum one must fold in Lockean "voluntarism" before one can begin to understand Rousseau's crucial insistence that "the general will is always right." Fénelonian antiquity and Lockean "will," subtly fused, do indeed provide the substructure of Rousseau's politics. Rousseau also captured his devotion to Fénelon's love of antiquity and to Locke's ardent modernism when he characterized himself, in a moment of brilliant insight, as one of those "moderns who has an ancient soul." No one ever saw this unorthodox and unexpected Rousseauian *rapprochement* between Fénelon and Locke as clearly as Judith Shklar. But then she was in the habit of seeing, not through a glass darkly, but face to face.

ENDNOTES

1 J. N. Shklar, *Men and Citizens*, 1.
2 *Ibid*. 4–5.
3 *Ibid*. 4–6.
4 Ely Carcassonne, *Fénelon: L'homme et l'oeuvre*, (Paris: Boivin, 1946), Chap. 1, and, above all, Jeanne-Lydie Goré, *L'itenéraire de Fénelon*, (Paris: P.U.F., 1957), *passim*.
5 Fénelon, *Maximes des saints*, edited by A. Cherel, (Paris: Libraire Bloud, 1911), 118–30.
6 Bossuet, *Avertissement* to *Quatre écrits sur les Maximes des Saints*, cited in M. Terestchenko, "La doctrine de Fénelon du pur amour," *Les études philosophiques*, 2 (1992).
7 Fénelon, "Lettre sur les occupations de l'Académie Française," in *Oeuvres de Fénelon* (Paris: Bonnot 1835), III: 248–50.
8 Bossuet, *Politics Drawn from the Very Words of Holy Scripture*, translated and edited by P. Riley (Cambridge: Cambridge University Press, 1990), Introduction; Fénelon, *Telemachus, Son of Ulysses*, translated and edited by P. Riley, (Cambridge: Cambridge University Press, 1994), Introduction.
9 J.-J. Rousseau, *Émile*, translated by B. Foxley, (London: Everyman, 1910), 431.
10 Fénelon, letter to Letellier, *Oeuvres*, III: 653–54.
11 Fénelon, *Telemachus*, 152–53.
12 *Ibid*. 109–10.
13 J.-J. Rousseau, "Government of Poland," in *Political Writings*, translated by F. Watkins (Edinburgh: Nelson, 1953), 174.
14 Fénelon, *Telemachus*, 252.
15 Fénelon, "Sur le pur amour," *Oeuvres*, I, 307–10.
16 B. Pascal, *Pensées*, edited by L. Brunschvicg, (Paris: Hachette, 1914), Nos. 473–83 and (above all) No. 792.
17 The notion that egoism is evil ties together figures as radically different as Plato, Augustine, Pascal, Fénelon, and Rousseau: In each of these there is a sublimated "ascent" from low to high. Here Kant is exceptional: For him all love is "pathological," and ethics needs "reason-ordained objective ends," not sublimated eros. See Kant, *Critique of Practical Reason* (Indianapolis, IN: Library of Liberal Arts, 1956), pp. 126–36.
18 Machiavelli, *Discourses*, Book I, Chap. 10 and Book II, Introduction.

19 See Rousseau's claim that "I am a modern who has an ancient soul" in "*Jugement sur la Polysynodie*," in *Political Writings*, edited by C. Vaughan, (Cambridge: Cambridge University Press, 1915), I, 421.

20 Fénelon, *Lettre sur l'Académie Française*, 248 ff.

21 *Ibid.*

22 Rousseau, *"Du contrat social"*, in *Political Writings*, II, 35–36.

23 *Ibid.* 105, 28.

24 Rousseau, *Émile*, 436.

25 J. Shklar, *General Will*, 275 ff.

26 J. Shklar, *Men and Citizens*, 184.

27 Rousseau, "Chronologie universelle," cited in P. Riley, *The General Will before Rousseau*, (Princeton, NJ, Princeton University Press, 1986), 206–207.

28 Rousseau, *Letters from the Mountain* (Edinburgh: 1764), 34–37.

29 Rousseau, *Political Economy* translated by R. Masters in *On the Social Contract* (New York: St. Martin's Press), 211–12.

5 Rousseau's Political Philosophy: Stoic and Augustinian Origins

It is well established that the philosophical writings of Jean-Jacques Rousseau were significantly shaped by his critical engagement with themes and arguments from the Stoic and the Augustinian traditions. Although Alasdair MacIntyre could write in 1983 that a "general blindness to the importance of the continuing influence of Augustinianism in the seventeenth and eighteenth centuries" had meant that "books of the highest importance about Rousseau tend with few exceptions to ignore the importance of *any* reference to Augustine,"[1] the situation is considerably changed today. MacIntyre's words served to introduce Ann Hartle's study of Rousseau's *Confessions*, in which she systematically compared the autobiographical techniques Rousseau used with those in Augustine's work of the same name; Patrick Riley's volume, *The General Will before Rousseau*, showed how the most important concept in Rousseau's political theory had first been elaborated for use in the theological arguments of the previous century by French Augustinian writers – including the Jansenist Antoine Arnauld (who may have coined the term), the Oratorian Nicolas Malebranche, and the Calvinist Pierre Bayle – as they sought to elucidate the Pauline claim that "God wills all men to be saved."[2] Owing to Rousseau's concerns to defend autonomy and to identify and attack relations of dependence, the Stoic strand in his thinking is much more readily apparent, and scholars have been alert to it for a lot longer: It is a theme in Jean Starobinski's classic study, for

For valuable conversation and helpful comments on earlier drafts of this chapter I am happily indebted to John Michael Parrish, Patrick Riley, Richard Tuck, Pratap Mehta, Amélie Oksenberg Rorty, and audiences at seminars held at the Center for Ethics and the Professions and the Department of Government at Harvard University and at the Department of Political Science at the University of Pennsylvania.

example[3]; among the more recent important works on the subject are a pair of articles by Amélie Oksenberg Rorty.[4]

Given the tasks Rousseau set himself, an engagement with certain aspects of Stoic and Augustinian philosophy was inevitable. On the one hand, as part of his project to improve on the political science he had inherited from Grotius and Hobbes, Rousseau was taking part in a discourse partially shaped by Stoicism, for it was Stoic philosophy that provided the moderns with the richest accounts of the natural inclination to self-preservation, which they used as the basis for the natural-rights theories that held out the possibility of an authoritative and universal theory of political legitimacy and international law. On the other hand, as part of his project to describe the moral psychology of his contemporaries, Rousseau gave a prominent place to the pathologies produced through *amour-propre*, or self-love, a concept that had hitherto been given most prominence with an Augustinian tradition that offered a powerful account of humans' prideful self-love as the fundamental vice that was responsible for actually existing human misery.

Yet the attempt constructively to engage both traditions posed a particular problem of its own. Stoic and Augustinian ideologies pull in quite different directions over a range of questions, and, in particular, Augustinianism in seventeenth-century France had itself been articulated precisely as a form of anti-Stoicism in an attempt to create an exclusive binary and compel a choice between the two standpoints. One of the significant challenges Rousseau faced, therefore, was to structure his own political theory in such a way as to be able to refuse this choice while still being able to work creatively with his Stoic and Augustinian inheritances, and the contention of this chapter is that it is through the interplay of the Stoic and the Augustinian thematics in Rousseau's work, and above all in the *Second Discourse*, "On the Origins of Inequality," that we see most illuminatingly why he arranges his political philosophy in the way that he does.

The fundamental antagonism between Stoicism and Augustinianism was well described by William J. Bouwsma in an important article from the 1970s.[5] He presented a distinctive interpretation of Renaissance humanism as, he wrote, a "singularly complex movement," but one with its own "underlying unity."[6] It was a single movement "in much the sense that a battlefield is a definable piece of ground," and he suggested that the "two ideological poles between which Renaissance humanism oscillated may be roughly labeled 'Stoicism' and 'Augustinianism.'"[7] Bouwsma was swift to concede that these were rather imprecise labels, but he emphasised that they did usefully serve to "designate antithetical visions of human existence"[8] that were peculiarly relevant to the understanding of humanism. For too long, he contended, scholars had thought of Renaissance humanism as an attempt to recover an authentic classicism embodied in the works of Plato or Aristotle, whereas it was the philosophy of the Stoics and of Augustine that represented "genuine alternatives for the Renaissance humanists to ponder."[9]

This opposition between "Stoicism" and "Augustinianism" had many dimensions.[10] A Stoic, for example, would emphasise that the human being partook of the substance rather than of the image of God, whereas for an Augustinian it is the other way around. A Stoic would insist that careful study of the natural world would render it intelligible to us, and help us discover how we should live, and would be optimistic about the possibilities of a natural theology. However, for the Augustinian the truths of religion are revealed in Scripture, not discovered in Nature. A Stoic would hold to the Socratic teaching that it is impossible to know the good and not to do it, that virtue is a kind of knowledge, that we come to virtue through reason; but an Augustinian would stress the frailty of human reason and its capacity to be led astray in the absence of divine illumination. Not only the weakness but also the corruption of the will makes it straightforward for an Augustinian that one can know what the right thing to do is, and why one ought to do it, and yet still be wholly unable to perform the required action. The Stoics teach that it is wholly in our power to determine whether we lead a just and virtuous life, to achieve a state *apatheia*, or of philosophical detachment, passionless existence and – therefore – of constant happiness. From an Augustinian perspective this is absurd, for such a view denies our almost total dependence on God, and the only tranquillity we will ever enjoy will be in a world to come.

Stoicism and Augustinianism did present rival and incompatible visions of human existence and human excellence, and yet what Bouwsma shows in his survey of Renaissance writings is the extent to which the humanists rarely put themselves in a position in which they felt forced to choose one set of ideals and commitments and to abandon the other. Owing to the unsystematic nature of much humanist reflection and the limited availability of the more technical Greek Stoic sources, the polarity between Stoic and Augustinian philosophies was not as clearly perceived as it would later become. As Bouwsma noted of the Renaissance, "Its Augustinianism consisted of a bundle of personal insights that had, indeed, legitimate affinities with Augustine himself . . . ; but its Stoicism was singularly confused."[11] Yet even as the humanists did come to understand some of the distinctive complexities of Stoic philosophy and of how it differed on the one hand from its rival systems of ancient philosophy and on the other from the claims of mainstream Christian theology, many writers continued to draw selectively on Stoic doctrines in pursuit of some kind of syncretism.[12]

Even the most extensively Stoic project of the late Renaissance shared in the syncretist ambition. Bouwsma notes that the Belgian humanist Justus Lipsius, who offered "the first fully systematic presentation of Stoicism" and was the first to recognise clearly that "the heart of Stoicism is not its ethics but its philosophy of nature," "recognised a number of Christian objections to Stoicism."[13] It might also be added that in his textbook presentations of Stoic doctrine, he also suppressed the elements he considered least compatible with Christian orthodoxy. Thus Lipsius argued that the Stoics' "divine fire," which they thought permeated the cosmos, in some sense existed above and beyond ordinary nature, whereas the Stoics themselves were straightforward materialists. For the Stoics, God was physically coextensive with nature, yet Lipsius tells us that this doctrine must be false and that instead we should merely understand that when the Stoics *say* nature, they sometimes *mean* God – "*naturam dixi, intellego Deum*" – which is a little different. Although the Stoics were determinists who denied anything we would recognise as a free-will doctrine, Lipsius nevertheless manages to find a free-will teaching in the Stoics' account of human action.[14]

If writers like Lipsius or Guillaume Du Vair had tried to defend a set of Stoic positions, Hugo Grotius by contrast was chiefly interested in one particular Stoic argument.[15] This was the rather simple thought that all creatures have a natural instinct towards self-preservation, that their behaviour is naturally guided towards the appropriate kinds of goods that will help them to secure their continuing existence.

In the "Preliminary Discourse" to *The Rights of War and Peace,* Grotius confronts a hypothetical objection posed by a Carneadean sceptic, that there is no such thing as justice and that individuals seek only their private advantage, and he invokes a Stoic argument in response:

> But what is here said by the Philosopher [Carneades], and by the Poet after him [Horace] must by no Means be admitted. For Man is indeed an Animal, but one of a very high Order, and that excells all the other Species of Animals much more than they differ from one another; as the many Actions proper only to Mankind sufficiently demonstrate. Now amongst the Things peculiar to Man is his Desire of Society, that is, a certain Inclination to live with those of his own Kind, not in any Manner whatever, but peaceably, and in a Community regulated according to the best of his Understanding; which Disposition the Stoicks termed Οικειωσιν [*Oikeiosis*]. Therefore the Saying, that every Creature is led by Nature to seek its own private Advantage, expressed thus universally, must not be granted.[16]

Here his focus is on Stoic *oikeiosis* as the basis of a natural sociability among men; but later in the same work, he returns to the same concept, this time putting the emphasis on self-preservation:

> Marcus Tullius Cicero, both in the third book of his treatise *On Ends* and in other places, following Stoic writings, learnedly argues that there are certain first principles of nature – "first according to nature," as the Greeks phrased it – and certain other principles which are later manifest but which are to have the preference over those first principles. He calls first principles of nature those in accordance with which every animal from the moment of its birth has regard for itself and is impelled to preserve itself, to have zealous consideration for its own condition and for those things which tend to preserve it, and also shrinks from destruction and things which appear likely to cause destruction....[17]

Grotius thus follows the Stoics in arguing that both the natural inclination to self-preservation and the the natural disposition to a social existence have a common source in the concept of *oikeiosis.* *Oikeiosis* can be translated into English as something like appropriateness, a word that is doubly suitable – or, indeed, appropriate – as it suggests both the *appropriate* goods that we need in order to flourish and our *appropriation* of them to do so.[18] The impulse to self-preservation is shared by all animals ("impulse," or *horme,* is what distinguishes animals from plants in Stoic philosophy[19]) and the same impulse is at the root of a parent's natural affection for its offspring. This impulse, furthermore, according to Cicero and emphasised by Grotius, is "the starting-point of the universal community of the human race" and of our being naturally suited "to form unions, societies and states."[20]

Grotius was more than a generation younger than Lipsius, writing at a time when the restatement of arguments drawn from ancient Scepticism was becoming extremely popular, and these arguments were being formulated with great skill and devastating results.[21] In particular, the exploration of much of the non-European world was nurturing the varieties of moral relativism that often accompany the serious contemplation of cultural difference. Grotius's distinctive contribution to modern moral philosophy – hailed by the eighteenth-century scholar Jean Barbeyrac as his "breaking the ice" of medieval moral philosophy[22] – was to claim that the natural *instinct* towards self-preservation served to ground a natural *right* of self-preservation, and that this natural right could be used as the foundation of a universally valid, nonrelativistic moral code. It might not be surprising that he used a Stoic idea to ground a post-Sceptical philosophy, for the Stoics had been the most sustained opponents of the ancient Sceptics and had fashioned their conceptual tools in opposition to Scepticism. (René Descartes would follow suit, using the "clear and distinct idea" – a variant of the Stoics' *phantasia kataleptike* – as his chief epistemological weapon against Sceptical doubt). Although Grotius drew carefully on Stoic arguments in fashioning this ethical theory, he stressed that none of the ancient schools would have objected to his emphasis on the right of self-preservation: "For on this point, the Stoics, the Epicureans and the Peripatetics are in complete agreement, and apparently even the Academics have entertained no doubt."[23]

Grotius was keen to emphasise that his moral theory could stand independently of the truth of revealed religion, becoming notorious for his claim that the argument would remain valid "[T]hough we should even grant [*etiam daremus*], what without the greatest Wickedness cannot be granted, that there is no God, or that he takes no Care of human Affairs."[24] The theory presented itself as self-sufficient, fully compatible with Christian religion but not necessarily dependent on it for its validity; and in presenting his theory in such a way, Grotius contributed to both the secularisation of moral theory and the differentiation and mutual insulation of the spheres of ethics and theology. However, the self-image of the modern theory of natural rights might be thrown into question when we ask how such a theory might appear from an Augustinian perspective?

In contrast to the tenor of the natural-rights theorists, whose arguments sought to provide criteria for the recognition of legitimate political authority, the tenor of Augustinianism was always to accept that rulers are sent by God and that we should for that reason obey them. If those who rule over us are brutal, then perhaps they are sent to chastise us for our sins, or perhaps their violence is inflicted on us in order to test our Christian commitment to not resisting evil:

> But the power of lordship is given even to such men as this [Nero] only by the providence of the supreme God, when He judges that the condition of human affairs is deserving of such lords....[25]

> Earthly kingdoms, however, He gives to the godly and the ungodly alike, as it may please Him, Whose good pleasure is never unjust.... He Who gave it to Augustus also gave it to Nero.... He Who gave it to the Christian Constantine also gave it to the apostate Julian.[26]

"Though the causes be hidden," Augustine asks, "are they unjust?"[27] Indeed, the most resolute Augustinians of the seventeenth century still tended towards absolutism in politics even when, as in the cases of Pierre Bayle and the Jansenists, they themselves were being persecuted by the King of France: Bayle, in particular, considered it contemptible that one should abandon one's principled absolutism merely because one's own people were suffering.[28]

We get closest to Augustine's views on the question of self-preservation in the opening book of his early dialogue, *On the Free Choice of the Will*, during a discussion of the possibility of a defensible killing.[29] Augustine and his interlocutor Evodius have established that "inordinate desire" or "cupidity" lies behind an instance of evildoing, and a distinction has been drawn between cupidity and "fear": The one desires its object, the other flees from it.[30] The way seems to be open for one of the pair to make a natural-rights-style argument – that killing someone because you fear that otherwise you will lose your own life could be an example of legitimate killing. Instead, the dialogue takes a different turn. Augustine asks whether a man would be a murderer who "kills someone, not out of cupidity for something that he desires to gain, but because he fears that some harm will come to himself . . . ?"[31] Evodius insists that this man *does* desire something, namely, to live without fear, and Augustine responds that this is not a *blameworthy* desire and that it is therefore outside the domain of cupidity. In what way, then, does this man do wrong? The question is still open.

Augustine takes a different example. "So consider someone who kills his master because he fears severe torture. Do you think that he should be classed among those who kill a human being but do not deserve to be called murderers?" Evodius first replies that "No law approves of the deed in your example," but Augustine denies that an appeal to authority will suffice, as they are trying to find out how it is that the law can be said to be just.[32] Both initially agree that the killing is unjust, and it is in order to establish why it is unjust that Augustine makes his key move:

Augustine: It follows that, since the master is killed by the slave as a result of this desire [to be free from fear], he is not killed as a result of a blameworthy desire. And so we have not yet figured out why this deed is evil. For we are agreed that all wrongdoing is evil only because it results from inordinate desire, that is, from blameworthy cupidity.

Evodius: At this point it seems to me that the slave is unjustly condemned, which I would not dream of saying if I could think of some other response.

Augustine: You have let yourself be persuaded that this great crime should go unpunished, without considering whether the slave wanted to be free of the fear of his master in order to satisfy his own inordinate desires. *All wicked people, just like good people, desire to live without fear. The difference is that the good, in desiring this, turn their love away from things that cannot be possessed without the fear of losing them.* The wicked, on the other hand, try to get rid of anything that prevents them from enjoying such things securely. Thus they lead a wicked and criminal life, which would better be called death.[33]

Instead of appealing to a Stoic principle of a natural inclination to self-preservation as the grounds of a lawful killing, Augustine appeals to another principle, familiar above all from the philosophy of the Stoic Epictetus: the distinction between things that are and are not "under our control," here presented as the distinction between things that can and cannot "be possessed without the fear of losing them."[34] This then is the distinction that provides Augustine with his basic criterion for distinguishing rightful from wrongful killing.

Evodius likes this distinction very much and seems to embrace it more strongly than Augustine himself. For the newly enlightened Evodius, killing in order to preserve "the things that one can lose against one's will" – one's life, for example – can*not* now be justified in any circumstances. He is unfazed by Augustine's objection that if this is so then the law is unjust that allows a traveller to kill a highwayman, for he confidently asserts that the law

permits lesser evils among the people that it governs in order to prevent greater evils.... The law does not force them to kill; it merely leaves that in their power. They are free not to kill anyone for those things which can be lost against their will, and which they should therefore not love..., I don't blame the law that allows such people to be killed; but I can't think of any way to defend those who do the killing.[35]

Augustine's reply is weak, given his previous comment about the appeal to legal authority: "And I can't think why you are searching for a defense for people whom no law condemns."[36] Both agree that there may be a hidden divine law that punishes those who act wrongly but who go unpunished by human law. The dialogue then takes another turn, to investigate the relationship between this eternal law and the temporal law, and then to the nature of the good will, which occupies the rest of the dialogue.

Although it is hard to say precisely where Augustine settles on the question of a wrongful killing, it is clear that he rejects considerations regarding self-preservation as being the right kind of criteria to use. Instead, the distinctively Augustinian question about the object of one's love occupies the centre of his attention. This is, of course, the question that underpins the political theory of *The City of God*, which also, in its most succinct formulation, asserts that "Two cities ... have been created by two loves: the earthly city by love of self extending even to contempt of God, and the heavenly by love of God, extending to contempt of self."[37] From an Augustinian perspective, once shaped by an appreciation of the divergent paths of the two cities, a natural-rights theory could indeed form a part of the earthly city's self-understanding. Those who aspire to membership of the City of God should accept natural rights and the law that rests on them as the law of the earthly city to which they submit in accordance with God's decree. However, they submit to that law because it is the temporal, positive law that they must put up with during their pilgrimage on earth, and not because it is thought to have any special, rational, universally valid authority of its own.

Stoic ideas had flourished in France in the early decades of the seventeenth century. In addition to the works of Lipsius, which were widely read across western Europe, the *Essais* of Montaigne did much to interest French authors in the ideas of the Stoics, and the works of Seneca remained extraordinarily popular throughout the period. Stoic philosophy fertilised discussions of moral psychology, shaped the curriculum of the Jesuit academies, and influenced both the drama and the political thought of the age.[38] However, as we might expect in light of Bouwsma's analysis of the "two faces of humanism," the backlash against this Neostoic current in French culture came as a part of the revival of militant Augustinianism in the middle of the century. Cornelius Jansenius's *Augustinus*, posthumously published in Louvain in 1640 and in Paris in 1641, provoked the most explosive debate among French theologians in the seventeenth century, but it was this book that also inaugurated a new round of anti-Stoic polemic.[39]

Convinced that much Catholic teaching on the key questions of grace and free will was insufficiently Augustinian, and in particular that the free-will teaching espoused by the Jesuits, who followed the doctrine of the Spanish theologian Luis Molina, was both false and dangerous, Jansenius presented in his *Augustinus*, a three-volume Latin treatise, what he asserted to be the authentic and authoritative teaching of Augustine on these questions. Predestination was reasserted; the role that divine grace played as a necessary cause of right action was emphasised,[40] as was the seemingly arbitrary distribution of this divine grace across the human species. Stoicism entered his account because of the argument, made in the opening part of the fifth chapter of the first volume of *Augustinus*, that Stoic philosophy is one stage in the historical development of the Pelagian heresy.

PEL.

The fifth-century British monk Pelagius had taught that sin was in its essence voluntary. He argued that we could always choose not to sin, and – relatedly – that Adam's disobedience in the garden of Eden could not have issued in inherited original sin that would afflict all his descendants. In the last great theological controversy of his life, which began in 411 and continued until his death in 430, Augustine had engaged Pelagius and his followers in vigorous polemic. Augustine defended the reality and the heritability of original sin, arguing that the church's practice of infant baptism would otherwise be unintelligible. He worried that the Pelagian teaching raised the possibility of a sinless life or of a human being for whom Christ's redeeming sacrifice on the Cross was in vain – and therefore of someone who could not with justice be damned to hell or someone to whom God would owe eternal life in paradise – yet it was axiomatic for Augustine that God could owe His creation nothing. The Church agreed with Augustine, and declared Pelagius's doctrine heretical in two condemnations in 416 and 417.

Jansenius argued in *Augustinus* that Stoic philosophy was a version of this Pelagian teaching. The Stoic account of the will that stressed the distinction between the things that were and that were not in our power and the ability that we always had to withhold our assent from any proposition was, he suggested, the precursor of the Pelagian will that could always choose to avoid sin. The mistake the Stoics made had been to assume that human nature was still that of Unfallen Man, whose sin had indeed been voluntary, and Pelagius's mistake had been to repeat this error.[41] This was not altogether new. Augustine himself never tried to pin the Stoic label on his Pelagian opponents – for example, in his unfinished polemic *Against Julian* – but it is clear from the fourteenth book of *The City of God* that Augustine understood the vocabulary and emphases of Stoic philosophy as a relevant guide to understanding what life must have been like for Adam and Eve before the Fall. There, for example, we find the following succession of chapters:

8: Of the three dispositions which the Stoics wish to find in the mind of the wise man, pain or grief being excluded because the virtuous mind ought not to feel it.

9: Of the things which disturb the mind, which become right feelings in the lives of righteous men.

10: Whether we are to believe that the first human beings were subject to emotions of any kind when they were placed in Paradise and before they sinned.

11: Of the fall of the first man, whose nature, created good and vitiated by sin, can be restored.

One of the stock Christian objections to Stoicism through the ages had always been that the Stoics attributed too much power to the unaided human will and seemed to deny human beings' dependence on God. Jansenius was in essence restating this traditional objection, but he articulated it in a new way. The connection between Stoicism and Pelagianism was made quite explicit. Pelagianism was not just any old deviation from Catholic orthodoxy, but the most dangerous heresy that the greatest of the Church Fathers had so strenuously opposed. And Augustine's (and Jansenius's) relentless concern to focus attention on the Fall was a powerful reminder that Adam's original sin was one of disobedience rooted in pride and that pride had always been taken to be the besetting sin of the Stoics.

Although Jansenism was condemned by the Pope in the 1653 encyclical *Cum Occasione* (which condemned five propositions defended by the book) and later again in the 1713 bull *Unigenitus*, the argument about Stoicism was never a part of the theological controversy between the party of Jansenius and their more orthodox Catholic opponents. Indeed, the anti-Stoic argument was taken up and restated by other Augustinian writers who were themselves opponents of the Jansenists. The best example of Augustinian Christianity being articulated precisely as anti-Stoicism is perhaps to be found in two prefaces written by the prominent Oratorian father Jean-François Senault.

Senault published a treatise, *De l'usage des passions*, in 1641, and an anti-Pelagian theological treatise on original sin, *L'homme criminel*, in 1644, each of which was accompanied by a preface that was more forthright than anything in the main text of the books themselves, and both took a hard line against Stoicism. The preface to the treatise on the passions, for example, stressed that the opinions of the Stoics

do infinitely differ from the beliefs of the Christians... [for] the Stoics thought virtue the only happiness; and Christians allow of no felicity but grace... [The Stoics] fill the soul with arrogance, and in the misery of their condition, they imitate the pride of devils; [whereas the Christians] acknowledge their weakness, and finding by experience that nature and reason cannot deliver them, they implore aid from grace....[42]

Elsewhere in the same text, the sharp distinction between Stoic nature and Christian grace is emphasised, and Senault also invokes Augustine's famous distinction between the two loves that created two cities: it is corrupt self-love that lies behind the Stoic philosophy, which therefore stands in direct contradiction to true Christian charity. Although the main text of his later treatise, *L'homme criminel*, barely touches on Stoicism at all, it is clear from its preface that an attack on Stoicism was a significant part of its purpose:

Pride has made so powerful an impression in the soul of man, as that all the pains he suffers are not able to efface it. . . . This error being the outmost of all our evils, religion labours only how to disabuse us therein. . . . Only the Stoics, whose whole philosophy is enlivened with vainglory, did believe that if man were irregular, it was only because he would be so. . . . Pelagianism may be said to have had it originally with this proud sect, and that diverse ages before Pelagius's birth, Zeno and Seneca had taken upon them the defence of corrupted nature; for they allotted all her disorders to man's constitution and education, nor knowing any other sins save such as be merely voluntary. . . . Not knowing that reason was blind and liberty a captive, they impudently affirmed that . . . their felicity depended upon their own proper power. . . .[43]

Considered as ideology, this aggressive anti-Stoicism proved quite flexible. It was not only directed against the Neostoics, the Jesuits, and the Molinists, but it could also be turned against François La Mothe Le Vayer and the *libertins erudits*.[44] Augustinian anti-Stoicism would continue to be developed in the second half of the seventeenth century, in particular in the hands of Blaise Pascal and Nicolas Malebranche.[45] However, the main outline of the Augustinian anti-Stoic argument was clearly discernible by the mid-1640s, and it is this argument that constituted an important criticism of the modern natural-rights project. It is not so much the case that the French Augustinians were setting out to discredit the natural-rights philosophy of Hugo Grotius and his followers. Writers in Catholic France were considerably less interested in modern natural-rights theory than those in Protestant countries. The French Augustinians' targets were who they said they were: libertines, Neostoics, Molinists, Jesuits, and Cardinal Richelieu. However, their argument did have a straightforward application to natural-rights theory.

The key claim of the natural-rights theorists, as we have seen, was something like this: that in the face of serious moral disagreement among peoples, and of widespread philosophical scepticism, one should look for a moral principle that all peoples must be assumed to share – to serve as a point of overlapping consensus, to use a contemporary idiom. If this were to be found, a moral code that could be developed from that principle might be minimal, but would be universal, and could then be used to regulate the otherwise lawless sphere of international relations and to ground a moral theory that could withstand sceptical objections. Grotius had suggested that a right of self-preservation was precisely a principle of this kind, and he had presented his arguments in distinctively Stoic terms, building on the idea of the natural instinct towards self-preservation, which was derived from the Stoics' concept of *oikeiosis*, or appropriateness.

If, however, the Stoics' impulse to self-preservation was to be theorised not as a universally shared foundation for a new moral science, but as a consequence of sinful self-love, the fruit of pride, an echo of original sin, or a symptom of the corruption of human nature – as the French Augustinians seemed to suggest – then it is not at all clear that the principle of self-preservation can be the starting point for a universal moral code. Instead, it seems to serve an opposite function, as the fountainhead of vice. In restating the Augustinian doctrine of two antithetical loves in uncompromising terms and deliberately locating Stoic philosophy on the prideful, self-loving, anti-God side of the stark binaries, the Augustinians assembled all the elements that were needed for a powerful attack on the Grotian enterprise, even if they did not make it themselves. Of all the Augustinian writers, it was Blaise Pascal who drew the connection between Augustinian self-love and Stoic *oikeiosis* most explicitly in a fragment that simply runs, "Thus we are born unjust, for each inclines towards himself."[46] If Grotius became notorious for his claim that his theory would be valid even if we were to grant (*etiam daremus*) that there is no God, it would seem to be the case in light of this objection that his theory most obviously loses all of its force if there is in fact a God and if He should turn out to be a French Augustinian.

The seventeenth-century French Augustinians were not themselves especially concerned with the question of the feasibility of a natural-rights theory. However, in seeking to establish a set of sound "principles of political right," Jean-Jacques Rousseau in the eighteenth century certainly was. For although Rouusseau denounced the principles of Grotius and his followers as false (*Émile*, p. 467), declared Grotius to be a "child in bad faith" in the field of "the science of political right" and denounced Hobbes for "bas[ing] himself on sophisms" (*ibid.*, p. 458), he showed himself to be a careful student of the natural rights and related social contract traditions, and his own political theory presents a radical and sophisticated development of these traditions rather than a fundamental alternative.[47] Given his reputation as the most effective Enlightenement critic of the classical Augustinian doctrine of original sin, we might therefore expect to find Rousseau fully embracing the dichotomies proposed by the seventeenth-century Augustinians and to take sides against them alongside the Stoics and the Pelagians and the modern natural-rights theorists. Yet this would be much too simple. For although Rousseau does indeed reject the central planks of Augustine's theology of grace and original sin, his own arguments retain deeply Augustinian elements with respect to both content and structure, and it is in the way in which he synthesizes the Stoic and the Augustinian traditions that his philosophy is at its most creative and original.

On matters concerning grace, Rousseau opposed the Augustinian claims of the Jansenists. Whereas Augustine had argued that divine grace was not and could never be merited by human action but was instead distributed across the human species in a way that could seem only arbitrary and mysterious to human intelligence, Rousseau presented a radically different doctrine. It is most strikingly expressed in a letter in the the sixth part of the epistolary novel *Julie, or the New Heloise*, in which Julie's lover St. Preux repudiates, piece by piece, Augustine's teachings on grace and free will:

In creating man he [= God] endowed him with all the faculties needed for the accomplishment of what he required of him, and when we ask him for the power to do good, we ask him for nothing he has not already given us. He has given us reason to discern what is good, conscience to love it, and freedom to choose it. It is in these sublime gifts that divine grace consists, and since we all have received them, we are all accountable for them.... I do not therefore believe that after having provided in every way for man's needs, God grants to the one and not to the other exceptional assistance, of which he who abuses the assistance common to all is unworthy, and of which he who makes good use of it has no need. This respect of persons is prejudicial to divine justice.

The arguments between the Jansenists and their opponents always turned on the precise interpretation of a small number of verses in the letters of St. Paul and St. Preux breaks with this method of conducting theological dispute by rejecting the authority of Scripture:

Were this harsh and discouraging doctrine deduced from Scripture itself, is not my first duty to honor God? Whatever deference I owe to the sacred text, I owe even more to its Author, and I would sooner believe the Bible falsified or unintelligible than God unjust or evil. St. Paul does not allow the vessel to say to the potter, why hast thou made me thus? That is all very well if the potter demands nothing more of the vessel than services he has made it capable of rendering; but if he rebuked the vessel for not being suited to a use for which he had not made it, would the vessel be wrong to say to him, why didst thou make me thus? [*Julie*, Dartmouth edition, pp. 561–2]

It was these passages that led Rousseau to his celebrated exchange with the official French censor Malesherbes, who rightly declared this to be "A most daring doctrine on grace, a revolt against the authority of holy scripture, an *ad hominem* argument against St. Paul" and, therefore, "more than is needed to require... excision." Rousseau's response, that "If St. Preux wants to be a heretic concerning grace, that is his business...," was disingenuous insofar as there are no strong reasons for thinking that the opinions put into the mouth of St. Preux were not his own. When it came to the privileged position of Biblical texts in theological argument, Rousseau dropped this insistence on the separation of author and his fictitious character:

As for what M. de Malesherbes calls revolt against the authority of Scripture, I call it submission to the authority of God and of reason, which must take precedence over the Bible's, and serves as its foundation: and as for St. Paul, if he does not admit of counter-argumentation, he ought not to argue himself, or at least he should do it better.[48]

Yet even as he asserted this heterodox theology Rousseau was not wholly abandoning Augustine, but rather marking a retreat from the older Augustine's obsession with grace to the younger Augustine's account of the nature of the free will presented especially in the dialogue *On the Free Choice of the Will*, a section of which was examined earlier in this chapter. For where this "young" Augustine, Stoicism (especially in its presentation by Epictetus), and Rousseau most strikingly converge – with intimations, furthermore, of the Kantian philosophy to come – is in their shared belief that a rightly-directed will is the only genuinely unqualified human good [Riley fns DLA 1.12]. Augustine's *bona voluntas*, directed to the proper love of God; the Epictetan *hegemonikon*, which learns to distinguish between that which is and that which is not truly under our control; and Rousseau's *volonté générale*, whereby the individual citizen enjoys freedom by living in accordance with the shared civic will of the political community: In each case the right kind of will is the one that transcends the narrow horizons of the self-centred agent to find fulfilment through aligning itself with something of universal, infinite, or general value.

Augustine ascribed such significant enough powers to the rightly directed freely choosing will in *On the Free Choice of the Will* that his Pelagian opponents quoted his own words back at him during their long-running polemic many years later. In the Retractationes, compiled at the end of his life, Augustine insisted not that the early account was wrong, but that it was incomplete[49]:

> In these and similar statements of mine, because there was no mention of the grace of God which was not the subject under discussion at the time, the Pelagians think or may think that we held their opinion. But they are mistaken in thinking this. For it is precisely the will by which one sins and lives rightly, a subject we discussed here. Unless this will, then, is freed by the grace of God from the servitude by which it has been made – 'a servant of sin' – and unless it is aided to overcome its vices, mortal men cannot live rightly and devoutly.

One of Augustine's main worries in his dispute with the Pelagians was that they seemed to deny the Fallen state of humankind, making nonsense of the Church's claims about the postlapsarian need for redemption through Christ. And if the early Augustine's account of the will is not coupled with his much later account of grace, he suggests, we may be very close indeed to Pelagianism.

As we have seen, Rousseau does indeed combine a strong account of the freedom of the will with a denial of Augustinian grace, but he joins to this Pelagian combination a secular narrative of Fall that provides a functional equivalent for the Augustinian account of original sin that is lacking in the Pelagian schema. Like its Augustinian alternative, Rousseau's conjectural history of the emergence and the entrenchment of ineqaulity in human society, presented in the *Discourse on the Origins of Inequality*, seeks to explain how humankind passed from an original state of contentment to one of degradation, corruption, and misery. To use Ernst Cassirer's phrase, Rousseau sought to transpose the traditional problem of theodicy onto the terrain of politics, locating the origins of evil not in any original sin by the First Couple but in the consequences of the organisation of human societies.[50] Yet with unmeritable grace denied and the problem transposed into a new register, Rousseau's account retains unmistakably Augustinian elements. First, in its form, the Discourse, like the fourteenth book of the *City of God*, presents an account of human life in its prelapsarian state, tells a story of how that state came to be abandoned, and in so doing teaches something about the contours of any possible redemption. Second, the story it presents is one in which self-reinforcing patterns of behaviour are attendant on the original corruption that serves to mire humankind ever deeper in its problems, foreclosing any nonradical solution to the problem presented by the Fall. Third, Rousseau's narrative agrees with Augustine's in having as its pivot a distinctive account of the nature and malign consequences of self-love, or, to use the word extensively discussed by the seventeenth-century French Augustinians, of *amour-propre*.

In Rousseau's account, primitive humans originally lived in a prepolitical, presocial state of nature in which "the produce of the earth furnished him with all he needed, and instinct told him how to use it." However, as these primitives began to encounter difficulties – whether they took the form of other animals, variable "soils climates and seasons" – and opportunities – such as the chance discovery of fire, for example – then

the way these different beings and phenomena impinged on him and on each other must naturally have engendered in man's mind the awareness of certain relationships ... which we denote by the terms great, small, strong, weak, swift, slow, fearful, bold, and the like ..." (p. 85).

They begin to understand the ways in which they are superior to animals – they know how to catch them, for example – and they begin to feel a certain pride.[51] As early societies form and humans interact one with another and do things together, they learn how to make comparisons, to form judgements about what is better and worse, and to acquire preferences. This is very bad, for as "each one began to consider the rest, and to wish to be considered in turn, ... thus a value became attached to public esteem." A reflexive characteristic enters human thinking for the first time: They came to think more highly of themselves if they thought themselves to be highly thought of by others, and this, says Rousseau, was "the first step towards inequality, and at the same time towards vice."[52] Comparative judgements, a sense of superiority, the desire for the approval of others: All are aspects of *amour-propre*, the self-love that comes to poison the simplicity of the primitive life and that leads to hierarchy, poverty, slavery, misery, property, and to the social division of labour.

This is all quite Augustinian, in its way, but Rousseau does not want to embrace all of the Augustinian argument, even in this radically secularised form. The implication of the Augustinian critique, especially in its strict Jansenist interpretation, as we have seen, is that self-love is always and everywhere bad, that the principle of self-love or of the natural instinct towards self-preservation could not serve as an adequate foundation of a natural-rights theory. It is this thought that brings us to the famous distinction between self-love as *amour-propre* and self-love as *amour de soi* in Rousseau's thought, and it also brings us back to Stoicism.

In the Preface to the *Second Discourse*, Rousseau writes:

[C]ontemplating the first and most simple operations of the human soul, I think I can perceive in it two principles, prior to reason, one of them [self-love as *amour de soi*] deeply interesting us in our own welfare and preservation, and the other [pity, *pitié*] exciting a natural repugnance at seeing any other sensible being, and particularly any of our own species, suffer pain or death.[53]

The famous distinction between self-love as *amour de soi* and as *amour-propre* appears in other books by Rousseau, notably *Émile*, and in important respects Rousseau's *amour de soi* closely resembles Stoic *oikeiosis*. For the Stoics as well as for Rousseau, for example, this principle had more content than merely being a mechanical instinct towards bodily self-preservation. Stoic *oikeiosis* helps to explain the care that parents have for children and the affection that the children have for them; in Rousseau's *Émile*, also, we are told that "we have to love ourselves in order to preserve ourselves" and that it therefore "follows from the same sentiment that we love what preserves us. Every child is attached to his nurse" (p. 213). *Amour de soi* is presented as "the source of all our passions" (p. 212), but Rousseau quickly qualifies this to note that the "gentle and affectionate passions are born of *amour de soi*, and . . . the hateful and irascible passions are born of *amour-propre*," reminding us of the distinction the Stoics drew between the harmful passions and the benign *eupatheiai* that would come to replace them. (Rousseau will often use the word sentiment to refer to the affectionate and desirable passions). The fit is not perfect: The Stoics would not, for example, have conisdered *oikeiosis* a principle "prior to reason," but rather one involving judgement or mental assent, however instinctive it might seem to be.

If Rousseau's *amour de soi* does serve as a version of Stoic *oikeiosis*, then what he is doing becomes clear. He accepts the full force of the Augustinian argument about the centrality of self-love – *amour-propre* – in accounting for the corruption of human society; but he denies what was implicit in the seventeenth-century Augustinian argument, that the baneful effects of self-love can serve as an indictment of a natural-rights theory resting on a principle of self-preservation. What the French Augustinians found to condemn in self-love speaks only to the domain of *amour-propre*, and this *amour-propre*, we might say, does not go all the way down. It is not the most fundamental principle of postlapsarian human nature, in the way that the Augustinians alleged. *Oikeiosis* – or, here, *amour de soi* – can still serve perfectly well as the foundation of a natural-rights philosophy as well as serve as the ground for Rousseau's belief in the natural goodness of humankind.

There is an obvious objection to this line of argument. In the passage immediately following the one cited above from the Preface to the *Discourse on Inequality*, Rousseau remarks that

It is from the agreement and combination which the understanding is in a position to establish between these two principles [amour de soi and pitié] without it being necessary to introduce that of sociability, that all the rules of natural right appear to me to be derived.[54]

At first glance, it looks as if Rousseau is here repudiating the Stoic foundation of natural-rights theory altogether. Grotius's approving discussion of Cicero on "sociableness" (*sociabilitas*) formed a part of the demonstration that there was a significant appeal to Stoic philosophy in the argument for natural rights. Yet what is going on in this passage is that Rousseau is denying a principle of the natural sociability of human beings that could be used to defend the naturalness of *political* society. Here, Rousseau follows Hobbes, whose contract theory is premised on the artificiality of political community, which has to be a radical construction of human will. In denying the principle of human sociability in the way that he does, Rousseau is not abandoning Stoic principles: His account of *amour de soi* might generate certain kinds of other-regarding activity, as it does in *Emile*, but it cannot generate the thicker account of human sociability that Hobbes's natural lawyer critics, including Pufendorf, were keen to defend.[55]

In positively valuing some form of self-love, is Rousseau abandoning the Augustinian tradition decisively? It is not clear that he is, for the French Augustinians of the seventeenth century often deployed more rigid distinctions than those that Augustine himself had used. Although Augustine taught that "two loves created two cities" and says much to condemn self-love, we should remember that, for Augustine, nothing in created nature is ever inherently bad and that the self-love he deplored was the prideful love of self that – crucially – leads one to despise God. Oliver O'Donovan's extensive discussions in his book, *The Problem of Self-Love in Augustine*, make it clear how nuanced – and how complex – Augustine's treatment of self-love was and how implausible it is to reduce his analysis to a single, negatively valued concept of *amour-propre*. Rousseau's whole argument is basically secular, and it is this feature of his argument that most clearly marks a break with the Augustinian tradition, not his positive valorisation of self-love as *amour de soi*.

It seems also that Rousseau developed this theory in opposition to an alternative Augustinian social theory, which was presented by the Jansenist Pierre Nicole. A natural question to pose to strict Augustinians is to ask how human society is able to function in any tolerably well-ordered way if humanity is as Fallen as they assert. Nicole had famously argued that although self-love – *amour-propre* – was indeed depraved, the ties of self-interest that bound one person to another worked to produce a kind of social cohesion.[56] These ties were generated by a disreputable cupidity, not be a worthy charity, to be sure, but the resulting society could *look* very similar to what a society might look like if all its inhabitants were to have been motivated by true charitable love of God and neighbour. On this account, it is when we begin interacting with other people, generating ties of interdependency through the exchange of goods and services, adjusting our behaviour to fit the expectations of others, that the depraved effects of self-love begin to be redeemed, in an earthly register, at least. Human action remains motivated by a sinful self-love and is to that extent deplorable, but a trick of divine providence brings about a certain kind of social harmony.[57] Rousseau's account in the *Discourse on Inequality* thus reverses Nicole's at a crucial moment. Although humans are substantially independent of one another, living in the state of nature, with their *amour de soi* guarding over their self-preservation, *amour-propre* is barely existent and poses no particular problem. However, when early societies begin to develop, the interactions among people provoke and inflame *amour-propre*, and it is these repeated social interactions that quickly are translated into relations of dependency, inequality, and oppression. For Nicole it is social existence that corrects some of the bad effects of self-love; for Rousseau it is the social existence that produces these bad effects in the first place, perverting natural *amour de soi* into awful *amour-propre*.

The problem facing Rousseau's political philosophy, then, is that of discovering a way in which *amour de soi* can be preserved and nurtured, minimising the influence of *amour-propre* as much as is possible, disciplining it, channelling it into productive outlets and generally preventing its growth. This problem is structurally analogous to the problem facing Stoic philosophy, too. The task of Stoicism is to find a way of living in accordance with nature, an important part of which involves extirpating the (harmful) passions, and especially anger; in Rousseau's vocabulary, *amour de soi* is presented as entirely natural, *amour-propre* as the origin of all the "hateful and irascible passions." Whereas the Stoics present their philosophical training and their programme of spiritual exercises as the most suitable means of attaining their goal, Rousseau turns to democratic politics instead.

The democratic citizen republic of the *Social Contract* describes the institutions within which a people may live together without inflaming their *amour-propre*. The rough economic equality of citizens prevents the development of hierarchies and of certain forms of dependence and oppression; so does the transparency of the majoritarian political process, which insists on the equal status of all citizens. Rousseau attacks oratory or partial associations – interest groups, factions, and parties – both of which are ways for individuals and groups to acquire more significance in the common life than they deserve to possess. A citizen's life under the general will is a disciplined life, as is the life of the Stoics' sage, lived in accordance with the universal law of the cosmos, but in both cases the discipline provides, paradoxically enough, the best chance of being able to live in accordance with nature or of living in freedom. Stoicism brings about the moral transformation of an individual; Rousseau's politics deals with the collective moral transformation of an entire people.[58] Just as Augustine himself once found Stoic philosophical vocabulary helpful for describing the condition of Unfallen Man, Rousseau's Stoic democracy aims to preserve an entire people in an Unfallen condition, safe from the miseries induced by too much *amour-propre*. It is not too much, perhaps, to call Rousseau's political theory a strikingly original piece of secular Augustinian Stoicism.

For those of us who want to be the friends of the Stoics, there is something exhilarating about this line of thought. Although the historical record itself is mixed on this point, the Roman Stoics acquired for themselves a reputation for being pillars of republican virtue and enemies to those who sought or occupied the Imperial throne. This Stoic pantheon includes Cato of Utica, Marcus Brutus, and Helvidius Priscus, who steadfastly refused to submit to the dictators or tyrants they opposed.[59] Lipsius and the early modern Neostoics, by contrast, had been theorists of a centralised, absolute monarchy; they opposed representative assemblies, and they denied popular sovereignty. Not the least part of Rousseau's Stoic achievement is to have articulated, at long last, the theory of a participatory republican politics, which many people through the ages have often believed was somehow implicit in the Stoics' philosophy of freedom.

I have introduced two alternative Augustinian social theories into this chapter. On the one hand, there was Pierre Nicole's argument about the unintended consequences of self-love, which is more familiar to us in Adam Smith's later version, in which it is known as the Invisible Hand argument. If everyone's behaviour is motivated by narrow self-interest – the secular version of Augustinian self-love – then the aggregate outcomes can still tend to the benefit of all, including the poorest members of the society.[60] As Smith secularises the Augustinian argument, interestingly enough, he also Stoicises it, too, for Smith was extremely interested in Stoic moral philosophy, and much of it finds its way into the pages of *The Theory of Moral Sentiments*.[61] Smith's other great book, *The Wealth of Nations*, inaugurated the tradition of the Classical Political Economy, which later included David Ricardo and John Stuart Mill. Although a revolution in value theory took place in the 1870s, beginning what we now call Neo-Classical Economics, which is still taught in universities today and is the basis of the rational-choice theory that is popular among political scientists, the Nicole–Smith argument was still retained right at the heart of the new economic science.

On the other hand, there was Rousseau's argument – also a form of secular Augustinian Stoicism, as I have suggested – that human society is corrupted and divided most severely by the results of precisely the kind of social and economic interactions that are valued in the Nicole–Smith approach. In unequal societies in which *amour-propre* runs rampant, people are alienated from their authentic or natural selves: Appearance and reality diverge. As Rousseau writes, "it ... became the interest of men to appear what they really were not. To be and to seem became two totally different things."[62] On his account, furthermore, human society is divided into brutal and entrenched class hierarchies: The poor are exploited by the rich, and the rich own great property, but their title to this property is despicable, for it rests ultimately on crime, on the seizure and private appropriation of the common land.[63] In Rousseau's political theory, only a rather severe form of democratic action can bring an end to this alienation and exploitation, holding open the possibility of the free, collective, moral development of the entire people.

I have just redescribed Rousseau, of course, in the language of alienation and exploitation, terms made familiar to us above all from the writings of Karl Marx, Rousseau's great successor in the tradition of European radical democracy. The occasional references to Rousseau in Marx's writings exhibit a variety of attitudes. There is the famous sneer of the *Critique of the Gotha Programme*: "In short, one could just as well have copied the whole of Rousseau." There is the approving quotation from the *Discourse on Political Economy* in the first volume of *Capital*:

"I will allow you," says the capitalist [Marx's replacement for Rousseau's "rich man"], "to have the honour of serving me, on condition that, in return for the pains I take in commanding you, you give me the little that remains to you."

There is his most persistent note, sounded both in the essay *On the Jewish Question* and in *The Grundrisse*, in which Marx links

Rousseau's "abstract notion of political man" to the radical individualism found in the later theorists of "civil society" and describes
his theory as the political analogy of the "Robinsonades" of the
eighteenth-century political economists. Nowhere, however, is
Marx's debt to the spirit and substance of the *Second Discourse* properly acknowledged, though it remained both deep and lifelong.[64]
    If this is a plausible sketch of the succession from Rousseau to
Marx, then the question of whether one is an apologist for liberal
capitalism on the one hand or sympathetic to the claims of radical
socialism on the other comes to turn in part on which secularising
and Stoicising transformation of the Augustinian problem of original sin one comes to prefer. If that is the case, to conclude, then the
legacies of the Stoic and Augustinian traditions are of crucial importance, not just for the political philosophy of Jean-Jacques Rousseau
in the eighteenth century, but for us all in the twenty-first.

ENDNOTES

1 Alasdair MacIntyre, writing in the Preface to Ann Hartle, *The Modern
  Self in Rousseau's* Confessions (Notre Dame, IN: Notre Dame Press,
  1983), p. x. An important exception would be Nannerl O. Keohane's
  Philosophy and the State in France (Princeton, NJ: Princeton University Press, 1980).
2 Patrick Riley, *The General Will before Rousseau* (Princeton, NJ: Princeton University Press, 1986): *New Testament*, 1 Timothy 2:4.
3 Jean Starobinski, *Jean-Jacques Rousseau: Transparency and Obstruction* (Chicago, IL: University of Chicago Press, 1971).
4 Rorty, A. O., "Rousseau's Therapeutic Experiments."*Philosophy* (1991):
  1–22. "The Two Faces of Stoicism in Rousseau and Freud." *Journal of
  the History of Philosophy* 34(1996): 335–56.
5 William J. Bouwsma, "The Two Faces of Humanism: Stoicism and
  Augustinianism in Renaissance Thought," in *A Usable Past: Essays
  in European Cultural History* (Berkeley, CA: University of California
  Press, 1990), pp. 9–73.
6 *Ibid.* 19.
7 *Ibid.* 20.
8 *Ibid.* 20.
9 *Ibid.* 22.
10 *Ibid.* 24–27.
11 *Ibid.* 58.
12 *Ibid.* 60.

13 *Ibid.* 63–4.

14 A. A. Long, *The Stoic Legacy on Naturalism, Rationality and the Common Good* (unpublished MS), (Harvard University Archives) pp.15–17.

15 J. B. Schneewind has a useful summary of the ways in which Grotius is not a Stoic in *The Invention of Autonomy* (Cambridge, U.K.: Cambridge University Press, 1998), p. 175.

16 Grotius, "Preliminary Discourse," in *The Rights of War and Peace*, (1738 London edition), Vol. VI, pp. xv–xvi.

17 From the excerpts from Grotius in J. B. Schneewind, *Moral Philosophy from Montaigne to Kant: An Anthology* (Cambridge, U.K.: Cambridge University Press, 1990). The relevant part of Cicero's *De Finibus* follows. The speaker is Cato. "He said, 'it is the view of those whose system I adopt, that immediately upon birth, for that is the proper point to start from, a living creature (*animal*) feels an attachment for itself and an impulse to preserve itself and to feel affection for its own constitution and for those things which tend to preserve that constitution (*ipsum sibi conciliari et commendari ad se conservandum et ad suum statum eaque quae conserventia sunt eius status diligenda*); while on the other hand it conceives an antipathy to destruction and to those things which appear to threaten destruction. In proof of this opinion they urge that infants desire things conducive to their health and reject things that are the opposite before they have ever felt pleasure or pain; this would not be the case, unless they felt an affection for their own constitution and were afraid of destruction. But it would be impossible that they should feel desire at all unless they possessed self-consciousness, and consequently felt affection for themselves. This leads to the conclusion that it is love of self (*se diligendo*) which supplies the primary impulse to action.' " Cicero, *De Finibus*, BK 3, Ch. V. Secs. 16–17; Loeb translation, Harvard University Press, pp. 232–4.

18 For the most significant surviving original Stoic passages on *oikeiosis* and a useful philosophical commentary, see A. A. Long and David Sedley, *The Hellenistic Philosophers* (Cambridge, U.K.: Cambridge University Press, 1987), Vol. 1, Section 57, pp. 346–354.

19 See Long and Sedley, *op.cit,* Vol. 1, p. 350.

20 *Coetus, concilia civitates.* Cicero, *De finibus*, 3.XIX.62–3. Loeb translation, pp. 281–5.

21 See, especially, Richard Popkin, *The History of Skepticism from Erasmus to Spinoza* (Berkeley; CA: University of California Press, 1979) for details of the nature and the extent of sceptical arguments in Europe in the early seventeenth century.

22 See Tuck, R., *Natural Rights Theories: Their Origin and Development.* Cambridge, 1979: 174–5.

23 Grotius, *Prolegomena* to *De Indis*, quoted by Richard Tuck, *Philosophy and Government* 1572–1651 (Cambridge, U.K.: Cambridge University Press, 1993), p. 173.

24 Grotius, "Preliminary Discourse" in *The Rights of War and Peace* (1738 London edition), Vol. XI, p. xix.

25 Augustine, *City of God*, Vol. 19.

26 *Ibid.* Vol. 21.

27 "*Et si occultis causis, numquid iniustis?*" *Ibid.* Vol. 21.

28 See the classic chapter on Bayle's dictionary article on "David" in Walter Rex, *Essays on Pierre Bayle and Religious Controversy* (The Hague: Martinus Nijhoff, 1965). Nannerl Keohane presents a good English summary of the main themes in Jansenist political thought in the ninth chapter of her *Philosophy and the State in France* (Princeton, NJ: Princeton University Press, 1980).

29 The same passage is also discussed by Richard Tuck, *The Rights of War and Peace* (Oxford, U.K.: Oxford University Press, 1999), pp. 55–56.

30 Augustine, *On the Free Choice of the Will* (Indianapolis, IN: Hackett, 1993), p. 6.

31 *Ibid.* 6.

32 *Ibid.* 7.

33 *Ibid.* 7–8 (emphasis added).

34 See Epictetus, *Enchiridion* 1 or *Discourses* 1.1 for this distinction and its importance.

35 Augustine, *op. cit.*, 8.

36 *Ibid.* 9.

37 Augustine, *City of God*, Vol. XIV, p. 28: "*de qualitate duarum ciuitatum, terrenae atque caelestis. fecerunt itaque ciuitates duas amores duo, terrenam scilicet amor sui usque ad contemptum dei, caelestem uero amor dei usque ad contemptum sui.*"

38 For the neostoic current in moral psychology, see, especially, Anthony Levi, *French Moralists: the Theory of the Passions*, 1585 to 1649 (Oxford, U.K.: Clarendon, 1964). For an important neostoic French political text, see the *Political Testament of Cardinal Richelieu*, trans. Henry Bertram Hill (Madison, WI: University of Wisconsin Press, 1961). The major neostoic dramatist was Pierre Corneille. For an enormous amount of detailed research on Stoicism in France in the first half of the seventeenth century, see *père* Julien-Eymard D'Angers, *Recherches sur le stoïcisme aux XVIe et XVIIe siècles* (New York: Georg Olms Verlag Hildesheim, 1976), whose first chapter provides a useful summary of his main claims about the period.

39 The most detailed account of the theology of Jansenius's book in English is Nigel Abercrombie, *The Origins of Jansenism* (Oxford, U.K.:

Clarendon, 1936). More sympathetic to the Jansenists, and also extremely useful, is Leszek Kolakowski, *God Owes Us Nothing* (Chicago, IL: University of Chicago Press, 1995), which provides an excellent and spirited account of the theological debate.

40 A good account of the structure of the metaphysical underpinnings of Jansenius's doctrine of the will is in the *Cambridge History of Seventeenth-Century Philosophy*, Vol. 2, pp. 1205–6.

41 Anthony Levi, *French Moralists*, Oxford: Clavendon Press 1964, op. cit., p. 207.

42 Senault, Preface to *De l'usage des passions* (Paris, 1641; reissued Paris: Fayard, 1987). The passage quoted is from the English translation by Henry, Earl of Monmouth, *The Use of Passions* (London: printed by W. G. for John Sims, 1671).

43 Senault, Preface to *L'homme criminel* (Paris, 1644). The passage quoted is from the English translation, again by Henry, Earl of Monmouth, *Man Made Guilty, or the Corruption of Nature by Sinne According to Saint Augustine's Sense* (London: William Leake, 1650), which I have slightly modernised. Note the word "vainglory": Hobbes's *Leviathan* would be published the following year.

44 François La Mothe Le Vayer had published his *De la vertu des payens* in 1642, against which Antoine Arnauld wrote his long treatise *De la necessité de la foi en Jesus-Christ pour-être sauvé*, which restated parts of the new anti-Stoic argument, and which is reprinted in the 1775 *Oeuvres de messire Arnauld*, Vol. X.

45 For Pascal, see especially the "Conversation with M. de Sacy" in Levi and Levi, eds, *The Pensées and Other Writings* and the scattered remarks on the Stoics in the *Pensées*. For a discussion that emphasises the significance of anti-Stoicism to the *Pensées*, see Anthony R. Pugh, *The Composition of Pascal's Apologia* (Toronto: University of Toronto Press, 1984). For Malebranche, see his attack on Seneca in Book Two, Part Three, Chapter Four of *The Search After Truth*, trans. Thomas M. Lennon and Paul J. Olscamp (Columbus, OH: Ohio State University Press, 1980) and the chapter by Lennon in Tom Sorrell, ed., *The Rise of Modern Philosophy: The Tension between the New and Traditional Philosophies from Machiavelli to Leibniz* (Oxford, U.K.: Clarendon, 1993).

46 Brunschvig, ed. *Oeuvres de Blaise Pascal*. Paris: 1914. Quoted in Riley, P., *The General Will Before Rousseau*: 19n47.

47 Richard Tuck, *The Rights of War and Peace*: sections on "The Hobbesianism of Rousseau." (Cambridge, U.K.: Cambridge University Press, 1993).

48 Émile too ran into trouble for similar reasons, the Cardinal Archbishop

of Paris Charles de Beaumont complaining that Rousseau's language was "at complete variance with the doctrine of Holy Scripture and of the Church concerning the revolution which has come about in our nature." Christophe de Beaumont, *Mandement, portant condamnation d'un livre qui a pour titre EMILE, OU DE L'EDUCATION...*, quoted in Timothy O'Hagan, *Rousseau* (London: Routledge, 1999), pp. 241–2.

49 St. Augustine, *Retractationes* (Washington, D.C.: Catholic University of America Press, 1968), Book I, Chap. 8, p. 32.

50 Ernst Cassirer, *Das Problem J.-J. Rousseau*, translated by Peter Gay as *The Question of Jean-Jacques Rousseau* (New York: Columbia University Press, 1954).

51 Rousseau, *Discourse on the Origins of Inequality*, Cambridge University Press ed. v. Gourevitch, pp. 85–86.

52 *Ibib.* 90.

53 *Ibid.* 47.

54 *Ibid.* 47.

55 See Richard Tuck, *The Rights of War and Peace*, pp. 151–152, pp. 197–200 (Cambridge, U.K.: Cambridge University Press, 1993).

56 See especially his essays "*De la grandeur*" and "*De la charité et de l'amour-propre*" in his *Essais de morale*. There is an English translation, *Moral Essayes: Contain'd in Several Treatises on Many Important Duties* (London: printed for Samuel, Manship, 1696).

57 E. D. James, *Pierre Nicole: Jansenist and Humanist* (The Hague: Martinus Nijhoff, 1972), pp. 148–161.

58 In the *Discourse on Political Economy*, Everyman edition p. 143, Rousseau compares the achievement of Socrates with that of Cato, to the latter's advantage. See also the unpublished *Discourse on Heroic Virtue*, Cambridge edition, pp. 305–6 for similar sentiments.

59 Cato of Utica killed himself rather than submit to Caesar; Brutus was one of Caesar's assassins; Helvidius Priscus was an imperial Senator and Stoic whose defiance of the Emperor Vespasian is marvellously recounted by Epictetus, *Discourses*, 1.2. 19–24. Loeb translation, pp. 19–21.

60 Adam Smith, *The Wealth of Nations*, IV.ii.9; *The Theory of Moral Sentiments*, Glasgow edition, (Nelson 1938) pp. 184–5. This edition reports H. B. Acton's judgement that the passage from *TMS* immediately preceding the invocation of the invisible hand was written deliberately to oppose Rousseau's account of inequality in the *Second Discourse*.

61 There is a considerable literature by now on Adam Smith's use of Stoicism, with recent contributions in books by Vivienne Brown, *Adam Smith's Discourse: Canonicity, Commerce and Conscience* (London: Routledge, 1994), Stewart Justman, *The Autonomous Male of Adam*

Smith (Norman, OK: University of Oklahoma Press, 1993), Charles L. Griswold, Jr., *Adam Smith and the Virtues of Enlightenment* (Cambridge, U.K.: Cambridge University Press, 1999), Athol Fitzgibbons, *Adam Smith's System of Liberty, Wealth and Virtue* (Oxford, U.K.: Clarendon, 1995).

62 Rousseau, *ibid.* 95.

63 Rousseau, *ibid.* 84, 97–8. For Marx on the expropriation of the commons, see Chaps. 27 and 28 of the first volume of *Capital.*

64 In his article on "The Marxist Critique of Rousseau," *New Left Review* 59 1970, Galvano Della Volpe finds a striking congruence between Rousseau's discussion of the ideal of equality in the *Second Discourse* and Marx's arguments for the inherent inegalitarianism of an ideology of "equal right" in the second half of the *Critique of the Gotha Programme* (pp. 101–109).

6   Rousseau's General Will

Had Rousseau not been centrally concerned with freedom – above all with the voluntariness of morally legitimate human actions – some of the structural features of his political thought would be (literally) unaccountable. Above all, the notion of "general will" would not have become the core idea of his political philosophy: He would just have spoken, *à la* Plato, of achieving perfect *généralité* through civic education, as in *Republic* 462b ("do we know of any greater evil for a state than the thing that distracts it and makes it many instead of one, or a greater good than that which binds it together and makes it one?"[1]), or would have settled for Montesquieu's republican *esprit général*[2]; he would never have spoken of generalizing the *will* as something central but as difficult as squaring the circle – difficult because one must "denature" particularistic beings without destroying their (ultimate) autonomy. However, one must (for Rousseau) have *volonté générale*, not a mere *esprit général*: for "to deprive your will of all freedom is to deprive your actions of all morality," and "civil association is the most voluntary act in the world."[3] That voluntarist side of Rousseau is brought out best by Judith Shklar, who has argued persuasively that the notion of general will "conveys everything he most wanted to say" precisely because it is "a transposition of the most essential individual moral faculty [volition] to the realm of public experience."[4] (By contrast, Bronisław Baçzko, in his mainly splendid essay, "*Moïse, legislateur ...*," overstresses *généralité* at the expense of *volonté*: "le chef d'oeuvre en politique [on the part of Moses or Numa or Lycurgus] c'est de reussir à attacher le citoyen à sa Cité par des liens indissolubles de telle façon que l'amour de la patrie façonne toute son existence."[5] In Rousseau, one needs not just *amour,* but *volonté*; it is not just a matter of quasi-Platonic erotic *ascent,* in the manner of *Phaedrus.*[6])

Moreover: were not generalized will – a will of a very particular kind – essential in Rousseau, the Great Legislator would not have to achieve his civic results (in *Du contrat social* II, 7) by such tortured means – such as "compelling without violence" and "persuading without convincing."[7] Plato (again) did not worry about this kind of difficulty because the philosopher king simply knew the eternal verities such as "absolute goodness" (*Phaedo* 75d) that even the gods know and love (*Euthyphro* 10d-e) and therefore deserved to educate and rule (*Republic* IV); for Rousseau what is needed for perfect politics (*Du contrat social* II, 6) is "a *union* of will and understanding," so that the Great Legislator's civic knowledge is finally, at the end of civic time, *absorbed* into an (originally ignorant) popular general will that is ultimately as "enlightened" as it was always "right."[8] (If Aristotle's critique of *Protagoras* is correct, Plato lacked any adequate notion of volition[9]; but one can only generalize a "will" that actually exists.)

Here the history of "the general will" before Rousseau is illuminating. In Rousseau, the general will is nonnatural: It is artificially produced (over time) through the "denaturing," counteregoistic educative ministrations of Lycurgus or Moses – though at the end of education informed, independent choice must finally be possible (as Émile ultimately says, "I have decided to be what you made me"[10]). However, in the seventeenth century, to the inventors of *volonté générale* – Arnauld, Pascal, Malebranche, Fénelon, Bayle, Leibniz – the general will of God (to "save all men" after the Fall[11]) is *naturally* general: How could one "denature" or transform the will of a perfect being, make him "become" over time what he "naturally" was not? (For Malebranche, e.g., the "generality," uniformity and simplicity of God's [Cartesian] operation expresses his perfection: "God acts by *volontés générales* ... in order to construct or to preserve his work by the simplest means, by an action that is always uniform, constant, perfectly worthy of an infinite wisdom and of a universal cause ... to act by *volontés particulières* shows a limited intelligence ... little penetration and breadth of mind."[12]) Rousseau – who knew intimately the entire seventeenth-century controversy over "general will"[13] – knew too that a nondivinity must be (to revise a phrase) "forced to be general." However, that nondivinity's freedom must finally arrive, as a child (in *Émile*) finally becomes what it was not. Indeed the central problem of all Rousseau's thought is to find a form of nonauthoritarian educative authority that will "make men what they ought to be" (*Économie politique*[14]) without (permanently) depriving them of the freedom without which "neither virtues, nor vices, nor merit, nor demerit, nor morality in human actions" is conceivable (*"Lettre à M. de Franquières,"* 1769[15]).

Nonetheless, even if Rousseau's aim is to "generalize" will over time without destroying freedom – which makes it crucial that he find a nonauthoritarian authority that can "compel without violence" – one can say that Rousseau has a more difficult time in *reconciling* freedom and "what men ought to be" than (most notably) Kant does; and here a comparison with Hegel will also be helpful. Rousseau, Kant, and Hegel – separated by whole universes as they are – are all "voluntarists" who make "will" ethically weighty (in the shape of "general will," "good will," and [so-called] "real will"[16]). All three are in search of a nonwillful will; all are in full flight from capricious *volonté particulière*, from what Shakespeare calls "hydra-headed willfulness" ("Henry V," Act I, Scene i[17]). However, for Rousseau the flight from egoism and *amour-propre* ends at the border of Sparta (with the "Spartan mother" on the opening page of *Émile*), whereas for Kant one "ought" to move on to a universal Kingdom of Ends or (failing that) at least to universal republicanism and eternal peace.[18] Kant more easily preserves freedom/autonomy than does Rousseau – or Hegel, who wants our "real" will to be "recognition" of the state as rational freedom concretely *realized*[19] – because what "generalizes" (or rather universalizes) will is reason-ordained "objective ends," not Lycurgus (or *Bildung*). What moves us away from "pathological" self-love, for Kant, is not a denaturing civic education within Spartan or Roman borders, but simply "seeing" – at the "age of reason" – a moral law that (as a "fact of reason"[20]) is just *there*. It is no accident that education (domestic and civic) is everything in Rousseau (and nearly everything in Hegel[21]), and (nearly) nothing in Kant: If "ought" is a fact of reason, Moses' heroic efforts are superfluous (and possibly autonomy endangering). Rousseau, of course, doubted that there could be a reason-ordained *morale universelle*; for him the crucial line should be drawn *between* the "general" and the "universal," the *polis* and the *cosmopolis*. Doubting (in advance of Kant) that a "Kantian" kind of autonomy was possible, Rousseau set himself the daunting task of generalizing will without recourse to "objective ends" – but with recourse to educative authority whose highest ambition is to wither away after injecting its (civic, *"politan"*) knowledge into beings who become free in the course of time.

In what follows there will be, first, an examination of the (particular) way in which Rousseau generalizes *volonté* – leaving it (he hopes) free but not willful; and second, a fuller comparison of Rousseau and Kant (and also Hegel) that will try to determine which of these three great modern voluntarists does best in "canceling and preserving"[22] the will.

Rousseau's reasons for using "general will" as his central political concept were essentially philosophical – however ready-made for his purposes the seventeenth-century theological notion may have been. (Does not the Spartan mother have a *volonté générale* to "save" the city, as God has a general will to save "all men"?) After all, the two terms of *volonté générale* – "will" and "generality" – represent two main strands in Rousseau's thought. "Generality" stands, *inter alia*, for the rule of law, for civic education that draws us out of ourselves and toward the general (or common) good, for the nonparticularist citizen virtues of Sparta and republican Rome.[23] "Will" stands for Rousseau's conviction that civil association is "the most voluntary act in the world," that "to deprive your will of all freedom is to deprive your actions of all morality."[24] Also, if one could "generalize" the will, so that it "elects" only law, citizenship, and the common good and avoids willful self-love, then one would have a general will in Rousseau's particular sense. The (originally divine) *volonté générale* of Pascal, Malebranche, Fénelon, and Leibniz corresponded closely to these moral aims: Hence why not use a term already rendered politically usable by Bayle in the *Pensées diverses sur la comète?*[25]

It is scarcely open to doubt, indeed, that the notions of *will* and *generality* are equally essential in Rousseau's moral and political philosophy. Without will there is no freedom, no self-determination, no "moral causality" (*Première version du contrat social*[26]), no obligation; without generality the will may be capricious, egoistic, self-obsessed, willful.

Rousseau shared with modern individualist thinkers (notably Hobbes and Locke) the conviction that all political life is conventional, that it can be made obligatory only through voluntary, individual consent. Despite the fact that he sometimes treats moral ideas as if they simply "arise" in a developmental process, in the course of socialization (*Lettre à M. de Beaumont*[27]), he often – particularly in his contractarian vein – falls back on the view that the wills of free men are the "causes" of duties and of legitimate authority. Thus in an argument against slavery in *Du contrat social*, Rousseau urges that "to deprive your will of all freedom" is to deprive your actions of "all morality," that the reason one can derive no notion of right or morality from mere force is that "to yield to force is an act of necessity, not of will."[28] (This shows in advance how carefully one must interpret the *deliberately* paradoxical phrase, "forced to be free.") In *Inégalité*, in a passage that almost prefigures Kant, he insists on the importance of free agency, arguing that although "physics" (natural science) might explain the "mechanism of the senses," it could never make intelligible "the power of willing or rather of choosing" – a power in which "nothing is to be found but acts which are purely spiritual and wholly inexplicable by the laws of mechanism."[29] It is this power of freely willing, rather than reason, that distinguishes men from beasts. In the (unpublished) *Première version du contrat social* he had even said that "every free action has two causes which concur to produce it: the first a moral cause, namely the will which determines the act; the other physical, namely the power which executes it."[30] Rousseau, then, not only requires the Kant-anticipating idea of will as "moral causality"; he actually uses that term.

All of this is confirmed by what Rousseau says about will in *Émile*, in which he argues (through a speech put into the mouth of the Savoyard vicar) that "the motive power of all action is in the will of a free creature," that "it is not the word freedom that is meaningless, but the word necessity." The will is "independent of my senses": I "consent or resist, I yield or I win the victory, and I know very well in myself when I have done what I wanted and when I have merely given way to my passions." Man, he concludes, is "free to act," and he "acts of his own accord."[31] Moreover, human free will does not derogate from Providence, but magnifies it, as God has "made man of so excellent a nature, that he has endowed his actions with that morality

by which they are ennobled." Rousseau cannot agree with those theologians (for example Hobbes) who argue that human freedom would
diminish God by robbing him of his omnipotence: "Providence has
made man free that he may choose the good and refuse the evil ...
what more could divine power itself have done on our behalf? Could
it have made our nature a contradiction and have given the prize of
well-doing to one who was incapable of evil? To prevent a man from
wickedness, should Providence have restricted him to instinct and
made him a fool?"[32]

To be sure, the pre-Kantian voluntarism of *Émile* and of *Inégalité*
is not the whole story; even in the *Lettres morales* (1757), which
were used as a quarry in writing *Émile*, the relation of free will to
morality is complicated and problematical. The opening of the fifth
Lettre – "the whole morality of human life is in the intention of
man"[33] – seems at first to be a voluntarist claim, almost prefiguring
Kant's notion in the *Grundlegung* that a "good will" is the only "unqualifiedly" good thing on earth.[34] However, this *intention* refers not
to the "will" of *Émile*, but rather to "conscience" – which is a "divine
instinct" and an "immortal and heavenly voice." Rousseau, after a
striking passage on moral feelings ("if one sees ... some act of violence or injustice, a movement of anger and indignation arises at once
in our heart"), goes on to speak of feelings of "remorse" that "punish
hidden crimes in secret"; and this "importunate voice" he calls an involuntary feeling (*sentiment involontaire*) that "torments" us. That
the phrase *sentiment involontaire* is not a mere slip of the pen (or of
the mind) is proven by Rousseau's deliberate repetition of "involuntary": "Thus there is, at the bottom of all souls, an innate principle
of justice and of moral truth [that is] prior to all national prejudices,
to all maxims of education. This principle is the involuntary rule [*la
règle involontaire*] by which, despite our own maxims, we judge our
actions, and those of others, as good or bad; and it is to this principle that I give the name conscience." Conscience, then, is an involuntary moral feeling – not surprisingly, given Rousseau's view that
"our feeling is incontestably prior to our reason itself."[35] Therefore,
although the fifth *Lettre morale* opens with an apparent anticipation
of *Émile*'s voluntarism, this is only an appearance which proves that
it is not straightforwardly right to "find" in Rousseau a predecessor
of Kant. Rousseau's *morale sensitive* (one strand of his thought) is not
easy to reconcile with rational self-determination (another, equally

authentic, strand) – for if Rousseau says that "to deprive your will of all freedom is to deprive your actions of all morality," he also says that conscience is a *sentiment* which is *involontaire*.

The fact remains, however, that while *Émile* was published, the *Lettres morales* were held back. (Perhaps Rousseau anticipated the judgment of Bertrand de Jouvenel that "nothing is more danger-ous" than the sovereignty of a conscience which can lead to "the open door to subjectivism"[36] – a judgment no less effective for be-ing borrowed from Hegel's attack on Lutheran "conscience" in the *Phenomenology*.[37]) And in *Émile* Rousseau insists on the moral cen-trality of free will: so much for the supposed "Calvinism" of one who was (often) closer to being a Pelagian – as Pascal would have pointed out.[38] Hence Rousseau can understand "will" as an inde-pendent moral causality with the power to produce moral effects. He definitely thought that he had derived political obligation and rightful political authority from this "power" of willing: "Civil as-sociation is the most voluntary act in the world; since every individ-ual is born free and his own master, no one is able, on any pretext whatsoever, to subject him without his consent." Indeed the first four chapters of *Du contrat social* are devoted to refutations of erro-neous theories of obligation and right – paternal authority, the "right of the strongest" (*à la* Thrasymachus), and obligations derived from slavery. "Since no man," Rousseau concludes, "has natural author-ity over his fellow men, and since might in no sense makes right, [voluntary] convention remains as the basis of legitimate authority among men."[39]

Even if "will" is plainly a central moral, political, and theological notion in Rousseau, this does not mean that he was willing to settle for just any will – such as a particular will or a "willful" will. His constant aim, indeed, is to "generalize" will[40] – either through civic education, as in the *Gouvernement de Pologne*, or through private education, as in *Émile*. In his view, ancient societies such as those of Sparta and Rome had been particularly adept at generalizing hu-man will: Through their simplicity, their morality of the common good, their civic religion, their moral use of fine and military arts, and their lack of extreme individualism and private interest, the city-states of antiquity had been political societies in the proper sense. In them man had been part of a greater whole from which he "in a sense receives his life and being"[41]; on the other hand, modern "prejudices," "base philosophy," and "passions of petty self-interest" ensure that "we moderns can no longer find in ourselves anything of that spiritual vigor which was inspired in the ancients by everything they did" (*Pologne*[42]). And that "spiritual vigor" may be taken to mean the avoidance – through identity with a greater whole – of "that dangerous disposition which gives rise to all our vices," self-love. Political education in an extremely unified ("generalized") state will "lead us out of ourselves" and provide us with a general will before the human ego "has acquired that contemptible activity which absorbs all virtue and constitutes the life and being of little minds" (*Économie politique*[43]). It follows that the best social institutions "are those best able to denature man, to take away his absolute existence and to give him a relative one, and to carry the *moi* into the common unity" (*Émile*[44]).

If these reflections on the pernicious character of self-love and particularism are reminiscent of Malebranche – who had urged that "to act by *volontés particulières* shows a limited intelligence,"[45] and whose love for divine *généralité* had led Rousseau to rank the great Oratorian Father with Plato and Locke[46] – it is in contrasting Rousseau with Malebranche that an important difficulty arises. In Malebranche, God's will is essentially and naturally general; in Rousseau, men's will must be *made* general – a problem that he likens (in the correspondence with Malesherbes) to that of squaring the circle.[47] However, one can reasonably ask, Is will still "will" (*qua* independent "moral cause") if it must be denatured, transformed? Do Rousseau's notions of education – private and civic – leave will as the autonomous producer of moral "effects" that he seems to want? One is tempted to say that this is *the* question for one who wants *volonté* and *généralité* to fuse so that (at the end of time) a perfect "*union* of will and understanding" will synthesize (Lockean) "voluntary agreement" and (Platonic) generalizing education, will blend antiquity ("Sparta") and modernity ("contract") in this "modern who has an ancient soul."[48]

To retain the moral attributes of free will while doing away with will's particularity and selfishness and "willfulness" – to generalize this moral "cause" without causing its destruction – is perhaps the central problem in Rousseau's political, moral, and educational thought, and one that reflects the difficulty Rousseau found in making free will and rational, educative authority coexist in his practical thought. Freedom of the will is as important to the morality of actions for Rousseau as for any voluntarist coming after Augustine's insistence (*De Libero Arbitrio*) that *bona voluntas* alone is good[49]; but Rousseau was suspicious of the very "faculty" – the only faculty – that could moralize. Thus he urges in the *Économie politique* that "the most absolute authority is that which penetrates into a man's inmost being, and concerns itself with his will no less than with his actions."[50] Can the will be both an autonomous "moral cause" and subject to the rationalizing, generalizing effect of educative authority? This is Rousseau's constant difficulty. Even Emile, the best educated of men, chooses to continue to accept the guidance of his teacher: "Advise and control us; we shall be easily led; as long as I live I shall need you."[51] How much more, then, do ordinary men need the guidance of a "great legislator" – the Numa or Moses or Lycurgus of whom Rousseau speaks so often[52] – when they embark on the setting up of a system that will not only aid and defend but also moralize them! The relation of will to authority – of autonomy to educative "shaping" – is one of the most difficult problems in Rousseau. The general will is dependent on "a union of understanding and will within the social body"[53]: but that understanding, which is provided (at least initially) by educative authority – rather than by a Kantian "fact of reason" giving (timeless) "objective ends" – is difficult to make perfectly congruent with "will" as an autonomous "moral cause."

This notion of the relation of educative authority to will appears not just in Rousseau's theories of public or civic education (particularly in the *Économie politique* and the *Gouvernement de Pologne*[54]), but also in his theory of private education in *Émile*. In educating a child, Rousseau advises the tutor, "let him think he is master while you are really master." Then, "there is no subjection so complete as that which preserves the forms of freedom; it is thus that the will itself is taken captive."[55] One can hardly help asking what has become of "will" when it has been "taken captive" and whether it is enough to preserve the mere "forms" of freedom. On this point Rousseau appears to have been of two minds: The poor who "agree" to a social contract that merely legitimizes the holdings of the rich "preserve the forms of freedom," but Rousseau (in *Inégalité*) dismisses this contract as a fraud.[56] Thus it cannot be straightforwardly the case – as John Charvet argues in his remarkable Rousseau study – that the *citoyen de Genève* simply was not "worried by the gap which opens up between the appearance and the reality of freedom."⁵⁷ And yet Charvet has something of a point, as will is "taken captive" in *Émile* and "penetrated" by authority in the *Économie politique*; and neither that captivity nor that penetration is criticized by Rousseau – despite his *dictum* about depriving one's actions "of all morality" if one deprives his will of "freedom." So one sees again why a general will would appeal to him: Capricious willfulness would be "canceled," will rationalized by authority, "preserved."⁵⁸

If will in Rousseau is generalized primarily through an educative authority, so that volition as "moral cause" is not quite so free as he would sometimes prefer, it is at least arguable that any tension between "will" and the authority that "generalizes" it is only a *provisional* problem. Rousseau seems to have hoped that at the end of political time (so to speak) men would finally be citizens and would will only the common good in virtue of what they had learned *over* time; at the end of civic time, they might actually be free, and not just "forced to be free."⁵⁹ At the end of its political education – no *more* "denaturing" or transformative than any true education – political society would finally be in a position to say what Emile says at the end of his "domestic" education: "I have decided to be what you have made me."⁶⁰ At this point (of "decision") there would be a "union of understanding and will" in politics, but one in which "understanding" is no longer the private possession of a Numa or a Lycurgus. At this point, too, "agreement" and "contract" would finally have real meanings: The "general will," which is "always right," would be enlightened as well, and contract would go beyond being the mere rich man's confidence trick (legalizing unequal property) that it is in *Inégalité*. At the end of political time, the "general will one has as a citizen" would have become a kind of second nature, approaching the true naturalness of *volonté générale* in Malebranche's version of the divine *modus operandi*. "Approaching," however, is the strongest term one can use, and the relation of will to the educative authority that generalizes it remains a problem in Rousseau – the more so because he often denied (in his more Lockean moods) that there is any natural authority on earth.⁶¹

One can still ask, How can one reconcile Rousseau's insistence on an all-shaping educative authority with his equal insistence on free choice and personal autonomy ("civil association is the most voluntary act in the world")? A possible answer is this: through his theory of education, which is the heart of his thought – the one thing

that can make Rousseauism "work." At the end of civic time, when
men have been denatured and transformed into citizens, they will
finally have civic knowledge and a general will – just as adults finally
have the moral knowledge and the independence that they (necessarily) lacked as children. For Rousseau there are unavoidable stages
in all education, whether private or public: The child, he says in
Émile, must first be taught necessity, then utility, and finally morality, in that inescapable order; and if one says "ought" to an infant
he simply reveals his own ignorance and folly. This notion of necessary educational time, of *becoming* what one was not – Aristotelian
potentiality-becoming-actuality, transferred from *physis* to the *polis* – is revealed perfectly in Émile's utterance, "I have decided to be
what you made me."[62] That is deliberately paradoxical (as many of
Rousseau's central moral–political beliefs are cast in the form of paradoxes); but it shows that the capacity to "decide" is indeed "made."
(It is education that "forces one to be free" – by slowly "generalizing" the will.) Similarly, Rousseau's "nations" are at first ignorant:
"There is with nations, as with men, a time of youth, or, if you prefer, of maturity, for which we must *wait* before subjecting them to
laws."[63] Waiting, however, requires time; autonomy arrives at the
end of a process, and the general will is *at last* as enlightened as it
was (always) right. On the most favorable reasonable reading, then,
Rousseau does not, as some critics allege, vibrate incoherently between "Platonic" education and "Lockean" voluntariness[64]; if his
notion of becoming-in-time works, then the *généralité* of antiquity
and the *volonté* of modernity are truly fused by this "modern who
has an ancient soul."

In the end, the "generality" cherished (variously) by Pascal, Malebranche, Fénelon, Bayle, and Rousseau turns out to occupy a place
midway between *particularity* and *universality*; and that *recherche
de la généralité* is something distinctively French. This becomes
visible if one contrasts French moral–political *généralisme* with the
thought of Kant, viewed as the perfect representative of German
rationalistic universalism ("I am never to act otherwise than so
that I could also will that my maxim should become a universal
law ... reason extorts from me immediate respect for such [univer-
sal] legislation"[65]), and with that of William Blake, seen as a typical
representative of English ethical "empiricism":

> He who would do good to another
> must do it in Minute Particulars,
> General Good is the plea
> of the scoundrel, hypocrite and flatterer.[66]

The discovery of an *ethos* that rises above "minute particulars," that moves toward universality but has its reasons (*le coeur a ses raisons*) for not building *on* reason, and for drawing up short at a more modest *généralité* – the advocacy of a kind of (free) willing that is more than egoistic and self-loving and *particulière* but less than a Kantian, universal, "higher" will[67] – that is the distinctively French contribution to practical thought worked out by Rousseau, who socialized the "general will" bequeathed to him by his greatest French predecessors. The genesis of "general will" is in God; the creation of the political concept – yielding a covenant and a law that is a mosaic of the Mosaic, the Spartan, the Roman, and the Lockean – is the testament of Rousseau.

But why should Rousseau – unlike Kant – have drawn the dividing line between *généralité* and *universalité*, between the *polis* and the *cosmopolis*, between the "citizen" and the "person"? And why does this particular "placing" of the line make it visibly easier for Kant to *reconcile* freedom with "what men ought to be" than for Rousseau? Here a fuller Rousseau–Kant comparison will be helpful; and after that a contrasting of Rousseau and Kant with Hegel may be illuminating.

No one has ever doubted that Kant begins his moral philosophy with an insistence on "good will"[68] – that is, with the idea of a "moral causality" (owed to Rousseau), itself independent of natural causality, which is the foundation of man's freedom and responsibility. That good will is crucial to Kant's understanding of politics is quite clear: "Public legal justice" is necessitated by the partial or total absence of a good will that would yield, if it could, a noncoercive, universal "ethical commonwealth" (or "kingdom of ends") under laws of virtue. Good will's absence necessitates politics' presence. And the *idea* of an ethical commonwealth generated by good will serves as a kind of utopia that earthly politics can "legally" approximate through eternal peacefulness, both internal and international.[69]

Kant was by no means the first moral philosopher to insist that a good will is the only unqualifiedly good thing on earth; on this point he simply reflects and repeats St. Augustine's *De Libero Arbitrio* I, 12, which argues that a *bona voluntas* is "a will by which we seek to live a good and upright life" and that "when anyone has a good will he really possesses something which ought to be esteemed far above all earthly kingdoms and all delights of the body."[70] (This is remarkably "pre-Kantian": indeed one can wonder whether Kant's kingdom of ends was not suggested by Augustine's denigration of earthly kingdoms.) However, Kant, given his radical distinction between "pathology" and morality, could not have accepted Augustine's further notion of moral "delectation," could never have said, with Augustine, that the "man of good will" will "embrace" rightness as the "object of his joy and delight."[71] The Augustinian notion of opposing higher "delectations" to lower ones, so that "concupiscence" is replaced with the love of temperance, prudence, justice, ultimately *God* – with quasi-Platonic sublimated (made-sublime) erotism (as in the *Phaedrus*)[72] – is alien to Kant (though not always to the Rousseau who could speak of *morale sensitive*). If, then, Kantian good will is not an Augustinian *delectio*, or "higher" love, what is it? If it is not to be "pathological," it must surely be the capacity to determine oneself to action through what ought to be, so that "ought" is the complete and sufficient incentive. If what ought to be is defined as respect for persons as members of a kingdom of ends, then Kantian good will will mean "determining oneself to act from respect for persons."[73] Surely this is a reasonable way to read Kant's moral philosophy; for at the outset one cannot know exactly what post-Augustinian *bona voluntas* actually involves.

If, however, good will begins in Augustinianism, Kant, in insisting on will as a kind of undetermined "moral causality" is still more closely related to Rousseau – who, as was seen, had actually urged (in the *Première version du contrat social*) that "... every free action has ... a moral cause, namely the will which determines the act."[74] And Rousseau had also insisted – in an already-examined passage from *Inégalité* – that although "physics" might explain the senses and empirical ideas, it could never explain "acts which are purely spiritual and wholly inexplicable by the laws of mechanism": above all "the power of willing or rather of choosing," and "the feeling of this power."[75] All of this – will as free "moral cause," as something spiritual and not mechanically determined – Kant could and did applaud. However, then Rousseau had gone on to say (in *Inégalité*) that one must draw a line between "free agency" and "understanding"; that "if I am bound to do no injury to my fellow-creatures, this is less because they are rational than because they are sentient beings."[76] This Kant could not accept at all. In Kant's view, if the duty not to injure others rests on "sentience," then one can have duties only if one feels (and sympathizes with) the pains and pleasures of sentient beings. For Kant this is a calamitous view of morality: It makes duty a mere reflection of psychological facts (feelings) that change from moment to moment.[77] Rousseau, in Kant's view, cannot have it both ways: It cannot be the case that "will" is an independent "moral cause" that freely determines moral acts, and the mere tip of an iceberg of feelings. For in the second case "good will" would once again become a quasi-Augustinian *delectio*; it would not be self-determination through a rational concept (e.g., "ought").

Indeed, had not Kant been so boundlessly devoted to the "Newton of the moral world" as the moralist who had "set him straight" and taught him to "honor" mankind[78] – had Rousseau's thought been a mere *objet trouvé* that Kant stumbled across – he would have dealt more harshly with Rousseau. He might easily have said that Rousseau gets the concept of "negative freedom" – not being determined by mechanism – right, but without knowing why. To use the arguments from the *Critique of Pure Reason*, negative freedom in Rousseau is not "critically" established by showing that although *phenomena* must be understood as caused, *noumena* or "things in themselves" are undetermined.[79] At best, from a Kantian perspective, Rousseau can offer an intuitive account of the *feeling* of freedom, as in *La nouvelle Héloïse*: "A reasoner proves to me in vain that I am not free, [for] inner feeling [*le sentiment intérieur*], stronger than all his arguments, refutes them ceaselessly."[80] For Kant this anti-Spinozist feeling, however eloquently expressed, must yield to the "Transcendental Deduction's" proof in *Pure Reason* that being an undetermined "moral cause" is conceivable.[81]

However, in the treatment of "positive freedom," Rousseau is still more problematical from a Kantian point of view. For positive freedom in Kant means self-determination through an objective moral law ("ought") enjoining respect for persons-as-ends. However, Rousseau (a strict Kant would say) is wholly sound neither on self-determination nor on "ought." He frequently undercuts real self-determination – true spontaneity or "autonomy" – by reducing morality to a natural, "pathological" feeling (such as sympathy), or by saying, as in the *Lettres morales*, that "conscience" is a *sentiment involontaire* that precedes both reason and will.[82] As for "ought," that shifts from work to work: In *Du contrat social* it is *généralité* and the avoidance of "particularism" in one's willing[83]; in the *Profession de foi du Vicaire Savoyard* it is an "order" that reflects the divine world order, making morality nature's "analogue"[84]; in the earlier books of *Émile* it is Stoicism or limiting one's desire's to match one's powers.[85] Only in the eighth of the *Lettres écrites de la montagne* (1764) does Rousseau get both negative and positive freedom nearly right from a Kantian perspective; there he speaks of not being determined and of not determining others:

> It is vain to confuse independence and liberty. These two things are so different that they even mutually exclude each other. When each does what pleases him, he often does something displeasing to others; and that cannot be called a free condition. Liberty consists less in doing one's will than in not being subject to that of another; it consists again in not submitting the will of another to our own. Whoever is master cannot be free; to rule is to obey.[86]

(This is one reason why the "great legislator" does not *rule*, but only helps a people to "find" the general will it is "seeking" – or would seek, if it "knew." If the legislator were a "master," he would not have to bend backwards to "persuade without convincing" – so that freedom can finally arrive.)

One wonders whether Kant did not have this passage from the *Lettres écrites de la montagne* in mind when he said that "Rousseau set me straight ... I learned to honor mankind." Rousseau's notion in *Montagne* that one should neither be subjected nor subject others comes closest to a Kantian "negative" freedom that allows one "positively" to respect persons as objective ends.

However, if this is Rousseau's closest approach to Kant, Kant still wanted to turn back Rousseau's claim that "free agency" is separated from understanding or reason. Against that, Kant wanted to show that a truly free will – finally *good*, not merely *general* – would be determined by "practical reason" itself. That is why Kant insisted in the *Grundlegung* that

> Everything in nature works according to law. Rational beings alone have the faculty of acting according to the conception of laws, that is according to

principles, i.e., have a will. Since the deduction of actions from principles requires reason, the will is nothing but practical reason. The will is a faculty to choose that only which reason independent of inclination recognizes as practically necessary, i.e. good.[87]

Had Rousseau (consistently) risen to this view of rational self-determination, in Kant's opinion, he would not (occasionally) have undermined his own distinction between "physics" and free agency by reducing good will to nonrational sympathy for sentient beings. For Kant, sympathy and sentience are, equally, "pathological" feelings caused by nature[88]; that being so, one does not escape from the very "laws of mechanism" that Rousseau himself rejected by placing a gulf (unreasonably) between reason and freedom. All of this suggests what Kant actually believed: that one cannot find a real duty *in* sympathy, feelings of pleasure and pain, or happiness, simply because the concept "ought" cannot be extracted from these facts of pathology. The concept of moral necessity cannot be derived from the bare *data* of psychology.[89] Why Kant thought that "ought" cannot be extracted from nature – even human "nature" or psychology – he made especially clear in a quasi-Platonic passage from *Pure Reason* that is the foundation of his whole practical philosophy:

That our reason has causality, or that we at least represent it to ourselves as having causality, is evident from the *imperatives* which in all matters of conduct we impose as rules upon our active powers. "Ought" expresses a kind of necessity ... which is found nowhere else in the whole of nature. The understanding can know in nature only what is, what has been, or what will be .... When we have the course of nature alone in view, "ought" has no meaning whatsoever.[90]

Precisely here – and equally in *Practical Reason*'s insistence that the moral law is just there as a "fact of reason," underivable from *anything* else (nature, custom, God)[91] – lies the gulf that separates Rousseau and Kant (antiwillful voluntarists though they both are). If, for Rousseau, reason had "causality," we would not stand in need of Moses' or Lycurgus' *educative* "causality": The will would be generalized (or rather universalized) by a Kantian "objective end" (respect for persons as members of a kingdom of ends) that is *unproblematical* for freedom because all rational beings simply "see" that end (at the age of reason). The whole Kantian "universalizing" operation is completely impersonal: There is no person (Lycurgus) bending backwards to be impersonal, nonauthoritarian, persuading without convincing. In Kant, one is not made free (in time): One simply knows "ought" and takes himself to be free (able to perform ought's commands) *ab initio*[92] – much as Meno's slave just "has" astonishing geometrical knowledge.[93] Of course – and Rousseau would (reasonably) insist on this – Kantianism works only if there are universal, reason-ordained "objective ends" that we "ought to have" (*Religion*)[94]; and Rousseau worried about every term in that sentence: whether we can know a *morale universelle* that is "beyond" the *générale*, whether "reason" ordains anything (morally), whether there are "ends" that all rational beings "see" (as facts of reason). Negatively, Kant and Rousseau are companions-in-flight from self-loving *volonté particulière*; positively, they offer the still feasible *contrasting* possibilities once that flight is over – rational, universal, cosmopolitan morality valid for *persons* versus educator-shaped, general, politan *civisme* valid for a *citoyen de Génève* or *de Sparte*. (Try to imagine Kant as a *citoyen de Königsberg*: that will measure very precisely the distance from Switzerland to Prussia.)

Without "waiting" (as it were) for the actual Kant, Rousseau treated "Kantian" moral universalism and rationalism in his great attack on Diderot, the *Première version du contrat social* – a work in which Rousseau says, in effect, that *of course* one can readily make freedom and "what men ought to be" congruent if autonomous rational agents just "see" the right and the good for themselves. But what if a moral or general standpoint has to be *attained*, over time, through a denaturing antiegoism that will nonetheless finally *cause* autonomy? That is the permanent "Rousseau-question" that "Kantians" *ought* (suitably enough) to keep in mind – as Kant himself certainly did.

Rousseau's radical doubts about the real existence of any universal, reason-ordained morality come out most plainly and brilliantly in the *Première version* – that remarkable refutation of Diderot's *Encyclopédie* article, "*Droit naturel*," arguing that there is a universal *volonté générale* of and for the entire *genre humain*, a rational *morale universelle*.

In "*Droit naturel*," Diderot had argued that "if we deprive the individual of the right to decide about the nature of the just and the unjust," we must then "take this great question ... before the human race," for the "good of all" is the "sole passion" that this most-inclusive group has. Paralleling Rousseau (initially), Diderot goes on to say that "*volontés particulières* are suspect," for they can be indifferently good or wicked, but that "the general will is always good," as it has never "deceived" and never will. It is to this always-good, never-deceiving *volonté générale* "that the individual must address himself," Diderot insists, "in order to know how far he must be a citizen, a subject, a father, a child, and when it is suitable for him to live or to die."[95]

So far, no great gap has opened up between Diderot and Rousseau. However, when Diderot begins to indicate where the general will is *deposited*, he moves in the direction of a proto-Kantian universalism that is (usually) foreign to the citizen of Geneva. The general will can be "consulted," he urges, "in the principles of the written law of all civilized nations; in the social actions of primitive and barbarous peoples; in the tacit conventions of the enemies of the human race between themselves; and even in indignation and resentment, those two passions that nature seems to have placed even in animals, to supply the defect of social laws and public vengeance." Diderot's nominal *généralité* is in fact a *morale universelle* (to use his own term); it relates to the whole *genre humain* and seems to extend even to "honor among thieves."[96] Rousseau's *volonté générale* – of Rome, of Sparta, of Geneva – is a great deal more *particulière*; indeed, in the *Gouvernement de Pologne* Rousseau insists on the importance of national peculiarities and particularities that should not be submerged in a cosmopolitan universalism.[97] For Diderot, then – as Robert Wokler has elegantly put it – the general will is to be found almost everywhere, whereas Rousseau doubts that it has ever been fully realized anywhere.[98]

In the next section of "Droit naturel," Diderot goes on to urge – after repeating that "the man who listens only to his *volonté particulière* is the enemy of the human race"[99] – that "the general will is, in each individual, a pure act of the understanding which reasons in the silence of the passions about what a man can demand of his fellow-man and about what his fellow-man has the right to demand of him."[100] It is at this very point that Diderot begins to be separated from Rousseau: The *citoyen de Génève*, as he styled himself, would have stressed precisely "citizenship" and "Geneva" and would never have urged that *volonté générale* is immediately dictated by understanding or reason (as distinguished from will-generalizing civic education). Had Rousseau thought that, the passions being "silent" (a phrase Diderot borrows from Malebranche[101]), understanding and reason could alone dictate what is right, he would never have made his famous claim that "the general will is always right" but "the judgment which guides it is not always enlightened." If reason alone dictated right (as in Kant it furnishes "ought"), Rousseauian men would have no need of a Numa or a Moses to help effect "a union of understanding and will."[102]

Book 1, Chap. 2 of Rousseau's *Première version* is a refutation of Diderot's rationalism and universalism; but it also provides more than a hint of what Rousseau *would* have said about Kant's distinctive way of combining "ought" and freedom. At one time, to be sure, Rousseau had himself stressed a roughly comparable *morale universelle*; in an early, unpublished fragment called *Chronologie universelle* (ca. 1737) he had appealed to Fénelon's notion of a universal Christian republic:

We are all brothers; our neighbors ought to be as dear to us as ourselves. "I love the human race more than my country," said the illustrious M. de Fénelon, "my country more than my family and my family more than myself." Sentiments so full of humanity ought to be shared by all men.... The universe is a great family of which we are all members.... However extensive may be the power of an individual, he is always in a position to make himself useful ... to the great body of which he is a part. If he can [do this], he indispensably ought to....[103]

Later, of course – most clearly of all in the *Première version* – Rousseau would abandon the *universelle* in favor of the *générale* and exchange the *respublica christiana* for more modest republics: Sparta, Rome, Geneva. Indeed his great difference from Diderot – and, "in advance," from Kant – rests precisely in the difference between the *universelle* (known to all by reason alone, in the "silence of the passions") and the *générale* (known to citizens of a particular republic through a civic education supplied by Numa or Moses or Lycurgus). Hence Rousseau's problem with freedom: He must find an authoritative person who is neither authoritarian nor personal, who generalizes will while leaving it voluntary. Diderot and Kant, different as they are, do not have this difficulty.

That Rousseau is not going to argue for a reason-ordained *morale universelle* that is valid for the entire human race – whether in a late-Stoic, Diderotian, or Kantian shape – is evident in the opening sentence of the *Première version*: "Let us begin by inquiring why the necessity for political institutions arises."[104] If a passion-silencing reason spoke to and governed all men, no mere particular political institutions would arise at all (as Locke had already shown in Section 128 of the *Second Treatise*, saying that only a "corrupt" rejection of reason keeps a unitary, unified mankind from being perfectly governed by natural law[105]). Rousseau is struck by the beauty of Diderot's *morale universelle*: "No one will *deny* that the general will in each individual is a pure act of the understanding, which reasons in the silence of the passions about what man can demand of his fellow-man and what his fellow-man has the right to demand of him." However, where, Rousseau immediately and characteristically asks, "is the man who can be so objective about himself, and if concern for his self-preservation is nature's first precept, can he be forced to look in this manner at the species *en général* in order to impose on himself duties whose connection with his particular constitution is not evident to him?" If reason is not directly morally efficacious (as it cannot be, if great legislators are to have the important formative function that is assigned to them in *Du contrat social*), and if "natural law" is scarcely natural (as *Inégalité* tries to prove), then the natural man who fails to find his particular good in the general good will instead become the enemy of the *genre humain*, allying himself with the strong and the unjust to despoil the weak. "It is false," Rousseau insists, "that in the state of independence, reason leads us to cooperate from the common good."[106]

So strongly does this current of thought sweep Rousseau along that he mounts a brief assault on *généralité* that would be fatal not just to Diderot, but to his own political aims as well: "If the general society [of the human race] did exist somewhere other than in the systems of philosophers, it would be ... a moral being with qualities separate and distinct from those of the particular beings constituting it, somewhat like chemical compounds which have properties that do not belong to any of the elements composing them." In such a *société générale* "there would be a universal language which nature would teach all men and which would be their first means of communication"; there would also be a "kind of central nervous system which would connect all the parts." Finally, "the public good or ill would not be merely the sum of private goods and ills as in a simple aggregation, but would lie in the liaison uniting them. It would be greater than this sum, and public felicity, far from being based on the happiness of private individuals [*des particuliers*], would itself be the source of this happiness."[107]

Plainly this argument goes too far, as Rousseau himself wants to argue for a general good that is more than a mere sum or aggregation of private goods and ills; it is no wonder that he suppressed the *Première version*. Nevertheless the dilemma remains that a general society cannot be produced by passion-silencing "reason" alone.[108] The only way out of the dilemma, *selon* Rousseau, is through denatured, nonnatural "new associations" (Sparta, Rome, Geneva) that take the place of well-meant but imaginary reason-governed *sociétés générales* and that, through rigorous civic education, draw natural beings out of their (equally natural) egocentrism, bringing them to think of themselves (finally) as "parts of a greater whole" – a whole less extensive, but more realizable, than a *respublica christiana* or a kingdom of ends. The particular social remedies designed to overcome *particularité* and self-preference at the end of the *Première version* are rather abstractly, even vaguely, characterized ("new associations," "new insights," "perfected art"[109]); but one knows from other works such as the *Économie politique* and the *Gouvernement de Pologne* how Rousseau proposes to produce, through an educative shaping that finally yields "enlightened" free choice, a civic *volonté générale* that is certainly no cosmopolitan *esprit universel*.[110]

In the end, for Rousseau, no *morale universelle* – not a Christian one based on universal charity, not a Diderotian one grounded in passion-silencing reason, not a Kantian one resting on reason-ordained "objective ends" – can help in the transformation of natural men into denatured citizens. The *générale* must be (somewhat) *particulière*. This explains the weight that Rousseau gives to education. For him, men do not naturally think of themselves as parts of a greater whole[111] – a *genre humain* or a *Reich der Zwecke* – and must therefore be *brought* to a nonnatural civic belief. However, at the end of civic time – if *volonté* is to be equal to *généralité* – they must finally see the force of Émile's "I have decided to be what you made me."

If one can illuminate Rousseau's "generalism" by contrasting it with Kant's "universalism" – and this makes it plain that for Rousseau freedom must be made congruent with *shaping* and *becoming*, whereas for Kant "ought" is just "there" and does not endanger autonomy – one can throw some further light on Rousseau's effort to find a generalized *volonté* that will be voluntary but not "willful" by contrasting the Rousseauian operation with that of Hegel.

Here the first thing to be said is that Hegel strives to place more distance between himself and the citizen of Geneva than is really warranted. After all, Rousseau would agree with Hegel's assertion, in the Preface to the *Philosophy of Right*, that human thought is "perverted into wrong" if it "knows itself to be free only when it diverges from what is generally recognized and valid [*allgemein-anerkannten*], and when it has discovered how to invent for itself some particular character."[112] That sounds like, and is, a Teutonic echo of the *Économie politique*. Rousseau, moreover, would find little to reject – though much to reword – in Hegel's further claim that in the "ethical substantial order ... the self-will of the individual has vanished together with his private conscience which had claimed independence and opposed itself to the ethical substance," so that there is finally an "identity of the general will with the particular will [*Identität des allgemeinen und besonderen Willens*]."[113] Rousseau would also surely approve Hegel's definition of hypocrisy as "knowledge of the true general" coupled with "volition of the particular which conflicts with this generality" – a particular willing that is "evil in character."[114]

However, if Hegel praises Rousseau for correctly "adducing the will as the principle of the state" (rather than falling back on "gregarious instinct" or "divine authority"), if he congratulates him for seeing that "the will's activity consists in annulling the contradiction between subjectivity and objectivity and giving its aims an objective instead of a subjective character, while at the same time remaining by itself even in objectivity," he also, quite surprisingly, accuses Rouasseau of deifying "the will of a single person in his own private self-will, not the absolute or rational will."[115] This seems unjust, even perverse, if it is true that Rousseauian *volonté générale* in neither merely "private" nor simply "rational" – that it is general rather than universal, Lycurgus shaped rather than reason ordained. Hegel speaks as if there were nothing between the private and the "capricious" on the one hand, and the rational and the universal on the other; but that simply rules out Rousseau's distinctive mediation between subjective egoism and objective "higher" will. Thus when Hegel says in Section 258 of the *Philosophy of Right* that Rousseau's "'general will' ... reduces the union of individuals in the state to a contract and therefore to something based on their arbitrary wills," he neglects (generally, willfully) Rousseau's heroic effort to transform traditional Lockean contractarianism into a notion of educated, no-longer-fraudulent consent at the end of civic time, after the general will is finally as "enlightened" (and free) as it was always "right." He does injustice to Rousseau's valiant striving to transcend arbitrariness by bringing each denatured citizen to think of himself as "part of a greater whole." To be sure, Hegel thought he saw in Rousseau the embryo of Robespierre, the germ of the Terror: "The phenomena which [Rousseauism] has produced both in men's heads and in the world are of a frightfulness parallel only to the superficiality of the thoughts on which they are based."[116] Despite the incomparable brilliance of Hegel's reading of the unfolding of western *Geist* – one thinks of his definitive interpretations of "Antigone" and "Hamlet" – this reading of Rousseau is itself "superficial": Rousseau, not unlike Hegel, wanted citizens to embrace a "concrete" universal (the polity), not mere Kantian universalizing of maxims through nonpolitical "good will."[117] In short, Hegel ought to have understood Rousseau better, but he (in Shklar's words) "refused to honor his debt to Rousseau."[118] (May it be the very fact that Rousseau, Kant, and Hegel are "antiwillful voluntarists" that leads Hegel to accuse Rousseau of "superficiality" and Kant of being an "arid formalist" who tries to torture substantive ethics out of bare logic ["universality"]? May the fact that Rousseau and Kant were half right – in opposing *volonté particulière* – have distressed Hegel, who wanted will to be "satisfied" with the modern state *qua* rational freedom concretely "realized"? Were Rousseau and Kant too close for comfort, but not *quite* right enough?)

Following these Kantian and Hegelian critiques of the precise way in which Rousseau balances freedom and "what men ought to be" – and what Rousseau always wants is a generalized *volonté* that is finally free because it finally "sees" ("I have decided to be ...") – one can give the final word to Rousseau himself.

Rousseau not only wanted to "secularize" the general will – to turn it (mainly) away from theology (and God's will to save "all men"); he wanted to endow human beings with a will, a really efficacious "power" of choosing, which can then be subjected to the generalizing influence of civic education – a republican education that Montesquieu eloquently described but took to have vanished from the modern (monarchical) world. First *real* will, then *general will*; that is what Rousseau would say to his great French predecessors. This is not to say that Rousseau thought he knew perfectly what *la volonté* is: But in his most extensive and important treatment of volition (*Émile*, Book 4) Rousseau never allowed (unavoidably incomplete) knowledge of will to cast doubt on either the real existence or the moral necessity of this "faculty." And so he has the Savoyard vicar ask

How does a will produce a physical and corporeal action? I know nothing about that, but I experience in myself [the fact] that it produces it. I will to act, and I act; I will to move my body, and it moves; but that an inanimate body at rest should begin to move itself by itself, or produce movement – that is incomprehensible and unexampled. The will is known to me by its acts, not by its nature. I know this will as motor cause, but to conceive matter as the producer of movement is clearly to conceive an effect without a cause, which is to conceive absolutely nothing.[119]

This doctrine, Rousseau has the vicar say, is admittedly "obscure"; but it "makes sense" and contains nothing repugnant to either reason or observation. "Can one say as much of materialism?" the vicar finally asks.[120]

The answer is clearly, "no." That answer remained constant, seven years after *Émile*, when Rousseau wrote his magnificent *Lettre à M. de Franquières* – in which he urges his correspondent to abandon a materialism and a determinism that are fatal to freedom and morality:

Why do you not appreciate that the same law of necessity which, according to you, rules the working of the world, and all events, also rules all the actions of men, every thought in their heads, all the feelings of their hearts, that nothing is free, that all is forced, necessary, inevitable, that all the movements of man which are directed by blind matter, depend on his will only because his will itself depends on necessity; that there are in consequence neither virtues, nor vices, nor merit, nor demerit, nor morality in human actions, and that the words 'honorable man' or 'villain' must be, for you, totally devoid of sense.... Your honest heart, despite your arguments, declaims against your sad philosophy. The feeling of liberty, the charm of virtue, are felt in you despite you.[121]

Here, more than anywhere else in Rousseau, *le coeur a ses raisons que la raison ne connaît point*. However, this Pascalian "heart" is used to defend a freedom of willing that Pascal himself would certainly have called "Pelagian." And if that will can be generalized by a nonauthoritarian educative authority, the final product will be the realization of Rousseau's highest civic ideal: the *volonté générale* one has "as a citizen."

Had Rousseau not been centrally concerned with freedom – above all with the voluntariness of morally legitimate human actions – he would never have made "the general will" the core idea of his political philosophy.

ENDNOTES

1 Plato, *Republic*, 462a-e. Compare the astonishingly "parallel" passage in I Corinthians 12:1–31 – which makes one wonder how completely St. Paul was rejecting "the wisdom of the Greeks."

2 Montesquieu, *Mes Pensées*, in *Oeuvres Complètes*, Pléiade edition (Paris: Pléiade, 1949), pp. 1134, 1144: "It is essential in republics that there be an *esprit général* which dominates. In proportion as luxury is established, the spirit of particularism is established as well." Here one has *généralité* – but not yet *volonté*.

3 Rousseau, *Du contrat social*, in *Political Writings*, ed. Vaughan (Oxford, U.K.: Blackwell, 1962), Vol. 2, pp. 105, 28.

4 Judith N. Shklar, *Men and Citizens: A Study of Rousseau's Social Theory* (Cambridge, U.K.: Cambridge University Press, 1969), p. 184. See also J.N. Shklar, "General Will," in *Dictionary of the History of Ideas*, ed. P. Wiener (New York: Scribner's, 1973), Vol. 2, pp. 275 ff.

5 Bronisław Baczko, "Moïse, législateur ... ," essay in the collection, *Rousseau* (Manchester, U.K.: Manchester University Press, 1982).

6 Compare Plato, *Phaedrus*, 252b ff.

7 Rousseau, *Du contrat social*, op. cit., II, 7.

8 *Ibid*. II, 6.

9 See A.W. Adkins, *Merit and Responsibility* (Oxford, U.K.: Oxford University Press, 1960).

10 Rousseau, *Emile*, trans. B. Foxley (London: Dent, 1910), p. 435.

11 See the author's *The General Will before Rousseau* (Princeton, NJ: Princeton University Press, 1986), pp. 4 ff.

12 Malebranche, *Traité de la nature et de la grâce*, in *Oeuvres complètes* (Paris: Vrin, 1958), Vol. 5, pp. 147–8, 166.

13 See the author's *The General Will*, op. cit., Chap. 5.

14 Rousseau, *Économie politique*, in *The Social Contract and Discourses*, trans. G. D. H. Cole (New York: Everyman, 1950), p. 297.

15 Rousseau, *Lettre à M. de Franquières* (1769), in *Lettres philosophiques*, ed. Henri Gouhier (Paris: Vrin, 1974), pp. 180–81.

16 See the author's *Will and Political Legitimacy: A Critical Exposition of Social Contract Theory in Hobbes, Locke, Rousseau, Kant and Hegel* (Cambridge, MA: Harvard University Press, 1982), *passim*, for a full account of "voluntarism" in Rousseau, Kant, and Hegel.

17 Shakespeare, "Henry V," Act I, Scene i. Because the phrase refers to the King's previous incarnation as Prince Hal, the word "willfulness" is most apt. Certainly in the final scene of "2 Henry IV" the new king subordinates a *volonté* that had been *particulière* on a Falstaffian scale to the *bien général* of the English state:

Presume not that I am the thing I was,
For God doth know, so shall the world perceive,
That I have turn'd away from my former self.

This "turn" is precisely from radical *particularisme* to civic *volonté générale*.

18 Kant, *Rechtslehre*, in *Immanuel Kants Werke*, ed. E. Cassirer (Berlin: Bruno Cassirer Verlag, 1922), Vol. 7, pp. 161–62. See also the author's *Kant's Political Philosophy* (Totowa: Rowman & Littlefield, 1983), pp. 167 ff.

19 Hegel, *Philosophy of Right*, trans. T.M. Knox (Oxford, U.K.: Clarendon, 1942), p. 105: "Ethical life [in modernity the state] is the Idea of freedom ... the good endowed in self-consciousness with knowing and willing and actualized by self-conscious action." For splendid appreciations of Hegel's version of voluntarism, see George A. Kelly, *Hegel's Retreat from Eleusis* (Princeton, NJ: Princeton University Press, 1978), pp. 113–114, and Michael Oakeshott, *On Human Conduct* (Oxford, U.K.: Clarendon, 1975), p. 160: "The only conditions of conduct which do not compromise the inherent integrity of a Subject are those which reach him in his understanding of them, which he is free to subscribe to or not, and which can be subscribed to only in an intelligent act of will."

20 Kant, *Critique of Practical Reason*, trans. L.W. Beck (Indianapolis, IN: Library of Liberal Arts, 1970), p. 48: "The moral law is given, as an apodictically certain fact, as it were, of pure reason...."

21 Hegel, *Phenomenology of Mind*, trans. F. Baillie (New York: Harper & Row, 1967), p. 89, in which Hegel urges that each individual must "go through the stages through which the general mind has passed."

22 *Ibid.* 234.

23 See, above all, Rousseau, *Gouvernement de Pologne*, in *Political Writings*, op. cit., Vol. 2, pp. 424 ff.

24 Rousseau, *Du contrat social*, in *Political Writings*, op. cit., Vol. 2, pp. 105, 28.

25 Bayle, *Pensées diverses, Écrites à un docteur de Sorbonne*, 4th ed.

(Rotterdam: Chez Reinier Leers, 1704), Vol. 2, pp. 452 ff. For Bayle's political–moral argument that *generalité* is good, *particularité* evil, see the author's *The General will before Rousseau*, op. cit., pp. 79 ff.

26 Rousseau, *Première version du contrat social*, in *Political Writings*, op. cit., Vol. 1, p. 499.

27 Rousseau, *Lettre à M. de Beaumont*, in *Oeuvres complètes* (Paris: Éditions du Seuil, 1971), Vol. 3, pp. 340 ff.

28 Rousseau, *Du contrat social*, in *Political Writings*, op. cit., Vol. 1, p. 26.

29 Rousseau, *Discourse on Inequality*, in *The Social Contract and Discourses*, op. cit., p. 208.

30 Rousseau, *Première version*, op. cit., p. 499.

31 Rousseau, *Émile*, op. cit., pp. 243–44.

32 *Ibid.*

33 Rousseau, *Lettres morales*, in *Oeuvres Complètes de Rousseau*, Pléiade ed., op. cit., Vol. 4, pp. 1106 ff. For the importance of the *Lettres*, see Shklar, *Men and Citizens*, op. cit., pp. 229–30.

34 Kant, *Grundlegung*, trans. T.K. Abbott as *Fundamental Principles* (Indianapolis, IN: Library of Liberal Arts, 1949), p. 11.

35 Rousseau, *Lettres morales*, op. cit., pp. 1111, 1107, 1108, 1109.

36 Bertrand de Jouvenel, "Essai sur la politique de Rousseau," in *Du contrat social* (Geneva: Éditions du Cheval Aile, 1947), p. 78.

37 Hegel, *Phenomenology*, op. cit., pp. 660–62.

38 Pascal, *Écrits sur la grace*, in *Oeuvres de Blaise Pascal*, ed. Brunschvicg (Paris: Librairie Hachette, 1914), Vol. 11, p. 134.

39 Rousseau, *Du contrat social*, in *Political Writings*, op. cit., Vol. 2, pp. 105, 27.

40 Rousseau, *Première version*, op. cit., pp. 472–73, in which he urges that every authentic "act of sovereignty" involves "an agreement between the body politic and each of its members," which is "equitable because it is voluntary and general." Here *volonté* and *généralité* are of equal weight.

41 Rousseau, *Du contrat social*, op. cit., p. 52.

42 Rousseau, *Gouvernement de Pologne*, op. cit., Vol. 2, p. 430.

43 Rousseau, *Économie politique*, op. cit., p. 308.

44 Rousseau, *Émile*, excerpt in *Political Writings*, op. cit., Vol. 2, p. 145.

45 Malebranche, *Nature et grâce*, op. cit., pp. 147–166.

46 Rousseau, "Le Persifleur," in *Les Confessions*, Pléiade ed., op. cit., p. 1111, in which Rousseau urges that *la plus profonde metaphysique* is that of "Plato, Locke or Malebranche."

47 Rousseau, letter to Mirabeau, in *Lettres philosophiques*, op. cit.

48 Rousseau, *Jugement sur la Polysynodie*, in *Political Writings*, op. cit., Vol. 1, p. 421.

49 St. Augustine, *De Libero Arbitrio*, Book I, Chap. 12.

50 Rousseau, *Économie politique*, op. cit., p. 297.

51 Rousseau, *Émile*, op. cit., p. 444.

52 Rousseau, *Gouvernement de Pologne*, op. cit., Vol. 2, pp. 427–430. See also Rousseau's early prize essay, *Discours sur la vertu du heros*, in *Oeuvres complètes*, du Seuil ed., op. cit., vol. 2, pp. 118–120.

53 Rousseau, *Du contrat social*, op. cit., p. 51.

54 Rousseau, *Gouvernement de Pologne*, op. cit., Vol. 2, pp. 437–443.

55 Rousseau, *Émile*, op. cit., p. 84.

56 Rousseau, *Discourse on Inequality*, op. cit., pp. 180–82.

57 John Charvet, *The Social Problem in the Philosophy of Rousseau* (Cambridge, U.K.: Cambridge University Press, 1974), p. 58.

58 Hegel, *Phenomenology*, op. cit., p. 234.

59 Rousseau, *Du contrat social*, op. cit., p. 36.

60 Rousseau, *Émile*, trans. Foxley, op. cit., p. 435.

61 Rousseau, *Du contrat social*, op. cit., p. 27.

62 Same as note 60.

63 Rousseau, *Du contrat social*, op. cit., p. 56.

64 Particularly Vaughan, in his "Introduction" to Rousseau's *Political Writings*, op. cit., Vol. 1, pp. 35 ff.

65 Kant, *Grundlegung*, op. cit., pp. 19–21.

66 Blake's lines are quoted by A. J. Ayer in *Part of My Life* (New York: Oxford University Press, 1977), p. 176.

67 Shklar's phrase in "General Will," op. cit., p. 279.

68 Kant, *Grundlegung*, op. cit., pp. 11–12.

69 The notion that the "ethical commonwealth" of *Religion within the Limits* should be viewed as Kant's "utopia" was suggested (*en passant*) by Judith Shklar.

70 St. Augustine, *De Libero Arbitrio*, trans. Russell (Washington, D.C.: Catholic University of America Press, 1968), pp. 95–96.

71 *Ibid.* 97.

72 Plato, *Phaedrus*, 253b–257b.

73 Kant, *Grundlegung*, op. cit., pp. 55–56.

74 Rousseau, *Première version*, op. cit., p. 499.

75 Rousseau, *Inequality*, op. cit., p. 208.

76 *Ibid.* pp. 208, 194.

77 Kant, *Grundlegung*, op. cit., p. 29: "... all moral conception have their seat and origin completely *a priori* in the reason ...."

78 Cited by Ernst Cassirer in *Rousseau, Kant and Goethe*, trans. Gutmann et al. (New York: Harper, 1963), pp. 1–2.

79 Kant, *Critique of Pure Reason*, trans. N.K. Smith (London: Macmillan, 1962), pp. 464–65 (A 533/B 561).

80 Rousseau, *La Nouvelle Héloïse*, ed. R. Pomeau (Paris: Garnier Freres, 1960) p. 671.

81 Same as 79.

82 Rousseau, *Lettres morales*, op. cit., p. 1107.

83 Rousseau, *Du contrat social*, op. cit., pp. 42–50.

84 Rousseau, *Émile*, Pléiade ed., op. cit., Vol. 4, p. 588: "Le mal général ne peut être que dans le desordre, et je vois dans le systeme du monde un ordre qui ne se dement point." See also André Robinet, "A propos d'ordre dans la Profession de Foi du Vicaire Savoyard," in *Studi Filosofici*, I (Olschki Editore, Naples 1978), pp. 39–76.

85 Rousseau, *Émile*, op. cit., pp. 303–306.

86 Rousseau, *Lettres écrites de la montagne* (Amsterdam: Rey, 1764), Part II, p. 57.

87 Kant, *Grundlegung*, op. cit., p. 30.

88 *Ibid.* 17, 58–59.

89 *Ibid.* 29.

90 Kant, *Pure Reason*, op. cit., A 547/B 575.

91 Kant, *Practical Reason*, op. cit., p. 48.

92 *Ibid.* 29. For Kant we *think* freedom because we *know* "ought."

93 Plato, *Meno* 82b ff.

94 Kant, *Religion within the Limits of Reason Alone*, trans. T.M. Greene and Hoyt Hudson (New York: Harper & Row, 1960), p. 6n.

95 Diderot, "Droit naturel," in *Rousseau: Political Writings*, op. cit., Vol. 1, p. 431.

96 *Ibid.* 431–32.

97 Rousseau, *Gouvernement de Pologne*, op. cit., Chaps. 1–4.

98 Robert Wokler, "The Influence of Diderot on Rousseau," in *Studies on Voltaire and the 18th Century* (Banbury, U.K.: Voltaire Foundation, 1975), Vol. 132.

99 Diderot, "Droit naturel," op. cit., p. 432.

100 *Ibid.*

101 Malebranche, *Recherche de la vérité*, in *Oeuvres complètes*, op. cit., Vol. 2, p. 490.

102 Rousseau, *Du contrat social*, op. cit., II, 6.

103 Rousseau, *Chronologie universelle*, in *Annales de la Société Jean-Jacques Rousseau* (Geneva: Jullien, 1905), Vol. 1, pp. 213 ff.

104 Rousseau, *Première version*, in *On the Social Contract*, trans. R. Masters (New York: St. Martin's, 1978), p. 157.

105 Locke, "Second Treatise," in *Two Treatises*, Section 128.

106 Rousseau, *Première version*, Masters edition, op. cit., pp. 159–60.

107 *Ibid.*

108 Rousseau, *Du contrat social*, op. cit., p. 48. Compare George A. Kelly,

"Rousseau, Kant and History," in *Journal of the History of Ideas*, Vol. XXIX, No. 3, 1968, p. 353: "Rousseau is not an irrationalist. But ... reason is highly corruptible; the passions distort it into self-serving 'raisonnements.' Though reason enables us to know the truth, only conscience can make us *love* it ...."

109 Rousseau, *Première version*, Masters edition, op. cit., pp. 162–63.

110 Rousseau, *Gouvernement de Pologne*, op. cit., p. 437: "Tout vrai republicain ... ne voit que la patrie, il ne vit que pour elle ...."

111 Rousseau, *Du contrat social*, op. cit., p. 52.

112 Hegel, *Philosophy of Right*, op. cit., Preface, p. 4.

113 *Ibid.* 142.

114 *Ibid.* Section 140.

115 *Ibid.* 156, 32–33.

116 *Ibid.* 157, 33.

117 See Kelly, *Hegel's Retreat from Eleusis*, op. cit., pp. 55 ff.

118 Judith N. Shklar, *Freedom and Independence* (Cambridge, U.K.: Cambridge University Press, 1976), p. 207.

119 Rousseau, *Émile* (Paris: Pléiade, 1959), p. 576.

120 *Ibid.* 576–77.

121 Same as note 15.

7 Rousseau's Images of Authority (Especially in *La Nouvelle Héloïse*)

INTRODUCTION

By nature men are free, but left to their own devices they will inevitably enslave each other. Of all the "bipolarities" in the thought
of Jean-Jacques Rousseau none is more striking than this tension
between natural freedom and the spontaneous march to inequality
and oppression in which all men participate.[1] None aroused more
conflicting reactions in his own mind. If men are the sole authors
of their ills and not the mere victims of some external force, be it
original sin, a malevolent nature, or a hostile environment, then
there is always hope for self-improvement.[2] On the other hand, if
men were alone responsible for inventing and maintaining their own
social misery, they could scarcely be expected to overcome conditions they had themselves chosen to create. One could hardly hope
that those who had devised and imposed their own chains would either wish or know how to liberate themselves. If there was no need
for cosmic fatalism, there was every reason to despair of mankind's
own social powers. And indeed it was perfectly clear to Rousseau
that every man left free to follow his own inclinations and every
society allowed to pursue its inherent tendencies would repeat all
the familiar errors of the past. It was this conflict between possibility and probability that inspired all of Rousseau's works. All of them
are attempts to show some way out of the horrors of history. And if all
are marked by a deep note of hopelessness, each one is also an act of
rebellion against the weight of the actual. The suggestions, the paths
he traced and held out, were numerous and various. Among them,
the hope of salvation through the personal authority of great men
was one of the most important. In almost all his writings, whether

philosophical or fictional, some such dominating figure appears. An account of the character and work of these authoritative individuals thus not only illuminates an important, though relatively obscure, part of Rousseau's thought, it also reveals much that is morally and psychologically most subtle in it.

DISPELLING ILLUSIONS

The march to self-enslavement is clearly spontaneous, even if ill-intentioned men force their weaker fellows along. Rousseau did not believe that in the normal course of events much could be done about it. Occasionally a small country like Switzerland or Holland, perhaps Corsica, might still retain some degree of freedom and justice. For most of Europe that was quite out of the question. The history that had produced nothing but servants and masters ensured a future that could only be worse than the past had been. Utopia was Rousseau's way of exposing the prevalent degradation. It showed how far men had departed from the possibilities that were open to them. Better opinions were not psychologically impossible. Spartan republics were imaginable. And the restoration of the Golden Age by individuals determined to escape from Paris was thinkable. Even the education of children who would grow up free from *amour-propre* was not inconceivable. The likelihood that any of these enterprises would succeed was minimal, but they were not impossible. More-over, the contrast between the probable and the possible was what these utopias were meant to show. As such they illuminated the misery of mankind's actual situation.

How was one to imagine a sudden break in the history of either a group or of a single person? Men's inner resources were too limited to make self-restoration a plausible notion. Only an outside force could rescue them. That force was the personal authority of a great man.

That man in general needs a master is clear enough when one considers the misery that he drifts into by passively reacting to his situation. What is needed is someone so extraordinary in intelligence and moral strength that he can restructure the environment in which men live and thus indirectly compel them to turn away from their present course. The Spartan republic and the household that a Great Legislator and a God–father, respectively, might build would be such settings. Possibly a great teacher might, as Émile's tutor does, devote his entire life to saving one child from the impact of society. Someone completely outside the prevailing system of opinions might cure and prevent the wounds that social life usually inflicts on men. Rousseau provided portraits of such men of authority in almost every one of his works. Clearly he found them fascinating and deeply attractive. They were far more than mere mechanical contrivances, invented to give utopia a start. The authority that radiates from great men was obviously a form of psychological power that appealed to Rousseau directly. That was due at least in part to his own sensitivity to relations of authority. He longed for a paternal protector and also feared such men. He was constantly and intensely aware of his own desire for dependence, as well as of the dangers of domination that he might thus invite. From the painful experience that inevitably came with these dispositions, he was, as always, able to draw a public message that his figures of authority embodied.

Paternal authority was not only a personal solution for Rousseau in moments of helpless weakness. Although his own experience made him sensitive to both the advantages and limitations of authority, he looked beyond the consumers of authority to those who exercised it. If the Greater Legislator is a figure that owes too much to Plutarch to arouse much psychological interest, Rousseau did draw one portrait of a man of authority that is unforgettable. M. Wolmar is the real hero of the *Nouvelle Héloïse*, because he is omnicompetent and perfect. He cures the ill, saves the weak, and builds a model estate. He is, in fact, as Rousseau makes perfectly clear, God, and he is better and kinder than God. God gave men a freedom that they are too weak to use well and then left them to suffer. It is only in a human image that the goodness ascribed to God can really be made manifest. It is not therefore only the catastrophic state in which most men find themselves that justifies authority. The history of men's vices shows the need for it also. The man of authority, the genuinely good and capable man, who educates, saves, and builds, is inherently admirable. He automatically arouses moral aspirations in those around him, because to know him is to become aware of morality. Without these qualities teachers are mere masters, fathers are domestic tyrants, and legislators are mere Hobbesian despots. The miracle of the true man of authority is that he subjugates the will of his pupils so that they may develop enough inner strength to throw off the yoke of personal servitude.

The most obvious difficulty would seem the impossibility of finding such men of authority. This, however, troubled Rousseau relatively little. He wanted to believe in his Plutarchian heroes, and such figures as the Legislator, Émile's tutor, and M. de Wolmar show how well he could imagine men capable of reordering the lives of others. All he had to show was that such men were possible. What *did* trouble him was the worth of even the most beneficent and necessary authority. On one hand he was completely convinced that a liberating form of authority was possible and the only means of helping men out of their present muddle. Good and wise chiefs know how to "prevent, cure and palliate" that mass of abuses and ills that overwhelm us.[3] The possibility of "forcing men to be free" through complex psychological devices (though not through the punitive means implied in the actual context of that famous phrase) was, for him, a real one. Yet Rousseau never forgot that authority meant submission. Even the most self-liquidating forms of authority involve subordination, and that is in itself the essence of evil. Rousseau therefore doubted whether authority could accomplish its true ends. It might cure and palliate, but once men needed a master, they would never be able to do without one. Authority may keep them from evil, but it does not liberate fully or permanently. It only perpetuates dependence. For all his belief in the creative powers of great men, Rousseau never quite overcame his fear of them. Nevertheless, these misgivings did not outweigh his acute sense of the self-destructiveness of untutored men. Here, as always, a negative impulsion, a critical rather than a reforming zeal, was his ultimate inspiration.

Personal experience, moreover, only added to Rousseau's perplexities. His view of authority grew directly out of his own inner confusions. His correspondence bristles with declarations of independence. "First of all I want my friends to be my friends and not my masters." He wanted to be happy in his way, not according to their ideas.[4] In the end he concluded that his need for personal liberty was such that he was simply not made for any civil society.[5] "He has ideas of independence," wrote the ever-observant Boswell, "that are completely visionary and which are unsuitable for a man in his position." Boswell did not refer merely to Rousseau's social station here. "Behold the man he is, and tell me if such a man does not need a great deal of affection from his fellows – and consequently if he does not depend on them as we all depend on one another."[6]

That was, of course, the trouble, and Rousseau knew it only too well. The Calvinist spinster who had raised him had seen to it that he became positively "fond of acts of submission." She had, as he knew perfectly well, crippled him morally and sexually.[7] Hume was not exceptionally perceptive when he noticed that Rousseau was at the mercy of those whom he loved, even of his little dog.[8] He ought also to have realized that Rousseau resented and feared those whom he suspected of exploiting his softness.[9] Eventually that fear led to exaggeration. And although Rousseau certainly was victimized, not everyone conspired to tyrannize over him, as he believed they did. He was, therefore, torn all his life between an urge for perfect freedom and a longing for submission and for a return to childhood under the parental care of Mme. de Warens or Maréchal Keith. If patronage was always rebuffed at first and the offer of every royal pension produced a crisis, Rousseau also longed for a supervising father. As Saint-Preux, Rousseau's imaginary self-portrait, had addressed Wolmar, so he later would call Maréchal Keith *mon bienfaiteur et mon père* and speak of himself as the *fils cadet*.[10] Patronage could be endured only if it was transformed into pseudopaternity. It was Hume's failure to recognize this that led to their dreadful quarrel in England. Thus Rousseau's first response to the approaches of his future patron, M. de Luxembourg, was an outburst of plebeian resentment. "I hate the great, I hate their estate, their hardness, their prejudices, their pettiness and all their vices."[11] This, however, presently changed to "Ah, M. le Maréchal, I hated the great before I knew you, and I hate them even more now that you have made me feel so well how easy it would be for them to make themselves adored."[12] He would have wanted to seek him out, Rousseau later wrote to his patron, even if they had been equals. How was he to treat him now, without forgetting himself?[13] For he did not wish to forget the inequality between them, little though it mattered to M. de Luxembourg. Rousseau only wanted to transform grandeur into paternity and to replace class distinctions with emotional subservience. Much as he hated inequality he did not want equality either, and positions of superior and inferior were to be maintained.

Deeply rooted as these psychological tendencies were, they were exacerbated by Rousseau's experiences with the powers that be. To be sure, his distaste for impersonal relationships in any form, and especially for those involving subordination, would have made it difficult for him to accept regular employment of the usual sort. However, Rousseau was also a man of supreme gifts forced to endure every social indignity that society could inflict. If in Rousseau's case apprenticeship, vagrancy, and domestic service did not lead to a rejection of all authority, they did fill him with a deep contempt for all the cruel and incompetent masters of this world, in fact for all actual masters. Being themselves corrupt, they can only maim and hurt those doomed to serving them. Had M. de Montaigu been a decent man, Rousseau, his secretary, imagined that he might have made a passable career for himself in the diplomatic service. Had M. de la Roque been a kind man, he would have given his valet, Rousseau, the courage to confess a theft rather than to callously allow an innocent girl to be blamed.[14] The reason why servants cheat and steal is that the masters are usurpers, liars, and fools.[15]

It was not difficult for Rousseau to draw the obvious conclusions from these experiences. Actual authority was exercised only to maintain a destructive and false order. "Wherever I look, I see only masters and slaves, not a people and its chief."[16] The result is that no communication and no genuinely binding relationships are possible at all. "Neither master nor slave belongs to a family, but only to a class."[17] His travels up and down the entire social ladder had shown him only too clearly that "the great know only the great and the small only the small."[18] Enforced class isolation means mutual hostility and irresponsibility – pride and cruelty at the top, envy, servility, and dishonesty at the bottom. What is astonishing is that in spite of these experiences and perceptions Rousseau should still have looked for "chiefs" and longed for individuals who possessed qualities that justified submission to their authority. Moreover, to a certain degree, he even expected such persons to come from those very upper classes whose vices he had so eloquently exposed. It is not the offended plebeian Saint-Preux, but his patron Lord Bomston, an English aristocrat of immense wealth and power, who delivers the most scathing of all Rousseau's denunciations of the hereditary nobility and who proclaims the cause of equality.[19]

This ambivalence emerges even in Rousseau's view of political authority. On the whole he thought monarchy completely vicious. Even elective kings tend to be tyrants.[20] Nothing amused him more than the Abbé de Saint-Pierre's belief that reform was in the "true" interest of kings. Far from it, replied Rousseau. Their interest lies precisely in exploiting and, oppressing their subjects.[21] Masters never prefer any interest to their own, and most statesmen are positively malevolent.[22] Rousseau was outraged by M. de Mirabeau's notion of a "legal despotism" as a cure for all political ills. What a contradiction in terms! There are only two alternatives, Rousseau replied. One might have the pure rule of law in which all personal authority is entirely eliminated. That is pure democracy. If this should be impossible (as he thought it was), then one should accept the most perfectly arbitrary, unlimited personal rule. That is the rule of a God. The trouble with this was that it would in fact bring on rulers like Tiberius and Nero, who could inspire only despair. However, there are only two options, democracy, which is for angels, or the most perfect Hobbism.[23] This stark either/or is very revealing. It is a genuine conflict between ideals, not a choice between the possible and the impossible. Neither one of the ideals is at all likely to be realized, but both are valid. The actuality of bad kings does not invalidate the ideal of beneficial personal rule any more than the actuality of illegality destroys the idea of the pure rule of law. They are merely part of different visions of salvation. The Spartan republic is the utopia of virtue; the rule of a paternal despot is what prevails within each one of the happy families of the Golden Age. Neither can be recreated, and indeed neither has ever existed. Both merely remind us of what we might be.

The choice between these two possibilities must be made, if only to understand what they imply and what men's potentialities are. In making his own choice Rousseau did not exactly prefer personal authority to impersonal law, but he thought that the latter was less effective in molding men. It does not reach deep enough into the human heart to divert men from their destructive inclinations and the empire of opinion.[24] A Great Legislator is needed not only for that, but to make law possible at all. Even if law is to rule, men must be educated to accept it.

It has occasionally been suggested that Rousseau, in providing Corsica and Poland with constitutional plans, imagined himself to be a real legislator.[25] In fact, he thought nothing of the sort. In a most revealing passage he explained that he could never fulfill the role, precisely because he lacked the necessary personal qualities.[26] He declined, for that very reason, to participate directly in Corsican affairs.[27] No one had a clearer view of the differences between the life of action and the life of observation, and he knew himself to be capable of only the latter. At most he might help to guide some future statesman.[28] At times he claimed that he did not even wish to lead his contemporaries, but only to warn them against false prophets.[29] Not that he was modest. He alone among authors had revealed the nature and history of the human heart.[30] Now knowing the human heart was certainly one of the main prerequisites of legislative as of all other authority, but it was not the only one. Rousseau certainly could dream of being a leader, but he knew that it was a mere fantasy. If he had the ring of Gyges he would certainly use it to make mankind happy. It would lift him above all partiality and weakness, but not even in a dream could it make him into a man of action. His force was bound to remain "negative." He would remain human, the equal, in spite of himself, of those over whom he should rule.[31] The personality that radiates authority cluded him. It was with Saint-Preux, not with Wolmar, that Rousseau identified himself.[32]

M. Wolmar is, in fact, Rousseau's most perfectly realized figure of authority. Just because Rousseau dreamt that he himself might be the beneficiary of such a man, he was able to bring out very clearly what he expected an omnipotent father to be and to do. Such a man does not tell people what they ought to do. Far from it. He draws them to himself because they long for his approval and to be at one with him. This alone is the source of every real form of authority, in politics as in personal life. The man who wants to mold a people in fact needs the same qualities as a father who rules his children or a tutor who is capable of raising a child properly. And in a sense all are soul surgeons, men who prevent or cure the diseases that affect the human heart in every society whether it be the family or the polity.

In his own lifetime Rousseau seems to have known only one such man. That was Claude Anet, Mme. de Warens' factotum, and Rousseau's immediate predecessor as her lover. This, Rousseau noted several times, was an extraordinary man, the only one of his kind that he had ever seen. Slow, composed, thoughtful, circumspect and cold, he treated those around him like children, and so made them happy. He managed to do what Rousseau could never do: to keep order in Mme. de Warens' affairs. He did this because she, like Rousseau, and everyone else, esteemed and feared him, and did so because they could not bear his disapproval. Rousseau knew exactly where Anet's power came from and why he could never emulate him. It was force of personality alone. He had neither the sangfroid nor the firmness of Anet. Though he was brighter and better educated, he lacked that quality that made people instinctively seek Anet's approval.[33] Even though he did not say so, Rousseau also resented Anet deeply. In his novel, the least attractive character, the worthless valet, is called Claude Anet.

It is a measure of what Rousseau thought real authority might be that no one resents M. Wolmar, the perfect man of authority. That is because, among other things, Wolmar is God. Saint-Preux does not want to love the man who has married Julie, but he nevertheless *does* love him.[34] Wolmar cures him of all his ills and restores his self-esteem because paternal love is irresistible, as Saint-Preux discovers.

Who is Wolmar and what does he do? Born somewhere in Eastern Europe, he is rich and a member of the highest nobility.[35] After an active and adventurous life of travel and soldiering he settles down in his later years to marriage and to running a model estate, Clarens. We are told nothing of his appearance in the novel, but in a letter to his illustrator Rousseau insisted that Wolmar's gaze must be *fin et froid*.[36] Along with his vast experience among every class of men, Wolmar is distinguished by a total absence of any passion. He needs no one, certainly not God. His only active love is for order; his one aversion, to see men suffer. His only interest in life is to read the hearts of men. That his penetrating eye has supernatural powers of looking into the hearts of others is frequently noted by all who know him.[37] This talent is the source of his unfailing judgment.[38] In Wolmar, alone among men, action and observation are not distinct. He acts to learn, and observes in order to act.[39] He not only knows men completely, but he identifies entirely with his plans for them, with the creation of order. In this he is indeed like God. The reason Wolmar does not believe in God is that he *is* God to all intents and purposes. Certainly he has all the attributes that Rousseau ascribed to God, self-sufficiency, justice, love of order. If he is not God, he certainly does God's work.[40] Not only does he create peace through justice on his estate, he returns corrupt or ill men to that natural moral condition in which God wants them to remain.[41] His power of attracting others has an immediate impact. To know Wolmar is to desire his approbation.[42] In this also he is like God.

Wolmar is capable not only of running a model estate, he is also the soul surgeon who heals the moral wounds of those whom society has in some way deformed. He undoes all that fantasy and false opinions have created, and so makes men out of mere victims. To see how great a man Wolmar is, one must appreciate the depth to which those whom he helps have sunk. The evils he erases are the best proof of his goodness.

Saint-Preux is Rousseau's portrait of man destroyed by society. "We are meant to be men, laws and customs thrust us back into infancy."[43] Saint-Preux remains a child because he has been victimized by his situation. The prejudices of an inegalitarian society prevent him from becoming either a citizen or the head of the family. His illusions and disordered passions keep him from developing a will. Lord Eduard, his friend and protector, pleads with him to emerge from childhood and to be a man before he dies. He has nothing to fear from his passions. Only his illusions distract him.[44] Saint-Preux cannot respond to this advice, because his natural passions have become distorted. It is not enough to tell a man of thirty to grow up. He must be made capable of it and given a motive for asserting his will. If he could help himself he would not be so utterly miserable. Evidently he needs more than good advice, and it is Wolmar who takes complete charge of Saint-Preux to liberate him from his obsessions. To understand why Wolmar has to assert such complete authority over Saint-Preux, indeed has to reconstruct his past for him, one has only to recognize the full extent of the younger man's illness. It is the evil that justifies the cure as much as Wolmar's inherent superiority.

What exactly is wrong with poor Saint-Preux? He is afflicted by a complete disorder of his erotic and intellectual powers. He cannot love without suffering, and he has an all-devouring memory that makes him incapable of self-awareness and of action in the present. The origin of both these troubles is that he is not, and cannot be, the master of his own destiny. To Saint-Preux and Lord Eduard this seems to be entirely the fault of the "barbaric" prejudices of Julie's father.[45] Why, however, should these prejudices make him feel that suffering is the true mark of love? Julie knows that there is more to Saint-Preux's misery than her father's humiliating refusal to permit their marriage. She frequently reproaches Saint-Preux for being led entirely by those around him, of having no willpower of his own.[46] She is certainly in a position to know. Whenever she tells him to go away, he goes. When she recalls him, back he comes, just as obediently.[47]

His submissiveness is, in his own eyes, his greatest claim on her love. At no time does he make a plan for both of them or suggest that she follow him. It is Lord Eduard who, behind Saint-Preux's back, tries to persuade Julie to elope with her lover. When the young man finally leaves her, he puts himself entirely into Lord Eduard's care. "Do as you please, milord. Rule me."[48] And for ten years Lord Eduard makes every decision for him.

Why is Saint-Preux so utterly lacking in self-esteem? He knows that true self-esteem is the source of real honor and morality, unlike the false pride of Baron d'Etange, which is based on mere opinion.[49] And he is firm and self-assertive whenever he confronts Julie's father directly. Why then does he grovel so before the daughter? Why does he suffer so, even at the moment of supreme felicity?[50] Why is his love, as Lord Eduard remarks, such an abuse of his powers?[51] There is more than class humiliation here, though that plays its part. There is also the suffering that men cause themselves when their desires exceed their capacities.[52] This cupidity is not directed at things. Indeed, domination is its primary aim. The baby's second cry is, after all, already an effort to subjugate his mother. The desire for power after power over people is the first and the chief source of our self-abuse. Saint-Preux knows from the beginning that he cannot possess Julie completely. That is because he does not really want to *live* with her, but to *die* with her. No sooner has he kissed her than he longs to die in her arms.[53] As soon as he leaves her he laments that "the image of death" is now all that he has before him, but that image accompanied him on his one night with her also.[54] When she decides to marry Wolmar, he admits that he wishes she were dead, but that he may not love her enough to stab her.[55] When he returns to see her, years later, they visit an isolated place where he used to dream of her. On the way back he barely restrains himself from throwing both of them into the lake.[56] And finally when he again spends a night at an inn where he stopped after leaving her for the first time, years earlier, he dreams that she is dead.[57] Wolmar knows what that means. In a cold letter he tells Saint-Preux that one only dreams of the death of people whom one wishes to kill.[58] That is what it means to have a penetrating eye that reads the hearts of men! In the end of course Julie does die, and that is a necessity because the whole novel moves to that end. Whether she be Christ or Woman, she is the spirit of love that everyone, except Wolmar, wants to sacrifice. And so it is done. When Saint-Preux has been liberated from his miseries and she has fulfilled her maternal functions no one needs her. She is indeed perfectly ready to die.

Saint-Preux's longing for death comes from a sense of futility. That is a social disease. There are no social tasks worthy of his real powers for him. He is neither a father, nor a citizen, nor a man. He is in fact a philosopher.[59] Unlike most, he is without any *amour-propre* or ambition, but he is not free from the other defects of intellectuality. Both Lord Eduard and Julie note the disparity between his intellectual and emotional powers. It is clear to both that Saint-Preux's absorption in speculative philosophy has atrophied his passions. Why does he write good books, instead of doing good deeds?, asks Lord Eduard.[60] Saint-Preux is kind and gentle, but his inability to really love is part of that emotional dissipation, that lack of real feeling, that Rousseau ascribed to all intellectuals. It is not merely an unjust society that denies Saint-Preux his proper place. He has chosen mutilating preoccupations. Reflection makes men miserable by keeping them from enjoying the present. They are torn between tormenting desires and regrets.[61] That is certainly poor Saint-Preux's trouble. Unlike most philosophers he does not take his malaise out on others. He turns all his anger back on himself. That is why he is a pure victim and worth saving. That, also, is why Julie loves him so, even when he exasperates her with his incessant jealousy, feebleness, and instability.

Lord Eduard, who is English and a political animal, thinks that all of Saint-Preux's troubles would disappear in a free republic in which he could marry his Julie and be a citizen. He is not wrong, but neither is he altogether right. There are pains created by association that go even deeper than those of injustice. Reflection can stimulate the imagination, foresight, and memory until the sense of reality is totally destroyed. Saint-Preux is not given to thoughts about the future, but his memory is completely out of control. The yearning for the past is for him what ambition is to harder men.

Enduring love between the sexes is never natural, as sexuality is. Love depends on memory, and that is a faculty that is not awakened until men leave the state of nature.[62] Nor does love normally last. Its natural course is to decline. Because Saint-Preux was separated from Julie at the height of his love, he keeps his feeling artificially alive in his imagination.[63] As soon as he leaves her he begins to live in the past. Eternal regret becomes his permanent torment.[64] He is the victim of an all-devouring nostalgia.

Although Rousseau disagreed with Locke's opinion that both love and memory were natural, it was from Locke that he and his contemporaries had learned to recognize the immense psychological importance of the memory. The association of ideas that create all knowledge and understanding is nothing but the work of that faculty. To Locke, personal identity, the sense of selfhood, itself depended on memory.[65] He was, moreover, deeply aware of the dangers of a distorted memory. Erroneous and obsessive patterns of association were at the root of all intellectual and religious errors and delusions.[66] Rousseau was inevitably more concerned with the moral suffering caused by aberrant associations. Moreover, he thought that self-awareness was an immediate sensation, a feeling resembling, though not quite like, Descartes' "I think, therefore I am," rather than a recollection. Moral self-consciousness was, however, wholly a matter of remembering. Man is a moral being and has a conscious moral life *only* when he has a memory. Without memory there is no conscience. Conscience is our ability to regret our misdeeds and to feel pleasure in remembering our good acts. Memory alone creates moral self-awareness.[67] This and our ability to enjoy pleasant memories are the positive aspects of the faculty of memory.[68]

The painful side of memory was, however, a more constant theme for Rousseau. Memory is a form of opinion, Wolmar observes, and so it is easily turned into illusion that can be an escape from selfhood for people who lack self-confidence. It keeps them from accepting themselves, from living in the present.[69] Happiness and health, however, are to be found only in the ability to live in the present, to take each day as if there were neither yesterday nor tomorrow. Memory induces reflection that is crippling, inhibiting, and destructive. It keeps us chained to a past that is illusory.[70] And it is not only guilt or a pleasant past that can force us back. Saint-Preux is not troubled by a bad conscience, but only by a dreadful sense of what might have been. Indeed the whole novel is suffused with nostalgia, as Saint-Preux sees life entirely filtered through regret. Like all artificial faculties, memory is not limited as our natural powers are. That is why it can lose all proportion. Most of our present ills would amount to little if the memory of past pleasures did not add regret to them.[71] Nostalgia that is overpowering can destroy all other emotions.

Rousseau was himself the victim of nostalgia, but he did not discover it as a distinct emotional affliction. It had been discussed for decades, especially in Swiss medical circles. Young Swiss mercenaries were known to suffer so severely from homesickness that they often could not perform their duties. The sound of native melodies, especially the *ranz des vaches*, would make them so nostalgic that they became ill. Indeed, it had been recognized for some years that this was a moral illness that brought about physical sickness, either directly or through complex physiological processes. Rousseau had heard of the learned works on this subject, and in one of his writings on music he noted that the *ranz des vaches* had no strong emotional qualities as music, but it deeply affected the Swiss abroad, because it was a *signe mémoratif*.[72] Saint-Preux is a perpetual victim to such mnemonic signs. Every object associated in any way with Julie immediately arouses his nostalgia. During the ten years of separation these objects have, in fact, tied him to her completely.

As soon as Wolmar sees Saint-Preux he realizes what is the matter with him. There is no romantic dramatizing of nostaliga here. There is nothing beautiful or significant about it as far as Wolmar is concerned. Saint-Preux is sick, and he should recover and put his life to some use. His self-confidence, and so his freedom, have to be restored. He must become "himself" again.[73]

The trouble with Saint-Preux, as Wolmar says, is not that he is in love with Julie de Wolmar, but that he is obsessed by his love for her as a young girl – who no longer exists. The hardest slavery, Rousseau wrote, is that imposed by a passion from which one would like to deliver oneself, but cannot.[74] Saint-Preux cannot forget. Wolmar's method is therefore to "cover the past with the present," so that Saint-Preux will recognize Julie as she now is, a wife and a mother, and himself as a man who has long had a life apart from hers. To bring about all this Wolmar begins by asserting a complete authority over Saint-Preux. He "takes possession of him," and Saint-Preux is only too delighed to find himself a child again, with Wolmar as his father rather than as his host.[75] And from the first Saint-Preux knows that Wolmar is the image of God. That is, he alone is really a man.

To release Saint-Preux from his memories, Wolmar makes him relive the past, step by step. Saint-Preux must see and touch everything that he saw and touched when he first knew Julie. He is forced to seek out everything that can arouse his memory and make him relive the past. He does so, however, in the present and in the company of a woman who is no longer the same woman as his former mistress. At each moment, profound though the mnemonic shock is, Saint-Preux realizes that he also has changed and he begins to be liberated from the past. The final, almost violent, trip that he and Julie take to the rocks upon which he once scratched her name finally shakes him free. That, he says, was the "crisis of his madness."[76] It passes, and Saint-Preux begins to live in the present, to enjoy Clarens, and to disentangle his destiny from his past.

It is all Wolmar' work. How does he proceed? He never preaches, never reproaches, never punishes. What he does is to arrange situations that force Saint-Preux to face reality: first the reality of Mme. de Wolmar as a woman whom he no longer loves, then himself as a man capable of making decisions for himself. These situations are created with infinite care, the environment being structured in advance.[77] Often it is done against the wishes of Julie and Saint-Preux, as when Wolmar departs, leaving them alone for several days.[78] Sometimes it involves deception, as when Wolmar's collaborator, Lord Eduard, puts Saint-Preux in a contrived situation in which he seems obliged to help his patron and to take charge of the latter's life and future.[79] In both cases Saint-Preux is forced into self-recognition and so into freedom. He is cured of nostalgia and of insecurity. As Julie says of herself, Wolmar "returned her to herself," and now Saint-Preux is again sane; Wolmar, she notes, has been his "liberator."[80]

It is a slow process. At first Saint-Preux becomes completely dependent on Wolmar and feels unsure as soon as the latter's watchful eye is removed.[81] After passing all the contrived tests arranged for him, he is, however, not only prepared to accept Wolmar's offer to bring up his children, but he no longer fears Wolmar's *"oeil éclairé"* when it reads his heart.[82] He does not become a second Wolmar, to be sure; such is not his bent nor his station in life. Even when he is restored to himself he remains in need of Wolmar's guidance. His first response to a difficult situation is to lament Wolmar's absence: "Where are your paternal cares, your lessons, your insight? What shall I do without you?"[83] When he finally does recognize that he is now a free and competent person, he is still aware that this has been Wolmar's work, not his own. It is then that he calls the former his benefactor and his father and notes that "in giving myself wholly to you I can offer you, only as to God himself, the gifts that I have received from you."[84]

In the final test in which Saint-Preux discovers his will, Wolmar forces him to protect Lord Eduard, who has for so many years looked after Saint-Preux. The young man is meant to prevent Lord Eduard's marriage to a prostitute. It would have been very much to Saint-Preux's advantage to let this happen, for it would force Lord Eduard to settle in Switzerland and Saint-Preux could then remain near him and Julie. He never thinks of it, but acts with great ingenuity and perseverance to save his patron. When he succeeds he knows that he is a man. He is now ready to assume the post that Wolmar had promised him. For Wolmar has given him a task sufficiently demanding and interesting to give purpose and direction to Saint-Preux's life. He is to bring up Wolmar's children. That is a lifetime's occupation. Saint-Preux will always need Wolmar, if not as a father, as a patron. Wolmar himself accepts responsibility in advance. "Live in the present," he tells Saint-Preux, "and I shall answer for the future," and that is also Julie's cousin's advice: let Wolmar manage.[85] Saint-Preux cannot expect to be Wolmar's equal, but he has been liberated from himself and from the need for a healing authority. As a member of the community that Wolmar has created at Clarens he remains under his penetrating eye, but not as a patient.

Although Wolmar has done much for his wife, he does not have the authority over her that he exercises over Saint-Preux. He does not even try.[86] Her regeneration is her own work, even if it is only a partial cure that is completed only when she commits sacrificial suicide. Neither Wolmar nor Saint-Preux can influence her, because she has a rare strength of character. She also exercises authority through her capacity to inspire what is really a very servile sort of love and devotion.[87] This all attracting, but also subtly hateful, portrait was entirely in keeping with Rousseau's general view of women. Women rule men and make of them whatever they please.[88] "Do you want to know men? Study women."[89] Clearly Rousseau did not like this monstrous regimen of women. Paris, the very epitome of modern corruption, was entirely ruled by women.[90] Indeed, women were responsible for most of the moral evils of this world, but Rousseau could not help admiring authority, even in this case. The result was a considerable uneasiness. He composed two brief essays to show that women had been important in the great events of history and that in civic virtue and military heroism women were really the equals of men.[91] This did not deter him from claiming that "the law of nature bids women obey men," because men are active and strong, whereas women are passive and feeble.[92] To be sure, husbands ought to treat their wives well, but just or unjust, women must submit to the commands of their spouses.[93] However, in the end Rousseau decided that this submission was itself only superficial. Julie also rules at Clarens, and when Emile's tutor resigns his authority over his pupil, he says, "My weighty task is now ended and another undertakes this duty. Today I abdicate the authority which you gave me; henceforth Sophie is your guardian."[94] If anything, her authority is greater even than that of the man who ruled Émile so completely, for she rules over an adult, not a child. It is not a blessing. Throughout his novel Rousseau put the joys of friendship into glaring contrast with the anguish that men and women in love cause each other. Claire and Julie are a support and comfort to each other. Lord Eduard and Saint-Preux are models of what human beings really owe each other. In the end Lord Eduard chooses to remain a bachelor on civic grounds. He does not wish to increase the already excessive number of peers.[95] But then Lord Eduard is English. He has political obligations. Wolmar wants Saint-Preux to marry Julie's cousin, but Claire refuses him out of devotion to Julie's memory.[96] In any case it is clear that everyone will be better off in the single state. Moreover, the duties of a tutor permit no other distractions. Certainly Saint-Preux does not need to be dominated by another woman.

If the authority of women over men is not good, their influence over their children is rarely wise. Though they desire the happiness of their young, most are too stupid to bring them up properly.[97] The ignorance of women is, however, not the only flaw in parental authority, a subject to which Rousseau gave much thought. Of all the actual and inevitable forms of authority it is the most important. In all corrupt, that is, in all contemporary, societies, parents are the agents who transmit false traditions and habits from one generation to the next. Children are sacrificed to social vanity, cast too early into the conventional mold and, thanks to the ambitions of their fathers, forced into unhappy marriages.[98] Rousseau was, moreover, anxious to minimize the legitimate scope of paternal authority in order to prove, as Locke had, that it could not serve as a model or justification for absolute monarchy.[99]

It is not just the socializing and political functions of the family that make it a suspect institution under present circumstances. It is also inherently inefficient as a way of educating the young. If a child is to be brought up for his own sake, to become a good and happy man, he needs constant attention. To be the perfect tutor of a single child is a lifetime's work.[100] It is a sobering thought. Nothing less than a full-time tutor for each child can bring about the regeneration of men through education. And where are tutors to be found? Rousseau doubted whether any man was really fit for it.[101] The tutor, to be sure, need not have the magnetic personality, the immense social experience, nor the wealth and rank of a Wolmar. A reformed Saint-Preux will do. Indeed, a tutor should be no more than a man and should show his pupil that he is only human, a person with weaknesses and needs.[102] Nevertheless, his talents, like his responsibilities, must be immense. Rousseau himself had been a wretched failure as a tutor. His inability to exercise authority had been his undoing, as he recognized perfectly clearly.[103] His *ideas* on education, however, were fully developed very early, and he adhered to them with unusual consistency. From his first to his last letter on the subject one point was, moreover, always emphasized: The tutor must have complete and absolute authority over his charge.[104] No one, not even the parent, may interfere.

Not only must one "be a man before [one] can train a man," so that one may "set a pattern he shall copy," one must also be able to control everyone around the child if one is to be his master.[105] The tutor, as a man, must also play God, for he must create an environment, a new "natural" situation in the midst of society for the child. Because the threats from within and without are so great, he must be able to exercise an unlimited preventive authority.

It is clear from the discussions between the Wolmars and Saint-Preux that the education he is to give their children is to be the same as Émile's. Saint-Preux even mentions that he has written something on education.[106] It is agreed that the main task is to prevent the empire of opinion from destroying nature. At Clarens the children will be isolated from society at large and their environment controlled. A benevolent authority will check their slightest inclination toward domination and vanity. They also will learn the true law of nature: to obey necessity and no one and nothing but that. Their tutor is to be guided by nature at every step, moreover. That means two things. First of all the character, the given self of each child, is to determine the exact upbringing most likely to allow him to flourish. That is also Émile's tutor's principle. He is, however, never called on to discuss Émile's personality, for Émile is not given one. Julie speaks of her boys' characters, but Émile is "child" in general. As Wolmar explains, each child does have characteristics that belong to man in general, as well as his personal traits. The former are set stages of growth through which all men must pass. Émile's education is specifically concerned with these, with the learning, physical, moral, and intellectual appropriate to each age, especially the earliest years during which nothing must be forced or imposed on him. There is to be neither retardation nor forced progress.[107] This is above all a preventive project. The young Wolmars and Émile are to be saved from all the miseries that Saint-Preux had to suffer. That is why he is such an ideal tutor and why he is so delighted when Wolmar offers him the job. It is at last a way of making good use of his talents.[108]

To become entirely unlike Saint-Preux, Émile is taught never to desire anything that he cannot reach single handed. He will not be allowed to develop any artificial passions and is to know nothing of habit and routine. Memory is not to be stimulated, and imagination is not to be aroused. He will grow up simple and direct without *amour-propre* but confident, as he has every reason to be, in his ability to take care of himself. Émile is not ignorant, but reading and speculation are not stressed. He has a useful trade to keep him busy and to protect him against reversals of fortune and the fear of such changes. In the end he marries a young woman who has been especially brought up for him. They settle down in the country to recreate the patriarchal Golden Age together. If his country should call on him to serve it he would do so, but that is most unlikely. Honest men are no longer in political demand. Emile need not expect to be called from his rustic retreat.[109]

To bring up children in this way demands, Julie explains, that a constant and absolute authority be exercised over them. "The laws of liberty" cannot otherwise be enforced. Moreover, the force of public opinion and the dangers of denaturation are so great that only an incessant control over a child's daily life can keep them at bay. A child is to be educated *against* society, and he must be protected against parents, neighbors, and servants who would press their false values on him. The tutor's direct authority over the child must be complete, because the child is always so defenseless, so exposed to external influences. The question is not, to rule or not to rule over the child, but who is to create his environment for him and to what end? Is convention or virtue to create the man? If the tutor is to replace society, he must have more than equivalent means to arrange the child's life, to structure his experiences, and to replace all other human examples and influences. "Negative education," which is the tutor's method, is far from being effortless or unplanned.

What then is "negative education"?[110] It differs from conventional education not only in its ends, but also, of necessity, in its entire method. Its aim is to make a self-sufficient adult who lives at peace with himself.[111] To achieve this, one must at all costs avoid trying to impose a foreign, social character on the child. His natural self must not be inhibited in any way. On the contrary, everything must be arranged so that the child may learn everything that he has to know, without losing his natural characteristics. "Fit a man's education to his real self, not to what is no part of him."[112] "Negative education" is negative in that it prevents the imposition of an artificial, socially devised and socially oriented self on the child. It prepares him for knowledge by protecting him against error.[113] If Émile is docile to a degree and if his will is at the mercy of his tutor, it is because the latter has made himself loved and has made himself the child's only model. He rules over the child's will by prearranging experiences and situations, not by any sort of direct imposition.[114] He never bullies and rarely, if ever, punishes.[115] He demonstrates and manipulates. Like Wolmar, he does not hesitate to employ stratagems and deceits. His whole art lies in "controlling events."[116] He does not give orders, and, again, like Wolmar, is everywhere without being seen.[117] If Émile is in this way buffeted and protected at every point, he is compelled to *do* only one thing: to learn for himself.[118] In this sense he is forced to be free by being negatively educated. That is, he is prevented from becoming weak and self-destructive, as he most certainly would have come to be without his tutor's care.

The tutor's authority is indeed immense, but so are the evils he must forestall. Far from relaxing with the years, moreover, his control must in fact increase as Émile becomes more exposed to both inner and external threats to his balance. During Emile's childhood the tutor had only to manipulate the environment in order to give nature a chance. Émile needs only challenges to help him grow, not orders or direct instructions. These would only stunt his spirit and encourage deceit. When Émile reaches sexual maturity the relationship alters drastically. Religion and book learning are introduced and, far more

important, he must now be subdued. As a young child he was allowed to be self-assertive and to learn by doing. At twenty he must
be made utterly docile. Now he is allowed only a mere "show of
freedom" so that the tutor can be the master of Émile's will.[119] Now
is the time when the young man enters society, and now more than
ever he must be kept "from being altogether artificial."[120] Because
he has never been forced to obey as a child Émile is, in fact, not re-
bellious now. He is obedient, meek, mild, and, in short, docile to a
frightful degree.

While Émile is a child one would not expect him to enjoy full freedom under any circumstances. However, he remains dependent on
the tutor's protective guidance even as an adult. At the end of *Émile*,
the pupil, now fully grown and about to become a father, still feels in
need of the protective presence of his tutor. "Advise and control us,"
he begs, "as long as I live I shall need you. I need you more than ever
now that I am taking up the duties of manhood."[121] As he had said
earlier, "Resume your authority. I place it in your hands of my own
free-will."[122] Even more revealing is the story of what happens to
Émile and Sophie once the tutor does leave. The sketch for a sequel
to *Émile* that Rousseau left unfinished begins with Émile's lament,
"If you had not left us, I should still be happy!"[123] As soon as the
tutor departs Émile and Sophie cease to be able to cope with the difficulties that beset them and commit one mistake after another until
their marriage and their happiness are destroyed. Émile's education
continues to stand him in good stead. He bears adversity admirably.
But he does not know how to avert or end the troubles that afflict
him and his wife. He cannot control his situation. What is impossible
for the perfectly reared Émile, who possesses every virtue except the
quality that controls men and events, is certainly not possible for
lesser men.

THE TRUE ART OF RULING

Wolmar's good works are not limited to curing lovesick youths. He
is also the creator and master of a model estate, Clarens. As befits a
man of his spiritual powers, enormous experience, and various skills,
he naturally exercises authority over an entire community.[124] The
end of Wolmar's managerial cares is not his property so much as
the peasants and servants who work for him. They must be kept on

the land and away from Paris. To that end rural life must be made more acceptable to them than it usually is. In running his estate Wolmar does not have political powers at his disposal. His people can leave his employment whenever they wish. If they are to stay at Clarens, Wolmar must gain authority over their wills. He must manage their lives in such a way that they will not want to go away. That is no great difficulty for Wolmar. He is a master of the art of ruling the wills of other men, as the helpless Saint-Preux discovered.

Wolmar certainly has all the qualities that would be needed to found a republic. He has all those suprahuman talents that the Great Legislator possesses, but there is no occasion for him to use them. A people is not available. Instead Wolmar tries to recreate the Golden Age. That also requires godlike powers. To be the head of a full household and to run it properly, not in order to increase one's possessions, but to enjoy them and to benefit one's dependents, is to be like God. In fact, it is to be better than God, who has left mankind to flounder so helplessly. At Clarens only does one forget one's century and feel that the Golden Age has been regained.

If Wolmar's personal qualities are not in any degree inferior to those of the great founders of republics, his task is very different from theirs. It is even remote from the office of a magistrate. Rousseau distinguished domestic economy very sharply from political economy or government. The talents required for the former are essentially those of a father who is wisest in following his inclinations. That would only lead to injustice in a republican magistrate. The head of a household should be partial to his own family and think of nothing but preserving his patrimony for his own children. They in turn will defer to him, at first out of weakness, then out of gratitude. No magistrate should count on such attachments. Law must guide him and the citizens, not personal feeling. The natural authority of a man over his wife, though clear, is not that of a sovereign. Pregnancy keeps her inactive often, and he must rule her to make sure that her children are really his also. It is an authority, however, that looks to unity and concord in running a family. And it is not complete. There is, as it were, semidivided sovereignty in the family. No such condition may prevail in a republic. Between the head of a household and those who work for him there is a relationship of exchanged services only. He has no direct coercive, military powers. In return for their work, he sees to their maintenance. They can quit

his employment, and he may dismiss them. Because this is an impersonal relationship justice does enter into it, as it does not among the
members of the family bound solely by ties of affection.[125] If the two
forms of authority differ, it does not follow that domestic government is less difficult than political rule. Nature speaks too feebly in
the actual world to guide most fathers. And in fact there are no good
landlords. Only Wolmar knows how to be a real father, and it is quite
clear at every step that his policy is always the exact opposite of that
of all the actual masters whom Rousseau had served.

The primary principle of Wolmar's rule at Clarens is autarchy.
Nothing is bought or sold. He does not try to increase his holdings;
he merely improves them so that his sons will inherit a model estate.
Autarchy is also a moral necessity. How else is Paris to be shut out
effectively? The Wolmars are good hosts, but they certainly do not
invite visitors. As many people as possible are given work on the
land. The going rate is accepted as the basic wage, but it is increased
in proportion to a man's efforts and length of service. There is no
caprice in all this. It is as certain as law would be. Work is distributed
according to talents and strength so well that equals could not have
arranged it more equitably. Moreover, there are no quarrels among
the workers, because they are each one so deeply attached to their
common master. This shared feeling serves to bind them, indirectly,
to each other. Servants always imitate their masters, and Wolmar
is alone a model worth emulating. Moreover, he tries to make life
reasonably pleasant for his people. In a republic citizens are ruled by
mores and principles of virtue that have been engraved upon their
hearts. Domestic servants and people who work for pay in general
can only be ruled by constraint. Wolmar knows that ultimately it
is fear of being dismissed or upbraided that moves his workers. He
therefore tries to cover their fear with "a veil of pleasure."

In these efforts Wolmar's guiding hand is felt, but never seen. It
is invisible yet omnipresent. He has to *do* very little, but he must
always *be* there. Without his example and his felt presence Clarens
would fall apart. All the disrupting temptations would flourish, and
justice would disappear among the people who live and work there.
For Clarens is just as artificial, just as "unnatural" as any other organized society. The division of labor, inequality, and constraint is
just as integral a part of this rural world as of any other society. What
makes Wolmar's rule beneficial is its palliative effect and its justice.

He prevents the peasants from rushing to their doom in Paris, and he saves his domestic servants from the corrupting vices of their situation. They are at least not consumed by envy, promiscuity, and dishonesty.

The immense authority that Wolmar exercises over his dependents and neighbors is justified by his method of ruling, which can be summed up in one word: justice. A rigorous system of rewards and penalties is administered by a man who is always "equitable without anger" to his servants. The neighboring peasants are helped to recognize that their situation, for all its hardships, is the best one open to mankind. No one is encouraged to change his social position, but justice renders social inferiority bearable and gives it a degree of moral validity.[126] Each man gets his deserts and respects those of others. However, at no time does Wolmar, or anyone else, claim that inequality and domestic service are natural or agreeable conditions. Wolmar's justice can only render them tolerable. He lessens the force of resentment, and his people endure their burdens without complaint. Certainly none of Wolmar's servants want to leave his estate. Life at Clarens, autarchical, isolated from the "great" world, without any disorder or luxury, and with some sense of common unity and justice, is not perfect, but at least there is less cause for dissatisfaction and hostility than in other societies. More than that even the semidivine Wolmar cannot do.

Order, regularity, security of expectations, and fairness: Everything in this stable, harmonious society reflects the soul of the master.[127] And although everyone seems to be doing what pleases himself, it is Wolmar who directs each one, for all are united in their attachment to him. That is not only because Wolmar wants to be well served, but because he is concerned with the moral welfare of his servants and with the order of his estate as a whole. It is his responsibility and he attends to it directly, never acting through, and thus depending on, intermediaries. That is the only way in which genuine authority *can* be exercised.[128] This personal involvement also marks the other efforts that Wolmar and Julie make to soften the anguish of inequality. From time to time they practice "togetherness" with their servants and neighbors. Festivities and celebrations in which all join are frequently held at Clarens in order that servants and masters might at least share some of the pleasures of life in a spontaneous way and occasionally recognize their common humanity. However, this is only palliative, a way of reducing the coldness imposed by inequality. The differences in rank are not forgotten.[129] The brute reality remains, and Rousseau was not disposed to forget it. Even when he was looking for ways of transcending its worst emotional and moral effects, he remained acutely aware of inequality: the heaviest of all chains that society imposes on us.

Infrangible inequality is the greatest single limit on Wolmar's powers. It is not the only one. Even he cannot undo what civilization has wrought. The recreation of the Golden Age, like that age itself, is fragile. Julie does not find her happiness there, because she is no longer capable of living in the present, as peasants might. The civilized cannot return to a presophisticated condition. That is the eventual discovery of Émile and Sophie. It is also Julie's. The peasant who needs no education other than that which his situation provides might well evade the impact of civilized life, as long as Wolmar is there to protect him against it.[130] Sooner or later history would no doubt roll over Wolmar's people just as it had destroyed all of Switzerland; "Neufchatel, unique on earth," was not long for this world, as Rousseau knew only too well. If the villager could only be warned and temporarily saved, the refugee from history was past hope. Escape was a psychological impossibility and the attempt to return to the land could end only in failure.

Wolmar must take men as he finds them and create an environment for them that will prevent their becoming even worse. That is a great achievement. It does not, however, compare in scope or depth with the task of the Great Legislator, the image of political authority. Lycurgus "turned [the human heart] from its natural course."[131] He and Numa and Moses each *created* a people. In this they were unique, semidivine figures. Calvin is mentioned only once, in a footnote and then as a legislator whose work did not endure any too well.[132] It was Plutarch who had fired young Rousseau's imagination and who continued to dominate it.[133] Perhaps historical imagination was not among Rousseau's strong points. Perhaps the Legislator is altogether too much the sum of all the qualities that modern leaders so conspicuously lacked. Certainly of all his images of authority the Great Legislator is the least genuine, the most wooden, one-dimensional figure. Rousseau admitted that "the comparison of that which is with that which ought to be had given him *l'ésprit romanesque* which had always drawn him far from actuality."[134] When he built a dream world out of familiar materials and scenes, a Swiss Clarens inhabited by men and women who emerged, however much altered, from his own experiences, Rousseau was totally convincing. Plutarch served him less well. Those ancient heroes were altogether too remote to come alive, much as Rousseau needed to believe in them. One can feel the force of Wolmar's penetrating eye, but one is merely told about the great deeds of the legislators.

Like Wolmar, the Great Legislator is a god. He also is a model for all other men and just as inimitably above them. He is a public tutor. If Émile's mentor merely prevents the growth of the diseases of association, the Legislator must provide perpetual antidotes for them. He cannot call on nature's helping hand. On the contrary he must defy her.

He who believes himself capable of forming a people must feel himself to be capable of changing, so to speak, the nature of men. He must transform each individual, who by himself is a complete solitary whole, into a part of a greater whole, of which that individual must, in some manner, receive his life and his being; he must mutilate, so to speak, the constitution of man.[135]

Without this transformation men cannot be subjugated in order to be made free. Without it they can never be expected to live in virtue under the rule of law.[136]

Indeed the rule of law itself is feeble at best. Without a strong will no people can be expected to possess the self-restraint to live in justice. Law in fact is more the expression than the cause of republican virtue. Above all, to structure the will that creates rules, to give a people its life in the first place, requires a single hand and a single voice. Hymns to the rule of law, of course, abound in Rousseau's writings. Only law is compatible with freedom.[137] Only law is a "joug salutaire."[138] Only under law can the dependence of man on man be ended.[139] Only law can subject men without constraining the will. Law liberates.[140] The great problem of politics is to make governments the guardians, rather than the enemies, of law.[141] That is only a small sample of a recurrent theme. However, there were qualifications. The first was that law is psychologically ineffective. It can condition only external behavior. Public opinion and mores alone can touch the heart.[142] And to be truly effective public authority must penetrate to the very heart.[143] To do this requires more than law, it depends on continuing education.[144] Second, laws do not grow spontaneously in society. The Great Legislator must not only invent them, but must create the moral climate that is needed for their acceptance. Last, and this is the greatest weakness, law is not self-perpetuating. Like all the works of men, even the best institutions decline under the inevitable impact of moral weakness. And once corruption has set in, there is no stopping it.[145] If Sparta and Rome fell, what can endure?[146] Law ultimately is what personal authority can give society for a while; it does not replace that force, of necessity a personal one, that can alone touch the human heart. That was the way of those ancient political paragons, Moses, Lycurgus, Numa, and Solon.[147] Of such men, alas, modern history knows nothing.[148]

The ancients who knew how to rule did not argue or appeal to the interests of the people. They controlled the affections of the heart especially by using nonverbal symbols to move people to civic emotions. Objects and music appealed to the eye and ear. Every sense was stirred to evoke thoughts and feelings associated with the fatherland. "The mind was forced to speak the language of the heart."[149] Language itself was sonorous and designed to arouse, in the open air, a sense of civic unity. The poetry of Homer, the drama, the melodious rhetoric of the public speech all spoke not to dry reason and calculation, but to the primary emotions. That is what is meant, no doubt, when Rousseau spoke of the Legislator's ability to "persuade without convincing" and of his acting directly on the will.[150] This is also that "inner force which penetrates the soul" without which the moral bond is too feeble to hold men together.[151] To say as monarchs do, "*tel est mon plaisir*," does not require an emotive language or a treasure house of symbols that call on every one of the senses.[152] The Legislator must need all of these if he is really to fortify the soul of his charges against all the awful evils that civilization holds in store for them. Without so profound a transformation, without calling on all the feelings of men, they cannot receive a new character and a new will. Without those they will inevitably fall victim to all the iniquities of association.

The main source of the Legislator's strength in this extraordinary enterprise is his own personality. He is a man–god who, though he knows our nature thoroughly, does not share it. His tasks and his powers have nothing in common with the more usual forms of political authority.[153] He neither coerces, nor argues. Everything is done by the force of personality. A magnetic personality transforms lesser men. The political future of Corsica could be left to the "soul and heart" of General Paoli.[154]

Force is self-defeating and reason is wasted on disoriented, simple people, as it is on children, like Émile. Only direct experience and the force of example can really touch men.[155] It is useless to say, "be good" to them; they must be made so. How are they to be reconstructed?[156] The great Legislator has only one means at his disposal: illusion and stage management. And indeed it is not everyone who can make himself appear an agent of God and speak for Him.[157] The altering of public opinion, the revolution in attitudes that impinge on behavior, can be done only by an example so impressive that it inspires the wish to imitate. Like Wolmar, the Great Legislator must change each individual directly, must impress himself on the inner life of each future citizen.[158]

To change public opinion, popular judgments of right and wrong, he must also engage in the most detailed stage setting. In all this the guiding hand must remain hidden. To rule over public opinion one must not only be above it, but out of its sight.[159] It is suggestive power that gives people new ambitions and social instead of private aspirations. That also is why festivals, ceremonies, and all other simple and striking ways of structuring the environment to press new feelings on the populace are so important. All are necessary to protect the public self against the alluring calls of the private self, of *amour-propre*, and the false empire of opinion.

Creative legislative authority that "mutilates the human constitution" and reduces each person to a particle of a greater whole cannot be effectively exercised at all times. It can only be attempted in the youth of peoples. That is why Brutus and Rienzi failed.[160] For legislation is foresight and prevention. Only very few people are in a material or psychological position to be able to bear this salutary yoke. An isolated people, small in number, just out of nature, that has reached a stage that is exactly like Emile's adolescence, might be educated. If to "the simplicity of nature the needs for society have been added without any of its vices," then there is some hope. Even so, the Legislator has much to destroy before he can give a people good opinions.[161] A young people has no memories; that is its main virtue. What nostalgia is to individuals, traditional prejudices are to a people. On occasion a Lycurgus could "wash away" the past.[162]

This itself was possible for peoples only if they suffered experiences so intensely shocking that they obliterated their past from memory. That is what happened to Sparta at the time of Lycurgus, to Rome after the Tarquins, and to Holland and Switzerland in the course of their liberation. For the large, old, decrepit nations of Europe no such prospect existed. Corsica might be saved from civilization; that was all.[163]

Even in Corsica Rousseau feared there might be no great inclination for eternal simplicity.[164] Nor was the absence of suitable subjects for legislation and the disappearance of great men in the modern age all. Rousseau's sense of the hopelessness of man's position reached its height in his conviction that even the best trained Spartans will eventually fall victim to the spiritual diseases that association always engender in men.

The conclusion that creative legislative authority would fail was not fortuitous. It was all but inevitable, given Rousseau's psychological assumptions. For it is not merely the fatal attractions of false social values that threaten the good republic. It is not only civilization that is bound to creep in. Perpetual denaturalization cannot be maintained except by perpetual tutorial vigilance. The difficulties of full socialization were so great because Rousseau was so deeply aware of the individuality of each person. Each one of us has a self that forms the core of our character. This personal self is not inherently hostile to other selves, nor does it thrive in permanent solitude. Indeed "our sweetest existence is relative and collective and our true self is not entirely our own,"[165] Solitude is not the answer, but neither is society. In fact, there simply is no solution.

The best education, whether civic or private, tries to establish a harmony between the self and the environment. Unfortunately, no environment, however well planned, can displace man's preexisting self, his inborn personality. Happiness lies precisely in avoiding injuries to this self. Independence and self-esteem can flourish only if one's integral character is preserved. To that end one must claim the ability to withdraw into oneself and to be oneself, even in the midst of society. "Let us begin by again becoming ourselves . . . by conserving our soul."[166] Only then can we find within ourselves that *moi humain* that is the essence of our selfhood and of our shared humanity. That is not only true for men living in corrupt society. The citizen, however much denatured, however conscious of his civic self, has still an individual self, an inner life of his own, and it is bound to assert itself as soon as the vigilant eye of the Legislator is removed. The Legislator can work only to postpone that dangerous hour, and that is what he does.

A cohesive community cannot be built by those who cherish the *moi humain*.[167] That is why civic education and the education of the individual have nothing in common. However, having invested the natural self with such deep roots and recognized its profound value, Rousseau was in no position to argue that the Legislator could easily supply the citizens with new communal selves. That is why the Legislator's task is in fact superhuman. It is because men would have to be re-created if society were to be just that he is both necessary and doomed to failure. For the *moi humain* that is the source of all our goodness is also the fountain of all our aberrations.

Civic man needs a new self to replace his feeble natural equipment for social life. He needs a character that can withstand the assaults of *amour-propre*. The wholly military education, the games, the ceremonies, and the other appeals to his senses are designed to achieve that. Instead of a weak and divided self the citizen is to have an inner strength that derives wholly from his sense of being a part of a greater whole and of having a *"patria"* that is genuinely his. He does not need knowledge for that. He needs only to be saved from error and illusion.[168] Self-esteem is the best protection against these.[169] Pride is what keeps a people attached to those mores and opinions that the Legislator has stimulated in them. It protects them against conspirators who would create inequality and against foreign enemies. There is, above all, no time for reflection, idleness, and intellectuality in the good society.[170] The Spartan situation keeps men moving. Perpetual public activity and stimulation by public objects prevent passivity, drift, illusion, and their social expression in exploitation, oppression, and deception.[171]

All this is created by that supreme illusionist, the Legislator. It is the force of a magnetic personality alone that forces a character on a disoriented multitude. For quite unlike later nationalists Rousseau did not believe that the national self had any basis in nature. On the contrary, its creation does violence to all our spontaneous tendencies. National character was, for him, no "soul" at all and in no sense a free emanation arising from the disparate selves of individuals. It was not even an historical accretion. There is no group mind apart from the Legislator. Moses *created* the Jews. He gave them their distinctive, national identity. Before him there was only an inchoate herd. This was the example the Poles were to follow in *giving* themselves "a national physiognomy."[172] This was just what Peter the Great had failed to do. By merely imitating others he had not been able to devise a collective personality suited to the human material in his hands. Not that he had destroyed the Russian soul, there being no national souls. He was merely a Pygmalion who had no talent.[173] Whatever national character a republic is to have, and it must have one, can be only an artificial imposition from above. This character and will, being alien, are always frail structures. Because the Legislator must do more than just integrate existing personalities into a more coherent whole, his work does not endure. Laws and mores cannot withstand the assaults of nature for long. For in the last resort the *moi humain* is indestructible.[174]

The sheer hypnotic power of a great personality can achieve what neither force, reason, nor inclination can produce, but it is not an enduring triumph. That was, indeed, exactly what Rousseau meant to say. If the enormity of men's errors justifies such immense authority, it also renders it, ultimately, ineffective.

Freedom is what puts man out of nature and freedom to "perfect" himself (how ironic that word is meant to sound!), puts man into a psychological position that prevents him from ever finding a real home on earth.[175] Because he is unlimited in his ability to develop every sort of artificial deformity of his powers, there is no way to control his capacity for self-destructive behavior. It is therefore because men are free that they need masters. It is when Émile reaches adulthood that he cries out for his tutor. The Polish peasants and burghers who are to be freed and raised in rank are chosen carefully for their merits, but it is just when they reach civic maturity that they need guidance most. They are to be watched, protected, and helped, not because they are poor subjects, but because they are *free*.[176] It is they who must have an orderly environment and a directing hand. After all, even that part of the public that really desires the common good needs guides.[177] How much more so the more feeble mass!

To Rousseau it did not appear that genuine authority limits freedom. The real tension was between authority and equality. Personal authority is not merely compatible with freedom; it creates the latter. In its healing form, in ordering the disrupted passions, it is psychologically liberating. In ordering the environment it allows men to retain an integrated self and to preserve their independence. Wolmar and Émile's tutor are nothing if not tolerant, especially in matters of faith and opinion.[178] Freedom, in any case, was for Rousseau not a matter of doing as one pleased, but of *not* being compelled, either from within or from without, to do what one does *not* wish to do.[179] Inner compulsion is thus a most severe form of enslavement. That is why an ordered existence is needed to support men in a free condition. That also is why moderate desires, a capacity to live in the present, and dependence only on things are the prerequisites of the very possibility of a free life.[180] All of them, however, depend on an educative, preventive, curative, and ordering authority. Authentic authority liberates. It gives liberty to those who are incapable of creating it for themselves. Better a will dominated by a tutor than no will at all.[181]

The strong then liberate the weak, but the distance between them remains. Nothing can alter the fact that Saint-Preux will never be Wolmar's equal, nor Émile his tutor's However, though its extent is no less than the difference between God and man, this inequality is a natural one, and, as such, relatively unproblematic. It is only the addition of social inequalities to those of nature that creates our great miseries. If Rousseau's images of authority show any one thing it is the intensity and consistency of his hatred for all forms of personal dependence and social inequality and for their psychological roots, weakness, and *amour-propre*. It is these that cause even loving parents to destroy the happiness of innocent young people like Julie and Saint-Preux. It is these that make even the best-constructed republic a fleeting palliative. It is these that render even the serene life at Clarens galling to most of its inhabitants. *Amour-propre* and inequality are, moreover, inseparable from social life as such. In society their worst consequences may be cured, palliated, and, in the case of a chosen few, prevented from arising. The evil itself remains ineradicable. In his last years Rousseau felt that under prevailing conditions peace was worth more even than freedom. For freedom existed only in the heart of the just man.[182] In short, things being what they are, peace, order, and quiet were the best anyone could hope for.

This resignation was not merely a matter of old age and exhaustion. It was implicit in Rousseau's work all along. Indeed, it is less Burke's traditionalist rhetoric than Rousseau's psychological insight that has set the most severe limits on all hopes of easy reform. *Émile* is anything but a manual for those eupeptic schoolmasters who imagine that it is possible to reconstruct society by fiddling with the curriculum and altering the atmosphere of the classroom. A regenerative education *against* society and apart from its strains and prejudices would require one perfect tutor for each newborn child. Apart from Swiss peasants, each child would need the constant attention of a man who was himself above society. Where are such teachers to be found? Yet this is the only way to cure denatured men through educative means. To be sure, it is neither morally nor psychologically impossible, but it is historically very unlikely. Society, being what men have made it, and expressing, as it does, the most deep-seated psychological deformities, is not readily altered. The great men, whose personalities can impinge on the consciousness of those whom they wish to improve, can effect some real, though never complete, alleviation. Such men, always rare, have now, however, ceased to exist altogether. In their absence nothing can be done to morally reconstruct the European world.

That made the need for a utopian vision all the more compelling. It alone could keep the sense of man's moral possibilities alive and it alone could warn those who were not yet wholly corrupt of the dangers that beset them. Only utopia could expose, judge, and shame the civilized world as it deserved to be.

To be sure, Rousseau's concerns were not limited to this single grand design. He was often deeply immersed in schemes for partial political reform, especially in Geneva. Moreover, the very act of devising standards for improvement, even excessively high ones, was an act of affirmation on his part. If disgust and distress were his immediate inspiration, the vision of equality was not a chimera. He was certain that he had known egalitarian societies in rural Switzerland, and he believed that such communities had existed in the remote past. If criticism, indeed denunciation of the most devastating sort, was all that his contemporaries received from him, he was not the prophet of withdrawal either. However, at no time did he allow himself the illusion of painless reform or of the possibility of effortless social regeneration. His images of men of authority are so interesting because they are his answer to the question "how do we begin?" That his reply should have been cast in psychological rather than in social terms is scarcely surprising. Indeed it was inevitable, as for Rousseau politics was but a part of that study of the human heart that he had made his province. That also is the chief reason for his enduring relevance.

ENDNOTES

1 I owe the felicitous term bipolarity to Jean Wahl's remarkable article, "La Bipolarité de Rousseau," *Annales Jean-Jacques Rousseau*, Vol. 33 (1953–1955), pp. 49–55.
2 "*Lettre à Voltaire*," 18 August 1756, *Correspondance générale de Jean-Jacques Rousseau* (ed. Théophile Dufour, Vrin, Paris, 1924–1932), II, 303–324. (Hereafter cited as C.G.)
3 Vaughan, I, 207 (*Inégalité*).
4 "*Lettre à Mme d'Epinay*," 26 March 1757, C.G., III, 44; "*Lettre à Diderot*," C.G., III, 50; *Lettres à Malesherbes*, II, 1137.
5 *Rêveries*, VI, 1059; *Confessions*, I, 38.
6 *Boswell on the Grand Tour: Italy, Corsica and France, 1765–1766*, eds. Frank Brady and F.A. Pottle (Mac Millan, New York, 1955), 300.
7 *Ébauche des Confessions*, 1157.
8 "Lettre à la Marquise de Barbantane," 16 February 1766, C.G., XV, 62–3.
9 *Lettres à Malesherbes*, III, 1141.
10 *Confessions*, I, 56; XII, 596–9; "*Lettre à Milord Marechal*," 8 December 1764, C.G., XII 122–4; "*Lettre à Mme. la Comtesse de Boufflers*," 28 December 1763, C.G., X, 278–80.
11 *Lettres à Malesherbes*, IV, 1145.
12 *Confessions*, X, 527.
13 "*Lettre à M. de Luxembourg*," 30 April 1759, C.G., IV, 231.
14 *Confessions*, VII, 327; II, 87.
15 N.H., Part IV, Letter X.
16 Vaughan, II, 31 (*Contrat social*).
17 *Émile*, 369.
18 *Ébauches des Confessions*, 1150.
19 N.H., Part I, Letter LXII.
20 Vaughan, II, 446–7, 461, 464 (*Poland*).
21 Vaughan, I, 244 (*Économie Politique*); 389–92 (*Jugement sur la Polysynodie*); II, 77 (*Contrat social*).
22 Vaughan, I, 358 (*Fragment*).
23 "*Lettre à M. de Mirabeau*," 26 July 1767, C.G., XVII, 155–9.
24 Vaughan, II, 64 (*Contrat social*).
25 For example, Jean Starobinski, "*La Pensée Politique de Jean-Jacques Rousseau*," in Samuel Baud-Bovy et al., *Jean-Jacques Rousseau*, Vrin, Paris 1962, pp. 83, 99.
26 *Rêveries*, VI, 1057–9.
27 *Confessions*, XII, 650.

28 Vaughan, I, 350–1 (*Fragment*).

29 Vaughan, I, 342 (*Fragment*).

30 *Rousseau Juge de Jean-Jacques*, I, 728.

31 *Rêveries*, VI, 1057–9.

32 *Confessions*, VIII, 355; *Rousseau Juge de Jean-Jacques*, II, 778.

33 *Confessions*, V, 177–8, 201–6, 264–5.

34 N.H., Part III, Letter XVIII.

35 *Ibid.* Part III, Letter XVIII.

36 "*Lettre à M. Coindet*," December 1760, C.G., V, 295. The coldness of the true sage was often noted; e.g., *Rousseau juge de Jean-Jacques*, II, 861–2.

37 N.H., Part IV, Letters XI–XII.

38 "What then is required for the proper study of men? A great wish to know men, a great impartiality of judgment, a heart sufficiently sensitive to understand every human passion, and calm enough to be free from passion." *Émile*, 206. Just so Wolmar.

39 N.H., Part V, Letter XII.

40 "La véritable Grandeur consiste dans l'exercice des vertus bienfaisantes, à l'example de celle de Dieu *qui ne se manifeste que par les biens qu' il repand sur nous.*" *Oraison Funèbre du Duc d'Orleans*, O.C., II, 1277. (My italics.)

41 "Dieu veut que nous soyons tels qu'il nous a fait," *Lettre à Christophe de Beaumont*, 88–9. God says to man, "*Je t'ai fait* trop *foible pour sortir du gouffre, parce que je t'ai fait assez fort pour n'y pas tomber.*" *Confessions*, II, 64. In a sense the Wolmars of this world do better than God. They retrieve men from the abyss, rather than leaving them to suffer the consequences of weakness.

42 As soon as Saint-Preux has met Wolmar he says, "*Je commençais de connoitre alors quel homme j'avois à faire, et je résolus bien de tenir mon cocur en état d'être vu de lui,*" N.H., Part IV, Letter VI.

43 *Émile*, 49.

44 N.H., Part V, Letter I.

45 *Ibid.* Part II, Letter II.

46 *Ibid.* Part II, Letter XXVII.

47 *Ibid.* Part I, Letters III, XVI, XLII, LXV; Part II, Letter XII.

48 *Ibid.* Part II, Letter X; Part III, Letter XXIV.

49 *Ibid.* Part I, Letter XXIV.

50 *Ibid.* Part I, Letter XXIII.

51 N.H., Part II, Letter II.

52 *Émile*, 44.

53 N.H., Part I, Letter XIV.

54 *Ibid.* Part I, Letters LXVI, LV.

55 *Ibid.* Part III, Letter XVI.
56 *Ibid.* Part IV, Letter XVII.
57 *Ibid.* Part IV, Letter XVII.
58 *Ibid.* Part V, Letter IX.
59 *'Préface' à Narcisse*, 967.
60 N.H., Part II, Letter LXXVII; Part V, Letter II.
61 *"Préface' à Narcisse,"* 970.
62 Vaughan, I, 215–16 (*Inégalité*).
63 N.H., Part III, Letter VIII; Part IV, Letter LXIV.
64 *Ibid.* Part III, Letter XX.
65 *Essay*, Book II, Ch. 27, ss. 9–25.
66 *Ibid.* Book II, Ch. 28, ss. 7–16.
67 *"Lettres Morales,"* 358–9, 362–3, 365, 368, 371–2.
68 Georges Poulet, *Études sur le Temps Humain* (Nelson, Edinburgh, 1949), 158–93. This is a remarkable account of the "good" that Rousseau ascribed to memory. It is not much concerned with the negative aspects.
69 N.H., Part IV, Letter XII.
70 Vaughan, I, 150, 178 (*Inégalité*); *Émile*, 44–5; *Rêveries*, V, 1046.
71 *Pensées*, XLVI, 1309.
72 I owe all my information to Jean Starobinski, *"La Nostalgie: théories médicales et expression littéraire,"Studies in Voltaire and the Eighteenth Century*, XXVII, 1505–18 (1963).
73 Much as M. Gaime once restored young Rousseau's self-confidence. *Emile*, 226–7; *Confessions*, III, 90–1.
74 *Pensées*, LXXI, 1313.
75 N.H., Part IV, Letter VI.
76 *Ibid.* Part IV, Letter XVII; Part V, Letter II.
77 For the best account of this see Etienne Gilson, *"La Méthode de M. de Wolmar,"* in *Les idées et les lettres* (Vrin, Paris, 1932), 275–98.
78 N.H., Part V, Letter XII.
79 *Ibid.* Part II, Letter XII; Part VI, Letter III.
80 *Ibid.* Part III, Letter XVIII; Part IV, Letter VII; Part VI, Letter XII.
81 *Ibid.* Part IV, Letters VI, XV.
82 *Ibid.* Part V, Letter VII.
83 *Ibid.* Part V, Letter XII.
84 *Ibid.* Part V, Letter VIII.
85 N.H., Part IV, Letters IX, XII.
86 *Ibid.* Part IV, Letter XIV.
87 *Ibid.* Part V, Letters III, X; for a religious interpretation of the relationship, see Pierre Burgelin, *La philosophie de l'existence de Jean-Jacques Rousseau*, Presses Universitaires de France, Paris, 1952, 447–55.
88 *"Lettre à Lenieps,"* 8 Nov. 1758, C.G., IV, 115–16.

89 *Letter to d'Alembert*, 82.

90 N.H., Part I, Letter XXI.

91 *Essai sur les evènements importants dont les femmes ont été la cause secrète*, O. C., II, 1257–9; *Sur les Femmes, ibid.* 1254–5.

92 *Émile*, 322, 370–1; *Pensées*, VII, 1300; *Letter to d'Alembert*, 87–8.

93 *Émile*, 333, 359.

94 *Ibid.* 444.

95 N.H., Part VI, Letter III.

96 *Ibid.* Part VI, Letters IV, XIII.

97 *Émile*, 5, 87. Rousseau regretted that the law gave them too little power over their children, mainly because he thought maternal affection less harmful than paternal harshness.

98 Vaughan, I, 205 (*Inégalité*); N.H., "*Second préface*"; *Émile*, 48, 149, 163.

99 Vaughan, I, 185 (*Inégalité*); I, 237–40 (*Économie politique*); II, 80 (*Contrat social*); *Émile*, 423.

100 *Émile*, 19.

101 *Ibid.* 17; N.H., Part IV, Letter XIV.

102 *Émile*, 208, 299–300. That is why a Saint-Preux would do.

103 *Confessions*, VII, 267–9; *Émile*, 18.

104 Rousseau made this point in his first essay on private education written in 1740, "*Mémoire presenté à M. de Ste. Marie pour l'education de son fils*," C.G., I, 367–99, and he repeated it many years later in advising a nobleman on the rules to be followed by the governess of the latter's daughter, "*Lettre au Prince de Wurtemberg*," 10 Nov. 1763, C.G., X, 205–17; *Émile*, 20. The tutor, not the father, Rousseau insisted, chooses a wife for *Émile, ibid.* 369.

105 *Émile*, 59.

106 N.H., Part V, Letter VIII.

107 *Ibid.* Part V, Letter III; *Émile*, 10–11, 157, 216–17.

108 N.H., Part V, Letter VIII.

109 N.H., Part V, Letter III; *Émile*, 15–16, 33–5, 44–9, 55–8, 65, 71–6, 124–6, 128, 155–63, 171, 217–18, 435–9.

110 *Rousseau juge de Jean-Jacques*, I, 687; *Émile*, 16, 57.

111 *Émile*, 6.

112 *Ibid.* 157, 216–17; N.H., Part V, Letter III. "Give nature time to work before you take over her business." *Émile*, 71.

113 *Lettre à Christophe de Beaumont*, 71.

114 *Émile*, 84–5.

115 *Ibid.* 55.

116 *Ibid.* 209.

117 *Ibid.* 84–5, 88–9, 107, 177.

118 *Ibid.* 169.

119 *Ibid.* 291–2, 295, 297–300.

120 *Ibid.* 281–2.

121 *Émile*, 444.

122 *Ibid.* 290.

123 *Émile et Sophie*, in *Émile*, op. cit.

124 N.H., Part IV, Letter X; Part V, Letters II and VII.

125 Vaughan, I, 238–40 (*Économie politique*).

126 See also, Vaughan, II, 497 (*Poland*).

127 N.H., Part III, Letter XX.

128 *Émile*, 47–8.

129 N.H., Part V, Letter VII. That also is the reason why Rousseau urged festivals so much on the Poles. And indeed his Polish project presents a strange mixture of domestic and political government. Vaughan, II, 434–5 (*Poland*).

130 *Émile*, 9.

131 *Ibid.* 8.

132 Vaughan, II, 52 (*Contrat social*); 427–30 (*Poland*).

133 *Confessions*, I, 9; VIII 356; *Rousseau juge de Jean-Jacques*, II, 819; *Lettres à Malesherbes*, II, 1134.

134 *"Lettre au Prince de Wurtemberg,"* 10 Nov. 1763, C.G., X, 217.

135 Vaughan, I, 324 (*Fragment*); 478 (*Première version*); II, 51–2 (*Contrat social*).

136 *Ibid.* I, 245–8 (*Économie politique*).

137 Vaughan, II, 37 (*Contrat social*).

138 *Ibid.* I, 126 (*Inégalité*).

139 *Émile*, 49.

140 Vaughan, I, 248 (*Économie politique*).

141 *Confessions*, IX, 404–5; Vaughan, I, 246 (*Économie politique*).

142 Vaughan, I, 322 (*Fragment*).

143 *Ibid.* I, 248 (*Économie politique*).

144 *Ibid.* I, 330–1 (*Fragment*); II, 426–7 (*Poland*).

145 "Lettre à Vernet," 29 Nov. 1760, C.G., V, 270–2.

146 Vaughan, II, 88, 91 (*Contrat social*). *"Le Corps politique, aussi bien que le corps de l'homme commence à mourir dès sa naissance."*

147 *Ibid.* II, 427–9 (*Poland*); I, 314–20, 330–2 (*Fragment*).

148 *Ibid.* I, 338 (*Fragment*).

149 *Émile*, 286–8; Vaughan, II, 429–30 (*Poland*).

150 Vaughan, II, 53 (*Contrat social*).

151 *Ibid.* I, 483 (*Première version*).

152 *Essai sur l'origine des langues*, 407–8.

153 Vaughan, I, 477–83 (*Première version*); II, 51–4 (*Contrat social*).

154 "Lettre à M. Buttafoco," 26 May 1765, C.G., XIII, 334–6.

155 "Lettre à M. l'Abbé de Raynal," June 1753, C.G., II, 49. The multitude, Rousseau wrote, are sheep; they need examples, not arguments.

156 Vaughan, I, 250–1 (*Économie politique*); 476 (*Premiére version*).

157 *Ibid*. II, 54 (*Contrat social*).

158 Vaughan, II, 51 (*Contrat social*).

159 *Ibid*, I, 246–7 (*Économie politique*).

160 *Ibid*. I, 331 (*Fragment*); 489 (*Première version*); II, 54–6 (*Contrat social*); *Letter to d'Alembert*, 74.

161 Vaughan, I, 491 (*Première version*); II, 60 (*Contrat social*).

162 *Ibid*. I, 183 (*Inégalité*).

163 *Ibid*. II, 55–6, 61 (*Contrat social*). Poland was a mere afterthought. Vaughan, II, 441 (*Poland*).

164 He feared that his ideas "differed prodigiously from those of the Corsicans," "*Lettre à M. Buttafoco*," 24 March 1765, C.G., XIII, 150–3.

165 *Rousseau juge de Jean-Jacques*, II, 813.

166 "*Lettres Morales*," 369.

167 Vaughan, I, 255–7 (*Économie politique*).

168 *Ibid*. 341 (*Fragment*); II, 429–30 (*Poland*).

169 *Rêveries*, VIII, 1079.

170 "*Préface*" à *Narcisse*, 970.

171 Vaughan II, 344–5 (*Corsica*).

172 *Ibid*. I, 355–6 (*Fragment*); II, 428, 432–3 (*Poland*).

173 *Ibid*. II, 56 (*Contrat social*); 487 (*Poland*).

174 One can constrain individual character, but one cannot change it, according to Wolmar. N.H., Part V, Letter III.

175 Vaughan, I, 149–50, 178–9 (*Inégalité*).

176 Vaughan, II, 501 (*Poland*).

177 *Ibid*. II, 51 (*Contrat social*).

178 Rousseau was proud of his tolerance. Only intolerance is prohibited by the civil religion, after all. Vaughan, II, 133–4 (*Contrat social*); N.H., Part V, Letter V; Part VI, Letter VII; *Rousseau juge de Jean-Jacques*, II, 811.

179 *Lettres à Malesherbes*, II, 1137; *Rêveries*, VI, 1059; *Lettres Écrites de la Montagne*, VIII, 227–8.

180 *Émile*, 48–59, 125–6, 436; *Pensées*, XXXI, 1305.

181 *Émile*, 196.

182 "Lettre à Moulton fils," 7 March 1768, C.G., XVIII, 147–50.

8   The Religious Thought*

Kant held that Newton and Rousseau had revealed the ways of Providence: "After Newton and Rousseau, God is justified, and Pope's thesis is henceforth true."[1]

Rousseau discussed Providence and Pope's thesis, that "Whatever is, is right," most fully in a long letter that he wrote to Voltaire in 1756, approximately a year after the publication of the *Discourse on Inequality* (1755), at a time when he is likely also to have done work on the *Essay on the Origin of Languages*. These three writings, the *Discourse*, – together with Rousseau's replies to the criticisms of it by the Genevan naturalist Charles Bonnet, writing under the pseudonym Philopolis, and by the Master of the King's Hunt, Charles-George Le Roy, writing under the name Buffon – the *Essay*, and the *Letter to Voltaire*, form a unit: They consider the natural order and man's place in it more specifically than do any of his other writings.[2] The *Discourse* is the only one of these publications that Rousseau himself initiated. The *Letter to Voltaire* differs from the other writings in this group by discussing man's place in the natural world in theological terms. Indeed, it is the only record we have of a theological discussion that Rousseau freely initiated with a near equal: "a friend of the truth speaking to a Philosopher" [2]. Still, his relations with Voltaire were already tense, and he clearly did not think even of this *Letter* as entirely candid and private: He omitted his boldest reflections from the copy that he sent to Voltaire, and its unauthorized publication, some years later, cannot have taken

---

*An abridged, earlier version of this study appeared in *Literary Imagination, Ancient and Modern: Essays in Honor of David Grene*, (Chicago, IL: University of Chicago Press, 1999), pp. 285–311. ©1999 by The University of Chicago. All rights reserved. This full version is published here by permission.

him by surprise. The fact remains that none of his numerous other discussions of religious issues is addressed to a near equal or to a "philosopher"; most of them are public; some are frankly apologetic; others are carried on by various characters of his invention, some of whom explicitly are and some of whom explicitly are not "citizens," and a number of whom appear in the guise of the first person. The reader is therefore not free simply to attribute to one of his characters the views that he attributes to another one of them; nor is the reader free simply to attribute to the author the views that he attributes to one or another of his characters; in his last writing he goes so far as to embed what little he says about his religious views in a discussion of lying, and even in that context he says of these views only that they are "more or less" the same as those that he had Émile's tutor attribute to the Savoyard vicar. In short, the *Letter to Voltaire* is Rousseau's most authoritative discussion of religious issues, the discussion in the light of which careful readers will assess his numerous other discussions of these issues.[3]

The immediate occasion for the *Letter* was a small booklet Rousseau received in early 1756, made up of two didactic poems by Voltaire, *Poem on Natural Law* – initially entitled *Poem of Natural Religion*, written in 1751/1752, and *Poem about the Lisbon Disaster*, written shortly after the terrible earthquake that struck Lisbon on Saturday, 1 November, All Saints' Day, 1755. The quake was followed by tidal waves and extensive fires, causing the death of thousands of people and destroying much of the city. The disaster made a deep impression throughout Europe.[4] Voltaire writes about it in impassioned tones and with none of his usual detachment or irony. His *Poem* is a sustained attack on "optimism," "the axiom," as its subtitle announces, "*Tout est bien*," Leibniz's thesis that this is the best world possible, and the thesis of Pope's *Essay on Man* (1733/1734) that "whatever is, is right."[5]

In 1737 the French Jesuit *Journal de Trévoux* coined the term optimism to mock Leibniz's "best (*optimum*) world possible." It mocks optimism because, as Voltaire points out in the Preface to his *Poem*, the theologians very correctly saw that the optimists' claim, that this is the best world possible, relegates the Fall, redemption, and salvation to a strictly subordinate role in men's lives. Initially, then, optimism referred to a philosophical position and not, as it does now, to the belief that things get better and better. The circumstances in which the term was introduced only underscore how closely the permanent problem of the origin of evil had become entangled with Christian theology. The discussion about optimism revolved around what Locke had called The Reasonableness of Christianity and around the relation between nature and grace, and it had engaged Bayle and Leibniz, Fénelon and Bossuet, and Malebranche and Arnauld, as well as innumerable lesser divines and literati. The point at issue between the optimists and their critics was not whether the world is free of evils – no one claimed it is – but whether it could ever be or had been free of them. The optimists held that it had not and could not ever be entirely free of them. Their critics held that it had or could have been.[6] In 1753 the Royal Academy of Berlin announced as the topic for its 1755 Prize competition a thorough discussion of Pope's thesis, of the relation between it and Leibniz's teaching, and of whether it is tenable or not. The competition was widely perceived as an invitation to write that Pope's and Leibniz's optimism is not tenable, because the Academy's President, Pierre Moreau de Maupertuis, had recently published an *Essai de philosophie morale* (1749) in which he had claimed to prove that the evils of men's lives outweigh their goods. Bayle had reviewed a number of earlier such comparisons, especially in his *Dictionary* articles "Manichéens" and "Xenophanes"; Leibniz had reviewed some in his *Théodicée* (I, Sections 12–19 and III, Sections 251–253); Rousseau had spoken to the issue and alluded to Maupertuis's argument in the *Discourse on Inequality* (I [34] and Note IX [1]); Kant considered entering the competition; Lessing and Mendelssohn wrote, but did not submit, a highly critical analysis of Pope's *Essay* under the ironic title *Pope a Metaphysician!*; and now Voltaire, writing under the impact of the earthquake, makes essentially the same claim Maupertuis had made: life's evils exceed its goods.

Voltaire's *Poem* is not particularly long, no longer than the first of the four Epistles that make up Pope's *Essay*. In form, as well as in content, it proceeds on two levels: in form, it is divided into the *Poem* proper, its prose Preface, and occasionally rather extensive Notes; in content, the *Poem* proper is an essentially theologico-moral meditation on divine Providence, whereas the prose Preface and especially some of the longer Notes summarize philosophical–scientific objections to the view that this is the best of all possible worlds. Voltaire leaves it to the reader to find the connection between the feelings he expresses in the *Poem* proper and the prose arguments he presents in the Preface and the Notes. He does not himself integrate them into a clear, coherent whole.

Voltaire claims not to want to take issue with Pope, "whom he has always admired and loved," or with the views of Shaftesbury and Bolingbroke and the thought of Leibniz that, he rightly notes, Pope wove together into the *Essay on Man*.[7] Rather, he claims to take issue with the defining tenet of "optimism," "*Tout est bien*," on the grounds that it might encourage "fatalism" and complacency in the face of imperfection and evil: "'Whatever is, is right' taken in an absolute sense and without hope for a future, is simply an insult to the suffering in our life." (Preface to the *Poem* [8]) His professed aim is to secure – or to restore – a place for hope. Hope, in this debate, is traditionally understood as hope for personal immortality.[8] He further claims to challenge the optimists' "Whatever is, is right" on the grounds that evil is incompatible with God's being all good and all powerful. He thus appears to side with the theologians.

The *Poem* opens with a description of devastation and an outcry at the horror and the injustice of it. How, in the face of such destruction, can the philosophers maintain that "whatever is, is right"? (*Préface* [1], *Poem* ll, 4ff, 122–124). The Lisbon disaster is not a unique occurrence. Strife and destruction threaten everywhere:

> *éléments, animaux, humains, tout est en guerre.*
> *Il le faut avouer, le mal est sur la terre* (ll, 125ff).

Evil(s) (mal, maux), in this debate, refers primarily to "physical" in contrast to "moral" evil(s), evils men suffer but do not themselves cause, foremost among them, death, but also such often great and undeserved losses as those of Job or of the victims of the Lisbon earthquake. Voltaire therefore adds to the traditional list of these "physical" evils the fact that we find ourselves forced to try to understand what apparently we simply cannot understand.[9] The quest for the origin of evil, in this debate is the quest for the general, overarching cause(s) of such evils(s).

Voltaire weaves into his *Poem* a brief review of the possible views regarding the origin of evil: Manicheanism, the view that the whole is subject to two principles, one good, the other evil (ll, 129ff, 138), which had recently been given renewed currency by Bayle;[10] the view that evil is divine punishment, either collective, for original sin (l, 149), or particular, for the sufferers' individual sins (ll, 17–23); the view that evil is a divine trial to determine whether and how much eternal bliss an individual may deserve (ll, 155–158); the view that evil is the inevitable by-product of the workings of nature's inexorable laws, either because God is indifferent to their workings (ll, 150–152, 15ff, 42–44), or, because evil is inevitable even in the best of all possible worlds and may therefore be said to contribute to the general good (ll, 169–174, 66–68); and, finally, the view that evil is the by-product of strictly material necessity that is not subject to divine control (ll, 153ff).

On the face of it, Voltaire appears summarily to reject the first alternative, Manicheanism: "God alone is master" (l, 138). The remaining four alternatives naturally form two classes: evils that are due to human failure or sin, what at the time was called "moral evil(s)"; and evils that are due to the constraints on the parts of wholes because they are parts, what Leibniz called "metaphysical evil(s)," and Newton's spokesman Samuel Clarke referred to by the traditional name of "evil(s) of imperfection."[11]

For all intents and purposes, Voltaire ignores "moral evil." His criticism of "optimism" deals exclusively with what the philosophers called "metaphysical evil(s)" or "evil(s) of imperfection": evil as the necessary consequence of the world order. He lists two versions of this alternative: Evil is a necessary consequence of inherent limitations matter imposes on intelligence and will (ll, 153ff)[12] or evil is the necessary consequence of God's initial decrees, which He lets run their course:

> sans couroux, sans pitié, tranquille, indifférent (1, 151).

In his *Poem about the Lisbon Disaster*, Voltaire says nothing about the first version of this alternative.[13] In *Poem about the Lisbon Disaster* he discusses in detail only the view that evil is the necessary consequence of the world order or of necessary laws, that, in an order made up of different parts or kinds, each part or kind must necessarily accommodate the whole of which it is a part, and such accommodation manifests itself as physical evil. On this view each thrives at the partial expense of the others, and the evils each suffers redound to the others' benefit.[14] For all intents and purposes, this is the only argument that Voltaire seriously considers.

He objects to this "metaphysical evil" argument on two grounds: on what might be called moral–theological grounds and on what might be called philosophical–scientific grounds. He spells out his moral–theological objections in the body of the *Poem*, and he relegates his philosophical–scientific objections to the Notes.

The optimists' necessary-laws argument is morally and theologically repugnant because it entails that we, as well as the rest of the world, would be less well off if there were no evils:

> "Tout est bien et tout est nécessaire."
> Quoi! L'univers entier sans ce gouffre infernal,
> Sans engloutir Lisbonne eut-il été plus mal? (ll, 42–44).

The optimists' necessary-laws argument is further morally and theologically repugnant because a necessity that visits evils on innocent and guilty alike is unjust and therefore reflects ill on an omnipotent God (ll, 173ff).

What is more, the necessary-laws argument is simply not morally effectual: Necessity is not a consolation, even if we did grant that our own evils are other people's goods.[15] It does not help to be told that the world was not made for us, or that to complain is to display pride, or to have Paul rebuke the pot that would ask its potter "Why hast thou made me thus?"(Romans 9:20ff). *This* pot is a sentient and a thinking vessel and so surely has a right to complain (ll, 58, 83–96); and surely pity for our fellows is not pride but simply the just claim to be recognized in the eyes of God as being worth more than sticks and stones.[16]

In the *Poem* proper, Voltaire maintains that an omnipotent God is not bound by natural or rational necessity and hence could dispose things differently:

> Non, ne présentez plus à mon coeur agité
> Ces immuables loix de la nécessité,
> Cette chaîne des corps, des esprits et des mondes.
> O rêves savants! ô chimères profondes!
> Dieu tient en main la chaîne, et n'est point enchaîné;
> Par son choix bienfaisant tout est déterminé (ll, 71–76).

In the lengthy note that he appended to this passage, he states his objection in philosophical–scientific rather than moral–theological terms. Evils cannot be due to the workings of general laws because phenomena do not conform to strict laws. There are "indifferent" phenomena in the realm of nature as well as in the realm of human affairs: Not all bodies are necessary to the order and preservation of the universe and not all events make a difference.[17] Even if the phenomena did conform to strict laws, we could not know that they do, because, speaking philosophically, we have no access to first principles (Note to l, 210), or, speaking theologically, the unaided human reason cannot fathom God's ways:

> La nature est muette, on l'interroge en vain
> On a besoin d'un Dieu qui parle au genre humain (ll, 163ff).

In short, whatever *is* does not conform to the principle of sufficient reason.[18]

Voltaire ends his review of the alternatives regarding providence by claiming that he cannot choose between them and that he therefore follows Bayle who, scales in hand, teaches doubt, but, he adds in a Note, never denies Providence or the immortality of the soul (*Poem*, Preface [10]; ll, 191–196; note to l, 192). Neither does Voltaire explicitly deny them. Although the argument of the *Poem* is not particularly rigorous, its ostensible aim is clear enough: to combine a physics and a cosmology that allow for some indeterminacy in nature and in conduct with a theology that appears orthodox because it allows for divine intervention in the course of nature.[19] Newton's cosmology appears to allow for such a combination, whereas the cosmology of the optimist Leibniz does not.[20] Now, Newton may be a respectable ally against Leibniz, but Voltaire's model is Bayle. His case against optimism closely parallels Bayle's case for Manicheanism: Both argue that the evils of life are proof – or at least very strong evidence – that an evil principle inheres in the very nature of things. The *Poem*'s clearly intended effect is therefore the very opposite of its ostensible aim, and Voltaire's protestation to the contrary – "I do not rise up against Providence" (l, 222) – only reinforces the reader's impression that this is a poem *against* Providence. For by ignoring evils that might be due to human failures properly so-called "moral evils," but especially by arguing *both* that there are no theoretical reasons why God cannot intervene in the course of nature *and* that there are strong moral reasons why He should intervene in it at least to the point of sparing the innocent, Voltaire leaves his reader under the impression that God is indifferent, arbitrary, even malicious. He was more candid with the Pastor Jacob Vernet: "... this business [i.e., the Lisbon earthquake] is a kick in the rear of Providence."[21] As for the immortality of the individual soul, the *Poem*, which ostensibly sets out to restore the hope for it, ends by bitterly and defiantly questioning it.[22] It would seem that the only hope Voltaire holds out is hope for a better, "future," a "new order of things" (Preface [8], [10]) in this life. He attacks what was then called optimism – the reasoned trust that this is the best world possible – in the name of what is now called optimism: the belief that things can and do keep getting better and better, and that the evils of this world can be reduced or even eliminated altogether. In the process he comes close to replacing Providence and the immortality of the soul with a project for a progressive history.[23]

By contrast, Rousseau, in the *Letter* that he wrote to Voltaire in response to his Lisbon *Poem*, defends optimism in the original sense of the term. The trust that this is the best world possible is perfectly consistent with what, in a text he had drafted just a short time before but never published, he described as his "sad...system" (*Preface of a Second Letter to Bordes* [6]). Most immediately, his defense of optimism in the *Letter to Voltaire* consists in once more arguing that most of the evils we suffer are of our own making[24] ([7], [8]) and to vindicate our common-sense trust in "the ordinary course of things" ([10], [12]; cf. [25]) and our belief or hope in the conformity between this "ordinary course of things" and our moral lives. The debate between Voltaire and Rousseau is framed by the question of whose view of providence is the least cruel and the most consoling (Voltaire, *Poem*, ll: 31, 59, 70, 102, 141–145, 155; Rousseau, *Letter* [4], [6], [10], [23], [28], [29], [30]).

Rousseau begins by briefly praising Voltaire's earlier *Poem on Natural Law* and noting that the views he expresses in it are sharply at odds with the views he expresses in the accompanying *Poem about the Lisbon Disaster*. He is perfectly right. In the Lisbon *Poem* Voltaire indignantly rejects every attempt to justify the ways of God to man, whereas in the earlier *Poem*–and, indeed, in most of his other writings – he is more resigned than indignant about the evils of this world.[25] Rousseau rather pointedly remarks that if Voltaire does not hesitate to contradict himself, then neither need he, Rousseau, hesitate to contradict him, and he devotes the longest part of his *Letter* ([6]–[22]) to a detailed criticism of the Lisbon *Poem*. He goes on briefly to discuss the distinction between universal and particular providence ([23]–[26]) and the premises of any belief in providence

([27]–[31]) and to invite Voltaire to add to the argument of his earlier *Poem on Natural Law* – which Rousseau describes as the "catechism of man" – a "kind of civil profession of faith" or the "catechism of the citizen" [35]. He ends the *Letter* by remarking, briefly but sharply, how much their differences about providence and the immortality of the soul reflect differences about this life. [36]

Rousseau does not deny that the Lisbon earthquake was a great calamity or that our lives are beset by innumerable evils. He denies that evils are all equal: He rejects Voltaire's putting mortality and great cataclysms on the same footing as evils that are wholly or largely due to a lack of prudence ([8], [9]) or to an excess of pride [21]; and he rejects Voltaire's attributing all evils to an omnipotent God's failure to prevent them. Voltaire's *Poem* leaves us questioning God's goodness and justice and feeling forsaken and dejected [5]. What is more, by couching his distressing message in verse, Voltaire only makes it more insidious ([10], [31]).

Rousseau, in contrast to Voltaire, sets out to show that the evils that beset us are either unavoidable but minor or are of our own making and hence at least partly avoidable ([4]–[8]). He sides with Leibniz and Pope, who leave us feeling reconciled and even hopeful because they have God combining the most good(s) with the fewest evils possible:

... or (to say the same thing even more bluntly, if need be), if he did not do better, it is that he could not do better" [5].

God is not omnipotent[26] ([6], cf. [27]). In short, Rousseau defends the traditional, rigorously rational necessary-laws argument against Voltaire's assault on it.

One reason why Voltaire rejects the necessary-laws argument is that in his view it fails to console us for the evils we suffer or to reconcile us to the course of things; one reason why Rousseau adopts it is that in his view it alone frees us from dependence on another's will, and so makes us rather bear those ills we have. Voltaire's poem leaves us discontented; Pope's poem buoys our spirits [5].

Voltaire backs his moral–theological objections to the necessary-laws argument with philosophical–scientific objections to it: Newton's cosmology and "the learned geometer" Crouzas prove that in the realm of nature as well as in the realm of human affairs there are "indifferent" phenomena, that some things or events could just as well be one way as another, that the dust a carriage raises makes no more difference in the scheme of things than it does whether Caesar spat to the left or to the right on his way to the Senate the day he was assassinated ([17]; and notes 17 and 18 in this chapter). Rousseau, in agreement with Leibniz, rejects Voltaire's and Samuel Clarke's "indifferent" phenomena. Everything makes some physical or moral difference in the long run [17].[27] As for Crouzas's criticism of Pope, he had considered and discussed it at length some fifteen years earlier. However, in his present discussion of Providence he chooses to cast himself in the role of the common man who has not read him and may well not be able to understand him [14] and who refuses to accept on authority scientific claims that fly in the face of common experience [18].[28] More generally, he mocks Voltaire for being so categorical about the nature of mathematics and claiming "demonstrated" knowledge about the movements of the heavenly bodies while professing to follow Bayle and to suspend judgment about Providence. "How likely is one to be believed when one boasts of knowing nothing while asserting so many things?" ([19]; cf. Rêveries VII, OC 1, 1069).

The point at issue between them here is not so much what may be the true scientific account of things, as it is what constitutes the familiar, shared, comparatively regular and stable world of common experience. The premise of the *Letter to Voltaire*, the starting point of all of Rousseau's thought, is that we take our bearings in our day-to-day existence by what twice in this *Letter* he calls "the ordinary course of things" ([10], [12], cf. [25]), the world of common experience in contrast to rational and scientific accounts of nature on the one hand, and to supernatural interventions and miracles on the other.[29] "The ordinary course of things" is "first for us." We trust it. All conduct and all inquiry rest on this trust and attachment.

Rousseau's privileging "the ordinary course of things" goes hand in hand with his so consistently presenting his thought dramatically, through the intermediary of a vast cast of characters among whom the first person is assigned a number of particularly prominent roles, with his repeated appeals to sentiment and the heart in contrast to reason, and with his consistent disparagement of "metaphysics."

Our trust and attachment to "the ordinary course of things" manifest themselves perhaps most conspicuously in our trust that all things somehow cohere and constitute a whole, and indeed the best of possible wholes or worlds; in other words, that whatever is, is right. It would appear to point to what might be called "cosmic support of man's humanity" or "Providence." Our trust in "the ordinary course of things" manifests itself most distinctively as our finding dependence on natural and impersonal necessity comparatively easy to bear – Rousseau calls it "consoling" – whereas dependence on another's will is the greatest evil, and we naturally chafe at it. Accordingly, Rousseau depersonalizes even God by denying Him omnipotence and subordinating Him to impersonal necessity. Voltaire, by contrast, says that dependence on necessary laws is "cruel." Yet he personalizes necessity as the will of an omnipotent God, and by turning his protests against the evils inherent in the human condition into protests against this omnipotent God, he only confirms Rousseau's view that what men resent and reject is primarily dependence on another's individual and arbitrary will.[30]

Even if all things do somehow cohere and constitute a whole, it can manifestly not be a homogeneous whole. It is made up of disparate parts. The good of one part or kind or species differs from the good of another and hence from the good of the whole ([21], [22]).[31] The goods of the various parts or kinds or species are not compossible, nor even are the goods of all the members of our kind.[32] There are then "evils" inherent in the very "system" or "constitution" of the universe ([8], [21], [22], [5], [23]).[33] God could, then, not do better [5] because of the nature(s) of things. The best world possible is not good without qualification. Evils cannot cease.

However, when Voltaire claims that nobody would be prepared to live his life over again (l, 210 and Note), Rousseau counters that this may be how swaggerers feel who make a show of scorning death by setting too low a stock by the goods of life, or the malcontent rich, or melancholy men of letters ([11], [12]). Such people who, like Voltaire himself, enjoy life and cling to it all the while they claim that we suffer more evils than we enjoy goods are manifestly in bad faith ([11], [36]). They fail to acknowledge "the sweet sentiment of existence" [11].[34] If Voltaire had instead consulted ordinary folk, tradesmen, artisans, or the mountain folk of the Valais, people whose attitudes carry weight if for no other reason than that they make up the greater part of mankind, he would have had to acknowledge that in the full context of our lives the goods we enjoy outweigh the unavoidable general evils we suffer [12].[35] "What! Because two or three madmen a day kill themselves in London, the English do not fear death?"[36] Rousseau levels at Voltaire's claim that the evils of life exceed its goods the same charge that he levels at Hobbes' account of the state of nature as a war of all against all: If life were as burdensome as Voltaire makes it out to be or as perma- nently threatened as Hobbes makes it out to be, the species could not long have endured [11].[37] The fact that it has endured alone shows that we would rather be than not be, and this alone suffices to jus- tify our existence. He allows that in some cases evils do outweigh goods and that the wise may then choose suicide, ([12], cf. *Nouvelle Héloise* III 21).

In short, Rousseau rejects the twin premises of Voltaire's *Poem:* that an omnipotent God could have prevented or altogether elimi- nated the evils of life and that our evils outweigh our goods.

Remarks such as "Man is by nature good [bon]" or "Whatever is, is right [bien] on leaving the hands of the author of things," are fre- quently taken to entail that, in Rousseau's view, human beginnings were good without qualification. However, this is evidently not his view.[38] "Man is by nature good" in the sense that by nature, "ini- tially" everyone's needs and powers are in balance and that therefore no one is irreversibly dependent on others to do his own good; "what- ever is, is right upon leaving the hands of the author of things" in the sense that things are in more or less stable balance (especially *Essay on the Origin of Languages* 9 [31]–[33]); the formula clearly echoes – and modifies – God's beholding His creation and seeing that parts of it were good – *les trouva bons*, as the eighteenth-century French text has it – and the whole of it very good, *très bon*; "everything degenerates in the hands of man" in the sense that even success- ful attempts to remedy existing evils inevitably introduce new ones. Gains necessarily entail losses.[39]

All Rousseau says about moral evil in the *Letter to Voltaire* is that its source must be sought "...in man free, perfected, hence cor- rupted..." [8]. He closely links being free with being perfectible, being perfectible with speech, and speech with moral conduct or "progress in good as well as in evil."[40] In short, the source of moral evil – and hence also of moral good – is "perfectibility," most par- ticularly the distinctive capacity for artifice and convention that is set in motion "with the aid of circumstances," in other words by the workings of nature's necessary laws.[41] In the *Social Contract*, Rousseau narrows his focus from artifice and convention in general to political society. Broadly speaking, the

... transition from the state of nature produces a most remarkable change in man by substituting justice for instinct in his conduct, and endowing his actions with the morality they previously lacked (I 8 [1]).

This and similar remarks are sometimes said to have radically altered the debate about the origin of moral evil by shifting it from necessary laws, or from human nature, or from original sin, to society and, more specifically, to political society (*Discourse on Inequality* II [35]–[39], *Social Contract* I 8 [3]).[42] However, political philosophy has from the very first coupled the origin of moral evil or of injustice with the introduction of political society,[43] and Rousseau consistently attributes the institution of political society to the workings of nature's necessary laws. More precisely, political society is by the workings of necessary laws as regards the "system" or "constitution" of the universe; it is "by accident" as regards human nature, because, in Rousseau's view, man is not a political animal or by nature inclined to form or to enter political society. Sometimes he makes this point by speaking of political society and its consequences as moral effects of physical causes.[44] The view that Rousseau attributes the origin of moral evil to society is frequently coupled – explicitly or implicitly – with the claim that in his view a political order can be devised that would prevent or eliminate most and perhaps all moral evils, or even that in his view political society should or could be eliminated altogether.[45] Yet he never holds out such a prospect. Like all political philosophers, he explores ways of reducing the "inconveniences" attendant on political society.[46] However, he categorically denies the possibility of eliminating them altogether [*Rousseau juge de Jean Jacques* III (OC I, 934ff)]. What holds with respect to the larger whole or the universe holds equally with respect to such smaller wholes as political societies: tensions, conflicts, "inconveniences" among the goods of the different parts or among the goods of the parts and the good of the whole, are inevitable. Even the best possible balance between their competing claims is precarious. Some rare individuals might be able to withdraw from political society altogether (*Discourse on Inequality*, N. XVI [1]) or to live well at its margins, *in* it without being of it [*Émile*, V, (OC IV, 858); *Nouvelle*

Héloise, VI, 5 (OC II, 657); *First Discourse* [59]]; the mass of mankind cannot, and, Rousseau holds, may not [*First Discourse* [39], *Émile*, III (OC IV 470); *Rêveries* I, V, VI (OC I, 1000, 1047, 1056)]. Yet only self-sufficient solitaries could possibly conform to the precept never to do their good at another's expense (*Émile* II (OC IV, 340*), cf. IV, 493, tr. 105*, 214; *Rousseau juge de Jean-Jacques*, II (OC I, 790, 823ff)]; and even solitaries would have to acquire – as do Émile and the first person of the Rêveries – the austere moral self-sufficiency that inures to the evils that others might visit on them and to slavery itself [*Emile et Sophie, ou les solitaires*, II, (OC IV, 905ff, 916ff); *Rêveries* I, IV, VI, (OC I, 1000, 1002ff, 1027, 1046ff, 1056)]. "Everything that is not in nature has its inconveniences, and civil society more than all the rest" (*Social Contract*, III, 15 [10]).

The "inconveniences" that inevitably attend on civil society are what the tradition calls "metaphysical evils." Rousseau does not use the expression. He is reluctant to call even inevitable inconveniences "evils." The optimist denies "general evil" [23]. The optimist's formula, "Whatever is, is right," is equivalent to saying "Providence is universal." It is emphatically not a formula of uncritical acquiescence to whatever may be the case.[47] The optimist does not deny particular evils. No philosopher ever has [23]. There is no particular providence [25].[48]

Voltaire fails to distinguish between general and particular evil and between universal and particular providence. His fallacy – Rousseau calls it the fallacy of the *philosophes* – is formally the same as the fallacy committed by the priests and the devout: The philosophers wrongly conclude, on the evidence of particular evils, that evil is general and, as a consequence, in effect deny providence altogether; the priests and the devout attribute even particular, natural events to Providence [24] and as a consequence in effect deny particular evils.[49] Rousseau, by contrast, proceeds on the premise that

...in the eyes of the Lord of the universe, particular events here below are nothing, that his Providence is exclusively universal, that he leaves it at preserving genera and species, and at presiding over the whole without worrying about how each individual spends this short life [25].

Compare *Discourse on Inequality* I, [33], [17]–[20]; *Reply to Charles-George Le Roy* [2], and *Essay on the Origin of Languages* 9 [31]–[34]; *Social Contract*, II 6 [2].

In this view of it, Providence is not "moral" in any sense of the term. Not even the greatest evils – or goods – men might visit on one another pertain to it.[50]

"Moral evils" in the sense of evils that may be said to be of our own making because they are due to our doing badly what it is within our power to do well or badly are "particular evils." Indeed, one of Rousseau's primary aims in drawing the distinction between general and particular evil as he does is to disentangle the permanent problem of moral evil from the theological, but primarily from the Christian theological doctrines about it, in order to reclaim a common-sense middle ground for the exercise of prudence, or human, personal providence. The need to set up civil society arises as a result of the inexorable workings of the laws of nature; how we structure civil society and arrange our lives is, within limits, up to us.[51] The Lisbon earthquake came about as a result of the inexorable workings of the laws of nature [9]; it was an evil because countless innocents suffered and died; but they suffered and died for want of human – not divine – providence or prudence. Divine Providence – Rousseau says "nature" – does not guide men to build cities or to build them in one place rather than another ([8]; cf. *Discourse on Inequality* N. XVII). To protest, as the Voltaire of the *Lisbon Poem* does, that the earthquake should not have struck Lisbon is to expect nature to adapt to man. Rousseau, by contrast, holds that man must adapt to nature {[9]; cf. *Émile*, IV (Savoyard vicar) (OC IV, 602) (tr. 292); and, again, *Essay on the Origin of Languages*, 9 [31]–[33]}. Optimism is emphatically not anthropocentric.[52]

This is, precisely, Voltaire's main objection to it: a Whole is not well ordered if beings endowed with sense, and in particular human beings, do not enjoy a privileged place in it:

Undoubtedly, everything is arranged, everything is ordered by Providence; but for a long time now, it has been all too evident that everything is not ordered for our present well-being. *Lisbon Poem*, Preface [1].

It is not a consolation to know that our mortal remains serve as food for worms (*Poem* ll, 99ff). Rousseau indicates, discreetly but clearly, that for earthlings to assume they are worth more in the eyes of God than are the inhabitants of Saturn is a thoughtless display of self-importance [21].[53] At the same time, he tries to meet Voltaire's objection head on: Insofar as we are parts of a whole, or even of a mere aggregate, and hence necessarily subject to evils, the question is not

...whether each one of us suffers or not; but whether it was good that the universe be, and our evils were inevitable in the constitution of the universe ([23], [8]).

Having stated the question in the most general terms, Rousseau answers it in the most general terms:

... the greatest idea of Providence I can conceive is that each material being be arranged in the best way possible in relation to the whole, and each intelligent and sentient being in the best way possible in relation to itself; which means, in other words, that for a being that senses its existence, it is preferable to exist than not to exist. ([26], cf. [11])

The "sweet sentiment of existence" may contribute to preserving the genera and species of sentient and intelligent beings [25],[54] and it may grant to them – and hence specifically to man – a privileged place among the beings. However, it does so on the most minimal terms. Earlier in this *Letter*, Rousseau had held up as exemplary the mountain folk of the Valais who are content to enjoy their sentiment of existence, to vegetate, and to lead an "almost automaton life" ([12], [13]; cf. *Discourse on Inequality*, I [21]). Voltaire understood him perfectly: in *L'histoire d'un bon bramin* (1759), he contrasts an "automaton" happy life with a thoughtful and therefore unhappy one.

The sentiment of existence suffices to justify our existence,

... even if we should have no compensation to expect for the evils we have to suffer, and even if these evils were as great as you depict them [11].

Rousseau goes so far as to claim that the sentiment of existence also establishes a presumption in favor of individual immortality: the "rule" that for a being that senses its existence it is preferable to exist than not to exist

...has to be applied to each sentient being's total duration, and not to some particular instant[s] of its duration, such as human life; which shows how closely related the question of Providence is to that of the immortality of [the] soul [26].[55]

The evidence for this "rule" would seem to be the well-nigh-universal belief in immortality. As Voltaire remarked in the concluding note to his *Poem*, men entertained this belief "even before enjoying the assistance of revelation." The concern with immortality may be one manifestation of the sentiment of existence (e.g., *Rousseau juge de Jean-Jacques*, OC I, 805). Another manifestation of it may be our feeling that justice calls for happiness in proportion to deserts.[56] No natural sanctions corroborate this feeling.[57] Yet our moral life rests on the trust that what is somehow conforms to what should be. We may therefore be moved to hope that merit unrewarded here and now might be rewarded hereafter and to hope – or fear – that wickedness unpunished here and now might be punished hereafter – but not to the point of eternal punishment "...which neither you nor I, nor any man who thinks well of God, will ever believe" [26] – and hence to hope or fear that the individual soul is immortal. The hope that it is immortal may sustain the righteous, and Rousseau therefore frequently speaks of his own hope for it; and the fear that it is immortal may deter the wicked, and curb the insolence of the powerful and the privileged.[58] In short, we may hope or fear that there is, in the strict sense of the term, a moral order with sanctions for particular actions.[59] Such a moral order might be called providential. However, it could clearly not be called providential in the sense in which Rousseau speaks of providence as "exclusively Universal,...preserving genera and species..." [25].

Rousseau acknowledges that the immortality of the individual soul is no more than an assumption: ... I am not unaware that reason can doubt it ... [26].

So is the necessary condition for universal providence, for our trust in the ordinary course of things, our trust that all things together constitute a whole, and indeed the best-ordered whole possible, no more than an assumption:

> ...instead of saying *Tout est bien* [Whatever is, is right], it might be preferable to say *Le tout est bien* [The whole is right], or *Tout est bien pour le tout* [All is right for the whole]. Then it is quite obvious that no man could give direct proofs *pro* or *con*; for these proofs depend on a perfect knowledge of the world's constitution and of its Author's purpose, and this knowledge is indisputably beyond human intelligence [23].[60]

In short, such formulas as "whatever is, is right," or "this is the best world possible" are systematically ambiguous: They may mean either that whatever is conforms to a standard of good or right, which leads to an infinite regress, or that whatever is, is this standard.

Rousseau therefore concedes that the sufficient condition for Providence, too, is no more than an assumption:

If God exists, he is perfect; if he is perfect, he is wise, powerful and just; if he is wise and powerful, all is well; if he is just and powerful, my soul is immortal . . . . If I am granted the first proposition, the ones that follow will never be shaken; if it is denied, there is no use arguing about its consequences [27].

Rousseau does not deny the first proposition; neither does he affirm it:

I candidly admit to you, that on this point neither the *pro* nor the *con* seems to me demonstrated by the lights of reason. . . . What is more, the objections, on either side, are always irrefutable because they revolve around things about which man has no genuine idea [29].

In short, the God of the *Letter to Voltaire* may be a premise and the Providence of the *Letter* a "great and consoling dogma" [23]. They are not conclusions.

Yet Rousseau professes to believe in God as firmly as he believes any other truth. He tells Voltaire that the fact that he cannot establish the existence of God by reason does not lead him to deny it or even to suspend judgment regarding it. For, he goes on to say, doubt is too violent a state for his soul to bear. When his reason wavers, his faith or belief [*foi*], incapable of remaining in suspense for long, decides on its own and without involving reason:

. . . to believe or not to believe are the things in the world that least depend on me . . . [29].

Reason is one thing; faith or belief is another. Reason leaves the scale in balance. Hope and a thousand objects of preference tip it in favor of the more consoling alternative [29].

In the copy of the *Letter* that he sent to Voltaire, Rousseau breaks off his discussion of this delicate subject at this point. He has been extremely radical: he has denied divine omnipotence, and he has denied particular providence; He well knows that in so doing he has tacitly rejected the possibility of revelation and of all other miracles and has undercut a major justification for prayer; he has gone so far as to say explicitly that the nature and the existence of God do not admit of rational proof any more than does the immortality of the individual soul; he has ignored or rejected outright many of the positive teachings of the Churches; he has not hesitated to allow for suicide; in his own name rather than in the name of one of his characters, as he does in the *Nouvelle Héloise*; he has rejected every version of predestination; he has rejected eternal punishments, and, by parity of reason, eternal rewards. In the following paragraph, which he omitted from the copy of the Letter that he sent to Voltaire as well as from the version of it which he later allowed to be published, he goes even further.[61] In it he spells out the argument against the existence of God and of universal providence. He tells that what most forcefully struck him in his entire life was Diderot's showing, in the twenty-first of his *Pensées philosophiques*, that the manifest order we behold can be accounted for by matter, motion, and chance, without invoking an ordering intelligence, prime mover, wisdom, or beneficence.[62] He finds both Diderot's argument and the arguments against it convincing, but he knows of no conclusive refutation of Diderot's argument. Once again, reason leaves the scales in balance.[63]

Diderot's *Pensée* sweeps aside the classical objection to Epicurean cosmology that both Diderot and Rousseau mention, that it seems even less likely that the universe came about by chance than that a poem might be "composed" by sufficiently many throws of the letters of the alphabet.[64] It makes the strongest case possible for discontinuity between "the ordinary course of things" and what might be the "true" account of them. Rousseau recognizes, indeed he stresses, that argument cannot overcome our finding it utterly implausible to have order arise by chance. He had made the same point regarding free will: Regardless of what may be the truth of the matter, we cannot help *feeling* that we act freely.[65] Diderot's argument may convince, it does not persuade [30].

The contrast Rousseau draws, here and in a number of other places, between being convinced and being persuaded corresponds to the contrast that he draws here, and in a number of other places, between reason proper and sentiment, as well as with the contrast that he goes on to draw between demonstration proper and proofs of sentiment. To convince and to demonstrate is to establish "physical" certainty; to persuade and to offer proofs of sentiment is to establish "moral" certainty. The lawgiver must invoke the gods in order to persuade the vulgar whom he cannot convince (*Social Contract* II, 7 [9]); the Savoyard vicar claims no more than that he is persuaded by his Profession of Faith [*Émile* IV (OC IV, 606ff), (tr. 295)]; by contrast,

Diderot's argument against the existence of God and Providence convinces Rousseau without persuading him.[66] In the *Letter to Voltaire* the first person claims that he – not his reason – yields to the merely persuasive "proof of sentiment," not of "religious sentiment," an expression that Rousseau does not ever use. Nor does he negate reason to make room for faith.[67] On the contrary, he very explicitly acknowledges the sovereignty of reason when he says that what he calls proof of sentiment could equally well be called prejudice [30].[68] He may claim nevertheless to yield to this proof of sentiment because he cannot refute it in thought or in deed. Diderot's *Pensée* is so utterly at odds with ordinary experience that to live and to act in terms of it would require a restructuring of our beliefs and ways that is beyond most, perhaps all, men's powers.[69] It is therefore likely only to undermine the trust and belief on which all conduct and inquiry are based, and to undermine them in the name of alternatives that are not certain and, Rousseau pointedly adds, not useful, is, as he repeatedly tells Voltaire, simply cruel ([6], [30], [31]). Once again sentiment tips the scale in favor of the more consoling alternative.

Rousseau's concession to sentiment honeys the cup, masking the wormwood taste that Diderot's – and Voltaire's – arguments leave.[70] It contributes to the shift away from physicocosmological arguments for the existence of God and from religion to religiosity, in which his thought played such an important part.[71] At the same time, the successive reflections by which he moves from reason's inability to prove the existence of God, and hence of Providence, to his being unable to remain in doubt about it and finding it cruel to cast doubt on it, to his therefore believing it out of sentiment or prejudice and inclination for the more consoling and disinclination for the more cruel alternative, clearly prepare the widespread contemporary rejections of belief in God in the name of "intellectual probity" or of "the refusal to make the sacrifice of the intellect."[72] Rousseau himself never publicly takes this step. On the contrary, he tries to check it. He reminds Voltaire that skepticism does not yield certainties [19],[73] and he presents arguments – or, more precisely, sentiments – against rejecting belief in God. The fact that he presents these sentiments in the first person does not entitle us to attribute them to him. The first person here may be, as it was earlier in this *Letter*, someone who cannot understand claims that fly in the face of common experience ([14], [18]). The paragraph he omitted from the copy of the

Letter that he sent to Voltaire thus raises anew the question of what, precisely, might be his own views and in particular the question of his materialism or of his Epicureanism.

Rousseau returns to the problem of materialism repeatedly. He consistently rejects reductionist materialism – he sometimes refers to it disparagingly as "modern philosophy" – if only because it so manifestly breaks with "the ordinary course of things," sentiment or "prejudice."[74] He is ever mindful that what is "first for us" is as constitutive of what is as is what may be "first in nature." When he restricts his reflections to materialism, narrowly so called, he does so in terms of the perennial questions: Are motion and/or sensation of the nature of matter, or not? He appears to hold that we cannot *conceive* of motion as essential to matter, but cannot *know* that it is not; if it is not, then, according to the received argument, an immaterial self-moving mover – soul or god – must at least initially impart it to matter; and if it does or did impart it, materialism, narrowly so called, is refuted. This would still leave open the question of whether and in what sense immaterial, self-moving soul or god is prior to matter, and how it acts on it.[75] Rousseau does not discuss these questions directly, but he does remark on how problematic dualism is, and he speaks of the action of our soul on our body as unintelligible, "the abyss of philosophy" (Émile IV, OC IV, 553; *Geneva ms.* I 4 [5]). He tends to recast questions about body and soul in terms of what he calls physical and moral causes and effects [17], and at one time he planned a *morale sensitive* or *matérialisme du Sage* that would explore the relation between them.[76] The relation between physical and moral causes and effects is, of course, as much an abyss as is the relation between body and soul. Rousseau repeatedly indicates as much: for instance, in his discussions of the pure state of nature, of the relation between "perfectibility," speech, and freedom, of the origin of language and of musical imitation; and, most dramatically, in M. de Wolmar's failure to cure his wife of her love for St. Preux.[77]

Regardless of whether or in what sense Rousseau's teaching may be "materialist," his account of human things is best understood as a form of Epicureanism. Its premises are the classical Epicurean premises: rejection of teleology at every level, and in particular of providence (*Observations* [39]) and of the view that man is a political animal and the political life is the good life, in favor of the view that political life is instrumental or ministerial, that human good consists in pleasure (*plaisir, volupté, jouir*), and that happiness consists in freedom from dependence on another's will, in tranquility of soul and hence in a soul at one with itself.[78] Classical Epicureanism is primarily a teaching about friendship and life in a small circle of friends. Rousseau conveys his conception of such a life most fully in the works in which he explores alternatives to political economy and citizenship in the strong sense of the term, in his depiction of the domestic economy of the Wolmar household in the *Nouvelle Héloise*, in his account of the domestic education of Emile, and in his autobiographical writings.[79] He did not write the *Art of Enjoying* (*Art de jouir*) that he had planned (OC I, 1173–1177 and ed. n. 1864ff), but he discusses his conception of enjoyment in all of his works, and he has one of the characters of the *Nouvelle Héloise*, St. Preux, describe the novel's heroine, the pious Julie, as rejecting "vulgar Epicureanism" in favor of what his remark implies is "refined Epicureanism:"

... the art of enjoying [*jouir*] is for her that of privations; not of those difficult and painful privations which offend nature and the senseless homage of which its author scorns, but of the transitory, moderate privations which uphold the empire of reason and which, by seasoning pleasure, keep us from spoiling our taste for it by abusing it. *Nouvelle Héloise* V, 2 (OC II, 541f, 552).

Julie's refined Epicureanism, like Rousseau's own, and like their classical model's, is temperate.[80] And, for all the differences between them, Julie, like Rousseau himself, and like their classical models, attains happiness in *this* life [*Nouvelle Héloise* VI 8 (OC II, 695); *Confessions* XII (OC I, 640); *Rêveries* V (OC I, 1046ff)] and *Rêveries* X (OC I, 1099).

Rousseau's Epicureanism is in large measure mediated by Lucretius. The direct influence of Lucretius is most evident in the *Discourse on Inequality*.[81] It is pervasive but more diffuse in the debate with Voltaire. Still, the very occasion of this debate, the shock caused by the Lisbon earthquake and the questions it raises about "optimism," brings to mind Lucretius's observation that earthquakes are the most vivid perceptible evidence that the walls of the world will crack and that there is no providence (V, 95–109, 1236–1240; VI, 596–607). Lucretius's poem remains *the* classical statement of the sober, somber "optimism" that Rousseau defends in the *Letter to Voltaire*. His Epicureanism diverges most conspicuously from classical and, in particular, from Lucretius's Epicureanism by attending far more to the many who do not find sweet solace (V, 21, 113; VI, 4) in its stark teaching, than to the few who do. It takes far more seriously than Lucretius would appear to do, that its

> argument (*ratio*) full often seems
> too bitter to those who have not tasted it and
> the multitude (*vulgus*) shrinks back from it.
>   I, 943–945; IV, 18–20.[82]

The Rousseau who sides with the vulgar who calls himself "an honest man who knows nothing and esteems himself none the less for it" (*First Discourse* [60], [4]), who told Voltaire that he had not read and probably could not understand de Crouzas [14], and who consistently attends to "the ordinary course of things," tends, by and large, to speak of political life and of religion as desirable in themselves rather than instrumentally, and to assign to them a far more central role than his Epicurean models do. Still, like them, he bases political society on a contract or convention, and even with respect to the place that he assigns to religion he is faithful to one Epicurean alternative:

It would be better to follow the story about the gods than to be a slave to the fate of the natural philosopher; for the former leaves the hope that the gods can be swayed by entreaties, whereas the latter confronts us with inexorable necessity.[83]

This is the spirit in which he speaks of the more consoling alternatives regarding Providence as "proofs of sentiment" and "prejudices," and it is the spirit in which he has Julie's husband, M. de Wolmar, describe his wife's religious devoutness as "an opiate of the soul" (*Nouvelle Héloise* VI 8, OC II, 697). M. de Wolmar is, so to speak, living proof that being a nonbeliever and being virtuous are compatible, whereas his wife is, so to speak, living proof that Epicureanism and piety are compatible. Rousseau consistently tries to do justice to both alternatives. (*To Vernes*, 24 June 1761; *Confessions* IX, OC I, 435ff). Still, M. de Wolmar occupies a unique place in his vast cast of characters. He is the only one of them explicitly to belong to the few who, Rousseau says, have no need of Divine Revelation or of God (*To Franquières* [8]). He never includes the first person in their number.

As regards political society, Rousseau has been mindful of it throughout this *Letter*, but he does not speak of it directly until late, and when he does, he does so only insofar as the issues that he has been discussing bear on it [31]–[35]. At the beginning of the *Letter* he had expressed his general agreement with the argument of Voltaire's *Poem of Natural Religion* or, as Voltaire prudently renamed it, *Poem on Natural Law* [2]. Voltaire had once referred to it as "the catechism of natural law."[84] In his *Letter* to him, Rousseau calls it "the Catechism of Man" [35], and he invites him to go on and elaborate a "Catechism of the Citizen." Such a catechism would be much more reticent than Voltaire's *Poem* or even than Rousseau's *Letter*. In the *Letter* he had left open many of the questions that he had raised about Providence, the existence of God, and the immortality of the soul, but he had drawn the line at including in it his reflections about Diderot's *Pensée* or at spelling out its consequences; he never speaks about "the cracking of the walls of the world," and he alludes to it only once, in a text left unpublished in his lifetime.[85] Instead, he sets down *the* principle that guides all of his writings about God, freedom, and immortality:

... there is something inhumane about troubling peaceful souls, and distressing men to no purpose, when what one is trying to teach them is neither certain nor useful [31].

And in one draft of the *Letter* he spells out the conclusion:

Thus I could not approve of reasoning about such subjects in public in popular language [*langage vulgaire*] and, if I may say so, still less in verse. ([31] ms. 2; cf. [10]).

By contrast, a Catechism of the Citizen, especially one in verse, would be the most useful work ever [35]. It might persuade without convincing.[86]

Political society requires religion; but not any religion. Rousseau claims only to be following Voltaire's lead in holding

... that one cannot too forcefully attack the superstition that disturbs society, nor too much respect the Religion that upholds it [31].

In the Lisbon *Poem* Voltaire had said nothing about "the superstition that disturbs society" or the religion that upholds it; however, he had spoken of "the unfortunate disputes of the school that disturb society" in the *Poem of Natural Religion* (IV, heading). Rousseau's "superstition" is entirely faithful to what Voltaire means by "the unfortunate disputes of the school." Within a few short paragraphs he is even more blunt: not only may the superstition that disturbs society be attacked, but the religions that attack its foundations must be exterminated [34]. "Exterminate" recalls Voltaire's "crush" (*écraser*).

However Rousseau, in contrast to Voltaire, also takes account of the religion that upholds political society, and hence of the need for "a kind of civil profession of faith" [35] that spells out "the principles of morality and of natural right" [34] or "the social maxims everyone would be bound to acknowledge" [35].[87] Everyone would be bound to acknowledge them in their conduct. Only conduct may – and can – be enforced. Beliefs may not – and cannot – be enforced ([32], cf. [29], [33]; *Social Contract* II, 7 [9]; *à d'Alembert*, OC V, 13.) For what counts in civil life is what one does. "When a man serves the State well, he owes no-one an account of how he serves God" [32]. M. de Wolmar attends religious services and conforms to the laws and practices of his community (*Nouvelle Héloise*, V 5, OC II, 592ff).

In any event, Voltaire never did take up Rousseau's suggestion to compose a catechism of the citizen. Rousseau's own later summary of the dogmas he thought indispensable in a civil religion was extremely terse. Its positive dogmas are

[T]he existence of a powerful, intelligent, beneficent, prescient and provident Divinity, the life to come, the happiness of the just, the punishment of the wicked, the sanctity of the social Contract and the Laws (*Social Contract* IV, 8 [33]).

Publicly to profess that the soul is mortal is subversive of sound citizenship (*Social Contract* IV, 8 [32]). For, in the absence of natural sanctions and of particular providence, would not a person acting justly to his detriment be a fool and only a person acting unjustly to his benefit prove rational? The positive dogmas of the civil religion promulgate a political equivalent of particular providence.[88]

The most important negative dogma of the "catechism of the citizen," and the only negative dogma of the "civil religion," is the prohibition of intolerance and, most particularly of religious intolerance ([34], *Social Contract* IV, 8 [33]). Rousseau rejects religious intolerance because, as he had said earlier in this *Letter*, it does not depend on ourselves to believe or not to believe in matters in which demonstration has no place. Besides,

I am quite sure... that he [God] will not deny eternal happiness to any non-believer who is virtuous and in good faith ([32], [33]).

In the *Social Contract* he rejects religious intolerance on the strictly political grounds that it is bound to be the instrument of the priests, and so to subvert popular sovereignty (IV, 8 [34], [35]).

His stand against religious intolerance aligns Rousseau with the party of the *philosophes* and of Voltaire. However, he is wary of parties. He suspects that the party of the *philosophes* opposes intolerance only because it is now the butt of it, and that if it ever gained the upper hand, it would be as ruthlessly intolerant of its opponents as they now are of it [34].[89] He therefore goes out of his way to tell Voltaire that he, himself, opposes intolerant nonbelievers as firmly as he opposes intolerant believers. Before long, Voltaire's conduct toward him will amply confirm his worst suspicions about intolerant nonbelievers.

Rousseau ends his *Letter* with a brief summary of the contrast he had drawn earlier between Voltaire's vantage point and his own. Voltaire speaks about Providence, the goods and evils of this life and the prospects for the next, from the vantage point of the powerful and the privileged, whereas Rousseau speaks about them from the vantage point of ordinary folk, the poor, the obscure. Voltaire is "assured of immortality" – at least in the sense of immortal fame – but holds out only a tenuous hope for immortality in any other sense of the term; Rousseau speaks on behalf of those who can only hope for their just rewards in a life to come and as one of them ([36]; cf. [11], [12]); *Nouvelle Héloise* V, 5, 592). Yet Voltaire sees only evil, whereas Rousseau finds that all is well. What accounts for these apparent contradictions between them?

You yourself have given the explanation: you enjoy [*vous jouissez*], but I hope...[36]

Voltaire had said nothing about enjoyment in the Lisbon *Poem*. But he had named his estate just outside Geneva *Les Délices*, and in private as well as in public he had long celebrated self-indulgent luxury, most notoriously in *Le Mondain* (1736), and in the *Défence du Mondain, ou l'apologie du luxe* (1737). Rousseau had just as consistently criticized it:

...what will become of virtue, when one has to get rich at all cost? The ancient political Thinkers forever spoke of morals and of virtue; ours speak only of commerce and of money. (*First Discourse* [41]; *Observations* [52]; *Narcissus* [27]; *Discourse on Inequality* N, IX [9]–[11]).

Epicureanism proper, "refined Epicureanism," is essentially private and austere; public and self-indulgent Epicureanism, by contrast, is "vulgar Epicureanism," and vulgar Epicureanism is inevitably subversive of civic virtue.

Voltaire's *Poem* had ended with the very faintest concession to hope (see nn. 19 and 22 in this chapter). Rousseau's *Letter* ends with a poem to it.

All the subtleties of Metaphysics will not make me doubt for one moment the immortality of the soul and a beneficent Providence. I sense it, I want it, I hope for it, I shall defend it to my last breath; and of all disputations I will have engaged in, it will be the only one in which my own interest will not have been forgotten [37].

He does need to repeat for the benefit of so attentive a reader as Voltaire what he had said in the body of his *Letter* about hope and belief. His concluding remark, that the case he has been making for Providence and for the immortality of the soul is the only case he has ever made in which he has taken his own interests into account, echoes a similar remark of Socrates's as he sets out to inquire into the immortality of the soul on the day on which he was to drink the hemlock (*Phaedo* 70c, 1f). However, Rousseau considers immortality solely in moral terms: Only an immortal soul might reap hereafter the just deserts that it was denied in this life, and only a beneficent Providence could secure this consummation.

ENDNOTES

1 *Bemerkungen über das Gefühl des Schönen und Erhabenen, Gesammelte Schriften, Akademie Ausgabe,* **XX**, 59.

2 For translations of these texts and details about them, see Jean-Jacques Rousseau, *The Discourses and Other Early Political Writings,* V. Gourevitch, ed. (New York: Cambridge University Press, 1997). All references to the works contained in this volume and in its companion volume, Jean-Jacques Rousseau, *Social Contract and Other Later Political Writings,* V. Gourevitch ed. (New York: Cambridge University Press, 1997), are by part or book and chapter number, followed by paragraph number in brackets.

   Otherwise unidentified references in brackets throughout this chapter are to the relevant paragraph of the *Letter to Voltaire* in *Discourses* (etc.) ed. Gourevitch, N.Y. 1997.

   All references to works by Rousseau not included in these two volumes are to the five-volume work, Jean-Jacques Rousseau, *Oeuvres*

Complètes, B. Gagnebin and M. Raymond, eds. (Paris: Pléiade, 1959–1995), abbreviated as OC, followed by a Roman numeral indicating the volume, and Arabic numeral(s) indicating the page(s). References to Rousseau's correspondence are to R.A. Leigh's magisterial *Jean-Jacques Rousseau, Correspondance complète* (Geneva: Institut et Musée Voltaire, Oxford, The Voltaire Foundation at the Taylor Institution, 1965–1989), abbreviated as CC, followed by a Roman numeral indicating the volume and Arabic numeral(s) indicating the page(s).

3 Rousseau recounts the circumstances surrounding his writing of the *Letter to Voltaire in Confessions* IX (OC I, 429–430) and the circumstances surrounding its publication in *Confessions* X (OC I, 539–542). For full details, see R.A. Leigh, "Rousseau's Letter to Voltaire on Optimism," *Studies on Voltaire and the Eighteenth Century*, **30**, 247–309, (1964), summarized in CC IV, 50–59, and in B. Gagnebin's *Notice bibliographique* (OC IV, 1880–1884). Voltaire acknowledged Rousseau's *Letter* in a brief note (12 Sept. 1756, CC IV, 102) that ignored the issues Rousseau had raised. Rousseau believed that *Candide* (1759) was Voltaire's full reply to his *Letter: Confessions* IX (OC I, 430). However, see also Voltaire's short tale *L' histoire d' un bon bramin*, published the same year as *Candide*. The *Letter to Voltaire* has most recently been edited by R.A. Leigh in CC IV, 37–84; by H. Gouhier in OC IV, 1059–1075; by Th. Besterman in his edition of the *Oeuvres complètes de Voltaire*, Vol. 101 (*Correspondance* Vol. XVII), The Voltaire Foundation, 1971, pp. 280–297; and by G. Fauconnier in *Etudes Rousseauistes et index J.-J. Rousseau*, Série B, Vol. 5 (Geneva: Slatkine, 1979), pp. 152–359.

On the distinction between private and public discussions of theological issues – or between discussions of theological issues with philosophers on the one hand and authors on the other – see also the *Letter à d'Alembert* (OC V, 10) (Bloom, tr., p. 11). On addressing the public regarding religious issues: *Social Contract* II, 6 [10], II, 7 [9]–[11]; on *Émile*, "Je l'ai choisi parmi les esprits vulgaires..." *Émile* IV (OC IV, 537) (Bloom, tr., p. 245); cf. *Émile* I (OC IV, 266) (Bloom, tr., p. 52); on Franquières, the comment about the nineteen-twentieths of mankind, in the *Letter* to him, [9] (OC IV, 1137ff); on the stage setting for the Savoyard vicar's profession of faith, *Émile* IV (OC IV, 558, 606, 635) and *Lettres Écrites de la Montagne* III (OC III, 749ff); on the parallels between the vicar's and Julie's professions of faith, *Lettres Écrites de la Montagne* I (OC III, 694) and *Confessions* VII (OC I, 407); on the error of attributing to an author the sentiments that he attributes to one of his characters: *Rousseau juge de Jean-Jacques* I (OC I, 751); and again in his last writing, *Rêveries* III (OC I, 1018); as well as the letters to Verne of 18 Feb. and 25 March 1758.

4 For example, T.D. Kendrick, *The Lisbon Earthquake* (London: Methuen, 1956).

5 *Tout est bien*, "all [or whatever is] is right [or well or good]," is how the contemporary French translators rendered Pope's "whatever is, is right": *An Essay on Man*, Epistle I, 1, 294, Epistle IV, 1, 394. Brockes' standard contemporary German translation of Pope's *Poem* rendered "whatever is, is right" as *alles was ist, ist gut*.

Tout est bien becomes a formula in its own right in Voltaire's *Poem*, but especially in Rousseau's *Letter* and, indeed, in his entire teaching: The opening of *Émile*, *Tout est bien en sortant des mains de l'auteur des choses...*, might therefore be translated as "Whatever is, is right [or well or good] on leaving the hands of the author of things..."; and the *Social Contract's* [c]e qui est bien et conforme à l'ordre est tel par la nature des choses... – "what is right [or well or good] and conformable to order is so by the nature of things..." (*Social Contract* II, 6 [2]). However, it is impossible to translate *bien* and *bon* consistently by the same two English words. This is one reason for preserving an explicit reference to "good" in translating *tout est bien*; another reason is that man's natural goodness, *bonté*, plays such a prominent role in Rousseau's doctrine; and a third reason for preserving it is that both Voltaire and Rousseau are concerned not only with Pope's dictum, but also with Leibniz's proposition that "this is the best [*optimum*] world possible": e.g., *Essais de Théodicée: Sur la Bonté de Dieu, la Liberté de l'Homme, et l'Origine du Mal* (1710): I, 8–10 *et passim*.

6 Patrick Riley explores much of relevant French background of these debates in *The General Will before Rousseau: The Transformation of the Divine into the Civic* (Princeton, NJ: Princeton University Press, 1986); Leslie Stephen surveys much of the English background in *History of English Thought in the Eighteenth Century*, 2 vols. (New York: Putnam's, 1902); A.O. Lovejoy surveys some of the English and of the Continental background in "The Parallel of Deism and Classicism" (1930), reprinted in *Essays in the History of Ideas* (Baltimore, MD: Johns Hopkins University Press, 1948), pp. 78–98, and in *The Great Chain of Being* (Cambridge, MA: Harvard University Press, 1948), Chap. VII and X.

7 "Préface" to the *Poème sur le désastre de Lisbonne* [7]. Two decades earlier, Voltaire had translated some lines from Pope's *Rape of the Lock* in the twenty-second of his *Philosophical Letters* (1733/34), and he had read Pope's *Essay* soon after it appeared [G.R. Havens, "Voltaire's

Marginal Comments upon Pope's *Essay on Man*," Modern Language Notes, **43**, 429–439 [1928]].

> ... *Pope*
> ... porta le flambeau dans l'*abîme de l'être;*
> Et l'homme avec lui seul apprît à se connaître.
> > "*Poème sur la loi naturelle,*"
> > *Exorde,* ll, 15, 17ff.

8   "Hope humbly then; with trembling pinions soar;
Wait the great teacher Death, and God adore!
What future bliss, he gives not thee to know,
But gives that hope to be thy blessing now.
Hope springs eternal in the human breast:
Man never Is, but always To be blest:
The soul uneasy and confined from home,
Rests and expiates in a life to come."
> Pope, *Essay,* Epistle I, ll, 91–98.

Compare I Corinthians 15:19–26.

9   *[L'homme] rampe; il souffre, il meurt; tout ce qui naît expire;*
De la destruction la nature est l'empire (ll, 181ff).
L'homme, étranger à soi, de l'homme est ignoré.
Que suis-je, où suis-je, où vais-je, et d'où suis-je tiré?
Atomes tourmentés sur cet amas de boue,
Que la mort engloutit, et dont le sort se joue,
Mais atomes pensants ...
Au sein de l'infini nous élançons notre être,
Sans pouvoir un moment nous voir et nous connaître (ll, 199–206).

10 *Dictionnaire historique et critique,* in *Oeuvres complètes* (The Hague, 1737) especially the articles "*Manichéens,*" "*Marcionites,*" "*Pauliciens,*" and "*Zoroastre,*" and the Appendix "*Éclaircissemens sur certaines choses répandues dans ce Dictionnaire*" II; cf. Leibniz, *Théodicée,* Amsterdam 1710, II, Section 136.

11 Leibniz, *Théodicée* I, Section 21; Samuel Clarke, *A Demonstration of the Being and Attributes of God* London [1705], (no pub), pp. 218–221.

12 A view that Voltaire stated in his *poem on Natural Law* as follows: "All the ancients, without exception, believed in the eternity of matter; it is almost the only point on which they agreed. Most of them believed that the gods had arranged the world; none believed that God had drawn it out of nothing. They held that the divine intelligence, by its own nature, had the power to order matter, and that matter existed by its own nature," Note to part I, l, 4; see also n. 75 of this chapter.

13 However, in a long Note to the *Poem on Natural Law,* which he published together with the Lisbon *Poem,* Voltaire defends Locke's notorious suggestion that an omnipotent deity could endow senseless matter with the power to perceive and to think; in other words, that

matter imposes no inherent limitations on intelligence or on divine omnipotence; and that it therefore does not necessarily make for meta-physical – and hence also not for physical – evil: *Poem on Natural Law*, Part III, 1, 87; note also: *Micromégas*, penultimate paragraph; Locke, *Essay Concerning Human Understanding*, IV, 3, Section 6. Two decades earlier, in his *Letters concerning the English Nation* (1733), Voltaire had done much to popularize Locke's suggestion. He knew that it was taken to entail materialism: "That Mr. Locke doubted whether the soul was immaterial or no, may justly be suspected from some parts of his writings..." Samuel Clarke, First Reply, #2, in the 1715/16 *Leibniz–Clarke Correspondence*, H.G. Alexander ed. (Manchester, U.K.: Manchester University Press, 1956), originally published in 1717; a French translation appeared in 1720. Voltaire was familiar with this *Correspondence*, and in the Lisbon *Poem* as well as in his other writings he relied heavily on Clarke's criticism of Leibniz. See also note 75 in this chapter.

14 Ainsi du monde entier tous les membres gémissent;
Nés tous pour le tourment, l'un par l'autre ils périssent:
Et vous composerez dans ce chaos fatal
Des malheurs de chaque être un bonheur général! (ll, 117–120).

Compare:

See dying vegetables life sustain,
See life dissolving vegetate again:
All forms that perish other forms supply..."
Pope, *Eassy*, III, 15–17

15 "Ce malheur, dites vous, est le bien d'un autre être."
De mon corps tout sanglant mille insectes vont naître;
Quant la mort met le comble aux maux que j'ai soufferts,
Le beau soulagement d'être mangés des vers! (ll, 97–100).

Consider also Preface to the *Poem* [3] and ll, 67ff.

16 C'est l'orgueil, dites vous, l'orgueil séditieux,
Qui prétend qu'étant mal, nous pouvions être mieux (ll, 35ff).
Quand l'homme ose gémir d'un fléau si terrible,
Il n'est point orgueilleux, hélas il est sensible (ll, 57ff).

In a very different context, St. Preux comments on Paul's remark: "That's all very well if the potter requires of it only offices he enabled it to perform for him; but if he blamed the pot for not being suited to a use for which he'd not fit it, would the pot be wrong to say to him: why hast thou made me thus?" *Nouvelle Héloise*, VI 7 (OC II, 684).

17 "The universal chain is not, as some have said, a gradual progression linking all beings. An immense distance probably separates man and brute, man and the higher substances; the infinite separates God and

all substances. The orbs revolving around our sun have nothing of these imperceptible gradations, in their size, or their distances, or their satellites....

"It is not true that if a single atom were removed from the world, the world could not subsist....

"This chain of events has been acknowledged and most ingeniously defended by the great philosopher Leibnitz; it deserves to be elucidated. All bodies, all events depend on other bodies, other events. This is true; but all bodies are not necessary to the order and conservation of the universe, and all events are not essential to the series of events. One drop of water, one grain of sand more or less cannot change anything in the general constitution. Nature is not subject to any precise quantity or precise form. No planet moves in an absolutely precise orbit; no known being has a precise mathematical figure; no precise quantity is required for any operation; nature never acts strictly [rigoureusement]. There is therefore no reason to maintain that one atom less on earth would be the cause of the earth's destruction.

"The same is true regarding events: each has its cause in the event that precedes it; this is something no philosopher has ever doubted. If Caesar's mother had not undergone a Caesarian section, Caesar would not have destroyed the republic, he would not have adopted Octavian, and Octavian would not have left the empire to Tiberius. Maximilian marries the heiress of Burgundy and the Low Countries, and this marriage becomes the source of two hundred years of war. But Caesar's having spat to the right or to the left, the heiress of Burgundy having her hair dressed one way or another, surely did not change anything in the general system.

"There are, then, events that have effects, and others that do not. The chain of events is comparable to a genealogical tree; some branches die out, and others perpetuate the race. A number of events remain without filiation. Thus in every machine some effects are necessary to its movement, and others, that are the consequences of this first movement, are indifferent to it, and produce nothing. The wheels of a carriage make it go; but the journey gets accomplished just as well regardless of whether they raise a little more or a little less dust. Such is the general order of the world that the links in the chain [of events] would not be disturbed by a little more or a little less matter, a little more or a little less irregularity.

"The chain is not an absolute plenum; it has been proven that the heavenly bodies perform their revolutions in a non-resisting space. Not all space, is filled. There is, therefore, not a [continuous] progression of bodies from atoms to the most distant stars; immense intervals can, therefore, separate sensible as well as insensible beings. Man can therefore not be said necessarily to occupy one of the links that are joined one to another in an uninterrupted progression. Everything is linked [or chained, *enchaîné*] means only that everything is orderly [*arrangé*]. God is the cause and master of this order [*arrangement*]. Homer's Jupiter is the slave of the fates; but in a more purified philosophy, God is master of the fates. See Clarke, *A Demonstration of the Being and Attributes of God*." (Note 1 to the *Poem*).

The mention of Caesar suggests that in this Note Voltaire is specifically taking issue with Leibniz's thesis that " ... the notion of an individual substance once and for all contains everything that can ever happen to it, and that in considering this notion one can see in it everything it will be possible truthfully to say about it, just as we can see in the nature of the circle all the properties that can be deduced from it" (*Discourse on Metaphysics*, Section XIII). Leibniz goes on, in this same section of the *Discourse*, to illustrate this thesis with Caesar as his example; also, *Theodicée*, e.g., Section 9.

The mention of "indifferent phenomena" is backed by a brief reference to the "learned geometer" Crouzas, and to some "proofs" of Newton's. Jean-Pierre de Crouzaz (1663–1750) published two volumes criticizing Pope's *Essay*. Here Voltaire is relying on his *Examen de l'essai de M. Pope sur l'homme* (Lausanne et Amsterdam, 1737), pp. 87–94. Not surprisingly, Pope reserved a place for Crouzas in the *Dunciad* (IV, 198).

Voltaire draws Newton's "proofs" that some phenomena are "indifferent" largely from Newton's spokesman, Dr. Samuel Clarke: "If the Supreme Cause is not a Being endued with Liberty and Choice, but a mere necessary Agent, whose Actions are all as absolutely and naturally Necessary as his Existence: Then it will follow, that nothing which is not, could *possibly* have been, and that nothing which is, could *possibly* not have been; and that no mode or Circumstance of the Existence of any thing, could *possibly* have been in any respect otherwise, than it now actually is. All which, being evidently false and absurd: it follows on the contrary, that the Supreme Cause is not a mere necessary agent, but a being endued with Liberty and Choice," Samuel Clarke, *A Demonstration of the Being and Attributes of God*, (1705), pp. 130ff. "The *Number and Motion of the Heavenly Bodies*, have no Manner of Necessity in the Nature of the Things themselves. The number of the Planets might have been greater or less; And the Direction of all their Motions, both of the Primary and the Secondary Planets uniformly from West to East, when by the Motion of Comets it appears there was no Necessity but that they might as easily have moved in all imaginable transverse Directions; is an evident proof these things are the Effect of Wisdom and Choice," *ibid.* pp. 137ff.

18 "Undoubtedly nothing is, without a sufficient reason why it is rather than not; and why it is thus rather than otherwise. But in things in their own nature indifferent, mere will, without anything external to influence it, is alone that sufficient reason. As in the instance of God's creating or placing any article of matter in one place rather than in another, when all places are originally all alike... it would be absolutely indifferent, and there could be no other reason but mere will why three equal particles should be ranged in the order a, b, c, rather than in the contrary order," Dr. Clarke's Third Reply, #2. "A mere will without any motive, is a fiction, not only contrary to God's perfection, but also chimerical and contradictory; inconsistent with the definition of will ..." Leibniz's Fourth Paper, #2; see *ibid.*, #3. *"Neuton soutenait que Dieu, infiniment libre comme infiniment puissant, à fait beaucoup de choses, qui n'ont d'autre raison de leur existence que sa seule volonté.*

"Par example que les planètes se meuvent d'occident en orient, plutôt qu'autrement, qu'il y ait un tel nombre d'animaux, d'étoiles, de mondes, plutôt qu'un autre; que l'univers fini, soit dans un tel ou tel point de l'espace, etc., la volonté de l'Etre suprême en est la seule raison.

"Le célèbre Leibnits prétendait le contraire, et se fondait sur un ancien axiome employé autrefois par Archimède, rien ne se fait sans cause ou sans raison suffisante, *disait-il, et Dieu à fait en tout le meilleur,* parce que s'il ne l'avait pas fait comme meilleur, il n'eût pas eu raison de le faire. Mais il n'y à point de meilleur dans les choses indifférentes, disaient les newtoniens; mais il n'y à point de choses indifférentes répondent les leibniziens," Voltaire, *Éléments de la philosophie de Newton* I, 3, ll, 1–15. "... *pourquoi ce mouvement à droite, plutôt qu'à gauche, vers l'occident plutôt que vers l'orient, en ce point de la durée, plutôt qu'en un autre point? Ne faut-il pas alors recourir à la volonté d'indifférence dans le créateur?" ibid.* ll, 63–66.

19 Voltaire succeeded so well in appearing orthodox that the distinguished neo-Thomist scholar Etienne Gilson cites the concluding verses of an intermediate version of the *Poem,*

> Le passé n'est pour nous qu'un triste souvenir:
> Le présent est affreux, s'il n'est point d'avenir,
> Si la nuit du tombeau détruit l'être qui pense.
> Un jour tout sera bien, voilà notre espérance;
> Tout est bien aujourd'hui voilà l'illusion (ll, 215–219),

as very close to what he, Gilson, calls "Christian optimism" in contrast to the philosophers' optimism that the *Journal de Trévoux* had mocked:

L'esprit de la philosophie médiévale[2] (1994), p. 111, note 1; see note 22 of this chapter.

20 Leibniz charged that, according to the doctrine of Sir Isaac Newton and his followers, "... God Almighty wants to wind up his watch from time to time; otherwise it would cease to move. He had not, it seems, sufficient foresight to make it a perpetual motion. Nay, the machine of God's making is so imperfect, according to these gentlemen, that he is obliged to scour it [*la décrasser*] every now and then by an extraordinary concourse, and even to mend it, as a clockmaker mends his work; who must consequently be so much the more unskillful a workman as he is oftener obliged to mend his Work and to set it right. According to my opinion, the same force and vigor remains always in the world, and only passes from one part of nature to another, agreeably to the law of nature, and the beautiful preestablished order." To which Clarke replies, "The notion of the world's being a great machine, going on without the interposition of God, as a clock continues to go without the assistance of a clockmaker; is the notion of materialism and fate, and tends, (under the pretense of making God a *supramundane intelligence*) to exclude providence and God's government in reality out of the world. And by the same reason that a philosopher can represent all things as going on from the beginning of the creation, without any government or interposition of providence; a skeptic will easily argue still farther backwards, and suppose that things have from eternity gone on (as they now do) without any true creation or original author at all, but only what such arguers call all-wise and eternal nature," *The Leibniz-Clarke Correspondence*, Leibniz's First Paper, #4; Clarke's First Reply, #4.

In Koyré's memorable formulation, "... the God of Leibniz is not the Newtonian Overlord who makes the world as he wants it and continues to act upon it as the Biblical God did in the first six days of Creation. He is, if I may continue the simile, the Biblical God on the Sabbath Day, the God who has finished his work and who finds it good, nay the very best of possible worlds, and who, therefore, has no more to act upon it, or in it, but only to preserve it in being. This God is, at the same time – once more in contradistinction to the Newtonian one – the supremely rational Being, the principle of sufficient reason personified ..." *From the Closed World to the Infinite Universe* (Baltimore, MD: Johns Hopkins University Press, 1957), pp. 240ff.

21 "... *de cette affaire* [sc. *le tremblement de terre de Lisbonne*] *la Providence en a dans le cul.*" Cited by H. Gouhier, *Rousseau et Voltaire*, (Paris: Vrin, 1983), p. 76. "While always appearing to believe in God,

Voltaire really always only believed in the Devil; since his supposed God is nothing but a maleficent being who, according to him, takes pleasure only in doing harm." Rousseau, *Confessions* IX (OC I, 429). Voltaire's *Oedipe* teaches that the gods force us to do what they then punish us for: *Lettre à d'Alembert* (OC V, 30).

22 The first, unauthorized, publications of the *Poem* ended

> Le passé n'est pour nous qu'un triste souvenir,
> Le passé est affreux s'il n'est point d'avenir
> Si la nuit du tombeau détruit l'être qui pense.
> Mortels, il faut souffrir,
> Se soumettre en silence, adorer et mourir (ll, 215–219).

Voltaire quickly recognized that the ecclesiastical authorities might find this ending too gloomy. He therefore inserted "hope" between the final "adore" and "die." Even this seemed inadequate, and he reworked the ending massively. He now summarizes his difference with the optimists as follows:

> Un jour tout sera bien, voilà notre espérance,
> Tout est bien aujoud'hui, voilà l'illusion.

This is the passage that Gilson quotes as coming close to expressing "Christian optimism" (see n. 19). However, in what appears to have been his own copy of the poem, Voltaire changed these lines to read

> Un jour tout sera bien, quel frêle espoir!
> Tout est bien aujourd'hui, quelle illusion.

See George R. Havens, "Voltaire's Pessimistic Revision of his Conclusion of his *Poème sur le désastre de Lisbonne*," *Modern Language Notes* 44, 489–493 (1929).

23 This is the view Kant proposes: *Idea for a Universal History*, Second Thesis, Third Thesis (last paragraph), Eighth and Ninth Theses (and see n. 45 below). Kant attributes this modern conception of optimism, as he himself calls it, to Rousseau: *Religion* (Book I, Paragraph 3), a context in which he cites the same passage from Seneca's *de irá* (Book II, Chap. 13, Sec. 1) that Rousseau chose as the epigraph of the *Émile*.

24 *Discourse on Inequality* I [9], Note IX [1]; *To Philopolis* [10]. In the *Confessions* Rousseau describes himself as calling out in the *Discourse on Inequality* "Fools, who constantly complain about nature, learn that all your evils [maux] are due to yourselves" (OC I, 389). This is also the guiding thought of *Émile*, which opens with the optimists' formula mocked in Voltaire's *Poem*: "Whatever is, is right upon leaving the hands of the author of things: everything degenerates in the hands

of man" (OC IV, 245) (tr. 37); and again: "Our greatest evils come to us from ourselves" (OC IV, 261) (tr., 48); and see note 5 of this chapter.

25   Tous les divers fléaux dont le poids nous accable
          Du choc des éléments l'effet inévitable,
          Des biens que nous goûtons corrompent la douceur,
          Mais tout est passager, le crime et le malheur.
                    Poème sur la loi naturelle, Part II, ll, 37–40.

          Quand de l'immensité Dieu peupla les déserts,
          Alluma les soleils, et souleva les mers:
          "Demeurez, leur dit-il, dans vos bornes prescrites."
          Tous les mondes naissants connurent leurs limites.
          Il imposa des lois à Saturne, à Vénus,
          Aux seize orbes divers dans nos cieux contenus,
          Aux éléments unis dans leur utile guerre,
          A la course du vent, aux flèches du tonnerre,
          A l'animal qui pense, et né pour l'adorer,
          Au verre qui nous attend, né pour nous dévorer.
                    Poème sur la loi naturelle, Part II, ll, 115–124.

Compare Job 38, and contrast with the Lisbon *Poem*, ll, 97–100, 125ff.
26 So, too, in the civil religion: One of its few positive dogmas is the existence of the powerful – *not* the all-powerful – Divinity (*Social Contract* IV, 8 [33]); in the letter to *Franquières* [14]; in Julie's guarded "the power of the God I serve astounds me," *Nouvelle Héloise* VI, 8, (OC II, 696); in her death-bed remark about God's being "very powerful, very good," *ibid.* VI, 11 (OC II, 716). This is perfectly consistent with Rousseau's general proposition about the relation between power and goodness, "whoever could do anything would never do evil," as well as with the Savoyard vicar's noncommittal "Whoever can do anything, can only want what is good. Hence the sovereignly good because sovereignly Powerful being, must also be sovereignly just," *Émile* I (OC IV, 288); IV (OC IV, 588ff) (Bloom tr. 67; 276ff).

Julie's husband, M. de Wolmar, in a private conversation, is more cautious: Faced with the choice between accounting for the existence of evil by "lack of intelligence, power, or goodness in the first cause," he refuses to choose, *Nouvelle Héloise* V, 5 (OC II, 595ff and n. (a) ad p. 596).
27 Also *Discourse on Inequality* I [53] and N X [1], Lucretius, *De rerum natura* I, 311–328, IV, 1286ff; and "History is in general defective in that it records only perceptible and manifest facts that can be fixed by name, place, date; but the slow and progressive causes of these facts, which cannot be specified in the same way, invariably remain unknown," *Émile* IV, (OC IV, 529) (tr. 239ff).
28 Rousseau's detailed discussion of Crouzas's criticism of Pope in a letter

to François de Conzié (17 Jan. 1742, CC I, 132–139) shows that he was perfectly capable of understanding it. He is likely also to have discussed both Pope's *Essay* and Crouzas's criticism of it with Diderot, who drew up an extensive *Observations sur la traduction de An Essay on Man de Pope par Silhouette*, A. Sezenac and J. Varloot: Diderot, *Oeuvres complètes* (Paris: Hermann, 1975) I, pp. 165–266. Voltaire had referred to Crouzas as a "learned geometer" (*Poem* n. 1, Paragraph 3); in a draft of his *Letter*, Rousseau said of him, "An ordinary geometer, a poor reasoner, a rigid and pedantic mind, an obscure and careless writer, this man acquired, I know not how, a modest reputation he would soon have lost if people had troubled to read him" (OC IV, 1064, var. e). He omitted this description from the final version of the *Letter*. However, he has Julie write, "M. de Crouzaz has just given us a refutation of Pope's Epistles which I have read with some irritation. Truth to tell, I do not know which one of these two authors is right; but I do know that M. de Crouzaz's book will never lead to a good deed's being done, and that there is nothing good one is not tempted to do upon setting down Pope's book. I have not, myself, any other way of judging what I read than to inquire how it leaves my soul disposed, and I can scarcely imagine what can be the good of a book that does not incline its readers to the good," *Nouvelle Héloise* II 18 (OC II, 261).

29 In the final analysis, "the ordinary course of things" is also the object of the quest of the *Discourse on Inequality*: consider I [6] (in conjunction with *Letter to Voltaire* [30] and *Essay on the Origin of Languages* 9 [32]), and I [21]; see also "the order of human things" [25] – cf. "the nature of human things," *Discourse on Inequality* ED [14].

As regards the expression "the ordinary course of things," compare Bacon's "common course of nature" and "common course of the universe," *Novum Organum*, The Second Book of Aphorisms, especially No. xvii; Spinoza's "common order of nature" *Ethics*, II, xxix, Scholium, and II, xxx, Proof; Leibniz, *Théodicée*, I, *Discours de la conformité de la foi avec la raison*, Sections 12, 18; Locke's "ordinary course of things," *Essay*, IV, 17, Sections xiii, xiv; Hume's "ordinary course of events," "course of nature," and "the common and experienced course of nature" in "Of the Immortality of the Soul," *Essays Moral, Political, and Literary*, (Green and Grose, eds., Vol. II (Edinburgh, 1889) p. 400), and *An Inquiry Concerning Human Understanding*, XI ("Of a Particular Providence and of a Future State") *passim*; see also the Leibniz passage quoted in n. 69 of this chapter.

On one occasion Rousseau speaks of asexual reproduction as "This irregularity so contrary to the ordinary march of nature...," *Dictionnaire de Botanique*, "aphrodites" (OC IV, 1212).

30 "As regards all evils that befall us, we look more to the intention than

to the effect. A tile that falls from the roof may hurt us more, but it distresses us less than does a stone deliberately cast by a malevolent hand. The throw may sometimes miss, but the intention never fails to hit its mark. Material pain is what one feels least in the blows of fortune, and when unfortunate people do not know whom to blame for their miseries they blame destiny which they personify and endow with eyes and intelligence that deliberately torments them. This is how a gambler distraught by his losses grows enraged without knowing against whom. He imagines a fate that deliberately sets out to torment him, and finding an object for his anger, he gets wrought up and infuriated by the enemy he created. The wise man, who sees the miseries that befall him as nothing but the blows of blind necessity, is not subject to this senseless excitement, he cries out in his pain but without being carried away, without anger, he feels only the material impact of the evil to which he is a prey, and while the blows that strike him may hurt his person, none reaches his heart," *Rêveries* VIII (OC I, 1078). Regarding the moral and political import of "necessary laws" and trust in them, consider "I thought that the most essential part of a child's education, the part that is never taken into account in the most careful educations, is to make the child feel fully its misery [*misere*], its weakness, its dependence, and... the heavy yoke of necessity which nature imposes on man; and this not only so that it might be sensible of what is being done for it in order to lighten this yoke, but above all so that it might know from early on the place that providence assigned to it..." *Nouvelle Héloise* V. 3 (OC II, 571); also "To demur against an useless and arbitrary prohibition is a natural inclination, but which, far from being in itself vicious, conforms to the order of things and to man's constitution; since he would not be able to attend to his preservation if he had not a very lively love of himself and of the preservation of all his rights and privileges as he received them from nature... a feeble being whose power is further limited and restricted by law, loses a part of himself, and in his heart he reclaims what he is being deprived of. To impute this to him as a crime is to impute to him as a crime that he is what he is and not some other being; it would be to wish that he both be and not be. For this reason the order infringed by Adam appears to me to have been not so much a true prohibition as a paternal advice...," À *Christophe de Beaumont* (OC IV, 939ff); note also, *Émile* on the contrast between dependence on men and dependence on things (OC IV, 311, 320) (Bloom tr. 85, 191), *Social Contract* II, 7 [10] on the laws of nature and of the state; *To Mirabeau* [4].

Hence, "I never believed that human freedom consists in doing what one wants, but rather in never doing what one does not want...," *Rêveries* VI (OC I, 1059). However, perfect freedom is something else:

"... I was perfectly free, and better than free, subject solely to my attachments, I did only what I wanted to do." Rêveries X, OC

31 "What misleads in this matter is ... that one is inclined to believe that the best in the whole is also the best possible in every part." "... the part of the best whole is not necessarily the best that could have been done with this part...," Leibniz, Théodicée III, Sections 212, 213. The problem harks at least as far back as the break with pre-Socratic philosophy, Socrates's criticism of Anaxagoras for claiming that reason rules and yet failing to show that what is the case is best both for each thing/being taken by itself and for the common good of all things/beings (Phaedo, 98B2ff). Leibniz quotes Socrates's comment in a somewhat free translation on several occasions, most conspicuously in Discourse on Metaphysics, Section 20. However, he breaks off the quote just before Socrates acknowledges that neither he himself nor anyone else could do what he charges Anaxogoras failed to do, namely to show that what is the case is indeed best both for each thing/being taken by itself and for the common good of all things/beings (Phaedo, 99C8ff).

32 "... enlightenment and the vices always developed in the same proportions, not in individuals, but in peoples; a distinction I have always carefully drawn, and which not one of those who have attacked me has ever been able to grasp." À Christophe de Beaumont (OC IV, 967); cf. Nouvelle Héloise V. 2 (OC II, 538). "... it is to this ardor to be talked about, to this frenzy to achieve distinction which almost always keeps us outside ourselves, that we owe what is best and what is worst among men, our virtues and our vices, our Sciences and our errors, our Conquerors and our Philosophers, that is to say a multitude of bad things for a small number of good things." Discourse on Inequality II [52]. See also the texts cited in n. 41 in this chapter.

33 "... if, as it seems to me, it is a contradiction for matter to be both sentient and insentient, they [i.e., physical evils] are inevitable in any system of which man is a part ... " [8] " ... the system of this universe which produces, preserves, and perpetuates all thinking and sentient beings, must be dearer to him [i.e., the author of this universe] than a single one of these beings; hence in spite of his goodness, or rather because of it, he may sacrifice something of the happiness of individuals to the preservation of the whole." [21]; "The constitution of this universe does not allow for all the sensible beings that make it up to concur all at once in their mutual happiness [;] but since the well-being of one makes for the other's evil, each, according to the law of nature, assigns priority to himself, regardless of whether he is working to his own advantage or to another's prejudice; straightaway peace is disturbed as

regards the one who suffers, [and] not only is it natural then to repel the evil that pursues us, but when an intelligent being perceives that this evil is due to another's ill-will, he gets irritated at it and tries to repel it. Whence arise discord, quarrels, sometimes fights." *War* [42]; see also *Origin of Languages* 9 [32]* and Editor's Note; *To Philopolis* [11] (cited in n. 47 in this chapter).

34 Also *Nouvelle Héloise* III, 22 (OC II, 389); so, too, Leibniz, *Théodicée* I, Section 12ff, III, Section 253.

35 He had made the same point in the *Discourse on Inequality* II [13]; see also Leibniz, *Théodicée* I, Section 13.

However, in *Émile* the prospect of death accompanied by the hope of a better life hereafter – in other words, of the immortality of the individual soul – alone makes this life and its burdens bearable: *Emile* II (OC IV, 306); so, too, the Savoyard vicar, *ibid.* 588.

36 *Idea of the Method in the Composition of a Book* [10].

37 *The State of War* [8].

38 "... peace and innocence escaped us forever before we tasted their delights; unsensed by the stupid men of the first times, having escaped the enlightened men of later times, the happy life of the golden age was always a state foreign to the human race, either for its having failed to recognize it when it could enjoy it, or for its having lost it when it could have recognized it.

"What is more; this perfect independence and this unregulated freedom, even if it had remained associated with ancient innocence, would always have had one essential vice, and been harmful to the progress of our most excellent faculties, namely the lack of the connectedness between the parts that constitutes a whole. The earth would be covered by men with almost no communication between them; we would have some features in common without being united by a single one; everyone would remain isolated amongst the rest, everyone would think only o himself; our understanding could not develop; we would live without sensing anything, we would die without having lived; our entire happiness would consist in not knowing our misery; there would be neither goodness in our hearts, nor morality in our actions, and we would never have tasted the most delicious sentiment of the soul, which is the love of virtue." *Geneva ms.* I 2 [6], [7]; cf. *Fragments politiques* (OC III, 477).

39 "... however diligent one might be, help that comes only after the harm, and more slowly, invariable leaves the state on sufferance: as one tries to remedy one inconvenience, another is already making itself felt, and the very correctives produce new inconveniences ...," *Political Economy* [50]; *Poland* V [1]; cf. Machiaveli, *Discoureses* II, Introduction

(Paragraph 2). The Abbé de Saint-Pierre "... claimed that human reason was forever perfecting itself, since every century adds its lights to those of the preceding centuries. He did not understand that the scope of human understanding is always one and the same, and very narrow, that it loses at one end as much as it gains at the other, and that ever recurring prejudices deprive us of as much enlightenment as cultivated reason might replace." *To Mirabeau* [1]; so, too, *Émile* IV (OC IV, 676) (tr. 343).

40 "It is, then, not so much the understanding that constitutes the specific difference between man and the other animals, as it is his property of being a free agent." "But even if the difficulties surrounding all these questions left some room for disagreement about this difference between man and animal, there is another very specific difference that distinguishes between them, and about which there can be no argument, namely the faculty of perfecting oneself; a faculty which, with the aid of circumstances, successively develops all the others...," *Discourse on Inequality* I [16], [17]. "...those who know that, although the organ of speech is natural to man, speech itself is not natural to him, and who recognize the extent to which his perfectibility may have raised Civil man above his original state...," *Discourse on Inequality*, N. X [5] "Conventional language belongs to man alone. This is why man makes progress in good as well as in evil, and why animals do not," *Essay on the Origin of Languages*, 1 [14].

41 "It would be sad for us to have to agree that this distinctive, and almost unlimited faculty [i.e., perfectibility] is the source of all of man's miseries; that it is the faculty which, by dint of time, draws him out of that original condition in which he would spend tranquil and innocent days; that it is the faculty which, over the centuries, causing his enlightenment and his errors, his vices and his virtues to flourish, eventually makes him his own and Nature's tyrant," *Discourse on Inequality* I [17]; cf. *ibid.* II [1], [32], [36].

42 One influential commentator has gone so far as to assert that Rousseau's teaching substitutes social for original sin: "Il n'y à donc pas, dans chaque âme humaine, un péché originel, qui s'oppose à son salut individuel, mais il pèse sur l'humanité un péché collectif: le péché social," P.M. Masson, *La Religion de Jean-Jacques Rousseau*, 3 vols. (Paris: Hachette, 1916), Vol. 2, p. 278. It is not at all clear what "social sin" might mean, especially as "sin" has no place in Rousseau's teaching.

43 Plato, *Republic* II, 372 d–e; 373 e.

44 See, e.g., *Discourse on the Origin of Inequality* E [3]; *To Philopolis* [9]. "Necessary law," e.g., "He who willed man to be sociable inclined the globe's axis at an angle to the axis of the universe with a touch of the

finger. With this slight motion I see the face of the earth change and the vocation of mankind settled: I hear, far off, the joyous cries of a heedless multitude; I see Palaces and Cities raised up; I see the birth of the arts, laws, commerce; I see peoples forming, expanding, dissolving, succeeding one another like the waves of the sea: I see men clustered in a few points of their habitation in order there to devour one another, turning the remainder of the world into a dreadful waste; a worthy monument to social union and the usefulness of the arts," *Origin of Languages*, 9 [23]; Also, "...in the first place, everything comes down to subsistence, and everything that surrounds man thus has a bearing on him. He depends on everything, and he becomes what everything he depends on forces him to be. The climate, the soil, the air, the water, the productions of the earth and the sea, form his temperament, his character, determine his tastes, his passions, his labors, his actions of every kind. If this is not strictly so regarding individuals, it is unquestionably so regarding peoples: and if fully formed men arose from the earth, then regardless of where this might happen, anyone who knew well the state of everything around them could accurately ascertain what they will become," *Fragments politiques* (OC III, 530). Again, "Earthquakes, volcanoes, conflagrations, inundations, floods, by all of a sudden changing the face of the earth and, with it, the course human societies were taking, re-arranged them in new ways, and these new arrangements – whose first causes were physical and natural – in time became the moral causes that changed the course of things, brought on wars, migrations, conquests and finally revolutions that fill history and have been attributed to men without going back to what made them act this way," *Fragments politiques* (OC III, 533); *Discourse on Inequality* N, X [1], *Languages* 8, 9, 10; *Social Contract* II, 10 [2]; III 8; *Rousseau juge de Jean Jacques*, II (OC I, 804–811); and "It is easy to see how the establishment of a single Society made unavoidable the establishment of all the others and how, in order to stand up to united forces, it became necessary to unite in turn," *Discourse on Inequality* II [33], and *To Voltaire* [13]–[19].

"Accident," e.g., *Discourse on Inequality* I [51], II [18], *Origin of Languages* 9 [27], *Social Contract* I, 6 [1]–[3].

45 Cautiously, Kant, e.g., *Conjectural Beginning of Human History*, Remark, and *Perpetual Peace*, First Supplement [1] (and see note 23 in this chapter); categorically, Cassirer, "Society in its form so far has inflicted the deepest wounds on mankind; but society also can and must heal these wounds by its transformation and reformation. This is the solution to the problem of theodicy provided by Rousseau's philosophy of right," *Die Philosophie der Aufklärung* (J.C.B. Mohr, Paris 1932), pp. 210, 361–367. So, too, Jean Starobinski, *J.-J. Rousseau: la*

transparence et l'obstacle (Gallimard, Paris 1971), pp. 33–35; with qualifications, 1989, *Les emblèmes de la raison* (Paris, Flammarion, 1979), pp. 175–179; and *Le remède dans le mal* (Gallimard, Paris, 1989) pp. 165–208, where, however, the wound (mal) and the cure have become part of an all-encompassing three-pronged "theocosmological" "myth of Telephus": pp. 195ff.

For a thoughtful Kantian reading of the Rousseau–Voltaire debate, see S. Neiman, "Metaphysics, Philosophy: Rousseau on the Problem of Evil," in *Reclaiming the History of Ethics, Essays for John Rawls*, A. Reath, B. Herman, Ch. M. Korsgaard, eds. (New York: Cambridge University Press, 1997), pp. 142–168.

For a comprehensive, illuminating study of the Rousseau–Kant relation, see R.L. Velkley's exemplary, *Freedom and the End of Reason*, (University of Chicago Press, Chicago 1989).

46 This is also all the *Émile* epigraph from Seneca's *de irā* says.

47 When the Genevan naturalist Charles Bonnet, writing under the pseudonym Philopolis, seemed to maintain that it is, Rousseau replied, "If whatever is, is right [or good; *tout est bien*] as you understand it, what is the point of redressing our vices, curing our evils, correcting our errors? Of what use are our Pulpits, our Courts, our Academies? Why call the Doctor when you have a fever? How do you know whether the good of the greater whole which you do not know, does not require you to be delirious, and whether the health of the inhabitants of Saturn or of Sirius would not suffer because yours was restored? Let everything go as it may, so that everything always go well. If whatever is, is as best it can be, then you must blame any action whatsoever. For since any action, as soon as it occurs, necessarily brings about some change in the state things are in, one cannot touch anything without doing wrong, and the most absolute quietism is the only Virtue left to man. Finally, if whatever is, is right [or good], then it is good that there be Laplanders, Eskimos, Algonquins, Chickasaws, Caribs, who make do without our political order, Hottentots who have no use for it, and a Genevan who approves them. Leibniz himself would grant this," *To Philopolis* [11]; cf. *Origin of Languages* 9 [32]–[34], *Social Contract*, I, 3 [3].

48 Kant succinctly spells out the formal argument in "Über partikuläre Providenz," *Sieben kleine Aufsätze aus den Jahren* 1788–1791, *Werke*, Cassirer edition, 4, 524ff.

49 Julie and St. Preux, the two main characters of the *Nouvelle Héloise*, discuss the question of universal and particular providence in terms of the specifically Christian debates about grace and election. Julie writes, "According to you, this act of humility [i.e., prayer] is without benefit to us, and God, having given us everything that can incline us to good

by giving us conscience, thereafter abandons us to ourselves and lets our freedom act. As you know, this is not the doctrine of Saint Paul nor is it that professed in our Church.... To listen to you, it would seem that it is a bother for it [i.e., the divine power] to watch over each individual; you fear that a divided and steady attention might tire it, and you find it fairer that it do everything by general laws, no doubt because they require less of its care." St Preux replies, "I... do not believe that, once He has provided in every way for man's needs, God grants to one person rather than to another some extraordinary assistance, which the one who abuses the common assistance does not deserve, and the one who uses it well does not need. This acceptance of persons does injury to divine justice. Even if this harsh and discouraging doctrine could be deduced from Scripture itself, is not my first duty to honor God? However much respect I may owe the sacred text, I owe its Author more, and I would rather believe the Bible falsified or unintelligible than God unjust or maleficent," *Nouvelle Héloise*, VI, 6 (OC II, 672) and VI, 7 (OC II, 684); *Lettre à d'Alembert* (OC, V, 12) (tr. p. 13). When the Censor's Office required that Saint-Preux's remark be struck, Rousseau replied "These pages must remain exactly as they stand. If Saint-Preux wants to be heretical regarding grace, that is his business. Besides, it is necessary that he defend man's freedom, since elsewhere he makes the abuse of this freedom the cause of moral evil: he absolutely has to be a Molinist if he is not to be a Manichean," to Malesherbes, March 1761 (CC VIII, 237); cf. *ibid.* p. 120; St. Preux "makes the abuse of... freedom the cause of moral evil" in *Nouvelle Héloise* V, 5 (OC II, 595); see also *Émile*, IV (Savoyard vicar) (OC IV, 587) (tr. 281.)

H. Gouhier, the Pléiade editor of Rousseau's *Letter*, claims not to be able to understand how denying particular providence can be more consoling than asserting that some are predestined to be saved and others to be reprobated without regard to merit or desert, many called and few chosen: *Rousseau et Voltaire* (op. cit.) p. 86.

50 This is also so on the Savoyard vicar's account: *Émile* IV (OC IV, 587ff) (tr. 281ff).

51 Regarding these limits, see especially *Discourse on Inequality*, P [6], *Geneva ms.*, I 2 [5], *Social Contract*, III, 8, 15 [9]–[10].

52 For example, "There is no reason to hold that God would upset the entire order of nature for the sake of somewhat less moral evil," Leibniz, *Théodicée*, II, Section 118.

53 "I die, I am eaten by worms; but my children, my brothers will live as I have lived, and by the order of nature, I do for all men what Codrus, Curtius, the Decii, the Philaeni, and a thousand others did voluntarily for a small number of men," [22]; also *To Philopolis* [12]; and the parallel

238   VICTOR GOUREVITCH

passages in Lucretius, *De natura rerum*, III, 931–963 and 1024–1035. However, in his *Poem on Natural Law* as well as, for example, in his *Micromégas* (last paragraph), Voltaire himself makes the point that for earthlings to assume that they are worth more than the inhabitants of Saturn is a thoughtless display of self-importance.

54 Also, *Discourse on Inequality* II [2]; and "... there is perhaps something fine in living just by itself, provided there is no great excess of hardships. It is clear that most men will endure much harsh treatment in their longing for life, the assumption being that there is a kind of joy in it and a natural sweetness," Aristotle, *Politics*, III, 6, 1275b 25–30 (C. Lord, tr.).

55 The context suggests that Rousseau is here speaking about the immortality of the individual human soul; but the wording in one manuscript of the *Letter* leaves open the possibility that here he is speaking about the immortality of the (unindividuated) soul: "*Mais il faut appliquer cette regle à la durée totale de chaque être sensible, et non à quelque instant particulier de sa durée, tel que la vie humaine...,*" (OC IV, 1780, n. (a) ad p. 1070); cf. Plato, *Phaedo*, 105D3–107B9. So far as I know, Rousseau does not pursue this line of inquiry in any of his writings. However, consider the discussion of immortality and resurrection, *Nouvelle Héloise* VI 11 (OC II, 727–729).

56 Rousseau has the Savoyard vicar state this feeling: "God, it is said, owes his creatures nothing; I believe that he owes them everything he promised them by endowing them with being. Now, to give them the idea of a good and to make them feel the need for it, is to promise it to them. The more I turn inward, the more I consult myself, the more do I read the following words inscribed in my soul: *be just and you will be happy.*" *Émile* IV (OC IV, 587); cf. Kant, *Kritik der Praktischen Vernunft*, I, 2.2, and the discussion in R.L. Velkley, *Freedom and the End of Reason*, op. cit., 104ff, 141–145, 153f, 161.

57 "Considering things in human terms, the laws of justice are vain among men for want of natural sanctions; they only bring good to the wicked and evil to the just when he observes them toward everyone while no one observes them toward him," *Social Contract*, I, 6 [2]; "Philosopher, your moral laws are very fine, but pray show me their sanction," *Émile* II (OC IV, 635*) (Bloom tr. 314*); *Nouvelle Héloise* III, 18 (OC II, 358ff).

58 "... the prejudices of childhood and the secret wishes of my heart tipped the scale to the side I found most consoling. It is difficult to help believing what one so ardently desires, and who can doubt that one's interest in accepting or rejecting the judgments in the other life determines most men's faith as to what they hope or fear [in this life],"

Rêveries III (OC I, 1017); cf. *ibid.* II (OC I, 1010). This is how Rousseau
has the Savoyard vicar describe the rewards and punishments in the
other life: "I could not recall after my death what I was in the course of
my life without also recalling what I felt, hence what I did, and I do not
doubt that this memory will some day make for the happiness of the
good and the torment of the wicked," *Émile* IV (OC IV, 590ff) (Bloom tr.
283), and the long concluding note to the vicar's "Profession": *Émile*
IV (OC IV, 632–635) (tr. 313ff.); also *Rousseau juge de Jean Jacques*
III (OC I, 968ff). Julie makes much the same point in much the same
terms: *Nouvelle Héloïse* VI, 11 [OC II, 729, together with note (a)].

59 "...the dogma of the moral order is restored in the other life...,"
Rousseau juge de Jean-Jacques III (OC I, 968); and see *Rêveries* III
[OC I, 1018ff, with variants (c) and (d)].

60 Again: "...the good of the greater whole, which you do not know...,"
To Philopolis [11].

61 The omitted paragraph was first published by George Streckeisen-
Moultou in his *Oeuvres et correspondance inédites de J.J. Rousseau*
(Geneva Chez Jullien, 1861), with a note explaining that it was part of
the manuscript of the *Letter* in his possession.

62 Diderot's *Pensées philosophiques* (1746) had been publicly condemned
a decade earlier, and contributed to their author's imprisonment at Vincennes (1749). Rousseau had included a discrete reference to them in
the *First Discourse* [51].

Hume entrusts the argument to Philo in the Dialogues Concerning
Natural Religion Part VIII; Shaftesbury summarizes it as "The Athe-
istic Hypothesis:" Characteristics, "The Moralists," Part II, Section
IV.

63 Although he repeatedly returns to the argument of this *Pensée*: in a
letter to the pastor Jacob Vernes, 18 Feb. 1758 (CC V, 32ff); in the Savoyard vicar's Profession of Faith, *Émile* IV (OC IV, 579) (tr. 275ff); in the
Fiction ou morceau allégorique sur la révélation (OC IV, 1046); and in
the *Letter to Franquières* [11], [13]. Rousseau never publicly acknowledged that he found it convincing or that he knows of no refutation to
it. H. Gouhier remarks "Il est curieux de constater que Rousseau n'a
pas retenu sa réfutation de l'argumentation de Diderot dans la lettre
qu'il envoie à Voltaire." Jean Jacques Rousseau, *Lettres philosophiques*,
présentées par H. Gouhier (Vrin, Paris, 1974) p. 53 n. 56. Gouhier's perplexity is perplexing: after all, Rousseau never so much as mentioned
Diderot's argument in the letter which he sent to Voltaire; what is
more, in the paragraph which he omitted from the letter he did send
him, he explicitly says "Je n'y sais pas la moindre réponse qui ait le
sens commun;" and a few lines later he adds that he finds both it and

its counter-argument equally convincing; so, too, in his remark, some twenty years later, about the atheists' argument: *Rêveries*, III, OC I, 1016.

64 Compare Lucretius, *De rerum natura* (Bailey edition), I: 196–198, 823–827, 906–914; II: 688–694, 1013–1021; I: 1021–1028; and V: 187–194, 416–431 with Cicero, *De natura deorum*, II, 37; also, e.g., Plato *Laws* X, 889b–892c; Aristotle, *Physics* II, 4, 196a24–196b4, II, 6, 198a5–13, II, 8, 199b5–7; also, Fénélon, *Traité de l'existence et des attributs de Dieu* I, 1, and Leibniz, the passages quoted in n. 69 in this chapter.

65 *Discourse on Inequality* I [16], [17] (quoted in n. 40 in this chapter) and *ibid.* [34]; so, too, the Savoyard vicar: *Emile* IV (OC IV, 585ff); *Nouvelle Héloise* VI, 7 (OC II, 683).

66 Persuade/convince: also *Preface to Narcisse* [2]; *Origin of Languages* 4 [4], 19 [2]; *Émile* IV (OC IV, 453, 606ff); *Nouvelle Héloise* V, 5 (OC II, 594ff) in the context of a discussion of the origin of evil; *Rêveries* III (OC I, 1016); *Letter to Mirabeau* (July 1767) [13]; C. Kelly considers the formula in "'To persuade without Convincing': The Language of Rousseau's Legislator," *AJPS* 31:321–335 (1987). Traditionally, to persuade is to move to action; to convince is to demonstrate or to prove; persuasion is properly the province of rhetoric; demonstration is properly the province of philosophy or science: e.g., Plato, *Gorgias* 454e2–455a4; Aristotle, *Rhetoric* I: 2, 1355b, 26ff; Cicero, *De finibus* IV, iii, 7; Berkeley, *Alciphron*, Dialogue 4, section 2; Hume, *Dialogues Concerning Natural Religion*, VIII (i.f.). The distinction persuade/convince is sometimes said to correspond to the distinction exoteric/esoteric; "arguments that admit of no answer and produce no conviction" are characteristically skeptical arguments: Hume, *An Inquiry Concerning Human Understanding*, Section XII, Part I (note).

67 "Ich mußte... das Wissen aufheben, um zum Glauben Platz zu bekommen..." Kant, *KdrV* B, *Critique of Pure Reason*, "B" Preface (1787 ed.), p. XXX.

68 See also the passage from the *Rêveries* quoted in n. 58 in this chapter; M. de Wolmar compares the contrast between his own way and his wife's to that between reason and sentiment: *Nouvelle Héloise* V, 5 (OC II, 595). Rousseau is likely to have been acquainted with Bayle's judgment: "Proofs of sentiment settle nothing.... Every people is imbued with proofs of sentiment for its religion: they are therefore more often false than true," *Continuation des pensées diverses* XX (p. 214b), *Oeuvres Complètes*, op cit., Vol. 3

69 Consider, "If I found myself transported to a new part of the universe in which I saw clocks, furnishings, books, buildings, I would boldly wager everything I have that this is the work of some reasonable creature,

although it is possible, in absolute terms, that it not be so, and that one may pretend that in the infinite expanse of things there is a country where books write themselves. It would nevertheless be one of the greatest chance occurrences in the world, and one must have lost one's mind to believe that this country in which I found myself is precisely this possible country in which books write themselves by chance, and one cannot blindly accept so strange – though possible – an assumption in place of what happens in the ordinary course of nature: for the likelihood of the one by comparison to the other is as small as a grain of sand is by comparison to a world. Hence the likelihood of this assumption is as infinitely small, that is to say morally nil, and it is consequently morally certain that providence governs things," Leibniz: Y. Belaval, *Pour connaître la pensée de Leibniz*, p. 257, quoting Foucher de Careil, *Oeuvres de Leibniz* II (Paris: Jadot, 1859–1875), p. 529. Yet; "... one can not only say with Lucretius that animals see because they have eyes, but also that they have been given eyes in order to see." Belaval, op. cit. p. 261, quoting Gerhardt, *Die philosophischen Schriften von Gottfried Wilhelm Leibniz* (Berlin: Weidemann, 1875–1890) VII, p. 273.

70 Lucretius, *On the Nature of Things* (I, 936–942 = IV, 11–17). Tasso adopts the metaphor "honeying the cup" at the beginning of *Jerusalem Delivered* 1681 (I, 3). Rousseau quotes Tasso's formulation in the Second Preface to the *Nouvelle Héloise* (OC II, 17) to explain why he wrote the novel and why he wrote it as he did. He translated portions of the first two books of Tasso's poem (OC V, 1277–1295).

71 For example, the advice to Franquières in the Letter to him [5]; cf. *Observations* [35]; and the cogent comments by Karl Barth, *Protestant Thought from Rousseau to Rischl*, Brian Cozens, tr. (New York: Simon and Schuster, 1969), pp. 91ff., and by Jean Guéhenno, *Jean-Jacques Rousseau: histoire d'une conscience* (Paris: Gallimard, 1962), Vol. II, pp. 109–111.

72 Nietzsche, e.g., *Fröhliche Wissenschaft* #357, *Jenseits von Gut und Böse*, #227; Max Weber, "Wissenschaft als Beruf," in *Gesammelte Aufsätze zur Wissenschaftslehre* (Tübingen: J.C.B. Mohr, 1922), pp. 551ff, 553, 554. Compare. Leo Strauss, *Philosophie und Gesetz* (Berlin: Schocken, 1935), pp. 25–28; Spinoza's *Critique of Religion* (New York: Schocken, 1965), Preface to the English Translation, pp. 29ff.

73 Rousseau has one of his characters, St. Preux, say in praise of another of his characters, M. de Wolmar, that he is not an atheist because he is a skeptic: *Nouvelle Héloise* V, 5 (OC II, 589); also, "... doubt is as rare among the People as assertion [*l'affirmation*] is among true Philosophers," *Discourse on Heroic Virtue* [13].

74 "Modern philosophy, which takes account only of what it can explain

...," *Emile* IV (OC IV, 595) (tr. 286); cf. *Discourse on Inequality* I [16]; *Origin of Languages* 15[6] and 13–17 *passim*.

75 "We cannot *know* whether motion is essential to matter; we can therefore not deny that it is; we can therefore not reject materialism or atheism": *Letter to Voltaire* [30]; "we cannot conceive of motion as a natural property of matter:" *Morceau allégorique* (OC IV, 1046); "motion cannot be of the essence of matter because we can conceive of matter at rest": author's note inserted into the Savoyard vicar's "Profession of Faith," *Émile* IV (OC IV, 574*); and the fuller discussion of this issue in the *Lettre à M. de Beaumont, Archevêque de Paris* that begins "... so many men and philosophers who throughout the ages have thought about this subject have, all of them, unanimously rejected the possibility of creation, except perhaps a very few who appear sincerely to have subjected their reason to authority; a sincerity which considerations of self-interest, security and repose render exceedingly suspect, and which cannot possibly be trusted so long as one runs a risk in speaking true," (OC IV, 955–957); see also n. 12 in this chapter.

The distinction Rousseau draws in the *Letter to Voltaire* between brute and sentient matter – "... if, as it seems to me, it is a contradiction for matter to be both sentient and insentient ... " [8] – is hypothetical and leaves open the possibility that one and the same principle might account for both; so does the proposition, later in the *Letter*, "... the greatest idea of Providence I can conceive is that each material being be arranged in the best way possible in relation to the whole, and each intelligent and sentient being in the best way possible in relation to itself ... " [26]. "Sense" and its cognates (sentient, sensibility, sentiment) are systematically ambiguous: e.g., *Rousseau juge de Jean-Jacques* II (OC I, 805); however, *Émile* IV (OC IV, 384).

In connection with Rousseau's reflections on materialism, consider also his reflections on "the harmony of the three realms" of nature, the mineral, the vegetal, and the animal, *Rêveries* VII (OC I, 1062).

Rousseau understandably raises questions about Buffon's "organic molecules" and about Lucretian "soul atoms" [30]: *Émile* IV (OC IV, 575) (tr. 273*), *To Franquières* [13]); but it is not clear that he rejects them out of hand, anymore than that he categorically rejects Locke's suggestion of thinking matter: author's note inserted into the Savoyar vicar's "Profession of Faith," *Émile IV* (OC IV, 575*) (tr. 273*) (and 584*) (tr. 279*), *Morceau allégorique* (OC IV, 1046). He might well have accepted Buffon's formulation, "... *le vivant et l'animé, au lieu d'être un degré métaphysique des êtres, est une propriété physique de la matière*," "Histoire générale et particulière," Vol. II (1749), ch. 1 i.f., in Piveteau, ed., Buffon, *Oeuvres philosophiques* (Paris: PUF, 1954), 238a51–238b3. For the parallel between Buffon's "organic molecules" and Lucretius's *primordia rerum*, see Jacques Roger's classic *Les sciences de la vie dans la pensée française du XVIIIè siècle* (Paris: Armand Collin, 1971), pp. 548–551, 581, as well his *"Diderot et Buffon en 1749,"* Diderot Studies IV, (1963), 221–236. Regarding the mid-eighteenth-century debates about Locke's suggestion, see John W. Yolton, *Thinking Matter: Materialism in Eighteenth Century Britain* (University of Minnesota Press, 1983), and his *Locke and French Materialism* (Oxford: Clarendon, 1991); also, n. 13 in this chapter.

For the view that Rousseau sought to remain "neutral" with regard to the conflict between materialism and antimaterialism, see L. Strauss, *Natural Right and History*, (Chicago: Chicago University Press, 1953), pp. 265ff; and C. Kelly, "Rousseau's Philosophic Dream," *Interpretation* **23**: 417–435, 420ff (1996).

76 "In searching within myself and looking in others for the causes of these different ways of being [able or unable to resist desires one ought to be able to resist], I found that they depended in large measure on the prior impression made on us by external objects, that we are constantly being modified by our senses and our organs, and that we introduced these modifications into our ideas, our sentiments and our very actions without being aware of it. The striking and numerous observations I had collected were unquestionable, and it seemed to me that their physical principle might provide an external regimen [*régime extérieur*] which, by being varied as circumstances varied, could put or keep the soul in the state most favorable to virtue. How many missteps reason would be spared, how many vices would be kept from arising if the animal economy could be forced to favor the moral order it so often disturbs! The climate, the seasons, sounds, colors, light, dark, the weather, food, noise, silence, motion, rest, everything impinges on our machine and hence on our soul; everything offers us a thousand almost certain holds by which to govern from their very inception the sentiments by which we let ourselves be mastered," *Confessions IX* (OC I 409); *also* Fragments politiques (OC III, 533) quoted in n. 44 in this chapter, Rousseau illustrates this *morale sensitive* in all works; E. Gilson discusses some aspects of it in *"La méthode de M. de Wolmar,"* in *Les idées et les lettres* (Paris: Vrin, 1932), pp. 275–298.

77 Discourse on Inequality P [4], I [26] and V. Gourevitch, "Rousseau's 'Pure' State of Nature," *Interpretation* (1988) 16: 23–59; Essay on the Origin of Languages 16 [6], Nouvelle Héloise I, 48; *Nouvelle Héloise* VI 12 (OC II 740); and more emphatically, var. (a) *ad*. OC II, 741.

78 *Discourse on Inequality* II [19], [57]; *Social Contract* IV, 8 [17]; *Émile* I (OC IV, 249ff) (tr. 39ff); *Fragments politiques*, OC III, 531; cf. *Languages* 9 [27], [28], [31]; *Rêveries* V (OC I, 1046ff). Bayle gives a fair and hence laudatory account of Epicurean morality: *Dictionnaire*, s. v. *"Épicure"*,

and *Pensées diverses sur la comète*, Chaps. clxxiv and clxxvi; Montaigne, *Essays* II, 11; Barbeyrac, in the Introductory Essay to his French translation of Pufendorf's *Right of Nature and of Nations*, cautions that Epicurean ethics is "very dangerous in Civil Society"; and he summarizes the arguments against Epicurus's placing happiness in tranquility of soul in this life; and against his view that justice is good not in itself but only instrumentally (cii–cv).

79 "I was born for friendship..." Confessions VIII, OC I, 362; "...I was never really suited for civil society..." Reveries VI, OC II, 1059. Emile will be "...a likeable stranger..." (Emile IV, OC IV, 670, tr. 339), brought up to enjoy (*jouir*): *Emile* V, OC IV 771; St. Preux frames his fullest account of the Wolmar household by remarking on the pleasure in its midst in the company of friends: *Nouvelle Héloise* IV 10, OC II 440, 470; and especially 466f.

80 Julie's description of pleasure [*jouissance*] through privation: *Nouvelle Héloise* III, 7 (OC II, 320); her cousin, Claire, describes Julie's "pleasure [*volupté*] of the wise" and her "Epicureanism of reason" in almost the same terms: it consists in "abstaining for the sake of enjoying [*jouir*]," *ibid.* VI, 5 (OC II, 662); Émile's tutor, right after giving voice to the Savoyard vicar's Profession of Faith, describes at length how he, himself, would be "temperate out of sensuality," IV, 678 and var. (d) (tr. 345); and this is also how the character "Rousseau" describes himself in *Rousseau juge de Jean-Jacques* II (OC I, 807 and 818). On temperance and moderation, see also *Discourse on the Virtue a Hero Most Needs* [31]–[33].

81 The *Discourse on Inequality* is also the writing of Rousseau's that Diderot most directly influenced and liked best (*Confessions* VIII, OC I, 389). The influence of Lucretius on the *Discourse* was noted from the first: J. de Castillon, *Discours sur l'inégalité parmi les hommes. Pour servir de réponse au Discours que M. Rousseau, Citoyen de Genève, a publié sur le même sujet* (Amsterdam, 1756); it is documented in Jean Morel's classical "*Recherches sur les sources du Discours de l'inégalité,*" in *Annales de la Société Jean-Jacques Rousseau*, Vol. V, pp. 119–198; see also L. Strauss, *Natural Right and History*, (Chicago: Chicago University Press, 1953), p. 271, n. 37; L. Robin, *La pensée hellénique* (Paris: PUF, 1967), pp. 550ff, n. 1; V. Goldschmidt, *Anthropologie et politique: Les principes du système de Rousseau* (Paris: Vrin, 1974), pp. 305, 436ff, 479; J.H. Nichols Jr., *Epicurean Political Philosophy* (Ithaca, NY: Cornell University Press, 1976), especially pp. 198–207; H. Meier ed., J.J. Rousseau, *Diskurs über die Ungleichheit/Discours sur l'inégalité*, (Schöningh, 1984), s.v. Lukrez. Rousseau mentions Lucretius's "formal denial of any kind of creation" (*De natura*

rerum, I, 150) in his *Lettre à M. de Beaumont* (OC IV, 957); and the classical difficulty regarding the strictly rectilinear movement of atoms (Lucretius, *De natura rerum* II, 216–293; Cicero, *De natura deorum* I, xxv; Montaigne, *Essays,* II, 12, D. Frame tr. p. 407) in the *Fiction ou morceau allégorique* (OC IV, 1046); Rousseau also occasionally cites or mentions Lucretius in his writings on music: OC V, 155, 331, 919. For the Lucretian echoes in the *Essay on the Origin of Languages,* see V. Gourevitch, "'The First Times' in Rousseau's Essay on the Origin of Languages," *Graduate Faculty Philosophy Journal,* **11**:123–146, 139–141 (1986), and "The Political Argument of Rousseau's *Essay on the Origin of Languages,*" in Cohen, Guyer, and Putnam, eds., *Pursuits of Reason: Essays in Honor of Stanley Cavell* (Lubbock: Texas Tech University Press, 1993), pp. 21–35.

82   *haec ratio plerumque videtur*
        tristior esse quibus non est tractata, retroque
        Vulgus abhorret ab hac.
           I, 943–945; IV, 18–20 (C. Bailey tr.).

83 Diogenes Laertius, *Lives* X: Epicurus, *Principal Opinions,* 33, 35, 36; Lucretius: V, 1155, cf. 1025; Epicurus: *Letter to Menoeceus,* 134 (C.D. Young tr.). This is the spirit in which Rousseau has an unidentified speaker address Moses:

"What are you doing among us, O Hebrew; it is with pleasure that I see you here [*je t'y vois avec plaisir*]; but how can you, who were so contemptuous of us, be pleased to be here [*t'y plaire*]; why did you not stay among your own?

"You are mistaken, I come among my own. I lived alone on earth, amidst a numerous people I was alone. Lycurgus, Numa, Solon are my brothers. I come to rejoin my family. I come to taste at last the sweetness of conversing with my fellows [*mes semblables*], to speak and to be understood [*entendu*]. It is among you, illustrious souls, that I come at last to enjoy myself [*jouir de moi*].

"You have certainly changed your tone, sentiments and ideas," *Fragments politiques,* OC III, 500.

84 *To Gauffecourt,* January 1756, as quoted in Gouhier, *Rousseau et Voltaire,* op. cit. p. 77.

85 *Essay on the Origin of Languages* 9 [33] (OC V, 404).

86 Compare *Deuteronomy* 31:19–22.

87 In the *Geneva ms.* Rousseau speaks of these as "civility" and "benevolence" toward fellow citizens, and "reasoned natural right" toward strangers (II, 4 [13], [14]). On his use of "natural right" and "natural law," see V. Gourevitch, "Introduction" to *Rousseau: The Social Contract and Other Later Political Writings,* op. cit. pp. x–xii.

88 *Social Contract* I, 6 [2]; *à d'Alembert*, OC V, 22; *Émile* II (OC IV, 334–337) (tr. 101ff) and IV (OC IV, 626) (tr. 307); *Nouvelle Héloise* III, 18 (OC II, 358ff); *Fiction, ou morceau allégorique sur la révélation*, OC IV, 1053; *Rousseau juge de Jean-Jacques* III (OC I, 968ff); *To Franquières* [23]; see Plato, *Republic* II, 358e–367e, cf. I, 330d–331b, X, 608d–621d, and *Phaedo*, 63Cc6; also Spinoza, *Political Treatise* II, Section 12, I, Section 5; and "...everything you tell me about the advantages of the social law might be fine if, while I scrupulously observed it toward everyone else, I were sure that everyone else observed it toward me; but what assurance can you give me on this score, and could I find myself in a worse situation than to be exposed to all the evils which the stronger might choose to visit upon me, without my daring to make up for it at the expense of the weak? Either give me guarantees against every unjust undertaking, or give up the hope of my refraining from them in turn. It makes no difference that you tell me that by repudiating the duties which natural law imposes on me, I simultaneously deprive myself of its rights, and that my own acts of violence will authorize all the acts of violence that might be committed against me. I accept this all the more readily as I do not see how my moderation might guarantee me against them. Besides it will be up to me to get the strong to side with my interests by sharing with them the spoils of the weak; this will do more for my advantage and my security than will justice. The proof that this is how the enlightened and independent man would have reasoned is that this is how every sovereign society accountable for its conduct solely to itself reasons," *Geneva ms.* I, 2 [10].

"As soon as men live in society, they must have a Religion that keeps them in it. Never did or will a people endure without Religion, and if it were not given one it would make itself one or soon be destroyed. In every state that can require its members to sacrifice their life, anyone who does not believe in the life to come is necessarily either a coward or a madman; but we know all too well how much the hope of the life to come can drive a fanatic to scorn this life. Deprive this fanatic of his visions and give him the same hope as the reward for virtue, and you will make a true citizen of him," *Geneva ms.*, OC III, 336.

89 Also, "...if ever again there came to be some few true defenders of Theism, tolerance and morality, there'd soon arise the most frightful persecutions of them; a philosophical inquisition more cunning and no less bloody than the other would soon mercilessly have anyone who believed in God burned," *Rousseau juge de Jean-Jacques* III (OC I, 968) (and context); also, *Confessions* XI (OC I, 567, 570).

9   *Émile*: Learning to Be Men, Women, and Citizens

In the history of the philosophy of education, Rousseau is renowned as one of the founders of what is often both admired and vilified as "progressive" education. Yet Rousseau remains the most vehement critic of the idea of progress that he so rapidly identified as having become the new received wisdom of the forces of modernity that had set themselves to overturn the authority of tradition. That he should readily and persuasively be interpreted both as a voice of liberation and of conservatism is one reason for the perennial fascination with an author whose very paradoxes have a quality of consistency throughout his apparently varied output. Within education his fame rests on his contribution to the development of "child-centred" education with its attendant emphasis on the freedom of the child to develop at its own appropriate pace and on learning by discovery rather than by forms of imposition. His belief that in education the guiding principle should be to do the opposite to what was the prevailing method of schooling[1] has often seemed to be the inspiration of many of the radical experiments in the rearing of children over the succeeding period. Yet any examination of Rousseau's writings on education will demonstrate that this advocate of child liberation was as deeply concerned with discipline, albeit in a different manner, as the most conservative of writers.

This combination of liberty and discipline was central to Rousseau's educational ideas, as they were to his moral and political thinking. Education was, indeed, at the core of his thought.[2] It has been a striking feature of histories of political and educational thought that the same philosophers have been so prominent in both streams. The names stretch, to mention only the front rank, from Plato through Locke and John Stuart Mill down to Dewey and

Oakeshott in recent times. Moral and political conduct has to be learned, and education is regularly invoked in an attempt to ensure the appearance on the adult stage of persons well prepared to play the roles of subjects or citizens. Most commonly, education is perceived as an effective force in the "reproduction" of prevailing social and political values.[3] It may also, by contrast, be a means of rectifying such values, the children being expected to repair the deficiencies of the older generation. Theories of political education may be divided into those that largely take existing human motivations as given and those that aim at their transformation. The first category seeks to teach pupils how to redirect their behaviour into more socially and politically acceptable paths. The works of Hobbes, Bentham, and James Mill are examples of this approach. The second group is more radical. They look to education to help achieve a transformation of attitudes to man and society. John Stuart Mill and, perhaps, John Dewey belong in this class, but its prime representative is Rousseau.

The significance of education for Rousseau is that it seems to offer a means of solving one of the central dilemmas of his social and political thought. A fundamental objective is to create a virtuous circle in which transformed human beings could live in a transformed society in which all could equally enjoy a sense both of self-fulfilment and community with others. Such a circle cannot be generated in the conditions of modern society dominated by competitive self-interested behaviour, resulting in inequality and social and economic exploitation. Social norms produce the conduct appropriate to advancement in that society. To break into such a cycle of degeneration appears a forlorn prospect. A transformed society presupposes a transformed humanity, yet it seems that this new humanity can appear within only a new society. As Rousseau expresses the puzzle in the *Social Contract*, the effect must become the cause.[4] Education promises, at first glance, a solution to the problem. If it were feasible to reeducate a new generation to understand the world and themselves differently it might be possible to make a new start. These pupils could be the effect that produces the cause that begins the new cycle.

Not dissimilar ideas prompted a host of Enlightenment pedagogues to produce a formidable number of treatises on education during the eighteenth century. Rousseau's distinctiveness consists in the intellectual honesty with which he recognises that this analysis was insufficiently radical and the proposed remedies were superficial and perverse. The ideas of contemporary educationists were part of the problem, not part of the solution. Although they purported to be rejecting the authoritarian pedagogic practices of the past, these apparent innovators were still reproducing the norms of existing human conduct. Their methods consisted in little more than accepting that humans were moved by emulation and the desire to be approved by elite opinion and seeking to teach future adults how to channel behaviour so as to conform to social expectations. They had merely adapted the principle of "imitation" in education by substituting imitation of newer bourgeois values for the imitation of aristocratic conduct. Their concern remained with educating children for society as they knew it.

Rousseau insisted that education could not consist in reproduction if the vicious circle was to be replaced with the virtuous. Education must not be contaminated by the corruption of present-day society or its ideological agents. "Imitation" was not to be rejected but it was to require the imitation of "nature" and not a version of nature that had been transmogrified by the effects of society.

Although Rousseau's educational thought is unified by this search for a means of achieving a total transformation in human conduct, he does not offer just one account of education but several. The sheer scale of his enterprise and the audacity of his onslaught on convention make him aware of the possibility, even the likelihood, of its failure. Much of his writing on education, arguably indeed the greater part, is concerned with examining ways in which some of the goals of a good education can be retrieved in the face of a world that has not been, and possibly cannot be, transformed. In *Émile* he produces an account of an education that is designed to allow persons to live an honest life even when surrounded by the pressures of a corrupt society. It is intended to portray an ideal of education that is as close to nature as it is possible to attain in the world as we now find it. In total and intended contrast is the education for citizenship that he describes in *On Political Economy, Considerations on the Government of Poland* and the *Letter to M. D'Alembert on the Theatre*. Here the reader is offered an alternative vision of an education that deliberately "denatures" human beings but allows them to live a satisfying communal life. Pieceable together from the *Social Contract*, episodes in *Émile*, and the *Letter to M. D'Alembert* is Rousseau's conception of how one might learn to be the good man in the good society. Finally, and standing in juxtaposition to all these, is Rousseau's account of the proper education for women.

Rousseau provides his readers with four "moments" of education. It is not that there are a number of different Rousseaus so much as an author who is addressing the same topic from distinct viewpoints. This sometimes gives the impression of self-contradiction. It is, however, more the consequence of that feature of Rousseau's style that has been the source of comment from enthusiasts and detractors alike since his own day – the readiness to push every idea to its extreme, to test it to the full, sometimes to the point at which he seems to be reducing it to absurdity. He is seldom a man of compromise intellectually. He leaves it to others to try to find the middle way. Rousseau possessed a remarkable imaginative capacity to address fundamentally contrasting social and political conditions, to enter into their manners of thinking and feeling, and to devise what he deemed to be appropriate institutional and behavioural responses. It is understandable that he denied that he was writing, even in *Émile*, a treatise of education to be followed in practice.[5] He was tolerant of the experiments carried out in his name (and there are few more bizarre experiments than those carried out in educating children), but his ultimate subject was the "idea" of an education that would not corrupt the natural goodness of humanity.

LEARNING TO BE A MAN IN CIVIL SOCIETY

Rousseau's aim in *Émile* is to show how a child can be turned into a man in civil society or, more accurately, *despite* civil society. The boy Émile stands for all children born within existing society. Although the striking feature of his upbringing appears to be that he is isolated from society, in fact society looms as the ever-present threat to his development as a human being. Existing schooling is merely a means of socialisation into the roles that society requires to be filled. Émile, by contrast, is to be brought up to be a "man," capable of fulfilling the range of responsibilities that may fall on him. Émile is always intended for society but he must be armoured against its baneful effects. The constant effort of his teacher must be directed to delaying entry into the social world. This necessitates a tutor not himself corrupted by that world – a person knowledgeable of its ways yet not part of it. That the tutor's name should turn out to be Jean-Jacques is not surprising. Not even the parents can be entrusted with the task – they may be sensitive enough to employ the ideal tutor but they remain themselves members of civil society with a role and a status. The tutor is "the minister of nature."[6] Later Jean-Jacques proclaims that he is Émile's true father as it is he who has made him a man.[7]

If Émile is not to be educated by society he must be educated by "nature." He must learn in a spontaneous, unforced manner. The secret of teaching, especially in the earliest stages, is to do nothing.[8] It would be entirely wrong to conclude from this that Rousseau can be invoked in support of an extreme libertarianism according to which the child is free to discover what it will. This is to ignore the context of Rousseau's critique of society and his fear of its contamination. The child is not free to learn what it will since, without guidance, it is as likely to explore corruption as discover goodness. Émile's education is intended to be highly disciplined, but the discipline is to come from nature, not society. A defining feature of the illiberalism of modern society is the dependence of men on the will, whim, and social and economic interests of others. Instead of growing up to be self-reliant, men must, actually or metaphorically, sell themselves to others – a relationship that demeans both buyer and seller.[9] Men are, however, dependent on nature and to the extent that they must be mutually dependent on one another the reason for that dependence should be as solid as that occasioned by nature itself.

The child must therefore commence by experiencing its dependence on nature. The difficulty, as so many critics have pointed out, is that, as Compayré put it, "nature does not consent to play the part of schoolmistress."[10] This is why the tutor is required to act as nature's minister. He must arrange his pupil's encounters with nature so that the appropriate lessons may be learned. At the same time the pupil must be unaware of these contrivances. He must believe that it is unmediated nature that is the teacher. Deception is justifiable in the interests of producing a man free of deception. Rousseau wishes the child to learn from the experience of his confrontations with nature that the world does not succumb to his will and that his liberty involves recognising that it has bounds against which it is pointless to complain and strive. These bounds are not to appear arbitrary but are to be set into the nature of "things." They are not the product of the assertion of an alien human will that is the typical constriction imposed by conventional education designed for the very purpose of habituating the child to the arbitrary opinion of established elites. Thus from an early age the child should come to appreciate that there is no use in wailing against reality. The answer that "there is no more" will be acceptable to a child,[11] whereas the capricious withholding of what is desired will only accustom him to a world of patronage in which favours can be variously granted, withdrawn, and, still worse, bargained over.

Here too, however, there is a disjunction between appearance and reality. The tutor's commands are to have the weight and semblance of necessity even if they do not have this character in fact. Like the lessons in which Émile is "lost" in the woods so that he can "find" his way home by the stars, the problem has been set by the teacher. It is this that has led commentators to argue that Rousseau's "natural education" is as artificial as any that he criticised and, moreover, that it has parallels with the subtle educative role of the Legislator in guiding the people to liberty in the *Social Contract*.[12] Although Rousseau constantly asserts that nature must not be represented and that the child must learn by direct experience of things and not their images, nature is being constantly represented by the tutor. However, Rousseau wishes the reader to accept that he, Jean-Jacques, is unlike any other representative, whether in the political realm or the theatre, in that he is never interpreting or interposing his persona between nature and man but is nature's direct delegate.

Rousseau's celebrated designation of his method of early education as "negative education"[13] and, still more, his alternative term, the "inactive method,"[14] are misleading if they are taken to imply that the tutor will do nothing and simply allow events to unfold. Even if he appears to do nothing he is actively involved in purging the environment of all vestiges of the social as it is understood by conventional opinion. A better term might have been "defensive" or "protective" education. However, Rousseau wished to oppose his approach to what, with justification, he termed "positive" education.[15] The positive method was that prevalent among Enlightenment thinkers on education who, from the standpoint of Rousseau's critique, were merely repeating the educational errors of their opponents. It might also be regarded as the policy preferred by those politicians who look to the educational system both to sustain social norms and to achieve economic progress by an improvement in "educational standards." Positive education consists, at its crudest, in treating the child's mind as a blank sheet on which can be printed, at as early an age as is feasible, the appropriate ideas about the world and society. The temptation of such a vision is that a child can quite rapidly acquire the skills that society considers it needs. Teaching becomes a technique of transmitting ideas, and the success of both teacher and child can be assessed by tests of achievement. In the eighteenth century, Priestley in England and Helvétius in France (one of Rousseau's implicit targets) were prime exponents of the positive method.[16]

Rousseau condemned positive education as externally imposed on the child and as designed to reinforce social convention. It ignored the manner in which the child developed and instead sought to force it to mature prematurely. Education became a form of equine dressage. The child was being expected to reason and to verbalise its impressions before it was ready. The result was at best to produce apparent prodigies of learning who had no real understanding but merely parrotted conventional ideas. Repetition of words actually impeded an appreciation of things. Even the wise Locke treated the child from the outset as a reasoning being.[17] In this Rousseau both exaggerated his difference from Locke and underestimated the extent that Locke had cautioned against treating the young child as capable of adult understanding. Nevertheless, Rousseau astutely recognised that Locke was the intellectual source of positive education and was not entirely mistaken in thinking that his educational method was predicated on producing the young man who could contribute to the rational administration of his father's estate.

Rousseau, in total contrast to the positive method, called on the tutor to delay rather than hasten the learning process. The great skill of teaching in its earliest stages consisted not in finding time to instruct the pupil in every subject that was supposedly required in a kind of national curriculum, but in losing time.[18] To rush to place the young child into formal instruction was totally misplaced. The same was true of attempts to instruct the child in morality, whether through systems of ethics or religion. By contrast, positive educationists such as Helvétius were calling for the production of ethical catechisms to replace those of the church. Rousseau insisted that children lack any understanding of notions of duty that they can come to grasp only when confronted with choices they are required to make for themselves. The most that could be achieved by positive intervention was a modification in behaviour that was not, however, grounded in a proper appreciation of the meaning of the action. Typical was the practice of using rewards as a bribe to induce the child to act charitably. The only consequence is that one learns to be economical with charity and to act solely when one can expect some return.[19] Such an identification of self-love and social duty might have been sufficient to sustain a society operating on principles of self-interest but was not a basis on which to inculcate a genuine sense of duty and respect for others. Modern education could scarcely be better designed to prevent the emergence of the true citizen who, rather than engaging in trading personal and sectional advantages, will self-consciously lay aside partial interests and impartially consult his general will in pursuit of the general good.

Rousseau's essential requirement was that education must be sensitive to the child in the child rather than constantly thinking about the future adult and its suitability to society, especially as it is currently conducted. The child must be allowed the time and room to develop at its own pace. Modes of learning and teaching must therefore proceed in line with the normal evolution of the child's capacities. Émile is portrayed as the ideal – typical boy without any distinctive qualities or abilities, although Rousseau insists that any practical scheme of education must also take into account the specific dispositions of the pupil. The extent to which children were entirely alike at birth and infinitely malleable by education was one of the contentious issues in eighteenth-century philosophy of education.[20] For Rousseau the existence of different natural dispositions should imply that an education according to nature should respect them and permit them to flourish – a view to wield a profound influence on subsequent educational thought. Nevertheless, Rousseau's mode of argument in Émile does not permit a full exploration of the limits to the plurality of lifestyles that might be expected to flow from this acceptance of human variation, even though it has major implications for the ease with which the recipients of a natural education can live together. It is possible to infer, however, that even the most idiosyncratic child will be pulled up short by the nature of things, by "necessity" as it is experienced first in the natural, then in the moral, and, ultimately though too rarely, in the political worlds.

Each stage in the evolution of the child demands an appropriate educative response. Rousseau distinguishes four periods in child development, or, more strictly, boyhood development, as girls must be treated differently in accordance with their nature. The stages are infancy, childhood, prepuberty, and adolescence. Although Rousseau does not intend to suggest that these constitute abrupt changes, with the possible exception of the last, he does wish the teacher to adjust the mode of instruction to the transitions in the child's capacities, which are often matters of degree.

Adopting much of post-Lockean epistemology, Rousseau held that the source of knowledge lay in experience of the senses.[21] The mind of the infant and the young child were entirely dominated by the sensations that they received from their environment. Rousseau and the positive educationists were on common ground in recognising that the inference for education was the necessity of controlling this environment so that the child received only those impressions that it was appropriate for it to experience. Where they differed, and the sceptic may cast doubt on the reality of this difference, was that the positivists sought to provide a learning environment that would lead the child to make its way in a society that they might hope, if they were liberals (like Helvétius) to reform but not transform or, if they were conservatives, they would aim to reproduce through the next generation. Rousseau's negativism consisted in avoiding any impact from the social environment that might divert the child from the path of discovering its own potential while, at the same time, also understanding the legitimate boundaries placed on self-enactment by nature and, eventually, by the equal entitlements of other human beings.

Rousseau presents this protective education as a liberation from the constrictions of conventional child care. It starts with infancy when the baby should be opened to the sensations of the outside world. It is true, as many commentators have pointed out, that Rousseau's strictures against the swaddling of infants and his calls for young children to be allowed to run and exercise were common-places among reforming educators rather than novelties. What is more novel is that these were not conceived merely as conducive to a healthy life, which was the concern of most of this literature, but were an aspect of liberation. The crowding in of sensations on the child posed problems that stimulated it to attempt the solutions that were in its power. Some of the puzzles it can learn to over-come, but it is also an essential part of education that one confronts difficulties that are insuperable, that one is at the limit of not only one's own but of human capacities. This is the significance of Rousseau's repeated insistence on the child's encounter with necessity and the nature of things. In this respect the education of the infant and the young child varies in only degree rather than in essentials. Infants and young children differ mainly in their strength to do what nature permits. Both in their own ways are subjugated to nature by being taught that there will be a response only to their genuine needs and not to their mere wills.

Deliberate exposure to the rigours of an outdoor life strengthens the child even if it may also occasionally suffer injury, which is an instance of nature teaching the limits of the child's capacity. It is true that the tutor moderates the lessons of nature – while permitting his charge to run barefoot he first checks that any broken glass is removed. Even serious illness can be nature's technique of teaching, which leads Rousseau to be ambivalent about inoculation against smallpox.[22] Most disease and illness are the products of social life, abetted by their agents in the medical profession.

Throughout Rousseau's educational programme the aim is to enable the child to work out for itself both its own capabilities and their limits. The liberating and the disciplinary objectives of the project are equally essential. Neither can be attained if this discovery – learning, as it came to be called, is subject to intermediation from others – or, more strictly, if the pupil becomes aware of intermediation's occurring. Without the child's realising it, the tutor leads him to handle objects and appreciate their qualities through the senses. In the form of "object learning" this entered modern education through the teaching of Pestalozzi. In play and in country walks he is brought to experience nature directly. In complete contrast to those who wish to develop the child's gifts rapidly, Rousseau delays the acquisition of reading and writing. Books interpose the ideas of the author between the matter and the reader, rendering it less possible for the child to think its own thoughts: "the child who reads does not think, he only reads; he is not informing himself, he learns words."[23] Speech and song are better vehicles for the expression of the child's own understanding of the world. This understanding will, if the education has gone well, be clear and exact. The child will attempt to satisfy its curiosity as to how the world works and this curiosity can be aroused by the tutor who can respond

to it by answering questions directly and at the child's level of understanding and without adding any interpretation.

The third stage of education is the prepubescent age from, by
Rousseau's estimation, twelve to fifteen. For the first time, and hardly
surprisingly from the standpoint of positive education, Rousseau is
in a hurry.[24] The onset of puberty and the passions will change everything and Rousseau now has a lot to pack into the curriculum.
Nevertheless his approach does not radically alter, even if the tutor
has to be more obviously interventionist in the way he steers Emile
towards the situations from which he is to obtain instruction. He
still builds on what has gone before. The tutor continues to stimulate the pupil's curiosity, relying on its self-interest to find out only
those things that are directly useful to its immediate concerns. This
will again concentrate attention on "facts." All forms of representation are to be avoided in favour of learning by direct experience.
The thing rather than its sign is to be shown. One does not teach
geography and the movement of the earth around the sun by globes
and maps but by allowing the child to see the sun appear on an early
morning walk and start to puzzle over the effect and its cause. What
Rousseau claims, in terms to be followed by "progressive educationists" ever since, is that he is not teaching science but how to do
science.[25] He is equipping the person to think for himself and not to
depend on any interpreter or representative – a lesson to be central
to Rousseau's conception of the man and the citizen. The only book
Émile is to be given is *Robinson Crusoe*, in which he will read of the
individual's lone struggle to come to terms with natural necessity
unencumbered with the judgments of others.[26]

Self-reliance in thought is to be matched by physical and economic
independence. Émile learns a manual occupation. Manual work as
an extension of the body is closer to nature than intellectual and
imaginative production are. These depend for their value on opinion
and are hence subject to social contamination and the fluctuation of
fashion.[27] Rousseau foresees an era of revolution at hand in which
all such values will be in confusion. In such a world the natural
skills will retain their enduring utility and enable Émile to face all
eventualities.[28]

A foundation has been laid at the end of Book III for Émile by the
age of fifteen as an autarchic being equipped to look after himself
and taught to view the world from an independent standpoint. He

does not need to follow the opinions of others about how the natural world works because his education has pemitted him to think these things out for himself. However, he now faces new challenges and his education must adapt, even if it retains certain fundamental features. Rousseau famously describes puberty as a "second birth" for men.[29] They begin to be driven by their inclinations to others – particularly female others – but they also become truly aware for the first time of others in general and of their alternative conceptions of the world. Emile has learned to exist but now he must learn to live, which means learning to live in society. Education must prepare him more fully for this novel experience and must continue to protect him from society's baneful effects until he can be trusted to act independently, yet precisely in the manner that he has been taught.

Education must become more positive, at least in the sense that the teacher must now be more open about the guidance he has been giving. He must explain more frankly how much he has been acting on behalf of nature in filtering out the contaminations of the social. The pupil can no longer be protected by ignorance but must come to rely on knowledge.[30] The natural instincts are to look benevolently on others and to sympathise especially with their misfortunes. However, Émile must be disabused of any naiveté concerning social men. Unlike Émile, they wear masks, and he needs enlightenment as to where his affections should truly be directed, especially in the case of love.[31]

In one major respect, however, the educational project remains unaltered. The prevailing attitude is defensive, and the policy is still to ensure that nothing is taught until the pupil is emotionally and cognitively ready. It is now a matter of urgency that the young man learn about human behaviour, but this knowledge must, as ever, be acquired in as pure a manner as possible. Opinion must be shunned. Therefore Rousseau desires that one learn from a study of remote rather than contemporary societies and recommends Thucydides as the historian who relies on reportage of facts and eschews interpretation and mediation.[32] This is to be followed by reading the lives of the ancients, not to be them – not even to be Cato – but to learn integrity from them.

By now Émile has learned what it means to be an autonomous human being. He recognises that one must think one's own thoughts. But he still lacks experience of the social world and, hence, his education is far from complete. This situation demands a transformation in the relations between master and student. If the teacher is to continue to instruct somone who possesses the basic elements of autonomy he must do so on the foundation of the consent of the pupil. Émile's tutor puts this openly to him and in response Émile contracts to place himself under his guidance. This is dependence but dependence which is consciously assumed. Émile asks his "protector and master" not to surrender his authority but, in terms reminiscent of the Social Contract, to "force me to be my own master and to obey not my senses but my reason".[33] Education can advance further since the disciplines proposed by the teacher as prerequisites for the attainment of full autonomy are now willed by the pupil. Self-discipline ostensibly replaces external manipulation. Émile eventually absorbs his teacher's lessons so completely that he can be safely let out of the master's sight with the total confidence that he will do what the master has taught him, which is to live according to nature even in the midst of society.

The educational contract entitles the tutor to prepare Émile for marriage, arrange his bride, Sophie, and instruct both partners in martial conduct. This is far from completing his education since before Émile can be a full mamber of society and a true moral agent he must mix more with others. A person can only claim to be a moral being if he is aware of alternatives and consciously chooses the right path. Émile's exposure to social alternatives has so far been deliberately limited. Although he is well armed against corrupting life-styles, he has not been truly tested. Accordingly, before his marriage Émile is torn away and sent on a tour of countries to experience the world. Book V of *Émile* is the story of man's encounter with the other, not only in the form of woman but of plural world views. Émile's travels are not merely a test of his commitment to Sophie but also of the teachings of his tutor or, in other words, of nature.

Yet again the tutor delays the point at which Émile can assume full responsibility. The travels are, it has been well said, Emile's descent into the Cave,[34] although, unlike Plato's philosopher, Émile is not to rule over others so much as to learn how to live with some personal integrity among them. On his tour he encounters worlds in which men constantly wear masks, desire what they do not need, are driven by opinion and not truth, and are at one and the same time exploiters and exploited. He also discovers that these worlds are sustained and reproduced by political orders. This is a political education provided by direct experience, but it is also supplemented by the tutor's succinct resumé of the *Social Contract* and its explanation of the true foundation of political right.[35] However, this political education is not necessarily intended to inspire Émile to political action. Émile has learned that there are no longer enough men like him to create a *patrie* and a citizenry. He has also learned, however, that some form of political order is necessary in the modern world as it is only within its framework that one can attempt to live a virtuous life. Accordingly the lesson of the lecture on political right is that a man should live quietly and do good at a local and personal level. He may even perform some of the duties of a civil life despite the fact that there is no true republic and therefore no genuine citizenship. Although states are not grounded on the social contract and although they can claim only the "simulacra of laws" they have some call on Émile's allegiance so long as the self-interest of the government, in a bargain typical of such societies, motivates it to protect the security of the subject.[36]

Émile's own education ensures that he, unlike others, will surmount self-interest and be motivated by the public good. In such a society he is not called on to be a leader or a hero – and it is unlikely that his fellow subjects would see him in such roles. Nor, in one of those typically poignant intrusions of the authorial presence, is he expected to try by his writings to contribute to his country's welfare from beyond its frontiers, as was Rousseau's own fate.[37] Beneath the apparently idyllic concluding pages of *Émile* there is the clear sense that Rousseau is offering his reader only a second best.[38] It is an education for a profoundly unsatisfactory world, and it largely consists in learning about it only to avoid it so far as is feasible. If Émile is not a hermit, he is far from being a citizen. Émile and Sophie play their own educative parts in setting an example by the governance of their household, but this form of benevolent despotism falls far short of teaching their "subjects" how to live the autonomous lives to which they are equally entitled according to Rousseau's principles of political right. *Émile* is in a sense, Rousseau's most practical contribution to educational thought in that, although not a treatise, it is supposedly adapted to social reality as he perceived it. In the past there had been an alternative of citizen education that is no longer available. Neither was an ideal.

LEARNING TO BE WOMEN

By giving his essay *On Education* the primary title of *Émile*, Rousseau was signalling that his chief interest was in the education of males rather than females. Sophie does not make her appearance until the final Book.[39] Nevertheless, Rousseau's views on the education of women were the subject of extensive comment as well as excoriation by even the mildest of feminist critics from the outset. The fact that Rousseau's ideas on the role of women were welcomed by contemporary conservatives and also by liberals whose concern for the rights of men did not extend to a similar conviction about the status of women has understandably led to the belief that, in this sphere, Rousseau was, most unusually for him, mouthing the male conventionalities of his time. However, it is important to recognise that Rousseau's conservatism was of a different order than that of his contemporaries and also that his views on female education were, certainly compared with those of many liberals, internally consistent given the acceptance of his fundamental premise that there existed distinctive feminine virtues – a premise denied from the beginning by such feminist critics as Mary Wollstonecraft and Catharine Macaulay.[40]

Rousseau opens his treatment of women in Book V in a manner that suggests that men and women are, with one exception, identical "machines." The exception is their sexual nature, but this proves to be all pervasive. In this crucial respect the two sexes are both opposites and complementary. Both require education for their respective sexually conditioned roles. The consequence is that the education of women is diametrically opposed to the education of men and yet, according to Rousseau, both are equally "natural."[41] From the assumption that woman's natural mission is to please, support, and, ultimately, influence men – and specifically their future husbands – Rousseau infers that the appropriate education for them will be the mirror image of that suited to men. The supportive role is the *telos* that determines the life of a woman from girlhood, whereas the sexual dimension becomes a factor in the life of men only with the second birth of puberty, and even then the object of education is to delay and limit its tendency to dominate.

Whereas the aim of male education is to negate societal conditioning and prepare for a life in which men will think their own thoughts, women should be subject to social constraint and supervision from infancy. Although they are naturally equipped, physically and emotionally, to attract men, girls still need training in how to use this equipment and, above all, they need to be disciplined to direct their attractions solely to gaining and retaining their husbands. To be faithful and to be considered faithful are essential. This implies that women must learn that they are always subject to the judgements of men. Parental education must insist on this from the early years. Whereas Émile's education is initially disguised surveillance succeeded by consciously authorised supervision as a step towards autonomy, Sophie's is open surveillance that continues into adulthood when Émile takes over this task from her father. Émile learns about "things"; Sophie must learn about people and opinions. Emile's tutor delays introducing him to religion and the precepts of morality until his experience permits him to understand for himself; Sophie should accept her mother's religion when a girl and her husband's when a woman. The female mind is incapable of sustaining abstract thought and should not attempt theology or philosophy, which merely lead them into forms of fanaticism.[42] Women should be taught to develop their specific sensitivity to the behaviour and sentiments of individuals – a trait that makes them the helpmeets of their own menfolk but renders them unsuited to politics that, ideally, requires a commitment to the general will and not to particular wills.

The female requires a training, from the mother, alongside an education in submission to social opinion, in the arts of pleasing men and persuading them to do, as if it were by their own accord, what the woman wishes. These skills include deception, sexual teasing, and emotional blackmail, summed up in the term "coquetry."[43] Such falsity is learned, yet is true to feminine nature. Again the contrast with the education of Émile is startling: He is brought up to be honest, plain dealing, and forthright, like Molière's austere Alceste.

In spite of some very obvious bows to the most prejudiced male stereotypes of female behaviour and capabilities, Rousseau does distance himself from some conventional views. The opinion to which Sophie, as the idealised woman, should be enslaved is not that of modern society. Modern female education distorts the natural talents of women for coquetry to produce the kinds of infidelity and cynicism that Rousseau would have found portrayed by Laclos in

Les Liaisons Dangereuses. The ease with which this can occur is indicated in *Émile et Sophie, ou Les Solitaires*, the fragmentary sequel to Émile in which Sophie, removed from her simple rural environment and the watchful supervision of her husband, is seduced literally and metaphorically by Parisian society and the marriage is destroyed. Female education is shown to be precarious, dependent as it is on constant surveillance. Émile, it seems, comes through the experience, sustained by an education that is internalised.

Modern education also produces the *savantes* of the salons to whom their liberal admirers would still, with less consistency in this regard than Rousseau, deny political and civil rights. In this respect he is again challenging the reproductive tendency of contemporary education, even if in favour of something more radically austere than a conventional conservative, wishing to uphold existing familial structures, would contemplate.

LEARNING TO BE A CITIZEN

Although, as has been argued earlier, Émile has to come to terms with a form of civil life, however inadequate, Rousseau insists that this is not the place to find an account of citizen education. Indeed, he declares at the outset of *Émile* that private and political education are at the opposite poles, and he refers readers who seek an account of the latter to Plato's *Republic* and the practices of Sparta.[44] Although Émile's is an education against society, a citizen is educated by society. The education of the individual treats the pupil as a distinct entity; the education of the citizen regards him as a fraction of a whole. More fundamentally still, whereas Émile is given an education in accordance with nature, the objective of citizen education is to "denature" men.[45]

Although Rousseau is unable to offer his readers a single account of citizen education comparable with that of Plato, he might, taking his *oeuvre* as a whole, have directed them to a number of expositions to be found mainly in the *Letter to M. D'Alembert, Considerations on the Government of Poland*, and the encyclopaedia article on *Political Economy*. What they would have read was a characteristically vivid and passionate portrayal of a manner of education that is a mirror image of that in *Émile*. Nevertheless, even if the education of *Émile* is a second best, it does not follow that his account of the education of the citizen presents the ideal, despite the warmth with which it is delineated. Rousseau is too aware of the shortcomings of even the most comprehensive attempts at political education for it not to be also an alternative second best to an ideal in which one learns to become at the same time an individual and a member of a true community of equals.

To form citizens is, Rousseau asserts, not the work of a day but must commence with the children. Hence, the office of public education is "the most important business of the state."[46] Despite his assurance that the teaching of citizens adheres to his belief in "negative education"[47] this is true only to the limited extent that the state, as tutor, should prevent vice before it seeks to instil virtue. Most of the other features of negative education are reversed, point by point. There is little sense that the state will seek to waste time. Rather, tuition starts early with the direction of the child's play into festivals that commemorate the nation's history and identity. The objective is, in contrast to that in bringing up Émile, to subject the child from the earliest days to the influence of public opinion. Children should be taught only by nationals, and they must learn national geography and history. There is no attempt, as with Émile, to eschew interpretation and present the unadulterated facts. Discovery–learning has no place in this scheme.[48] Travel beyond the country's borders is discouraged, cosmopolitanism is resisted, and distinctiveness reinforced through the wearing of national costume.

Citizen education has to be continuing education. The pupils learn in the course of active life. It is sustained through participation in public sports and festivals and involvement in the citizen militia.[49] The runners in the races, the soldiers in the regiment, the dancers in the festivals are learning to be men of political action and decision. Simultaneously they are imbibing from their fellow participants the distinctive *mores* of their nation. The denaturing process is achieved by the subjecting of all conduct to constant surveillance. Because political education is at the opposite pole to individual education this has the curious effect that such submission to opinion has more in common with the education of women in *Émile* than with the education for self-sufficiency of Émile himself. Not that women escape from denaturing and, in this respect at least, they take on some of the attributes of citizenship even where they lack any direct franchise. The Spartan mother who places the victory of her country ahead of the death in battle of her five sons is a *citoyenne* in her very unnaturalness.[50]

Whereas independence from other men is the goal for Émile, the citizen must learn to recognise his dependence on his fellows. He has to be taught that he is a fraction of the state and that his life gains meaning only from his participation in the state's maintenance. The state has responsibility to persuade him of this relationship. Rousseau confers the office of public education on the elderly and on heroic warriors who teach as much by example as by precept. These would "transmit from age to age, to generations to come, the experience and talents of rulers, the courage and virtue of citizens, and common emulation in all to live and die for their country."[51]

Whatever the attractions of such a political education, it was not available in Rousseau's time as there were no longer the small autarchic states that produced citizens and depended, in turn, on them. The modern state commands subjects instead of ruling over citizens able actively to participate in shaping their own laws and manners. The Hobbesian state that ensured a framework of security for the competitive pursuit of individual advantage was an accurate portrayal of political reality. However, not only could one no longer go back to the ancient past in which there were fatherlands, this was no longer a relevant ideal for modern man. Rightly or wrongly, autonomy, independence, and individual liberty were part of a modern consciousness that could not contemplate the dependence demanded by Spartan citizenship. If there were ever to be a possibility of anything comparable with ancient citizenship it would have to be grounded on conceptions of individual self-determination foreign to the old models and not cultivated by a pure political education.

LEARNING TO BE GOOD MEN *AND* GOOD CITIZENS

If both the individual education of Émile and the political education of the citizen are second bests, can one infer from them what might be required, and in what conditions, for teaching an individual to be both a man and a citizen? In the *Social Contract*, the society that exemplifies political right is one that is founded on the free choice of individuals to bind themselves to uphold law that they have participated in making. The law is the manifestation of the general will that emerges when each individual consciously sets aside his private advantage in favour of what he has concluded to be the public good. This determination is reached after deliberation uncontaminated by the personal or sectional interests of others and unaffected by their rhetoric and arts of persuasion.[52] The qualities of self-reliance, self-assertion, and self-respect that such political will requires are, in many ways, those that Émile's education is designed to encourage. They have been, however, intended to arm Émile against a corrupting society rather than assist him in contributing to a just one. They allow him to safeguard his own integrity more than encourage him to act collectively.

More seems to be required, therefore, than, as Peter Gay has suggested, a society of Émiles if there is to be a reintegration of the good man and the good citizen.[53] Émile in contemporary society has the character of Molière's Alceste but he needs to add the features of Cato. This is feasible within only very particular social, economic, and cultural conditions. It requires an economy in which people can live largely self-sufficient lives such that noone is dependent on another for his livelihood and, by inference, noone fears to think his own thoughts.[54] In settled conditions of equality, Rousseau argues, there will be less occasion for the emergence of a politics of interests and factions. Citizens will enjoy a shared experience that they draw on when considering the general needs of the community. Such experience arms each citizen with a general will stronger than the particular will that tends to triumph in modern unequal societies.[55] The manners of the community in which children and adults are educated come to take on the inevitability of nature. The civil laws should appear to grow out of these manners in such a way that they acquire something of the necessity of natural laws. Though the laws are manmade, dependence on them becomes comparable with the dependence on things, which was the first lesson Émile had to learn.[56]

Émile's tutor made him free by teaching him to yield to necessity, and when he reaches the point at which he can take up the role of citizen Émile "chooses" to reject the chains of opinion and accept those of nature and the laws.[57] Although the chains of nature are to be accepted by any properly educated man regardless of his society, the chains of law are fully legitimate only when one can be confident that they proceed from the free decision of men who are equal with oneself in their knowledge and understanding of the community and in their commitment to the public good. On this basis one can have some assurance that the outcome of one's vote in an assembly is likely to coincide with what is right for the community and with one's own will as a citizen.[58] If the laws are those the wise man would recognise as right and has participated in making, they can be defended as one's own. Only then can one unite the virtue that Socrates taught with the sense of fellowship taught by Cato.[59] It might be possible for Émile, even in modern society, to learn to aspire to the virtue of Socrates who himself lived in a country already ruined. The inspiration of a Cato, however, was incommunicable in a society of strangers.

It is only in these ideal conditions that Rousseau can envisage the reconciliation of an education for autonomy with an education for community. For many the twin goals are unreconciled and, perhaps, unreconcilable. They would be sceptical as to whether a homogeneous community could provide the environment in which an individual could learn to develop autonomy. This might require a critical distance from political institutions that may more readily be the means of social reproduction than of innovation. John Stuart Mill perceived this when he stated that the "national education existing in any political society" was "at once the principal cause of its permanence as a society and the chief cause of its progressiveness."[60] Like Rousseau, Mill also looked to an ancient model for an example of the formation of citizens, but it was to Athens, with its active and educative participation and its variety of ideas, and not to Sparta with its homogeneity and discipline.[61] Helvétius believed that Rousseau was an excessive admirer of Sparta and that he remained "trop fidèle imitateur de Platon."[62] Rousseau was, however, more convinced that closely knit communities did not necessarily suppress individuality and inventiveness. The basis of this conviction lay in Rousseau's vision of a polity in which each citizen could play an equal part in shaping the laws and, through them, in the mutual education of fellow citizens. Equal participation was, he supposed, the best guarantee against mastery by others and against their attempts to use positive techniques of education in furtherance of their domination.

At the same time, the forlorn nature of this aspiration to equality offered sound reasons for exploring the second best of an education designed to assist a person to live a passable imitation of a virtuous life in the midst of a society bent on teaching vice. In this sense *Émile* is a practical work of education and also a tragic one. Some follow-ers of Rousseau have detected a glimmer of hope and have wished to transform society by means of a new generation that, through a process of discovery – learning, can work out for itself a way of liv-ing in communal harmony, and, it has to be acknowledged, others have been tempted into programmes of political reeducation from above that Rousseau would surely have disavowed. In education, even more than in other areas in which he has exerted such an im-pact on subsequent imagination, his successors have continued to face Rousseau's own central dilemma of how to turn "effect" into cause.

ENDNOTES

1 Rousseau, *Émile, or On Education.* Introduction, Translation and Notes by Allan Bloom, Penguin, Harmondsworth, 1979, p. 94. (Henceforth cited as *Émile*); French edition cited will be from *Oeuvres complètes*, eds. Bernard Gagnerin and Marcel Raymond, Bibliothèque de la Pléiade, Gallimard, Paris, 1969, Vol. IV, p. 324. (henceforth cited as OC, followed by volume number and page).

2 The centrality of education to Rousseau's concerns means that much of the vast secondary literature refers to the subject. Particularly sig-nificant treatments of the educational thought include Peter Jimack, *Rousseau, Émile*, London, Grant and Cutler, 1983; Jimack, "*La genèse et la rédaction de l'Emile de J-J. Rousseau: Étude sur l'histoire de l'ouvrage jusqu'à sa parution*," in *Studies on Voltaire and the Eighteenth Cen-tury*, ed. T. Besterman, Vol. XIII, Voltaire Foundation, Geneva, 1960; N.J. Dent, *Rousseau*, Blackwell, Oxford, 1988; G.H. Bantock, *Studies in the History of Educational Theory*, Vol. I, *Artifice and Nature*, 1350–1765, London, Allen and Unwin, 1980 and Vol. II, *The Minds and the Masses*, 1760–1980, London, Allen and Unwin, 1984; W. Boyd, *The Ed-ucational Theory of Jean-Jacques Rousseau*, London, Longman, 1911; J. Shklar, *Men and Citizens: A Study of Rousseau's Social Theory*, Cam-bridge, U.K., Cambridge University Press, 1969; D. Steiner, *Rethink-ing Democratic Education*, Baltimore, MD, Johns Hopkins Press, 1994; J. Château, *Jean-Jacques Rousseau: Sa philosophie de l'éducation*, Paris, Vrin, 1962; P. Burgelin, *La philosophie de l'existence de J-J. Rousseau*, Paris, Presses Universitaires de France, 1952.

3 See P. Bourdieu and J-C. Passeron, *Reproduction in Education, Society and Culture*, 2nd ed., London, Sage, 1990.

4 Rousseau, *The Social Contract*, translated by G.D.H. Cole, revised and augmented by J.H. Brumfitt and John C. Hall, Dent, Everyman's Library, 1986, p. 216; *Du contrat Social*, OC III, 383, 1963.
5 Letter to Philibert Cramer, 13 Oct. 1764, *Correspondance complète de Jean-Jacques Rousseau*, édition critique, établie et annotée par R. A. Leigh, The Voltaire Foundation, Banbury, 1974, Letter 3564, Vol. XXI, p. 248.
6 *Émile*, p. 317; OC IV, 639.
7 *Émile*, p. 407; OC IV, 765.
8 *Émile*, p. 93; OC IV, 323.
9 *Discourse on the Origin of Inequality*, translated by G.D.H. Cole, revised and augmented by J.H. Brumfitt and John C. Hall, Dent, Everyman's Library, 1986, p.92; OC III, 171; *Social Contract*, p. 181; OC III, 351.
10 G. Compayré, *Jean-Jacques Rousseau and Education from Nature*, London, Harrap, 1908, p. 30.
11 *Émile*, p. 91; OC IV, 320.
12 For a shrewd assessment of the artificiality of Rousseau's educative methods see G.H. Bantock, *Studies in the History of Educational Theory*, Vol. I, Chap. 12 and Vol. II, Chap. I Oxford, 1974.
13 *Émile*, p. 93; OC IV, 323; *Lettre à Christophe de Beaumont, Archevêque de Paris* , OC IV, 945.
14 *Émile*, p. 117; OC IV, 359.
15 *Lettre à Christophe de Beaumont*, OC IV, 945.
16 Joseph Priestley, *Miscellaneous Observations Relating to Education*, Cork, Burleish, 1780; Claude Helvétius, *De L'Esprit*, Paris, 1758; the posthumous *De l'homme, de ses facultés intellectuelles et de son education*, London, 1773 contains a critique of Rousseau in Section V.
17 *Émile*, p. 89; OC IV, 317.
18 *Émile*, p. 93; OC IV, 323.
19 *Émile*, p. 103; OC IV, 338-9.
20 See John Passmore, *The Perfectibility of Man*, London, Duckworth, 1970.
21 See discussions by Peter Jimack, *Rousseau: Émile; La Genèse, etc.*
22 *Émile*, p. 131; OC IV, 378-9.
23 *Émile*, p. 168; OC IV, 430.
24 *Émile*, p. 172; OC IV, 435-6.
25 *Émile*, p. 207; OC IV, 487.
26 *Émile*, pp. 184-5; OC IV, 455.
27 *Émile*, p. 186; OC IV, 456-7.
28 *Émile*, pp. 194-6; OC IV, 468-471.
29 *Émile*, pp. 211-2; OC IV, 489-90.

30 *Émile*, p. 318; OC IV, 641.

31 *Émile*, p. 214; OC IV, 493–4.

32 *Émile*, p. 239; OC IV, 528–9.

33 *Émile*, p. 325; OC IV, pp. 651–2.

34 Burgelin, *La philosophie de l'existence*, p. 487.

35 *Émile*, pp. 458–67; OC IV, 836–49.

36 *Émile*, p. 473; OC IV, 858.

37 *Émile*, p. 474; OC IV, 858–9.

38 See Peter Jimack, *Rousseau, Émile*, pp. 20–21.

39 Accordingly some of the most perceptive interpreters of *Émile* have tended, for various reasons, to devalue the significance of Rousseau's discussion of female education: see P. Jimack, *Rousseau, Emile*, p. 12; Jimack *La Genèse*, etc., pp. 199–207; N. Dent, *Rousseau*, p. 153. One of the shrewdest assessments remains Pierre Burgelin, " *L'éducation de Sophie*," in *Annales de la société J-J Rousseau*, Vol. 35, 1959–62, pp. 113–37. See also Joel Schwartz, *The Sexual Politics of Jean-Jacques Rousseau*, University of Chicago Press, Chicago, 1984; Margaret Canovan, "Rousseau's Two Concepts of Citizenship" in eds. E. Kennedy and S. Mendus, *Women in Western Political Philosophy*, Wheatsheaf, Brighton, 1987, pp. 78–105; Ursula Vogel, "'But in a republic, men are needed': guarding the bounds of liberty" in ed. R. Wokler, *Rousseau and Liberty*, Manchester University Press, Manchester, 1995, pp. 213–30.

40 Mary Wollstonecraft, *A Vindication of the Rights of Woman*, ed. S. Tomaselli, Cambridge University Press, Cambridge, U.K., 1995, pp. 124–5: Catharine Macaulay, *Letters on Education, with Observations on Religious and Metaphysical Subjects*, London, 1790, Letters XXII–XXIV.

41 *Émile*, p. 365; OC IV, 703.

42 *Émile*, p. 377; OC IV, 721.

43 *Émile*, pp. 384–7; OC IV, 733–7.

44 *Émile*, p. 39–40; OC IV, 248–50.

45 *Émile*, p. 40; OC IV, 250.

46 *Political Economy*, translated and edited by G. D. H. Cole, Everyman's Library, London, 1986, pp. 147–9; OC III, 258–61.

47 *The Government of Poland*, translated, with an introduction by Willmore Kendall, Hackett Indianapolis, In, 1985, p. 21; OC III, 968.

48 *Poland*, pp. 18–22; OC III, 966–8.

49 *Politics and the Arts; Letter to M. D'Alembert on the Theatre*, translated with notes and introduction by Allan Bloom, Cornell University Press, Ithaca, NY, 1968, pp. 126–7, 135–6; OC V, 115–6, 123–5.

50 *Émile*, p. 40; OC IV, 249.

51 *Political Economy*, p. 150; OC III, 261.

52 *Social Contract*, pp. 203–4; OC III, 371–2.
53 Peter Gay, *The Enlightenment: An Interpretation. Vol II: The Science of Freedom*, Weidenfeld and Nicolson, London, 1970, p. 549.
54 *Social Contract*, p. 225; OC III, 391–2.
55 *Émile*, p. 85; OC IV, 311.
56 *Émile*, p. 85; OC IV, 311.
57 *Émile*, pp. 471–2; OC IV, 855–6.
58 For a further discussion of Rousseau's conditions for reaching a decision conformable to the general will based on conditions of equal education and information, see Geraint Parry, "Thinking one's own thoughts: autonomy and the citizen" in ed. R. Wokler, *Rousseau and Liberty*, pp. 109–12; B. Grofman and S.L. Feld, "Rousseau's General Will: A Condorcetian Perspective," *American Political Science Review*, 82, 567–76 (1988).
59 *Political Economy* , p. 143; OC III, 255.
60 J.S. Mill, "Coleridge." in *Collected Works*, Toronto University Press, Toronto, 1969, Vol X, p. 140.
61 J.S. Mill, "On Genius," in *Collected Works*, Vol I, 1981, p. 336.
62 Helvétius, *De l'homme*, II, p. 1 Paris 1751 (no pub).

10 *Émile*: Nature and the Education of Sophie

Woman has more wit [*esprit*], man more genius [*genie*]; woman observes, and man reasons. From this conjunction results the clearest insight and the most complete science regarding itself that the human mind [*esprit*] can acquire – in a word, the surest knowledge of oneself and others available to our species.[1]

Émile is the canvas on which Rousseau tried to paint all of the soul's acquired passions and learning in such a way as to cohere with man's natural wholeness. It's a *Phenomenology of the Mind* posing as Dr. Spock.[2]

Almost from *Émile*'s first appearance, Rousseau's treatment of the ideal education of women has provoked charges that it is both unjust and inconsistent with his own underlying principles. Mary Wollstonecraft dismissed his views on female education as "the reveries of fancy" and a "refined licentiousness" by which woman is falsely made "the slave of love." "According to the tenour of [Rousseau's] reasoning, by which women are to be kept from the tree of knowledge, the important years of youth, the usefulness of old age, and the rational hopes of futurity, are," she claims, "all to be sacrificed, to render women an object of desire for a *short* time."[3] And, as Susan Okin has stated more recently, "Rousseau ... failed to apply in the case of women [the] types of argument he used to define the natural man, instead finding her naturally located in her subordinate role in the patriarchal family."[4] In Okin's hands, Rousseau's treatment of women emerges as an aberration fundamentally at odds with his general philosophic understanding, and, in particular, his insistence on the natural equality and independence of all human beings.

That as radical and skeptical a thinker as Rousseau should remain shackled to the assumptions of the traditional patriarchal order is, for Okin, a sign of the latter's singular intractability and perniciousness. Alternatively, critics like Sarah Kofman understand Rousseau's treatment of women as a sign of an underlying pathology infecting all his work. For Kofman (following Jean Starobinski), Rousseau's peculiar elevation and debasement of women is inextricably bound up with his valorization of absolute independence and individuality (in men), and a consequence of his own unresolved feelings for a mother who, in sacrificing her life for him, also abandoned him.[5]

In what follows I take a somewhat different tack. Briefly stated, my argument is that Rousseau's treatment of female education in *Émile* follows with rigorous consistency from his position, in that work and elsewhere, on human nature and its implications for the modern human condition. Far from being an aberration, Rousseau's views on feminine perfection are a necessary correlate of his fundamental views concerning human freedom and the causes of and potential remedies for the current disorder in human affairs. Although it may be tempting to reduce these views to symptoms of "pathologies" (of attachment, and the like) on his part, it seems more useful and fruitful, at least initially, to enter into Rousseau's arguments with enough critical sympathy to be able to engage them on the merits. In doing so, we may find, however, that we cannot reject his views on women without calling into question other, superficially more attractive assumptions we may be reluctant to part with.

Rousseau, who once called *Émile* his "best" and "most important" book,[6] also indicated that it is best understood in light of two major writings that precede it: the *Discourse on the Arts and Sciences* and the *Discourse on the Origin of Inequality*.[7] Seen in that light, *Émile* emerges as a (tentative) answer to the fundamental predicament laid bare in those earlier works. Victims of an historical development of latent powers, unplanned and unprovided for, we are neither men nor citizens, neither wholes unto ourselves nor parts of some greater whole.[8] In the ensuing disorder, each seeks wickedly to advance his own happiness by promoting the unhappiness of others, and all are brought down. Among natural men and among fellow citizens, by way of contrast, order and harmony reign, thanks mainly to the mutual indifference (or goodness) of the former and the mutual identification (or virtue) of the latter. In Rousseau's striking image, at the beginning of *Émile*, we are neither like wild trees that naturally extend our branches, nor like those pollarded varieties in which art, through perfect constraint, supplies a second nature. Instead, we resemble bushes that grow unattended in a busy highway – stunted, distorted, and barely alive.[9]

Whereas classical thinkers traced disorder in human affairs to the intrinsic complexity of human nature, early modern thinkers tried to overcome it by reducing human behavior to its simplest elements: All men are naturally motivated by self-interest, they assert, and we can best promote the collective well-being of mankind by giving up our illusions to the contrary. What Rousseau saw was the impossibility of constructing society on the basis of self-interest alone. Members of society willy nilly take an interest in one another. Society is necessarily a complex whole, which – depending on the way in which that interest is expressed – can make happy or unhappy the individuals who constitute it. Rousseau joined earlier modern thinkers in denying that men are characterized by a natural sense of reverence or prohibition. Unlike earlier modern thinkers, however, he concluded that if man was naturally asocial and motivated solely by self-interest, he also could not have actively desired to do injury to others. Without society, he would also have lacked language, and with it the abstract concepts necessary for the pursuit of goals other than those resulting from pressing material need. The desire to dominate and shine – so manifest, and manifestly destructive, in actual society – must have arisen, along with other yearnings for a good beyond immediate satisfaction of the senses, in the course of an historical process. Rousseau understands that process as the accumulated effect of human choice in response to climate and other random natural events, such as the cataclysms that repeatedly caused human groupings to disperse and reunite.[10] The essential quality of man, so understood, is not reason, as ancient thinkers insisted and early modern thinkers still in part assumed, but the freedom or perfectibility that allows us to connect man in the present age with man as he must have been originally.[11]

However, what is that freedom or perfectibility? Man must have had both positive capacities that lay dormant in the rude state of nature (e.g., a capacity to construct abstract ideas and other abilities necessary to the formation of human language) and a negative freedom from instinctual determination of the kind that limits other species to a single and unchanging way of life. The very flexibility that allows men to adapt to different circumstances also allows them to adopt ends independent of nature's own direction. The perfectible species is also the only species intrinsically subject to depravity, as accumulated errors and follies remove us ever further from the simplicity that originally favored our individual serenity and collective happiness.

Given the supposition of these dormant capacities, the condition most favorable to our happiness "as a species" would not be the state of nature at its crudest (whose general bleakness, underplayed in the *Second Discourse*, is given greater prominence in the [unpublished] roughly contemporaneous *Discourse on the Origin of Languages*).[12] Instead, it would allow human faculties to become active without the vitiating weaknesses and vices that have historically accompanied their awakening. Rousseau associates that age with a period following the first formation of families, but before the discovery of metallurgy and agriculture and consequent emergence of private property. The "best age" of man was neither nature at its crudest (when human beings were, for all practical purposes, mutually indifferent) nor ancient civic life (in which each human being was reduced to a mere fraction.) The "happiest and most durable epoch" for man was instead one in which the emergence of family and tribal life made possible sentiments of conjugal and paternal love,[13] and ideas of beauty and esteem, unknown to isolated savages[14]:

The first developments of the heart were the effect of a new situation that united the husbands and wives, fathers and children in one common habitation; The habit of living together gave rise to the sweetest sentiments known to men: conjugal love and paternal love. Each family became a little society all the better united because reciprocal affection and liberty were its only bonds; and it was then that there established itself the first difference between the two sexes' manner of living.... Women became more sedentary and grew accustomed to watch over the hut and the children, while the man went to seek their common subsistence.[15]

Finally, with permanent habitations appearing in closer proximity, there arose ideas of merit and beauty that produced new feelings of sexual preference. In the wake of these new preferences, violent rivalries now occurred, whose cruelties, however, did not negate the overall desirability of a way of life, that was, according to Rousseau, "the best for man." The emergence of such sentiments and ideas more than compensated, in his view, for a certain loss of individual strength, as well as for the bloody jealousies to which men were simultaneously subjected. Here – midway between "the indolence of our primitive state and the petulant activity of our *amour-propre*" – men "lived as free, healthy, good and happy as they could according to their nature."[16] In such conditions, families were sufficiently united to allow young men and women to break from relations of dependence on their parents. At the same time, families were self-sufficient enough to protect adults from a vicious dependency on other adults. What made the mutual dependence of spouses, actual or potential, other than vicious, was its connection with love. It is not peace or independence that Rousseau most values in the natural condition but the possibility it opens for a sweetness and intensity of sentiment unknown to ruder times. The lover feels, and hence is, more fully alive than the rude savage, who exists only in the moment and in whom love, imagination – even fury – remain dormant.[17]

At the same time, however, the lover does not desire more from the beloved than he or she is happy and willing to give in turn. Love, as Rousseau later puts it, is an intrinsically "equitable" passion.[18] In the condition Rousseau calls the best for man, *amour-propre* arises with imagination to expand man's sense of self in harmony with love's peculiar justice – preempting the impossible demand, ordinarily associated with *amour-propre*, that others esteem us more than they esteem themselves.[19] In these early times, *amour-propre* intensifies rather than depresses the natural sentiment of existence, and thus heightens rather than destroys the healthy love of self (or "*amour de soi*") to which *amour-propre* is generally so fatal.

However, this happy compromise between "indolence and petulant activity" is upset by technological advances from which arises a division of labor and the land. These spawn, in turn, new needs that make it both possible and necessary to profit at the expense of others. Soon one finds "all [man's] faculties developed, memory and imagination in play, *amour-propre* aroused, reason rendered active, and the mind having nearly reached the limit of which it is capable...[in short] all the natural qualities put into action."[20] Yet the consequence is precisely to destroy the last vestiges of man's simple natural goodness: Unhinged from its primary source in sexual love, rivalry becomes "consuming ambition." The desire to raise the level of one's fortune "less out of real need than in order to put oneself above others," inspires in all men "a wicked inclination to harm one another, [from which there arises]... competition and rivalry on the one hand, opposition of interest on the other, and always the hidden desire to profit at the expense of someone else."[21]

Despite its fatalistic tone, the *Second Discourse* does not represent man's situation as altogether hopeless. Incipient government, which might have eased if not erased our ills, failed, according to Rousseau, owing to "a lack of philosophy and experience." "Despite all the labors of the wisest legislators, the political state always remained imperfect, because it was practically the work of chance.... People were always patching it up, whereas they should have begun by clearing the air... as Lycurgus did in Sparta."[22] Yet the happy exception of Sparta suggests that modern men – given a "philosophy and experience" lacking in earlier times – might also do better. What Lycurgus accomplished for the Spartans by extraordinary wisdom or good luck might be approximated if not exceeded, could human perfection be freed from the disabling vices that have historically accompanied its progress.

The *Discourse on the Arts and Sciences* confirms this clear, if feeble, hope. Though the arts and sciences historically "owe their origin to our vices," we might be less in doubt about their advantages, Rousseau grants, "if they owed it to our virtues."[23] The true "tutors of mankind" – men like Bacon, Newton, and Descartes – need no guides or teachers other than nature and are compensated solely by their contribution to the happiness of others. Only when such minds are allowed to influence "peoples" with their wisdom, "will we see what can be done by virtue, science, and authority" for the "felicity of mankind." Until then, "learned men will rarely think about great things, princes will more rarely do fine ones, and peoples will continue to be vile, corrupt, and unhappy."[24]

These general considerations frame the project of *Émile*. Absent the possibility of citizenship of a Spartan sort (or of the public education of Plato), Rousseau experiments with a "domestic" education that suits man for society without mutilating his nature or destroying his chance for individual happiness.[25] The guiding idea of that experiment is to mentally recover and improve on man's "golden age," on the basis of a "philosophy and experience" that was not available to the men and women who enjoyed living in that age. Specifically, Rousseau aims both to overcome the inherent vulnerability of that age – made manifest in the susceptibility of contemporary savages to the conquests of an enlightened Europe – and to preserve its goodness while allowing for a more complete development "of all men's faculties." Rousseau thus offers to private, post-Christian men a version of what Lycurgus offered the Spartans. The "romance" of Émile and Sophie, as Rousseau puts it, "ought to be the history of [our] species."[26] If Lycurgus, in denaturing Spartans, preserves them from the general decline of history, Rousseau allows us imaginatively to rewrite it. He thus remedies the greatest defects of the golden age by "Platonic" recourse to a new rational and poetic ideal erected on the basis of that age's *ex post facto* (re)construction.

Rousseau's general pedagogical method, in keeping with this aim, is to cultivate the pupil's natural powers and capacities to the maximum while minimizing the weaknesses and vices historically associated with their development. In the case of Émile, Rousseau's model boy, the primary task is to promote the development of all his physical and most of his mental capacities while retarding the socially engendered desire to be esteemed by others. Before Émile's natural puberty, the goal is to perfect his physical and intellectual faculties without jeopardizing his happiness and goodness, i.e., his natural "oneness" with himself. Young Émile is guided, first, by his immediate appetite and later (when he is in a position to understand it) by utility, understood as the ability to satisfy physical desire, both present and future, with the least possible effort. Émile's own bodily economy thus provides the basis for a physical mechanics based on real, if limited, knowledge.[27] At no time is he permitted to regard himself as subject to another's will, which would provoke his indignation and engender a motive to dissemble. (Rousseau gradually emends this rule to allow for the reciprocal return of favors in accord with what appears to be man's natural sense of gratitude [*reconnoissance*][28] and a primitive understanding of property rights that serves to preempt their negative historical consequences).[29] Émile's reason, i.e., his power actively to judge, arises out of (rather than in opposition to) the cultivation of his senses. Yoked to and guided by his real material needs, Émile's "higher" faculties of active comparison are in this way brought to a kind of perfection at the same time that they are inoculated against speculative fantasy.

The object, in thus teaching Émile to philosophize, is to not to make a philosopher, but to ensure that all he thinks he knows is true and that he has the wherewithal to learn more that is no less sound. At fifteen, he philosophizes without ceasing to be as solitary and resourceful as a savage and as robust and industrious as a peasant.[30] Finally, with puberty and the concern with others that, given society, necessarily accompanies it, Émile receives instruction – fueled by his nascent capacity for (sexual) love – in morality, religion, and good taste.[31] Unlike his savage counterpart, he is open to erotic sentiments unblemished by cruel and violent jealousy, and he will guard his social independence with greater prudence and clearer foresight. In sum, he has developed his active mental powers "almost to their limit" without relinquishing his natural goodness.

Émile's education is accomplished through a hidden regulation on the tutor's part that is so radical and comprehensive as to strain credulity if not altogether exceed the limits of the possible. Émile can be kept honest only by being surrounded by benevolent deception. What, then, is one to make of Sophie's education, which is mired in the proprieties and conventional, it seems, in almost all respects? Must one conclude, with Okin, that whereas Rousseau's "definition of the natural man is totally open-ended," that of woman is unjustifiably "teleological"? Is the education that he proposes for women "based on principles that are in direct and basic conflict with those that underlie his proposals for the education of men"?[32] And if not, how *does* Rousseau justify a feminine education so seemingly opposed in its ordering principle from that afforded to Émile? To answer this question, it is necessary to return to the natural condition from which the education of Émile also takes its bearings. Rousseau's first and fundamental recourse, for Sophie no less than for Émile, is to "nature" in its most primitive and physical sense. In everything not connected with sex, "woman is man." In everything that is connected with sex "woman and man are in every respect related and in every respect different."[33] The opposed yet complementary educations of Emile and Sophie flow directly from this perplexingly – and vexingly – related difference.

To be sure, a reading of the *Second Discourse* might lead us to conclude that the primitive experiences of the two sexes, in this regard, were very much alike. In the crudely natural condition, Rousseau tells us, "each man peacefully await[ed] the impetus of nature, [gave] himself over to it without choice and more pleasure than frenzy; and once the need [was] satisfied, all desire [was] extinguished."³⁴ Sexual desire was "a blind inclination, devoid of any sentiment of the heart," and producing "a purely animal act." "Once this need had been satisfied, the two sexes no longer took any cognizance of one another [ne se reconnoissoient plus], and even the child no longer meant anything to the mother once it could do without her."³⁵

It must be noted, however, that this description presumes an early age of natural bounty and thinly scattered population – an era in which pregnancy and child rearing did not appreciably detract from women's individual well-being or undermine their self-sufficiency. Yet this idyll of independence, according to Rousseau, did not last long. "Difficulties... soon presented themselves," challenging human beings to overcome them. It was soon "necessary to become agile, fleet-footed and vigorous in combat." Competition for resources forced men to occupy new climates and soils, provoking new and greater efforts at resourcefulness.³⁶ "The more the mind was enlightened, the more industry was perfected," leading to the building, by those who were physically strongest, of the first huts from cut wood and branches.³⁷

However, how did these huts, originally built for one, become the domiciles of families? Rousseau makes it plain that the original impetus for these new arrangements must have come from women.³⁸ Physically weaker and less able to support themselves then formerly because of a greater density of population that made food scarcer and pregnancy more frequent, women alone had the motive to bring about what Rousseau calls the first "domestic" revolution. Unable to force men to help them, they must have possessed other means of getting what they wanted.

That women alone had an initial motive to establish settled family life follows from Rousseau's basic assumption that human beings are, by nature, selfishly asocial. Women's desire for male support is a direct consequence of their own need, given the newly straitened circumstances in which they found themselves. Men's familial attachment, by way of contrast, has no immediate basis in self-interest. This asymmetry points to an important difference in the sexual economy of men and women that Rousseau's discussion in the Second Discourse only hinted at. The putative natural pacificity of human beings³⁹ goes hand in hand with a natural moderation of sexual appetite in human males that borders on indifference. The same human freedom from instinctual constraint that unleashes feminine desire protects human males from sexual conflict without binding them monogamously.[40] If human beings are free in the way that he insists, the sexual appetite of women cannot help but exceed the physically limited potency of men.[41] Hence – precisely if Rousseau's assumptions about the primary self-sufficiency of man are to remain intact – feminine desire must be coupled with a means of stimulating the desire of others. That means, which he calls "modesty," is necessary, given these assumptions, both to bring about the sexual act and (strange as it may seem) to ensure that men survive it. Both a stimulant and a depressant to desire, modesty is thus, like the natural psychology of woman, intrinsically divided and complex. Without modesty, women in the crude state of nature could not arouse men; without modesty women at a later time would arouse men so frequently that they would fatally exhaust them.[42]

The earliest expression of modesty would outwardly have differed little from the "coquetry," or feigned and provocative refusals, that Rousseau observes "even among animals, even when they are most disposed to give themselves."[43] The males of most species, Rousseau suggests, are aroused by a female's ritual refusal. That this is especially the case with human beings follows from a female sexual appetite without physical or instinctual limits. Freed from the instinctual cycles that govern females of other species, women will naturally want more of a pleasure that, unlike men, they can enjoy continuously. More, even, than is the case with other species, human females are the sexual instigators. Unlike Lucretius, whose depiction of the early conditions of man he otherwise follows rather closely, Rousseau denies that rape is natural.[44] However, woman's psychology is complicated by the fact that, desiring sex more frequently than do other females, she can also disguise and thus restrain her sexual impulse freely (rather than on the prompting of instinct) if only, in the end, the better to appease it.

We may readily surmise that under conditions of increased scarcity and denser population, women found it increasingly difficult to manage on their own and were increasingly attracted by the huts, occupied by the strongest and most physically resourceful males, for their promise of domestic comfort. Domestic life offered women nourishment and protection from the elements for them and their children and a permanent outlet for their sexual appetites. More needy and already naturally directed toward and practiced in a kind of self-control, they would have been less likely than men to regard domestic confinement as a painful limitation on their freedom. Moreover, already skilled in manipulating male desire by controlling the signals of their own, they had the necessary tools to complete the revolution for which men's physical inventiveness prepared. Men, for their part, readily became habituated to the pleasures that co-occupation now regularly afforded them. Cooperative ventures, previously rendered unstable by the inability of men to bind themselves to future action, now flourished, thanks to an injection of female prudence.[45] In short, women's calculating (and calculated) modesty enabled them to become as skillful in controlling the mechanisms of the heart as men were in coping with the forces of brute nature. Had women lacked this endowment, the human species, given the natural asociality that Rousseau presupposes, must surely have perished. Only the juncture of man's greater relative strength (and related physical inventiveness) combined with women's complex sexual reserve (and related intellectual precocity in using others to achieve naturally given ends) can explain our present circumstances without doing violence to that starting point.

Yet the same revolution to which the complex phenomenon that Rousseau calls "modesty" [*pudeur*] gave rise also managed to transform it. Domesticity changes the primary form of feminine modesty, which serves to stimulate desire, into "shame" [*honte*] and *modesté*, which serve to dampen it.[46] As self-restraint becomes less necessary to arousal, it finds new use in assuring women's partners of their faithfulness. Whereas monogamous female animals instinctively repel other males, women, by their own voluntary confinement, freely resist the attentions of other men. (Women, in short, imitate not only the feigning gestures of female animals, but also their real refusal during times of pregnancy.)[47] It is this secondary manifestation of modesty that truly founds the family and allows men and women to enter into monogamous relations of the heart that were not, in the first instance, natural to them.[48]

Women's aptitude for controlling men by appearing to submit to them has a further corollary: the susceptibility of men's desire to such (unnatural) manipulation. Both mankind's natural goodness and its capacity for evil are ultimately rooted, for Rousseau, in the indeterminacy of male sexual energy – its lack of directedness to or by a clear natural goal. Whereas savage woman's goal (though not her means of arriving at it) is directed by her natural needs, the aims of savage men are inherently more fluid and open ended. If women, bereft of their "reserve," are abandoned to "limitless desires," men, bereft of their natural moderation, are abandoned to "immoderate passions."[49] This erotic indeterminacy makes men, for better and for worse, the sex more prone to fantasy and infatuation.

The absence of any natural attachment on the part of fathers to their children is one sign of men's greater detachment generally from naturally imposed ends. Savage woman exploits the susceptibility of male sexual desire – less fixed than her own to a given purpose – by connecting it with other goals, for example, and in the first instance, the male's pleasure, fueled by a nascent *amour-propre*, in imagining his own strength.[50] This pleasure is soon followed by that of imagining the desire of the female for himself, a desire or preference that is most agreeable, however, when it is veiled by doubt.[51] Absent that doubt, males are, it seems, brought uncomfortably close to a premonition of their own mortal depletion. Sensing the capacity of women to arouse them in a way that men cannot control and conscious of the weakness that follows the act of love, savage men (but not women) might well find in sex a first intimation of their own death. Thus the attractiveness to men of female modesty, however paradoxical, is not an accident. Men (but not women, for whom the sexual act is not immediately so costly) are naturally put off by too direct an expression of sexual desire.[52] It is tempting to conclude that the lure of "victory" distracts men from an otherwise disturbing sense of being made use of, and, indeed, used up, however pleasurably.[53] The distinct association in Rousseau's mind between sex and death becomes, on such a view, not just a symptom of an underlying pathology, as Kofman suggests,[54] but intrinsic to his comprehensive understanding of the human soul as both rooted in animal nature and transcendent.[55] The sublimation of natural desire is a work (however mysterious) of seminal "fermentation."[56] However, that fermentation is possible only because woman freely (or unnaturally) resists desire in the first instance.

Despite its usefulness to human happiness and indispensability to human perfectibility, shame has a vitiating weakness that the education of Sophie will have to actively counter. The historically derivative character of shame makes it psychologically more fragile than the natural coquettishness from which it stems.[57] Every woman is a born coquette; *domesticating* modesty, on the other hand, must be learned, either through a calculation on the woman's part of her own advantages, or through taste, i.e., a habituation to domestic life that makes it "dear" to her, or, most likely, through both.[58] The "golden age" of isolated domesticity, which leavens mutual dependence with affection, born partly of gratitude, is thus intrinsically vulnerable. As soon as families congregate, preferences arise that override simpler habits. In the second domestic state Rousseau calls the "best for man," flirtation emerges without, however, entirely supplanting a more primitive shyness.[59]

With the advent of private property, on the other hand, all shyness vanishes.[60] Stripped of shame, woman's coquetry is generalized. Within corrupted society, a merely *natural* female modesty (i.e., raw coquettishness, bereft of *modesté*) becomes *im*modesty. Men, recognizing for the first time how much their own pleasures (which they had previously attributed, naively, to their own power and/or authority) depend on women's will, themselves grow calculating and insinuating. Women, who previously indirectly governed men, become the dupes of their own flatterers.[61] The task with Sophie will thus be to shore up shame (or its equivalent) without giving up the perfections of taste and sentiment ordinarily associated with corrupt society – to make coquettishness and shame, in other words, cooperate without frustrating the development of her essential talents.

We are now in a better position to reply to Rousseau's feminist critics. The pedagogies that inform the education of Émile and Sophie appeal to the same standard and are guided by the same goal. Her education, too, aims to develop natural strengths and talents to the fullest, with a view to maximizing the pupil's happiness, both now and in the future, consistent with the happiness of others. If Sophie is raised, in the first instance, "to suit [the natural man],"[62] it is not to sacrifice her happiness but to secure it. That less must be done, in Sophie's case, than in Émile's (a decent upbringing by conscientious and loving parents mostly suffices) is, as we shall see, due less to her subordinate standing in Rousseau's eyes than to woman's peculiar role in the "rewriting" of human history that he here plays with in all seriousness.

No less than Émile's, Sophie's education is guided as much by her natural constitution as by the social function that she ought someday to fulfill. Hers, like his, is a compromise that aims to

reconcile the indications and necessities of nature with the requirements of social order.[63] No less than Émile's, hers looks to the domestic age of human history as a benchmark, albeit one capable of
enhancement.

The earliest education of young girls is devoted, like that of young
boys, to developing the body. [64] That in the case of girls this education
aims more at attractiveness than sheer physical strength follows directly from woman's natural talent for and interest in pleasing. That
so essential a capacity manifests itself very early is confirmed by
Rousseau's observations of little girls, who "love adornment almost
from birth" and can be governed "by speaking to them of what will
be thought of them" at a time that little boys care only for their independence and their pleasure.[65] With girls, cultivating the body has
an immediate social (and moral) content that can be engaged more
easily and safely than is the case with little boys. This is so, in the
first instance, because women do not have or need as much absolute strength. Girls should have freedom to move, jump, shout, and
play with a view less to their overall physical strength than to their
grace and a robustness adequate for performing their domestic duties
charmingly, and – above all – giving birth to healthy children.[66] Girls,
then, do not need the bodily physics to which the early education
of Émile is largely devoted – either to develop their natural physical
strengths or to provide a healthy means of cultivating their reason.
Thanks to girls' natural intellectual precocity, their prudence can be
stimulated more easily and without such insistent (and deceptive) recourse to immediate bodily pleasure.[67] Most important of all, girls'
natural concern with the opinion of others makes the suppression
of *amour-propre* – a task that dictates much of Émile's early education – as unnecessary as it is futile. Unlike young boys, whose indignation at this age is almost fatally corrupting, girls can and should
be allowed to "indulge in the petulance natural to their age,"[68] for
they will learn soon enough, and without much effort, to suppress it.
The aim with girls is less to forestall their anger than to teach them
to control and redirect it – a task for which they are naturally well
suited. Girls are more inclined to use their anger "constructively,"
as we now say, to seek means of overcoming opposition other than
by violence or its threat. A conventional domestic childhood is in
this respect closer to the natural condition of women than to that of
men and, accordingly, less dangerous.

Equally consistent with their respective natural constitutions, boys and girls have "similar amusements" (for otherwise, how could the domestic revolution have taken place?) but very different primary tastes. Whereas boys prefer movement and noise, girls favor "what presents itself to sight and is useful to ornamentation." Hence the special entertainment girls find in dolls:

Observe a little girl spending the day around her doll, constantly changing its clothes... continually seeking new combinations of ornaments – well or ill matched.... Her fingers lack adroitness, her taste is not yet formed, yet already the inclination reveals itself. In this eternal occupation time flows without her thinking of it.... She even forgets meals. She is hungrier for adornment than for food.... She sees her doll and does not see herself. She can do nothing for herself.... She is still nothing. She is entirely in her doll.[69]

Unlike Émile, who is readily guided by his love of food, the girl naturally occupies and amuses herself in developing tools for the satisfaction of appetites of which she is only dimly aware. Young girls are naturally directed toward the future in a way that boys are not. Dolls serve Sophie, much as the figure of Robinson Crusoe serves Émile at a much later age – each habituating the child to labor through imaginative identification with a fictional (future) self. The little girl, who is "nothing" inasmuch as she can do nothing for herself, becomes "someone" through her doll; she constructs herself by becoming her own audience. *Amour-propre* is thus inseparable from a girl's earliest sentiment of her own existence. Woman's primary response to her lack of self-sufficiency is to compensate by attracting others to herself. Primitively equipped to stifle her crude physical desires when it is useful and primitively equipped with a taste that makes doing so pleasant, Sophie happily ignores the demands of her stomach long before puberty – the point at which Émile is finally (and naturally) liberated from his.[70]

Less jealous of their independence, little girls do not find submission to the wills of others very irksome, so long as they are provided with alternative means of satisfying their inclinations: The girl who wants "with all her heart how to adorn her doll" is "put in such a harsh dependence on the good will of others for this that it would be far more convenient for her to owe everything to her own industry." "In this way emerges the first reason for the lessons she is given.

They are not tasks prescribed to her, they are kindnesses done for her."[71] Even more than boys, who "love to move," little girls are naturally lazy. They are habituated, against the grain, to busy themselves by an appeal to their convenience that would not move boys at a similar age. Like Émile, Sophie is never asked to do anything whose use she cannot immediately sense, but her sense that what is useful may differ from what is immediately pleasant naturally arises sooner.[72] Sophie's never altogether free attendance to her "cares" replaces the alternation of labor and restorative recreation to which Émile is acclimated at a similar age. "Idleness and disobedience" are girls' "most dangerous defects"[73] because their acquisition marks the weakening or loss of their capacity to set their (future) needs against their (current) pleasures. As boys are hardened by habituation to endure the vicissitudes of nature, girls are taught to "conquer themselves" so that taming their caprices to the will of others later "costs them nothing."[74]

The young girl's first experience with property is, for similar reasons, an extension of her doll playing. She secures rights against her sisters to the dainty underwear she already calls her own, much as she will later secure, through marks equally conventional, the bonds of her own family.[75] Managed anger is the beginning, rather than the end, of her first juridical lessons. Whereas Émile learns to call a patch of beans his own by bestowing his labor on them, Sophie "owns" whatever embellishes a sense of self projected backward from her doll. Whereas Émile's aroused indignation (and love of melons) allows him first to comprehend, and much later, to approve, the indignation of the gardener, whose melons he disturbed, Sophie is easily reconciled to, and grateful for, the limited kindness she is offered. Sophie applies herself to learning difficult skills such as embroidery, not because she is imagines herself on Crusoe's island (where embroidery would hardly be wanted) but because it is the easiest way to reconcile her natural tastes with the recalcitrance of others – preparing her to manage such recalcitrance all the more effectively when she is older.

The same factors that make girls more docile (i.e., less inclined to take opposition as a slight) also make them more affectionate, provided that they are not dealt with harshly. Slower to flare up when they are thwarted, they are also quicker to take the attentions of others for a kindness, especially when it reminds them of the care they lavish on their dolls. "Attachment, care, and mere habit make the mother loved by her daughter, if she does nothing to make herself hated." This ready pleasure in the company of their mothers compensates girls for constraints that boys would find intolerable. Whereas little boys are made restless by whatever resists their immediate impulses, a little girl who loves her companion "will work beside her all day without... boredom," especially if she is allowed to "chatter freely."[76]

The verbal precocity of little girls recalls Rousseau's discussion elsewhere of the development of human language in southern regions, where nature is relatively bountiful. There language begins with love and favors the peculiar animation that women bring to interchange between the sexes. In such climates, where need did not impel people beyond their own immediate huts, "it took all the vivacity of agreeable passions to make the inhabitants begin to speak."[77] In contrast, Émile's early language, elicited and limited by need, mimes the rustic simplicity and clarity of language formed in harsher regions. There, speech first arose around industry rather than sentiment: The first words were not "love me" but "aid me," and the point of speaking was not to make others feel but to make them understand.[78] The joint speech of Sophie and Émile will thus combine the best features of man's social awakening – features that were in historic time geographically divided. A voluptuous southern tone, born of love and lassitude, will balance the harshly emphatic clarity of the austerer north, where "strong articulation" substitutes for the accents "that the heart does not provide."[79] The linguistic intercourse of Émile and Sophie calls to mind the blended male and female voices of "Le devin du village" – voices that reecho in Beethoven's "Fidelio" and other great romantic operas. Tender without fanaticism and clear without harshness, their language will jointly reconstitute, on a higher and more universal level, the poetry that once constituted the "cradle of nations."[80]

Perhaps no element of Rousseau's teaching is more galling to readers like Wollstonecraft and Okin than his insistence that girls learn to endure "even injustice" and "to bear a husband's wrongs without complaining."[81] His claim that gentleness will triumph in the end (unless the husband be a monster) is, indeed, rhetorically overstated if not hyperbolic.[82] At the same time, the natural docility of women (so central to his story of the race and to the psychology underlying it) makes enduring such injustice both less painful to women and less destructive of the bases of their moral self-respect. Docility in women is not meek submission (as it would be in men) but another means of conquest.

The gift accompanying woman's docility and compensating for her weakness is propensity for guile and indirection that can be safely cultivated so long as it is balanced by an simulataneous cultivation of her incipient conscience. Though she may never lie or disobey, Sophie is permitted to find ways around these strictures so long as she does not openly defy them. "Wit [esprit] alone is the true resource of the fair sex ... and consists in an art of exploiting man's position and putting [his] peculiar advantages to their use."[83] Both dishonesty and disobedience are especially dangerous in women. As the primary emotional link between her husband and her children and the sole witness to their paternity, she is primary guardian of the affection and trust on which the family (given Rousseau's assumptions) is founded. Sophie will cultivate her reason (or faculty of making comparisons), not, as with Émile, by ascending from sensible representations to ideas based on the mind's construction. She rises, instead, from skill in reconciling her desires and the commands of others, to skill in pleasing others without lying,[84] to skill in managing the proprieties without doing violence to her conscience.[85] Her natural intellectual talent for discovering means is thereby broadened, without a clear-cut break, from a concern with immediate satisfaction to an ability to sacrifice her personal desires to the larger family concerns with which her interests are ultimately interwoven. Her conscience is an extension of the gratitude she feels toward those who have cared for her. Her ingenuity pays tribute to the wit of those maternal ancestors who were the family's natural founders.

The obverse of girls' natural docility is their "extravagance" or lack of natural moderation: Once their desire is unleashed, it tends to run on, undiminished by natural limits. Hence girls must not only be kept from "boredom with their work," but also from "enthusiasm in their entertainment."[86] Even a woman lacking in sensuality, like Rousseau's beloved Madame de Warens, is rendered vulnerable to extravagance by her relative inability to frame ends of her own by which to regulate her actions.[87] Rousseau saw first hand, in the person of his first mistress, this essential defect of the sex, however otherwise estimable and worthy.[88] Though "good sense" – mankind's "universal instrument"[89] – belongs "equally" to men and women,[90] women's judgment is honed within the social world, whereas men's is best sharpened through encounters with nature and developed through study of the abstract sciences. Women's conscience should address duties they can readily sense, based on their natural advantages and tastes. Otherwise, given the weakness of the female mind in formulating its own abstract ideas, women become fanatically susceptible (as with Madame de Warens) to the groundless and morally corrupting fantasies of others. Sophie's conscience is not, as with Émile, a constructed generalization based on natural pity, nor does she take her primary moral bearings from an abstract concept of justice. By the same token, conscience does not demand of her the sublime self-conquest that marks Émile's education at its peak. Self-command is properly the foundation of Sophie's moral education, rather than its crown. Conscience is, instead, a supplement to shame, supplying Sophie with a touchstone, grounded in familial affection and gratitude,[91] to offset the mere regard for reputation into which shame – given a corrupt society – is otherwise likely to decline.

Sophie's introduction to religion is therefore not the late culmination of a physics and an ethics marked by progressively more abstract ideas, but an early reinforcement of her devotion to her family. If Émile's love of God is an extension of his own self-love and the gratitude to his Maker that derives from it, Sophie's builds on, and modifies, her childish attachment to and gratitude toward her mother. Sophie receives early, concrete intimations of her own mortality (her outgrown clothes, her grandfather who is no more), the better to wean her from too great a pride in her mother's (and her own) generative power and to provide solace and comfort for a life of care that might otherwise prove unendurable.[92] Less independent than men by nature (given the passing of the era of natural abundance), women should acquire the rudiments of religion at an earlier age, not only because it would be futile to wait for them to acquire facility with general ideas, and because they are so soon called on to guard their chastity, but also, and most importantly, because they need it more to protect their peace of mind in facing the misfortunes to which mankind is generally susceptible.

It is time to tackle head on Rousseau's doubts concerning feminine creativity, along with his corollary insistence that men are better than women at constructing or discovering ends. As he famously puts it,

Women's reason is a practical reason that makes them very skillful at finding means for getting to a known end, but not at finding that end itself. The social relationship of the sexes is admirable. From this society there results a moral person of which woman is the eye and man the arm, but they have such a dependence on one another that the woman learns from the man what must be seen and the man learns from the woman what must be done. If woman could ascend to principles as well as man can, and if he had as well as she does a mind [esprit] for details, they would always be independent of one another, they would live in eternal discord, and their society could not exist. But in the harmony which reigns between them, everything tends to the common end; one does not know who contributes more. Each follows the impulsion of the other; each obeys, and both are masters.[93]

Rousseau's position is not the conventional complaint that women are too passionate but rather that they are not passionate enough and thus less able to perform a task – the discovery and/or projection of ends – that is more poetic in its essence than it is calculative.[94] His reasoning follows directly from his basic understanding of the human condition and the sexual divergence that it implies. Both men and women are human and hence free of the instinctual determination that governs the behavior of beasts. Yet whereas men's sexual freedom essentially expresses itself in the plasticity of their desire, women's manifests itself mainly in their ability to mask and otherwise control the stronger impulses that incline them toward a fixed natural end. Only by virtue of this basic division of sexual labor can the kind of human freedom that Rousseau postulates be reconciled with mankind's survival or serve to explain the manifest phenomena of civilized life. Okin is thus right to note the more "teleological" character of his account of women, but wrong to find it inconsistent with his overall direction as a thinker. Male sexual desire is both weaker than women's and more free wheeling or, alternatively, more open to perversions (from its immediate natural object) of all kinds. However, this openness also leaves men freer to tap their sexual energies for purposes distant from their immediate physical needs. Male desire, more readily directable toward fantastic goods, is the easy ally of imagination, fueling the latter even as it is sustained by it. The Sophie who succumbs to ideal love was a woman of extraordinary constitution. The Émile who reaches equal heights of imaginative transport is an altogether ordinary male. To be sure, for such transports to be undertaken safely, he must first be led, by a most devious route, to replicate in his own need-based inquiries the basic course of modern natural science. The point of this laborious exercise is less to expand his knowledge than to guard him from pernicious error as he ascends beyond the immediate witness of the senses. Only then will he capable of a love that suits a loving and virtuous woman.

Men are, for good or ill, the "sublimer" – hence the more poetic – sex. For the same reason, they are also the sex better able to construct abstract ideas out of given particulars. Granting Rousseau's metaphysical assumptions about the essentially constructed character of all general concepts, men will also be the more philosophic sex – the one better able to think "systematically" and to formulate the fundamental ends of human life that it is mankind's glory and burden to have to discover on its own and without nature's immediate guidance.

Most men, however, are not philosophers, and must rely, like most women, on the discoveries of others. The difference is that they will more eagerly and readily "take" to studies that women find intrinsically more boring. Émile (on his knees!) will fill Sophie in on the basic principles of science, theology and ethics, that her own early education pointedly omitted. We are also told, however, that whereas she makes rapid progress in ethics and taste, she absorbs the rest only superficially.[95]

Sophie, for her part, will teach Émile how to love – first, insofar as he is led by his tutor to imagine her and thus attach his still free-floating sexual energy to a general idea of physical and moral beauty, and second, insofar as she herself inspires him to self-conquest by her own (misperceived) example. Rousseau is very direct in his insistence on the illusory character of sexual love,[96] which makes of its object more than it really is. He is also equally direct in his indications that Sophie's powers of self-conquest (along with that of women generally) are weaker than a besotted Émile (and well-brought-up men generally) takes them to be.[97] However, the truth does not lie in "what is" but in the "imperishable beauty" that our errors allow us to discover or construct for ourselves. If here again, woman, attracted almost from the start by the image of her own beauty, is less transported by love, this too, is to her own advantage and in accordance with her fundamental constitution.

The joined education of Émile and Sophie represents a single education of the human race; it is "the most complete science regarding itself that the human mind can acquire" and "the surest knowledge of oneself and others available to our species."[98] As such, it is less a practicable goal (for who could educate a real Émile?) than a constructed model against which actual efforts at amelioration can be measured. Émile and Sophie will combine the loyalty and peaceful affection of the first domestic age with the liveliness and heightened sentiment that characterized the second. Alert to, or otherwise protected from, the illusions and other pitfalls that seduced historic man, they will recapitulate the "golden age" of man on a higher level and more surely.

Rousseau presents the "novel" of Émile and Sophie as an ideal "history of the species" – the way history might have been had "philosophy and experience" been on hand when it first was needed, and the way our history might (perhaps) be written in the future. Rousseau replaces Plato's ideas with the negative ideal of man's irrecoverable (asexual) wholeness. The division of the human species into male and female marks the unmendable breach that opened when human intelligence – rebelling against or falling short of instinctual desire – began to determine, and thus broke free of, its own object.

The basis of Rousseau's guarded longings – for himself, if not humanity – is inscribed, perhaps most deeply, in his own extraordinary person. Owing to a unique natural form (when she made me nature "broke the mold")[99] and the peculiar accidents that shaped his early education, Rousseau himself combined perfections of the masculine and feminine, not just sequentially (as in the ideal marriage) but simultaneously.[100] The recovery of his own "wholeness" is inseparable, for Rousseau, from an overcoming of the fundamental division of the race into male and female. (It is unlikely that any philosopher has yearned with greater intensity for a union of both sexes within a single body.)[101] The (partially) actualized "form" of marriage, and with it, the ideal history of the race, is thus anticipated in the very science that Rousseau has painfully discovered and himself (tentatively) embodies.

Later thinkers, from Kant and the Romantics to Hegel and beyond, were inspired by Rousseau's example. The unification of subject and object – prefigured in the union of the sexes – is the aim of Fichtean striving[102] and the very substance of Hegelian spirit.[103] The teleology of human reproduction furnishes a natural/moral basis for an attempted recovery of natural wholeness without prejudice to human freedom.[104] (The poet–philosopher Novalis, who claimed his own Sophie, famously declared "we *live* in a colossal novel.")

Rousseau's diagnosis of the human problem – and tentative prescriptions for recovery – are inseparably linked to his understanding of the vexed relation between male and female. That men and women are so much alike and yet so different is at once nature's "marvel"[105] and the ongoing engine of our troubled history as a species. Female modesty, in Rousseau, takes over the functions once ascribed to man's natural sense of reverence or prohibition. Female modesty proportedly explains both man's depravity and his capacity for self-transcendence without disturbing the assumption that man is naturally asocial. However, the price of this explanation may be a burden greater than modesty, as Rousseau equivocally construes it, can bear.

No thoughtful person would claim that Rousseau's portrait of men and women is entirely false or that his prescriptions for education and a happy family life are altogether unconvincing. Still, it seems doubtful that the natural qualities of men and women can be "incompatible"[106] as he maintains and yet constitute a living whole[107] as he insists. (Men and women, for Rousseau, can be lovers or affectionate companions but rarely, if ever, friends.) The ambition of German Idealism and Romanticism to make good those claims received perhaps its most decisive refutation in the sexual politics of Nietzsche. Before succumbing to the sexual and moral pessimism to which these doubts, abetted by their failure, are likely to lead, it may be wise to revisit Rousseau's assumption that mankind is essentially defined by our perfectibility or freedom.

ENDNOTES

1 *Émile* [IV: 737; 387]. All references to Rousseau are to the Pléiade edition of his works (*Oeuvres complètes* [Paris: Galimard, 1959]), followed by reference to an available English translation: here, *Émile: Or On Education*, tr. Allan Bloom [New York: Basic Books, 1979].

2 Allan Bloom, Introduction, *Émile: Or On Education*, p. 3. Translations are mostly my own.

3 Mary Wollstonecraft, *A Vindication of the Rights of Woman*, in *The Vindications*, eds. D. L. Macdonald and Kathleen Scherf [Peterborough, Ontario: Broadview Press, 1997], pp. 213–15.

4 Susan Moller Okin, *Women and Western Political Thought* [Princeton, NJ: Princeton University Press, 1979], p. 139.

5 Sarah Kofman, *Le respect des femmes (Kant et Rousseau)* [Paris: Éditions Galilée, 1982]; see also Jean Starobinski, *Jean-Jacques Rousseau: Transparency and Obstruction*, tr. Arthur Goldhammer [Chicago: University of Chicago Press, 1971].

6 *Confessions* [I: 573]; *The Confessions and Correspondence, Including the Letters to Malesherbes* [*The Collected Writings of Rousseau*, Vol. 5], tr. Christopher Kelly [Hanover, NH: University Press of New England, 1995], p. 480.

7 *Letter to Malesherbes* [I: 1136; 575].

8 *Émile* [IV: 249; 39]; cf. *Discourse on the Origin of Inequality* [III: 178–80]; *Discourse on the Origins of Inequality* [*The Collected Writings of Rousseau*, Vol. 3], tr. Judith R. Bush [Hanover, NH: University Press of New England, 1992]. pp. 54–5.

9 *Émile* [IV: 245; 37].

10 *Discourse on the Origin of Inequality* [III: 162, 164–5; 42, 43–5]; *Discourse on the Origin of Languages* [V: 402]; *On the Origin of Language*, tr. John H. Moran and Alexander Gode [Chicago: University of Chicago Press, 1966], p. 40.

11 *Discourse on the Origin of Inequality* [III: 141–2; 25–6].

12 See *Discourse on the Origin of Languages*, Chaps. 9 and 10 [V: 395–408; 31–48].

13 *Discourse on the Origin of Inequality* [III: 168; 46].

14 *Discourse on the Origin of Inequality* [III: 170–1; 47].

15 *Discourse on the Origin of Inequality* [III: 168; 46].

16 *Discourse on the Origin of Inequality* [III: 170–1; 48].

17 Compare *Émile* [IV: 252; 42]: "To live is not to breathe; it is to act; it is to make use of all our organs, our senses, our faculties, of all the parts of ourselves which give us the sentiment of our existence. The man who has lived most is not he who has counted the most years but he who has most felt life."

18 *Émile* [IV: 798; 430].

19 To be sure, if these "sweet sentiments" meet resistance they are likely to become "an impetuous fury." Still, what is sought is merely a return in kind of what one is happy to give – not, as with *amour-propre* in its more noxious form, triumph over one's beloved and one's rivals for its own sake.

20 *Discourse on the Origin of Inequality* [III: 174; 51].

21 *Discourse on the Origin of Inequality* [III: 174–5; 52].

22 *Discourse on the Origin of Inequality* [III: 180; 56].

23 *Discourse on the Sciences and the Arts* [III: 17]; *Discourse on the*

Sciences and Arts [*Collected Writings of Rousseau*, Vol. 2], tr. Judith
R. Bush, et al. [Hanover, NH: University Press of New England, 1992],
p. 12.
24 *Discourse on the Sciences and the Arts* [III: 30; 22].
25 *Émile* [IV: 250–1; 40–1].
26 *Émile* [IV: 777; 416].
27 *Émile* [IV: 444–57; 178–86].
28 *Émile* [IV: 520–2; 233–5]: "One loves that which does one good; it is
so natural a sentiment! Ingratitude [*ingratitude*] is not in the heart of
man; but interest [*interêt*] is.... If, then, gratitude [*reconnoissance*] is a
natural sentiment, and you do not destroy it by your error, be assured
that your student, beginning to see the cost [*prix*] of your cares, will be
sensible/aware [*sensible*] of them – provided that you yourself have not
put a price [*prix*] on them.... Nothing has such weight on the human
heart as the voice of clearly recognized [*reconnu*] friendship; for one
knows that it never speaks to us of anything other than our interest
[*interêt*]." The French "*reconnoissance*" denotes both recognition and
gratitude; it also can refer to economic debt (as with an "IOU" note).
Human beings, who naturally return interest with interest, might enjoy
an economy of supererogatory abundance if they did not demand what
others are inclined to give freely. "Recognition," one could say, is, for
Rousseau, at once an economic and a moral act. Compare *Discourse on
the Origin of Inequality* [III: 164; 43].
29 *Émile* [IV: 328–34; 97–105].
30 *Émile* [IV: 443, 483–8; 177, 205–8].
31 See *Émile*, Book IV.
32 Okin, p. 135.
33 *Émile* [IV: 692–3; 357].
34 *Discourse on the Origin of Inequality* [III: 158; 39]; cf. *Émile* [IV: 694;
359] for a different account of natural desire in women.
35 *Discourse on the Origin of Inequality* [III: 164; 43].
36 *Ibid.*
37 *Discourse on the Origin of Inequality* [III: 167; 45–6].
38 Rousseau could not state this point more blatantly without undermining
the benign deception on women's part that he is trying to cultivate.
39 However, cf. *Discourse on the Origin of Languages*, chapters nine and
ten.
40 All other peaceful species cited by Rousseau are naturally monogamous.
The lack of natural attachment between men and women is reconcilable
with natural human peacefulness only if female desire exceeds male capacity to satisfy it. Rousseau explicitly links the relative peacefulness
of the crude state of nature with men's relative lack of sexual potency:

Unlike males of other nonmonogamous species, men do not fight over females because, unlike those other males, they do not take their potency to be unlimited (*Émile* [IV: 796–7; 429–30]).

41 *Discourse on the Origin of Inequality* [III: 159; 40]; *Émile* [IV: 694; 358].

42 *Émile* [IV: 694; 359].

43 *Émile* [IV: 694n; 359n]. Rousseau is coy throughout as to the precise origin and status of modesty in women, and, in particular, the degree to which it arises from, or implies, free choice as distinguished from determination by instinct. See, for example, [IV: 695; 359]: "The Supreme Being wanted to honor the human species in everything; in giving man inclinations without measure he gives him at the same time the laws that regulate them so that he might be free in commanding himself; in delivering him to immoderate passions he joins reason to these passions in order to govern them: in delivering women to limitless desires he joins modesty [*pudeur*] to these desires in order to contain them. In addition, he adds a real recompense to the good use of one's faculties – the taste that one acquires for decent things when one makes them the rule of one's actions. All this is worth more, it seems to me, than the instinct of beasts." Women, in this account, are only indirectly included in submission to the law and the capacity for self-command that seems to honor mankind generally; and their modesty is only ambiguously distinguished from instinct. Modesty, to be sure, is not the "instinct of beasts." Is it, then, instinct of another sort? Compare Rousseau's (rhetorical?) attribution of "freedom" of female animals [IV: 797; 429] who also, evidently, have their "wiles" [*manège*] [IV: 694n; 359n]. The least one can say is that women's wiles, unlike those of other females, involve an incipient taste for beauty. "Little girls love adornment almost from birth.... From whatever part this first lesson comes to them, it is very good" [IV: 703–4; 365].

44 Compare Lucretius, *De Rerum Natura*, V, 962–5; cited and discussed in Joel Schwartz, *The Sexual Politics of Jean-Jacques Rousseau* [Chicago: University of Chicago Press, 1984], pp. 16–20.

45 *Discourse on the Origin of Inequality* [III: 165–7; 45–6].

46 On the specifically social context of shame [*honte*] as distinguished from modesty [*pudeur*] see [IV: 497; 735; 217; 386].

47 *Émile* [IV: 695; 359].

48 Rousseau uses the word *mènager* to refer both to women's running of the household and to their managing of multiple lovers. By way of contrast, women are said to be unable to manage ["*mènager*"] male and female qualities without losing their advantage over men. Compare [IV: 701; 364] and [IV: 734; 384]; see also the animal *mènage* discussed

in note 42 of this chapter. (*Mènage* means both "wile" and "house-hold.")

49 *Émile* [IV: 695; 359].

50 *Émile* [IV: 694; 358].

51 *Émile* [IV: 696; 360].

52 Compare his claim in the *Confessions* that women must indeed be "fas-cinated," inasmuch as they are not "horrified" by the unveiled sight of (male) desire [I: 661; 56].

53 If there were some unfortunate place with an excess of females over males and in which philosophy had abolished female modesty, then – "given the facility with which women arouse men's senses, and reawaken in the depths of their hearts the remains of ardors that are almost extinguished" – "men would finally be [women's] victims and see themselves dragged to their death without being able to defend them-selves" [IV: 694; 359]. Under such conditions, the almost limitless mal-leability of male desire becomes a fatal one for men. In the crude state of nature, by way of contrast, a surplus of women is associated with male contentment. The difference between these two conditions lies in the heightened susceptibility of male desire, under civilized conditions, to stimulus, by means of the imagination, beyond bodily limits. The same quality in men, i.e., the detachability of their erotic energy from its pri-mary, natural source, also makes possible a nearly limitless expansion (or sublimation) of erotic energy almost unknown in women.

54 Kofman, pp. 62–70.

55 See, for example, *Confessions* [I: 218–19; 183]: "my passions have made me live, and my passions have killed me ... if ever a single time in my life I had tasted all the delights of love in their fullness, I do not imagine that my frail existence would have been able to bear it; I would have died in the act."

56 See *Émile* [IV: 502, 662; 220, 333]: Men are made sexually desirous either by the presence of the desired object or by the same object called to mind by the imagination. Absent women (present or imagined) and the "fer-mentation" of the blood their image causes, men's sexual capacity would remain undeveloped. For similar reasons, Émile must be protected from the "dangerous supplement" that permits him to use imagination to trick his senses [IV: 663; 334].

57 "Woman is a coquette by virtue of her state; but her coquetry changes its form and object according to her views" [IV: 703: 365].

58 Compare the *Second Discourse* [III: 164; 60] with *Émile* [361]: "There is no parity between the two sexes in regard to the consequences of sex. The male is male only at certain moments. The female is female her whole life or at least during her whole youth. Everything constantly

recalls her sex to her; and, to fulfill its functions well, she needs a constitution which corresponds to it. She needs care... , rest... , a soft and sedentary life... ; and she needs patience and gentleness, a zeal and an affection that nothing can rebuff in order to raise her children. She serves as the link between them and their father; she alone makes him love them and gives him confidence to call them his own. How much tenderness and care is needed to maintain the union of the whole family! And, finally, all this must come not from virtues but from tastes, or else the human species would soon be extinguished." In the *Discourse on the Origin of Languages* [V: 395; 31], Rousseau's (more Biblically correct) tracing of the family to "the [first] dispersion of men" is not inconsistent with the account given in *Émile* if one assumes a prefamilial (and asocial) point of origin.

59 Compare Rousseau's climatic derivation, in his *Discourse on the Origin of Languages*, of the difference between languages of the "north" and the "south." In the harsher north, language arises, in the first instance, from physical need and is clear, sonorous, and uninflected; in the milder south, language arises from and in response to sentiments of love and is rhythmic, melodious, and full of feeling. It seems that in the north, the "golden age" of isolated, independent households would have tended to last longer, whereas conditions in the south (greater leisure and a surplus of women) would have precipitated that second era of domestication that Rousseau calls "the best for man." Émile learns first to speak the "northern" way, and only later adopts the inflected speech that Sophie acquires early and more easily. The combined "languages" of Emile and Sophie represent a happy compromise between the primitive linguistic extremes, fitting them for a similar compromise between the two historical stages of human domesticity. Their relations will be as monogamous as the first, and as sentimentally heightened and lively as the second.

60 See *Émile* [IV: 659; 331].

61 See, for example, Rousseau's gloss on "modern gallantry": "Finding that their pleasures depended more on the will of the fair sex than they had believed, men have captivated that will by attentions for which the fair sex has amply compensated them" (*Emile* [IV: 696–98; 360]).

62 [IV: 700; 363].

63 [IV: 692; 357].

64 [IV: 704; 365].

65 [IV: 703–4; 365].

66 And, one might add, for surviving the ordeal. On the death of Rousseau's own mother in giving birth to him and his own strangely analogous malady, see *Confessions* [I: 7; 6–7] and *Émile* [IV: 499; 218].

67 [IV: 708; 368].

68 [IV: 704; 366].

69 [IV: 706–7; 367].

70 [IV: 410; 152].

71 [IV: 707; 367–8].

72 Compare [IV: 492; 213]; girls' precocious grasp of future utility lessens their rebelliousness against the wills of others – a trait to which boys, who lack this early ability, are necessarily more subject.

73 [IV: 709; 369].

74 Ibid.

75 [IV: 708–9; 369].

76 Ibid.

77 Essay on the Origin of Languages [V: 407; 46].

78 [V: 408; 47–8].

79 [V: 408; 48].

80 See [V: 406, 410; 45, 50–1].

81 Émile [IV: 710–11; 370].

82 Compare Émile [IV: 696n; 360n]; Le lévite de'ephraïm [II: 1208–1223].

83 Émile [IV: 713; 371–2].

84 [IV: 719; 376].

85 [IV: 730; 382].

86 [IV: 709; 369].

87 "Unable to draw the rule of their faith from themselves alone, women cannot set limits of evidence and reason to their faith" [IV: 721; 377].

88 Confessions [I: 195–200; 164–9].

89 Émile [IV: 445; 178].

90 [IV: 708; 368].

91 "The reason that leads man to knowledge of his duties is not very complex [composée]; the reason that leads women to knowledge of hers is even simpler. The obedience and fidelity she owes her husband, the tenderness and care she owes her children, are consequences of her situation so natural and readily sensed that she cannot without bad faith refuse consent to the inner sentiment that guides her, nor fail to recognize duty if her penchant is still unaltered" [IV: 731; 382]. On gratitude as a primary foundation of conscience in men and women alike, see note 28 in this chapter.

92 [IV: 729; 381].

93 [IV: 720; 377]. In one manuscript, according to the Pléiade editors, Rousseau speaks of women's knowledge as a "practical metaphysics."

94 See Letter to D'Alembert [V: 94–5n]; Letter to D'Alembert, tr. Allan Bloom [Ithaca, NY: Cornell University Press, 1960], p. 103 n. (I am indebted to Christopher Kelly for drawing my attention to this passage.)

95 *Émile* [IV: 791; 426].

96 [IV: 798; 430].

97 [IV: 795; 428].

98 [IV: 737; 387].

99 *Confessions* [I: 5; 5].

100 See, for example, *Confessions* [I: 8; 8]; on Rousseau's strong identification with his mother, see note 65 of this chapter.

101 See *Confessions* [I: 414; 348]: "The first of my needs, the greatest, the strongest, the most inextinguishable, was entirely in my heart: it was the need for an intimate society and as intimate as it could be; it was above all for this that I needed a woman rather than a man, a lover rather than a friend. This peculiar need was such that the closest union of bodies could not even be enough for it: I would have needed two souls in the same body; since I did not have that, I always felt some void."

102 See Johann Gottlieb Fichte, *Grundlage des Naturrechts; Erster Anhang; Grundriss des Familienrechts*.

103 See G.F.W. Hegel, *Elements of the Philosophy of Right*; # 158 (trans. T.M. Knox, Oxford, 1942): "The family, as the *immediate substantiality* of spirit, has its determination the spirit's *feeling* of its own unity, which is love."

104 The central concern of Rousseau's botanical studies is sexual reproduction in plants, whose "common order" is hermaphroditic (*Dictionnaire de botanique* [IV: 1230]). (According to the new system proposed by Linnaeus, which Rousseau largely endorses, plants are mainly classified by the various "nuptial" forms that they express.) The close analogy between the sexual parts of plants and our own is sometimes stated with a startling frankness (see, for example, [IV: 1238]). Rousseau at least toys with the notion that the *only* difference between plants and animals is the former's lack of feeling, as in his definition of "vegetable" [*végétal*] as "an organized body endowed with life and deprived of sentiment" [IV: 1245]. Male agency, according to Rousseau's scheme, furnishes the "*poussière prolifique*" (in animals, the "*liquour séminale*"); the female furnishes the receptive organs, along with the "fruit" or "*germe*," the latter of which Rousseau also compares (puzzlingly) to the "uterus" or "matrix" [IV: 1238]. How, precisely, in plants, life reproduces life remains, in the last analysis, as much a mystery as the sexual relationship of humans.

105 *Émile* [IV: 693: 358].

106 *Émile* [IV: 701; 364].

107 *Émile* [IV: 720; 377].

11   Rousseau's *Confessions*

The *Confessions* has almost certainly been Rousseau's most consistently popular work. *Julie, or the New Heloise,* which became the literary sensation of the eighteenth century immediately on publication, fell out of popularity in the next century. *On the Social Contract* is Rousseau's most famous work and maintains its status as one of the crucial texts in the history of political philosophy, but has never really been a popular favorite. Interest in the *Confessions,* however, is sustained by the persisting interest in autobiography that it did much to inspire. It is Rousseau's most accessible work and the one most closely tied to an enduring popular taste.

This is not to say that all readers have found it to be a likeable work. For every reader who reacts to it with enthusiasm, there is one who is repulsed by it. These diametrically opposed responses are inspired from the very beginning of Book I with Rousseau's insistence on his goal of showing "a man in all the truth of nature; and this man will be myself," a declaration directly followed by his claim that he will appear at the last judgment with this book in hand.[1] As part of his general denunciation of Rousseau, Edmund Burke referred to this opening, saying, "It was this abuse and perversion, which vanity makes even of hypocrisy, which has driven Rousseau to record a life not so much as chequered, or spotted here and there, with virtues, or even distinguished by a single good action. It is such a life he chooses to offer to the attention of mankind. It is such a life, that, with a wild defiance, he flings in the face of his Creator, who he acknowledges only to brave."[2] At the opposite end of the spectrum, the protagonist of William Boyd's novel *The New Confessions* describes first reading of the same opening by saying, "I have never read such an opening to a book, have never been so powerfully and immediately engaged.

Who was this man? Whose was this voice that spoke to me so directly, whose brazen immodesty rang with such candid integrity? I read on mesmerized."[3] These two reactions share little except their intensity, and other reactions to the *Confessions* have been similarly intense.

Living as we do in an age that incessantly pries into the most personal details of the lives of every notable person, many of whom are upset only when the spotlight on them fades, we are likely to take it for granted that a famous man would write an autobiography. Rousseau, however, insisted on the novelty of his enterprise, which he boldly proclaimed to be unique. Book I begins with the statement, "I am forming an undertaking which has no precedent, and the execution of which will have no imitator whatsoever. I wish to show my fellows a man in all the truth of nature; and this man will be myself."[4] To be sure, in an early draft of a preface he admitted that he did have apparent predecessors in Girolamo Cardano, the Italian mathematician and astrologer, who had written a *De Vita Propria*, and in the more illustrious Montaigne. Nevertheless he taxes the latter for his lack of sincerity and the former for the lack of useful instruction to be found in his book.[5] Rousseau insists that he alone can combine Montaigne's intelligence with Cardano's sincerity. The insistence on the need for both sincerity and intelligence is but one indication of the overarching goal of the *Confessions*, which is to combine the deeply personal with the universally significant.

Rousseau's contemporaries were inclined to agree that there was something shockingly novel in this enterprise. They were well accustomed to biographies of and memoirs by people of high social status: great heroes and famous captains. Moreover, it was readily apparent that, in spite of Rousseau's silence about his most famous predecessor in autobiography, his *Confessions* were to be set in opposition to those of St. Augustine, which had engendered a body of confessional literature in which people of all walks of life gave accounts of their sins and conversions. Rousseau's book, however, was something different. Far from being a glorification of heroic deeds, noble birth, or divine providence, it was the account of the life of a social misfit who had lived among the lowest as well as the highest elements of society and who confessed his misdeeds without attributing them to his sinfulness or presenting them as a preface to God's forgiveness.

That Rousseau would tacitly usurp the title of the most famous autobiography written before his own is a fairly characteristic indication of the scale of his literary ambition. [6] Throughout his career he willingly set himself into opposition with the leading lights of intellectual life of his day and of preceding centuries. He quarreled bitterly with Diderot and Hume. He was not afraid to confront Rameau on the nature of music or Voltaire on the proper way to confront religious issues. He did not hesitate to condemn the peaks of French drama as found in Molière and Racine. In his major writings he set the highest targets for himself. *Émile* is an attempt both to correct Locke and to rewrite Plato's *Republic. Julie or the New Heloise* is a recasting of one of history's most famous love stories in an effort to revise its lessons about seduction, romantic love, and religion. The *Confessions* joins these efforts to revisit decisive events in intellectual history and set them on a new footing.

THE GENESIS AND PURPOSE
OF THE *CONFESSIONS*

That Rousseau's choice of a title was a well-considered one in spite of his failure to refer explicitly to Augustine as a predecessor is indicated by how long it took him to settle on it. Rousseau frequently found his inspiration for a literary work in suggestions made by others, which he then turned in unanticipated directions. The two *Discourses* and *Émile* are examples of this; the former works resulting from questions posed by an academy and the latter being suggested by a mother seeking advice about raising a child. In the *Confessions* itself, Rousseau says that by 1759 his publisher, Marc-Michel Rey, whom he had met in 1754, had been urging him for several years to write a sketch of his life that could be used as an introduction to a collected version of his writings. He seems to have begun seriously collecting materials to use for this "life" around 1759, but continued to vacillate over the project for several years. His autobiographical letters to Malesherbes (written in January of 1762) were intended as a substitution for his memoirs, which he had temporarily abandoned. That Rousseau did not easily arrive at a clear view of the goal of this work is indicated by the fact that through this period he did not use the term "confession" as opposed to life, memoir, or portrait in connection with his autobiographical project.[7]

After fleeing from France following the condemnation of *Émile* in 1762, Rousseau settled in Môtiers and seems to have started writing what became the *Confessions* in 1764. The *Letter to Beaumont* written immediately before his resumption of the autobiographical project contains a short intellectual autobiography as well as numerous references to St. Augustine, including one rather long quotation from his *Confessions*.[8] Thus there is some reason to link Rousseau's final resolution to write an autobiography with his reading of Augustine's works.

Even at this point, however, Rousseau hesitated over the problem of how to be completely open about himself without compromising people with whom he had had relations. His qualms disappeared with the appearance at the end of 1764 of the pamphlet *Sentiments des citoyens* (written by Voltaire, but which Rousseau attributed to the Genevan clergyman Jacob Vernes) that, in addition to simply fabricating slanders, attacked him by revealing personal secrets he had confided to a few friends. At this point Rousseau concluded that he was no longer under any obligation to those former friends and resolved to draw the line only at revealing secrets that had been told to him in confidence.[9] One example can illustrate Rousseau's principle on such matters. Although he relates a fair amount of information about Mme. d'Epinay's love life, everything he says was either told to him by an outside party or not as a confidence. He explicitly says that he knows other things that he is obliged not to tell. For example, it appears from Mme. d'Epinay's pseudomemoirs that one of these things was that she had given her lover Francueil a venereal disease that she had contracted from her husband. As further protection for the reputations of living people he decided not to permit publication until after the death of all parties mentioned in it. It is only after his resolution of these issues that Rousseau began writing in earnest.

In deciding to write a book that could be published only after his death, Rousseau departed completely from Rey's intention. He indicated as much to Rey in a letter in 1764 in which he says, "I will do something unique, and I dare say something truly fine. I am making it into such an important object that I am devoting the remainder of my life to it."[10] By this point, what had begun as a publisher's request for a sketch to help stimulate sales had turned into a grand enterprise meant to rival that of St. Augustine. Rousseau's first reference to the *Confessions* under that title appears in a letter to his friend Du Peyrou written in July of 1765. Rousseau says, "I will employ this leisure by running through the events of my life and by preparing my confessions."[11] Certainly one of his new goals was the personal one of countering the portrait of his character being publicized by his enemies, but this was far from his only purpose. When he discusses his decision to write an autobiography in the *Confessions* itself, Rousseau also refers to the broader purpose of exercising an unprecedented frankness "so that at least once a man could be seen as he was inside."[12] In the *Neuchâtel Preface* he indicates that the detailed and accurate portrait of one man was meant to lay the foundations for the philosophic study of human nature.[13] The interplay of the personal and the philosophic purposes permeates every part of the *Confessions*. Rousseau attempts to invest the most intimate details of his personal life with a universal significance and, at the same time, attempts to make the most general intellectual issues into profoundly personal ones.

The completion of this project did not follow smoothly after Rousseau's decision to undertake it. He continued to work on Part One during his stay in England, which began in 1766, and completed it after returning to France in 1767. As he indicates at the beginning of Part Two, he then put the work aside for two years. He completed Part Two and a second copy of the entire manuscript near the end of 1770. Shortly thereafter he decided not to write the third part he had envisioned, and therefore the *Confessions* breaks off its account in October of 1765. In sum, Rousseau considered his enterprise on the *Confessions* for a period of between five and ten years before he began to write. He then took another half-dozen years to bring the work to its final state. Later he undertook two very different autobiographical works, the *Dialogues* and *Reveries*, both of which differ greatly from the *Confessions* in form.

Although the two complete manuscripts of the *Confessions* (as well as the partial manuscript that breaks off in the middle of Book IV) closely resemble each other, there are variations between them, some of which can be attributed to the different purposes for which they were intended. One manuscript was saved for the proposed publication after Rousseau's death. The other was held in reserve in case something happened to the first, but was also used for readings that Rousseau gave for a few select audiences until such readings were prohibited by public authorities at the insistence of Mme. d'Epinay, who was concerned about what Rousseau might be saying about her. The latter manuscript contains changes in word order evidently made with an ear to the demands of reading aloud.

In spite of Rousseau's insistence that his work not be published until at least 1800, the heirs of his literary executor yielded to the great public interest in Rousseau and to the hopes for a good profit and published the first part in 1782, five years after Rousseau's death. They waited only until 1787 to publish the more controversial second part. Out of an effort to respect the spirit, while violating the letter, of Rousseau's wish to delay publication, the earliest editions expurgated parts and omitted some names. The first complete version of the *Confessions* appeared in 1798, but the publishers compiled it by filling in gaps in the earlier editions by using the second rather than the first manuscript, thereby yielding a composite version. The *Confessions* was reprinted many times, but the first complete version based on a single manuscript (while taking account of the others) was not published until the twentieth century.

In sum, Rousseau clearly had a number of purposes in writing the *Confessions*. It is impossible to deny either the personal character of the work or that public attacks on Rousseau's character made by people like Hume and Voltaire spurred him on. He certainly wished to provide an accurate account of his life and to defend his character against the attacks of his enemies. In spite of the fact that the *Confessions* admittedly embellishes and regularly departs from exact chronology, it is quite successful in providing an accurate account.[14] The excellent biography of Rousseau by Maurice Cranston has demonstrated that, on the whole, Rousseau's version of the facts of his life in the *Confessions* is much more reliable than has ever been generally acknowledged.[15] Nevertheless, Rousseau repeatedly insisted that he could not bring himself to begin writing until he saw a more generally significant goal. He wishes to offer a new model of what sort of person is worth reading about and which aspects of human life are most important. As he indicates in the *Neuchâtel Preface*, the significance of his life lies in his thoughts and feelings rather than in his deeds.[16] This autobiographical enterprise must be seen in relation to Rousseau's literary project as a whole. As preparation for a glance at the body of the *Confessions*, one should consider the autobiography in relation to some fundamental philosophic questions posed by the works that lead up to it.

THE *CONFESSIONS* AND ROUSSEAU'S LITERARY PROJECT

In important respects the reading of the *Confessions* suggested here could be regarded as the inverse of the fascinating account given of Rousseau by Jean Starobinski. Starobinski interprets Rousseau's thought in the light of his personality as revealed in his writings, whereas the present reading interprets his presentation of his personality in the light of his thought.[17] In different ways each approach follows Rousseau's own lead. In fact, the claim that there was a strong connection between Rousseau's works and the personality of their author did not begin with the *Confessions*. It was first made, not by Rousseau himself, but by the opponents of his *Discourse on the Sciences and the Arts*. It is not surprising that these opponents should see the issues raised in the *First Discourse* in personal terms. In it Rousseau accuses even "the most enlightened of our learned men" of being essentially useless to society and condemns lesser figures, "that crowd of obscure Writers and idle men of Letters" in much stronger terms.[18] Many of the writers who responded to the *Discourse* reacted to what they took as an attack on their own integrity and devotion to the truth by insisting that Rousseau himself lacked these very qualities.

These countercharges took two forms. First, it was claimed that Rousseau's own behavior contradicted his argument. The *Discourse* itself is paradoxical in that it is a very learned work devoted to attacking learning. From what they took as a glaring contradiction, Rousseau's opponents derived a second countercharge, namely, that Rousseau did not believe his own stated position. As King Stanislaus of Poland said, his work is like an "ingenious novel" in which the "author gives fiction the color of truth."[19] In short, such critics claim that Rousseau's arguments against other intellectuals need not be taken seriously because he gives no sign of believing them himself.

The charges of inconsistency and bad faith were to follow Rousseau throughout his career. They were raised when he contributed articles on music to Diderot's *Encyclopédie* and were

repeated after the success of his opera *"Le devin du village"* and
the performance of his play *"Narcisse."* Rousseau himself conceded
that his publication of the novel *Julie* left him open to the charge
of self-contradiction after his numerous attacks on novels. Fifteen
years after the publication of the *First Discourse* Voltaire summed
up Rousseau's career as a combination of paradox and bad faith by
saying, "Judicious admirer of the stupidity and brutality of savages,
you have cried out against the sciences, and cultivated the sciences.
You have treated authors and philosophers as charlatans, and you
have been an author in order to prove this by means of an example.
You have written against the theater with the devoutness of a ca-
puchin monk, and you have composed bad plays."[20] The dismissal
of Rousseau's works as simply manifestations of a perverse character has persisted and characterizes a good portion of the scholarly
literature over the past two centuries.

Rousseau's response to the earliest personal attacks is rather complex. Most importantly, of course, he denies that the perceived contradictions exist and asserts that his readers have simply failed to understand his position. Second, he claims that, even if it were granted,
a contradiction between his doctrine and his conduct would prove
only that, like almost everyone else, he failed to live up to his principles. It would indicate nothing about either the soundness of those
principles or the sincerity of his attachment to them. "Jean-Jacques
may behave badly, but that doesn't make the behavior of Learned
men better."[21] In short, far from refuting him, the claim by opponents that Rousseau indulges in paradoxes he does not believe is
evidence of their own inability to given solid reasons against his
position. Their willingness to substitute personal attacks for argumentation is ample testimony of their own bad faith, and therefore
supports Rousseau's condemnation of intellectual life.

At first glance, Rousseau's early responses to the claim that his
doctrine and conduct were in contradiction with each other appear
very far removed from the intensely personal tone of the later autobiographical works. Although the *Confessions* begins by pointing
boldly to the singularity of Rousseau's character and his project of
revealing it to the world, the *Observations by Jean-Jacques Rousseau
of Geneva on the Reply Made to his Discourse* asserts, "Nothing is
ever gained by talking about oneself, and it is an indiscretion which
the Public rarely forgives, even when one is forced to do it. Truth is

so independent of the those who attack it and those who defend it, that the Authors who dispute over it ought to forget each other."[22] One would never guess that this statement came from the pen of the man who would later so boldly hold up the most intimate details of his life to public inspection. Nevertheless, Rousseau does not leave matters at the attempt to remove personal attacks from a philosophic dispute; rather, he follows a course that binds his positions and his public persona as an author ever more tightly.

Even in the works in which he most strongly argues against paying attention to the author at the expense of his reasoning, Rousseau indicates that the relation between personalities and arguments is a complex matter. For example, one of the features of the corruption he identifies as accompanying the spread of learning is the ability of the learned to hide their own vices behind the empty but high-sounding words of their books.[23] Furthermore, although the vices or weaknesses of the defenders of the truth do not refute what they argue, these moral failings deprive the truth of its effectiveness by undermining faith in it. Although Rousseau can denounce personal attacks on him as begging the real question, he also concedes that "it matters to the truth I have maintained that its defender not be justly accused of having lent his aid to it only out of caprice or vanity without loving and knowing it."[24] The existence of truth may be independent of the reputation of authors, but its effectiveness in the world is not.

In sum, Rousseau insists that the truth persists in spite of the weaknesses of its supporters. Nevertheless, without these supporters the truth has no ability to move or convert. For the personal authority normally accorded to kings and those with reputations for learning, Rousseau attempts to substitute a new authority based on personal conviction and exemplary behavior. His attempt to embody this new type of personal authority is exemplified by his adoption of the motto *vitam impendere vero*, to consecrate one's life to the truth.

It is in the light of this line of reasoning that one should judge Rousseau's very public personal reform undertaken a few years af-ter the publication of the *First Discourse*. Throughout the account of the launching of his literary career in Books VIII and IX of the *Confessions* he pays special attention to his attempt to embody in his public activities the principles he taught in his books. He sees a connection between his achievement of a status an a new kind of author – one who owes his success to his personal character – and the triumph of his doctrine. His view of the need to stand as a model of behavior in his public life accounts for numerous public actions such as his abandonment of Paris, his refusals to accept royal pensions and lucrative honorary positions, and other conspicuous examples of behavior that emphasize his disinterestedness and independence. He presents his "personal reform" as the effort to set an unprecedented example of independence.[25] This effort also accounts for Rousseau's ever-increasing willingness to identify his doctrine with himself. As he finally proclaims in the *Dialogues*, he is the man of his books.[26]

This insistence on the link between his character and his books both contributed to Rousseau's acute sensitivity to personal attacks and no doubt encouraged his opponents to make such attacks. This should be kept in mind in any attempt to interpret the *Confessions*. Behind Rousseau's personal quarrels is almost always a dispute over a principle involving how an author and philosopher should live his life. Whatever might be true about Rousseau's purely personal decision to defend his reputation and excuse his failings, his defense of his character is also part of his broader literary project. Having concluded that most readers remain unmoved by philosophic arguments, he hopes to win them over to his position through the effect of his example.

GOODNESS AND VIRTUE

This is not to say that Rousseau presents himself as a paragon of virtue, far from it. In fact, in many ways his account of himself corresponds to Burke's claim, referred to in the opening of this chapter, that the life described in the *Confessions* is completely devoid of virtues. In his defenses of the *First Discourse*, Rousseau presents himself as a man who loves virtue, who is its only public defender in a corrupt age, but who also knows that he himself fails to live up to the highest standards of virtue. This continues to be his self-portrayal in the *Confessions*. In fact, in many ways he presents himself as an exemplary case of corruption as he traces his acquisition of passions such as anger, vanity, and acquisitiveness.[27] This aspect of the book is well captured by the epigraph *Intus et in cute* (inside and under the skin), which in Rousseau's source, Persius, is applied to a man who is looking back sorrowfully at his loss of virtue. This admission of his own weakness, illustrated by many details in the autobiography, establishes Rousseau's candor and puts him within reach of readers who can easily identify with him. Thus even his confessions of lies help to establish Rousseau's trustworthiness.

In addition to foregoing a bond between Rousseau and his readers, this admission of lack of virtue quickly takes them to one of the central issues of his thought: that of the natural goodness of man.[28] It is well known that one of the distinctive marks of Rousseau's thought is the "great principle" described in the *Dialogues*, "that nature made man happy and good, but that society depraves him and makes him miserable."[29] The *Confessions* raises the question of the meaning of this principle from the very beginning when Rousseau issues a challenge to his readers. Proclaiming to God that he will arrive at the Last Judgment with the *Confessions* in hand for his fellows to hear, he concludes, "Let each of them in his turn uncover his heart at the feet of Thy throne with the same sincerity; and then let a single one say to Thee, if he dare: *I was better than that man.*"[30] That Rousseau would think poorly of his contemporaries comes as no surprise to readers of the *First* or the *Second Discourse*, but his claim here is more sweeping. He implies that even the virtuous heroes of antiquity whose praises he was always ready to sing do not surpass him in goodness. This is a disconcerting claim at the beginning of a work in which Rousseau is going to confess that he has made a false accusation out of a sense of shame, that he abandoned a friend in need, and that he put his own children into a foundling hospital, to mention only the most prominent of the admissions he makes in the *Confessions*.

Understanding, to say nothing of accepting, Rousseau's claim that no one is better than he depends on grasping the distinction made consistently throughout his writings between virtue and goodness. In the *Second Discourse* Rousseau enunciates what he calls the "maxim of natural goodness," which is "Do what is good for you with the least possible harm to others."[31] It takes little reflection to see that this maxim is quite compatible with harming others in those circumstances in which one's own good conflicts with theirs. Rousseau's claim for the moral status of natural goodness amounts to the assertion that it is not natural for humans to wish harm to others as a primary goal and the observation that it is only society that multiplies the naturally rather rare circumstances in which our interest is at odds with that of our fellows. The immorality caused by society is increased by the development of social passions such as anger and vanity, which demand the submission of others to ourselves independent of any tangible benefit coming to us from this submission. Natural goodness consists largely in the absence of these artificial passions.

Virtue is very different. In the *Social Contract* Rousseau asserts that the great transformation brought about by socialization is that "the voice of duty replaces physical impulsion and right replaces appetites."[32] Whereas a natural man follows his inclination to pursue his own interest, a virtuous one is able to subordinate his inclinations to what is right. Thus virtue in this strong sense of the term, just as much as vice, is a product of society. From the foregoing it is reasonable to infer that when Rousseau says in the *Confessions* that no man is better than he, he is implying essentially that no one has better maintained his natural inclinations while living in society. He is surely not implying that no one is stronger in combating his inclinations.

In fact, the *Confessions* is Rousseau's most effective illustration of his "great principle" of natural goodness. Time and again it dramatizes both the goodness of Jean-Jacques's spontaneous impulses and the way complex social relations turn these impulses to misdeeds. As he says at the beginning of Part Two, his life shows "enormous faults, unparalleled misfortunes, and all the virtues, except strength."[33] His lack of strength is both the cause of his faults and the sign of his essential goodness. The lesson of the *Confessions* is not that Jean-Jacques never did anything morally wrong, which would amount to saying that he can find an excuse for all of his misdeeds. It is, rather, that good people can have moral failings that lead them to misdeeds without their necessarily losing their fundamental goodness.

One out of many possible examples can illustrate this point.[34] In Book I Rousseau tells the story of his "first step toward evil," his theft of asparagus instigated by a journeyman who worked under the engraver to whom Jean-Jacques had been apprenticed.[35] Earlier Rousseau described the genesis of some of the other passions that predisposed him to vice. In the immediate context he stresses the covetousness and dissimulation stimulated by his mistreatment at the hands of his master. Even after the development of these corrupting

passions Rousseau persists in ascribing his vulnerability to being seduced into a career of petty theft to "good feelings badly directed."
Quite simply, out of a desire to be obliging to someone who claimed
to be a friend he gives way to coaxing and steals some asparagus.
Rousseau insists that greed played so little a part in this that the
proceeds all ended up in the hands of his seducer.

The narration of this seemingly trivial youthful indiscretion is in
fact extremely important in that it is one of the passages of Rousseau's
Confessions that invites direct comparison with a corresponding passage in Augustine's *Confessions*. In Book I of the latter Augustine
tells the story of his own youthful theft of pears.[36] In his story about
childhood theft, Augustine, like Rousseau, emphasizes that greed
played no role. Also, like Rousseau, he indicates that pressure from
his friends did play a part. Nonetheless, unlike Rousseau, Augustine
attributes responsibility for his sin to no one but himself. Moreover,
he explicitly claims that a sinful desire to harm someone else played a
decisive role. In short, whereas Rousseau looks for an explanation in
good feelings misdirected by social forces outside himself, Augustine
gives his example as an illustration of his own and humankind's great
propensity toward sin. In comparison with Augustine's explanation,
Rousseau's certainly leans in the direction of absolving humans of
responsibility for their own wicked actions. At the very least it suggests that a naturally good man should be pitied when unjust social
institutions lead him astray.

In spite of this tendency, however, Rousseau does not simply allow
his residual natural goodness to serve as an excuse for everything he
does. For example, when he describes his conversion to Catholicism
at age fifteen he says, "I could not dissimulate that the Holy work
that I was going to perform was at bottom only the action of a
scoundrel. Still very young I felt that whichever religion might be the
true one I was going to sell mine."[37] Although he claims that weakness rather than outright wickedness was at the root of his action,
he insists that this weakness was itself blameworthy. He says, "The
sophism that ruined me is the one made by the majority of men who
complain about lacking strength when it is already too late to make
use of it." Having allowed themselves to fall into perilous situations,
people then blame God for making them too weak to resist temptations they could easily have avoided. In sum, although Rousseau does
consistently attempt to absolve human nature, he is quite ready to
blame himself for some of his misdeeds. The corruption of natural

goodness by society explains the source of evil; it does not entirely excuse it.

The same sort of effort to attribute responsibility to a combination of social causes and a weakness that is all too ready to accept sophistic excuses occurs repeatedly in the *Confessions* from the account of the false accusation of Marion in Book II to the description of the placing of Rousseau's children in the foundling hospital in Book VIII. In each of these cases Rousseau insists on the goodness of his motives – he had no desire to injure anyone. Nonetheless, he also insists that his actions were wrong and that he is plagued with remorse for them. The issue posed by Rousseau's presentation of these events is not so much whether he is hypocritically absolving himself from deserved blame as whether his theoretical account of natural goodness and its corruption by society is defensible.

It is worth pointing out that throughout the *Confessions* Rousseau uses this same standard to evaluate the behavior of people other than himself. For example, he explains his father's negligence in terms of the unconscious triumph of self-interest over duty in a tender and otherwise virtuous father.[38] Moreover, he explains the many faults of his mistress, Mme. de Warens, as the result of false principles imbued in her during her education that often led astray her inclinations, which were themselves "upright and virtuous."[39] Such good, but weak, characters can be contrasted with more actively wicked ones such as Friedrich Melchior Grimm, whose reputation in society as a man of deep sensitivity is belied by his calculating and manipulative efforts to advance himself. In sum, one can look at Rousseau's depictions of a wide variety of characters as a catalog of the different ways in which social life can modify or destroy natural goodness. He invites his readers to examine their own misdeeds to see whether they, too, might be examples of natural goodness gone awry.

In sum, a proper assessment of the *Confessions* cannot come simply from sympathy for or revulsion at Rousseau's actions. Many readers have been profoundly moved by these passages, whereas others have found them to be appallingly self-serving. Their general significance, however, lies in the way they illuminate a fundamental theme of Rousseau's thought. In other words, Rousseau writes these passages in such a way that a thoughtful judgment about his character depends on an equally thoughtful judgment of his theoretical accounts of morality and human psychology.

KNOWING NATURE

The *Confessions* brings to a resolution of a sort a second issue posed by Rousseau's earlier writings. This issue involves the philosophic status of Rousseau's system or, to put it more simply, how he can know the truth of what he claims to know. In the *First Discourse* and writings in defense of it Rousseau expresses very strong doubts about the possibility of settling ultimate philosophic questions. At the height of his attack on philosophy he asks, "Even with the best of intentions, by what sign is one certain to recognize [the truth]? In this multitude of different sentiments, what will be our *Criterium* in order to judge it properly?"[40] Such passages with their appeal to the technical terminology of ancient skepticism caused Rousseau to be attacked, with some plausibility, for attempting to reinstate Pyrrhonian skepticism.[41]

Whatever might be the case about Rousseau's ultimate commitment to some sort of skepticism, the *Second Discourse* makes much of a very specific barrier to attaining knowledge of human nature in particular, precisely the sort of knowledge that is at the heart of Rousseau's system. In the Preface of the *Discourse* Rousseau poses a particularly radical version of the very old question of how one can separate what is natural in humans from what is merely the result of conventional, accidental, or historical accretions. He concludes his statement of the problem by saying that "as all the progress of the human Species continually moves it farther away from its primitive state, the more new knowledge we accumulate, the more we deprive ourselves of the means of acquiring the most important knowledge of all; so that it is, in a sense, by dint of studying man that we have made ourselves incapable of knowing him."[42] In other words, because fully developed reason is not natural to humans, the person who develops a sophisticated ability to study human nature has progressively moved himself away from the nature he wished to study. The most truly natural humans are in no position to understand anything, including their own nature, and the most fully rational humans are so far removed from nature as to be incapable of seeing it clearly.

To support his claim about the difficulty of knowing human nature Rousseau cites a similar discussion by the great naturalist Buffon that argues that humans are possessed of an "internal sense" by means of which they can know themselves, but that remains unexercised because the concern for self-preservation focuses their attention outside of themselves and leaves the internal sense undeveloped.[43] Buffon's statement of the problem suggests that the solution lies only in developing this internal sense. Rousseau's evaluation is more radical in that he argues that precisely developing this internal sense makes it unnatural. We can see the consequences of this argument in Rousseau's frequent assertions that his contemporaries are not able to understand anything but themselves and tend to identify what is only European with what is natural.

That these and related issues were always of central importance to Rousseau can be seen from his regular predictions that, precisely if what he says about the corrupting effects of civilization is true, his corrupted readers will either fail to understand or refuse to accept what he says. His epigraph for the *First Discourse*, "*Barbarus hic ego sum quia non intelligor illis*" [Here I am the barbarian for no one understands me], is only the first of numerous assertions to this effect, and Rousseau gave the identical epigraph to the *Dialogues* more than twenty years later. A persistent feature of his works is his acute awareness of the immense barrier between his readers and the lessons they must learn in order to help themselves.

Rousseau explicitly pointed to this problem of self-understanding at the beginning of the *Neuchâtel Preface* to the *Confessions*. He observes that virtually all people fail to understand both others and themselves. He says: "One makes oneself into the rule of everything, and this is precisely where the double illusion of amour-propre is waiting for us; either by falsely attributing to those we are judging the motives that would have made us act as they do in their place; or – in that same assumption – by deceiving ourself about our own motives."[44] The *Confessions* is meant to solve this problem by offering an example for comparison. By coming to understand Jean-Jacques on his own terms, readers will be cured of the vice of making themselves the rule and, moreover, by seeing how carefully he scrutinizes himself, they will be encouraged to stop deceiving themselves. Of course, the presupposition of this process is that Rousseau has in fact avoided deceiving himself without the aid of an example for comparison.

Although Rousseau can claim that he is unusual in the degree to which he maintained his natural goodness in civilized life, it is clear that in his development of passions and intelligence he has departed very radically from simple human nature. Accordingly, a simple act of introspection cannot be expected to show him human nature in its unaltered form. How, then, was he able to discover precisely what all other civilized humans miss? If his readers cannot be expected to understand the truth about human nature when it is presented to them, how could Rousseau himself have been capable of discovering this truth all by himself?

Book VIII of the *Confessions* provides the famous account of Rousseau's sudden discovery of his system while on the road to visit Diderot, who was imprisoned at Vincennes. This is not the first place in which Rousseau attempted to describe the discovery of his system. In the *Letter to Beaumont*, for example, he refers to his "ordinary method" of responding to critics, which consists in giving "the history of my ideas." The "history" given in the *Letter* is a sort of sketch of an intellectual autobiography. Rousseau says, "As soon as I was in a position to observe men, I watched them act and I watched them speak; then, seeing that their actions bore no resemblance to their speeches, I looked for the reason for the dissimilarity, and I found that, since for them being and appearing were two things as different as acting and speaking, the second difference was the cause of the other and itself had a cause that I still had to look for."[45] The process of the discovery of his system moves from an initial observation of a disproportion between what people say and what they do to the discovery of a more fundamental disproportion between being and appearing. The system itself is an account of the still more fundamental cause of this latter disproportion.

What this passage, which was written at precisely the time Rousseau was beginning to work on the *Confessions* in earnest, presents in purely intellectual terms, the autobiography presents as an account of Jean-Jacques's feelings as he lives these experiences rather than as a description of his reasoning about them. With this emphasis on feelings rather than thoughts, Rousseau ensures that the *Confessions* will be accessible to a wide range of readers, not merely to those interested in the philosophic issues he raises. Although the *Confessions* provides a wealth of information about what Rousseau studied while he was educating himself – listing philosophers such as Locke, Malebranche, Leibniz, and Descartes and subjects such as geometry, chronology, and astronomy – it provides this information rather unobtrusively without saying much about the substantive issues that captured his interest.[46] These issues emerge through the more elaborate and concrete discussions of his experiences and feelings. Nevertheless, in general terms the personal history of the *Confessions* follows the pattern laid out in history of ideas given in the *Letter to Beaumont*.

By presenting Rousseau's intellectual development only through his emotional development, the *Confessions* gives both a case study illustrating his understanding of human nature and an account of precisely what is involved in the discovery of this understanding. Although Rousseau indicates in the *Reveries* that the project of self-knowledge undertaken in the *Confessions* proved to be even more difficult than he had thought, the earlier work does provide a thoroughgoing concrete example of what is entailed by such a project. One can follow the structure of this project in the *Confessions* by examining the themes of (1) the opposition of words and deeds, (2) the opposition of being and appearing, (3) the discovery of the cause of these oppositions, and (4) the effect of this discovery on the one who made it.

The various disproportions between what people say and what they do and between appearance and reality cause the drama of the first seven books of the *Confessions*. Jean-Jacques's discovery of the key to these disproportions and the consequences that follow this discovery form the drama of the last five books. At the beginning of the *Confessions* Rousseau introduces the history of his feelings by proclaiming, "I felt before thinking; this is the common fate of humanity. I experienced it more than others."[47] He traces the extent of the priority of feelings to thinking to his early reading, first of novels and then of Plutarch's lives. In the first place, then, what people say means the books in which they interpret events both fictional and historical. This precocious reading had two major effects on Jean-Jacques. First, it stimulated the development of feelings that corresponded only to the images in books and had no relation to real experiences. Second, it gave him "bizarre and romantic concepts about human life." Feelings severed from their natural objects and an understanding ready to misinterpret the world because it is derived from books rather than real experiences are the hallmarks of Jean-Jacques's character in the early books of the *Confessions*. With alternately comic or tragic consequences, he is constantly ready to see himself as the lead character in a romance or as one of Plutarch's heroes. For example, after running away from Geneva at the age of fifteen, he sings outside the windows of every house he passes, hoping to attract the attention of a princess. He is unaware of the difference between what is said about human behavior in books and what really happens in the world.

The *Confessions* is a powerful warning against the seductive power of reading by the author who declared in *Émile*, "I hate books" and proceeded to limit their role in the education of his fictional student.[48] At the same time, the autobiography makes us aware of this very tendency of readers to write themselves into the books they read, or rather to evaluate their own experiences in the light of those books – as Rousseau says, to become the character about whom they are reading. Rousseau makes it easy for his readers to identify with his experiences and therefore to avoid identifying with those recorded by novelists or by Plutarch or by St. Augustine, for example. His promise is that the view of life contained in his book is more engaging, more realistic, and more wholesome than the alternatives.

As a result of being torn between the world as his imagination (which is guided by books) depicts it to him and his constantly disappointed experience, the young Jean-Jacques is also constantly perplexed by the fact that things are never quite as they appear to be. He fails to see the world as it is and the people he meets also refuse to show themselves as they are. Accidental and deliberate misrepresentations of oneself are constant themes in the *Confessions*, as they are in all of Rousseau's writings. For example, as a result of being falsely accused Jean-Jacques moves from seeing his teachers, the Lamberciers, as gods who could read his innermost thoughts to seeing them as willful torturers. In neither case does he see them as they are. Later he becomes fascinated by the charming confidence man Venture de Villeneuve, who possesses the ability to pass himself off as a Parisian music master in spite of his heavy Provençal accent. This fascination inspires the young Jean-Jacques to seek success through a similar imposture that is exposed to great comic effect when, in his new anagrammatical identity as Vaussore de Villeneuve, he conducts a public performance of a musical composition he has written in spite of an almost total lack of knowledge of music. His later pose as an Englishman named Dudding helps him in his virtually unique

amorous conquest, but even this success is constantly threatened by
Rousseau's almost total lack of knowledge of the English language.
Moreover, the young Jean-Jacques is constantly meeting people who
turn out not to be what they seem. His friend Venture is a charming confidence man, his acquaintance M. Simon conceals a sensitive
heart beneath a ridiculous exterior, Jean-Jacques becomes a translator for a swindler who claims to be raising funds to reestablish the
Holy Sepulchre, and so on. He seems fated to be both the tragic dupe
of other people's impostures and the comic dupe of his own.

Ultimately this issue of the relation between appearance and reality takes a new turn by becoming linked to more general questions
concerning the social order as a whole. Jean-Jacques is a young man
whose appearance promises much, but whose awkwardness invariably leads to disillusionment from this first impression. As Rousseau
says, "I would love society as much as anyone else if I was not sure of
showing myself, not only to my disadvantage there, but completely
different from the way I am."[49] Combined with his unsettled existence, this inability to show himself as he is leaves him without any
well-defined place in the social world. What he imagines himself to
be is one thing, what he is in fact is another, how he appears to others
is a third, and the position he occupies in the world is a fourth. His
book-fueled romantic dreams, his genuine natural abilities, his lack
of social skill, and his low status put his life into a turmoil relieved
only occasionally by what he calls "those too rare moments that put
things back into their natural order and avenge debased merit for the
insults of fortune."[50]

The role of the social order in reinforcing this confusion becomes
clearer and clearer as the *Confessions* progresses. Jean-Jacques's first
insight into this occurs when, during his wanderings, he comes across
a French peasant who at first takes him as a spy for the tax collectors,
but then manifests the rare ability to see his basic decency. This peasant is able to avoid being reduced to extreme poverty by concealing
every sign of prosperity. This sort of split between appearance and
reality is the result of a social order that encourages it. This experience, Rousseau says, "was the seed of that inextinguishable hatred
that has developed in my heart since then against the vexations
suffered by the unfortunate people and against its oppressors."[51] This
seed, however, was slow to develop into understanding as opposed to
mere feeling, and it is only in retrospect that Rousseau can declaim

against "foolish social institutions" that sacrifice the public good and justice to apparent but not real order.[52]

The real crisis in Jean-Jacques's understanding of the tensions among imagination, nature, and society occurs in Book VII. One of the distinctive features of the *Confessions* is that it would present a deep and genuine philosophic crisis of understanding in the recounting of a visit to a prostitute. Coming on this account after reading several hundred pages, we are surprised to find Rousseau exclaiming that it is the next three pages that most fully reveal him to us. This puzzling story is the genuine heart of the blending of the personal and philosophic character of the *Confessions*.[53]

After years filled with many misadventures and few accomplishments, Jean-Jacques finds employment as secretary to the French ambassador to Venice. In spite of a promising beginning in what could be a first step in a career as a diplomat, he quarrels with his employer and leaves his position in disgrace. After narrating these events Rousseau stops his chronological account and writes a digression about his manner of life during his entire stay in Venice. This digression consists of several stories about what he calls the "celebrated amusements of Venice," i.e., disreputable women. In the most important of these stories Jean-Jacques is the guest of honor at a dinner given by a French sea captain for whom he had performed a service. Although the captain fails to show Rousseau all of the conventional signs of honor, he does introduce him to the most beautiful woman he has ever seen, Zulietta, who has been paid in advance to give her attention to the ambassador's young secretary.

Rousseau emphasizes the goodness and the generosity of this courtesan as well as her immense beauty and charm. In fact, his active imagination embellishes her genuine attractiveness to the point that he sees "the divinity in her person." He finds it inconceivable that such a being could take an interest in him because his real merit is invisible whereas his lack of both wealth and social status is all too visible. In Zulietta he sees only imaginary perfection, and he believes that in him she must see only an impoverished secretary to an ambassador, not the talented and good man he is underneath. In his attempt to solve the puzzle posed by their relationship, Jean-Jacques arrives at the conclusion that her willingness to lower herself to what she thinks is his level proves that her apparent beauty must conceal a natural vice that makes her a "monster, the outcast of nature, men, and love," rather than a divinity. After extended examination he finds this flaw in a malformation of the nipple. In sum, he concludes that once again he has been the dupe of a false appearance and simultaneously once again has been unable to show himself as he really is. Nevertheless, it is clear that his transformation of Zulietta into a monster of natural vice is as problematic as his initial transformation of her into a divinity. In fact, in both cases his imagination has caused him to see her incorrectly. Even at the time Jean-Jacques feels acutely that he has failed to resolve the contradiction he feels. He says that he left her, "still uneasy in spite of everything I could do to reconcile the perfections of that adorable girl with the unworthiness of her condition." He dimly perceives, or rather, feels that it is not really nature that consigns Zulietta to her low social status.

It is this event that sets the stage for Rousseau's discovery of his system, reported a few pages later at the beginning of the next book of the *Confessions*. In his encounter with Zulietta the crucial elements of nature, the corruption of nature by society, the tendency of imagination to construct false accounts of monsters and divinities are all present, but not yet fully conscious. Rousseau's sudden revelation on the road to Vincennes showed him the source of "all the contradictions of the social system" including the contradictions he experienced between his own merit and his low standing and between Zulietta's real goodness and her prostitution. Zulietta is neither a goddess nor a monster, she is a naturally good woman who has been debased by a corrupt social order. Moreover, the religious terms in which Rousseau's imagination – itself corrupted by the social world – interprets her mirrors the way religion can help mystify the real causes of corruption. This revelation allowed Rousseau to discover the real cause of "the abuses of our institutions" and launched him on a literary career that attempted to demonstrate "that man is naturally good and that it is from these institutions alone that men become wicked."[54] The *Confessions* shows this to have been a sudden, accidental, and unpredictable revelation. Nothing in Rousseau's life made his discovery inevitable. Nevertheless the *Confessions* also shows in great detail the experiences that lead up to this revelation and therefore answers the question of how it happened that Rousseau could recognize the truth about human nature when he happened on it in spite of his own denaturing education. It is not, of course, a phenomenology of mind in the Hegelian sense, but it is the phenomenology of Rousseau's feelings as he moves toward his discovery.

The last several books of the *Confessions* are concerned with the implications of Rousseau's system both for his personal life and his public life as an author. Although Rousseau claims that his "illumination" instantaneously made him into "another man," the discovery of what is natural and how it is deformed by social life does not lead immediately and directly to a return to natural life. These books show only a gradual and incomplete stripping away of artificial passions such as shame and desire for reputation and a constant lapse into being controlled by imagination rather than a clear perception of things. Moreover, Rousseau's public teaching about the social causes of wickedness leads him into ever-deepening conflicts with those who profit from the current state of things. Thus the book concludes with Rousseau wandering through Europe in search of a place of refuge.

In summary, the *Confessions* clearly illustrates in a concrete fashion three important features of Rousseau's thought. First, it is the culmination of his effort to institute a particular understanding of what it means to be an author. He insists that, for practical purposes, the authority of books depends, or should depend, on their connection with an author of good faith and sincerity who takes public responsibility for what he writes. Second, in establishing the connection between the sort of man Rousseau is and his books, the *Confessions* shows what he means by the central doctrine of his system that man is naturally good, but men are corrupted by social institutions. Rousseau presents himself as what he wants us to see ourselves as, good but weak people who struggle to maintain that goodness. Finally, the *Confessions* attempts to explain how it can come about that someone can be transformed or denatured by his social experiences and nonetheless find himself in a position that allows him to capture the true understanding of human nature. Again Rousseau hopes that his account of his own experience will help to reproduce that experience in some of his readers.

In the final analysis the *Confessions* should be numbered among both Rousseau's popular works intended to influence a wide audience and his theoretical works intended for a philosophic audience.

Perhaps we could reverse King Stanislaus's characterization of the *First Discourse* mentioned at the beginning of this chapter and say that the *Confessions* reads like an "ingenious novel" and its author gives truth the color of fiction. At the same time it embodies a deeply philosophic teaching about human nature. Although it is not as bold as the *Second Discourse* in disclosing Rousseau's theoretical principles or as comprehensive as *Émile* in elaborating these principles, it nonetheless gives concrete illustrations of the central concepts of Rousseau's understanding of human nature and shows the connection between this understanding and the life of its discoverer. As Rousseau says about this most personal of his books, "By its object it will always be a precious book for philosophers."[55]

ENDNOTES

1 Jean-Jacques Rousseau, *The Confessions and Correspondence Including the Letters to Malesherbes*, Vol. 5 of *Collected Writings of Rousseau*, eds. Roger D. Masters and Christopher Kelly (Hanover, NH: University of New England Press, 1995), p. 5 [Pléiade Vol. I, p. 5]. Citations from the *Collected Writings* will be given as C.W. with volume number. They will be accompanied by the corresponding citation from *Oeuvres complètes* (Paris: Bibliothèque de la Pléiade, 1959–1996) identified as Pléiade in brackets.

2 "Letter to a Member of the National Assembly," in *The Works of the Right Honourable Edmund Burke* (London: Henry G. Bohn, 1845) Vol. III, p. 306.

3 William Boyd, *The New Confessions* (London: Hamish Hamilton, 1987) p. 161.

4 *Confessions*, C.W. Vol. 5, p. 5 [Pléiade Vol. I, p. 5].

5 *Neuchâtel Preface*, C.W. Vol. 5, p. 586 [Pléiade Vol. I, p. 1150]. See also Book X, C.W. Vol. 5, p. 433 [Pléiade Vol. I, pp. 516–17].

6 For a reading of Rousseau's *Confessions* as a response to Augustine's, see Ann Hartle, *The Modern Self in Rousseau's "Confessions": A Reply to St. Augustine* (Notre Dame, IN: University of Notre Dame Press, 1983).

7 The brief account of the genesis of the *Confessions* should be supplemented by the detailed reconstruction in Hermine de Saussure, *Rousseau et les manuscrits des " Confessions"* (Paris: Editions de Boccard, 1958).

8 Pléiade Vol. IV, pp. 967–8.

9 C.W. Vol. 5, p. 290 [Pléiade Vol. I, pp. 345–6].

10 *Correspondance complète de Jean Jacques Rousseau*, ed. R.A. Leigh (Oxford, U.K.: The Voltaire Foundation, 1976), Tome XXV, p. 189.

11 *Correspondance complète*, op. cit., Tome XXVI, p. 68. There is a minor confusion over the date of this letter. In *Rousseau et les manuscrits des "Confessions"*, Hermine de Saussure, following Rousseau's indication that it was written on Wednesday, 4 July 1765, cites it in accordance with that date. Noting that July 4 was on a Thursday that year, Leigh gives July 3 as the actual date of the letter.

12 *Confessions*, C.W. Vol. 5, Book X, p. 433 [Pléiade Vol. 1, p. 516].

13 *Confessions*, C.W. Vol. 5, p. 589 [Pléiade Vol. 1, p. 1154].

14 For Rousseau's admission that he embellished in the *Confessions*, see Promenade Four of the *Reveries*, Pléiade Vol. I, 1037–8.

15 Maurice Cranston, *Jean-Jacques: The Early Life and Work of Jean-Jacques Rousseau, 1712–1754; The Noble Savage: Jean-Jacques Rousseau, 1754–1762*, and *The Solitary Self: Jean-Jacques Rousseau in Exile and Adversity* (Chicago: University of Chicago Press, 1991–1997).

16 *Confessions*, C.W. Vol. 5, p. 586 [Pléiade Vol. I, 1151].

17 Jean Starobinski, *Jean-Jacques Rousseau: Transparency and Obstruction*, trans. Arthur Goldhammer (Chicago: University of Chicago Press, 1988).

18 *First Discourse*, C.W. Vol. 2, p. 13 [Pléiade Vol. III, p. 19].

19 C.W. Vol. 2, p. 28.

20 *Lettre au Docteur Pansophe*, in *Mélanges de Voltaire* (Paris: Bibliothèque de la Pléiade, 1961), pp. 850–1.

21 *Letter to Lecat*, C.W. Vol. 2, p. 178 [Pléiade Vol. III, p. 101].

22 *Observations*, C.W. Vol. 2, p. 40 [Pléiade Vol. III, p. 40]. See also, *Letter by Jean-Jacques Rousseau of Geneva about a New Refutation of His Discourse by a Member of the Academy of Dijon*, C.W. Vol. 2, p. 177 [Pléiade Vol. III, p. 100].

23 See *Letter from J.J. Rousseau of Geneva to Mr. Grimm on the Refutation of his Discourse by Mr. Gautier*, C.W. Vol. 2, p. 86 [Pléiade Vol. II, p. 62].

24 *Preface to Narcissus*, C.W. Vol. 2, p. 186 [Pléiade Vol. IV, p. 959].

25 *Confessions*, C.W. Vol. 5, p. 304 [Pléiade Vol. I, p. 362].

26 *Dialogues*, C.W. Vol. 1, 214 [Pléiade Vol. I, p. 936].

27 For a treatment of the development of these passions in the *Confessions* see Christopher Kelly, *Rousseau's Exemplary Life: The "Confessions" as Political Philosophy* (Ithaca, NY: Cornell University Press, 1987), pp. 95–107.

28 The most sustained analysis of this fundamental principle can be found in Arthur M. Melzer. *The Natural Goodness of Man: On the System*

of Rousseau's Thought (Chicago: University of Chicago Press, 1990). This theme in the *Confessions* is treated in the Introduction to the *Confessions*, C.W. Vol. 5, pp. xxi–xxvi.

29 *Dialogues*, C.W. Vol. 1, p. 213 [Pléiade Vol. I, p. 935].

30 *Confessions*, C.W. Vol. 5, p. 5 [Pléiade Vol. I, p. 5].

31 *Second Discourse*, C.W. Vol. 3, p. 38 [Pléiade Vol. III, p. 156].

32 *Social Contract*, Book I, Chap. 8, C.W. Vol. 4, p. 141 [Pléiade Vol. III, p. 364].

33 *Confessions*, C.W. Vol. 5, p. 233 [Pléiade Vol. I, p. 277]. On the significance of strength of soul in Rousseau's thought more generally see Christopher Kelly, "Rousseau's Case for and Against Heroes," *Polity*, Vol. xxx, No. 2 (Winter 1997) pp. 347–365.

34 Other examples can be found in the introduction to the *Confessions*, C.W. Vol. 5, xxi–xxvi and Kelly, *Rousseau's Exemplary Life*.

35 *Confessions*, C.W. Vol. 5, pp. 27–28 [Pléiade Vol. I, p. 33].

36 This example is also discussed in Kelly, *Rousseau's Exemplary Life*, 104–105.

37 *Confessions*, C.W. Vol. 5, p. 53 [Pléiade Vol. I, p. 63].

38 *Confessions*, C.W. Vol. 5, pp. 46–47 [Pléiade Vol. I, pp. 55–56].

39 *Confessions*, C.W. Vol. 5, p. 165 [Pléiade Vol. I, p. 165].

40 *First Discourse*, C.W. Vol. 2, p. 13 [Pléiade Vol. III, p. 18].

41 "Refutation of the Discourse Which Won the Prize of the Academy of Dijon in 1750" by Gauthier, C.W. Vol. 2, 78.

42 *Second Discourse*, C.W. Vol. 3, 12 [Pléiade Vol. III, p. 123].

43 *Second Discourse*, C.W. Vol. 3, p. 68 [Pléiade Vol. III, pp. 195–196].

44 C.W. Vol. 5, p. 585 [Pléiade Vol. I, p. 1148].

45 Pléiade Vol. IV, p. 966. For a discussion of this see "Introduction to the *Confessions*, C.W. Vol. 5, p. xxvi.

46 See especially Book VI for an account of Rousseau's studies. For the philosophic pre-history of some of Rousseau's key concepts see Patrick Riley, *The General will before Rousseau: The Transformation of the Divine into the Civic* (Princeton: Princeton University Press, 1986).

47 *Confessions*, C.W. Vol. 5, p. 7 [Pléiade Vol. I, p. 8].

48 *Emile*, trans. Allan Bloom (New York: Basic Books, 1979) p. 184 [Pléiade Vol. IV, p. 454].

49 *Confessions*, C.W. Vol. 5, pp. 97–98 [Pléiade Vol. I, p. 116].

50 *Confessions*, C.W. Vol. 5, p. 80 [Pléiade Vol. I, p. 96].

51 *Confessions*, C.W. Vol. 5, p. 138 [Pléiade Vol. I, p. 164].

52 *Confessions*, C.W. Vol. 5, p. 274 [Pléiade Vol. I. p. 327].

53 *Confessions* C.W. Vol. 5, pp. 267–271 [Pléiade Vol. I, pp. 317–322]. For very suggestive interpretations of this section of the *Confessions* see

Madeleine B. Ellis, *Rousseau's Venetian Story: An Essay Upon Art and Truth in "Les Confessions"* (Baltimore: The Johns Hopkins Press, 1966) pp. 128–140 and Edward Duffy, *Rousseau in England* (Berkeley and Los Angeles: University of California Press, 1969) pp. 135–137. See also Kelly, *Rousseau's Exemplary Life*, pp. 177–184.
54 "Letter to Malesherbes," C.W. Vol. 5, p. 575 [Pléiade Vol. I, pp. 1135–6].
55 *Confessions*, C.W. Vol. 5, p. 589 [Pléiade Vol. I, p. 1154].

12 Music, Politics, Theater, and Representation in Rousseau

[Melody] does not only imitate, it speaks, and its language – inarticulate but vigorous, burning and passionate – has a hundred times more energy than speech.

Essay on the Origin of Languages, 14 OC v 416.[1]

Some people think music a primitive art because it has only a few notes and rhythms. But it is simple only on the surface; its substance on the other hand, which makes it possible to interpret this manifest content, has all the infinite complexity that's suggested in the external forms of other arts and that music conceals. There is a sense in which it is the most sophisticated art of all.

Wittgenstein, *Culture and Value*, pp. 8–9

There are two commonly accepted, seldom scrutinized, claims about Rousseau. The first is that he opposed representation in politics and was an advocate of direct democracy; the second is that he was opposed to the theater on the grounds that is distanced citizens from moral understanding.

There is a third fact about Rousseau's theory of representation that has also received too little attention. Rousseau first found a voice of his own in music, which he knew naturally and learned formally after running away from Geneva at the age of 16. It shapes the account he gives of himself. The *Confessions* are, from their first pages, filled with music – the songs of his aunt Suzon, Swiss folk songs that drive him to tears, a grandiose and disastrous concert he organizes in Lausanne for a piece he composed at a time when he is almost completely ignorant of music, his pretense to be an itinerant Parisian composer. The cadence of the book is itself operatic, with dramatic changes in tempo, recitative alternating with action.[2] In the *Dialogues*, that strange work of an ecstatic author, he has the character "Rousseau" say of the character "Jean-Jacques" who is the subject of the dialogue: "He was born for music....He discovered approaches that are clearer, easier, simpler and facilitate composition and performance.... I have seen no man so passionate about music as he."[3]

Despite his dubious beginnings as a musician, such self-promotion was not without a certain justification. The concern with music sounds throughout his life. His first published work – *Project concernant de nouveaux signes pour la musique* – was a proposal in 1742 to the Academie des Sciences for a new system of musical notation, all on one line with numbers rather than symbols; it would, he averred, permit a more natural relation of the performer to the musical vocabulary. It is worth noting that Rousseau begins his career by proposing nothing other than a complete reworking of an entire language, with the explicit goal of making it more human, less professional.

Curiously the relation between these two claims about representation and Rousseau's musicianship have rarely been critically examined. This raises a number of questions, the most important for our purposes being, does music escapes Rousseau's strictures on imitation that apply to the other representative arts? And if it does, of what importance is that fact?

We argue below that these matters are in fact related and that understanding that relation is important to understanding Rousseau. Let us look at the first of these claims, that of representation in politics. At the beginning of Book III of the *Social Contract* Rousseau warns his readers to pay careful attention in what follows as he does not know how to be clear to those who do not read carefully.[4] Rousseau then insists on a clear-cut distinction between sovereignty and government. Whereas government is an intermediate body between sovereign and citizens, charged with what Rousseau calls administration, sovereignty might be thought of as the agent of the soul of a political body. Its manifestation is what Rousseau calls "law."[5] For "without law an existing state (*l'état formé*) is only a body without soul, for it is not enough for each to be subject to the general will; one has to know how to follow it."[6] A law, says Rousseau, has the quality of ecstasy, that is, of being beside oneself. He writes,

...[W]hen an entire people gives a law for the entire people (*statue sur tout le peuple*), it considers only itself. And if a relation [between the people as enacting the law and the people as subject to the law] is then established it is of the entire object from one point of view with the entire object from another point of view, without any division of the whole. Thus the matter for which a law is given (*sur laquelle on statue*) is general just as is the will which gives the law. It is this act that I call a law.[7]

Generality is thus the object of a law. That is, any act of the sovereign – thus any element of the general will – must have the quality of applying to each member of the body politic in exactly the same way. It is thus my will and at the same time, and as exactly the same, it is your will. The *general* will is thus the knowledge of what it means to be a citizen in/of a body; sovereignty is the action undertaken that embodies that knowledge. We might think of this as similar to what Wittgenstein calls grammar or as what Stanley Cavell has termed "categorical descriptives."[8] Such terms function both normatively and descriptively, or, more accurately, they make such a distinction misleading. Such terms are not just right but are the very determinant of what it means to be right in a particular speech situation. They make speech possible. This is why, for Rousseau, the General Will is either right or does not exist.

It is at this stage that the problem of political representation intervenes. Rousseau argues, famously, that sovereignty cannot be represented, that is, given over to someone else. Why, one might ask? If something is mine – and Rousseau is clear that nothing is more completely mine than the general will – can I not give it away, or at least lend it?

Rousseau's answer is complex. He argues first that sovereignty does not exist in time. In a draft of his thoughts on politics, he writes that each moment of sovereignty is "absolute, independent of the preceding."[9] From an examination of his notes, we see that Rousseau clearly spent some time getting this claim exactly right. Finally, in the *Social Contract*, this idea appears as the extraordinary claim that "yesterday's law carries no obligation today."[10] This amounts to saying that sovereignty has the quality of existing only in the present and as present to us. To say that something exists in the present means (at least) that we have no way of encountering it except as what it is.[11] To say that the general will is what it is is to say that the judgments of the general will cannot be references to analogous (but not identical) situations; each judgment expresses a claim that holds unambiguously for the exact circumstances and citizenry at hand. As they are constitutive of a given political actuality they tell us what the nature or (to be a little too high-faluting) being of politics is.[12]

(We should note here, although we cannot pursue the question, that none of this gives any reason to think that Rousseau is against representative *government*. Government deals with precisely that which is not the same for and in each: At times Rousseau calls it administration. Government makes rules, not what Rousseau calls laws[13]).

It is important to note here how different this idea of sovereignty is from our usual one. The usual image of sovereignty that we have is derived from Hobbes: It is that of the frontispiece to the *Leviathan*, a picture of the great benevolent giant severely but gently encompassing the land with the embodiment of regularity. For Rousseau, on the contrary, sovereignty is designed to show precisely the contingent and yet atemporal nature of our relation to a political body. Rousseau writes in the chapter on the sovereign, "There is not nor can there be any kind of fundamental law which is obligatory for the body of the people, not even the social contract.[14] So what Rousseau is after is an understanding of the political that is constitutive but not therefore obligatory.

This is why sovereignty cannot be represented. Representation gives a temporal dimension to sovereignty, something that could not but make it not what it is. In this sense sovereignty has the quality of an aesthetic object: We cannot help but respond to it, in that we cannot but find ourselves in it.[15] It is part and parcel of the context in which we find ourselves, present arguments, and render decisions. As such, response to the General Will or to an aesthetic object is required by the very act of political or aesthetic deliberation.

The difficulty for political theory is obvious: If there are no fundamental or universal statements that can be made about our political life, how is theory possible? A political theory is a representation of a generalized political context or set of issues, but this generality removes individuals from the present. An aesthetic object, on the other hand, is at once fully present and particular, but also universal in scope. Such art objects "demand" a critical response; insofar as these object are art, we cannot remain dead to them. What remains mysterious here is how this relation can be established in the political realm. In the aesthetic realm, we have artists – individuals who rely on imagination to create the response-requiring works of art. We might formulate the question of sovereignty as "how is creativity possible in the political realm?" or, taking the problems of representation seriously, "how is democratic political theory possible?"

To begin to get an idea of this problem with political representation, let us turn to Rousseau's other consideration of the perils of representation, this time in the aesthetic realm per se. We refer of course to his analysis of theater in the *Letter to d'Alembert*. d'Alembert, the coeditor of the *Encyclopédie*, had written the entry on "Geneva" for his project with Diderot. His article was generally admiring of the city–state but he had included a passage in which he had complained of the lack of a theater and urged the Genevans to establish one in order to "join the wisdom of Lacedaemonia to the grace of Athens."[16]

Rousseau responds to d'Alembert's proposal along two lines. His first concern is with the audience. He argues that no matter what the emotions on stage actually are, the fourth wall of the theater keeps us from them such that they are merely represented and not authentically ours. To the obvious counter that one can be moved to tears in the theater, he responds that these emotions are cheap, in that in the theater "nothing is required" from the spectator. By "nothing is required" Rousseau means that in the theater our emotions have no life consequences. Being a member of an audience is, in these circumstances, irresponsible, as if one were on holiday from one's ordinary life with others.

This raises his second concern. For Rousseau it is precisely the individuality of each one's response in the theater that makes it, at best, the "will of all" rather than the "general will." When Rousseau wrote a preface to his comedy *"Narcisse"* in 1752 (just after the success of the *Discourse and on the Arts and Sciences*, therefore), he suggested a link among philosophy, the theater, and the arts and sciences in general in that each takes us away from our commonalty with others.[17] Theater might in these conditions give us at most the appearance of public virtue, the clothing of the human so to speak, but this would be merely a simulacrum of virtue.

The problem with theater for Rousseau lies in the fact that although the emotions of characters may be repeated in the members of the audience, the goal of these emotions perforce cannot be. Hence what I experience in theater will never be *mine*, it will always be a representation, never the result of my will. If a just political society must always rest only in the present and if those human qualities that are essential to such a society can exist only in the present, then theater is, for Rousseau, a medium that cannot acknowledge those virtues.

Those who have worked with Rousseau's thought on these matters have generally felt a kind of doubleness. On the one hand, one sees what he means; on the other there seems to be an insistence that is too strong, as if Rousseau were trying to convince himself of something here. There is an interesting exception to this stance, and it occurs in a long footnote in the *Letter to d'Alembert*. In the *Letter*, he famously footnotes a passage recounting a childhood memory of the epitome of free citizenship.

Rousseau describes a scene in which he and his father looked down on the square in the St. Gervais quarter of Geneva and watched a militia regiment. After dinner, the band plays and they begin to dance; soon they are joined by others in along serpentine chain; women come to the windows and then down to the celebration. The mood is one of unmitigated joy at being there (or should we say *Dasein*?). Rousseau's father turns to him and recalls to him, as it were in a baptism, that "You are a Genevan." Rousseau continues:

They wanted to pick up the dance again, but it was impossible. They did not know what they were doing any more; all heads were spinning with a drunkenness sweeter than that of wine.... I am well aware that this entertainment, which moved me so, would be without appeal for a thousand others; one must have eyes made for seeing it and a heart made for feeling it. No, the only pure joy is public joy, and the true sentiments of nature reign only over the people.[18]

Here we have a festival without invidiousness. This extraordinary description of what one might call the bacchanalia of the political contains a number of elements that shed light on the possibility of political representation. First, the dance comes from the music and is both coordinated and formless: All work together as if all knew the same steps even though (perhaps because) the steps change all the time.[19] This is not the coordination of Rameauian harmony, in which each plays a different part and the whole is experienced only in the listener. Here each member performs the whole and hence, while requiring others, experiences the other as he or she experiences himself or herself. It is worth the reminder here that in the *Essay on the Origin of Languages* Rousseau indicates that music degenerates by "imposing new rules on itself" and by assuming a "fixed form" in which the "rules of imitation were multiplied."[20]

Second, the effect of the gaiety is to lose all sense of self-consciousness ("they did not know what they were doing") in the revelry of one's public identity. Hence the players are not looking at themselves or others in the potentially dominating way noted above. This is the only space for true theater: life. In the *Letter*, Rousseau had complained of the Frenchman's proposal to establish a theater in Geneva. However, here we see that Geneva, at its best, was itself a broad and universal theater.[21] Rousseau does not so much want to keep theater out of life, but to experience life as theater. Molière makes this impossible when, as in "*The Misanthrope*," he leaves us as an audience off the stage laughing at Alceste: This is the source for Rousseau's attack. Molière gives the audience the pretense of being superior: His theater thus reinforces domination.[22]

Third, the quality of this experience is that it is "eternal," that is, is completely in the present. Time past does not affect, nor is it affected, by the course through time. Rousseau, in his *Confessions*, presents himself as a person obsessed by his past: Crimes of his childhood, oversights and omissions of his youth haunt him and lie, as Marx and Joyce were to say in similar contexts, on him like a nightmare. The boldness of the *Confessions* lies in the claim that by bringing his past into the present he will make himself available as a human being to those around him. The complete picture of a person is everything that person has been: No wonder humans are multiple beings. (All of us [can] have been everything).[23] Similarly, a representation in politics must not hide the past or avoid the present, but make the entirety of the context exist in the moment.

Hence, the quality of presence in the St. Gervais festival is an encounter with, a being-in, the world as it is, with its being and not its historicity. As Hannah Arendt, following Martin Heidegger, was to argue 175 years later, it is this experience that is at the source of human identity, with being a people. The movement from music to dance to the theatricalized political realm makes forgetting unnecessary: One can simply be what one is, naturally, as it were.

Last, and most important, it is central to remember that there are two citizens who do not participate in this great dance of remembering. They are the young Rousseau and his father, framed in a window, framing the natural stage of life. The theorist must always be a spectator, for theory must "overlook" in order to represent the political context. The question becomes, we then think, how to be a theorist of the public without being an aloof spectator, that is, how to make sense of what it means to be a member of a/the public without claiming for oneself a privileged position in relation to it. To approach Rousseau's answer to this we have to look elsewhere.

REPRESENTATION'S DANGERS: THEATER

Rousseau's short essay "On Theatrical Imitation" has been neglected by interpreters, perhaps understandably so. Written as a part of (but never included in) the *Letter to d'Alembert* on theater, Rousseau himself says it is "only a kind of extract from diverse places where Plato treated dramatic imitation."[24] Because this work claims no originality beyond translation and compilation – Rousseau says, "I have hardly done anything other than gather together these [diverse remarks] and bind them in the form of a coherent discourse"[25] – no real act of *interpretation* seems required. However, this is too hasty an assessment. Any act of translation can be revealing, both in the subject matter chosen and in the understanding of a work a translator's choice of words display. In the case of "On Theatrical Imitation," the interpretive potential increases because, in grappling with Plato's texts, Rousseau makes a handful of emendations and additions. Rousseau's text is a rendering of the Platonic understanding as modified to fit the modern world.

Despite Rousseau's claim in a letter to Madame de Warens that he is learning Greek, his texts do not appear to have been translations but drew from existing French editions.[26] Considered simply as a summary, "On Theatrical Imitation" follows almost exactly the order and sense of the *Republic*, Book X (595a–608b), with additional amendments from other Platonic texts (*Republic*, Book III, the *Gorgias*, and the *Laws* are most obvious). In Book X of the *Republic*, Plato has Socrates return to the discussion carried on in Books II and III on the place of poetry in the education of the Guardians. Socrates argues in Book X that imitative ("mimetic") artists do not display an understanding of their subject's fundamental nature (its *eidos* or form), but instead present only a deceptively one-sided perspective on that subject. They do not represent being, but appearance. Not only is this presentation deceptive, but such art evokes passions in the audience that interfere with both reason and the perception of truth. Individuals beholding such art come to identify with the passions they witness and lose the ability to constrain their passionate side.

Rousseau follows this general sketch and makes little attempt to reorganize Plato's material.[27] We might therefore think of this work as the preliminary argument that makes possible the more extended argument in the *Letter to d'Alembert* that imitative art – dramatic poetry in particular – had a profound effect on its audience and needed to be censored or eliminated for political reasons. The longer argument presupposed answers to a distinct set of questions about imitative representation. First, what is an imitation or representation and what does it do? Second, who makes these representations and how do they do it? Last, who perceives and judges these representations, and how can Rousseau's adjustments of Plato's text best be understood as arising from his own answers?

WHAT IS AN IMITATION AND WHAT DOES IT DO?

As does Plato, Rousseau starts by trying to define "imitation." For both, imitation involves the representation of an object or action, often by means of a different medium than the original. Although Rousseau accepts Plato's claim that an imitation requires an original model that is "abstract, absolute, unique and independent,"[28] he immediately brings the whole matter down to earth by dropping the suggestion that this form had originally been designed by a divinity. Rousseau's example is an architect who uses a preexisting model of a palace in order to construct such a building. The architect "does not construct the model, he follows it, and this model is in his mind beforehand."[29] Here Rousseau substitutes the architect for Plato's carpenter who builds beds. This changes the sense of the metaphor slightly: Whereas it is acceptable to claim that a carpenter (a) uses no representative models to guide his work and (b) manufactures several beds based on the same mental idea, neither of these claims works well for the architect. The irony of this substitution is obvious

338   C.N. DUGAN AND TRACY B. STRONG

when Rousseau writes that "the architect can make several palaces based on the same model."[30] Rousseau, in his choice of example, has changed the sense of imitation from an artistry based on a practical understanding of an object's use to a technical act of design based on formal principles.[31] Bearing out the more technical sense of imitation, Rousseau later compares the architect to the philosopher in his obedience to principles – a comparison much less appropriate to a carpenter.[32]

Rousseau makes several other important amendments to the concept of imitation. They concern the effect on the character of the persons who must deal with imitations or "real" things. In Plato's text, Socrates asks whether anyone who had knowledge of the object of imitation would choose merely to represent it or would choose instead to act on that knowledge. If poets have real knowledge about heroism and courage, why would they present imitations of those virtues rather than becoming memorialized heroes themselves? (*Republic*, 599ab) Rousseau instead asks whether anyone presented with an image of his mistress would prefer that image to the possession of the real thing, or whether an artist capable of both creations would choose to create a simulacrum rather than the model (a house rather than a painting of a house). For Plato the contrast had been between imitating virtuous action and acting virtuously; for Rousseau, the distinction lies between possessing an imitation and possessing an object that exists in the real world. In his play "*Narcisse*," he had suggested that Valère, having postponed his marriage because he had fallen in love with a portrait (unrecognized) of himself as a woman, was in risk of removing himself from genuine society with others altogether – the threat of a kind of solipsism.[33] Rousseau's distress here is with the human temptation to prefer imitations over actuality and the effect of that preference on human society.

In part this subtle manipulation of the original sense of imitation must relate back to the distinct dangers that each author sought to address. Two other amendments develop this distinction. Plato was concerned that dramatic poetry continued to be used as a baseline for virtuous behavior in morality and politics because the emotionally appealing combination of music and words interfered with the individual's ability to develop and scrutinize a moral code on the basis of rationality.[34] Rousseau, on the other hand, was not threatened by the presence of poets and dramatists in his society, but was instead concerned with the corruption of social behaviors that resulted from witnessing such spectacles. It was suggested in the *Republic* that if poetry is allowed in the city, "pleasure and pain will be monarchs in your city contrary to both law and rationality which is always in common believed to be best"[35] (*Republic*, 607a). Rousseau adds to this, "the excited passions will dominate instead of reason; the citizens will no longer be virtuous and just men, always submitting to duty and fairness, but will be sensitive and weak men who will do good or evil indifferently, according to where the are led by their penchant."[36] Rousseau is at pains to emphasize the feebleness and incontinence that results from exposure to drama; and in fact he appears to be much more concerned than Plato with what one must call a perceived *feminization* of the citizens.

This concern is presaged by another of Rousseau's interpolations. Plato's text notes that it is customary to praise an individual for being emotionally restrained in the face of personal losses, and that a lack of restraint is considered womanly (*Republic*, 605e).[37] He opposes the social custom of restrained emotions to the suspension of restraint on stage and the praise such displays receive. Rousseau here launches into a long digression on the ways that this contradiction corrupts a proper sense of what is praiseworthy and how feminine (weak) behavior becomes valued at the expense of masculine virtues.[38] He suggests that, because of the influence of theater, we treat as good-natured

those who, always praised by the sex that subjugates them and which they imitate, have no other virtues than their passions, nor other merit than their weakness. Hence equality, force, constancy, the love of justice, the empire of reason, imperceptibly become detestable qualities, vices which they decry; men make themselves honored by all the things which make them worthy of scorn; and this reversal of healthy opinions is the infallible effect of the lessons which they are go to the theater to take.[39]

The performance of "feminine" behavior – being overly passionate (*vivement affectés de tout*), visibly mourning losses (*pleurent comme des femmes*), failing to look to rationality in decision making (*ne connaissent d'autre règle que l'aveugle penchant de leur cœur*) – changes the character of both audience and actor.[40]

The major point here is that Rousseau is applying gendered terms of autonomy and self-control to theatrical experience. Being

"feminine" means, in Rousseau's estimation, that control of perception and judgment is given up for the experience of a representation
and accepting that representation's partial perspective as the entire
truth. Poetic and dramatic representations enhance our desire that
there be a single truth such that we hand our judging faculty over to
the poetic author, depriving the audience members of their will to
evaluate the representation.

Who Can Make a Representation, and How Should It Be Done?

Rousseau makes this more clear in his amendments to Plato's answer to the second prevailing question. As noted above, Plato's text
insisted that poets must not have knowledge of how to be virtuous
and heroic, for if they did they would choose to be virtuous heroes
and serve the city in that capacity. The failure was of knowledge
and not of character. Rousseau had changed this sense slightly by
focusing on possessing real objects rather than doing real actions.
He further digresses from the original text by suggesting that it is
ridiculous to entrust the right to make poetic models of behavior to
those whose character makes it impossible for them to understand
the world as it is. He asks,

what to think of the one who wishes to teach us that which he could not
learn? And who wouldn't laugh to see a foolish group going to admire all the
forces of politics and of the human heart brought into play by a twenty year-
old scatterbrain, to whom the least sensible person in the assembly would
not wish to confide the least of his affairs?[41]

In the same way that a person might allow another to manage his
or her accounts, an audience puts its faith in the poet. This situation is worsened by the fact that the author is usually hidden from
the audience during performance – in effect, for Rousseau, the poet
entrusted by the audience could be anyone.

This is a truly dangerous situation because the artist is able to
constrain the audience's faculty of judgment. Plato had suggested
that an artist is only capable of representing one perspective at a
time of any given image (*Republic*, 598a). Rousseau makes this a
much more willful decision on the part of the artist, adding that the
artist

choosing this point of view according to his wishes, renders, following what suits him, the same object as agreeable or deformed to the eyes of the spectators. Thus never does he depend on them to judge the thing imitated in itself; but they are forced to judge them based on a certain appearance, and as the imitator pleases: often too they judge them only by habit, and *he brings arbitrariness right up into the imitation.*[42]

This is the sense in which the audience becomes "feminized" in Rousseau's terms: passive vehicles that merely accept the (masculine/active) imposition of the artist's judgment.

Rousseau reinforces this view by continuing to amend Plato's text to fit this assertion. In the midst of Plato's claim that though an artist paints craftsmen, he or she has no knowledge of the craft (*Republic*, 598c), Rousseau adds that the artist *abuses* the audience:

he abuses us doubly by his imitations, both in offering us a vague and deceptive appearance, in which neither he nor we knows how to distinguish error, and in employing false measures in order to produce this appearance, that is to say, in altering all the veritable dimensions according to the laws of perspective: in this way, if the spectators senses doesn't apprehend the change and limit itself to seeing the painting for what it is, they will be *fooled about all the relationships of the things presented to them*, or will find them all false.[43]

Similarly, further on Rousseau alters Plato's description (*Republic*, 602d) of optical illusions, adding that

all these errors are evidently in the judgments precipitating from the mind (*esprit*). It is this weakness of human understanding, always pressed to judge without knowledge, which gives a hold to all the prestige of magic by which optics and mechanics abuse our senses.[44]

The artist and poet capitalize on the weaknesses inherent in human perception, and through these devices disable the audience's faculty of judgment. This view, completely consistent with Rousseau's argument in the *Letter to d'Alembert*,[45] is notably lacking in Plato's text.[46]

WHO JUDGES AND HOW?

For Rousseau, preserving the possibility of judgment in a modern and social world was of primary importance. So it is not surprising that in answering this Rousseau most aggressively modifies Plato's text. One of Rousseau's first acts of revision was to abandon the classic Platonic tripartite soul. Instead of the Socratic discussion of the parts of the soul we find a focus on "the nature of man." This was a useful revision because it allowed Rousseau much more forcefully to argue for a proper relationship between reason and passion. He strays from Plato's text again in insisting that art arouses passions and that pleasures deny reason, whereas measured instruction connects with reason but ignores passion. "The art of representing objects is very different from the art of making them known. The first pleases without instructing; the second instructs without pleasing."[47] Rousseau wishes for neither the passions nor for reason to be directed by themselves towards anything. This would produce necessarily a limited and – Rousseau indicates – self-serving judgment. Human nature itself – mostly self-love – drives the potential judge to favor the pleasure of beholding a singular perspective granted by the artist. The contrast is starkly set by Rousseau's addition to *Republic*, 598c (cf. *Republic*, 602d):

Add to this [Rousseau had been attacking the use of perspective] that measurement, giving us successively one dimension and then another, slowly instructs us in the truth of things; instead appearance offers us everything all at once, and, under the opinion of a larger capacity of spirit, flatters the senses by seducing self-love (*l'amour-propre*).[48]

Moreover, his solution to this problem of passionate seduction of self-loving nature is much more drastic. Plato had suggested that instead of resorting to impassioned lamentation, one should concentrate on rationally balancing that inclination with emotional healing[49] Rousseau writes instead that one should find profit in bad fortune, and one should know how to "take, if it is necessary, a healing iron to his wound, and make it bleed so as to heal it."[50] Also one is to do this work by not allowing the passions to make an end run, as it were, around reason.

It is the relationship between author and audience that affects the possibility of judgment. In our experience of theater, we lose control over properly ourselves; our purely sentimental attraction to the portrayals "delivers us to our tender emotion for objects that are foreign to us."[51] In this state of suppressed rationality, the audience cannot dispassionately judge the presented characters.[52] The attraction to elements not within our own character proves almost irresistible: "in leaving us thus subjugated to the sadness of others, how do we resist our own?"[53] In the end, experiencing the emotions of others as our apparent own costs one the capacity to resist one's own emotions.

Part of the irresistible attraction to others' emotions, even when those passions or individuals are thought contemptible, is a problem of recognition. The witnessed passions need to connect with the audience's emotions and manners, and as such the audience is never simply a spectator. In responding emotionally to a performance, the audience admits its own similarity with the characters represented. To Plato's discussion of the ineffectiveness of presenting a temperate and well-adjusted character on stage (*Republic*, 604e), Rousseau adds that the vulgar

have difficulty getting interested in an image which is not their own, and in which they do not recognize their manners or their passions: never does the human heart identify itself with objects which it feels are absolutely foreign to it.[54]

Any sympathy with a performance is an admission of one's own character as well as a future endorsement.

There are, it appears, no criteria by which to judge a work of art other than those that the work gives us. As poetry and theater give us works that are not our own, we enter, quite happily, into dependence on others. As Rousseau remarks in the *Discourse on Inequality*, "All ran to their chains, thinking to preserve their liberty."[55] Here as in his social and political thought, Rousseau firmly rejects the idea of any preexisting natural standard by which representations can be judged. Instead, the ability to judge and evaluate is a product of habituation. Rousseau notes in a long footnote insertion that our perception of the world is shaped by our environment and our experience. He notes that pushing standards of interpretation back to natural dispositions is a flawed strategy; remarking on music in particular, he states that

we still do not know if our system of music isn't founded upon pure conventions; we do not know if the principles aren't totally arbitrary, and if any other system substituted for that one wouldn't through habituation succeed in pleasing us equally.[56]

He goes on to set up the challenging proposition that because painters currently attempt *trompe l'œil* works that appear to be bas-relief, it should be possible to make a bas-relief appear to be flat. Exposure to representations accustoms us to recreate similar acts of creation and judgment. The problem that Rousseau brings out here in his discussion of imitation is that neither in representational art nor in politics are there natural foundations. The problem for theater and poetry was that we were taken over by someone else, not against our will but without our wills or judgment. The reference to the nonfoundational quality of music will be essential for our subsequent discussion of music, for music is of all the arts the least representational. For now, it is important to note that judgment in music, art, or poetry does not work on the level of natural sentiments; instead a habituated sensibility or taste[57] is essential to proper evaluation of representations.

The essence of Plato's assault on poetic and artistic representation is that the audience is forced to turn its powers of judgment over to the artist. The essence of Rousseau's is that we as spectators are taken over by the characters, by our desire not to be ourselves. A representation that sought to maintain the dignity and authority of the individual members of the audience would have to find a way to avoid the traps that these forms of representation suffer. At this point Rousseau interjects with a defense of the philosophical perspective, and an explanation of why the philosopher, who is also ignorant, is a better judge.[58] He responds that

the philosopher does not profess to know the truth, he searches for it; he examines, he discusses, he expands our views, he instructs even while making mistakes; he offers his questions for our questions, his conjectures for our conjectures, and affirms only what he knows. The philosopher who reasons submits his reasons to our judgment; the poet and the imitator makes himself the judge.[59]

We suggest in the next subsection that music held out for Rousseau the possibility of avoiding this trap, as well as offering a model for moving beyond the problems created by modern language and communication.

As a final note, one small emendation of Plato's text that would not otherwise merit attention looks more important in light of the larger changes addressed above. Rousseau makes some changes with regard to the tone of Plato's criticism of representational art. In the *Republic* (601de), Plato had suggested that the standards for evaluating an object or action arise from the practices that put that object or action into use: Thus the flute player is the best judge of whether the flute maker has created a good product.[60] However, Rousseau refuses the flute player/maker analogy; the standards for evaluating musical representations (and the objects used to make the sounds that compose these representations) are more obscure. Instead of the flute, Rousseau writes elegantly of the

painting of the horses harnessed to Hector's chariot; the horses have harnesses, bits, reins; the goldsmith, the blacksmith, the saddle-maker made these diverse things, and the painter represented them; but neither the worker who made them nor the painter who drew them knows what they must be; it is up to the horseman or the driver who uses them to determine their form according to their usage; it is up to him alone to judge if they perform well or badly, and to correct their errors.[61]

However, who "uses" a poetic or artistic representation? Painting clearly, and poetry to a lesser extent, still rely on an attachment to a fundamental end user: Each refer mimetically to objects and actions in the world that permit of expert judgment based on utility. Music for Rousseau sidestepped this peril of representation by basing the evaluative standards *within the audience* rather than with the artistic creator or a imagined end user. For this reason, music provided a model through which Rousseau could conceive of a form of representation that was not politically or morally detrimental.

REPRESENTATION ABSOLVED: MUSIC

Rousseau thus keeps music intentionally separate from theatrical representation. Rousseau clearly indicated his dissent from Plato on this issue: In lamenting the decline of musicality in language, Rousseau remarks that "in cultivating the art of convincing we lost the art of arousing. Plato himself, jealous of Homer and of Euripides, decried the former and could not imitate the latter."[62] Although Plato's assessment of poetic and theatrical imitation had been useful for Rousseau, he distances himself from Plato's interpretation of music. This will have important political consequences. Theatrical representation is held out as analogous to oppressive attempts to represent the general will; the way in which such representation stimulates wrong passions wrongly and removes judgment from the audience is similar to the problematic nature of modern language. Music on the other hand offers the possibility of signification and performance that invoke passions that can be simultaneously judged and experienced by the listener. It holds out the hope of communication when words fail us. Most importantly music does not by its nature require that we give ourselves over to that which is not our self. The considerations on music should thus lead to a revision of the conclusions advanced by Jacques Derrida in *Of Grammatology*.[63] There Derrida argues that Rousseau's text undermines that which it claims to support, viz. the possibility of imitation (*mimesis*) and all the binary oppositions that such a concept requires. In fact, as we argue below, Rousseau is either in effect or consciously trying to overcome classical notions of imitation (and its accompanying metaphysics).

One way to mark this distinction is to look at Rousseau's plan for a collected edition of his works on theater – comprising *Essay on the Origin of Language in which melody and musical imitation are discussed, Of Theatrical Imitation*, and *The Levite of Ephraim*.[64] Though such a compilation was never published, Rousseau's intention to publish all three works together puts an interesting spin on the interpretation of each. The first work tells us that language has become separated from music, and this prohibits the possibility of persuasion in the modern world. The second, as we discussed above, defines theatrical representation as a model for all forms of spectacle that steal the capacity for and right to judgment from an audience. The final work, derived from the *Bible* (Judges, XIX–XXI), ties these two works together by illustrating the potentially redeeming function of poetic representation.

Rousseau calls *The Levite* "a little poem in prose"[65] and focuses in both prefaces (written at different times) on the special character of the work.[66] As a work of art composed in a time of great anger and sadness, it shows above all the possibility of transcending injustice, sublimating vengeful passions, and creating beauty through redirected passion. The story itself describes the improper expression of anger and vengeance, only to conclude with a redeeming act that moves the community beyond the cycle of injustice. The Bible details an event in which a Levite under guest protection in a foreign city is forced to hand over his concubine to be ravaged by the Benjaminite residents. In retribution the man cuts her corpse into twelve pieces and sends them to the tribes of Israel calling for revenge. The Israelites absolutely decimate the entire tribe save 600 men, even though only a handful were involved in the incident. Regretting their severity they commit another injustice by slaughtering another town to provide wives for the 600 remaining Benjaminites. Rousseau adds in his version that the last 200 abducted women were given a choice to stay with family and prior loves or marry the remaining Benjaminites. Following the example of one woman, all choose to marry in order to restore peace.

The decision of these women and Rousseau's own act of poetry stand in opposition to the savage responses of the Levite and Israelites. An excess of passion betrays their judgment: "Unfortunate humans who do not know what is good for you, you would be well to sanctify your passions; they always punish you by the excesses the make you commit...."[67] Rousseau explicitly calls for moving beyond such passions: "know how to pardon the guilty rather than punish the innocent."[68]

What we have to remember in this tale is that these events happened in the time before law:

In the days of liberty where nothing reigned over the people of the Lord, it was a time of license where each, without recognizing either magistrate or judge, was alone his own master and did all that seemed best to him. Israel, then scattered in the country, had few large cities, and the simplicity of their manners rendered the empire of law superfluous.[69]

This "simplicity of manners," which recalls the precivilization of the *Essay on the Origins of Inequality*, also permitted the creation of a spectacle to represent injustice (the dismemberment of the corpse) that required a response and judgment from the witnesses. Whereas written law encodes judgments beforehand,[70] spectacle summons the audience to make an evaluation in the present case alone. Rousseau encourages the people, in the face of the crime at hand, to

assemble yourselves; pronounce on this horrible act, and decide the price that it merited. In such crimes, one who turns away his glance is a coward, a deserter from justice; true humanity envisages them in order to know them, to judge them, and to detest them.[71]

However, in spite of the rational language of this passage, the Israelites own response was too harsh and too impassioned. What is needed is a way of composing a representation in words so as to evoke the passions but restrain them. A language that combines reason and passion is necessary; and reuniting words and music is the only hope for this nondespotic language.

To understand this, one must look at what Rousseau says about language in its most elemental appearance. (What he says will apply also to music, for there was no distinction originally). The first expressions used by human beings were "tropes." In eighteenth-century rhetoric tropes signified a displacement of a word onto something not its own and from which the meaning came only by virtue of the displacement.[72] Hence language was figurative before it was literal. Rousseau gives this example:

A savage man, in meeting others, will be first of all scared. His fright will make him see these men as bigger and stronger than he; he will give them the name of *giant*. After many experiences, he will have recognized that these supposed giants, as they are neither bigger nor stronger than he, the stature was not appropriate to the idea which he first attached to the word *giant*. He will thus invent another name common to them and to him, for example the name of *human*, and will leave that of *giant* to the false object which had struck him during his illusion.[73]

Rousseau then extends this to phrases. The following observations seem noteworthy. First, our fears in relation to the other lead us to misuse language, or more accurately, to respond from the desire to do away with the other; second, the literal or correct use of language is attained socially and through experience – it is learned; third, it consists in coming to accept commonalties, a shared world, that one had first refused or not acknowledged. There is, one might say, five years of psychoanalysis between *giant* and *human*. What is important is to realize that what makes the word human literal is the fact that is embodies the feeling of commonalty with the other. Humanity is something achieved. Thus although language is conventional it nonetheless has reality. Last, and most important, it does not appear that one can arrive at the literal or correct use of language without having the figurative or illusory use. The illusion is necessary to the capacity to develop the literal. It is always retained along with our literal use. Our capacity for the literal depends on our capacity for the figurative. Our use requires that we can misuse.

How do we come to use language as human beings use it, as the source of our commonalty and thus our difference? Most important, what is or can be the role of music in this process? Three ideas are to be avoided if we are to understand this.[74] To grasp this, let us look at a passage that Rousseau repeats three times in his writings of this period.

Music acts more intimately [than simple noise] on us by in a sense arousing in us feelings similar to those which might be aroused by another.... May all nature be asleep, he who contemplates it does not sleep, and the art of the musician consists in substituting for the insensible image of the object that of the movements which its presence arouses in the heart of he who contemplates... he [the musician] will not represent objects [*des choses*] directly, but will arouse in the soul the same pulsions that one might have in seeing them [Rousseau has been talking of storms and such].[75]

Music has for Rousseau a much wider range than the other arts: indeed, it takes in all the senses. Whereas painting deals not with the imagination but only with one of the senses, music "paints everything, even those objects which are not visible... she seems to put the eye in the ear." The point is, as Rousseau continues, that music can "arouse in our heart the same pulsions as one feels in seeing the [objects]."[76] It is important to recognize that when Rousseau speaks of musical imitation he does not mean "depiction"; he means that music makes us have the same feelings that we would were a particular person or object present to us. Music makes a world present. What is important about music is that it can give us the correct feelings – that is, those feelings that are appropriate to and part of the experience of what is present to us. Music is thus cognitive, not in the sense of saying what something is, but in the sense of establishing an appropriate relation to it – like learning to say "man" above.[77] Humans and music and language are what they are in that they are social: Transparency is not the aim here.[78]

Rousseau thus rejects one common device for explaining music's potency. He does not refer to its "natural" ability to give pleasure or to point toward a sort of mystical reverence based on its alleged imitation of the divine. Instead he argues that music is first and foremost a human and a social practice.[79] Music was born in the same instant as speech, for the first words spoken by humans were sung.[80] However, as languages became less and less bound to the force of the musical accent that gave words their passionate force, music itself became less effective in representing passion. Music comes to need the supplement of pleasure to bolster its moral force.[81] With this separation of language and music, words become the vehicle of rational communication, whereas music becomes the means of representing the passions.[82] Indeed, whereas d'Alembert had placed music in "the last place in the order of imitation," Rousseau places it highest.[83]

Music makes the passions available in three related ways. These three facets are clearly stated when Rousseau argues that "sounds in a melody do not act on us solely as sounds, but as signs of our affections, of our sentiments; it is in this way that they excite in us the movements which they express and in which we recognize the [represented] image."[84] First, music acts as a signifier for a set of objects or actions that are not currently present. Instead of using characters (as theater or novels) or images of objects (as painting or sculpture), music signifies through memory.[85] The sounds operate through hearing to evoke responses that had once been experienced by other senses and uses the individual auditor's imagination as the backdrop for representation.[86] Music is thus our own, in a way that painting is not.

In the second place, music creates depictions in the imagination of the audience by evoking passions within each individual. Melody, the heart of music, takes its potency "from the moral effects of which it is an image; knowing the cry of nature, the accent, number, measure and emotional and passionate tone which the agitation of the soul gives to the human voice."[87] The third part of this imitation is the recognition of the represented object because it imitates passions known to the audience. Music in effect makes the audience hear things that the senses associate with particular actions, objects, and passions. These are, for Rousseau, part of what it means to understand what something is. Melody is akin to the passions insofar as "in imitating the inflections of the voice expressing complaints, cries of sadness or of joy, threats, groans; all the vocal signs of the passions are in its jurisdiction."[88] The audience does not just recognize the passions being represented (as one might discern the passions represented on stage without actually *feeling* them), it becomes implicated and submerged within the experience of those passions. Rousseau writes that "the *chef-d'œuvre* of Music is to make itself forgotten, so that in discarding the disorder and trouble in the soul of the Spectator it hinders him or her from distinguishing tender and emotional Songs of a moaning Heroine, from the true accents of sadness...."[89]

One must not misunderstand this compound idea of representation as a substitution of emotional signs for actual passionate states. Olivier Pot has, for instance, suggested,

as Diderot's reflections on the forms which representations take in the deaf or blind – the senses can only perceive by substitution of other senses following an infinite metaphor or a metonomy of corporeal perceptions – , music is only able to imitate by means of associative displacements of ideas, in the end dismissing the art of sound to a signification always deferred and distinctive (différée et propre).[90]

Although it is certainly true that music for Rousseau relies on a metonymic substitution, this does not mean that its signification is necessarily deferred. Rousseau's argument is that there is no natural standard or language to which we can refer in order to understand the significance of music. Instead, human interaction in society and through language provides individuals with the grammar for properly experiencing musical communication.[91]

However, for this representation to be comprehensible, its signification must be clear and singular. Rousseau repeatedly argues against the danger of "double representation" in music. This phrase is used in particular to describe the contemporary situation in opera in which the sense communicated by the visual spectacle of staging and characters is distinct from the sense of the accompanying music.[92] This dissonance between content and music was the key point of attack in the quarrel between the partisans of Italian and French music of the time.[93] However, this problem is manifest in several different forms throughout Rousseau's writings on music. The most frequently assailed obstacle to clean musical communication is harmony.[94] Beyond this, potential doubleness arising from the contrast of melody and harmony, dance and poetry might also come into conflict – or at least appear redundant.[95] In essence in all these conflicts what is missing is "unity of melody." Rousseau notices this ideal in all arts:

all of the fine Arts have some *Unity* of object, source of the pleasure they give to the mind: for shared attention doesn't settle at all, and when two objects occupy us, this is proof that neither of the objects satisfies us. There is, in Music, a successive *Unity* which relates to the subject, and by which all the Parts, well connected, compose a single whole, by which one perceives the ensemble and all the relationships. But there is another *Unity* of object [which is] finer and more simultaneous, from which is born, without one thinking of it, the energy of Music and the force of its expressions.[96]

Although the former kind of unity operates on the level of sensual pleasure, the second, more potent unity is achieved through communication with the audience. This unity "is a pleasure of interest and of sentiment which speaks to the heart."[97] This singular representation of emotion communicates to the auditor by giving him or her a stake in listening (appealing to the "interest") and by offering emotions for which one is not wholly responsible (the pleasure of sentiment).

For Rousseau, music can represent and communicate only when it strives for this singularity of expression. Music and language are already drastically separated, almost beyond hope of repair. In fact, attempts to repair this state of affairs is more likely to lead to worse decay: In attempting to reunite itself with language, music is forced to resort to the monotonous languages that further deprive it of emotional force.[98] Because modern languages are no longer capable of sustaining the appropriate passionate force, composers come to rely on harmony to provide musical pleasure. However, this development further cripples music by separating

song and speech to such an extent that the two language combat each other, oppose each other, mutually deny each other all character of truth and cannot reunite themselves without absurdity in an emotional subject.[99]

With these two complementary languages kept wholly distinct, the expressivity and range of representation of each were lessened: Music could no more than conjure emotions without communicating a moral, and language could only make statements without the possibility of persuasion.[100] Because these two modes of expression are both limited, judgment of music and speech is similarly limited–reason has no place in the former, and passion none in the latter. This said, the matter is not without hope. Rousseau is also clear that whatever the distance be between music and language in the contemporary world, the original unity between them persists sufficiently to be at the source of music's continued ability to speak to that modern world.[101] The fact of music is testimony to the existence or the possibility of the existence of a truly human social bond. "As soon as vocal signs (*signes*) strike your ear, they herald (*annoncent*) a being similar to yourself; they are, so to speak, the organs of the soul and if they depict solitude they tell you that you are not alone."[102]

It is for this reason that national musics express the noble memory of self-creation. Rousseau notes that Swiss officers forbade the playing of the "*Rans des Vaches*" to troops as it led them to desert, "so much did it excite in them the burning desire to see their homeland."[103] Music is thus for Rousseau the mode by which we acknowledge the presence in our lives of other humans as humans. "One feels that [music] concerns us more than [painting] precisely because it makes one person closer to another (*rapproche plus l'homme de l'homme*) and always gives us some idea of those who are as we are (*nos semblables*)."[104] If humans were not capable of music – if it were not natural to them in the same way that language is – the acknowledgment of others that is a prerequisite for a truly human, just society, such as that Rousseau depicts in the *Social Contract*, would not be possible.

A society that has a language for political life will value eloquence over the use of public force. However, the only form of speech appropriate to a people to whom it can be said "such is my pleasure" is a sermon, and such people are taxed rather than assembled. The acknowledgment of others that arises naturally from a language that retains its connections to music is absent in a society that knows politics only through the language of decree. In a society with no musical language for politics, no one can hear. In fact, their language will have degenerated to the point that no one will be able to be heard in public:

Herodotus read his history to the people of Greece assembled out of doors, and he met with universal applause. Nowadays an academician who reads a paper in public session can hardly be heard at the back of the hall.[105]

This extraordinary analysis of Greece, complete with its Nietzschean condemnation of Plato, reveals a central quality that free society must have for Rousseau. There is to be no disjuncture between emotion and expression, between weeping and words, between meaning and saying. When the two are available to each other, there is no possibility of taking the speaker as other than he or she is. Furthermore, this experience of availability happens only in a manner that makes it available in the same manner to any other person.

The conditions of my freedom, as presented here musically, are the same conditions as yours.

This brings us back to the central questions of this essay. We began by considering the common assertion that Rousseau was averse to representation in politics and art and looked to the curious exception of music to grasp this supposed rejection more clearly. By drawing out the distinctions between representation in theater and representation in music, we isolated the problematic nature of improper representation in the theatrical removal of judgment from the audience. So long as the audience is merely given decisions to swallow or, in politics, given decrees to obey, there can be no individual autonomy. More importantly, without the possibility of recognizing others in one's own practice of judgment, one's human potential as a social creature is unfulfilled. We asserted that this was the key implication of Rousseau's ubiquitous attention to the relationship between music and language. A language that has lost its musicality – its ability to represent emotion while making rational arguments – will be unable to persuade or create real social bonds.

We posed the question of representation as an issue about creativity in politics and about the possibility of political theory more generally. Representation in politics, both in the sense of the presumption to speak for others and in the sense of generalizing about different political contexts, appeared problematic because it denied the presence that Rousseau insisted was essential for sovereignty. What we found, however, was that Rousseau provides us with models of a legitimate sort of political representation. The political theorist can remain a spectator, and political theory can be abstract, but only if the language used does not remove the means by which the theory can be judged. A theory that works only in logical terms is insufficient, not only because it is not persuasive – a characteristic essential to a *democratic* theory – but also because in neglecting passion it fails to make itself available to us as our own. Music holds our attention because it is part of who we are; similarly, political theory must find a language that makes its audience know its assertions as the audience's own. Otherwise, democratic theory remains an elusive impossibility: "all language with which one can not make oneself heard by the assembled people is a servile language; it is impossible that a people should remain free and speak this language."[106]

ENDNOTES

1 We have cited from Jean-Jacques Rousseau, *Oeuvres Complètes* (Paris: Gallimard, 1964ff) in five volumes. All translations are our own, unless otherwise noted. Citations are by key to the work, internal division number and/or section title, OC (for *Oeuvres Complètes*), volume number (roman), and page number (arabic). We use the following key:

C = Confessions (*Les confessions*)
D = *Dialogues. Rousseau judge of jean Jacques* (*Dialogues. Rousseau juges de Jean-Jacques*)
DM = *Dictionary of Music* (*Dictionnaire de musique*)
DOI = *Discourse on the Origin of Inequality* (*Discours sur l'origine de l'inégalité*)
E = *Émile* (*Émile, ou de l'education*)
ESOL = *Essay on the Origins of Language* (*Essai sur l'origine des langues où il est parlé de la mélodie et de l'imitation musicale*)
IT = *Of Theatrical Imitation* (*De l'imitation théâtrale*)
LdA = *Letter to d'Alembert* (*Lettre à M. d'Alembert concernant les spectacles*)
LE = *The Levite of Ephraim* (*le Lévite d'Ephraïm*)
LFM = *Letter on French Music* (*Lettre sur la musique françoise*)
LM = *Letters Written from the Mountain* (*Lettres écrites de la montagne*)
OM = *The Origin of Melody* (*l'Origine de la mélodie*)
SC = *Social Contract* (*Du contrat social*)

2 Beatrice Didier, *La musique des lumières: Diderot, L'Encyclopédie, Rousseau* (Paris: PUF, 1985), Chap. 5 and passim.
3 *Dialogues* 2 OC i, 872–3.
4 SC iii 1 OC iii 295. See also LM 5 OC iii 244.
5 The manifestation of government is *la police*, general bureaucratic administration and regulation.
6 SC first version i 7 OC iii 310.
7 SC ii 6 OC iii 379. For a more extended discussion see *Tracy B. Strong, Jean Jacques Rousseau. The Politics of the Ordinary* (Thousand Oaks, CA: SAGE, 1994), Chap. 3.
8 Stanley Cavell, *Must We Mean What We Say?* (New York: Scribners, 1969), p. 39.
9 *Fragments politiques* OC iii 465.
10 SC iii 9 OC iii 485.
11 The best description of this is that of Michael Fried. See *inter alia* his *Art and Objecthood* (Chicago: University of Chicago Press, 1998),

especially the title essay (pp. 148–172) and the essays on Anthony Caro.

12 On this see also the dissertation by Steven Affeldt, "Constituting Mutuality: Essays On Expression And The Bases Of Intelligibility In Rousseau, Wittgenstein, And Freud" (Cambridge, MA: Harvard University, 1997).

13 See the discussion in Strong, *Jean Jacques Rousseau*, op. cit., pp. 94–101. See also G.D.H. Cole, *Essays in Social Theory* (London: Macmillan, 1950), pp. 113–131.

14 SC I 7 OC iii 362. The French reads *"nulle espèce de loi fondamentale obligatoire pour le corps du peuple."* We read this as indicating that the kind of fundamental law that there cannot be is one that *obliges* the body of the people (note: not each person) in order to reconcile this with the passage in E 5 OC iv 840: "...[W]e see that there cannot be any other fundamental law, properly speaking, but the social pact." There can be a fundamental law, but not one that has the quality of obliging people. This was one of the aspects of the *Social Contract* that drew the angry attention of the Genevan prosecutor, Jean-Robert Tronchin. On the matter of the place of obligation in society generally see Hanna F. Pitkin, "Obligation II," *American Political Science Review* XXXX.

15 As Nelson Goodman has argued (*Languages of Art*, New York: Bobbs-Merrill, 1968), works of art may be allographic (in which the copy is a different entity, like a painting) or autographic (in which the copy is the same as the original, like a music score). However, in neither case can a work of art be represented and still be a work of art. The beginning of thought on this seems to us Walter Benjamin's classic essay, "The Work of Art in the Age of Mechanical Reproduction" in his *Illuminations* (New York: Schocken, 1968).

16 LdA preface OC v 4 [English translation in Allan Bloom, *Politics and the Arts. Letter to M. D'Alembert on the Theatre* (Ithaca, NY: Cornell University Press, 1989), p. 4 – henceforth given as Bloom. Bloom gives "prudence" for "wisdom" (*sagesse*) and "urbanity" for "grace" (*politesse*).] Some of the following paragraphs draw on Strong, *Jean-Jacques Rousseau*, op. cit., 92 ff.

17 *Narcisse preface* OC I 965–966.

18 *Letter to D'Alembert* OC v 123–4.

19 I am reminded of Gilles Deleuze's idea of a perfect game in *Logique du sens* (Paris, Minuit, 1971), in which the rules change all the time and are nevertheless rules.

20 ESOL 18 OC v 424.

21 Compare Plato's *Laws*, VII 817b, in which poets are told that "our entire constitution has been established as an imitation of the noblest and

best life, which we say is really the most true tragedy (*tragôidian tên alêthestatên*)." See note 58 of this chapter.

22 Whether or not Rousseau was right about Molière, it is worth noting that what he found in the St. Gervais festival is remarkably like what Nietzsche says can be or was realized in classical Aeschylean tragedy. There the chorus permits the audience to "overlook" (in both senses of the word) the "entire realm of culture." See Tracy B. Strong, *Friedrich Nietzsche and the Politics of Transfiguration* (Berkeley and Los Angeles, CA: University of California Press, 1988), Chap. 6, and Tracy B. Strong, *The Idea of Political Theory* (Notre Dame, IN: University of Notre Dame Press, 1990), Chap. 2.

23 See George Kateb, "Whitman and the Voice of Democracy," in Tracy B. Strong, ed., *The Self and the Political Order* (Oxford, U.K.: Blackwells, 1991), also revised as the last chapter in his *The Inner Ocean* (Ithaca, NY: Cornell University Press, 1992).

24 IT preface OC v 1195.

25 IT preface OC v 1195.

26 It should be noted that Rousseau was unlikely to have made translations from Greek. As to Rousseau's claim "*J'apprens le Grec!*" (*Correspondence Complète* 146 II 113), this probably meant he was able to write the Greek characters as a good copyist, but did not have mastery of the language. We know that he had access to a copy of Plato's *Œuvres* published in 1550 by Jean de Tournes, on a page of which he transcribed with some occasional commentary ten short phrases (reprinted in OC v 1297–8; see OC v cccvi.

27 For the sake of accuracy, it should be pointed out that the exact order is violated three times: part of 602d is imposed between 598b and 598c; 603c is imposed before 602d; 604c is imposed in the middle of 603d.

28 IT OC v 1196.

29 IT OC v 1196.

30 IT OC v 1197.

31 And probably as well based on contemporary taste: the architect is building *palaces*, not mere houses.

32 IT OC v 1204: "The Poet is the Painter who makes an image, the Philosopher is the Architect who lifts up the plan: the one doesn't deign to approach the object to paint it; the other measures before drawing."

33 See the discussion in Strong, op. cit., pp. 46ff,

34 For several different views of Plato's rejection of poetry, see E. Havelock (*Preface to Plato*, Cambridge, MA: Harvard University Press, 1963), I. Murdoch (*The Fire & the Sun: Why Plato Banished the Artists*, New York: Oxford University Press, 1977), S. Rosen (*The Quarrel Between Philosophy and Poetry: Studies in Ancient Thought*, New York:

Routledge, 1988), Alexander Nehamas ("Plato on Imitation and Poetry in Republic 10" in Moravscik and Temko, eds., *Plato on Beauty, Wisdom, and the Arts*, Totowa, NJ: Rowman and Littlefield, 1982) and H.-G. Gadamer ("Plato and the Poets" in *Dialogue and Dialectic: Eight Hermeneutical Studies on Plato*, P.C. Smith, trans. New Haven, CT: Yale University Press, 1980).

35 *Republic*, 607a. All translations of Plato are by Dugan, following Burnet's text [*Platonis Opera*, v IV, New York: Oxford University Press (Clarendon), 1902].

36 IT OC v 1210.

37 Plato had previously (*Republic* III, 411b) mentioned that excessive attention to music leads to a weakening of masculine strength – such a musical fanatic becomes a *malthakon aichmêtên*, a "gentle warrior" or "effeminate spearman." Apollo had called Menelaus this when urging Hektor to battle him (*Iliad*, XVII, 588).

38 The editors of the OC correctly note that this passage borrows from *Republic* III in its aversion to lamentation; the language used, however, is Rousseau's own – as is the strong emphasis on effeminate qualities.

39 IT OC v 1208. Wingrove ("Sexual Performance as Political Performance in the *Lettre à M. d'Alembert sur les spectacles*," *Political Theory* **23**:4, 1995:587) argues that "Rousseau considered nature an imperfect determinant of gender difference. In his sexual politics, bodies are originary signs only to the extent that they are political sites, where the enactment of meaning and the showing of difference depends more on theatrics than on science." One's "gender" was based less on anatomical reference (the new scientific mindset), than on performative gestures and representations of the self. This meant that theater could have a devastatingly potent effect on both the actor (who portrays the feminine) and the audience (who sympathetically experiences the feminine, and comes to find it within themselves).

40 In her article (op. cit., 616 n. 110), Elizabeth Wingrove attacks one of us (Strong, *Jean-Jacques Rousseau and the Politics of the Ordinary*) for an argument that whereas the male and the female sexes and have political meaning for Rousseau, man and woman do not. In Strong's analysis, Rousseau's consideration of citizenship finds a problem with sexual desire in that sexual desire makes impossible the acknowledgment of the common that Rousseau requires for the realization of political justice. Men are, according to Rousseau, only intermittently possessed by sexual desire whereas women, up to a certain age, are constantly. We recall, here that the Spartan woman who has had five children is presumably too old to have more and is the model of the citizen in Book XX. In a

fragment on women that has too rarely received attention, Rousseau notes that the small number of examples of women in positions of political preeminence is due to the "tyranny of men" for "all [power] is in their hands." Were this not the case, he continues, we would also see "in the other sex models of all the kinds of civic and moral virtues" (OC ii 1254–1255). Excellence of citizenship is thus not necessarily gender differentiated. Like Plato, Rousseau is trying to make *citizens* regardless of physical gender, it is sexuality and the dynamics of desire that are problems for him. One might recall also that Plato thought that the perfect city would fall when the guardians had "children out of turn," i.e., yielded to desire.

41 IT OC v 1200–1.

42 IT OC v 1197–8.

43 IT OC v 1199 (our italics). This last phrase suggests something of a *gestalt* shift that takes place in the audience: Either it sees the work as the author intended it to (i.e., submit to his or her judgment), or it does not understand the work at all. In neither case is the audience's judgment called into action.

44 IT OC v 1205.

45 Reason has no effect when one is watching a performance, so exposure to the dramatized passions forbids evaluation of whether those passions are proper or virtuous (LdA OC v 17–20). See the tirade against Molière (LdA OC v 31–42).

46 In a sense this is necessitated by the different author's view of truth and judgment. Plato was concerned that the representations made by artists who lacked knowledge would not cohere with absolute truth (except by accident). A well-made, truth-coherent representation could thus be quite effective for Plato (e.g., *Laws* II, 658e–660a, VII, 811cd; see C.N. Dugan ("Reason's Wake: Political Education in Plato's *Laws*," University of California at San Diego). Rousseau is less concerned with universal truth than with the possibility of rendering authentic judgments, a power that is renounced in watching theatrical representations. So although Rousseau is deeply dependent on several aspects of theatricality, theater itself is a deeply problematic institution.

47 IT OC v 1198.

48 IT OC v 1199. See Wokler, *Social Thought of J.J. Rousseau* (New York: Garland Publishing, 1987), p. 258: "Measure provided the structure of the song... bearing the same relation to melody as syntax to speech"; M.-G. Pinsart, "Musique – Texte – Passion dans les œuvres théoriques et musicales de J.-J. Rousseau," in *Annales de l'institut de philosophie et des sciences sociales*, Bruxelles, 1988, pp. 21–31, p. 24: "La déclamation chantée s'attache en priorité à suivre pas à pas et à souligner

l'accent grammatical, c'est-à-dire à se modeler sur les règles propres d'une langue. ... "

49 "But instead always habituating the soul to move quickly to healing and correction of the fallen and sick parts, thus obscuring threnody with healing (*iatrikêi thrênôidian aphanizonta*)" (*Republic*, 604d).

50 IT OC v 1207. The centrality of this theme in Rousseau has been explored by Jean Starobinski, *Le remède dans le mal* (Paris: Gallimard, 1989), pp. 165–232.

51 IT OC v 1209; amends *Republic*, 606a.

52 Compare LdA OC v 21: "I question whether all men to whom one exposes in advance the crimes of Phaidra or of Medea, will detest them more at the beginning than at the end of the play: and if this questioning is founded, what needs to be thought of this so vaunted effect of the theater? I would like very much for someone to show me clearly and without verbiage, by which means it could produce in us the sentiments which we do not already have, and make us judge moral beings otherwise than we judge them by ourselves."

53 IT OC v 1210; amends *Republic*, 606d.

54 IT OC v 1207.

55 DOI ii OC iii 177

56 IT OC v 1198.

57 Note the emphasis Rousseau places on the social and political importance of "taste" in the LdA: I say taste (*le gout*) or customs (*les mœurs*) indifferently: since even though one of these things might not be the other, they always have a common origin, and suffer the same revolutions. Which does not mean that good taste and good customs always reign at the same time, a proposition which demands clarification and discussion; but it is incontestable that a certain state of taste always responds to a certain state of customs (OC v 18).

58 The editors of the OC see inspiration for the following passage to *Laws*, 817bd. Again, this is accurate insofar as it reflects the sense, but not the wording, of Plato's text. Plato in this location requires that all poets entering the city compose in keeping with the city's customs. He notes that the new constitution the three discussants are drafting is a form of poetry – the best form since "this constitution just constructed is an imitation of the most beautiful and best life" (*hê politeia sunestêke mimêsis tou kallistou kai aristou biou*, *Laws*, 817b). If we assume that the three discussants are meant to be considered *philosophers*, then the OC may be justified in seeing a source of inspiration for Rousseau (but philosophy, per se, is mentioned only twice in the *Laws*).

59 IT OC v 1204.

60 This suggestion has been difficult to reconcile with Plato's apparent

commitment to eternal Forms that exist outside of (and even in spite of) actual practices. See Christopher Janaway, *Images of Excellence: Plato's Critique of the Arts* [New York: Oxford University Press (Clarendon), 1995], and Dugan, op. cit.

61 IT OC v 1203.

62 ESOL 19 OC v 425.

63 Jacques Derrida, *De la grammatologie* (Paris: Minuit, 1967), esp. pp. 203–34. [Trans by G.C. Spivak, *Of Grammatology* (Baltimore, MD: Johns Hopkins University Press, 1976).] Derrida sets music aside in his analysis.

64 The projected preface for the three can be found in OC v 373. See OC v cxciii. The matter is made more complex in that Rousseau planned in the 1765 edition of his works to place the *Essay on the Origins of Languages* after his *Lettre sur la musique française* and the *Examen de deux principles*. See Jean Starobinski, *Introduction*, OC v cc.

65 LE first preface OC ii 1205.

66 Rousseau thought quite highly of the work: He hopes his elegy will be "In the most cruel moments of his life, he created *The Levite of Ephraim*" (LE first preface OC ii 1206) and he notes in the *Confessions*, "If it is not the best of my works, it will always be the most dear of them" (C 12 OC i 1074).

67 LE 3 OC ii 1220.

68 LE 1 OC ii 1208. Compare from the earlier version of this passage: "learn to reign over your passions" (LE variant OC ii 1922).

69 LE 1 OC ii 1208–9. Compare Judges XXI:25.

70 Breaking a law defines the offender as unjust and the penalties are known before the crime, so no judgment beyond an assessment guilt is necessary.

71 LE 1 OC ii 1208. Compare Judges XIX:30, in which the display of the dismembered body *requires* the Israelites to render a judgment and decide on a course of action.

72 See Bernard Lamy, *La rhetorique ou l'art de parler*, art: Trope (1675). See Starobinski's discussion in his introduction to ESOL, OC v.

73 ESOL 3 OC v PAGES. See Strong, *Rousseau*, op. cit., pp. 86–88; Compare the discussion of this passage in Stanley Cavell, *The Claim of Reason* (Oxford, U.K.: Clarendon, 1979), pp. 466–457. Cavell reminds us that Freud notes somewhere that our first experience of others is fear, "a scream."

74 Compare with Jean-Jacques Rousseau, *Essai sur l'origine des langues*, edited and introduced by Catherine Kinstler (Paris: Flammarion, 1993), pp. 35ff.

75 DM s.v "Imitation" OC v 860–1. See Philip E.J. Robinson, *Jean-Jacques*

Rousseau's Doctrine of the Arts (Peter Lang, Berne, New York, 1984).
The other references are in the article on Opera and the first part of
ESOL, Chap. 15. Compare the letter to D'Alembert, 26 June 1751 (CC
ii p. 160) in which the same point is made.

76 DM, s.v. Imitation OC v 860–1. We use the somewhat rare pulsions to
translate *mouvements*.

77 See the excellent discussion in Downing Thomas, *Music and the Origins of Language: Theories of the French Enlightenment* (New York:
Cambridge University Press, 1995), pp. 103–5.

78 Here we avoid a long argument with Jean Starobinski (op. cit.) and Catherine Kintzler, *Poétique de l'opéra francais de Corneille at Rousseau*
(Paris: Minerve, 1993), p. 28.

79 On the one hand he battles against Rameau's theory of natural harmony,
which is universally appealing. On the other he scorns the "vague and
general definitions" the Ancients gave to music (DM, s.v. *Musique*, OC
v 915); regarding the connection between music and the divine muses,
he writes "whatever the etymology of the name, the origin of the Art is
certainly closer to man... " (OC v 916).

80 ESOL 12 OC v 410, OM OC v 333. However, cf. DM, s.v. *Chant*, OC
v 695, in which Rousseau claims that "song does not seem natural to
man. ... Melodious and appreciable song is only a peaceful and artificial imitation of the accents of the speaking or passionate Voice. ... "
Speech may be natural to humans, but music separated from its original
connection with spoken words is artificial imitation.

81 DM, s.v. *Opéra*, OC v 951: "From this is born the necessity of bringing
physical pleasure to the aid of the moral and of substituting the attraction of Harmony for the energy of expression," LMF OC v 293: "The
impossibility of inventing agreeable songs obliged Composers to turn
all of their concern to the side of harmony, and lacking real beauties,
they introduced beauties of convention, which have almost no other
merit than the *vanquished difficulty*; instead of a good Music, they
imagined a learned Music. ... "

82 OM OC v 337: "It seems that as speech is the art of transmitting ideas,
melody would be the art of transmitting sentiments. ... "

83 D'Alembert, *Preliminary Discourse to the Encyclopedia of Diderot* (Indianapolis, IN: Bobbs Merrill, 1963), p. 38. Thomas cites this passage
also, op. cit., p. 125.

84 ESOL 15 OC v 417.

85 With certain familiar songs and melodies "Music does not act precisely like Music, but like a reminding sign (*signe mémoratif*)," DM,
s.v. *Musique*, OC v 924.

86 ESOL 16 OC v 421: "music acts more intimately on us in exciting

by one sense affections similar to those which could be excited by another...."

87 OM OC v 342.

88 ESOL 14 OC v 416.

89 DM, s.v. *Opéra*, OC v 954.

90 Introduction to LMF, OC v cxxi.

91 This relates as well to the then-raging debate over the nature of the French and the Italian language. Rousseau saw French as the language of reason and philosophy (LMF, 2nd ed, OC v 1448n.a), but Italian was better suited to music and emotion (LMF OC v 297). Italian therefore works less by displacement of emotional sense by rational signs than by conjoining the two. However, of course, as a modern language the degree to which this power has degenerated is always in question. On Rousseau's contrast between Italian and French languages in music, see O'Dea, *Jean-Jacques Rousseau: Music, Illusion and Desire* (New York: St. Martin's, 1995), pp. 28–31.

92 DM, s.v. *Opéra*, OC v 957: Painting, "in the manner which it is used in Theater, is not as subject as Poetry to make with Music a double representation of the same object..."; 958: "it would be a great error to think that the regulation of Theater has nothing in common with that of Music, if it is not general propriety that they draw from the Poem. It belongs to the imagination of the two Artists [the musical composer and the stage designer] to determine between them what the imagination of the Poet left to their disposition, and to accord themselves so well with this that the Spectator always senses the perfect accord between that which he sees and that which he hears."

93 The accusation of "*contresens*"; see O'Dea, op. cit., p. 24. Compare M.-G. Pinsart, op. cit., p. 23: "*De par son origine commune avec le langage, la musique ne peut avoir que la déclamation comme modèle, elle doit en exacerber les ferments expressifs. Le travail du musicien est de souligner les inflexions d'un texte, de mettre les mots en valeur et non de les cacher sous les sons.*" The relevant texts for this quarrel have been gathered in *La querelle des bouffons*, 2 vols., Denise Launay, ed. (Genève: Minkoff, 1973).

94 On the failure of harmony to stimulate emotions or achieve imitation, see *Fragmens d'observations sur l'Alceste italien de M. le Chevalier Gluck*, OC v 449: "... harmony by itself, being only able to speak to the ear and imitating nothing, can only have very weak effects... It is by the accents of the melody, it is by the cadence of the rhythm that music, imitating the inflections which give the passions to the human voice, can penetrate all the way to the heart and move it by sentiments...."

95 DM, s.v. *Opéra*, OC v 961.

96 DM, s.v. *Unité de mélodie*, OC v 1143.

97 DM, s.v. *Unité de mélodie*, OC v 1144.

98 ESOL 19 OC v 426.

99 ESOL 14 OC v 416.

100 ESOL 20 OC v 428–9. Some hope of productive expression is held out though: "The quantities of Language are almost lost under those of our Notes; and Music, instead of speaking with speech, borrows, in some part from Measure, a separate language. The force of *Expression* consists, in this way, in reuniting these two languages as much as possible, and in insuring that, if Measure and Rhythm don't speak in the same manner, they at least say the same things."

101 ESOL 12–14 OC v 410–17, esp. 416: "l'empire des chants sur les coeurs sensibles."

102 ESOL 16 OC v 421. This entire chapter is filled with the superiority of music to all other forms of representation.

103 DM s.v. *Musique*, OC v 924.

104 ESOL 16 OC V 421.

105 ESOL 20 OC v 429.

106 ESOL 20 OC v 429.

13 The Motto *Vitam impendere vero* and the Question of Lying

TRUE CAUSES

In a lengthy note to the *Letter to d'Alembert* (1758), Rousseau declares that he has taken as his motto *Vitam impendere vero*.[1] The announcement is solemnly accompanied by an address to the reader and by an invocation to truth:

Readers, I may deceive myself, but not willingly deceive you; fear my mistakes and not my bad faith. Love of the public good is the only passion that makes me speak to an audience, so I am able to forget myself [...] Holy and pure truth to whom I have devoted my life, never shall my passions sully my sincere love for you, neither self-interest not fear will be able to change the homage it pleases me to pay you and never shall my pen refuse you anything but what it fears to grant to vengeance![2]

These are the words of an oath. Rousseau takes comfort in an allegiance to truth alone at the time of his break with Diderot and at which he becomes convinced that he must live without friends. At this time, Rousseau wants to serve that truth that contributes to the "public good," that is to say, to all individuals. After the publication of *Émile* and the *Social Contract*, in 1762, and without Rousseau's renouncing the goal of usefulness animating his "system," his profession of truth will increasingly take the self as its object. His insistence at the beginning of the *Confessions* is well known: "Here is the only portrait of man, painted exactly according to nature and in all its truth [...] I want to show my peers a man in the full truth of nature; and that man shall be myself."[3]

His autobiography is an account. Rousseau develops it in the finest details of his actions in order to make their deepest motives tangible. These actions were perhaps "bizarre," but they were never based on malice. The pleasure of recounting and multiplying images of the past is obvious, and this pleasure is seconded by a calming certainty: The more complete the narrative will be, the more it will become apparent that Jean-Jacques never intended to do ill, contrary to the slander he feels weighing on him. Because he believes himself innocent, it is in his best interest to reveal everything.

His first great autobiographical text, the four letters written to Malesherbes in the beginning of 1762, is an exposition of "motives" for Rousseau's conduct. He has taken up the pen, he assures the reader in the first of the letters, in order to enlighten his correspondent who, like everyone who "interprets his actions," is mistaken about those motives. Correction first turns on the "true cause" of his choice of solitude. The real cause was neither melancholy nor disappointed vanity, but "a natural love of solitude."[4] As far as the "invincible disgust" [...] that he has "always felt in human intercourse," Rousseau declares that he had "long [...] been mistaken about its cause." He discovers late that it came to him from "the indomitable spirit of freedom that nothing has been able to overcome."[5] For a long time, he had been unaware of it himself. He was to need to concentrate on better reading within himself, which means that his personal "dictionary" is constantly under revision.[6]

By Rousseau's own admission, there are, then, private motives that are immediately perceptible and others that are far less so and that require further attention. When he writes, at the beginning of the *Confessions*, "I feel my heart," he takes advantage of an immediate certainty that does not seem to call for the effort of a difficult deciphering. The task, in principle, is thus only to fix in writing everything that immediately forces itself on consciousness, whether it is a question of remembered images or current feelings. However, many pages of the *Confessions*, and subsequently the *Rêveries*, attest to the fact that the ascribing of his actions to their "real cause" was to remain for Rousseau not only a problem but a duty that he did not believe he fulfilled sufficiently. Thus it is that throughout the *Dialogues*, the two characters staged – Rousseau and the Frenchman – try to decode the "impenetrable mystery" of persecution and agree to seek out, as if by conjecture, the real Jean-Jacques. The character named Rousseau resolves to visit Jean-Jacques in order to "fathom him in his very interior, if possible."[7] The Frenchman, for his part, shall read Rousseau's works. We are certainly confronted with an expository endeavor. They shall then debate, in the Third Dialogue, their respective findings. Yet how revealing is this distancing, which allows the real Jean-Jacques and his "real motives" to be grasped only at the price of a double, painstaking external approach. There is a long way to go until the truth is ensured.

Precisely contrary to the distancing that is the formal premise of the *Dialogues*, the *Rêveries* lay claim to extreme closeness, the renunciation of any relation to a hypothetical reader. They try to be an absolute monologue, claiming even to exclude any reader. The *Rêveries'* agenda, as is well known, is only in part an immediate transcription of the wanderings of thought. The project is also to complete, for oneself alone, an examination that remained unfinished, in order to illuminate fully anything that might still be hidden. The *Rêveries* are not whimsical flights of fancy. Each of them maps out the work of a liberation from agony, even as occasions for agony are renewed. In the obstinate plan of finding compensation for his sufferings, Rousseau pursues the deciphering of the self in order to find an inner shelter from universal hostility. The role of euphoric reveries is limited, but these ecstatic moments are all the more intense by contrast.[8]

One has only to reread the first Promenade, in which Rousseau sets out the project of examining himself and of "reflecting upon [his] inner arrangements," by applying "the barometer to [his] soul." Two distinct levels can be seen mapping themselves out. The first is the soul subjected to unforeseeable affective variations. The second is the observer reading atmospheric variations on the barometer. This observer tries to be precise and clear sighted. The image of the barometer does not only imply (as Marcel Raymond has shown[9]) a meteorological perception of an inner world given over to sudden mood swings, but it also expresses the utopia of a numbered, graduated translation of changing passions. The observing subject becomes another for himself. Too far away not to be a traitor to himself, too close not to be his own accomplice. When one applies the barometer to the soul, metaphor and grammatical structure bring about an instrumental relationship between the self as observing subject and the self as object of observation. This is the paradox of introspection, which opens private space only at the cost of a split. The person who examines himself must transport himself from one level to the other, by means surpassing in precision those of a dictionary that

permits moving from a term to its definition in the same language
or to its counterpart in a foreign language. Rousseau, by this entirely
artificial effort, hopes to acquire "a new knowledge of [his] nature."[10]

THE INNOCENCE OF NATURE

Discerning causes, motivations, and arrangements in the secrecy of
souls: Such was the work of the moralists of the previous century,
informed by the philosophical doctrine of the passions and by the
morality taught by the Church, which tried to be faithful to the
teachings of Augustine. Their unfailing method was to oppose being
to appearance in order to make the masks of appearance fall. They
concentrated most often on denouncing false virtues, false brilliance,
on uncovering the "mechanisms" that "truly" determined an action,
or the "ends" that the action sought. "It is important first and foremost," writes Augustine, "to know by what cause, for what goal and
with what intention one acts."[11] This moral questioning, as we shall
see, resembles that which judicial rhetoric had long recommended.

La Rochefoucauld and his friends detect the dominant power of
self-love in the depths of the heart: In it they see the cause of causes
tirelessly at work. It is *through* it that we act. It inspires our motivations, that is to say, the satisfactions *for* which we form our enterprises. Like Pascal and his friends from Port-Royal, La Rochefoucauld
et al. become the accusers of the intentions and desires of which
we are puppets. What is honorable according to the rules and conventions of the "world" turns into sin according to revealed truths,
which teach that human nature is wounded, because it is marked
by the inheritance of Adam's disobedience. On the worldly stage are
strewn glories and prestige that lose all their brilliance in the eyes
of faith. This confrontation is an act of interpretation, which reads
the reality of the profane order by the light of the supernatural order. If one follows the suspicions of the religious moralists (or of the
laymen who echo them), the self-interest that moves us never has
the nerve to express itself directly: It uses trickery, it disguises itself,
it lies in order to make itself palatable. It uses devious means, like
the symptom in Freudian theory. The possessive desire inhabiting us
does not let go, but changes its language, deceiving its way into our
own conscience. The astuteness of the moralist–observer is distinguished by carrying out an operation of discerning the hidden cause.

To have recourse to a simple expression, one should designate this operation as a causal retroversion.

What grid of reading did the thought of the Christian moralists apply to apparent conduct, to explain it by its prime movers? Their method consists in essentializing a first "intention" or "disposition" by giving it an almost autonomous status. The target they wish to attain is original desire, generative of all subsequent passions. They denounce a desire [*appétition*] of which all the vices and apparent virtues of men are the altered appearance. This ailment [*affection*], in the language of French theologians of Augustinian inspiration, is named concupiscence, in which the creature, breaking off from its Creator, favors itself. According to these writers, the creature has been, from the moment of the first sin, prey to the triple libido – *libido sentiendi, libido sciendi,* and *libido dominandi.*[12] The moralists refer to it in each particular case by appealing to explanatory operators and reductors (adverbs or conjunctive locutions) such as "is," "only," or "because." "Our virtues most of the time *are only* disguised vices"; "the holiest and most sincere friendship is *only* a trade [*trafic*]" (La Rochefoucauld). Our gaze is thus turned back toward a reality that not only precedes appearances but has produced them.

To show the vices of society, as we know, Rousseau used the arguments of the religious critique of the human heart. With one important correction: Self-love is not innate; it was introduced over the course of the history of the human race, because of the socialization of an initially sparse human population. Perfectly innocent self-interest is its natural precursor. It is on this "genealogical" consideration and on this great qualitative distinction that Rousseau allows practically his entire philosophy of history to rest: Self-love, to which all the vices of social man can be imputed, is a late modification – an alienation and a straying of an initial self-interest, present in natural man, and close to the instinct of self-preservation common to all animals. In his doctrinal writings, Rousseau expressly combated the dogma of original sin. From that point on, the responsibility for evil no longer weighs on original human nature, but on men such as they have made themselves. Rousseau therefore refuses to inscribe at the base of human nature the guilty *libido* condemned by the Christian moralists. Leaving "the hands of nature," man is "naturally good." Something of this earliest innocence remains in those who would be able (as Rousseau claims the privilege for himself) to consult their conscience. The psychology of Augustinian inspiration saw through the ruses of self-love behind apparent human virtues and retranslated concealed virtues and vices. Rousseau, on the other hand, faced with evil, gives himself the advantage of making the responsibility weigh on society, while at the same time absolving certain people presumed guilty (and himself first of all) by returning to a native goodness. This doctrine authorizes anyone not profoundly disfigured by social life, therefore Rousseau first and foremost, to *retranslate* any guilty deficiency such that it can be reduced to misguided innocence, to frustrated goodness. When Rousseau declares that he is seeking a refuge in his "heart" and in his "earliest" feelings, it is in order no longer to find any trace of the evil into which social life may have led him. He boldly assures the reader that never has there been a better man than he. Henri Gouhier has shown convincingly how Rousseau substituted "nature" for "grace." By defining himself as the "man of nature," Rousseau seeks to keep open a path leading back to a clear origin, that is to say, to the possibility of annulling guilt and of giving himself as a homeland an uncorrupted [*inaltéré*] world.[13]

THE CASE OF THE STOLEN RIBBON AND JUDICIAL ELOQUENCE

In a famous episode from the *Confessions* (Book II), Rousseau in turn incriminates and exculpates himself. It is the story of the stolen ribbon, and then the false accusation of a servant, in the house in which he was a lackey in Turin, immediately following his conversion. The reflection on truth and lying developed in the fourth Promenade will again return to this error of his seventeenth year. The two evocations of these events show us how Rousseau practiced causal retroversion, that is to say, the way in which he retranslated a moment of his own history on which he feels the weight of an accusation of a "crime."

Let us recall the broad outlines of the episode. In the disorder following the death of Madame Vercellis, Jean-Jacques stole a ribbon lost by Mademoiselle Pontal, the dead woman's chambermaid. Temptation is initially the only alleged cause of the theft, as if it had only been a question of a self-centered compulsion: "This ribbon alone tempted me, I stole it. . . ." The theft having been easily noticed, Rousseau now appears before a domestic tribunal. He denies the theft and charges Marion, a young servant in whom he is interested: "Blushing, I say that Marion gave it to me." Worse than that, he remains unmoved by the girl's reproaches. He continues lying "with an infernal impudence." Marion and Jean-Jacques are both dismissed: "prejudice was in my favor."[14]This false accusation is thus a "crime," a "heinous act": these are the terms in which the text of the *Confessions* avows it. For in the case of Marion, dismissed and no longer able to find "a good position," the "consequences" of the mendacious accusation (Rousseau assumes) were no doubt dire. "Who knows, at her age, where the discouragement of debased innocence may have led her."

On examining closely the pages relating to the lie and its consequences, one can easily believe that they conform to a model. That model is none other than that which classical judicial rhetoric recommends to the orator.[15] Rousseau, faced only with himself, appears once again in the case that was so badly judged in the domestic tribunal of the Vercellis household. We are present at a long-distance case that the autobiographer brings against himself, and in which the crime of which he accuses himself is less the theft of a ribbon than the slanderous accusation of which he has made himself guilty. He therefore begins, against himself, a review of the trial held forty years earlier, in which he had insisted on denying his guilt. The Jean-Jacques of yore, who at that time had benefited from the doubt concerning the theft, is accused by Rousseau on the grounds of his lie's slandering Marion. He pleads by the rules. He acknowledges his error. He was indeed the guilty party. However, he next evokes a series of circumstances that make his fault lesser than that with which he originally reproached himself. In the final analysis, the Rousseau holding the pen acquits the adolescent Jean-Jacques: "However great my offense against [Marion] may have been, I have little fear of carrying the guilt for it with me." The word "guilt" [*coulpe*] belongs to religious vocabulary, and, as we know, it is indeed with the certainty of the heavenly tribunal's indulgence that Rousseau concludes the examination of his "crime."[16] Might it not have been only a peccadillo?

In what respect is the structure of the text in conformity with the prescriptions of the past masters of the art? First and foremost, by the order of its parts, by its composition, by its *arrangement*. One sees several distinct, successive parts. An *exordium* summarily defines the case: a "crime" and its debilitating "consequences" for Jean-Jacques's conscience. Then a *narration* reveals the details of the events (answering the questions *ubi* and *quando*). Following this, there intervenes an *argument*, which carefully evaluates the facts provided by the narration. One finally arrives at a *peroration*, in which the required sentence is formulated.[17]

In the narrative development, Rousseau evokes damning facts while taking on himself all the reproaches that a prosecuting attorney might make against him. The facts are related and interpreted as if before the gaze of an unbiased witness. The narration does not stop with the scene from Turin. It continues with the story of the reproaches that Rousseau, later on, continued to make against himself. Several elements of the accusatory narration will thus be able to be reused at the time of the defense argument. The evocation of a "terrible impression" left by "the only" "crime" he committed will make it easier to excuse the mistake. The underscoring of the heroism of the confession will also be important. Rousseau, who could never commit himself to a full admission of this "atrocious action," makes it one of the main reasons for writing the *Confessions*. The desire to "free" himself of it, he declares, "has greatly contributed to my resolution to write my confessions." The autobiographical endeavor is thereby justified. Christian morality, as we will see, does not permit one to talk about oneself unless it is necessary, *sine debita causa*. We are asked to believe that the book we hold in our hands exists for that reason. The word "free," at the end of the narration, has a very wide scope: of course it concerns revealing a secret, but also, already, pleading for the remission of the error.

The argument that follows recapitulates the facts of the narrative and matches them up with a why (*cur*) and a how. It works toward qualifying the offense (toward establishing its *qualitas*, according to the rules of the art) in order to allow for a decreased responsibility. Rousseau begins by turning to his advantage the resolution that led him to this terrible admission: Noone can reproach him for having lessened the impact of the "heinousness" of his "crime." This is a good methodological procedure; thus declares Quintilian (V, 12).[18] The assurance with which one says "Yes, I did that" (*ego hoc feci*) is a proof by affirmation (*probatio ex affirmatione*). The entire narration was already such an affirmation of the offense. As the remainder of the argument for the defense develops, one can recognize the different "grounds" [*lieux*] provided for by classical rhetoric. As we know, these "grounds" are classified into two categories by the author of the *Institution Oratoire*: persons (*persona*) and things (*res*). Priority must be given, Quintilian prescribes, to proofs derived from persons, because they are more convincing (V, 10). "The proofs that I regard as the strongest are those built upon the personhood of everyone" (*ex sua cujusque persona*, V, 12). Among the latter may be counted age (*aetas*) and the permanent dispositions of the soul (*animi natura*) or fleeting emotion (which is named *commotio*, or *temporarium animi motus*, such as anger or fear). In the case of these "inner dispositions," classical rhetoric associates the *locus a persona* and the *locus a causa*.

It is indeed thus that Rousseau pleads. Not only was Jean-Jacques "barely [...] beyond childhood," but in addition he had become like a stranger to himself when he was publicly confronted with Marion. This was, according to one of Rousseau's favorite expressions, one of those moments of "confusion" and disorder that he often experienced, from which he was later obligated to "return" to himself. A moment of alienation, and therefore of irresponsibility:

But I would not fulfill the goals of this book if I did not reveal at the same time my inner dispositions, and if I were afraid to excuse myself in matters in conformity with the truth. Never was maliciousness further from my heart than in this cruel moment, and when I charged this unfortunate girl, it is strange but it is true that it was caused by my friendship for her. She was present in my thoughts, I excused myself upon the first object that presented itself. I accused her of having done what I wanted to do, and of having given me the ribbon because it was my intention to give it to her. When I saw her appear next, my heart was rent asunder, but the presence of so many people was stronger than my repentance. I feared the punishment little, I feared only shame; but I feared it more than death, more than crime, more than anything in the world. [...] I saw only the horror of being found out, publicly declared in my own presence a thief, a liar, a slanderer. Total confusion took all other feelings away from me. If I had been allowed to return to myself, I would have declared everything without fail.[19]

The chain of the argument seeks to make clear the consistency of the latent motivations behind the differing stages of his manifest behavior. By what mechanisms was the young liar moved? Rousseau applies to himself the dictionary that he constantly invites his correspondents to learn more fully. All of the terms put forth in the argument for the defense negate a previous term. In the narration, written according to the order of appearances, Rousseau speaks of his "barbarous heart." In the argument, on the other hand, Rousseau pushes aside any maliciousness. The real causes were completely different. "My friendship for her was the cause." Cruelty is imputed to the moment – to "this cruel moment." Friendship for Marion inspired the thought of the gift, but Jean-Jacques, in his confusion, saw double – or rather he *inverted* the gesture of giving by claiming that it came from her. He apologizes for it in the way one apologizes for a *lapsus linguae*.[20] The retrospective look at his "inner dispositions" organizes the syntax in an astonishingly effective way. Let us examine more closely the two juxtaposed clauses:

She was present in my thoughts, I excused myself upon the first object that presented itself.

They are two independent, successive clauses in a paratactical arrangement. The comma between them indicates the speed with which a main subject is substituted for another main subject. It is not, however, in this case, a true anacoluthon, a term suggested by Paul de Man in this context.[21] The movement of the first phrase is from "she" to "my thoughts." The movement of the second phrase goes from "I" to Marion, designated as "the first object that presented itself." The self, at first absorbed inside itself ("my *thoughts*"), then turned toward the outside ("the first *object*"), is thus in the central position. At first in a passive, receptive situation, subjectively welcoming a feminine image; then, in an active role, formulating an excuse pointing toward this "she" that has become the "first object" encountered outside. A very exact balance is achieved around the subjective center. Rousseau, for the success of his argument, gives priority to "she" as the subject of the first phrase and as the object of thought, to make her reappear in the final position, in the second phrase, as the *indirect* object of the act of excusing.[22] The device put into practice here, in the group formed by the two phrases, is commutative (forming a "*chiasmus*"). In the relationship between "she" and "I," this device causes any aggressive element to disappear. The argument moves to a reassignment of roles, as if "she" had taken the initiative, to become in return implicated in the excuse. In the subsequent sentence, it is the desire for the gift that is alleged. Certainly, Rousseau lied by claiming to have received the ribbon, but in truth, he claims, he wanted to give it. Rousseau's sentence says this through doublings and inversions, as if in a play of mirrors. Let us reread it:

I accused her of *having done* what I *wanted to do* and of having *given* me the ribbon because my intention was to *give* it to her.

The sentence is constructed in symmetries and parallelisms. The active verb "I accused her" has as its object two infinitive phrases, the second explaining the first ("of having done". . . then, more explicitly, "of having given me". . .). Then each of these two object verbs in the infinitive echoes itself ("done" calling out "wanted to do"; "having given me" calling out "to give it to her"), through an object (*what*) or an explanation (*because*) that clears the way for the statement of Rousseau's true intentions. The two parallel statements, at the end of the concatenation of objects and subordinates, finally return to the initial "I" of the motivating *intention, before* the "crime": "What *I wanted* to do," and "*my intention* was to give it to her." The accusation was an "infernal" action. The giving is an innocent action, and it is put forward as the original meaning of the entire scene. From the initial position to the final position, the "I" has been transformed from an accuser (in fact) into a giver (by intention). The sentence has performed a qualitative transmutation at the same time as a temporal regression. If there has been, despite everything, straying from this good intention, Rousseau has just given the reason for it, which is on the level of an observation. Not the slightest malice enters into it: "She was present in my thoughts." Marion, "the first *object* that presented itself," was at base only a circumstance, as fortuitous as the theft itself. The accusation was the unfortunate translation of the desire for giving. At the time of the new trial he brings against himself and the judgment intended as definitive, Rousseau retranslates dishonest speech into the primitive language of feeling: Marion had crept into Jean-Jacques's *thoughts* and he allowed himself to be seduced.

Rousseau, in the first book of the *Confessions*, had offered an explanation of his juvenile propensity for stealing. He spoke of it as a "flight of fancy" of which he was unable "fully to cure himself." He also explained it in a way that absolved him. To justify his habit of "coveting in silence," to make understood his petty thefts of tidbits and objects (never money!), he offers as a reason his timid nature, the influence of a friend, the ban imposed on the expression of desire. Above all, Rousseau made frustration the source of his envy: "Everything [...] I saw became an object of envy for my heart, simply because I was deprived of everything. [...] Nothing I coveted was safely *within my reach*.[23] The feeling of *lack*, which marks the beginning of the series of thefts – "because I was deprived of everything" – links the temptation and the offense to the consequence of a wrong suffered. It is also very nearly the case that the stolen objects, as well, are to blame for being in his sight and within his grasp.

The justification for the first thefts of adolescence holds for Pontal's ribbon, which is accompanied by the same lexical index of "reach": "A lot of other, better things were *within my reach*; only the ribbon tempted me."[24] Frustration also plays a role in this new story of theft. Mademoiselle Pontal is the niece of the Lorenzys, who were "at the head of the household" in their capacity as stewards. She was their accomplice in monopolizing the good graces of the dying Madame de Vercellis. Jean-Jacques was no longer allowed to see the latter. (Already the idea of a plot!) In her will, she forgot her little valet. "I got nothing."[25] This mortified him. The narrative of the theft follows one of privation; it is as if Jean-Jacques had wanted to avenge himself symbolically by blaming a possession of the person who had passed him over.

The argument next invokes shame: "Invincible shame conquered all; shame alone caused my impudence." Rousseau knew the definition of "self-consciousness" [*"mauvaise honte"*] according to Plutarch's treatise, in which it is called in Greek *dysopia* and in which it is defined as the opposite of impudence. To take responsibility for shame, rather than impudence, and to make shame carry the burden of his guilty demeanor, is to effect, on Rousseau's part, a reversal from one opposite to the other, from a hateful vice to an excusable shortcoming resulting from fear.[26] No, he does not accept the reproach of "infernal impudence" that he leveled against himself in the narrative portion of his discourse!

Without a doubt, Rousseau also knew the definition theologians gave of "self-consciousness" [*"mauvaise honte"*]. A chapter is devoted to it in Pierre Nicole's *Instructions théologiques et morales*.[27] It is defined as "the fear of men's judgments, of being condemned by them, of displeasing them, of being the butt of their jokes. [...] It is this self-consciousness that prevents the confession of sins and makes it so difficult." For Nicole, there are three kinds of sinful passions (the love of pleasure, the love of science, the love of loftiness [*élévation*]) that are born of concupiscence, and there are three others that are rooted in fear and that can hold us back on the path leading to God. The reference to Augustine is very precise: *Peccata duae res faciunt in homine, cupiditas et timor* (*In Psalmos*, 79). Self-consciousness, which does not result from concupiscence (or "bad love"), resembles the "fear of human evils," or "sadness." Still evoking Saint Augustine, Nicole grants that certain sins inspired by fear are venal and do not incur eternal punishments.[28] For Rousseau, in the *Discourse on Inequality* and *Émile*, fear of others' judgment is a result of restless self-love, which supplants self-interest when man leaves the state of nature. Thus social life breeds self-love, and the fault becomes collective. Whether it be according to the code proposed by Plutarch (shame or impudence) or according to that of Augustinian-inspired morality (fear or concupiscence) or according to the grid of reading of his own "system" (social vice or, by some remote chance, natural maliciousness), Rousseau opts on all occasions for the least severe interpretation of his youthful error and attributes the "true cause" of his old misdeed to a lesser evil. Translation works to the advantage of transparency, not of heinousness.

Thus the relative banality of the feelings that Rousseau substitutes for aggravating assumptions discolors the "atrocious action" he has just avowed. The procedure of the excuse consists in returning to the psychical antecedent until one runs up against, in the final step, a childhood distress, such as the "fear of being found out." The evil committed was not "true heinousness," but "weakness." The reductive, minimizing "*only*" so often used accusatorially by the moralists, functions here as an expression of exculpation. "In youth true heinousness is even more criminal than in adulthood; but that which is *only* weakness is much less so, and my mistake at base was *scarcely* anything else." Thus reread in and translated into the language of intentions and "inner" feelings, Rousseau's mistake is considerably reduced. The feelings *through* which, the reasons *for* which he lied and persisted in the lie are strange, perhaps, but there is no longer anything "infernal" or monstrous about them. This is the case, according to Thomist casuistry, in which the accuser can receive the pardon of the accused, when false witness results not from a desire to defame, but from thoughtlessness. "The accused, if he is innocent, can pardon the wrong that was done to him, above all if he was maligned not in a slanderous way, but through thoughtlessness of the soul. *Accusatus, si innocens fuerit, potest injuriam suam remittere, maxime si non calumniose accusavit, sed ex animi levitate.*[29]

Rousseau has us know that he could have acted differently if the *circumstances* had been different. It is therefore a question of an argument that, according to the oratorical code, invokes "things" (*argumentatio a rebus*). Among the many preambles that such an argument may invoke are the place and the time (*ubi, quando*) and, more broadly, the circumstance (*peristasis, circumstantia*).[30] Rousseau does not forget them. Jean-Jacques was summoned before a "numerous [...] assembly." He was impressed by the "presence of so many people." Was he not thus forced to fail? Rousseau, as we have seen, declares with confidence; "*If* I had been allowed to return to my senses, I would unfailingly have declared everything." In this way, a new *if*, a new hypothetical clause, evokes other circumstances in which the more confidential attitude of the domestic judge would have made him drop his accusations. Rousseau replays another scene in the imaginary, in which other words would have been said to him and in which a different version of himself would have admitted his petty theft. These are impossible hypotheses, in the vein of those of melancholic regret, that express the exasperation of not being able to make the fait accompli reversible:

If M. de la Roque had taken me aside, would that he had said: do not ruin this poor girl. If you are guilty admit it to me; I would have thrown myself at his feet at that very moment; I am perfectly sure of it. But they only intimidated me when what I needed was to be provided with courage.

Here then, part of the guilt is turned on the judge himself and on an outside "they." Jean-Jacques was intimidated, that is, a victim of fear, in the strong meaning that the verb has in the eighteenth century. It is thus clear how closely argument by things is linked to argument by persons and by their emotions (*commotio, temporarium animi motus*). Shame, earlier in the text, was already accompanied by "terror" and "horror." Little by little, Rousseau has thus disarmed the accusation of effrontery and audacious maliciousness of which he had become the spokesperson in the preceding narration, to the point of presenting himself as a demon facing an angel whom he slanders.

A last argument: This mistake has certainly had consequences that Rousseau was unable to foresee at the moment.[31] He was distressed about them, less because of the "evil in itself" than the evil "it must have caused" in Marion's destiny. However, was it not also a fortunate mistake? *Felix culpa.* The evil, having provoked moral pain, turns into a good. The memory of it, Rousseau assures the reader, "even did me the good of preventing me for the rest of my life from any action tending toward crime, by the terrible impression left on me by the only one I ever committed, and I believe I can feel that my aversion to lying is derived in large part from my regret at having been able to tell such a heinous one."[32] It is no longer the feelings before the mistake that are brought to the fore, but the resulting effects, which finally become benefits.

One can consider the final three sentences to be a peroration. A long sentence, followed by two concluding statements:

If this is a crime that can be atoned for, as I dare to believe, it should be through all the misfortunes weighing on the end of my life, through forty years of rectitude and honor in difficult circumstances, and poor Marion finds so many avengers in this world, that however great my offense against her may have been, I have little fear of carrying the guilt for it with me. That is what I had to say on this subject. May I be allowed never again to speak of it.

The final enthymeme, the irregular syllogism in an admirably formed sentence, begins with a hypothetical (which calls for an affirmative answer), and ends with a consecutive. With light having been shed on the motive, the sin can be considered "atonable" (and therefore relatively venal), and the narrator can turn confidently toward the hereafter. His misfortunes have not been lesser than the offense against Marion. There has been compensation. From forty years' distance, without absolving the Jean-Jacques of yore, the author of the *Confessions* pronounces himself no longer in debt: His subsequent good behavior and his "misfortunes" are signs of sufficient attrition. "Atonement," sufferings undergone "in this world," "guilt": the peroration is inscribed within the religious register. Certainly he has not righted the wrong done to Marion, but he is squared away with his own guilt.

Such is the interpretation Rousseau proposes. It rests on events about which he is our only source of information. It is commonplace today to take as "real" events such as they are narrated and to contest the interpretation that the author gives of them in order to suggest a more convincing reading. The most radical attitude, which we have adopted, consists in considering the narrative of the events and the interpretation offered by Rousseau as an indissoluble whole: a literary creation concerning a memory now inaccessible to any verification. We do not look for reasons for Rousseau's action other than those he declares. If historians find the psychological self-commentary constructed by Rousseau to be suspect, they are free to construct a metacommentary, according to a different grid of reading, particularly the one that today psychoanalysis provides. The result can never be confirmed, in the absence of new documentary evidence or of details given by the main interested party that had remained unknown. Psychological metacommentary can be expanded and multiplied infinitely without encountering any resistance. Rereadings of the "real reasons" are entirely dependent on the facts and explanations that Rousseau saw fit to transmit to posterity. There are here, at one and the same time, an exposition and a retreat that are insurmountable. The writer, henceforth silent, remains the master of the game, despite being prey to the maenads that tear him apart. About the "true feelings" of an author from the past who has claimed to have reported them truthfully, anything can be said because nothing can be assailed. 33 When one speculates on the unconscious forces that may have led the game at the time of the event or those at work at the time of the belated composition of the story of the mistake, one remains dependent on the existing text. The interpretive code through which it is deciphered gives it the causal object that fits it. A system of necessities (of necessary conditions) is thus calculated, with a seriousness that does not take into account the text's contingency. The only possibility consists in accepting the text just as it is presented, as we have chosen it, and in trying to understand it independently of the unavowed reasons that presumably precede it. In place of these reasons, our attention is sufficiently occupied with the text's internal relations, with the links it establishes with the other parts of the author's *oeuvre*, with the explicit or implicit relationship that it establishes with the outside world. One can imagine various interpretive proposals about the theft of the ribbon and about the ensuing lie, all of which are as difficult to prove as to refute. If one rejects the two versions successively proposed by Rousseau – a simple temptation immediately satisfied or the desire for a gift for Marion – the choice is broad, now that psychoanalysis has perfected the code of the libido's variants: the disorder caused by the feeling of mourning, compensation for the earliest affective frustrations, fetishism (the ribbon becoming a substitutive object), the desire to see women take the lead in love relationships, difficulty in establishing a real relationship with women, uninhibited by sadomasochistic fantasies. No one will ever know whether the memory of Marion, the servant, was not latent at the time of the encounter with the laundress, Thérèse Levasseur. Was Marion, driven away, prostituted, in Rousseau's thinking, the persecuting victim, the Erinys fueling the long chain of remorse and torment?[34] He asks us to believe him on this page of the *Confessions*, all the while asking us also to believe that he has paid the price for his mistake.

TRUTH AND LYING: GROTIUS, PUFENDORF, AUGUSTINE

At the end of the second Book of the *Confessions*, Rousseau solicits permission never again to speak of his "crime" of Turin. This is a resolution that he was not to keep. He returns to the memory of Marion at the beginning of the fourth Promenade, to begin the long examination of truth and lying in order better to judge himself. Among his papers he found a correspondent's allusion to his motto: *Vitam impendere vero*.[35] Rousseau suspects that the allusion is ironic. His mind goes to work. He also revives, by way of a postscript to the *Confessions*, the explanation of his mistake through his "inner dispositions." This time, since he impugns any outside addressee and claims to deliberate only in dialogues with himself, he no longer adopts the resource of judicial eloquence and he no longer takes the reader as a witness: the work of writing patiently develops an entire general casuistry of true speech and duty to truth. For his defense, Rousseau still puts forward the same moral and "psychological" arguments, but in an entirely different textual organization. He had no "intent to harm" Marion. His lying was a "delirium," which resulted from his "timid nature" and from "self-consciousness." The feeling *by* which his very singular behavior was prompted therefore had nothing guilty about it in itself and moreover his action left him with "undying regrets." He may have been able to lie again in other circumstances, but it was "neither *out of* self-interest nor out of self-love, even less *out of* envy or malice, but solely *out of* embarrassment and self-consciousness" (p. 1034). The mechanisms *by* which his lies were created were never substantial vices. "Embarrassment" is what constrained him, socially, to "speak before thinking," to talk "non-sense" that "[his] heart disavowed as it issued forth" (p. 1033). As when he argued in the *Confessions* on the subject of the circumstances of his "crime" against Marion, the etiology he proposes is not a vice attached to its "nature," but a lack of force: "Never did falseness dictate my lies, they all came from weakness, but that is a very poor excuse. With a weak soul one can, at the most, protect oneself against vice, but it is being arrogant and rash to claim to profess great virtues" (p. 1039). Here are, together, his line of defense and his base for regular counterattacks. Force being the condition necessary for virtue, Rousseau does not declare himself "virtuous," but all the while assures the reader that there has never been a better man than he.

No longer having anyone but himself as main interlocutor, Rousseau, in the fourth Promenade, no longer pleads his case according to the methods of judicial eloquence, but he has not for all that forgotten the notions of religious morality and philosophical reflection. His dictionary, for reading within himself, is not of his own invention: It is a code that he receives from tradition and that he adjusts for his personal use. To be sure, Rousseau pronounces himself hostile to the lesson of books and to the bad example given by worldly people. However, Rousseau remembered works of philosophy. Proof of it is soon found.

At the beginning of his long casuistic deliberation, Rousseau evokes a "book of philosophy," whose title he does not cite. In it he found a definition and a deduction to which he replies with a series of questions:

I remember having read in a book of Philosophy that to lie is to hide a truth that one *ought to* make public. It follows from this definition that keeping a truth silent that one is not *obligated* to tell is not lying; but someone who, not content in such a case with not telling the truth, says the opposite, does he or does he not then lie? According to the definition one cannot say that he lies; for if he gives counterfeit money to a man to whom he owes nothing, he no doubt deceives this man, but he does not rob him.[36]

Not without reason, it has been supposed that the "book of philosophy" mentioned by Rousseau could be Helvétius's *De l'esprit*, of which Rousseau criticized, in a marginal commentary, a note to Chap. VI, which defined lying by referring to a comment of Fontenelle.[37] However, Rousseau could have encountered the same question much earlier, in the *Droit de la nature et des gens* (1672) by Samuel Pufendorf. He had also encountered it in the *Droit de la paix et de la guerre* (1625) by Hugo Grotius, of which Book III (11–20) systematically treats the legitimacy of lying in times of conflict.[38]

Pufendorf, at the beginning of the fourth book of his work, devotes to language a long chapter he entitles "Of the *obligation* concerning the use of speech." Pufendorf, after having recalled that the signs of language were not established by nature, but by convention, adds "But that is not enough to impose the obligation upon us to reveal to everyone, by means of these signs, everything that we have in our minds. It is also necessary to be committed by a *specific convention: or that a general law of natural right* prescribes it to us." The contract of truthfulness is therefore neither universal nor unconditional. The preponderant demand is not to "do harm" and not to "cause damage to someone who does not deserve it." There are certainly transactions that call for truthfulness, so that one may "contract [*conclure*] in a valid way," and reciprocally, count "on the word of others." However, in practice this type of relationship is not unfailingly established. Pufendorf observes,

But as one does not always find oneself bound by one of these reasons to reveal what one thinks, above all concerning our private affairs: it must be admitted that one is also not obligated to tell everyone everything that is in one's mind, but only to those who have a right [. . .] to know our thoughts, and that therefore one may innocently keep silent things that no one has the right to make us explain, and that one is moreover not held to reveal on one's own volition. Much more: when there is no other way to procure for oneself or to procure for others some advantage, or one could not otherwise protect oneself or protect others from a clear and present danger, it is permissible to use external signs in such a way as to make them express anything but what one thinks, provided that in so doing one does not however threaten anyone's rights.[39]

One may therefore lie "to procure for oneself or to procure for others an entirely innocent usefulness." Depending on whom one is speaking to, to tell a falsehood (*falsiloquium*) is not always reprehensible.

"If they have no right to know our thoughts, and in hiding them from them or in disguising them from them, one does no wrong to anyone, I do not see why, when one finds doing so advantageous, one would conform one's speech to their desire rather than to our own. Thus all lies are indeed falsehoods; but all falsehoods are not lies" (Section IX). The criterion of usefulness from which we or others may benefit allows us to weight [*pondérer*], indeed to suspend, the demand for truthfulness. With "moral truth" (different from "logical truth") being thus placed within a contractual frame, exceptions to the truth can arise, so long as they do not contravene the implicit stipulations of the contract. Grotius had already said that "according to the common opinion of peoples," lying "can only be an attack made against a real right remaining without diminishment, of the person to whom one is speaking, or towards whom one uses some other sign equivalent to speech."[40] Rousseau's whole development of the circumstances in which truth is owed to others and of the usefulness that makes it a *debt* toward others, only reprises the considerations Pufendorf had been formulating in a language that remained that of the philosophy of right. Moreover, Rousseau's vocabulary, in the fourth Promenade, is striking in its juridical nature:

As for those truths that have no sort of usefulness, neither for instruction nor in practice, how could they be an owed good, since they are not even a good, and since property is founded only on usefulness, where there is no possible usefulness there cannot be property. [...] Thus the truth owed is that which concerns justice, and it is to profane the sacred name of truth to apply it to vain things whose existence is indifferent to everyone and the knowledge of which is in every way useless. Truth, stripped of any kind of even possible usefulness, cannot therefore be a thing owed, and as a result whoever keeps it silent or disguises it does not lie.[41]

Rousseau goes further in the following part of his text. However, these initial considerations have nonetheless limited the number of circumstances in which his lies could have been injustices. A second question, according to Rousseau, is formulated as follows: Can one "innocently deceive"? He recalls that on this point "the books" recommend "the most austere morality." As for him, he wonders. Are there not indifferent facts? "Anywhere the truth is indifferent, the contrary mistake is also indifferent; from which it follows that in such a case the person who deceives by telling the opposite of the truth is no more unjust than the person who deceives by not declaring it. [...] How could someone be unjust who does harm to no one, since injustice consists only in the wrong done to others?" (p. 1027).

But what are these books that Rousseau mentions? What is this austere morality? He encountered them, in a diffuse way, in the culture of the moment. Rousseau could have found this morality, for example, in Pierre Nicole's *Instructions théologiques et morales* [...], who declares, following Augustine, that all lying is a sin because "the truth [...] is God himself," and that "it is necessary to love God as truth." (Fifth Instruction, I, Chap. VI). It is not certain that Rousseau knew directly Augustine's *De mendacio* and *Contra mendacium*, from which all the moral theology of the eighteenth century still drew inspiration on the issue of lying. The religious moralists recall Augustine's general definition, "Whoever lies speaks against what he thinks in his soul, with the intention to deceive. *Omnis qui mentitur contra id quod animo sentit loquitur voluntate fallendi*."[42] Duplicity and the will (intention) to deceive are never absent from lying according to Augustine's definition. The liar must be judged according to his intention (*ex animi sui sententia*). Rousseau knows this and repeats it. "It is solely the intention" of the person who engages in speech that "determines [his] degree of malice or goodness."[43] This definition allows for putting aside simple jokes, from which "perfect souls" (*De mendacio*, II, 2) should, however, abstain. On the other hand, "it is not lying to say something false if one has formed the opinion that it is true. *Non enim omnis qui falsum dicit mentitur si credit aut opinatur verum esse quod dicit*" (*De mendacio*, III, 3). Austere Augustinian morality permits an exception for error and countertruth told in good faith. Rousseau is quick to broaden the exception to his own advantage: "...In the matter of useless truths, error is nothing worse than ignorance. Whether I believe that the sand at the bottom of the ocean is white or red, that concerns me no more than not knowing what color it is. [...] When it is absolutely necessary to speak, and when amusing truths do not present themselves quickly enough to my mind, I tell fables in order not to remain silent."[44]

In a similar way to Pufendorf's text, the Augustinian treatises on lying contribute to making the fourth Promenade more readable. It is striking to observe that the different types of lying or nontruth discussed by Rousseau in the casuistry of the fourth Promenade could easily be classified into one or another of the categories Augustine inventories in decreasing order of seriousness. One lies, according to Augustine, first, in religious teaching, to lead someone to faith; second, to wrong one's neighbor; third, to serve someone while prejudicing another; fourth, for the simple pleasure of lying and deceiving; fifth, to make conversation agreeable; sixth, to be useful to someone without harming anyone; seventh, to save someone's life; and eighth, to allow someone to avoid being subjected to an impure attack.[45] Augustine's first category, concerning religious truth, finds its secularized version in Rousseau when, at the beginning of the fourth Promenade, the latter declares that "general and abstract truth is the most precious of all goods." It is a good that all men may demand. Everyone has a right to it, for this kind of truth is "necessary for everyone's happiness." To prevent one from it is "to commit the most iniquitous of all thefts." The interdiction against lying, in this area, is absolute. Rousseau, without opening the slightest debate on the subject of "general and abstract truth," makes communicating it an almost apostolic duty. It is an entirely different affair concerning "private and individual truth" (p. 1026), which therefore concerns individuals and their thoughts, their feelings, their actions, the contingent circumstances of their existence. That kind of truth can be "indifferent," and it may not interest "justice"....

Medieval theologians, notably Thomas Aquinas, taking into account the various categories distinguished by Augustine, had established three fundamental groups of lies: (I) pernicious lying, *mendacium perniciosum*, which covers Augustine's categories 1–4; (II) jocular lying, *mendacium jocosum*, which corresponds to Augustine's fifth category; and (III) officious lying, *mendacium officiosum*, discussed in Augustine's categories 6–8.[46] For Thomas Aquinas only sins contrary to charity are mortal. Humorous lying ("in which one seeks mild delight, *in quo intenditur aliqua levis delectatio*") and officious lying ("in which one seeks to be useful to one's neighbor, *in qua intenditur etiam utilitas proximi*") are not mortal.[47] It must be recalled that Aquinas made truthfulness (*veritas*) into a moral duty (*debitum morale*), inasmuch as the latter is one of the virtues that are part of justice (*veritas est pars justitiae*). "It emerges from this duty that man should show himself to others, in his words and deeds, such as he is. *Ad hoc debitum pertinet quod homo talem se exhibeat alteri in verbis et in factis qualis est.*"[48] Aquinas also added this important remark, Aristotelian in inspiration, on the fact that the social bond can subsist only on the basis of a refusal to lie: "[...] Because man is a social animal, a man naturally owes another that without which human society cannot be safeguarded. Men could not live communally if they could not trust each other, inasmuch as they show one another the truth. *Quia homo est animal sociale, naturaliter unus homo debet alteri id sine quo societas humana servari non posset. Non autem possent homines ad invicem convivere nisi sibi invicem crederent, tanquam sibi invicem veritatem manifestantibus.*"[49] In the fourth Promenade Rousseau defines the "true man" – that is to say, himself – in terms that conform to Church doctrine, whatever may be the debt we have in other regards made clear with respect to Grotius and Pufendorf. Contrary to worldly people, Rousseau's "true man" does not distinguish between "justice and truth": the essential part therefore remains intact. However, for that which does not derive from justice, he allows himself to invent, he gives free rein to his imagination, he supplements the facts lacking to his memory with fictions and fables. If Rousseau has lied in conversation or writing, it was "*out of* the embarrassment of speaking or *for* the pleasure of writing."[50] In his fictions, contrary to Montesquieu, he says he always had in sight the moral usefulness that his readers could derive from them. It is the category of *mendacium jocosum* that he tries to make compatible with moral duty (*debitum morale*), that invites the individual to "show himself as he is," following Aquinas' recommendation. A whole portion of the fourth Promenade works to *amalgamate* the permission for the freest use of fiction "in perfectly indifferent things," and the demand of absolute devotion to truth, including even self-sacrifice, when the latter implies respect for justice. Attention should be paid, in the following excerpt, to the way in which the denegation of unjust lying is interwoven with the (almost provocative) claim on fictional speaking. The repetition makes this attempt at synthesis even more noticeable. We see Rousseau speaking here of "alloying":

The man I call true [...] would scarcely have any scruples about amusing his company with fabricated facts from which no unjust judgment results for or against anyone living or dead: but any speech that produces profit or blame against justice and truth is a lie that will never approach his heart, nor his lips, nor his pen. He is solidly true, even against his own interest, although he cares precious little about being so in idle conversations. [...] But, it might be said, how could this laxity be reconciled with the ardent love of truth with which I glorify him? Is this love, then, false, because it allows itself to be so alloyed? No, it is pure and true: but it is only an outgrowth of the love of justice and never seeks to be false even though it is often incredible [*fabuleux*]. Justice and truth are in his spirit two synonymous words that he substitutes for one another without distinction. The holy truth his heart worships does not consist of indifferent facts and useless names, but in faithfully rendering unto each what [is] due to him in things that are truly his [...] He will therefore lie sometimes in indifferent matters without scruple and without believing that he lies, never for the harm or profit of others or himself.[51]

In a gesture of severity that theologians would not disavow, Rousseau sees an injustice in "officious lying," that is to say, in lies that impress "for the advantage either of others or of oneself." [...] "Whosoever praises or blames against the truth lies when it concerns a real person."[52]

Yet the fourth Promenade ends on the stories of two lies of which Jean-Jacques has reason to be proud. He told them in his childhood, both times to spare from punishment a playmate who has hurt him. These are two perfect examples of officious lying. One should certainly not neglect to underline in the passage the masochistic inflection with which the wounds are recounted. If Rousseau evokes these feelings from his childhood, it is in order to explain the "bizarre [...] silences" that made him omit from the *Confessions'* narrative these episodes, which could have been included to his own advantage. These silences "made him keep the good silent more often than the bad."

According to the Augustinian classification, the lies told by Rousseau in two circumstances in which a playmate spilled his blood could illustrate the case of lying with the intention "of being useful to someone without harming anyone." In this regard, Rousseau evokes the episode of Olindo and Sophronia recounted by Tasso, and he cites the poet's admiring exclamation before a lie that demonstrates greatness of soul:

Magnanima menzogna! or quando è il vero
Si bello che si possa a te preporre?

Magnanimous lie! When is truth
So beautiful that it can be preferred to you?[53]

Sophronia, blaming herself before the sultan for the theft of a holy statue that she did not commit, is willing to die herself to save the Christians from death. In his turn, in a surfeit of generosity, Olindo falsely blames himself in order to take the place of the one he loves and whom the tyrant has led to the stake. Rousseau leaves to his hypothetical reader the task of uncovering the disproportion between this heroic example and his refusal to denounce his playmates. The main point is that Rousseau here refers himself to *officious* lies, which precede in his life the *pernicious* lie of the stolen ribbon episode. Here indeed, then, he persuades himself, are his *first* impulses! In these same concluding pages of the Promenade, he says that he was constantly guided by his conscience and his feelings: Again he appeals to a prior occurrence on which no guilt can weigh. The personal *dictamen* to which he always tried to submit himself is prior to reasoning and to still possible mistakes. To be entirely strict, it would have been necessary to avoid all lying, as Augustine demands: to be "true to oneself," as the "gentleman" must pay homage "to his own dignity." Rousseau acknowledges that he should have avoided even "fiction" and "fable," about which he carefully demonstrated in the preceding pages that they ought not to be confused with lies. It is at this point that the final argument of weakness intervenes, an argument that does not solve the mistake, but creates a vacuum in the subject itself.

Does he finally admit that they are right who reproach him with having contradicted his motto and with being a liar? Yes, he resigns himself to that. However, he reduces his mistake to a disappointed hope. He shifts responsibility for it by linking it to the fault of having expected too much of himself. With a weak soul, "it is being arrogant and rash to dare to profess great virtues." He restates this many times: Virtue is accessible only to the strong. If Rousseau, finally, accepts the reproach of having failed the promises of his motto, it is by taking a resolution of modesty that henceforth has nothing heroic about it. Indeed, he pronounces himself incapable of the effort to which the absolute service of the truth obligated him. The last sentence of this fourth Reverie evokes a final "reform," with neither brilliance nor challenge: "[...] It is never too late to learn, even from one's enemies, to be wise, true, and modest, and to presume less of oneself." He thus declares that without suspecting it, his persecutors have done him a very great favor. Being "true"! That is what still remains for him to learn at the end of his life. This last resolution certainly implies self-criticism, but should not be viewed as a disavowal. The last effort of truthfulness, for Rousseau, consists in the admission of the peril that existed – for him – in proclaiming himself the spokesperson of truth.

ENDNOTES

1 *Oeuvres complètes* (hereafter OC), vol. V (Paris, collection Pléiade, Gallimard, 1995), p. 120. The motto is borrowed from Juvenal, *Satires*, IV, 91. Rousseau had a seal made bearing this motto. In the conserved correspondence, it is first seen applied on a letter from 18 March 1759. The motto appears as the epigraph to the *Letters Written from the Mountain* (1764).

2 *Ibid.*

3 *Confessions*, OC I, 3, 5.

4 *Letters to Malesherbes*, OC I, 1131. As concerns the word "motive" [*motif*], see in particular its use on pp. 1130 and 1142.

5 *Ibid.*, 1132.

6 Rousseau uses the word "dictionary" in writing to Madame d'Epinay: "learn my dictionary better." [...] *Correspondance complète*, ed. R. A. Leigh (Geneva: Institut et Musée Voltaire, subsequently Oxford, U.K., Voltaire Foundation, 52 volumes), Vol. III, No. 389, pp. 292–293.

7 *Dialogues*, OC I, 783.

8 I refer the reader to our study entitled "Rêverie et transmutation," in *Jean-Jacques Rousseau. La transparence et l'obstacle* (Gallimard, Paris, 1970), pp. 415–429.

9 Marcel Raymond, *Jean-Jacques Rousseau. La quête de soi et la reverie* (Paris: Corti, 1962).

10 *Rêveries*, First Promenade, OC I, 1000.

11 See Augustine, *Contra mendacium;* III, 18: "*Interest* [...] *plurimum qua causa, quo fine, qua intentione quid fiat.*" For example, giving charity to the poor may be done out of mercy (*causa misericordiae cum recta fide*) or out of boastfulness (*jactantiae causa*).

12 Pascal denounces this concupiscence, following the first Epistle of John II:16: "Everything in the world is concupiscence of the flesh, or concupiscence of the eyes, or pride of life: *libido sentiendi, libido sciendi, libido dominandi*" (*Pensées*, Brunschvicg edition, fragment 458).

13 Henri Gouhier, *Les meditations métaphysiques de Jean-Jacques Rousseau* (Paris: Vrin, 1970).

14 *Confessions*, Book II, OC I, 85. In the narrative of the unjust punishment at Bossey, Rousseau writes, "Appearances condemned me" (Book I, p. 19). There are similarities in vocabulary between the two recollections

(in the *Confessions* and the *Rêveries*) of Jean-Jacques' lying at Turin and
the narrative relating the false accusation of lying of which he was the
object in the episode of the broken comb. The vocabulary of religious
morality is present in these different texts. The Lamberciers wrongly reproach him for a "diabolical stubbornness" (Book I), while he ascribes to
himself an "infernal impudence" in the accusation of Marion (Book II).
Fifty years after the incident of the broken comb, he "declared in the face
of Heaven" that he was innocent; in the fourth Promenade, he swears
"in the face of heaven" that he would "joyfully" have given all of his
blood to "divert" on himself alone "the effect" of his lie at Turin.

15 On the situation of the autobiographer as accused, see my study "The
Style of Autobiography," in *La relation critique* (Paris, Gallimard, 1970),
pp. 83–98, in which I examine Rousseauean and Augustinian confession.
See also Gisèle Mathieu-Castellani, *La scène judiciaire de l'autobiographie* (Paris: PUF, 1996).

16 Acad., 1798: "Guilt [*coulpe*]: Error, sin. It is only used in matters of religion. It signifies besmirchment, the stain of sin that deprives the sinner
of God's grace. *By confession guilt is remitted, but not punishment.
God's great love, his perfect charity, takes away guilt and punishment,
delivers from guilt and punishment.*" Rousseau uses the same term in
the third Promenade to exculpate himself in the hypothesis whereby the
philosophical system he elaborated in full good faith might be marked
by error: "If in spite of that we fall into error, we cannot in full justice
bear the punishment for it, since we in no way bear the guilt [*coulpe*]
for it" (OC I, 1018).

17 On the precepts of *inventio*, I refer the reader to Heinrich Lausberg,
Handbuch der literarischen Rhetorik (M. Hüber, Munich, 1960), Vol. I,
Chap. II, Sections 255–442. In the text of the episode, the exordium contains a paragraph, beginning with "Why have I not concluded" (p. 84);
the *narration* contains three paragraphs, beginning with "It is indeed
difficult that the dissolution of a household," and concluding with:
"of writing my confessions" (pp. 84–86). The *argument* begins with
"I have proceeded briskly in [the confession] that I have just made"
and concludes with "of the regret of having been able to commit such
a heinous one" (pp. 86–89). The *peroration*, conveying a moving enthymeme, begins with: "If it is a crime that can be atoned for." These
are the concluding lines of Book II of the *Confessions*, which ends with
a wonderful optative: "May I be allowed never again to speak of it"
(p. 87).

18 Rousseau knows Quintilian well through Rollin's Latin abridgment
(M. Fabii Quintiliani, *Institutionum oratorium libri duodecim, ad usum
scholarum accommodati* [...] *a Corolo Rollin*, 2 vols., Paris, Viduann

JEAN STAROBINSKI

Estienne, 1754). In 1742, he recommends that the son of M. de Mably learn it by heart (which is asking a lot!). See the *Mémoire présenté à M. de Mably*, OC IV, 29.

19 *Confessions*, Book II, OC I, 86–87. In the fourth Promenade, Rousseau will call the state in which he found himself "delirium."

20 "As if it were a slip," Paul de Man quite correctly writes in *Allegories of Reading* (New Haven, CT: Yale University Press, 1979), p. 288.

21 Paul de Man, *op. cit.*, p. 289. The two short phrases admitting to the theft have a structure exactly similar to those explaining the lie: "Only the ribbon tempted me, I stole it" (OC I, 84). The term "anacoluthon," which refers to a fragmentary construction in the syntax of a single sentence, cannot be applied to short, juxtaposed independent clauses with different subjects. See the article "Anacoluthia" in B. Dupriez, *Les Procédés littéraires* (Union Générale d'Editions, Paris, 1980). A change in subject in two juxtaposed clauses, even if they were separated by a comma, and not by a stop, cannot be analyzed in that way. Rousseau is not unaware of anacoluthia and does not fear true breaks in syntax. Here is an example: "But born for true attachments, the communion of hearts and intimacy shall be precious to him" [...] (*Dialogues*, II, OC I, 820). In the narration of the theft and then that of the confrontation in the domestic tribunal, the thoughtlessness of the behavior and the rush of events are indicated by a series of short clauses, juxtaposed without coordinating conjunctions, and whose subjects are different from moment to moment. The reader may be the judge of it: "She was called; the gathering was large, the Comte de la Roque was there. She arrives, they show her the ribbon, I charge her boldly; she is unable to speak, is silent" [...], *op. cit.*, p. 85.

22 Contrary to what Paul de Man supposes, the expression "to excuse oneself upon" is in no way uncommon in the eighteenth century. It indicates the reason or the alleged pretext of those who excuse themselves. See in particular the *Dictionnaire de Trévoux*, Veuve Delaune (1771). It is undeniable that this expression is well chosen here. Through its indirect character, it softens the effect of the verbs with a direct object that surround it, such as "to accuse," "to charge."

23 *Confessions*, Book I, OC I, 32–3. Previously, in his family, before this subjection, Rousseau assures the reader that he had known no pleasure that was not "within his reach," no unavowed *desire* (*op. cit.*, p. 31).

24 Another element of the excuse: it was the smallest theft. This "pink and silver colored" ribbon was "small" and "already old" (*op. cit.*, p. 84).

25 *Ibid.*

26 *Les oeuvres morales et meslees de Plutarque*, translated by Jacques

Amyot (Geneva: Stoer, 1603), Treatise XI, p. 77 r. "We understand by shameful one who blushes with shame, excessively and in any circumstance." It is a change in the look or the face before others. With "self-consciousness" [*"mauvaise honte"*], according to Plutarch, one lacks courage before others. One tries to please them, rather than standing up to them. Self-consciousness "yields and gives in to all requests, to the point of not daring to look head-on at those who ask [...] For those who are excessively ashamed, when they ought not to be, often make as many mistakes as those who are brazen and impudent, except that they are grieved and unpleasant in their failings, and the others are delighted about it: for the impudent person is not displeased with having done something dishonest, and the shameful person becomes easily flustered by things that appear to be dishonest but are not." I am grateful to Alain Grosrichard for having called my attention to this text. Montaigne evokes Plutarch on the subject of "self-consciousness" [*"mauvaise honte"*] (*Essais*, III, 10, Paris: Félix Alien, 1923, Villey, ed., p. 1019).

27 Pierre Nicole, *Instructions théologiques et morales* [...], (Paris, Chez C. Osmont, 1723), Vol. II, Chap. V, Section 2, "Of the fear of men's judgments, or of self-consciousness," pp. 56–62.

28 *Op. cit.*, p. 55.

29 Thomas Aquinas, *Summa theologica*, II, II, Quaestio 68, articulus 4.

30 Quintilian, *Institution Oratoire*, V, 10.

31 On the question of uncontrolled consequences, I refer the reader to my study, "The Dinner at Turin," in *La relation critique* (Gallimard, Paris, 1970).

32 Rousseau, *Confessions, op. cit.*, p. 87.

33 The same is true when it is a question of psychological "cases" described in psychiatric literature, above all for psychoanalysis. In the immense literature devoted to Freud's classic case studies, too numerous are those who claim to complete or revise Freud's interpretations and too rare are those who take into account the complete circularity between the "factual" or narrative elements reported by Freud and their interpretations. The clinical history has been constructed *for* and *by* that interpretation, which appears to have been applied to it after the fact.

34 Of course, my entire analysis depends on a modalization, which I ought perhaps to signal more often, by expressions such as according to Rousseau, judging by Rousseau's text, on the faith of the *Confessions*, the *Dialogues*, the *Rêveries*, etc. I anticipate readers who do not need such signals. They understand that I am not arguing about Rousseau's "real" reasons: I am content with analyzing the text in which Rousseau names his reasons.

35 On the literature devoted to the fourth Promenade, see Bartolo Anglani, *Le maschere dell'io* (Fasano: Schena, 1995), pp. 317–332.

36 "Fourth Promenade," OC I, 1026. Emphasis added.

37 [*Notes on Helvétius' "De l'esprit"*], OC IV, 1126. See Jean Deprun, "Fontenelle, Helvétius, Rousseau and the Casuistry of Lying," in *Fontenelle. Actes du colloque* Rouen, 1985, Paris, PUF, 1989), pp. 423–431. The definition of lying attributed to Fontenelle by Helvétius – "keeping silent a truth one must" – could not be referenced by Deprun in Fontenelle's published works. In fact, the casuistry of truth, such as it was found in *De l'esprit*, passed on a traditional doctrine that Rousseau may have known, for his part, completely independently. In *De l'homme* (posthumous, 1772), Helvétius includes a chapter entitled "That one owes men the truth" (Section IX, Chap. XI), without the slightest reference to Fontenelle. The chapter begins with quotations from Augustine and Ambrose, which clearly indicate the source of the issue. "Does truth become a subject of scandal? Let scandal be born and the truth be told" (Augustine, quoted without reference); "One is not the defender of truth, if at the moment one sees it, one does not tell it without shame and without fear" (Ambrose, quoted without reference). For Helvétius, public interest is the measure of the duty to truth: ... "If all men must, as citizens, contribute with all their power to the happiness of their countrymen, is the truth known? It must be told. To ask if it is owed to men is, by an obscure and devious turn of phrase, to ask if it is permissible to be virtuous and to contribute to the good of one's fellow men." [Helvétius, *De l'homme*, Section IX, Chap. IX, in *Oeuvres* (Servieres et Bastien, Paris, 1792), Vol. V, pp. 54–55].

38 In the dedication to the *Discourse on Inequality*, Rousseau writes "I see Tacitus, Plutarch and Grotius mingled before him with the instruments of his trade" (OC IV, 118).

39 Samuel Pufendorf, *Le droit de la nature et des gens* (1672), French trans. by Jean Barbeyrac, 2 vols. (Chez G. Kuyper, Amsterdam, 1706), Vol. I, Part IV, Chap. I, "Of the obligation concerning the use of speech," pp. 386–413. This chapter is also important as regards the use of signs. It is one of the sources of Rousseau's theory of language. This book of Pufendorf is among the books that Jean-Jacques finds in his room, in Annecy, on his return from Turin (*Confessions*, Book III, OC I, 110). Pufendorf and Grotius are among the readings that the 1740 *Projet d'éducation*, prescribes to M. de Sainte-Marie, of whom Rousseau is the tutor (OC IV, 31). These are more advanced readings, which lead to "a bit more of an ordered knowledge of morality and natural right." These authors are necessary "because it is worthy of a gentleman and of an intelligent man to know the principles of good and evil, and the

foundations upon which the society of which he is a part is established" (*ibid.*).

40 Hugo Grotius, *Le droit de la guerre et de la paix*, trans. Jean Barbeyrac, 2 vols. (Leiden dépens de la Compagnie, 1759), Book III, Chap. I, Section 11, Vol. II, pp. 720–721. He adds "It is also necessary that the right that one attacks be the right of the person to whom one is speaking, and not that of another: similarly as in the matter of contracts, injustice consists only in the violation of the right of the contracting parties."

41 Rousseau, *Rêveries*, fourth Promenade, *op. cit.*, pp. 1026–1027.

42 Augustine, *Enchiridion de fide*, 286.

43 Rousseau, *Rêveries, op. cit.*, p. 1029.

44 Rousseau, *Rêveries, ibid.*, pp. 1027, 1033.

45 Saint Augustine, *Oeuvres*, First Series, *Opuscules*, II, Moral Problems, ed. Gustave Combes (Desclée de Brouwer, Paris, 1937), p. 233. See above all *De mendacio*, XIV, 25. Augustine devotes a great deal of attention to lies that compromise or protect the chastity of others. It must be recalled that what Rousseau reproaches himself with, regarding the consequences of his slanderous accusation, concerns the chastity that Marion, dismissed, was probably unable to preserve.

46 There is the same classification in Bonaventure, cited by Jean Pontas in the article "Lying" from the *Dictionnaire des cas de conscience*, 3 vols. (Sevestre, Paris, 1734): *Mentiens autem aut intendit prodesse, aut delectare, aut laedere. Secundum quod intendit prodesse, est mendacium officiosum. Secundum quod intendit delectare, est mendacium jocosum. Secundum quod intendit laedere, est mendacium perniciosum.* The person who lies has the intention of serving, amusing, or harming. If he has the intention of serving, it is an officious lie. If he has the intention of amusing, it is a jocular lie. If he has the intention of doing harm, it is a pernicious lie.

47 Thomas Aquinas, *Summa theologica*, II, II, Quaestiones CIX (*De veritate*) and CX (*De vitiis opposites veritati, et primo de mendacio*).

48 *Op. cit.*, II, II, Quaestio LXXX, articulus unicus. To speak about oneself can be an act of vice, even in speaking the truth, if it is not for "due cause." Spontaneous confessions are suspicious: *Dicendum quod confiteri id quod est circa seipsum, in quantum est confessio veri, est bonum ex genere. Sed hoc non sufficit ad hoc quod sit virtutis actus: sed ad hoc requiritur quod ulterius debitis circumstantiis vestiatur: quae si non observentur, erit actus vitiosus. Et secundum hoc vitiosum est, quod aliquis sine debita causa laudet seipsus etiam de vero: vitiosum est quod aliquis peccatum suum publicet, quasi se de hoc laudando, vel qualitercumque inutiliter publicando* (q. CIX, art. I). Thomas takes confession of sin, when it is not due (*sine debita causa*), as an act of vice,

or at least as useless. The morality he teaches does not therefore pave the way for a good reception of avowals like Rousseau's. Is it because he remembers received doctrine that Rousseau declares at the beginning of the fourth Promenade that "private and individual truth" is useless to other men? He does not, for all that, persevere any less in the undertaking of the *public* examination of oneself, according to his "private and individual" truth.

49 *Op. cit.*, II, II, article 3. Montaigne reprises the idea at the end of the chapter "Du démentir" (*Essais* II, 18).

50 *Rêveries*, fourth Promenade, p. 1038.

51 *Ibid.*, p. 1033.

52 *Ibid.*, pp. 1030–1.

53 "Magnanimous lie! When could the true be so beautiful that it can be preferred over you?" We know that Rousseau translated this episode, which appears at the beginning of Canto II of Torquato Tasso's *Jerusalem Delivered*. The cited verses are from strophe XXII. See OC V, 1287–95, and the remark on p. CCCV.

14   Rousseau's *The Levite of Ephraim:* Synthesis within a "Minor" Work

Understanding the unity or, if one prefers, the abiding obsessions of Rousseau's works has often been compromised by the drawing of borders that have little to do with Rousseau or the contexts in which he wrote. One such border is a creation of the modern university. Working in distinct academic disciplines, even Rousseau's most astute critics have collaborated in producing the mirage of two separate and often incommensurable Rousseaus: one for political scientists and historians of philosophy, another for students of literature and psychology. As inevitable as that border may appear, it has led to a fragmentation that can compromise our understanding of his work as a whole. The real challenge in reading Rousseau is to appreciate how his political vision depends on his literary and autobiographical writings while at the same time recognizing the extent to which his literary representations of subjectivity flow from a dialectic of self and other at the core of his political writings. Our study of Rousseau must not foreclose the possibility of grasping in his work the complex paradoxes that balance the literary with the political, the psychological with the anthropological.

Another border hampering our understanding of Rousseau is that between works designated as major and minor. On the one hand, such a division is understandable in the case of someone who, between the *Second Discourse* of 1755 and the *Rêveries* left unfinished at his death in 1778, produced at least six works incontestably qualified as major within the western tradition. On the other hand, the preponderance of that subset too easily leads to the neglect of other less crucial and less influential works that can reveal with singular economy and clarity the abiding concerns and tensions at work in Rousseau's thought. In some cases, a work qualified as minor brings together in one text themes leading to the most divergent aspects of Rousseau's reflection while clarifying otherwise unrecognized relations among them.[1]

Crossing the borders separating the literary from the political as well as the major from the minor, I would like to examine a work that, although unpublished during Rousseau's lifetime, held a particular importance for him from the time he first composed it in 1762 to the year of his death, when he took great pleasure in reading it to Bernardin de Saint-Pierre.[2] In Book 11 of the *Confessions*, speaking of *The Levite of Ephraim*, Rousseau goes so far as to say "if it is not the best of my works, it will always be the most cherished."[3] In addition to declaring his great pleasure in writing and rereading this text, the short preface to *The Levite* Rousseau wrote in 1762 assigns to it a function that as the years pass will become uppermost in his mind: "Should some just man one day take my defense against so many outrages and libels, I ask only these words of praise: 'In the cruelest moments of his life, he wrote *The Levite of Ephraim*.'"[4]

This work's intimate connection to *Émile*'s condemnation and the order for Rousseau's arrest makes *The Levite* singularly important as an expression of Rousseau's abiding concern with his portrayal of himself as a sacrificial victim whose statement of truth reestablishes justice in the threatened community. As the preface of 1762 makes clear, Rousseau asks the reader to relate *The Levite*'s genesis to "the cruelest moments of his life": the threat of arrest and his ensuing flight to Switzerland. Book 11 of the *Confessions*, however, offers a more complex and intriguing description of the circumstances in which the work was composed – a description, in fact, so detailed and so nuanced that we seem to know more about the writing of this short text than we do about many of the major works in which, more often than not, a strong element of retrospective justification qualifies much of what Rousseau has to say about their composition.

In early June of 1762, having lived for almost five years at Montlouis, the small country house provided by the Duc and the Duchesse of Luxembourg on their estate at Montmorency, Rousseau has taken to combating his nightly insomnia by reading from the Old Testament. On the evening of June 8, finding it more difficult than usual to fall asleep, Rousseau extends his nocturnal reading to the whole of what he calls "the book that ends with the Levite of Ephraim and which, if I am not mistaken is the Book of Judges"

(*Confessions* 1, 580). Finally falling asleep, yet at the same time drawn back to the story he has been reading, Rousseau begins to dream: "That story greatly moved me, and I was pondering over it in a sort of dream when suddenly I was aroused by a noise and a light" (*Confessions* 1, 580).

At two o'clock in the morning, awakened from his dream, Rousseau finds a servant standing at his bedside with a note from the Duchesse enclosing a letter she has just received from the Prince de Conti. The message is as simple as it is alarming. Nothing more can be done. Tomorrow morning, in a few hours, the *Grand'Chambre* will not only issue its condemnation of *Émile* but will decree Rousseau's arrest and dispatch *huissiers* to Montmorency. Maneuvering as best he could in overwhelmingly hostile circumstances, Conti could obtain only the assurance that, if Rousseau is not at Montmorency when the *huissiers* arrived, he will not be pursued.

Rousseau decides immediately to flee, insisting, however, that it was not any concern for his own safety that motivated his decision. He so readily accepted the idea of flight to spare his hosts, the Duc and the Duchesse, the embarrassment of harboring a man whose arrest had been ordered by legitimate civil authority. The rest of the morning is taken up with an incredible scene in which the aged Duc helps Rousseau sort through his accumulated papers, deciding what will be burned, what Rousseau will take with him, and what will be left at Montmorency. During these frantic preparations, when Thérèse is finally summoned to receive the news of his departure, Rousseau presents his departure as separating their life together into two distinct parts: a *before*, now recognized as lost felicity, and an *after*, announcing itself as relentless woe: "My child, you must arm yourself with courage. You have shared the good days of my prosperity. It now remains for you, since you wish it, to share my miseries. Expect nothing but insults and disasters henceforth. The fate that begins for me on this unhappy day will pursue me till my last hour" (*Confessions* 1, 583).

With the same lamentation, addressed not to Thérèse as a premonition but to all his readers as a factual résumé of the period from June 1762 to the time he wrote the *Confessions*, Rousseau begins Book 12: "Here begins the work of darkness in which I have been entombed for eight years past, without ever having been able, try as I might, to pierce its hideous obscurity" (*Confessions* 1, 589). As with his departure from Geneva, as with his separation from Madame de Warens, Rousseau organizes his life around a radical break separating past happiness from future suffering, a break over which he has no control.

Once alone in the coach, Rousseau returns to the abruptly interrupted dream of the previous night: the story of the Levite of Ephraim. He spends the first days of his journey to Yverdon in an ambiguously motivated prolongation of that singularly pleasant dream. To understand both how *The Levite* functions as a text and why it is more significant than the pedestrian variation on a biblical story to which some critics have reduced it, we must examine how Rousseau's conscious continuation of the dreamwork responded to the trauma of his flight. In fact, Rousseau offers two different versions of the relation between his flight and the composition of *The Levite*. In Book 11 of the *Confessions*, the global narration I have been following, he insists that he wrote *The Levite* without concern for his personal situation. The Levite's story, Rousseau claims, returned to his mind only *after* he had completely forgotten the events of the previous day: "The day after my departure I so completely forgot all that had just happened... that I should never have given it another thought during my whole journey if it had not been for the precautions I was obliged to observe. One memory which came to me *in place of all these* was that of the book I had been reading on the eve of my departure" (*Confessions* 1, 586; italics mine). By what might be described as a process of total substitution, Rousseau presents his decision to rewrite the end of *Judges* as replacing and excluding all sterile handwringing over his personal fate.

Should we hesitate to recognize the strong element of denial in Rousseau's insistence on such complete forgetting, we have only to examine the other version of this scene in a text the Pléiade edition titles *Second projet de préface* to The Levite and usually dated to June or August 1768. This second preface makes clear that rewriting the Levite's story did provide Rousseau with a gratification of desires born of his misfortune, but even more important, it reveals a form of substitution whose implications extend far beyond this single work: "Those sad ideas pursued me in spite of myself and made my trip an unpleasant one. I tried as hard as I could not to think of them since there is nothing my mind less willingly concerns itself with than wrongs done me. I am far more upset by the injustices I witness than by those I suffer. I decided it would be wise to end my daydreaming by forcing myself to think of other things" (*Second préface*, 2, 1206). Obsessed by a particularly painful series of mental representations, trying to force them from his mind, Rousseau substitutes for them an even more strongly cathectic image of his fate: "I am far more upset by the injustices I witness than by those I suffer." Taken in context, this passage suggests that the force and importance of Rousseau's consciously elaborated status as a *witness* denouncing social injustices derives from the sublimation of a more profound, properly unconscious, need to consolidate his status as *victim*. This second preface, a short text of roughly one printed page, alerts the reader to the question why, in the *Confessions*, Rousseau so strongly insists on a radical break between his anxiety as a fugitive and the writing of *The Levite*. In a sense, we have already seen the beginnings of an answer to this question in the short quotation from the first preface, the one written at the same time as *The Levite*, in which Rousseau proclaims what he sees as the best refutation of his many detractors: "In the cruelest moments of his life, he wrote *The Levite of Ephraim*."

Rousseau was willing to stake a great deal on a text. The stake in *The Levite*, however rides on what is absent from the text: Anyone doubting Rousseau's obliviousness to the evil done him, his inveterate unconcern with resentment and retaliation, has only to read this work and think for a moment of when he wrote it. This claim is, to say the least, surprising. *The Levite of Ephraim*, a faithful retelling of the events narrated in the last three chapters of *Judges*, is the story of the gang rape and murder of an innocent woman whose body, cut up into twelve pieces and dispatched to the tribes of Israel, initiates a holy war of vengeance with no fewer than 65,000 casualties. Given what Rousseau recognizes as the "atrociousness" of his subject matter, the reader cannot help but admire the audacity of his claim that the three days spent mulling over variations on these events irrefutably prove his irenic nature.

Rousseau's argument for this interpretation does have a certain logic. He insists that, without eliminating a single episode from this macabre story, he has managed to transform the somber biblical episode into a "prose poem" characterized by "a naïve and rural style [*un style champêtre et naïf*]" in the manner of Salomon Gessner's *Idylles*.[5] He has, Rousseau continues, never written anything "where there reigns a more touching sweetness of manners." His point, then, is that in personal circumstances justifying paralysis in the darkest despondency he was able, with astounding facility, to meet the challenge he had set himself and transform his rendition of the Old Testament story into something distinctly different from the original: "It was hardly to be supposed that my situation at that time furnished me with such cheerful ideas as might enliven it. I made the attempt, however, simply to amuse myself in my carriage and without any hope of success. The moment I began it I was astonished at the pleasant flow of my ideas and the facility I found in expressing them" (*Confessions* I, 586).

The logic at work in Rousseau's claim is like that behind Proust's suggestion that beautiful women should be left to men without imagination. How simple it would have been, and how insignificant, to have taken as the point of departure for his prose poem an innocent, lighthearted story whose characters and situations would have set the tone for his own work. However, with such a choice the possibility of distinguishing between the influence of the source and the specific creative impulse of the author would have disappeared. The real test of an author's serenity, Rousseau seems to claim, comes not when he is asked to tell a story that portrays and solicits such calm but when, setting himself to telling the most violent and somber tale, he suffuses even such recalcitrant material with a spirit of peace and benevolence. In fact, the baroque challenge Rousseau sets himself will transform what began as a justification of self into an implicit accusation of others: "Let all those great philosophers be brought together who, in their books, are so superior to the adversities they have never sustained. Let them be put into a position like mine. Let them try to undertake a work like mine in the first violence of their outraged honor. We should soon see what they would make of it" (*Confessions* I, 587).

It is not surprising that Rousseau found himself fascinated by the story of the Levite. A man whose birth was redefined by the death of his mother, Rousseau had every reason to be drawn to this story of a man whose fate, along with that of his entire nation, is redefined by the death of a much-loved woman, which he was powerless to prevent.[6] Only by examining the strange logic of Rousseau's psychic investment in this text can we evaluate what he has actually done in his variations on this biblical narrative of violence and retribution. The four cantos of Rousseau's *Levite* represent a return of the repressed: the reappearance, in a significantly transmuted form, of precisely those desires whose absence the work is presented as proving. As a microtext, this short work of roughly fifteen printed pages reveals an obsession with violence and victimage that is very much at work in the macrotext of Rousseau's major writings: the political and the pedagogical as well as the literary and the autobiographical.

A short summary of the Levite's story as told in *Judges*, Chaps. 19–21, will help identify and evaluate Rousseau's additions, deletions, and transformations. Breaking Chapter 19 at the reunited couple's departure from Bethlehem, Rousseau's four cantos otherwise parallel the chapter divisions of the Bible. In the valley of Mount Ephraim, Chap. 19 begins, there lived a Levite and his concubine from Bethlehem. When she returned to her father's house, the Levite went there to bring her back. On their return they stopped in the Benjaminite town of Gibeah. An old man living there with his daughter took them in, but that evening the townsmen surrounded the house and demanded that the Levite be handed over to them for their sexual pleasure. After refusing the old man's offer that they take instead his virgin daughter, the men of Gibeah took the Levite's concubine, raped her, and killed her. The Levite brought her body back to Mount Ephraim, cut it into twelve pieces, and sent one to each of the tribes of Israel. Chapter 20 opens with the Israelites assembled at Mizpah, where they decide to form an army to punish the evildoers. Because the Benjaminites refuse to turn them over, a war ensues. On the third day of the war, after losing 40,000 men, the Israelites are victorious and kill all but 600 of the 25,000 Benjaminites. With the war over, Chap. 21 shows the Israelites' realizing that the oath they had taken before the battles never to give their daughters in marriage to a Benjaminite has condemned an entire tribe of Israel to extinction. Because, however, the town of Jabesh had shirked its duty to send soldiers for the holy war, the Israelites decide to destroy it and order its 400 virgins to become wives for the surviving Benjaminites. The remaining 200 Benjaminites are sent to Shiloh to kidnap an equal number of maidens. All retaliation by the men of Shiloh is prevented when the Israelites explain to them that this is the only way to avoid breaking the collective oath while ensuring that the tribe of Benjamin survives.

Even this summary allows us to recognize a number of elements that explain, at least on a conscious level, Rousseau's fascination with the story. The Book of Judges is so named because it describes a period of Israel's history when the twelve tribes were not yet unified within a single monarchy. The biblical text ends with a statement sure to appeal to the author of the *Second Discourse*: "In those days there was no king in Israel and each man did what was right as he saw it" (*Judges* 21:25). Rousseau, in fact, transposes to the very beginning of his narrative an expanded version of this Thelemic observation, adding implications nowhere present in the biblical text. "In those days of freedom when no man reigned over the people of the Lord, there was a time of liberty when each man, recognizing neither magistrate nor judge, was himself his own master and did all that seemed right to him. The nation of Israel, spread out over the fields, had no large towns, and the simplicity of its ways made laws superfluous" (*Le Lévite* 2, 1209).[7] As much as it is the story of a crime, the episode of the Levite is also the story of an entire community's achieving unity and discovering a unanimous general will in its decision to go to war. The biblical text is punctuated by phrases such as "all as one" (Judges 20:1) and "all the people rose as one man" (*Judges* 20:8). Evoking still another of Rousseau's works, the Levite's dispatching a piece of the concubine's corpse to each of the tribes served as an important example for Rousseau when, in the *Essay on the Origin of Languages*, he argued that "the most energetic language is that in which what is seen says everything before anyone speaks."[8] It would be easy to continue this list of themes and incidents from the last chapters of *Judges* that echo preoccupations scattered throughout Rousseau's work. The point, however, is clear: Rousseau's obsession with this story justifies our approaching his text as an overdetermined symptom condensing into one short narrative elements at work in all the major works.

In analyzing Rousseau's version of the Levite's story we can best apprehend his purposes and preoccupations at those points where his narrative most clearly deviates from the story as told in the Bible. As it happens, the most substantial and significant deviations occur at three points: at the beginning of the story, where Rousseau describes the Levite and his concubine before their arrival in Gibeah; in the middle section, where he deals with the discovery of the crime and its social ramifications; and at the close of the narrative, where Rousseau adds an entire cast of characters to the biblical narrative.

The first canto represents that part of *The Levite* in closest harmony with Rousseau's claim that his treatment proves his distance from any concern with hatred or revenge. The biblical text begins with four short, purely narrative sentences, free of descriptive detail, that introduce the two characters and bring us to the Levite's arrival in Bethlehem to retrieve his concubine. Rousseau expands this sober statement of events into a pastoral love story in four acts. Act I opens with the Levite, well before the start of events in *Judges*, passing through Bethlehem and discovering there a young girl whose beauty moves him to a declaration of love as passionately made as it is quickly accepted. She does not become the Levite's "wife," Rousseau points out in the text's sole footnote, only because the injunctions of the Mosaic Law regarding the intertribal circulation of property forbid her that legal status. Act 2 takes the couple to the valley of Mount Ephraim, where their life consists of love songs accompanied by the Levite's golden zither and gifts of wild honey, roses, and turtle doves pressed to the girl's bosom. Act 3 casts a shadow over the idyll as the girl surrenders to her growing nostalgia for the childhood joys of her father's house. Rousseau motivates her departure with the observation that "she grew tired of the Levite, perhaps because he left her nothing more to desire" (*Le Levite* 2, 1210). This is, it should be pointed out, a substantial deviation from the biblical explanation. The Ostervald Version offers "she committed an impurity [*elle commit une impureté*]," whereas André Chouraqui, in a translation that prides itself on its fidelity to the original Hebrew, gives "his concubine played the whore [*sa concubine putasse*]."[9] Act 4 focuses on the Levite, now inconsolable, who assumes the romantic posture of one condemned to live in a world that has become a poeticized memorial to his absent beloved.

I enumerate these elements of Rousseau's first canto because, aside from the bare statement of facts, none of them is present in *Judges*. Rousseau emphasizes the simple joys of rustic family life during the Levite's stay in Bethlehem and the attempts by the girl's loving father to prolong it by stretching out meals until it is too late in the day to travel. Although the biblical text mentions only the father, Rousseau adds a mother and a number of *folâtres soeurs*. Moreover, Rousseau heightens the melodramatic potential of the ultimate departure so that the father's grief – "his mute embraces were lugubrious and convulsive; piercing sighs lifted his breast" (*Le Lévite* 2, 1211) – functions as a premonition of his daughter's fate.

We might conclude from this first cluster of deviations that Rousseau clearly identifies with the character of the Levite. All his expansions derive from a clearly pleasurable imagining of what might have been the Levite's actions and reactions within the bare skeleton of the biblical narrative. It should also be noted that a period of shared happiness abolished by the woman's longing for reintegration in the paternal order is not a theme to which the author of *Julie* was indifferent. Confirming Rousseau's identification with the Levite, the Neufchâtel manuscript contains, in Rousseau's hand, instructions for a series of illustrations he intended for this work. All three of them, even though they are destined for a story that continues far beyond the Levite's disappearance from it, have this character as their central focus: the Levite offering a turtle dove to his beloved, the Levite discovering her body in Gibeah, the Levite addressing the assembled Israelites. The longest and most detailed of the three not only has no biblical counterpart but represents a rare foray on Rousseau's part into an imagery of rococo eroticism easily associated with Boucher: "A pleasant valley traversed by a stream and lush with roses, pomegranates and other bushes. A young and handsome Levite has offered to his beloved a turtle dove that he has just caught in a net. The delighted maiden caresses the dove and clasps it to her bosom" (Notes to *Le Levite* 2, 1926).

The second cluster of modifications occurs in the sequence beginning with the Levite's discovery of his concubine's body and extending to the transformation of her murder into the gravamen of a holy war. This cluster in a text turning on the relation of the individual to the community reveals with a clarity unique in Rousseau's works how the operation of the general will relies on an act of expulsion and victimage. *The Levite* speaks of what might be called the "dark side" of the general will, a side that the political works repress in favor of a more serene view of how unanimity is achieved within society.

This second cluster opens and closes with significant departures from the biblical text. At the end of Rousseau's second canto, the Levite, having brought his concubine's body back to Mount Ephraim, dissects it and sends one piece to each of the tribes of Israel. In and of itself this is a message whose immediate eloquence convokes the tribes to the assembly at Mizpah: "With a firm and sure hand, he cuts the flesh and the bones, separating the head from the limbs. After having dispatched these terrifying gifts to the twelve tribes, he goes before them to Mizpah, rends his garments, strews ashes on his head, prostrates himself as they arrive and, with great lamentation demands justice from the God of Israel" (*Le Levite* 2, 1215–16). *Judges* has the Levite sending the tribes not only the dissected body parts but also emissaries carrying messages that define the corpse's significance. Whereas in Rousseau's text the body alone is an eloquent and self-sufficient message, the biblical account presents it as a token, a proof, a particularly horrifying answer to the *habeas corpus* the Israelites are sure to formulate as a response to the emissaries' narrations: "And the men whom he sent he commissioned as follows: 'Thus you shall say to every man of Israel, "Has there ever been such a thing as this from the time the Israelites came up from the land of Egypt to this day, Put your mind to it! Take counsel and speak!"'"(*Judges* 19:29–30).

The assembly at Mizpah listens to the Levite's story and, responding to his plea for justice, resolves unanimously to punish Gibeah. At this point the Levite disappears from the biblical text, never to be mentioned again as the narrative takes up the story of a holy war. *Judges* is the story of a particular period in the history of Israel as a nation and the Levite is one of a number of characters, always secondary to the nation as such, who fade from view once they have played their limited roles in that history. Rousseau, however, adds a final and particularly important scene centered on the Levite as an individual: his falling dead before the assembled Israelites and his burial beside the reconstituted body of the concubine. "The Levite then cried out in a loud voice: Blessed be Israel as she punishes infamy and avenges innocent blood. Maiden of Bethlehem, I bring you good news: your memory shall not be dishonored. In saying these words he fell forward onto his face, dead. His body was accorded a public funeral. The pieces of his wife's body were brought together and placed in the same tomb. And all Israel shed tears upon them"

(*Le Lévite* 2, 1216). The literal and figurative reunion of these two bodies in their burial, an act carried out as a public ceremony, reaffirms the threatened social order.

Rousseau's text tells the story of an individual who finds himself the focal point of a criminal and profoundly transgressive desire shared by the men of Gibeah. From their midst emerges only one person, himself a foreigner – the Levite's host – who opposes that group. His opposition, however, fails and the crime is committed. The Levite, in the person of the concubine with whom he will be buried, is its victim. The men of Gibeah, by reason of their criminality, form a community. However, Rousseau makes clear, their community is a sham, an anticommunity leagued in their shared transgression, first, of the law of hospitality, and, more profoundly, of the law of Israel. Their crime reduces them to a level below the human. The men become a horde or, as Rousseau's metaphor puts it, a pack of predatory animals: "In their brutal fury they are like a pack of famished wolves as they surprise a weak heifer at the foot of the frozen Alps and throw themselves upon her.... Your cries are like those of the horrible hyena, and like it you devour cadavers" (*Le Lévite* 2, 1214–15).

However, this is only part of the story. In reaction to the crime committed by the men of Gibeah, all the Israelites assemble at Mizpah. The criminal conspiracy by a subgroup is referred to the larger community in its entirety. Once brought before this court of last appeal, the narrative, the crime as narrative, becomes itself a force ensuring a true and just unification that animates the community in its punishment of the conspirators. In rewritring *The Levite*, Rousseau fulfills, in other words, the abiding and constantly reiterated wish that motivates the *Second Discourse*, the *Confessions*, and the *Dialogues*.[10] In all these works Rousseau presents before the court of society as a whole, before the court of posterity, his denunciation of a conspiracy that has vitiated the community. In so doing, this conspiracy has leagued itself against him as its elected victim, as the one voice of truth that would force all to contemplate the sad reality of what the criminal acts of some have made of that community. The league devoted to his persecution has, as it were, become a monstrous parody of the general will with Rousseau himself as its designated victim. What some critics dismiss as the delirious paranoia of a text like the *Dialogues* is, as Michel Serres has argued, another version of the *Social Contract*: "Toward the end of his life Rousseau describes as fact what he had earlier, in his political writings, proposed as abstract theory. As a bloc, the others are bound together by a pact. This pact is the expression of their general hatred, a derivation from and perversion of what he had earlier called their general will. Jean-Jacques, split in two, rewrites the *Social Contract*."[11] No matter how large that conspiracy might become, no matter how closely it might coincide with society as a whole, Rousseau's denunciations testify to his unswerving faith that a more just community will one day render an informed judgment of him and, recognizing his truth, will denounce and avenge the violence of which he has been the victim. As will be the case in the *Social Contract*, Rousseau's readers are called on to recognize his as a voice speaking from afar, a voice situated outside their congeries of violence, deceit, and criminality. Only by speaking alone and from afar can he avoid the threat of compromise with their conspiracy. His status as martyr becomes a precondition of his maintaining so absolute a vision of the truth that he can denounce and unmask all the lies and stratagems that have systematically deceived mankind.

Only by distinguishing these two movements and understanding their complementarity can we begin to grasp the full implications of Rousseau's claim that hatred and vengeance were the emotions farthest from his mind as he composed *The Levite of Ephraim*. In writing this work, Rousseau identified fundamentally with the Levite, the innocent victim. Strictly speaking, it is not the Levite who carries out any act of vengeance. That will be the concern of the community as a whole, the nation of Israel, once it is informed of the truth. The Levite's story is a story of unshakable faith in the community, in the collectivity of all as a force capable of righting the wrongs suffered by an innocent victim who finally asks only to speak and to die.

This act of faith in the community's ability to recognize truth and avenge evil manifests itself from the text's opening words. The first paragraphs of the first canto form a prologue, invoking the muse of virtuous anger and defining the lesson to be drawn from the story that will follow. The diction of these two paragraphs, standing outside of yet summarizing the narration to come, is curiously ambiguous. At some points these paragraphs read like quotations from the Levite addressing the assembled Israelites at Mizpah. At others we hear Rousseau's own voice speaking to his readers of their duty to look on the spectacle of his own persecuted innocence and to judge, to punish, to avenge: "O you men of meekness, enemies of all inhumanity; but who, for fear of looking upon your brothers' crimes, prefer to leave them unpunished, what horrors shall I offer your eyes? ... O sacred people, come together, judge this horrible act and accord it the response worthy of it. The man who turns away from such crimes is a coward, a deserter from the service of justice" (Le Lévite 2, 1208).

This prologue is also important because it focuses attention on the story's crucial moment, the moment when the innocent victim of a conspiracy presents his truth to the community as a whole. If, as is clear in a text like the Essay on the Origin of Languages, Rousseau was obsessed with the semiology of truth, his concern with that subject arose from his acute need to find some other system of signs that, breaking through the endless lies spoken and written about him, might at last figure forth and adequately represent his unjust victimization. Rousseau's abstract reflections on the degeneration of human sign systems in progressively more calcified forms of social organization must be read as an attempt to explain why, in spite of his many and repeated messages, his truth continued to go unrecognized.

Rousseau's fascination and identification with the figure of the Levite comes at least in part from that character's ability to achieve an act of perfect self-representation. A theoretical work like the Essay makes clear that, for Rousseau, the Levite had access to a system of representation no longer conceivable in French society as he knew it. In the Essay Rousseau emphasizes how ineffective the Levite's dispatching of the dismembered body would be in his own day: "In our day this affair, recounted in court pleadings and discussions, perhaps in jest, would be dragged out until this most horrible of crimes would in the end have remained unpunished" (Essai 5, 377). For Rousseau, contemporary society offered only a vitiated language that had long ago accommodated itself to a political organization in which relations of force and domination had become sclerotic. His contemporaries, a debased hierarchy of interlocking masters and slaves, need only a language suited to the secret consolidations of self-interest: "Our languages are made for whispering on couches.... I say that any language with which one cannot make oneself understood to the people assembled is a slavish language. It is impossible that a people remain free and speak that language" (Essai 5, 428–9).

The third cluster of Rousseau's modifications comes at the end of the narration. It involves the addition of an entire cast of characters, none of whom have equivalents in the biblical text. *Judges* ends with the attempt to resolve the problem of finding wives for the 200 Benjaminites still without spouses after the 400 virgins from Jabesh have been handed over to the 600 survivors at Rimmon Rock. *Judges* presents this solution in two moments. The first is a general council of the elders. They decide that the abduction of the daughters of Shiloh by the 200 Benjaminites is the best way of getting around their oath. Anticipating the one problem sure to arise, they assure the Benjaminites that they will head off any counterattack by explaining to the men of Shiloh that this abduction is the only way to save the tribe of Benjamin while avoiding anyone's breaking his oath. The second moment is a rapid "And thus it was done" that leads directly to everyone's return to his home and clan.

Rousseau segments this ending into a number of distinct scenes, each with specific characters embodying the major conflicts. At the council of the elders, one man, the Old Man of Lebona, presents the plan to have the Benjaminites kidnap the maidens at Shiloh. Following this scene there is a direct narration of the ambush in the vineyards. The tumult as the maidens are overpowered by the Benjaminites brings the entire population of Shiloh to the vineyards and another general assembly is formed. Moved by the fathers' indignation at their daughters' being carried off like slaves by the Moabites, the assembly relents and decides that the captured maidens are free to do as they wish. At this point Rousseau focuses on one couple: Axa and her fiancé Elmacin, who is among the men just arrived from the town. Axa's choice seems obvious. At that point, however, Axa's father steps forth. He is, Rousseau points out, none other than the Old Man of Lebona, the same elder who first suggested the kidnapping of these women by the Benjaminites. Taking his daughter by the hand, he calls on her to accept her duty to the nation of Israel as twelve tribes. Closer to death than life, Axa lets herself fall into the arms of the Benjaminite who had captured her. Elmacin, the fiancé, then steps forward and, taking a vow of chastity, proclaims that he will consecrate the rest of his life to the service of the Lord. Following this example worthy of Corneille, all the maidens choose their Benjaminite abductors and a cry of joy rises from the people.

The importance for Rousseau of this final reconstitution of the nation becomes clear when we contrast it with the earlier assembling of the tribes, in which Rousseau affirmed his faith in the capacity of the community to ensure justice once it knows the truth. Justice for the crime of Gibeah began with an act of denunciation: the larger community, the assembled tribes of Israel, denounced as criminal the conspiracy of a smaller group to appropriate authority through violence. This final scene, however, presents a different situation. The problem the community now confronts cannot be resolved by the uncovering of a hidden truth. The moments of truth and justice are past. The crime of Gibeah has been punished, and we are now in the phase of pity and pardon for the surviving Benjaminites.

The community finds itself in a double bind: Because all have taken a collective oath, none may give his daughter to a Benjaminite; because all are the chosen people of the Lord, none may tolerate the extinction of an entire tribe. If the community is to survive, some element within it must step outside established law and, as an anomaly, provide a solution that will allow the continued existence of the whole. The Old Man of Lebona, in presenting his plan to the council of elders and in overcoming his own paternal affection, becomes a variant of the ultimate foundation of the just community in Rousseau's political works. The Old Man of Lebona, as he speaks and as he acts, represents the same incarnation of the impossible within the possible as the Lawgiver described in Book 2 of the *Social Contract*: "The discovery of the best rules of society suited to nations would require a superior intellligence, who saw all of men's passions yet experienced none of them, who had no relationship at all to our nature yet knew it thoroughly, whose happiness was independent of us, yet who was nevertheless willing to attend to ours."[12] The Old Man of Lebona, the final avatar of the father in *The Levite*, is an agent of salvation and continuity. Thanks to his extraordinary action, on himself as much as upon the community, the social order is saved, the tribe of Benjamin will survive, and this entire narrative of crime and vengeance can draw to a close in peace and justice enforced and protected by the community.

The importance of this superhuman figure should not, however, lead us to overlook the equally significant roles played by the other characters Rousseau introduces into his ending of the Levite's story: Axa and her fiancé, Elmacin. The Old Man of Lebona's decision to rise above the human by choosing to act as the savior of his nation rather than as the father of his daughter changes the status of both Axa and Elmacin. In obeying the father, they embrace a sacrifice, proving their allegiance to a duty extending beyond individual desire to the community as a whole. Faced with the impossibility of the love they had pledged each other, Axa and Elmacin choose to accept and perpetuate their separation, not as a depravation, but as the apotheosis of a virtue that will now be preserved both as the indelible memory of their love and as the consecration of their persons to a higher principle. Even as she obeys her father, Axa accords to Elmacin an ultimate recognition as the true object of her love by pronouncing his name in a voice broken by tears signifying the inevitability of their separation. Unable to become Axa's husband, Elmacin vows to embrace an eternal chastity and to devote his life to the service of the living God as the Nazarene of the Lord.

This final scene imagined by Rousseau stands as a free transposition of the central conflict in *Julie*. Acting out of deference both to a promise made and to the social order, the father declares impossible the union of his daughter with her originally chosen beloved. Like Julie at the moment of her death, Axa obeys the father's command but makes it clear that the love she renounces has never died. Like Saint-Preux, Elmacin will consecrate what remains of his life to the service of an ideal virtue, forswearing the possibility that he might love any other woman. At the same time, a number of echoes link this closing scene to the earlier episodes of *The Levite*. Both the Levite as he faced the men of Gibeah and Elmacin as he arrived before the Benjaminites remain passive at the spectacle of violence. Both the Levite's concubine and Axa are described with similar turns of phrase in their respective plights: "They immediately surround the half-dead young girl" (*Le Lévite* 2, 1214) and "turning around half-dead, she falls into the arms of the Benjaminite" (*Le Lévite* 2, 1223). Elmacin's decision to live on as a priest presents him as assuming the sacerdotal function formally assigned to the tribe of Levy.

When these three clusters are brought together, it becomes clear that Rousseau's modifications of the biblical text turn on the expansion or addition of elements grouped around two central figures: the Levite and the Old Man of Lebona. Each of them has, as we saw, one or more doubles in the narrative: Elmacin for the Levite; the host at Gibeah and the concubine's father for the Old Man of Lebona. This proliferation of doubles undermines their treatment as distinct psychological presences while justifying their interpretation as successive representations of one primordial pair: the son and the father. The son, it emerges, is son because he continues to address himself to the father, because he preserves his faith in a paternal order from which, no matter how heinous the crime committed against him, he may expect justice.

What this configuration reveals is the status of *The Levite of Ephraim* as a synthesis that brings together the registers of the literary and the political within Rousseau's work. Standing between the categories of a minor and a major work, *The Levite* was Rousseau's almost immediate response to the order issued by *Parlement* for his arrest. As such, it is a work firmly grounded in and determined by the event through which a hostile society most explicitly and most aggressively declared his status as victim. At the same time, this concise, overdetermined narrative weaves together, in a fabric as intriguing as the dream it continues, strands linking it to the entire spectrum of Rousseau's major works. As in the *Second Discourse*, the past from which everything begins is an idyllic pastoral marked by self-sufficiency and immediately gratified desire. Abolished by an event "that might well never have taken place" but which, once having happened, irremediably separates him from that past, the Levite, like the author of the *Confessions*, addresses himself to and asks justice of a higher tribunal that he identifies with society as a whole, with the community of readers from which the truth of his victimization cannot remain forever hidden. In order that the social order be preserved once justice has been administered, one axial figure, a human yet superhuman Lawgiver, must, as in the *Social Contract*, step beyond and restructure the laws of society so that it might incorporate the truth revealed by the victim's act of self-representation. Finally, as in the *Dialogues* and the *Rêveries*, the sacrifice of this secular Christ is intended neither as a radical defiance of the community nor as a calling into question of its authority to judge. The victim's plea is instead that society recognize and punish the wrongs done him. He, like Elmacin, may linger on, but only as a consciousness for which felicity exists as a cherished, ineradicable memory sustaining a life lived in recollection. Rousseau's role in fashioning the sense of self that characterizes our modernity derives in large part from the tragic dimensions of the individual consciousness we find so compelling expressed within his rewriting of the

Levite's story. Confronted with an imperfect community whose understanding seems little more than a fleeting moment in an endless temporality of incomprehension, Rousseau solicits in his writing some recognition of his truth by a larger and more just community that will redress the scandal of his victimization.[13]

ENDNOTES

1 Speaking of the interest of Rousseau's "minor" works, Robert J. Ellrich argues that "As a rule, minor works provide more ready access to obsessions, tensions, and contradictions often painted over in the crafty process of producing a coherent, 'finished' masterwork," Richard J. Ellrich, "Rousseau's Androgynous Dream: The Minor Works of 1752–62 " *French Forum* **13**(3), 319 (1988).

2 The *Levite of Ephraim* was first published in 1781 in the first volume of the Geneva edition of the *Œuvres posthumes*. Relatively few critical studies have given more than passing consideration to this text. François Van Laere's *Jean-Jacques Rousseau, du phantasme à l'écriture* (Paris: Minard, 1967) presents this work as a transposition of Rousseau's complex relation to Thérèse. Madeleine Anjubault Simons's *Amitié et passion: Rousseau et Sauttersheim* (Geneva: Droz, 1972) devotes part of one chapter to the *Levite* as a work that allows her to organize a number of reflections on what she sees as Rousseau's repressed homosexuality, his ambiguous attitudes toward women and sexuality, and the appearance of these same themes in his other works. Susan K. Jackson's *Rousseau's Occasional Autobiographies* (Columbus, OH: Ohio State University Press, 1992) offers a provocative analysis of this text as one of a series of works anticipating and preparing the autobiographical effort the *Confessions*.

3 Jean-Jacques Rousseau, *Les confessions, oeuvres complètes*, eds. Bernard Gagnebin and Marcel Raymond (Paris: Gallimard, Bibliothèque de la Pléiade, 1959–1995), I, 586. All subsequent quotations will be cited parenthetically in the text. My translations follow J.M. Cohen, *The Confessions* (London: Penguin, 1953).

4 Jean-Jacques Rousseau, *Le Lévite d'Ephraïm, oeuvres complètes*, eds. Bernard Gagnebin and Marcel Raymond (Paris: Gallimard, Bibliothèque de la Pléiade, 1959–1995), 2, 1205–1206. Quotations from *The Levite* and its two prefaces are cited parenthetically in the text. The translations are my own. *The Levite* has recently been the subject of a useful critical edition providing a facing-page presentation of the work's draft and final versions as well as a bibliography and interpretation of the work as a controlled and impersonal *conte philosophique*. See Frédérick S.

Eigeldinger, ed., *Le Lévite d'Ephraïm, by Jean-Jacques Rousseau* (Paris: Honoré Champion, 1999).

5 In fact, Rousseau's memory of Gessner had as much to do with his choice of subject as it did with the style of the *Levite*. The first of Gessner's works with which Rousseau was familiar through Michel Huber's translation was titled *La mort d'Abel*. Like the *Levite*, it is the adaptation of a biblical story meant to support the thesis that the Old Testament was particularly suitable for pastoral treatment because it depicted a rural, agrarian society. In his translator's preface to the *Idylles*, Huber, referring to that earlier work, speaks of "the analogy of pastoral life and that of the ancient patriarchs." See Salomon Gessner, *Idylles et poèmes champêtres*, trans. Michel Huber (Lyon: Librairie Bruystet, 1762), p. xxiii.

6 Jean-François Perrin points out how the death of the mother also relates Rousseau to the figure of Benjamin in Genesis. His mother, Rachel, concerned that she would not survive the pain of his birth, named him Benoni or "son of my suffering" before Jacob changed the name to Benjamin. See his "La Régénération de Benjamin: Du *Lévite d'Ephraïm* aux *Confessions*," in *Autobiographie et fiction romanesque: Autour des Confessions de Jean-Jacques Rousseau*, ed. Jacques Domenech (Nice: Association des Publications de la Faculté des lettres de Nice, 1996), pp. 45–57. Pierre-Paul Clément in his *Jean-Jacques Rousseau, de l'éros coupable à l'éros glorieux* (Neuchâtel: La Baconnière, 1976) argues for another parallel between the Levite's story and the circumstances of Rousseau's life at the time he wrote this text. The Levite's inability to protect his concubine from the men of Gibeah is, he claims, similar to Rousseau's leaving Thérèse behind at Montmorency.

7 Comparing the description in the Book of Judges of how a group of nomadic tribes moves toward becoming the nation of Israel united under a king with the stages of social development in Rousseau's anthropology, Aubrey Rosenberg argues that Rousseau saw *Judges* as an example of the golden age of familial clans, a stage of social organization described more extensively in the *Essay on the Origin of Languages* than in the *Second Discourse*. See Aubrey Rosenberg, "Rousseau's *Lévite d'Ephraïm* and the Golden Age," *The Australian Journal of French Studies* **15**, 163–172 (1978). This argument is summarized in the entry on *Le Lévite d'Ephraïm* written by Rosenberg in the recent *Dictionnaire de Jean-Jacques Rousseau*, ed. Raymond Trousson and Frédéric S. Eigeldinger (Paris: Champion, 1996), pp. 544–547. Judith Still examines this same chronology and the same configuration of Rousseau's works from the perspective of what she sees as an exploitation of women through the imposition upon them of a series of paternalistic "meanings." See Judith

Still, "Rousseau's *Lévite of Ephraïm*: The Imposition of Meaning (on Women)," *French Studies* **43**, 12–30 (January 1989).

8 Jean-Jacques Rousseau, *Essai sur l'origine des langues, oeuvres complètes, eds. Bernard Gagnebin and Marcel Raymond (Paris: Gallimard, Bibliothèque de la Pléiade, 1959–1995), 5, 376. All subsequent quotations from this work are cited parenthetically in the text. My translation follows On the Origin of Language, ed. and trans. John H. Moran and Alexander Gode (New York: Unger, 1966).

9 Interpreting Rousseau's motivation of the woman's return to her father's house is further complicated by the differences between the Reformed and the Catholic versions of this biblical passage. Whereas the Reformed version, basing itself on the Masoretic text, translates from the Hebrew *wtznh 'lyw* to arrive at the sense of "played the whore," the Catholic version used the Codex Alexandrinus, whose Greek *orgisthe auto* translates as "became angry." In any case, Rousseau's decision to have nostalgia motivate the woman's return represents a departure from both versions. The English translations throughout this text are from *The Anchor Bible: Judges*, ed. Robert G. Boling (Garden City, NY: Doubleday, 1975). The Chouraqui translation is from André Chouraqui, ed., *La Bible: Josué et Juges* (Paris: Desclée de Brouwer, 1974), p. 188.

10 Jean Starobinski has underlined how the Levite's dispatching of the dismembered body parts accomplishes what Rousseau always saw as the crucial function of his writing. "The central episode in the history of the Lévite (...) may have taken on the value of a metaphor for Rousseau, a mythic and hyperbolical representation of writing activity (...); for Rousseau, writing was first and foremost the denouncing of evil, the naming of crime and vice." See his "Rousseau's Happy Days," *New Literary History* **11**, 147–66 (1979).

11 Michel Serres, *Le Parasite* (Paris: Grasset, 1980), p. 159. The translation is my own.

12 Jean-Jacques Rousseau, *Du contrat social, Oeuvres complètes*, eds. Bernard Gagnebin and Raymond (Paris: Gallimard, Bibliothèque de la Pléiade, 1959–1995), 3, 381. All subsequent quotations from this work are cited parenthetically in the text. My translations follow Roger D. Masters and Judith R. Masters, *On the Social Contract* (New York: St. Martin's, 1978).

13 For a more extensive development of this interpretation in terms of Rousseau's other works, see my *Writing the Truth: Authority and Desire in Rousseau* (Berkeley, CA: University of California Press, 1987).

15 Ancient Postmodernism in the Philosophy of Rousseau

Unless it was Immanuel Kant, who declined to believe it, practically no one who lived in the age of enlightenment ever took note of that fact.[1] The term The Enlightenment made its inaugural appearance in only the late nineteenth century, The Scottish Enlightenment was first ushered into print in the early twentieth century, and the Enlightenment Project, about which virtually every contemporary social philosopher now speaks with authority, is an expression invented more than thirty-five years after the demise of the Manhattan Project, whose adherents, by contrast, at least knew its name. Throughout its relatively brief history, The Enlightenment has largely assumed the identity assigned to it by its inventors determined to denigrate its achievement. *The Oxford English Dictionary* still defines The Enlightenment as an age of "superficial intellectualism," marked by "insufficient respect for authority and tradition," adding, for good measure, that a *philosophe* is "one who philosophizes erroneously." In the French language, matters are, if anything, worse still, as no Frenchman has ever managed to coin a term for The Enlightenment at all. At least God, even if He never existed either, somehow managed to get Himself invented, as Voltaire famously remarked, but not, alas, The Enlightenment. Frances Hutcheson in Glasgow observed that he was called New Light there, but no sparkling luminary in Paris, so far as I know, ever noticed that he was one of *les lumières*.

Of course a concept is not the same as a word, and it may have meaning without a name. Monsieur Jourdain in Molière's *"Bourgeois gentilhomme"* realised that he had been speaking prose all his life without ever knowing exactly what it was, and so too I think, just by virtue of their campaigns, were Voltaire and the international brigade

of *engagés volontaires* he mobilised to *écraser l'infâme* thereby en-
listed in the service of enlightenment, albeit ignorant of its name.
Not only was Voltaire the chief spokesman of The Enlightenment,
but, to my mind, he may even be described as the principal adher-
ent of the Enlightenment Project in precisely the sense that Alasdair
MacIntyre defines it in *After Virtue*. Who else but MacIntyre could
Voltaire have had in mind when, in his *Lettres philosophiques*, in
the most celebrated of all Enlightenment pleas for toleration, he
portrayed a London Stock Exchange in which Muslims, Jews,
Anabaptists, and Presbyterians exchange a common currency before they go off to practise their religions quietly in their diverse
churches, denouncing as an "infidel" only those who go bankrupt?
When, however, they are at home, in Scotland, he continues, when
Presbyterians form what is currently called a moral majority, they
adopt a solemn bearing and preach through their nose, denouncing
the spirit of cosmopolitan enlightenment, if I may here add my own
gloss on Voltaire's remarks, by way of Scottish Nationalist Party
broadcasts of the songs of Ossian.[2]

Rousseau, likewise, without ever inventing a term for it, was similarly well acquainted with the Enlightenment Project, by which I do
not just mean the *coterie holbachique* or international conspiracy
he supposed was plotting to defame him, but rather that intellectual
world constituted by its holy writ (as it can surely be so described),
the *Encyclopédie*, dedicated to the promotion of freedom and virtue
through the advancement of knowledge. Although they are unfortunately seldom noticed, there are many features of Rousseau's philosophy that address the empty formalism and abstract foundationalism
of seventeenth- and eighteenth-century metaphysics in terms later
to be embraced by Michel Foucault, Jacques Derrida, Jean-François
Lyotard, and their followers. In denouncing the cosmological framework and universalist pretensions of Rameau's acoustical theory
of harmony allegedly based on the resonance of a *corps sonore*,
Rousseau put forward a theory of musical expression that allowed
for aesthetic diversity, difference, and uniqueness in embracing ancient Greek, Persian, and Chinese melodies as well as the octave
of the relatively modern Western scale. In combating Diderot's notion of the *volonté générale* based on a premise of common humanity, Rousseau, above all in his *Manuscrit de Genève*, deconstructed
the myth of the natural society of the human race on which that

cosmopolitan notion depended, much in the manner adopted by Hegel in his critique of the abstract formalism of Kant and later by postmodernists in their objections to the so-called metanarratives of Enlightenment philosophy as a whole.[3]

Notions of circumscribed specificity as against generic definitions of human nature, wrongly presumed to be everywhere the same, inform Rousseau's objections to Hobbes' theory of the state of war, Locke's notion of the family, and indeed virtually every one of the natural jurisprudential doctrines – of Grotius, Pufendorf, Cumberland and others – he attempted to explain with reference to the peculiarly local and deliberately manufactured contexts in which alone they might have validity. Rousseau was both the Heidegger and the Foucault of the eighteenth century, anticipating Heidegger's ontological puns and the playfulness of his language, on the one hand, and Foucault's brutally sharp cleavage of the categories of knowledge to the disciplines of order and punishment, on the other. Whereas Heidegger introduces the linguistic turns of *Das sein* and *Wass sein* and *Wahr sein* and *Dasein*, in his, *Sein und Zeit*, Rousseau offers an account of the corruption of civilization as a whole in terms of the corruption of language, as the savage languages of passion would have been transfigured into barbarian languages of need and then, in commercial society, the languages of exchange; so that *aimez-moi* would have been superseded by *aidez-moi* and finally, today, when we are utterly estranged at once from ourselves and everyone around us, all that we say to each other, he contends, is *donnez de l'argent*.[4]

What else is Rousseau's whole philosophy of history, moreover, but a portrayal of mankind's self-inflicted incarceration in the great Panopticon of our civilization as a whole? The connection between *savoir* and *pouvoir* is not just a Marxist or Nietzschean or postmodernist and Foucauldian theme. It forms the kernel of the critique of what may be termed the Enlightenment Project itself by one of its main protagonists who, to use Hegelian language, was *an sich aber nicht für sich*, that is, who was part of it but in large measure did not subscribe to it. How else but with respect to *pouvoir's* determination of *savoir* are we to understand the central theme of his first *Discours*, in which Rousseau portrays our arts, letters, and sciences as "garlands of flowers round the iron chains by which [mankind] is weighed down?"[5] His understanding of the trappings of civilization is, to my mind, even richer than Foucault's, not least because, in Heideggerian fashion, he understood the force of language and metaphor and the ways in which, through language, individuals became the victims not just of one another's abuse of power but also of their own ideals, subjugated by their own conjugations, as it were, running headlong into their chains, thinking themselves free. In his fragment on *L'Etat de guerre*, probably drafted in the mid-1750s, he remarks that "With a tranquillity like that of the imprisoned companions of Odysseus waiting to be devoured by the Cyclops, we can only groan and be quiet." Here is Rousseau's myth of the cave. No postmodernist critic of the Enlightenment Project ever plumbed the depths of his deconstruction of *Homo sapiens* into *Homo deceptus* more deeply.[6]

I take Rousseau to have well understood what the Enlightenment Project was about and to have recognised his own philosophy as shaped by it, even when in defiance of some of its central aims. His was not a grotesque caricature such as, soon after his death, would embrace his own philosophy together with Voltaire's, as if these two fiercest ideological enemies of the whole eighteenth century were some homogeneous Gilbertonsullivan compound, pointing arm in arm to the new dawn of civilization, projecting the Enlightenment together. But just as Voltaire managed to refute Alasdair MacIntyre before the inventor of the expression The Enlightenment Project was born, so, for his part, did Rousseau manage to portray the ethnic cleansing of Bosnia and Kosovo even before Yugoslavia was created. Here are some more lines from the same passage of *L'Etat de guerre*. "I lift my eyes and look into the distance," he writes,

There I see fire and flames, a countryside deserted, villages pillaged. Monstrous men, where are you dragging these poor creatures? I hear a dreadful noise, such uproar, such screams! I draw near. I bear witness to a murderous scene, to ten thousand slaughtered men, the dead piled together, the dying trampled by horses, everywhere the sight of death and agony. All of this is the fruit of peaceful institutions! Pity and indignation rise up from the depths of my heart.[7]

One of the reasons why this passage, and indeed *L'Etat de guerre* in general, has been less frequently considered by Rousseau's readers than perhaps should have been the case is that his philosophy, by way of its alleged confusion of ancient liberty or popular sovereignty, on the one hand, with modern liberty or the protection of individual rights, on the other, has itself been blamed for many of the horrors it decries. According to his fiercest critics, his conjunction of absolute freedom with absolute power even engendered the Terror in the course of the French Revolution, giving rise to both the Jacobin and the Bonapartist dictatorships, as if the *volonté générale* or general will must always be translated as the *volonté du général*, the general's will. His interpreters who stress the extent to which the modern state has apparently been shaped by his own political doctrines thereby contrive to overlook his philosophy of history and the critique of modernity that it embraces, as it points uncomfortably in much the same direction as they do against him and is indeed often couched in images they would come to adopt themselves. From different ends of the political spectrum Paul de Man and Jacques Derrida have each written at some length about Rousseau's linguistic turns in several of his writings,[8] without ever addressing his reflections on the corruption of language in the *Essai sur l'origine des langues* and elsewhere as a measure of the failure of an Enlightenment Project whose principles postmodernists have frequently opposed for reasons not dissimilar to his own. Foucault has introduced Rousseau's tortured *Dialogues* as an anticonfessional autobiography, but where he might have been expected to find common cause with Rousseau's attack on modernity, he instead, as in his course of lectures on the idea of "governmentality" at the Collège de France, identified the political doctrine of the *Contrat social* with the institutions of totalitarian surveillance he had earlier associated with Jeremy Bentham.[9]

I mean to address just a few of these themes, and in particular Rousseau's conceptions of ancient and modern liberty, in a moment. However, in commenting here on the abiding pertinence and topicality of both Voltaire and Rousseau, I must not regard them as authors of a fresh Book of Revelations. I must not adopt the stance of those admirers of *Émile* who lay undue emphasis on Rousseau's remark there to the effect that Europe is approaching a century of revolutions that will ensure that its monarchies do not have long to survive, or of readers of the *Confessions* who note that in this work Rousseau uses the expression "*Qu'ils mangent de la brioche,*" which Marie-Antoinette herself never uttered.[10] Rousseau's reflections on war in *L'Etat de guerre* are not addressed to the recent crisis of the Balkans but to the writings of Hobbes and indirectly to the natural jurisprudential tradition that formed the nexus both of modern politic thought, as he understood it, and of the modern state insofar as its subjects also imagined themselves to be its rulers. That is its proper focus, or as we might say in Cambridge, its context. In contending that the state of war is a social and not a natural state, Rousseau set out to explain that our political institutions were themselves responsible for the crimes they were purported to solve, providing solutions to problems of which those solutions were in fact the cause. This is how the work begins, not as it is inaccurately assembled in all French editions including the Pléiade *Œuvres complètes*, but quite recently by Grace Roosevelt, who found that the creases in the original manuscript in the Bibliothèque de la Ville de Neuchâtel had somehow been turned inside out. "I open the books about law and morality," Rousseau remarks,

I listen to wise men and jurists and, moved by their penetrating words, I deplore the miseries of nature, I admire the peace and justice established by the civil order. I bless the wisdom of public institutions and take comfort from my being a man in seeing myself as a citizen. Well instructed in my duties and my happiness, I shut the book[s], leave the class, and look outside. [There] I see unfortunate people trembling under an iron yoke, the whole of humanity crushed by a handful of oppressors, a starving multitude racked by pain and hunger, of whom the rich peacefully lap up the blood and tears, and throughout the world nothing but the strong holding sway over the weak, armed with the redoubtable strength of the laws.[11]

As against modern notions of absolute sovereignty put forward by these wise men and jurists – that is, by men such as Bodin, Grotius, Hobbes, and Pufendorf – Rousseau elaborated an alternative idea of sovereignty that also embraced an ancient republican commitment to civil liberty. Before its use in his philosophy, the concept of "sovereignty" had been connected by its interpreters to the idea of force or empire, and it characteristically pertained to the dominion of kings over their subjects rather than to citizens' freedom. For both Bodin and Hobbes, in particular – the best-known advocates of absolute sovereignty before Rousseau – the terms *souveraineté* or sovereignty were derived from the Latin *summa potestas* or *summum imperium*, which defined the prevailing power of the ruler. For Rousseau, by contrast, the idea of sovereignty was essentially a principle of equality, which identified the ruled element, or the subjects themselves, as the supreme authority, and it was connected with the concepts of will or right rather than force or power; it expressed *le moral* of politics and not *le physique*. To my mind, it is precisely because of his innovative conjunction of an altogether unlikely pair of terms – *liberté*, as drawn from an ancient republican tradition of self-rule, and *souveraineté*, from a modern absolutist ideology addressed to the need for predominating power – that liberal critics have judged his doctrine more sinister than any other collectivist conception of freedom. How can absolute force and perfect liberty possibly go hand in hand? To be "forced to be free," as Rousseau stipulated in one of the most famous passages of the *Contrat social*,[12] seems the vilest deception imaginable from one who made the idea of liberty the most central principle of his political philosophy.

On this subject Rousseau has a case to answer, and as a matter of fact he answered it. The absolute authority of the sovereign, he wrote, must both come from all and apply to all. The voice of the *volonté générale* it enacts cannot pronounce on individuals without forfeiting its own legitimacy, as it articulates in law the common interest of every citizen, whereas the exercise of force over individuals is reserved exclusively for a nation's government. Rousseau's sovereign never implements its own laws and never punishes transgressors against it,[13] nor indeed forces anyone to be free.

Beyond all major political theorists before or after him, Rousseau distinguished right from power, the formulation of principle from its application – in this context the moral will that determines laws from the physical force that implements them – by placing each in different hands, here, respectively, the legislative power and the executive power. His point about force and freedom means scarcely more than that citizens must always be bound by their own agreements, even when they feel inclined to disregard them. No force is exercised except over persons who have reneged on their decision to abide by laws they enact themselves, and no force is exercised at all by the sovereign. The tyrannical abuse of power that liberal critics impute to Rousseau's sovereign was actually perceived by him to be a misappropriation of the powers of government, against which the absolute sovereignty of the people was the only real safeguard. With the executive power of the Republic of Geneva (that is, the *Petit Conseil*) substituted for the popular will of the assembly of all citizens (that is, the *Conseil Général*), absolute right had been corrupted into unfettered force. And "where force alone reigns," as Rousseau remarked in his *Lettres de la montagne*, "the state is dissolved. That...is how all democratic states finally perish."[14] Rousseau's conception of absolute sovereignty was thus designed to ensure civil liberty by virtue of an infrastructural separation of powers, exactly contrary to the notions of sovereignty put forward by Bodin and Hobbes. Liberty was made secure, in his view, by the very institution that, his liberal critics have since alleged, can only destroy it. So long as the general will of a community remained general, citizens kept their freedom under the rule of its laws.

I take this novel association of the ideas of sovereignty and freedom to have informed the meaning of what he termed *la liberté civile* in Book I, Chap. viii of the *Contrat social*, though it should not be forgotten that the same chapter also introduces a second idea of liberty gained by citizens in their membership of the state, which Rousseau called *la liberté morale* or "obedience to the law we prescribed to ourselves."[15] That concept is also drawn from Rousseau's understanding of ancient hisory and philosophy, but whereas *la liberté civile* is inspired fundamentally by the same Roman republican sources that enthralled his beloved Machiavelli, *la liberté morale* is essentially Greek in origin, as is plain from the word autonomy that we will still use to define it. Both in his use of the political and moral meanings of *liberté* and in his novel use of the expression *la volonté générale*, Rousseau articulated classical ideals of liberty in a modern vocabulary that may, at first glance, seem as alien to them as is his invocation of ancient liberty in justification of modern sovereignty. Some of his most striking images indeed derive their force from just such attempts to illuminate the values of old cultures in a new language commonly thought to have dispensed with them, and much may be learnt about his political ideals if we regard him, to use his own words from his *Jugement sur la Polysynodie*, as one of those "moderns who had an ancient soul," although he is not speaking of himself there but of the Abbé de Saint-Pierre.[16]

Perhaps the most distinctive feature of his concept of *la liberté morale* is its peculiarly reflexive element of self-prescription. Every morally free agent, Rousseau insisted, was required to follow rules established only within the depths of his own conscience in a self-reliant manner, free from the influence of all other persons. The most absolute authority, he observed in his *Discours sur l'économie politique*, "is that which penetrates into man's innermost being,"[17] incorporating him into the common identity of the state, as he put it in the *Contrat social*.[18] Liberal critics recoil in horror from these claims, insofar as they take them to imply the complete submergence of our separate wills under the collective will of the body politic that envelops and moulds us. Yet what Rousseau meant by his conjunction of moral liberty with the general will was designed to avert rather than achieve the social indoctrination of individuals. Not only did he insist on the fact that a nation's general will could be realised only through opposition to the particular wills of each of its members, with the constant tension between two kinds of will or interest – instead of the suppression of one by the other – indispensable to the achievement of the common good. He also stressed that the same opposition was present in the minds of all citizens, so that every person was motivated by both a particular will and a general will, dividing his judgment of what was beneficial to himself from what was right for the community.

Especially in the modern world, Rousseau believed, our general will was much weaker than our particular will, and it was to be strengthened and animated not by our imbibing the collective opinions of our neighbours in a public assembly, but just the reverse – by all citizens expressing their own opinions alone, "having no communication amongst themselves," as he put it in the *Contrat social*, which might render their separate judgments partial to this or that group interest.[19] To ensure that in the assembly there were as many votes as individuals, every member must act without regard to the rest, consulting his own general will as a citizen, thereby still obeying himself alone. Our personal identity was lost only when in legislation we echoed the opinions of an unreflective, undiscriminating multitude. For Rousseau, the more perfect our independence from others – the more profoundly we turned into ourselves for guidance – the more likely were our deliberations to yield the common good.

In the social contract state that he envisaged, deep introspection was therefore the corollary of the outward pursuit of that common good or public interest. The idea of will in this context expresses the voluntarist, contractarian strain of modern political thought – or, if I may put my point another way, it mediates a fundamentally Greek notion of "autonomy" through the language of "conscience" drawn from the Protestant Reformation – whereas what is general encapsulates the Roman republican idea of a public good towards which each person's will should be aimed. It follows that according to Rousseau's philosophy, in order to be a citizen of a *res publica* one must look deep within oneself for a personal commitment to a collective goal, which alone renders our *liberté morale*, as he conceived it, so much grander than the *liberté naturelle* he claimed men forfeit when they enter into civil society. In the eighth chapter of Book I of the *Contrat social*, and again, as I mean to show presently, in the fifteenth chapter of Book III, Rousseau puts forward his case on behalf of ancient as opposed to modern liberty – in an exposition that might well have borne the title *De liberté des anciens contre celle des modernes*, so as to refute in advance the case made by Benjamin Constant on behalf of modern liberty conceived as personal freedom and the protection of individual rights, in his celebrated lecture of 1819 designed to show the inappropriateness to the modern age of principles such as those of Rousseau.[20]

We have only to turn to the *Considérations sur le gouvernement de Pologne* to note how passionate was Rousseau's commitment to ancient political liberty as against this alternative, individualist, notion. In a chapter of that work entitled *"Esprit des anciennes institutions,"* itself anticipated in his fragmentary *Parallèle entre les deux républiques de Sparte et de Rome*,[21] and before that by many contributors, including Fenélon, to the late-seventeenth- and early-eighteenth-century *Querelle des anciens et des modernes*,[22] Rousseau grieved over the civil and moral liberty we had lost in passing from antiquity into the modern world. "Modern men," he wrote, "no longer find in themselves any of that spiritual vigour which inspired the ancients in everything that they did." Ancient legislators sought to forge links that would attach citizens to *leur patrie* and to one another, in religious ceremonies, games, and spectacles. The laws that rule modern men, by contrast, are solely intended to teach them to obey their masters.[23]

The continually assembled citizens of Sparta, as he portrayed them in his *Lettre à d'Alembert (sur les spectacles)*, consecrated the whole of their lives to amusements that were great matters of state. Why should it not be so in modern republics as well? he exclaimed, in which the people could be "forever united" through festivals held "in the open air, under the sky." Yet what do we find instead? "Private

meetings (les tête-a-tête)...taking the place of public assemblies."
Where today, asks Rousseau in the same passage, is the concord of
citizens from which the men of antiquity derived all their strength?
"Where is la fraternité publique? ...Where is peace, liberty, equity,
innocence?"[24] The term fraternité cited here in conjunction with
liberté does not figure often in Rousseau's works, however much its
meaning seems so obviously infused in his conception of the general will and, indeed, resonates throughout his political writings as a
whole. However, it is used as well, once again, in his Gouvernement
de Pologne, in which he calls on Polish youth to follow the example of the people of Rome rather than emulate the decadence of the
French, so as to become accustomed to égalité and fraternité as citizens of a truly free state, "living under the eyes of their compatriots,
seeking public approbation."[25]

By so linking hand in hand the ideas of liberté, égalité, and fraternité, Rousseau – in this as in so much else – heralded the French
Revolution whose advent he anticipated in Émile, just by fixing his
gaze upon an ancient world that of course had never really existed
any more than did l'état de nature, similarly pieced together out
of his own imagination. In La Nouvelle Héloïse, moreover, he drew
all three principles together by way of depicting an exultant feast of
grape harvesters in which all partake freely, equally, and fraternally,[26]
thereby evoking an image of freedom radically different from the
ideal of personal liberty that would be elaborated by Constant and
other modern liberals virtually at the moment that their intellectual
movement was formed, and for that matter when the world liberal
was coined, largely by way of reaction to Rousseau's alleged abuse of
the term.

I have already mentioned the passages of his Essai sur l'origine
des langues in which he complained that whereas our ancestors had
once sung aimez-moi to one another, we now only mutter donnez
de l'argent. The same expression, donnez de l'argent, repeated in
Book 15 of the Contrat social, is described there as the harbinger of
a society in chains, ruled by the slavish institution of "finance," unknown to the men of antiquity, who also had no grasp of our modern
notion of "representation," he adds for good measure.[27] Representation, on the one hand, and finance or public taxation, on the other,
were for Rousseau the most centrally defining features of the political world of modernity as a whole, whose adoption of these principles

and their attendant institutions had marked the demise of ancient liberty as he understood it. We moderns have been transformed into mute auditors of declamations from the pulpit and proclamations from the throne, our collective voice stilled, he lamented in the concluding chapter of his *Essai sur l'origine des langues*.[28] Whereas once our interests were openly shared and inscribed in our hearts, he added in the *Contrat social*, now they are in conflict, secreted away in the linings of our purses. Have we forgotten that, once we aspire to serve the state with our purses rather than our person, it is on the edge of ruin? Have we forgotten that "in a well-ordered city everyone flies to the assemblies?"[29] Modern liberty, shorn of its ancient associations with fraternity, on the one side, and equality, on the other, stands exposed as nothing more than "private gain." However, so far from it embracing the only proper use of the term *liberté*, the contemporary ethos of private gain was for Rousseau just ancient slavery in a modern form, all the more psychologically insidious for our pursuing it as if it were real freedom. Turned inward on himself and outward against his neighbours, modern man in fact, like primeval man in fiction, had run headlong into chains that he supposed had made him free.

By focusing on Rousseau's vision of ancient liberty, I have here addressed the impassioned rhetoric that his French Revolutionary admirers came to love, the imagined community of *Roma redivivus*, whose utter unsuitability for the modern era would prompt Mme. de Staël and other liberals who did not welcome it to charge that Rousseau "*n'a rien découvert, mais il a tout enflammé*"[30] the passions, the senses, the Terror. Voltaire formed a similar judgment of the incendiary prose of Rousseau's *Lettre sur la musique française*, the first of his works that made him appear to be a threat to the French nation, even if Rousseau himself was convinced that it actually had merited the King's gratitude because, as he relates in his *Confessions*, the public outcry it provoked in the autumn of 1753 diverted an impending revolution against the state into a revolution against him alone.[31] There are indeed close parallels between Rousseau's political tributes to republican Rome over monarchical France, on the one hand, and his endorsement in the *Querelle des Bouffons* of the melodious Italian language over the bark and bray of French, on the other. Recognising that link, d'Alembert, in his essay *De la liberté de la musique* of 1759, asserted that if we wish to conserve the kingdom we must preserve opera as it is, as the terms *bouffoniste* and *republican* may be used inter-changeably.[32]

I should like, however, to conclude these reflections on Rousseau's ancient postmodernism by addressing not his role in the French Revolution that failed to occur but rather the significance of his classical republican ideals with respect to the Revolution that *did* take place, whose greatest successes and failures alike were to earn for him the status of chief poet and acknowledged legislator of the age of modernity we still inhabit. I regard as manifestly false all the arguments known to me – including those of Hegel, Constant, Proudhon, and Talmon – to the effect that it was Rousseau's political philosophy above all others in the Enlightenment that engendered the collectivist or totalitarian tyranny of the modern nation-state, and in the little space that remains available I mean to show that his critique of modern despotism by way of invoking ancient liberty remains as trenchant today, with respect to political institutions un-heralded by his doctrines, as it was in his own lifetime.

As is implied in the very title of Mercier's work of 1791, *Rousseau, considéré comme l'un des premiers auteurs de la Révolution,* Rousseau was of course the spiritual guide of a regenerated France. He pointed the way to the promised land. However, although his *Contrat social* would come to be esteemed as if it formed the French Revolution's first commandments, its most central tenets were in fact to be repudiated in the age of modernity launched by the politi-cal upheavals of 1789. Even in adopting much of Rousseau's rhetoric, France's revoutionary leaders deliberately abandoned most of his principles and, at each stage of their deliberations, triumphantly op-posed everyone who endorsed them. In the course of its gestation the political system they devised suffocated the most fundamental stricutres of that system's putative founder. Like Freud's conception of the birth of the Jewish people through an act of primal parricide as outlined in his *Moses and Monotheism* – even like Rousseau's birth, which cost his mother her life – the first modern nation-state that ostensibly embraced his doctrines suppressed them.[33] In the act of its self-creation, if I may so put this point, modernity killed the Rousseauist ideals to which it purportedly subscribed. Let me try to explain what I mean, by way of pursuing the logic of Hegel's treatment of "Absolute Freedom and Terror" in his *Phänemonologie des Geistes*, in order to refute the case he makes himself against Rousseau in his *Philosophie des Rechts*.

On 17 June 1789, the deputies of the *Estates-Général*, which had been convoked the previous autumn by King Louis XVI, resolved that they were no longer assembled at the monarch's behest but were rather agents of the national will (*le vœu national*), entrusted with the task of representing the sovereignty of the people of France. The three estates thereby constituted themselves as a single *Assemblée nationale*, bearing sole authority to interpret the people's general will. It is in this way, Hegel suggests, that political modernity was born, with a unicameral legislative system corresponding to a unitary will, a unified state speaking on behalf of an undifferentiated nation.[34]

Because the motion that was carried had been put to the National Assembly by the Abbé Sieyès in the light of principles already enunciated in his famous pamphlet of the previous winter, *Qu'est-ce que le tiers état?*, Sieyès himself may with some justice be deemed the progenitor of the modern nation-state. Hegel, who had witnessed modernity's birth and was to devote much of his life to portraying its childhood, came eventually to reflect on Sieyès' paternity of modernity, as it were, in his essay, *Über die englische Reformbill*, of 1831, in which he remarked that Sieyès had been able to extract out of his own papers the plan that was to give France the constitution it came to enjoy.[35] For my part, as I interpret the extent of Sieyès' influence not only on the course of the French Revolution, but also on the development of the state in both theory and practice, no one, including Rousseau, has ever contributed more to shaping the modern world's political discourse.

In pursuit of the reasoning that had led to the formation of the National Assembly, Sieyès insisted that the King of France must be denied any kind of veto, absolute or suspensive, over legislation that could not articulate the nation's sovereign will if the monarch stood above the people's representatives. Both in the spring of 1789 in the Estates-Général and again in the National Assembly at the end of July, he also argued, in this case successfully, that the people of France must similarly be denied a binding mandate, or *mandat impératif*, over their own delegates, because such a mandate, just like a royal veto, would deprive the people's representatives of their freedom and would accordingly substitute the multifarious particular wills of scattered citizens for the collective will of the nation as a whole. The act of creation of the National Assembly that Sieyès had sponsored declared that the Assembly was *une et indivisible*. If the general will was to speak with one voice in a unitary nation-state, he insisted, it could no more be accountable to the people at large than to a king.

At the heart of his conception of modernity lay an idea of representation that in Sieyès' eyes was to constitute the most central feature of the French state. The modern age in its political form, which he termed *l'ordre représentatif*, depended for its prosperity on a system of state management that adopted the same principle of the division of labour as was necessary for a modern economy. This system entailed that the people must entrust authority to their representatives rather than seek its exercise directly by themselves, their delegates articulating their interests on their behalf while they acordingly remain silent. In thus distinguishing the effective agents of state power from its ultimate originators, Sieyès merely pursued the logic of his own differentiation of *active* from *passive* citizens, whose separate identification for a brief period under the French Constitution of 1791 was to prove one of the crowning achievements of his career.[36]

There could be no confusion in France between representation and democracy such as inspired Paine and others to imagine that the hybrid form of government established in America had nourished a classical principle of self-rule in a large state. For Sieyès, who sometimes spoke of direct democracy as a form of *démocratie brute*, it would be tragic for the first genuinely modern state of human history to make a retrograde step. In establishing a political system that was without precedent, France could not hesitate between ancient and modern principles of government. Despite his endorsement of other constitutional safeguards against the sovereign assembly's abuse of its powers, Sieyès did not permit any allegiance to Montesquieu with respect to such matters to overcome his mistrust of Rousseau, as he was adamant that the people themselves, lacking discipline, must be deprived of such means as would put public order at risk. Democracy, he thought, was no more fit for modernity than was the mixed constitution that would issue from the preservation of a royal veto. Sovereignty thereby passed from the nation's multifarious fragments to the people's delegates constituted as one body, the populace ceasing to have any political identity except as articulated through its representatives, who by procuration were granted authority to speak for the electorate as a whole.

Although the conception of the modern state put forward by Sieyès thus required that both the King, on the one hand, and the people, on the other, should be marginalized from the government of France, the implementation of his plan did not proceed as smoothly as he might have hoped. Apart from the King's disinclination to yield all his powers to an assembly that he had originally called into being himself, the people had their revolutionary champions as well. The Jacobins, in particular, regarded Sieyès' distinction between active and passive citizenship as anathema and, opposing his principle of the indivisibility of the general will as articulated by the nation's representatives, they sought to return directly to the people, in their districts and through their communes, the indivisible sovereignty of the whole nation which had been expropriated by their independently minded political delegates. *Their* notion of sovereignty, conceived as residing with the people as a whole, thus seemed to contradict the logic of modernity pursued by Sieyès and his associates, insofar as the Jacobins portrayed themselves as standing for the people rather than for the nation that had been substituted for them.

As Hegel correctly perceived, however, the Jacobins' contradiction of Sieyès' logic of modernity was fundamentally illusory, as the nation that they envisaged to comprise all its people was to prove as monolithic as Sieyès' conception of a nation represented by the state. When they came to power within the Convention in the autumn of 1793, they behaved as Sieyès and his associates had done earlier, but in reverse – that is, they attempted to root out the people's enemies within the state, just as Sieyès had sought to silence the enemies of the state within the nation. Pure democracy was to prove as incompatible in practise with Robespierre's populism as it was alien to Sieyès' notion of representative government, so that in 1793, no less than in 1789, when these two enemies had last been in agreement in their opposition to the royal veto, they could once again be of one mind. The Terror of the Jacobins was to follow directly from their idea of the sublime unity of the nation, which required a lofty purity of public spirit that made the vulgar purity of democracy seem an uncouth substitute for virtue. Popular sovereignty was not only to be given voice but actually created by the nation's genuine representatives. The greatest enemy of the people for whom they stood, and who had still to be manufactured in the image of what they might become, were all the fractious people cast in recalcitrant moulds resistant to such change, who thereby stood in the way of the agents of the people of the future. In concluding this section of his *Phänomenologie*, Hegel thus contends that in its abstract existence of unmediated pure negation, the sole work of freedom is death, a death without inner significance, the coldest and meanest of deaths, like splitting a head of cabbage.[37]

However, Hegel's attribution, in his *Rechtsphilosophie*, of ultimate responsibility for the Terror to Rousseau, is altogether misconceived. Rousseau was convinced, contrary to Hegel, Sieyès, and Robespierre, that to express their general will citizens must deliberate together and then heed their own counsel; they could not just vote for spokesmen who, as their proxies, would determine the nation's laws. In large states, he observed, there must be means whereby the true sovereign could exercise its will even when assemblies were entitled, over prescribed periods and subject to general ratification, to speak with the consent of the people as a whole. There must in such circumstances be plebiscites, he believed, such as had been enjoyed by the citizens of the Republic of Rome, entitled to dispense with their tribunes at will, for in the presence of the represented, as Rousseau put it, there could be no representation.[38]

For all his misgivings about democracy as a form of government, Rousseau believed more passionately than any other eighteenth-century thinker in the idea of popular or democratic sovereignty. It was principally this doctrine, which was presumed to have been inscribed in the *Déclarations des droits de l'homme* and the constitutions of the revolutionary years, that ensured his renown as the patron saint of a regenerated France. However, the doctrine was upheld by him in its pure form, embracing the people as a whole,[39] whereas the purity of purpose sought by Sieyès, Robespierre, and their associates with respect to the sovereignty of the nation was always of another, contradictory, sort. As is perhaps plainest from his *Gouvernement de Pologne*, Rousseau subscribed to just that notion of a *mandat impératif* that in the modern world most closely approximated the full legislative authority of citizens acting collectively, such as he understood to have prevailed in the free republics of antiquity.[40] He was a democrat against representation, he stood for the direct and unmediated sovereignty of the people against all forms of delegated power, and not once in the course of a revolution said to have been framed by his ideas did the advocates of his philosophy – in the National Assembly, the Commune of Paris, the Jacobin Club, or the Club of the Cordeliers – come to prevail.

Hegel's conceptual history of political modernity, within which Rousseau's idea of absolute liberty is portrayed as having engendered both the National Assembly and the Terror, was thus only made possible, to my mind, by the category mistake of his confusing Rousseau's political doctrine with the philosophies of both Sieyès, whom he supposed to have put Rousseauism into practice, and Robespierre, whom he regarded as having brought Rousseauism to its dreadful climax. As the father of modernity, Sieyès was of course no more likely to assume responsibility for the Terror than was God ever inclined to accept blame for original sin. If he was aware of it, he was never persuaded by Hegel's reading of the French Revolution and always remained convinced that the Terror had actually sprung from the betrayal of his own ideas on the part of populists who could not abide the principle of indirect sovereignty which his theory of representation prescribed. From his point of view, a form of Rousseauism had indeed been responsible for the Terror, in dissolving all his achievements in the National Assembly through its successful implementation of just that brutish form of direct democracy which was unfit for the modern world. For their part, in their advocacy of one nation, the Jacobins likewise proved as little democratic as was Sieyès in upholding the integrity of one state.

The inappropriateness of democracy for modernity was as striking to Sieyès as was the unsuitability of modernity for democracy in the eyes of Rousseau. With regard to *his* grasp of the meaning of Rousseau's political principles, Sieyès was as clear as was Hegel obscure, and he devoted much of his career to combatting those democrats of the National Assembly who espoused them. As against Rousseau's democratic notion of sovereignty he turned instead to that of Hobbes. Rousseau's followers in the National Assembly had no understanding of the system of representation required in a modern state, he supposed, but at least a sketch of it could be drawn from the sixteenth chapter of the *Leviathan*.[41] To the Hobbesian theory of representation, the nation-state as conceived by Sieyès adds the dimension of the comprehensive unity of the people, the representer and represented jointly forming an indissoluble whole, the state and nation bonded together, each understood through the other.

Much like Hegel himself, but contrary to Rousseau, Sieyès sought to establish the foundations of a new and progressive political order that would embrace rather than destroy the trappings of commercial society, in a state whose legislative system could express the solidarity of a national community only indirectly through representatives. Finance and representation lie at the heart of both Hegel's and Sieyès' conceptions of the modern state, as indeed they are embraced by all governments that preside over what are now termed representative democracies – that is, the exact opposite of democracies as guardians of their subjects' civil and moral liberty in the sense explained by Rousseau. The triumph of systems of representative democracy in this age of so-called democratic republics may be said to mark the abandonment, and, in the case of France, the suppression, of the most central ideals of Rousseau's social contract state.

Let me, finally, return to Rousseau's own portrayal of modernity in *L'Etat de guerre*. In opposing the democratic *mandat impératif*, Sieyès resisted what he perceived to be the threat to the expression of the nation's general will that might be constituted by the people. It was of the essence of his plan that the nation in assembly spoke for all the people and must never be silenced by the people themselves. Over the past 200 years the nation-state has characteristically achieved that end because it represents the people, standing before them not just as monarchs had done earlier, as the embodiment of their collective will, but rather by assuming their very identity, bearing the personality of the people themselves. With some notable exceptions – the United States of America, of course, foremost among them – most of the world's population now live in nation-states. All peoples that have accredited identities form nation-states. What Sieyès did not foresee was that in the age of modernity heralded by his political philosophy, a people might not survive except by constituting a nation-state. In the age of modernity, it has proved possible for the nation-state to become the enemy of the people.

As Hannah Arendt rightly noted in her *Origins of Totalitarianism*, it has been a characteristic feature of the nation-state since the French Revolution that the rights of man and the rights of the citizen are the same.[42] By giving real substance and proper sanction to the various declarations of the rights of man within the framework of its own first constitutions, the French revolutionary nation-state invented by Sieyès joined the rights of man to the sovereignty of the nation.[43] It defined the rights of man in such a way that only the state could enforce them and only members of the nation could enjoy them, thereby ensuring that henceforth only persons comprising nations that formed states could have rights. Yet the history of modernity since the French Revolution has characteristically been marked by the abuse of human rights on the part of nation-states that alone have the authority to determine the scope of those rights and their validity. Not only Rousseauism but the Enlightenment Project itself has been largely abandoned in an age in which so many nation-states have collectively rescinded that Project's eighteenth-century restoration of the Edict of Nantes, if I may so put it, whose first revocation in 1685 had given rise to the ethnic cleansing of France and thereby heralded, by way of their response to religious bigotry, the genesis of the Enlightenment Project and Rousseauism together.[44]

Throughout our century whole peoples that comprise nations without states have found themselves comprehensively shorn of their rights. Thanks ultimately to the political pioneers of the French Revolution, ours is the age of the passport, the permit, the right of entry to each state, or right of exit from it that is enjoyed by citizens that bear its nationality alone. For persons who are not accredited as belonging to a nation-state in the world of modernity, there are few passports and still fewer visas. To be without a passport or visa in the modern world is to have no right of exit or entry anywhere, and to be without a right of exit or entry is to risk a rite of passage to the grave. That above all is the legacy bequeathed to us, not by way of our adoption of a Rousseauist reversion to ancient republican ideals, but from the political inception of the modern age, on 17 June 1789. "We now enter into a new order of things," Rousseau had remarked in *L'Etat de guerre*, "in which we shall see men united by an artificial accord coming together to cut one another's throats, and in which all the horrors of war arise from the efforts that were taken to prevent it."[45]

At the moment of Rousseau's illumination on the road to Vincennes in the summer of 1749 that was to spark the composition of most of his major works, he managed to retain an impression of just the smallest sliver of the thunderbolt that struck him, which he then conveyed to Diderot in prison. It was the *Prosopopœia of Fabricius*, inspired by Plutarch's *Life of Pyhrrus*, in which he called on two eminent kings of France to recognise, as "the noblest sight that ever appeared beneath the heavens," the 200 virtuous Senators of the ancient republic of Rome.[46] In attempting to exculpate Rousseau from responsibility for the new modes and orders of the first modern republic of the Old World which put an end to the *ancien régime*, I must not just blame Sieyès and Robespierre instead, even if their revolutionary careers and aspirations make them far better candidates for scrutiny. However, I believe that, more than any other figure of the eighteenth-century Enlightenment, Rousseau glimpsed the heart of darkness beneath civilization's new dawn. "*Où veux-tu fuir?*" he asked in *La Nouvelle Heloïse*, recalling some of Satan's lines in Milton's *Paradise Lost*. "Le Phantôme," he answered, "est dans ton cœur."[47] Across what would now be termed different disciplines, Rousseau managed to probe and uncover some of modernity's deepest faults, and, to my mind, the flawed world that he portrayed throughout his writings was not only his but also ours.[48]

ENDNOTES

1 With respect to Kant's and other eighteenth-century German treatments of the question *"Was ist Aufklärung?"* see especially Werner Schneiders, *Die wahre Aufklärung* (München: Karl Alber, 1974) and James Schmidt (ed.), *What is Enlightenment?: Eighteenth-Century Answers and Twentieth-Century Questions* (Berkeley, CA: University of California Press, 1996). For an analysis of Michel Foucault's varied interpretations of Kant's seminal essay, see Christopher Norris, "Foucault on Kant," in Norris, *The Truth about Postmodernism* (Oxford, U.K.: Blackwell, 1993), pp. 29–99; Maurizio Passerin d-Entrèves, "Critique and Enlightenment: Michel Foucault and 'Was ist Aufklärung?'", in Norman Geras and Robert Wokler (eds.), *The Enlightenment and Modernity* (New York: St. Martin's, 2000), pp. 184–203; and Schmidt and Thomas Wartenberg, "Foucault's Enlightenment: Critique, Revolution and the Fashion of the Self," in Michael Kelly (ed.), *Critique and Power: Recasting the Foucault/Habermas Debate* (Cambridge, MA: MIT Press, 1994), pp. 283–314. Foucault had edited and provided the first French

translation of Kant's *Anthropologie in pragmatischer Hinsicht* as the *thèse complémentaire* he submitted for his doctorate in 1960.

2 I have addressed MacIntyre's notion of the Enlightenment Project in "Projecting the Enlightenment" in J. Horton and S. Mendus (eds.), *After MacIntyre* (Cambridge, U.K.: Polity Press, 1994), pp. 108–26. Having originally imagined that the expression The Enlightenment Project dates from the 1930s, I should be grateful to any reader who may have located it in print before the publication of *After Virtue* in 1981. For Voltaire's description of the London Stock Exchange, see the sixth of his *Lettres philosophiques* on the Presbyterians.

3 Rousseau's critiques of Rameau and Diderot along these lines are addressed in my "Rousseau on Rameau and Revolution" in R.F. Brissenden and J.C. Eade (eds.), *Studies in the Eighteenth Century*, IV (Canberra: Australian National University Press, 1979), pp. 251–83, and "The Influence of Diderot on the Political Theory of Rousseau," *Studies on Voltaire and the Eighteenth Century* **82**, 55–112 (1975), respectively.

4 See the *Essai sur l'origine des langues*, Chaps. x and xx, in Pléiade Vols. 408 and 428.

5 Rousseau, *Discours sur les sciences et les arts*, Pléiade III, 7.

6 This is one of the main themes of my "Perfectible Apes in Decadent Cultures: Rousseau's Anthropology Revisited" in *Rousseau for our Time*, *Daedalus* (Summer 1978), pp. 107–34.

7 Rousseau, *L'Etat de guerre*, Pléiade III, 609.

8 See De Man, "Rousseau's Theory of Metaphor," *Studies in Romanticism* **12**, 475–98, (1973); De Man, *Allegories of Reading: Figural Language in Rousseau, Nietzsche, Rilke and Proust* (New Haven, CT: Yale University Press, 1979); and Derrida, *De la grammatologie* (Paris: Les Éditions de minuit, 1967).

9 See Rousseau, *Juge de Jean Jaques: Dialogues, texte présenté par Michel Foucault* (Paris: Librairie Armand Colin, 1962); Foucault, *Résumé des cours*, 1970–1982 (Paris: Julliard, 1989); Graham Burchell, Colin Gordon, and Peter Miller (eds.), *The Foucault Effect: Studies in Governmentality* (Chicago: University of Chicago Press, 1991); Lawrence Kritzman (ed.), *Politics, Philosophy, Culture* (London: Routledge, 1988); Dean Mitchell, *Governmentality: Power and Rule in Modern Society* (London: Sage, 1999); and Jon Simon, *Foucault and the Political* (London: Routledge, 1995).

10 See Rousseau, *Émile*, Book III, Pléiade IV, 468n., and *Confessions*, Book VI, Pléiade I, 269.

11 Rousseau, *L'Etat de guerre*, Pléiade III, 608–9. On the reconstitution of this text, see Grace G. Roosevelt, *Reading Rousseau in the Nuclear Age* (Philadelphia: Temple University Press, 1990), introduction, pp. 13–17.

12 See Rousseau, *Contrat social*, I, vii, Pléiade III, 364. A notable treatment of this passage is provided by John Plamenatz in his "'*Ce qui ne signifie autre chose sinon qu'on le forcera d'être libre,'*" in Maurice Cranston and Richard Peters (eds.), *Hobbes and Rousseau: A Collection of Critical Essays* (New York: Doubleday Anchor, 1972), pp. 318–32.

13 See the *Contrat social* II, iv, II, v and III, i, Pléiade III, 373, 377, and 397.

14 Rousseau, *Lettres de la montagne*, Septième Lettre, Pléiade III, 815.

15 Rousseau, *Contrat social* I, viii, Pléiade III, 365.

16 Rousseau, *Jugement sur la Polysynodie (de l'abbé de Saint-Pierre)*, Pléiade III, 643.

17 Rousseau, *Discours sur l'Économie politique*, Pléiade III, 251.

18 See the *Contrat social* I, vi, Pléiade III, 361.

19 See the *Contrat social* I, vii and II, iii, Pléiade III, 363, 371, and 371n.

20 In Chap. 1 of his *Benjamin Constant and the Making of Modern Liberalism* (New Haven, CT: Yale University Press, 1984), pp. 28–52, Stephen Holmes usefully discusses that lecture with respect to Constant's divergence from Rousseau.

21 Pléiade III, 538–43. See also Claude Pichois and René Pintard, *Jean-Jacques entre Socrate et Caton* (Paris: Librairie José Corti, 1972).

22 A classic treatment of this subject can be found in Hubert Gillot, *La querelle des anciens et des modernes en France* (Nancy: A. Crépin-Leblond, 1914).

23 See the *Gouvernement de Pologne*, Chap. ii, Pléiade III, 958 and 959. Wide-ranging treatments of Rousseau's passionate attachment to the civic spirit of ancient institutions are provided by Denise Leduc-Fayette in *Jean-Jacques Rousseau et le mythe de l'antiquité* (Paris: Vrin, 1974) and Paule-Monique Vernes in *La ville, la fête, la démocratie: Rousseau et les illusions de la communauté* (Paris: Payot, 1978).

24 See the *Lettre à d'Alembert*, Pléiade V, 114, 121, and 122.

25 Rousseau, *Gouvernement de Pologne*, Chap. iv, Pléiade III, 968.

26 See *La Nouvelle Héloïse*, Cinquième partie, lettre vii, Pléiade II, 607–9.

27 See the *Contrat social*, III, xv, Pléiade III, 429. Compare the *Projet de constitution pour la Corse* and the *Gouvernement de Pologne*, Chap. xi, Pléiade III, 929 and 1004.

28 See the *Essai sur l'origine des langues*, Chap. xx, Pléiade V, 428.

29 See the *Contrat social*, III, xv, Pléiade III, 428–9.

30 Germaine Necker, Mme. de Staël, *De la littérature considérée dans ses rapports avec les institutions sociales* (Paris: Maradan, 1800), 2.33.

31 See Voltaire's letter to Charles Borde of 4 January 1765 (Leigh 3835) and Rousseau, *Confessions*, Livre VIII, Pléiade I, 384.

32 See d'Alembert, *De la liberté de la musique*, in Denise Launay (ed.), *La querelle des bouffons* (Genève: Minkoff, 1973), III, 2217.

33 See Freud, *Moses and Monotheism* (London: Hogarth, 1939), pp. 58–64 and 130–45, and my "The Enlightenment, the Nation-State and the Primal Patricide of Modernity," in *The Enlightenment and Modernity*, pp. 161–83.

34 See Hegel, *Phänomenologie des Geistes*, Wolfgang Bonsiepen and Reinhard Heede (eds.), in Hegel's *Gesammelte Werke* (Hamburg: Felix Meiner Verlag, 1968–), IX, 315, lines 14–15 and 27–28.

35 See Hegel, *Über die englische Reformbill*, first published in the *Allgemeine preußische Staatzeitung*, in his *Politischen Schriften*, Nachwort von Jürgen Habermas (Frankfurt: Suhrkamp, 1966), p. 310. It must be noted that Hegel here refers, not to Sieyès' role in establishing the National Assembly in 1789, but to his authorship of the constitution of the year VIII, which he drafted as provisional consul a decade later, following the bloodless *coup d'état* of the eighteenth Brumaire of Napoleon Bonaparte that marked the transition of France's revolutionary government from the *Directoire* to the *Consulat*. As First Consul, Bonaparte altered Sieyès' scheme to suit his own advantage and ambition.

36 See William Sewell, Jr., "*Le citoyen/la citoyenne*: Activity, Passivity, and the Revolutionary Concept of Citizenship," in *The Political Culture of the French Revolution*, forming Vol. 2 of François Furet et al. (eds.), *The French Revolution and the Creation of Modern Political Culture* (Oxford, U.K.: Pergamon, 1987–89), pp. 105–23.

37 See Hegel, *Phänomenologie des Geistes*, p. 320, lines 9–13.

38 See especially the *Contrat social*, III, xiv and xv, and the *Gouvernement de Pologne*, Chaps. ii and vii, Pléiade III, 427–31, 957–59, 975–89.

39 By which Rousseau of course meant just the citizenry, or the whole of the electorate eligible to serve public office. As opposed to sovereignty, which must be exercised directly by the people and from which no one could be excluded, government, he argued, was inescapably representative and therefore could never be democratic.

40 See the *Gouvernement de Pologne*, Chap. vii ("*Moyens de maintenir la constitution*"), Pléiade III, 978–85. On the implications of Rousseau's critique of representation as perceived in the constitutional debates of 1789, see Keith Michael Baker, *Inventing the French Revolution: Essays on French Political Culture in the Eighteenth Century* (Cambridge, U.K.: Cambridge University Press, 1990), Chap. 10, pp. 224–51.

41 With respect to Sieyès' debt to the Hobbesian theory of representation, see especially Murray Forsyth, "Thomas Hobbes and the Constituent Power of the People," *Political Studies* 29, 191–203 (1981). In a notable treatment of Sieyès' conception of the nation-state [see "The Permanent Crisis of a Divided Mankind: 'Contemporary Crisis of the Nation-State in Historical Perspective,'" *Political Studies* 42, 203 (1994)] Istvan Hont

concludes that "as a political definition of the location of sovereignty, Hobbes's 'state' and Sieyès' 'nation' are identical. Sieyès' 'nation' is Hobbes's 'Leviathan'. Both are powerful interpretations, in a sharply converging manner, of the modern popular *civitas*." With respect to the contrast between Sieyès' and Rousseau's conceptions of representation, but also the apparent convergence of their ideas of the general will and indivisible sovereignty, see Bronisław Baczko, "Le contrat social des Français: Sieyès et Rousseau," in Baker (ed.), *The Political Culture of the Old Regime*, forming Vol. I of *The French Revolution and the Creation of Modern Political Culture*, pp. 493–513.

42 See Arendt, *The Origins of Totalitarianism*, first published in 1951, 2nd ed. (London: Allen and Unwin, 1958), pp. 230–1. Arendt here comments on what she terms "the secret conflict between state and nation," arising with the very birth of the nation-state on account of its conjunction of the rights of man with the demand for national sovereignty. Her reflections on this subject have occasioned extensive comnmentary. See, for instance, Julia Kristeva, *Étrangers à nous-mêmes* (Paris: Fayard, 1988), pp. 220–9, and Hont, "The Permanent Crisis of a Divided Mankind," pp. 206–9.

43 The phrasing of the third article of the declaration of the rights of man and of the citizen, which begins, 'Le principe de toute souveraineté réside essentiellement dans la Nation," is owed principally to Lafayette. For the fullest histories of the sources and drafting of the whole document and of the deliberations leading to its endorsement by the *Assemblée nationale* on 26 July 1789, see Stéphane Rials' commentary on *La déclaration des droits de l'homme et du citoyen* (Paris: Hachette, 1988), and Marcel Gauchet's *La révolution des droits de l'homme* (Paris: Gallimard, 1989).

44 I have recently addressed this subject in an essay on "Multiculturalism and ethnic cleansing in the Enlightenment," in Ole Peter Grell and Roy Porter (eds.), *Toleration in Enlightenment Europe* (Cambridge, U.K.: Cambridge University Press, 2000), pp. 69–85.

45 Rousseau, *L'Etat de guerre*, Pléiade III, 603.

46 See the *Discours sur les sciences et les arts*, Pléiade III, 14–15. On Rousseau's appreciation of the career of Fabricius as recounted by Plutarch, see George R. Havens' edition of this text (New York: The Modern Language Association of America, 1946), n. 152, pp. 203–4, and Jean Starobinski, "*La prosopopée de Fabricius*," *Revue des sciences humaines* **41**, 83–96 (1976).

47 Pléiade II, 770. As is noted by Philip Stewart [see his "*Julie et ses légendes*," *Studies on Voltaire* **260**, 275–6 (1989)], this inscription for Gravelot's tenth plate of *La Nouvelle Héloïse* does not figure anywhere

in the novel itself; it is a textual addition. See also Rousseau's remark in the *"Profession de foi du vicaire Savoyard,"* Émile, Livre IV, Pléiade IV, 588: "Homme, ne cherche plus l'auteur du mal, cet auteur c'est toi-même." The passage from Milton I have in mind comprises lines 73–5 in Book IV of *Paradise Lost*: "Me miserable! Which way shall I fly? ... Which way I fly is Hell; myself am Hell."

48 This text develops the keynote address I delivered, at Duke University in May 1999, to the eleventh colloquium of the North Amercian Association for the Study of Rousseau on the subject of "Rousseau and the Ancients." In that format, entitled "Ancient postmodernism in the philosophy of Rousseau," it is scheduled to appear eventually with other conference papers in *Pensée libre* no. 7. It is also partly recast from some of my earlier writings on Rousseau, including "Rousseau on Rameau and Revolution" (see n. 3 above); "La Querelle des Bouffons and the Italian Liberation of France: A Study of Revolutionary Foreplay," in *Studies in the Eighteenth Century* 6, *Eighteenth-Century Life* n.s. 11. (1987), pp. 94–116; and, above, all, "Rousseau's Two Concepts of Liberty," in George Feaver and Fred Rosen (eds.), *Lives, Liberties and the Public Good*, London (Macmillan), 1987, pp. 61–100; on the other hand, it incorporates passages from some of my most recent work on the conceptual history of modernity and Hegel's interpretation of the French Revolution, including "The Enlightenment and the French Revolutionary birth pangs of modernity," in Johan Heilbron, Lars Magnusson and Björn Wittrock (eds.) *The Rise of the Social Sciences and the Formation of Modernity: Conceptual Change in Context*, 1750–1850, Sociology of the Sciences Yearbook 20 [1996] (Dordrecht: Kluwer,1998), pp. 35–76; "Contextualizing Hegel's Phenomenology of the French Revolution and the Terror," *Political Theory* 26 (1998), pp. 33–55; and "The Enlightenment, the nation-state and the primal patricide of modernity" (see n. 1 above). I am grateful to Patrick Riley both for granting me more time to revise and submit this text than it or I merited, and for prompting my reflection on Rousseau's classical sources and modern identity intermittently over many years.

BIBLIOGRAPHY

Works of Rousseau (in French)

Oeuvres complètes, eds. B. Gagnébin and M. Raymond et al. (Paris: Gallimard [Pléiade], 1959–1995) (the "standard" edition), 5 vols.

Oeuvres complètes, ed. M. Launay (Paris: Éditions du Seuil, 1967–1971), 3 vols.

Correspondance complète, ed. R. A. Leigh (Geneva and Banbury, U.K.: Voltaire Foundation, 1965–1989), 50 vols.

Lettres philosophiques, ed. H. Gouhier (Paris: Vrin, 1974).

Le Lévite d'Ephraïm, crit. ed. by S. Eigeldinger (Paris: Honoré Champion, 1999).

Works of Rousseau (in English)

Collected Writings of Rousseau, eds. R. D. Masters and C. Kelly (Hanover, NH and London: University Press of New England, 1990 –), 7 vols. (to date).

Political Writings, trans. and ed. F. Watkins (Edinburgh: Nelson, 1953 [reprinted with new Preface by P. Riley, Madison, WI: University of Wisconsin Press, 1986]).

Political Writings, ed. C. E. Vaughan (Cambridge, U.K.: Cambridge University Press, 1915 [reprinted Oxford: Blackwell, 1962]), 2 vols. (French texts, English apparatus, and notes).

Confessions, trans. J. M. Cohen (Harmondsworth, U.K.: Penguin, 1954).

Discourses and Other Early Political Writings, trans. and ed. Victor Gourevitch (Cambridge, U.K.: Cambridge University Press, 1998).

Émile, trans. A. Bloom (New York: Basic Books, 1979 [reprinted London: Penguin, 1991]).

Émile, trans. B. Foxley (London: Everyman, 1910).

Letter to d'Alembert on the Theatre, in *Politics and the Arts*, trans. and ed. A. Bloom (Ithaca, NY: Cornell University Press, 1960).

Religious Writings, ed. R. Grimsley (Oxford, U.K.: Clarendon, 1970) (texts in French, apparatus and notes in English).

Social Contract and Discourses, trans. and ed. G. D. H. Cole (London: Dent, 1973 [revised ed.]).

Social Contract and Other Later Political Writings, trans. and ed. Victor Gourevitch (Cambridge, U.K.: Cambridge University Press, 1998).

The Reveries of a Solitary Walker, trans. and ed. C. Butterworth (Harmondsworth, U.K.: Penguin, 1964).

Works on Rousseau (a highly selective list)

Baczko, Bronisław, *La cité et ses langages*, in R. A. Leigh (ed.). *Rousseau after 200 Years* (Cambridge, U.K.: Cambridge University Press, 1982).

Berlin, Isaiah, "Two Concepts of Liberty," in H. Hardy et al. (eds.), *The Proper Study of Mankind* (New York: Farrar, Strauss, Giroux, 1998).

Bréhier, Émile, "Les lectures malebranchistes de Jean-Jacques Rousseau" (1938), in *Études de philosophie moderne* (Paris: Presses Universitaires de France, 1965).

Burgelin, Pierre, *La philosophie de l'éxistence de J.-J. Rousseau* (Paris: Presses Universitaires de France, 1952).

Canovan, Margaret, "Rousseau's Two Concepts of Citizenship," in E. Kennedy and S. Mindus (eds.), *Women and Western Political Philosophy* (Brighton, U.K.: Wheatsheaf, 1987).

Cassirer, Ernst, *Rousseau, Kant and Goethe*, trans. P. Gay (Bloomington, IL: Library of Liberal Arts Press, 1963).

Cassirer, Ernst, *The Question of Jean-Jacques Rousseau*, trans. P. Gay (New York: Columbia University Press, 1954).

Cobban, Alfred, *Rousseau and the Modern State* (London: Croom Helm, 1934).

Charvet, John, *The Social Problem in the Philosophy of Rousseau* (Cambridge, U.K.: Cambridge University Press, 1974).

Cooper, Laurence D., *Rousseau and Nature: The Problem of the Good Life* (University Park, PA: Penn State University Press, 1999).

Cranston, Maurice and R. Peters, eds., *Hobbes and Rousseau: A Collection of Critical Essays* (New York: Anchor, 1972) [essays by Strauss, Plamenatz, Shklar, Masters, Grimsley, Charvet, de Jouvenel].

Cranston, Maurice, [*A Rousseau Biography*]: *Jean-Jacques* (Vol. 1), *The Noble Savage* (Vol. 2), *The Solitary Self* (Vol. 3) (London: Allen Lane and Viking, 1983–1997).

Crocker, Lester G., *Jean-Jacques Rousseau: The Quest (1712–1758); The Prophetic Voice (1758–1778)* (New York: Macmillan, 1973 [2nd ed.])

Della Volpe, Galvano, "The Marxist Critique of Rousseau," in *New Left Review*, Vol. 59 (1996).

Dent, N. J. H., *Rousseau* (Oxford, U.K.: Blackwell, 1988).

Dérathé, Robert, *Jean-Jacques Rousseau et la science politique de son temps* (Paris: Vrin, 1970).

Domenich, Jacques, ed., *Autobiographie et fiction romanesque: Autour des Confessions de Jean-Jacques Rousseau* (Nice: Faculte des lettres de Nice, 1996).

Fetscher, Iring, *Rousseaus Politische Philosophie* (Neuwied: Luchterhand Verlag, 1962).

Gilson, Étienne, "La méthode de M. de Wolmar," in *Les idées et les lettres* (Paris: Vrin, 1932).

Goldschmidt, Victor, *Les principes du système de Rousseau* (Paris: Vrin, 1974).

Gossman, Lionel, "Time and History in Rousseau," in *Studies on Voltaire and the 18th Century* (Banbury: Voltaire Foundation 1964), Vol. XXX.

Gouhier, Henri, "Ce que le vicaire doit à Descartes," in *Annales de la société Jean-Jacques Rousseau* (Geneva: Droz, 1962), Vol. XXXV.

Guehenno, Jean, *Jean-Jacques Rousseau* (London: Routledge, 1966).

Hartle, Ann, ed., *The Modern Self in Rousseau's Confessions* (Notre Dame, IN: Notre Dame Press, 1983).

Hendel, C. W., *Jean-Jacques Rousseau, Moralist* (London: Oxford University Press, 1934), 2 vols.

Hoffmann, Stanley, et al., *Rousseau et la philosophie politique* (Paris: Presses Universitaires de France, 1965) [essays by Barth, Burgelin, Dérathé, Fetscher, Friedrich, de Jouvenel, Plamenatz].

Hoffmann, Stanley, ed., *Rousseau and International Relations* (Oxford, U.K.: Clarendon, 1991).

Hulliung, Mark, *The Autocritique of Enlightenment* (Cambridge, MA: Harvard University Press, 1995).

Jimack, Peter, *Rousseau: Émile* (London: Grant and Cutler, 1983).

Jouvenel, Bertrand de, "Essai sur la politique de Rousseau," introduction to *Du contrat social* (Geneva: Droz, 1947).

Kant, Immanuel, "Conjectural Beginning of Human History," in L. W. Beck (ed.), *Kant on History*, (Indianapolis, IN: Library of Liberal Arts, 1963).

Kavanagh, Thomas, *Writing the Truth: Authority and Desire in Rousseau* (Berkeley, CA: University of California Press, 1987).

Kelly, Christopher, "Rousseau's Case for and Against Heroes," in *Polity*, Vol. XXX, No. 2 (Winter 1997).

Kelly, Christopher, *Rousseau's Exemplary Life: The Confessions as Political Philosophy* (Ithaca, NY: Cornell University Press, 1987).

Kelly, George A., *Idealism, Politics and History* (Cambridge, U.K.: Cambridge University Press, 1969).

Kelly, George A., "Rousseau, Kant and History," in *Journal of the History of Ideas*, Vol. XXIX, No. 3 (1968).

Keohane, Nannerl, *Philosophy and the State in France* (Princeton, NJ: Princeton University Press, 1980).

Leigh, R. A., ed., *Rousseau after 200 Years: Proceedings of the Cambridge Bicentennial Colloquium* (Cambridge, U.K.: Cambridge University Press, 1982) [essays by Baczko, Charvet, Dérathé, Gagnebin, Grimsley, Starobinski, Wokler, inter alia].

Leigh, R. A., "Rousseau's Letter to Voltaire on Optimism," in *Studies on Voltaire and the 18th Century* (Banbury Voltaire Foundation: 1964), Vol. XXX.

Levine, Andrew, *The General Will: Rousseau, Marx, Communism* (Cambridge, U.K.: Cambridge University Press, 1993).

Lovejoy, Arthur O., "Rousseau's supposed Primitivism," in *Essays on the History of Ideas* (Baltimore, MD: Johns Hopkins University Press, 1948).

MacIntyre, Alasdair, "Preface" to *The Modern Self in Rousseau's Confessions* (Notre Dame, IN: Notre Dame University Press, 1983).

Marso, Lori Jo, *(Un)manly Citizens: Jean-Jacques Rousseau's and Germaine de Staël's Subversive Women* (Baltimore, MD: Johns Hopkins University Press, 1999).

Masters, Roger D., *The Political Philosophy of Jean-Jacques Rousseau* (Princeton, NJ: Princeton University Press, 1968).

Miller, James, *Rousseau: Dreamer of Democracy* (New Haven, CT: Yale University Press, 1984).

Mornet, Daniel, *Les origines intellectuelles de la revolution française*, 5th ed. (Paris: Presses Universitaires de France, 1954).

O'Hagan, Timothy, *Rousseau* (London: Routledge, 1999).

Plamenatz, John, *Man and Society* (London: Longman, 1962), Vol. 2.

Postigliola, Alberto, "*De Malebranche à Rousseau: Les apories de la volonté générale et la revanche du 'raisonneur violent'*," in *Annales de la société Jean-Jacques Rousseau* (Geneva: Jullien, 1980), Vol. 39.

Rawls, John, *A Theory of Justice* (Cambridge, MA: Harvard University Press, 1971), pp. 189–90, 402–3.

Raymond, Marcel, *Jean-Jacques Rousseau, la quête de soi et la rêverie* (Paris: Corti, 1962).

Riley, Patrick, *The General Will before Rousseau: The Transformation of the Divine into the Civic* (Princeton, NJ: Princeton University Press, 1986 [Italian trans., *La volontà generale prima di Rousseau*, Milan: Giuffre, 1995]).

Riley, Patrick, *Will and Political Legitimacy: A Critical Exposition of Social Contract Theory in Hobbes, Locke, Rousseau, Kant, and Hegel* (Cambridge, MA: Harvard University Press, 1982).

Riley, Patrick, "General Will," in A. Ryan et al. (eds.), *Blackwell Encyclopedia of Political Philosophy* (Oxford, U.K.: Blackwell, 1988).

Robinet, André, "*À propos d'ordre dans la Profession de foi du vicaire savoyard*," in *Studi Filosofici* (Florence: Olschki, 1978), Vol. 1.

Schwartz, Joel, *The Sexual Politics of Jean-Jacques Rousseau* (Chicago: University of Chicago Press, 1984).

Schneewind, Jerome, *The Invention of Autonomy* (Cambridge, U.K.: Cambridge University Press, 1998).

Shklar, Judith N., "General Will," in P. Wiener (ed.), *Dictionary of the History of Ideas*, (New York: Scribner's, 1973), Vol. 2.

Shklar, Judith N., *Men and Citizens: A Study of Rousseau's Social Theory* (Cambridge, U.K.: Cambridge University Press, 1969 [reprinted 1985]).

Starobinski, Jean, *Jean-Jacques Rousseau: La transparence et l'obstacle* (Paris: Gallimard, 1971 [expanded ed.]); English trans., University of Chicago Press, Chicago, 1988.

Strauss, Leo, *Natural Right and History* (Chicago: University of Chicago Press, 1953), "Rousseau" chapter.

Strong, Tracy B., *Jean-Jacques Rousseau and the Politics of the Ordinary* (Thousand Oaks, CA: Sage, 1994).

Temmer, Mark, *Time in Rousseau and Kant* (Paris and Geneva: Droz, 1958).

Trousson, Raymond, and F. S. Eideldinger, eds., *Dictionnaire de Jean-Jacques Rousseau* (Paris: Honoré Champion, 1996).

Van Laere, Francois, *Jean-Jacques Rousseau, du phantasme à l'écriture* (Paris: Minard 1967).

Velkley, Richard, *Freedom and the End of Reason* (Chicago: University of Chicago Press, 1989).

Wahl, Jean, "La bipolarité de Rousseau," in *Annales de la société Jean-Jacques Rousseau* (Geneva: Jullien, 1955), Vol. XXXIII.

Wokler, Robert, *Rousseau* (Oxford, U.K.: Oxford University Press, 1995),.

Wokler, Robert (ed.), *Rousseau and Liberty* (Manchester: Manchester University Press, 1995).

Wokler, Robert, *Rousseau on Society, Politics, Music and Language* (New York: Garland, 1987).

Wokler, Robert, "The Influence of Diderot on Rousseau," in *Studies on Voltaire and the 18th Century* (Banbury: Voltaire Foundation, 1975), Vol. 132.

INDEX